*When should I tr*
*Where do I go for answers to my travel questions?*
*What's the best and easiest way to plan and book my trip?*

# frommers.travelocity.com

**Frommer's**, the travel guide leader, has teamed up with **Travelocity.com**, the leader in online travel, to bring you an in-depth, easy-to-use resource designed to help you plan and book your trip online.

At **frommers.travelocity.com**, you'll find free online updates about your destination from the experts at Frommer's plus the outstanding travel planning and purchasing features of Travelocity.com. Travelocity.com provides reservations capabilities for 95 percent of all airline seats sold, more than 47,000 hotels, and over 50 car rental companies. In addition, Travelocity.com offers more than 2,000 exciting vacation and cruise packages. Travelocity.com puts you in complete control of your travel planning with these and other great features:

**Expert travel guidance from Frommer's** - over 150 writers reporting from around the world!

**Best Fare Finder** - an interactive calendar tells you when to travel to get the best airfare

**Fare Watcher** - we'll track airfare changes to your favorite destinations

**Dream Maps** - a mapping feature that suggests travel opportunities based on your budget

**Shop Safe Guarantee** - 24 hours a day / 7 days a week live customer service, and more!

Whether traveling on a tight budget, looking for a quick weekend getaway, or planning the trip of a lifetime, Frommer's guides and Travelocity.com will make your travel dreams a reality. You've bought the book, now book the trip!

# A New Star-Rating System & Other Exciting News from Frommer's!

In our continuing effort to publish the savviest, most up-to-date, and most appealing travel guides available, we've added some great new features.

Frommer's guides now include a new **star-rating system.** Every hotel, restaurant, and attraction is rated from 0 to 3 stars to help you set priorities and organize your time.

We've also added **seven brand-new features** that point you to the great deals, in-the-know advice, and unique experiences that separate travelers from tourists. Throughout the guide look for:

| | |
|---|---|
| **Finds** | Special finds—those places only insiders know about |
| **Fun Fact** | Fun facts—details that make travelers more informed and their trips more fun |
| **Kids** | Best bets for kids—advice for the whole family |
| **Moments** | Special moments—those experiences that memories are made of |
| **Overrated** | Places or experiences not worth your time or money |
| **Tips** | Insider tips—some great ways to save time and money |
| **Value** | Great values—where to get the best deals |

We've also added a **"What's New"** section in every guide—a timely crash course in what's hot and what's not in every destination we cover.

## Other Great Guides for Your Trip:

*Frommer's London*

*Frommer's Portable London*

*Frommer's England*

*Frommer's England from $75 a Day*

*Frommer's Memorable Walks in London*

*Frommer's Europe*

*Frommer's Europe from $70 a Day*

# Frommer's®

# London
## from $85 a day

## 8th Edition

## by Harriot Lane Fox

**Here's what the critics say about Frommer's:**

"Amazingly easy to use. Very portable, very complete."
—*Booklist*

"The only mainstream guide to list specific prices. The Walter Cronkite of guidebooks—with all that implies."
—*Travel & Leisure*

"Complete, concise, and filled with useful information."
—*New York Daily News*

"Hotel information is close to encyclopedic."
—*Des Moines Sunday Register*

"Detailed, accurate, and easy-to-read information for all price ranges."
—*Glamour Magazine*

Hungry Minds™

Best-Selling Books • Digital Downloads • e-Books • Answer Networks
e-Newsletters • Branded Web Sites • e-Learning
New York, NY • Cleveland, OH • Indianapolis, IN

## About the Author

**Harriot Lane Fox** is a native Londoner and has lived in the city all her life. Her interest in travel began with an epic three-month adventure in the United States after she left school. At university, she spent a year living and studying in France. Harriot's first job was as a public relations consultant, but 10 years ago she swapped sides to become a journalist. A former features editor of a business magazine, she is now a freelancer and writes on subjects as diverse as hotshot entrepreneurs and mouthwatering homes.

Published by:

## Hungry Minds, Inc.

909 Third Ave.
New York, NY 10022

ISBN 0-7645-6524-9
ISSN 1055-5331

Editor: Christine Ryan
Production Editor: M. Faunette Johnston
Cartographer: Nick Trotter
Photo Editor: Richard Fox
Production by Hungry Minds Indianapolis Production Services

## Special Sales

For general information on Hungry Minds' products and services please contact our Customer Care department; within the U.S. at 800-762-2974, outside the U.S. at 317-572-3993 or fax 317-572-4002. For sales inquiries and reseller information, including discounts, bulk sales, customized editions, and premium sales, please contact our Customer Care department at 800-434-3422.

Manufactured in the United States of America

5  4  3  2  1

# Contents

## 5  Great Deals on Dining    110

## 6  Exploring London    160

## 7  Shopping    217

## 8  London After Dark                                236

## 9  Easy Excursions from London          261

### Appendix: London in Depth                 277

### Index                                        295

# List of Maps

## An Invitation to the Reader

In researching this book, we discovered many wonderful places—hotels, restaurants, shops, and more. We're sure you'll find others. Please tell us about them, so we can share the information with your fellow travelers in upcoming editions. If you were disappointed with a recommendation, we'd love to know that, too. Please write to:

*Frommer's London from $85 a Day*, 8th Edition
Hungry Minds, Inc. • 909 Third Avenue • New York, NY 10022

## An Additional Note

Please be advised that travel information is subject to change at any time—and this is especially true of prices. We therefore suggest that you write or call ahead for confirmation when making your travel plans. The authors, editors, and publisher cannot be held responsible for the experiences of readers while traveling. Your safety is important to us, however, so we encourage you to stay alert and be aware of your surroundings. Keep a close eye on cameras, purses, and wallets, all favorite targets of thieves and pickpockets.

### New! Frommer's Star Ratings & Icons

Every hotel, restaurant, and attraction listing in this guide has been ranked for quality, value, service, amenities, and special features using a star-rating scale. In country, state, and regional guides, we also rate towns and regions to help you narrow down your choices and budget your time accordingly. Hotels and restaurants are rated on a scale of zero (recommended) to two stars (very highly recommended); exceptional "worth a splurge" options may get three stars. Attractions, towns, and regions are rated according to the following scale: zero stars (recommended), one star (highly recommended), two stars (very highly recommended), and three stars (must-see).

In addition to the rating system, we also use seven icons to highlight insider information, useful tips, special bargains, hidden gems, memorable experiences, kid-friendly venues, places to avoid, and other useful information:

*Finds*  *Fun Fact*  *Kids*  *Moments*  *Overrated*  *Tips*  *Value*

The following abbreviations are used for credit cards:

| | | | | | |
|---|---|---|---|---|---|
| AE | American Express | DISC | Discover | V | Visa |
| DC | Diners Club | MC | MasterCard | | |

## FROMMERS.COM

Now that you have the guidebook to a great trip, visit our website at **www.frommers.com** for travel information on nearly 2,000 destinations. With features updated regularly, we give you instant access to the most current trip-planning information available. At Frommers.com, you'll also find the best prices on airfares, accommodations, and car rentals—and you can even book travel online through our travel booking partners. At Frommers.com, you'll also find the following:

- Daily Newsletter highlighting the best travel deals
- Hot Spot of the Month/Vacation Sweepstakes & Travel Photo Contest
- More than 200 Travel Message Boards
- Outspoken Newsletters and Feature Articles on travel bargains, vacation ideas, tips & resources, and more!

# What's New in London

London was losing one of its most famous photo opportunities last year as Mayor Ken Livingstone finally began to rid Trafalgar Square of its pigeons. It took two tragi-comic trips to the high court to oust the last licensed feed-seller. Animal activists in the Pigeon Alliance defiantly brought corn dinners for the thousands of "rats with wings," as the mayor affectionately called them. But that couldn't compete with the official starve 'em out policy and the birds began to get the message. Yippee! I've never understood why tourists flock here to turn themselves into perches for flying poop-machines.

Apparently, controlling pigeon poop is the first sign that London's great urban renaissance is finally underway. The ambitious plan to pedestrianize part of the square, and make the capital's busiest roundabout fit for humans again, could start this spring. Except, I have this *Groundhog Day* feeling that this has all been said before—we'll have to wait and see if this is more than just civic hot air!

To be fair, Mayor Ken hasn't had long to get things moving. He took office in July 2000, doesn't even move into his new glass display-case HQ until 2002, and has been fighting tooth and nail against Tube privatization in between. But he has found the time to jot down a 20-year plan for the capital to cope with a population forecast to grow from 7.4 million to over 8 million by 2016. London is a low-rise city so he's heading for a punch-up with the heritage lobby with his push for Manhattan-style skyscrapers, and an end to the 12 protected clear views of St. Paul's Cathedral, where the Queen commemorates her Golden Jubilee this year.

He faces opposition on all sides. The local council was planning to give the same legal protection to views of the British Airways London Eye, which it would like to stay put after the putative 5-year lifespan comes to an end. And no wonder. The giant observation wheel recovered brilliantly from its dysfunctional start to become the second most popular attraction in Europe after that Mickey Mouse operation, Eurodisney. By the time it celebrated its first birthday, the Eye had been hijacked twice by protesters, hosted its first exchange of bodily fluids between a couple of randy teenagers on a night-time ride, and become *the* enduring symbol of this gold-rush town.

London is still enjoying the aftershocks of the millennial BANG, when £6 billion poured into celebrating modern achievements and redeveloping the institutions of the distant and not-so-distant past—museums, galleries, and theaters. The Tate Modern is a perfect example. It's been such a hit that there's already talk about throwing out a new wing, or even building a hotel!

Londoners are as proud of their city as ever. That old empire-building arrogance was never dead, just dormant in the decades of Britain's declining power. But buttons are polished, chests puffed out, and they're standing by their beds ready to conquer the world. You can't blame them. Ever since Tony Blair wiped the Tories' eyes the first time in 1997, people everywhere have been lauding Britain's capital as *the* happening place: with the hottest fashion designers; the most entrepreneurial restaurateurs starring in a bubbling dining scene; fabulous theater, music, and dance; and megastar DJs, who tour the world for bigger fees than many of their rock star rivals.

Except for Madonna, of course, or "Madge" as the Brits like to call her now that she's married to Guy Ritchie and an honorary local. More than 100,000 people a year move to London from overseas. Recently, Kensington has been basking in the reflected glow of new residents, the glamour couple Christiane Amanpour, CNN's chief international reporter, and her husband, hot-spot buster, James Rubin. And Eminem has been house-hunting in leafy upscale Hampstead, or so his granny told breakfast TV. In addition to these celebs, there are armies of imports, long-stay, short-stay, and stopover, whose names don't sell papers. So don't be surprised if you go several hours without hearing an English voice.

*Note:* Usually, the millions of out-of-town Britons get cross because London hogs all the attention. But last year, it was the countryside that lit up TV screens worldwide with the hellish glow of foot and mouth animal pyres. It cost the capital alone £1 billion in revenue, as tourists voted with their feet and stayed away. Contrary to reports, however, life in London was as normal. No pall of smoke hung over the city. Nor did everyone wear rubber booties and wash in Lysol every night. And British food is safe to eat. At the time of writing, the wildfire spread had stopped though there were still new cases needing drastic remedies. If foot and mouth remains an issue when you are planning your trip, check out the latest on the Guardian newspaper's website (**www.guardian. co.uk/footandmouth**) and the official **www.openbritain.gov.uk**, and with your national Customs department.

Following are some more highlights of changes that New Labour, the new millennium, and a new mayor are bringing to London.

**PLANNING YOUR TRIP** The London GoSee card has gone (RIP) but some clever marketing types have come up with a new discount deal called the **London Pass** (✆ **0870/ 242-9988;** www.londonpass.com). It's worth it to cock a snook at the queue as you sweep past to swipe your card at each attraction. This comes with a **London VisitorCard,** the cheap travel pass only available outside the U.K., so buy it before you fly. See chapter 2 for details.

**GETTING AROUND** The Underground needs £12 billion worth of refurbishments and leaves regular passengers like me, and irregular ones, in a permanent state of fury. The only good news is that you can now surf for updates on escalator breakdowns at **www.thetube.com** to avoid booking a hotel near a walk-up station. Mayor Ken has set up one good deal, too—all travel cards, including the London VisitorCard, get you a third off the price of Thames boat trips. That will include the river hoppa between the two Tate galleries once the spacey Millbank pier is built, hopefully by summer 2002. See chapter 3 for details.

**ACCOMMODATIONS** Worried about their rip-off image, hotels and B&Bs held prices steady until cancellations because of foot and mouth dented their wallets so badly in 2001 that they've bumped rates up by a few pounds. After a year of indecision about how to run its accommodation booking service, and who should run it, the London Tourist Board has a new hotline (© 020/7932-2020).

The ever-expanding Choice Hotels has added another London franchisee, so there's now a Notting Hill Gate **Comfort Inn** at 6–14 Pembridge Gardens, W2 (© 020/7229-6666). Happily for budget travelers, these guys are rather sneaky, offering much better rates if you deal direct with them rather than through central reservations. At the other end of the bed budget, **St. Christopher's Village** has opened a hostel on Shepherds Bush green (© 020/7407-1856; www. st-christophers.co.uk), a scruffyish neighborhood, west of Notting Hill, home to the BBC and squads of young travelers from overseas. See chapter 4 for details.

**DINING**  You'd think Londoners had never tasted curry before, instead of growing up on it, from the fuss everyone is making about Indian cuisine. But then so few Indian restaurants win stars from the snobby Michelin men, as **Zaika** (257–259 Fulham Rd., SW3; © 020/7351-7823) did last year for its innovative fusion cuisine. Not what Ronnie Biggs was dreaming of for all those years on the lam in Brazil. Even more innovative is the move down-market (and down-budget) to reinvent street food at **Masala Zone,** 9 Marshall St., W1 (© 020/7287-9966), and **Mela,** 152–156 Shaftesbury Ave., WC2 (© 020/7836-8635). This reaction against flash dining is a familiar one— witness the waning popularity of Sir Terence Conran's restaurants. But few people would have predicted it from *the* gourmet grandee, Nico Ladenis, despite his resignation of his Michelin stars. Yet his new **Incognico,** 117 Shaftesbury Ave., WC2 (© 020/7836-8866) is pitched at brasserie prices. Thank you Nico! See chapter 5.

**SIGHTSEEING**  Getting sacked by Tony Blair after the election seems a poor reward for ex-culture secretary Chris Smith after he pulled off his big culture coup. It took months of negotiations, but all London's major national museums agreed to drop their admission charges by the end of 2001. That includes the **Victoria & Albert Museum,** Cromwell Rd., SW7 (© 020/7942-2000), which has unveiled a £31 million refurbishment of its British Galleries. London is still enjoying the tail end of the millennial splurge of investment that brought such new excitements as Tate Modern. **Tate Britain** at Millbank, SW1 (© 020/7887-8000), opened its centenary development last year—35% more hanging space, which it must be hoping will lure back some of the visitors who put the new Tate at the head of their visiting list. Americans will be interested to hear that the house where **Benjamin Franklin** lived between 1757 and 1775 is due to open to the public in early 2002 after a lengthy restoration. To find out more, call (© 020/7930-9121). See chapter 6 for details on all of London's museums.

**SHOPPING**  It's the ultimate reverse snobbery but fashion babes like Stella McCartney and Kate Moss are deep into thrift-shop chic, allegedly. As well as trawling Portobello and Camden markets, **Oxfam Originals** at 22 Earlham St., WC2 (© 020/7836-9666; Tube: Covent Garden), is a hotspot for retread threads. Otherwise, for great 1970s gear, head to **Pop Boutique,** 6 Monmouth St., W1: my suede sweater cost less than £20 ($29) yet people always assume it's this season's Bond Street bank-breaker. See chapter 7.

**AFTER DARK**  London is agog to see what the **Royal Shakespeare Company** gets up to after April when it quits its home at the Barbican to hot-stage it around the West End. Lips are smacking already as the company has lured Ralph Fiennes and Kenneth Brannagh into performing with it this year.

The days of superclubs being hot news just for being big is well over. For example, **home** in Leicester Square lost its cool even before it lost its license because the police discovered flagrant drug dealing. But club nights are still a big deal. Only in England could you find **SchoolDisco.com**—a Saturday nighter for which 2,000 allegedly cool dudes dress up in school uniform! A cooler crowd, at least to my mind, heads for intimate club bars like **Cargo,** Kingsland Viaduct, 83 Rivington St., EC2 (© **020/7739-3440**), where the cover is cheap for live music and DJs, dancing, and food—like a nightclub in the 1950s. See chapter 8 for details.

# The Best of London from $85 a Day

London is one of the most expensive cities in the world, more so even than New York. But that doesn't mean you can't enjoy a marvelous, affordable vacation here; that's the raison d'être for this guidebook. Here are some of the best sightseeing, lodging, and dining options for travelers who want a great vacation without breaking the bank.

## 1 Frommer's Favorite London Moments

- **Roam Along the River.** I'm torn between two favorite strolls. A newly spruced-up walk runs uninterrupted along the south bank of the Thames from the British Airways London Eye, opposite the Houses of Parliament, to Southwark, past a score of must-visit sights, including the Tate Modern and the Millennium Bridge. On the flip side, the toll-path heading west from Putney along the river could hardly be more different. The luminous tunnel of trees leads past the world's biggest urban wetland sanctuary to Hammersmith Bridge. Cross over there for a pint at one of the pubs between the string of north-bank boathouses.
- **Do That Continental Thing and Take to the Streets.** Now, it's not just Covent Garden where strollers and outdoor eaters can watch the street entertainment. Millions have gone into refurbishing the courtyard at Somerset House, on the other side of the Strand, and there's nearly always something going on there. The summer cafe on the river terrace is one of the most delightful cheap

lunch spots in town. My other favorite thing is to pick up the Sunday paper and head to Soho for a late breakfast at one of the tempting patisseries. With the throngs of locals and visitors, it's like a Spanish *paseo.*
- **Get a Rooftop View.** The giant British Airways London Eye lifts you, at a crawling pace, 135 feet in the air for a staggering 25-mile view across the city. There are also stonking panoramas from the dome of St. Paul's Cathedral, from the tower of Westminster Cathedral, and from the just tarted-up Wellington Arch at Hyde Park Corner. But you have to get out your wallet to enjoy all of these. Savvy travelers head for an unofficial picnic spot—the glass-walled corner room on level 7—at my favorite freebie, Tate Modern. See chapter 6.
- **Time-Travel into Pageantry from the Past.** The Brits have had centuries to practice their pomp and circumstance, which is why they've got ceremonies like the Changing of the Guard at Buckingham Palace, Horse Guards Parade, and St. James's Palace,

# Central London

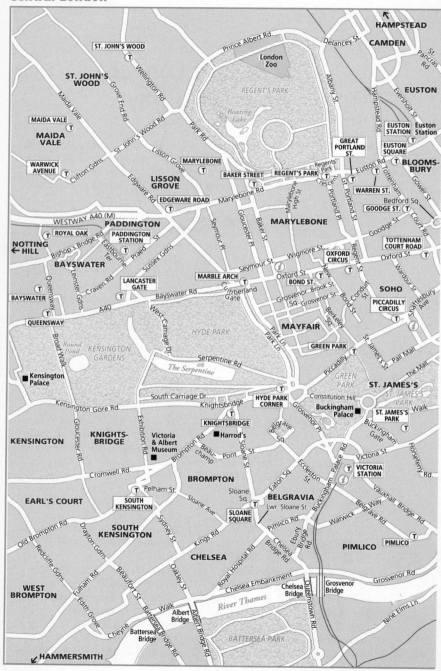

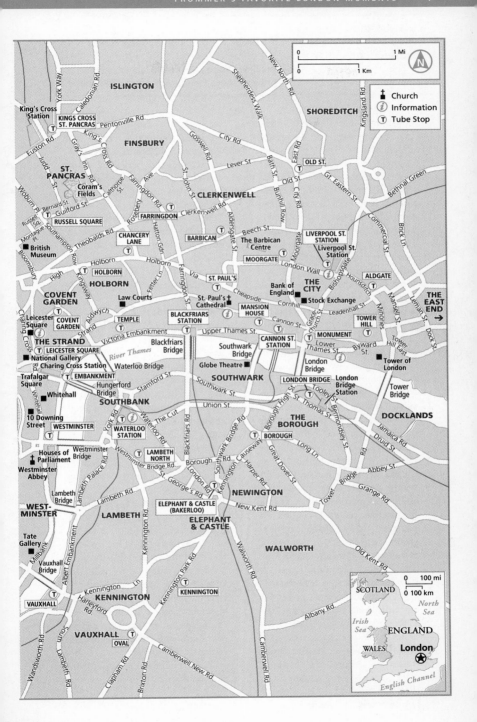

## Impressions

*Anybody who enjoys being in the House of Commons probably needs psychiatric care.*

—Ken Livingstone MP, now Mayor of London,
in the *Evening Standard,* February 26, 1988

down to a fine art. Prime Minister's Question Time, on Wednesday afternoons at 3pm, is another example. See chapter 6.

- **Take in a Show with "Auntie."** That's the nickname for the BBC among Brits of a certain generation. The Beeb, as it's also known, is always keen to recruit audiences for its TV and radio shows, and tickets are free. If you're a fan of quirky British humor, try and catch my Radio4 favorites, *The News Quiz* and *I'm Sorry I Haven't a Clue,* the latter hosted by famous jazzman Humphrey Littleton. Some of the references will be pretty obscure to out-of-towners, but I can guarantee a good giggle. See chapter 6.

- **Make like a Modern Mary Poppins.** Nannies have always taken their charges to the park for a dose of healthy fresh air before afternoon tea. Today, you're more likely to see stay-at-home dads in charge, or young Aussie travelers saving up the cash to hop to another European country. They'll be heading for the scramble-on pirate ship at the Peter Pan playground in Kensington Gardens, a memorial to Princess Diana. The other Mary Poppins treat is watching the keepers feed the pelicans, descended from a pair given by the Russian ambassador in the 17th century, by the lake in St. James's Park. See chapter 6

- **Drool over Aspirational Antiques.** London is a fantastic place to browse for antiques. Go to a free pre-auction viewing of rare treasures and weird arcana at

one of the big salerooms—Christie's, Sotheby's, Phillips, or Bonhams. Serious treasure-hunters should set their alarm clocks for a dawn raid on Bermondsey market, where dealers come to sniff out bargains at 5:30am. Portobello market is on Saturday—not quite such an early start, but bolt your breakfast to beat the tourist hordes. Camden Passage is best on Wednesday and Saturday when stalls set up outdoors. See chapters 6 and 7.

- **Label Yourself for Less.** If you love the funky Burberry brand—it even does tartan bikinis these days—but hate the astronomical prices, you'll do what I do and head for the factory shop in Hackney. For wannabe it-girls and -boys, there's one stop—Top Shop at Oxford Circus. It has persuaded a gang of great designers to create exclusive collections that even show up in the pages of Vogue—in the cheap, cheap shopping section. See chapter 7.

- **Be a Good Sport.** Horseracing is much less snobby than you'd imagine from watching the Derby or Ascot on TV. One of my favorite ways to spend a summer Monday evening is to take the boat from the local station up the river to Windsor Racecourse, with a picnic and a bottle of fake champagne—you can buy a glass of the real stuff there. Greyhound racing at Wimbledon is a more raucous evening's entertainment, and the dogs an even dodgier bet. So stick to a pound each way. See chapter 7.

- **Steal a Musical Moment.** Lots of London's major arts venues do giveaways, perhaps to prove that they're worth all those millions of pounds from the public purse. Check out the Commuter Jazz in the foyer of the Royal Festival Hall, and the Monday lunchtime sessions at the Royal Opera House. And I've persuaded lots of friends to ditch their pay-up ethics and enjoy the summer opera at Holland Park Theater for free while sitting on the grass outside. See chapter 8.

- **Invest in the Theatrical Future.** The productions you'll see at the Royal Court Theatre could be on Broadway next year—it was the first to stage Conor McPherson's *The Weir.* Why wait and pay mortgageable ticket prices, when all seats here go for a fiver on Monday nights? If you're prepared to gamble, here's an even better deal: last-minute standbys at the downstairs stage cost a token 10p (16¢). The Soho Theatre also charges £5 ($8) a seat on Mondays and specializes in new writing. See chapter 8.

- **Go Early-Bird Clubbing.** Lots of London's nightspots start the evening as bars. Go before the DJ plugs in, and there's no cover charge. You could even find that it's happy hour. That's the deal at Bar Rumba, where drinks are two for the price of one between 5 and 9pm Monday to Thursday. A hot 'n' cool crowd comes for a different funky sound every night of the week. It's where I learned to salsa, at the pre-club classes. See chapter 8.

- **Raise Your Elbow.** A pub crawl is the best way to re-educate anyone who thinks beer is that anemic yellow stuff, aerated, and antarcticly chilled. For a really good pint of real ale head for Jerusalem Tavern in Clerkenwell, which is stocked with over 20 different ones to try from St. Peter's Brewery in Suffolk. If it's a pint of the black stuff you're after, then crawl over to the always-crowded Toucan in Soho. See chapter 8.

## 2 Best Hotel Bets on a Budget

Turn to chapter 4 for a full review of these hotels.

- **Best Overall Value: Arran House,** 77 Gower St., WC1 (© **020/7636-2186**), isn't a ritzy place at all. Indeed, the rooms are simple, and some are quite small. But look at what it offers at extremely competitive rates: roses rambling across a beautiful private garden; double-glazing masking traffic noise; a truly enormous full English breakfast (two types of bacon, sausages, fried bread, French toast, scrambled eggs, baked beans, tomatoes, grapefruit, toast and jam, orange juice, tea, and coffee); use of the kitchen to make supper; self-service laundry facilities; and a very friendly welcome.

- **Best for Families:** The British Airways London Eye is right next door. The Houses of Parliament are on the opposite bank of the river. The London Aquarium is in the basement. And there's a restaurant with robot waiters. Do not pass go. Head straight for **Travel Inn Capital, County Hall,** Belvedere Rd., SE1 (© **020/ 7902-1600**).

- **Best for Travelers with Disabilities:** Sadly, there aren't a lot of rivals for this recommendation. **Regent Palace Hotel,** Piccadilly Circus, W1 (© **020/7734-7000**) has 32 units, and it is right in the thick of things. The **Citadines Trafalgar Square,** 18–21 Northumberland Ave., WC2 (℃ **800/ 528-3549**) is a bit of a splurge, but good for people on longer visits who prefer the flexibility of self-catering. It has 16 adapted studios and a 1-bedroom apartment.

- **Best for Nonsmokers:** The filthy weed is banned outright at **Jenkins Hotel,** 45 Cartwright Gardens, WC1 (℃ **020/7383-2067**), where the strokable Labrador hosts are a good substitute if you're missing your four-legged friend!

- **Best for Gay Travelers:** The **Philbeach Hotel,** 30–31 Philbeach Gardens, SW5 (℃ **020/ 7373-1244**) is a home away from home, only louder, with its famed Friday club nights. Pack light— it's got a trannie dressing service.

- **Best for Romantics:** You may have to forge a marriage certificate but it's worth it because honeymooners can sometimes jump the queue for a four-poster bed at **Wigmore Court Hotel,** 23 Gloucester Place, W1 (℃ **020/7935-0928**).

- **Best Jumbo Breakfast:** The Davies family cooks a huge fat-boy breakfast, *and* gives guests free run at a buffet of fruit, yogurt, croissants, and cereals, at **Harlingford Hotel,** 61–63 Cartwright Gardens, WC1 (℃ **020/ 7387-1551**). Take a doggy bag! For a local treat, check into **Vicarage Private Hotel,** 10 Vicarage Gate, W8 (℃ **020/7229-4030**). It's the only budget guesthouse I've seen with kippers (smoked herring) and porridge on the menu. As befits a Frommer's top tip, **Arran House** (see above) also sets out a bumper feast.

- **Best for Serious Shoppers:** Put a padlock on your wallet if you're staying at either of these. The **Willett Hotel** (℃**020/7824- 8415**) is just round the corner from Peter Jones in Sloane Square and a 5-minute walk to Chelsea's King's Road. **The Ivanhoe Suite Hotel,** 1 St. Christopher's Place, W1 (℃ **020/7935-1047**), is in a little pedestrian enclave off Oxford Street, crammed with boutiques.

- **Best for Theater Buffs:** An Abba-esque 1970s timewarp, **The Fielding Hotel,** 4 Broad Court, WC2 (℃ **020/7836-8305**) is right by the Royal Opera House, in the heart of theatrical Covent Garden, which is why so many of its guests are performers and their groupies.

- **Best for Interior Design Tips:** The **Rushmore Hotel,** 11 Trebovir Rd., SW5 (℃ **020/7370- 0274**), is an extravaganza of muraled ceilings and stage-set bedrooms. It is only rivaled for va-va-voom by a less refined, even more over-the-top splurge, **The Pavilion,** 34–36 Sussex Gardens, W2 (℃ **020/7262- 0905**)—the fash-pack's fave, allegedly.

- **Best for Party-Animals on a Shoestring:** For only £14-a-night ($20.30), **St. Christopher's Village,** 165 Borough High St., SE1 (℃ **020/7407-1856**), offers you a sauna and hot-tub on the roof, a basement nightclub, and subsidized grub.

- **Best for Net Addicts:** Guests pay £5 ($7.25) to have a computer in their room, then surf for free at **InterneSt@Portobello Gold,** 97 Portobello Rd., W11 (℃ **020/ 7460-4910**). Or they can just pop along to the cyber bar at this old converted pub, which is right in the middle of the antiques stalls during the Saturday market.

## 3 Best Dining Bets on a Budget

See chapter 5 for a full review of these restaurants.

- **Best Overall Value:** This year, the top $-a-day award goes to a top-dollar celebrity restaurateur. The name of Nico Ladenis has been synonymous with splurgey London dining for decades, so it's a shock and a delight to find the ambrosial three-course lunch and early-bird menu at his new eaterie, **Incognico,** 117 Shaftesbury Ave., WC2 (© **020/7836-8866**) costs a mere £12.50 ($18.15). A superb budget blow-out.
- **Best Fixed-Price Bargain:** Indian food is the hot thing, again, so it seems fitting to split this accolade between a new restaurant and an old friend. **Masala Zone,** 9 Marshall St., W1 (© **020/7287-9966**), restyles traditional street food, offering thalis from £6 ($8.70): this meal on a tray includes a curry, bowls of vegetables, dal, yogurt curry, rice, popadum, chapatis, chutneys, and raita. Or try a South Indian feast at long-time budget favorite, **Diwana Bhel Poori House,** 121 Drummond St., NW1 (© **020/7387-5556**) for just £6.20 ($9), and you can bring your own wine with no charge. Gobsmacking and certainly gob-filling!
- **Best for Families:** Talking drink trolleys circle the restaurant like R2D2 while the food circles on a long conveyor belt. So tell me **YO! Sushi** isn't kid heaven! The restaurant's many branches are heaven for Mom and Pop, too, because the kids eat for free from Monday to Friday. There are scaled down and toned-down dishes for them, from chicken nuggets to cigar-shaped fish fingers.
- **Best for a Grand Entrance:** The sweeping staircase down into the multileveled **Vong,** Berkeley Hotel, Wilton Place, SW1 (© **020/7235-1010**), could have been made for a royal entrance. And the £22.50 ($32.65) early- and late-bird menu is a fair deal for a "black plate" filled by Euro-celebrity chef Jean-Georges Vongerichten. Eat your heart out, Queenie.
- **Best of Britain I:** Lily Langtry and Edward VII used to tryst at **Rules,** 35 Maiden Lane, WC2 (© **020/7836-5314**), and it still specializes in feathered and furred game—farmed now, rather than blasted onto the plate with a 12-bore shotgun, as it would have been in the King's day.
- **Best of Britain II:** Cabbies know everything, and they're always right, as you'll find out if you travel by taxi. Their vote goes to **North Sea Fish Restaurant,** 7–8 Leigh St., WC1 (© **020/7387-5892**), for the national dish, fish & chips.
- **Best Pub Grub:** The beef-and-ale pie at the **Museum Tavern,** 49 Great Russell St., WC1 (© **020/7242-8987**) is a hearty bite. Or, if you want to go gastro, check out the **Atlas,** 16 Seagrave Rd., SW6 (© **020/7385-9129**), where the chef likes to apply a Spanish or a North African twist to his Mediterranean cuisine.
- **Best for Sunday Lunch:** The three-course Sunday lunch at **Maggie Jones's,** 6 Old Court Place, off Kensington Church St., W8 (© **020/7937-6462**) is like granny used to make it, offering such national culinary treasures as roast beef with Yorkshire pudding and yum-scrum apple crumble.

- **Best Barbecues:** Enjoy the sizzle and smells of steaks, lamb, sausages, and corn-fed chicken cooked to order by the Hellbergs, who run **Arkansas Café,** Old Spitalfields Market, E1 (*©* **020/ 7377-6999**). Keir gets up at dawn to choose the best meat from Smithfield Market and posts up the life story of each cut.
- **Best for Vegetarians:** Amid the fleshpots of Soho, **Mildred's,** 58 Greek St., W1 (*©* **020/ 7494-1634**) can do magical things with a pinto bean and organic wine.
- **Best for Nonsmokers:** You can't light up at **Wagamama,** 4a Streatham St. (off Coptic Street), WC1 (*©* **020/7323-9223**), and most smokers don't mind—the atmosphere is so frenetic, it probably won't even occur to them to do so. Nor is nicotine allowed to yellow the shelves at top shop 'n' lunch spot, **Books for Cooks,** 4 Blenheim Crescent, W11 (*©* **020/7221-1992**).
- **Best for a Romantic Dinner:** No restaurant can rival the cozy candlelit charm of **Andrew Edmunds,** 46 Lexington St., W1 (*©* **020/7437-5708**), where young locals whispering sweet nothings make up the bulk of the clientele. Afterward, wander the buzzy streets of Soho hand in hand. Aaaaaah.
- **Best View:** Raise yourself above the hoi polloi in Covent Garden Piazza at **Chez Gerard at the Opera Terrace,** First Floor, Covent Garden Central Market, WC2 (*©* **020/7379-0666**). Even the stilt-walkers can't reach that high to interrupt your meal.
- **Best for the Morning After: The Star Café,** 22 Great Chapel St., W1 (*©* **020/7437-8778**) does a fantastic all-day breakfast. And if the situation is grave enough, you can get a Bloody Mary from the pub downstairs.
- **Best Gory Story:** The 17th-century it-girl Lady Elizabeth Hatton was murdered in Bleeding Heart Yard in the middle of her annual winter ball. Who can say she's not a see-through regular at **Bleeding Heart Tavern,** off Greville St., EC1 (*©* **020/7404-0333**), which you'll find in the yard today. This restored 1746 tavern serves earthy regional English cuisine and robust real ale.

# Planning an Affordable Trip to London

Planning an affordable trip to one of the most expensive cities in the world is a challenge, but it's certainly not impossible, especially if you make arrangements in advance. Your trip will be much more fun—and certainly a lot smoother—if you plan it properly. This chapter is designed to help you do that, step by step.

## 1 The $85-a-Day Premise

Our premise is that two people traveling together can have a great time in London for only $85 a day per person. That will cover the price of a decent double room, a lunchtime refueling stop at a pub or cafe, and a fine feast at an ethnic restaurant in the evening. It's likely that you'll get a free, full breakfast at your hotel.

After searching the streets of London, we've come up with the best of the budget deals. And don't worry—this doesn't mean you'll have to stay at dingy dives or eat nasty food. You can do it for less than $85 if you want to, of course, and you can certainly do it for more. Included in the book are recommendations on how to do both.

We've found some gem hotels in hot locations. Bloomsbury, for example, is a real hot spot for typically English guesthouses catering to modest travelers. We've even found a couple of brilliant deals in hotels so central, just off Oxford Street in Marylebone, in Soho, and off the Strand, that you'll want to cut your credit cards up before venturing out the door. If you're on a very strict budget, check out both the YHA hostels and the funky commercial ones for the snowboarding generation.

We've also reviewed the best student halls.

The biggest revolution for savvy travelers, though, has taken place on the eating scene. The Brits have discovered food, as the rest of the world knows it, in a big, big way. And it isn't just the high end that's changing. New cuisines and revamped old ones—Thai one year, sushi the next, and now new-wave Indian—are storming through budget eateries. Healthy food, from freshly squeezed this to organic that, is converting the meat-and-two-veg crowd all across the city. Even pubs tend to offer much better fare, replacing congealed, prepacked sludge with hearty homemade dishes. Some have even turned into understated but stylish restaurants, known rather unfortunately as "gastropubs." The selections in this book are designed to guide you to the best value options and point out some of the locals' favorites. Take a break from sightseeing on at least 1 day, because it's at lunchtime that some of the celebrity chefs lower their prices enough to let in hoi polloi.

As for sightseeing, you can't get around the fact that some of the stock-in-trade sights are overpriced—Madame Tussaud's and Buckingham Palace, particularly. The good news is that London's major national museums introduced free admission for all towards the end of 2001, and many other exhibitions and galleries already were free. So you can enjoy a splendidly rich vacation at these and the street and antiques markets, the rituals and ceremonies that make up London life, and just by strolling through the city.

## 2 Fifty Money-Saving Tips

### PRETRIP PLANNING AND TRANSPORTATION SAVINGS

1. Information pays. Read as much as you can about London before you go. Talk to people who've been there recently. Check in with the **British Tourist Authority** offices in New York or Chicago (see "Visitor Information," later in this chapter) for a wealth of free information. The BTA pack has details about several discount deals: the **London Pass,** a 1-, 2-, 3- or 6-day saver pass to major museums and galleries (see tip 11, below); the **London for Less discount card and guidebook,** and **Great British Heritage Pass** (see tips 8 and 9, below). You'll also be able to get maps and helpful booklets like *Britain for Cyclists, Britain for Walkers,* and more.

2. Make a note of the London fun that requires months of forethought. For instance, you'll need to write in for tickets to see Prime Minister's Question Time (see p. 170), the Ceremony of the Keys at the Tower of London (see p. 178), Trooping the Colour (see "Calendar of Events," below), or visit the Lord Chancellor's rooms and Mansion House (see p. 187). The ballot for Wimbledon tickets closes in December.

3. Travel off-season. Airfares and B&B rates are cheaper and easier to get if you travel from late fall through early spring. Hotel/flight packages plummet by hundreds of dollars. And, unlikely as it sounds, London is great in the winter. Cultural life is at full throttle, and sightseeing is more rewarding without the summer hordes. You don't have to go in darkest February—in March or October, you'll still reap financial benefits.

4. Reserve and pay in advance, especially if you plan to rent a car. If you book with an agency like **Europe by Car, (℗ 800/223-1516** in the U.S., or 212/581-3040 in New York; www.europebycar.com), or the broker **Holiday Autos (℗ 800/576-1590** in the U.S., 0870/400-0099 in the U.K.; www.holidayautos.com), you'll pay much less than with a local hire company, except the online-only **www.easyRentacar.com**. Its rates fluctuate according to demand: from £9 ($13.05) a day, even on a peak-season weekend if you book several weeks ahead, to £28 ($40.60), plus £5 ($7.25) car-prep fee, and 20p (29¢) for every mile over 75 miles. Great value for day-trips into the English countryside.

5. Fly during the week and early in the morning and save big money. Shop around for your airfare. This will be the most expensive part of your trip, so it pays to do some legwork. Surfing the Internet will turn up some great bargains. Alternatively, scour the newspaper for consolidators like **Cheap Tickets (℗ 212/570-1179,** 800/377-1000; www.cheaptickets.com), which sells airline seats at a substantial—as much as 60%—discount. Certainly consult

your travel agent, who will often be privy to special deals and package rates. Air carriers want to fill every seat on every flight, so they're constantly adjusting the pricing. Also investigate charter flights on scheduled airlines offered by reliable operators like **Travac** (© **800/872-8800,** 888/872-8327 for fare quotes; www.the travelsite.com). For information on all of these, see "Getting There," later in this chapter.

6. Consider buying a **holiday package:** one low price that includes airfare, transfers, accommodations, and some sightseeing discounts. For example, in 2001, **Cosmos** (© **800/556-5454;** www.globusandcosmos.com) was offering a week in a smartish hotel in London for $1,223 (per person, peak season). The airlines have all put packages together, too. (See section 9 of this chapter for more information.)

7. Pack light. You won't need a porter, and you're less likely to succumb to the desire for a taxi. But pack small, too: no space just aching to be filled with shopping. *Note:* Luggage carts are free in London's airports.

8. Buy a **London for Less card and guidebook** for $19.95, valid for up to four people for 8 consecutive days. It gets you a 20% to 50% discount at many different attractions, on theater and concert tickets, in restaurants and shops, on tours, car rental, hotels, fees at Travelex foreign currency exchanges, and telephone calls. With money off at the Almeida, the English National Opera and Ballet, and the Royal Philharmonic, *plus* savings on admissions or tours at the Tower of London, Westminster Abbey, Hampton Court Palace, Kensington Palace, and Kew Gardens, you're sure to

cover the sign-on cost. The card and book are available in London at any tourist info center for £12.95 ($18.80). To buy before you leave home, call © **888/ GO-FOR-LESS** in the U.S., or 937/846-1411 (www.for-less. com), or visit Britrail's **British Travel Shop,** 551 Fifth Ave., 7th floor, New York, NY, next to the BTA office.

9. The **Great British Heritage Pass** is great if you're planning any daytrips. You get free entry into almost 600 public and private historic properties owned by bodies including the National Trust, English Heritage, and Historic Royal Palaces. That means Hampton Court Palace, Kensington Palace State Apartments, Royal Ceremonial Dress Collection (plus half-price at the Tower of London), and Windsor Castle. Passes are valid for 7 days ($54), 15 days ($75), or a month ($102), no discounts for children. In the U.S. call **BritRail** © **866/ BRITRAIL** or 877/677-1066 (www.britrail.net). In London, take your passport to the Britain Visitor Centre, 1 Regent St., SW1, or any tourist information center. At press time, the exchange rate favored that approach—£32, £45, and £60 ($46.40, $65.25, and $139.20) respectively.

10. Before you leave, also get a 3-, 4-, or 7-day **London VisitorCard,** which offers virtually unlimited travel on public transport and is not available in the United Kingdom. Contact your travel agent or BritRail (© **866/BRITRAIL** or 877/677-1066; www.britrail.net). It comes with a bunch of discount vouchers and has other advantages over buying a local pass in London: You don't have to provide a passport photo and can travel at any time (in London,

many passes only work after 9:30am: see "Getting Around," in chapter 3). You can choose all zones or just Central London, which will cover most of what you need, even stretching as far as Greenwich: Central zone (zone 1 and 2) adult passes cost $20 for 3 days, $25 for 4, and $30 for 7; child equivalents cost $9, $10, and $13. All-zone cards are $29, $39, and $58 for adults, $13, $16, and $25 for children.

11. Buy a **London Pass** (© 0870/ 242-9988; www.londonpass. com). This beat-the-queue swipe-card is worth £300 in free admissions to over 60 attractions. Then there's the guided walks, boat trips, commission-free currency exchange, free and discounted telephone calls, and an all-zone London VisitorCard for untramelled travel on the Tube and buses. The London Pass costs £22 ($31.90) for 1 day, £39 ($56.55) for 2 days, £49 ($71.05) for 3, and £79 ($114.55) for 6; or £14 ($20.30), £24 ($34.80), £30 ($43.50) and £42 ($60.90), respectively, for kids. Like any pass, you have to be pretty energetic to make it pay. The Visitor-Card is only available to travelers from overseas, so you will need to buy the London Pass online before you leave home. Other-wise, you can buy it without the transport element from Exchange International bureaux de change, the London Transport Informa-tion Centre and London Tourist Board office at Heathrow, and at the London Visitor Centre at Waterloo station. Without the transport element, it costs £17.50 ($25.40) for 1 day, £26.50 ($38.45) for 2, £31 ($44.95) for 3, and £43 ($62.35) for 6 for adults; or £12 ($13.05), £19

($27.55), £22.50 ($32.65) and £27 ($39.15) for children.

12. International phone calls are exorbitant. Though using a calling card overseas usually carries a surcharge, it's worth checking it out before leaving home: American Express cardholders should ask about the charges using the company's "Connections" plan. Also see what AT&T, MCI, and Sprint have to offer and whether it's worth switching your residential service to one of them.

Much less hassle is the traveler's friend, **eKit** (www.ekit.com)—both the Youth Hostel Association and Council Travel offer their own branded versions. Join for free on the Web, and you'll get free e-mail, cheap access to voice-mail and to a "travel vault"—a secure place online to store passport and credit-card details, medical records, and so on—and super-cheap international calling rates. The lowest BT charges are only available on weekends. eKit has one rate 24 hours a day, but you will have to pay for a local call to access the cheapest discount price. I've totaled that up, assuming you'll probably be using a pay-phone, in this per-minute comparison: 21p (BT) and 11p (eKit) to the U.S., 21p (BT) and 21p (eKit) to Canada, 44p (BT) and 21p (eKit) to Australia and 44p (BT), and 29p (eKit) to New Zealand. The only catch is that lines do get jammed, usually just when you want to call home.

## ONCE YOU ARRIVE

13. Take public transport from the airport into the city. The Pic-cadilly Line on the Underground runs directly from Heathrow to Central London and costs only £3.60 ($5.20), instead of the £40

($58) or more that a taxi would cost. That saves you over half a day's budget.

14. Don't use traveler's checks or moneychangers like American Express and other bureaux de change. Instead, go to an overseas ATM and withdraw money from your account at home (if you can). You'll get a much better deal on the exchange rate. Do check with your bank first to find out what kind of fee you'll be charged for this service. Above all, don't draw cash on a credit card; you'll pay exorbitant interest rates.

## ACCOMMODATIONS

15. When you're looking for a hotel, try a university area like Blooms-bury first. Other London neighborhoods worth investigating for a good supply of budget hotels are Paddington, Bayswater, Victoria, and Earl's Court. Many options in these and other budget neighborhoods are listed in the London Tourist Board's free publication, *Where to Stay on a Budget.* It's available from British Tourist Authority offices (see "Visitor Information," below) or by calling ✆ **020/7932-2000.**

16. Think about what you really want in a hotel room. If a private bathroom isn't crucial to you, you can save anywhere from £10 to £20 ($14.50 to $29) a night.

17. Negotiate the price. Check if the management will give you a discount for staying 3 nights or more. Suggest trade-offs—a lower price for a smaller room or a room minus TV, and so on. Ask for an old-style per-person (not room) rate: On a tight budget, a couple may be able to downgrade to a 4-foot-wide bed normally used as a single; with a bit more cash, you could get a good rate on a triple. If you're on a hotel-lined street like

Sussex Gardens in Paddington, or Ebury Street near Victoria, keep checking out rooms until you find one you like for your price.

18. Think about alternatives to hotels and guesthouses. Many Londoners offer bed-and-breakfast in their homes, a cozy option that costs as little as £40 ($58) a night for two people in attractive West London through **Host and Guest Service** (✆ **020/7385-9922;** www.host-guest.co.uk). Other similar services include **At Home in London** (✆ 020/8748-1943; www.athomeinlondon.co.uk), which offers rooms from £52 ($75.40) in West London, and **Uptown Reservations** (✆ 020/7351-3445; www.uptownres.co.uk), with rooms from £90 ($130.50) in central London.

19. Or be even braver and do a house swap, which costs nothing once you've paid the matchmaking service's fee: $30 a year through U.S.-based **HomeExchange. COM** (✆ **805/898-9660;** www.homeexchange.com).

20. Depending on your threshold of pain, consider staying at a youth hostel, or at one of the dozens of university dorms. **High Holborn Residence** charges £57 to £67 ($82.65–$97.15) for a twin, and provides two TV lounges, a bar with two pool tables, table tennis, 24-hour Laundromat, and a computer room.

21. Don't call home from a hotel phone unless you can access USA Direct or a similar company, and even then, check to see if there's a charge for the connection. Similarly, don't call direct from a pay phone, which may connect to carriers charging super-high prices.

## DINING

22. Stay at a hotel providing a full breakfast, not the continental one

that hotels are switching to now. We've noted which still serve the traditional cereals, bread, fruit, bacon, eggs, sausage, mushrooms, and tomatoes. That would cost you at least £6 ($8.70) a head outside the hotel.

23. Bring a knife, fork, plate, and corkscrew so that you can feast on delights from the splendid food halls at Harrods, Fortnum & Mason, and Selfridges; on simpler fare from Tesco Metro and Marks & Spencer; or the super-fresh produce from the city's farmers' markets.

24. If spreading your own butter is not your style, then check out the ever-expanding range of budget eating options, such as one of the four SOUP Works branches around Soho and Covent Garden, where prices start at £1.50 ($2.20) a cup.

25. At many a London restaurant, you'll find fixed-price and pre-theater menus. Depending on the neighborhood, a two-course meal could cost as little as £6 ($8.70), and many are £10 to £15 ($14.50–$21.75). Even Nico Ladenis does lunch and early-bird supper at his new Incognico restaurant for £12.50 ($18.15). Note, though, that most of these menus offer a limited choice— that's why they're the price they are.

26. At many restaurants, service is included—don't make the mistake of tipping twice.

## GETTING AROUND TOWN

27. Walk—it's the best way to explore the city and meet the locals. London is big, but it only takes a little forethought to schedule sights, shops, and meals by neighborhood. That way, you can explore on foot and save on Tube costs, as well as on wasted downtime.

28. If walking's not for you, take advantage of any discounts on public transport. Travelcards (see tip 10, above, and "Getting Around," in chapter 3) allow you to ride the buses and Underground throughout the two zones of Central London for £4 ($5.80) a day and £18.90 ($27.40) a week. They make sightseeing so much more spontaneous, too.

29. For London's cheapest tour, ride the no. 11 bus from Liverpool Street to Fulham Broadway, or the new **R1 Riverbus** service from Covent Garden to the British Airways London Eye, Tate Modern, the Globe, and over Tower Bridge to the Tower of London. Or any other route, for that matter. With a travelcard, you can go wherever you please inside the zones to which it applies.

## SIGHTSEEING & ENTERTAINMENT

30. Surf **www.londonfreelist.com**. It lists 1,500 permanently good deals and diary date specials, most of which are free, and none costing more than £3 ($4.35), from famous London attractions to local neighborhood events— jumble and car boot sales; fetes and festivals; and so on.

31. From the end of last year, all the national museums have ditched their admission charges, for students, seniors, children, and generally expensive adults! In addition, many museums and galleries put on tours, talks, hands-on workshops and other entertainment to engage the public's interest. It's like sightseeing with knobs on, and lots of it is free.

32. Make creative sightseeing choices. Some of the best things in life are free. A walk down any street in London is bound to turn up several buildings marked with blue plaques, showing someone famous once lived there. No one

can charge you for looking, so enjoy the architecture. Oh, and do make sure to walk across the marvelous Millennium Bridge (assuming they've sorted out the swinging hammock effect!).

33. If you go to the park, opt for the classic iron bench, not a deck chair where bum-space costs money.

34. Stand and stare at the host of festivals and ceremonial events: the Changing of the Guard at Buckingham Palace, St. James's Palace and Whitehall; the Lord Mayor's Show; the Notting Hill Carnival; and a year-long list of many more (see "Calendar of Events," for details). You can enjoy the entertainment in the Piazza at Covent Garden any day—fire-eaters, mime artists, a jazz trio, who knows what.

35. Take a seat in the galleries at the Old Bailey in the City, the Royal Courts of Justice in the Strand, and of course, the Houses of Parliament. They're all free and will give you a glimpse both into the past and into the institutions and social issues of contemporary London.

36. Visit a legion of long-dead celebrities at London's cemeteries. And not just High Gate—Brompton Cemetery on Old Brompton Road, Hampstead Cemetery on Fortune Green Road, and the Dissenters' Graveyard at Bunhill Fields in the City. The Pet Cemetery in Kensington Gardens was the fashionable place to bury noble and not-so-noble cats and dogs, from Victorian times until 1867. Call ahead for permission to visit (© **020/7298-2117**).

## NIGHTLIFE

37. Go to nightclubs early or very late to get a discount. For instance, **Bar Rumba** has a happy hour Monday to Thursday, 5 to 9pm, and there's no cover charge then. Also clip out the Privilege Pass, printed weekly in listings magazine *Time Out.* And check Tower Records in Piccadilly Circus for cheap-deal flyers, which some of the clubs also post on their websites.

38. Queue at the **tkts** kiosk in Leicester Square for half-price West End theater tickets. Or pop into an Internet cafe, and surf **www.lastminute.com** for right-now discounts. There are five handy branches of **easyEverything** (see "Surf 'n' Slurp @ the Best Internet Cafes," in chapter 5).

39. Go to matinees instead of evening performances. A top-price matinee will cost at least £5 ($7.25) less than a top-price evening ticket.

40. On Monday nights, when all tickets are only £5 ($8), go to the Royal Court Theatre, which offers some of the city's most exhilarating and controversial contemporary drama.

41. Think laterally about what constitutes an entertainment venue! **Borders** stages live music, readings, and talks usually at 6:30pm. Events at **Waterstone's** bookstore tend to start around 7pm and most are free too. (For both, see chapter 7).

42. Hunt down those free concerts. In churches at lunchtime, in the foyers of the Royal Festival Hall, at the Royal Opera House, and at London's many drama and music schools. For example, students of Trinity College give free concerts in Hinde Street Church on most Thursday lunchtimes during term. Call these places for information: the **Guildhall School of Music and Drama,** the Barbican, EC1 (© **020/7628-2571;** www.gsmd.ac.uk); **Royal Academy of**

**Music,** Marylebone Rd., NW1 (© **020/7873-7373;** www.ram. ac.uk); or **Trinity College of Music,** 11–13 Mandeville Place, W1 (© **020/7935-5773;** www. tcm.ac.uk).

43. At many a jazz or other music club, sitting at the bar instead of at a table can save you anywhere from £6 to £12 ($8.70–$17.40) cover charge.

44. London has developed a happy-hour culture. Many bars offer discounted drinks—cocktails are the hip tipple these days—usually between 5:30 and 7:30pm, with prices slashed by 30% to 50%.

## SHOPPING

45. Hang out at the outdoor markets: Camden Town on the weekends for a youth-oriented avant-garde experience akin to Canal Street in New York City; Bermondsey and Portobello for antiques; and Borough Market and the city's new farmers' markets for mouthwatering fresh produce.

46. Come to London in January, and shop in the sales. Virtually every store of every description knocks down its prices, and Londoners indulge in a frenzy of post-Christmas spending.

47. Check if there's one of the grab-and-shop designer sales on during your stay. Mens- and womenswear is 40% to 80% off during these warehouse-style jamborees, put on by one company at a photographic studio near King's Cross and another at the Old Truman Brewery in Brick Lane (see "Regular Sales" under "Fashion," in chapter 7).

48. Check out department store Debenhams (see chapter 7), as well as high street fashion chains like Top Shop: They've invited big name designers to create exclusive collections for them, at unexclusive prices.

49. Trek a few extra Tube stops to find 25% to 80% discount on ends of lines at the Burberry factory shop, or, for china and glass, Villeroy & Boch.

50. Get your VAT refund—a whopping 17.5%. Fill out the appropriate forms in the shop; get the form and your receipt stamped at customs; and mail them back to the retailer.

## 3 Visitor Information

Information about London and traveling elsewhere in the country can be obtained from the **British Tourist Authority (BTA).** The BTA has two offices open to the public in the United States. The main one at 7th Floor, 551 Fifth Ave., at 45th St., New York, NY 10176 (© **800/ GO2BRITAIN** or 212/986-2266), operates Monday to Friday from 9am to 6pm. Office hours at 625 N. Michigan Ave., Suite 1001, Chicago, IL 60611 (© **800/462-2748**) are 9am to 5pm. The BTA website has sections tailored to each visitor nationality, so surf **www.visitbritain.com.**

You can also buy the following passes at the **British Travel Shop** next to the Manhattan BTA office: **London for Less** discount card to major London attractions (See tip 8, above) or order this by credit card from © **888/GO-FOR-LESS** (www. for-less.com); the **Great British Heritage Pass** (See tip 9, above), which gives you free entry into around 600 historic properties across the country, or call BritRail (© **866/ BRITRAIL** or 877/677-1066; www. britrail.net).

The BTA also has offices in **Australia,** at Level 16, Gateway, 1

Macquarie Place, Sydney, NSW 2000 (© **02/9377-4400**); in **Canada,** at 5915 Airport Rd., Suite 120, Mississauga, Ontario, L4V 1T1 (© **888/ VISITUK** or 905/405-1840); in **Ireland,** at 18–19 College Green, Dublin 2 (© **01/670-8000**); and in **New Zealand,** at 17th floor, 151 Queen St., Auckland 1 (© **09/ 303-1446**).

In London, visit the main British Tourist Authority office in the **Britain Visitor Centre,** 1 Regent St., SW1 (no phone). It's open Monday to Friday 9:30am to 6:30pm, Saturday and Sunday 10am to 4pm (Saturday 9am to 5pm, June to October). It has a Globaltickets booking service for theater, sightseeing, and events; a bureau de change; and a Thomas Cook hotel and travel reservations office.

## 4 Entry Requirements & Customs

### DOCUMENTS

Citizens of the United States, Canada, Australia, and New Zealand need only a valid passport to enter Great Britain.

### CUSTOMS

**INTO THE U.K.** Overseas visitors are allowed to import duty-free either 200 cigarettes, or 100 cigarillos, or 50 cigars, or 250 grams of tobacco; 2 liters of still table wine plus 1 liter of alcoholic drinks over 22% volume, or 2 liters of alcoholic drinks under 22%; 60cc of perfume and 250cc of eau de cologne. Other items can be imported free of tax, provided they're for personal use or, in the case of gifts, do not exceed £145 ($336) in value. Live animals, plants, and produce are forbidden. So are counterfeit and copied goods, and anything made from an endangered species: Leave your fake Rolex and your ivory jewelry at home.

**FOR U.S. CITIZENS** Returning **U.S. citizens** who've been away for 48 hours or more are allowed to bring back, once every 30 days, $400 worth of merchandise duty free, plus 100 cigars, 200 cigarettes, and 1 liter of alcohol. You'll be charged a flat rate of 10% duty on the next $1,000 worth of purchases. Be sure to have your receipts handy. Pre-register on a form 4457 any valuable personal items you're taking with you, especially those not made in the U.S. (a Japanese laptop, for instance), to smooth the

journey back through United States customs. On gifts mailed home, the duty-free limit is $100. You cannot bring fresh foodstuffs into the country; tinned foods, however, are allowed. The **U.S. Customs Service** publishes a useful free pamphlet *Know Before You Go*: call © **202/354-1000,** or read it on the website (www. customs.ustreas.gov/travel/know.htm).

**FOR CANADIANS** For a summary of **Canadian** rules, read the booklet *I Declare* (publication no. RC4044), issued by **Revenue Canada** (© **800/ 461-9999;** www.ccra-adrc.gc.ca). The personal exemption is C$750, and you can bring back duty free 200 cigarettes, 200 grams of tobacco, 50 cigars, and 1.5 liters of wine or 1.14 liters of liquor. In addition, you're allowed to mail gifts worth up to C$60 per package to Canada from abroad, provided they're unsolicited and don't contain alcohol or tobacco (write on the package "Unsolicited gift, under $60 value"). You should declare all valuables on the Y-38 form before leaving Canada, including serial numbers on things like expensive foreign cameras. *Note:* The C$750 exemption can be used only once a year and only after an absence of 7 days.

**FOR AUSTRALIANS** The duty-free allowance in **Australia** is A$400 or, for those under 18, A$200. Personal property mailed back from England should be marked "Australian goods returned" to avoid duty. Upon returning to Australia, citizens can bring in 250 cigarettes or 250 grams of loose tobacco, and 1,125 milliliters of alcohol. If you're returning with valuable goods you already own, such as foreign-made cameras, you should file form B263. And you must declare all foodstuffs, even tins. There's a helpful booklet, *Know Before You Go,* available from **Australian Customs Services** (© **1/300-363-263;** www.customs. gov.au/travel/know.htm) and overseas consulates.

**FOR NEW ZEALANDERS** The duty-free allowance for **New Zealand** is NZ$700. Citizens over 16 can bring in 200 cigarettes, or 50 cigars, or 250 grams of tobacco (or a mixture of all three if their combined weight doesn't exceed 250 grams); plus 4.5 liters of wine or beer, and 1.125 liters of liquor. Any excess will be subject to duty and GST, where applicable, but Customs will only collect combined charges of over NZ$50. Most questions are answered in a free pamphlet, *Advice to Travellers,* available at consulates, and from New Zealand Customs: (© **0800/428-786** or 9/300-5399; www.customs.govt.nz/ travhome/advice1.htm).

## 5 Money
## CURRENCY
**POUNDS & PENCE** January 1, 2002, is €-Day, when the 12 countries that have signed up for European Monetary Union launch the euro as legal tender. There will be a phasing in period, but within 2 months their respective national currencies will all have ceased to be legal tender. Some posher London shops, such as Selfridges and Harrods, say they may have to accept the devilish new European currency. Otherwise, nothing is changing here because Britain is still treating EMU like a spectator sport. The British **pound** (£), a small, thick, pale-yellow coin, is divided into 100 pence (pennies). These come in 1p

### The British Pound & the U.S. Dollar

At the time of writing, $1 = approximately 70p (or $1.45 = £1), and this was the rate used to calculate the dollar values in this book (rounded to the nearest nickel). Exchange rates are volatile. If you have access to the Web, you can get the right-now equivalents at **www.xe.net/currency**.

| U.K.£ | U.S.$ | U.K.£ | U.S.$ |
|-------|-------|-------|-------|
| .05 | .07 | 6.00 | 8.70 |
| .10 | .15 | 7.00 | 10.15 |
| .25 | .36 | 8.00 | 11.60 |
| .50 | .73 | 9.00 | 13.05 |
| .75 | 1.10 | 10.00 | 14.50 |
| 1.00 | 1.45 | 15.00 | 21.75 |
| 2.00 | 2.90 | 20.00 | 29.00 |
| 3.00 | 4.45 | 25.00 | 36.00 |
| 4.00 | 5.80 | 30.00 | 45.00 |
| 5.00 | 7.25 | 35.00 | 50.75 |

| What Things Cost in London | U.S.$ |
|---|---|
| Taxi from Heathrow Airport to London | 58.00 |
| Underground from Heathrow to central London | 5.20 |
| Local telephone call | .29 |
| Double room at Hart House (splurge) | 152.25 |
| Double room at Travel Inn, County Hall | 108.70 |
| Fish and chips for one, at The Rock & Sole Plaice | 10.15 |
| Lunch for one at most pubs | 7.25 |
| Celebrity-chef set lunch for one, at Criterion Brasserie | 21.70 |
| Pint of beer | 2.60 |
| Coca-Cola in a restaurant | 1.45 |
| Coca-Cola in a can | .75 |
| Roll of ASA 400 film, 24 exposures | 5.80 |
| Admission to Tate Modern | Free |
| Walking tour | 7.20 |
| Movie ticket | 12.35 |
| Cheapest evening seat at *Mamma Mia!* in the West End | 26.85 |
| Can of Heinz Baked Beans | .50 |

and 2p copper coins, and the silvery 5p, 10p, and 7-sided 20p and 50p coins. There are also large two-tone £2 coins. Notes are issued in £5, £10, £20, and £50 denominations.

## CREDIT CARDS/ATMS

All major credit cards are widely accepted. However, be aware that budget hotels and restaurants often refuse American Express and Diners Club because of the merchant charges. In England, MasterCard is also called Access. Using plastic can be economical as well as convenient. Credit cards eliminate commissions for currency exchange. They also allow for delayed billing, which can work out to your advantage or disadvantage, depending on whether the dollar goes up or down with time.

Similarly, today you'll save money if you use an ATM rather than convert your home currency at a traditional bureau de change. The fees are generally lower and also the exchange rate is the "wholesale" rate, which is better.

Check with your bank before you leave about any charges, daily withdrawal limit, and whether you need a new pin number. It will also supply a list of overseas ATMs. To find out which overseas banks belong to the **CIRRUS** network, call © **800/ 424-7787** (www.mastercard.com/ atm). For **Visa Plus,** call © **800/ 843-7587**(www.visa.com/pd/atm).

## TRAVELER'S CHECKS

Although ATMs are an easier and cheaper way to get cash, some more safety-conscious travelers may prefer to stick to traveler's checks in foreign currencies, which are still easily exchanged in London. Banks and companies like American Express and Thomas Cook offer the best rates. *Beware:* Private currency-exchange businesses that stay open late charge high commissions.

Sterling traveler's checks are accepted at most shops, restaurants, hotels, theaters, and attractions, except the smaller ones of all the

> **Tips   No Commission, Thank You!**
>
> Another benefit of the London Pass is free currency swapping at any branch of Exchange International, of which there are 17 in central London, and one each at Gatwick and Heathrow. There is also a commission-free deal with a London for Less card and guidebook, at Travelex.

above. But there are two drawbacks to carrying them. First, you'll have to exchange your money into pounds at home, where the transaction usually proves more expensive than it would in London. Second, you'll have to re-exchange unused pounds after the trip and pay again.

## 6 When to Go

Spring and fall are the best seasons for avoiding the hordes that descend on the major sights in summer. In winter, the weather in London can be very dreary—January and February are particularly grim—but the cultural calendar is rich, and the attractions much more peaceful.

If you're traveling with kids, it's a good idea to aim for English school holidays, including the 1-week mini-break in the middle of each of the three terms, as museums, galleries, and attractions put on extra fun. And there are lots of fairs, festivals, and special events. Not every school operates to exactly the same calendar but these dates for 2002 cover the spread of options: spring half-term, February 18 to February 22; Easter holidays, March 25 to April 5; summer half-term, May 27 to June 7; summer

holidays, July 19 to September 4; winter half-term, October 21 to November 1; and the Christmas holiday starts on December 20.

### THE CLIMATE

London's infamous Jack the Ripper–friendly fog was never fog at all. It was the mucky exhaust from coal fires. Air-pollution controls long ago made it an offense to use anything but smokeless fuel, so "fog" is no longer in the forecast. Rain, drizzle, and showers are, of course. A typical weather forecast any time of year predicts "scattered clouds with sunny periods and showers, possibly heavy at times." Temperatures are mild and rarely go below freezing in winter or above 75° Fahrenheit in summer—although there've been some major heat waves recently.

### London's Average Daytime Temperature (°F) & Rainfall (inches)

|          | Jan | Feb | Mar | Apr | May | June | July | Aug | Sept | Oct | Nov | Dec |
|----------|-----|-----|-----|-----|-----|------|------|-----|------|-----|-----|-----|
| Temp.    | 40  | 40  | 44  | 49  | 55  | 61   | 64   | 64  | 59   | 52  | 46  | 42  |
| Rainfall | 2.1 | 1.6 | 1.5 | 1.5 | 1.8 | 1.8  | 2.2  | 2.3 | 1.9  | 2.2 | 2.5 | 1.9 |

### PUBLIC HOLIDAYS

Businesses are closed on Christmas Day, for Boxing Day on December 26, and on New Year's Day, January 1. If any of these dates fall on a Saturday and/or Sunday, then the following Monday and/or Tuesday becomes a public holiday. A high proportion of offices, though not stores, actually close for the whole week between Christmas and New Year. In Britain, Good Friday is a public holiday as well as Easter Monday. There are also three bank holidays, on the first and (usually) last Mondays in May, and the last Monday in August. In 2002, however, the second May bank holiday has been put back to the first weekend in June, with Tuesday tacked onto the end of it, to celebrate the Queen's Golden Jubilee. In London, shops, restaurants, museums, and other attractions tend to be much less quick to shut down, but there's no fixed policy. So call to check. For school holidays, see the introduction to this section above.

## LONDON CALENDAR OF EVENTS

Dates given below are current for 2002 as of press time, but are subject to change.

### January

**New Year's Day Parade.** The biggest in the world, apparently, as 10,000 musicians, dancers, acrobats, cheerleaders, clowns, and carnival floats set off at noon from Parliament Square. January 1.

**Charles I Commemoration.** Banqueting House, Whitehall. Hundreds of men march through Central London, starting at 11:30am at St. James's Palace, dressed as cavaliers to mark the anniversary of the 1649 execution of King Charles I. January 27.

### February

**Great Spitalfields Pancake Day Race.** Teams of four run in relays, doing that pancake-tossing thing. Noon on Shrove Tuesday (40 days before Easter) at Old Spitalfields Market, Brushfield St., E1 (📞 020/ 7375-0441). Why not join in? February 12.

**Chinese New Year Parade.** Chinatown, at Gerrard and Lisle streets. Festive crowds line the streets of Soho to watch the famous Lion Dancers and browse stalls crammed with crafts and delicacies. February 17.

### March

**The Oxford & Cambridge Boat Race.** The dark and light blues compete over a 4-mile course along the Thames from Putney to Mortlake. The race has been held since 1829, and crowds line the towpaths for the 3pm start to cheer the teams on (**www.theboatrace. org**). March 30.

### April

**Flora London Marathon.** Almost 30,000 serious athletes and nutcases dressed up as chickens run 26 miles, from Greenwich to The Mall, SW1. The start is staggered from 9am (📞 020/7620-4117; www.londonmarathon.co.uk). April 14.

### May

**Museums & Galleries Month.** Thousands of attractions all over Britain put on special exhibitions and events linked to common guiding themes (**www.24hourmuseum. org.uk**). All month.

**May Fayre & Puppet Festival.** Procession at 10am; service at St. Paul's Covent Garden at 11:30am; then Punch & Judy until 6pm at this church where Samuel Pepys watched England's first show in 1662 (📞 020/7375-0441). Usually second Sunday in May.

**BOC Covent Garden Festival.** A celebration of the singing voice from cabaret to opera, in lovely old venues around the neighborhood (📞 020/7413-1410; www.cgf.co. uk). Last 3 weeks of May.

**Chelsea Flower Show.** This international spectacular features the best of British gardening, with displays of plants and flowers for all seasons, set in the beautiful grounds of the Chelsea Royal Hospital. For ticket information, write Shows Department, Royal Horticultural Society, Vincent Square, London SW1P 2PE (📞 020/7834-4333; www.rhs.org. uk). Tickets go on sale in late November. May 21 to 24.

## June

**Royal Academy Summer Exhibition.** The world's largest open art exhibition and a great time to hear the critics at their catty best. Call ✆ **020/7300-8000** for info (www. royalacademy.org.uk). June through July.

**Queen's Golden Jubilee.** To celebrate the 50-year reign of Elizabeth II, the powers that be have shunted the Whitsun bank holiday back one week and tacked the Tuesday onto the end of it, to make a really long weekend. For full details of how London and Her Maj plan to mark the occasion, check out chapter 6. June 4 and 5 (2002 only).

**The Derby.** Pronounced "darby," this is one of the highlights of the flat racing season, at Epsom Racecourse in Surrey. Posh frocks, corporate suits, and much too much champagne, darling. (✆ **01372/ 726311;** www.epsomderby.co.uk). June 7 and 8.

**Meltdown.** The Royal Festival Hall on the South Bank invites a celebrity artistic director (Robert Wyatt last year) to host his or her dream festival, pulling together any art forms and performers they choose. (✆ **020/7960-4242;** www. sbc.org.uk). Usually the last 3 weeks of June.

**Spitalfields Festival.** Hawksmoor's Christ Church, Spitalfields, is the principle venue for a 3-week festival of medieval and early chamber music, new choral commissions, and much more, including walks and talks, some of which are free (✆ **020/7377-1362;** www. spitalfieldsfestival.org.uk). Usually starts 2nd week of June.

**Trooping the Colour.** Horse Guards Parade, Whitehall. On the Saturday closest to her official birthday, Elizabeth II inspects her regiments from an open carriage and receives the salute as they parade their colors before her. Quintessential English pageantry that still draws big crowds—many of them waiting to see a wretched young soldier faint in the heat under his ridiculous bearskin hat. Tickets are free and are allocated by ballot. Apply in writing between January and the end of February, enclosing an International Reply Coupon (available at most post offices) to: The Ticket Office, HQ Household Division, Chelsea Barracks, London SW1H 8RF. Canadians should apply to Royal Events Secretary, Canada House, Trafalgar Square, London SW1Y 5BJ. June 16.

**Royal Ascot.** A 4-day midweek event held at Ascot Racecourse in Berkshire. The glamorous event of the racing season, as renowned for its fashion extravaganzas as for its high racing standards. The royal family attends. (✆ **01344/876456;** www.ascot.co.uk). June 18 to 21.

**The Covent Garden Flower Festival.** A free extravaganza of flowers, arts, and entertainment in Covent Garden Piazza, celebrating the rich local cultural life (✆ **09064/ 701777;** www.cgff.co.uk). June 19 to 23.

**City of London Festival.** A 3-week extravaganza of over 100 events, covering the whole musical spectrum, at venues from St. Paul's Cathedral to City livery company halls not normally open to the public (✆ **020/7377-0540;** www.colf. org). Usually from the 3rd week of June.

**London Mardi Gras.** A huge gay and lesbian costumed march and parade from Hyde Park to Parliament Square is followed by live music, dancing, and general over-indulgence, plus a blessing tent, at a ½-day party in Finsbury Park. Note, this venue may change in 2002 (© **020/7494-2225;** www. londonmardigras.com). Usually last Saturday of June.

**Wimbledon Lawn Tennis Championships.** This is a thrilling event where the posh and the people rub shoulders, and you can get right up close to the world's top tennis players. For full admission details, see "Spectator Sports," in chapter 6. June 24 to July 7.

### July

**Greenwich & Docklands International Festival.** Ten days packed with music, dance, and theater in historic buildings by the Thames (© **020/8305-1818;** www.festival. org). Usually from the end of June.

**Henley Royal Regatta.** A serious international rowing competition—the course covers more than a mile, against the current—with serious champagne socializing on the side. Held at Henley-on-Thames, Oxfordshire. Tickets are obtainable from the Secretary (© **01491/ 572153;** www.hrr.co.uk). July 3 to 7.

**Henry Wood Promenade Concerts.** Famous summer musical season at Royal Albert Hall. Dating back to 1895, it runs the gamut from ancient to modern classics, and jazz, too. It's only £3 ($4.35) to rough it with the promenaders on the floor of the hall (© **020/ 7589-8212;**www.royalalberthall. com or www.bbc.co.uk/proms). Mid-July to mid-September.

### August

**Teddy Bears Picnic.** Around 1,000 kids and their furry friends enjoy free entertainment, from face-painting to workshops, at Battersea Park (© **020/8871-7117**). Usually 1st Friday afternoon in August.

**Great British Beer Festival.** Organized by the Campaign for Real Ale. Olympia Exhibition Centre overflows with over 500 different ales, beers, ciders, and perries, brewed the traditional way. (© **01727/867201;** www.gbbf. org). Usually 1st week of August.

**The Notting Hill Carnival.** One of the largest street festivals in the world, attracting more than half a million people. Expect live reggae, steel bands, and soul music, great Caribbean food, and a charged atmosphere—sometimes over-charged because it is much too big a crowd crammed into too small a space. Moves to alter the route failed last year, but they haven't gone away. Check the listings magazines for details. August 25 to 26.

### September

**Thames Festival.** Fireworks, theatrical shows, sculpture, art exhibitions, bankside entertainment, a river pageant, and torch-lit procession (© **020/7401-2255;** www.coinstreetfestival.org). September 15.

**London Open House Weekend.** A pat on the back for centuries of British architecture, as over 400 London buildings usually closed to visitors throw open their doors for the weekend, for free! Call © **09001/600061** (www. londonopenhouse.org). September 21 to 22.

**Soho Jazz Festival.** Eleven-day feast of jazz in local bars, cafes, and clubs (© **020/7434-3995;** www. sohojazzfestival.co.uk). September 26 to October 6.

### October

**Pearlies Harvest Festival.** London's famous Pearly Kings and Queens, with their fabulous coats encrusted with buttons, celebrate Harvest Festival at St. Martin-in-the-Fields, in

Trafalgar Sq., SW1 (© **020/ 7766-1100**). Usually 1st Sunday in October.

**Chelsea Crafts Fair.** The largest such fair in Europe: contact the Crafts Council for details (© **020/ 7278-7700**; www.craftscouncil. org.uk). Takes place during the last 2 weeks of October.

### November

**State Opening of Parliament,** Whitehall and Parliament Square. Although the ceremony itself is not open to the public, crowds pack the parade route to see the royal procession (© **020/7291-4272**; www. parliament.uk). Late October or early November.

**London to Brighton Veteran Car Run.** More than 300 veteran cars compete in this 57-mile run from London's Hyde Park to Brighton. Staggered start from 7:30 to 9am (© **01753/681736**). November 3.

**Fireworks Night.** Hyde Park, Battersea Park, and other public space in London. Commemorates the "Gunpowder Plot," a Roman Catholic conspiracy to blow up King James I and his parliament in 1605. Huge bonfires are lit to burn effigies of the most famous conspirator, Guy Fawkes. Free. November 5 and closest Saturday.

**London Film Festival.** Two-week fest of movies from all over the world, including big name premieres, at the National Film Theatre on South Bank and in West End cinemas (© **020/7928-3232**; www.lff.org.uk). From early November.

**The Lord Mayor's Procession and Show.** Over 100 floats follow the new Lord Mayor in his gilded coach from Guildhall, in the City, to his inauguration at the Royal Courts of Justice in the Strand (© **020/ 7332-1456**; www.lordmayorsshow. org). November 9, from 11am.

### December

**Spitalfields Festival.** A little Christmas sister to main 3-week festival in June, with magical music by candlelight in Christ Church, Spitalfields, (© **020/7377-1362**; www.spitalfieldsfestival.org.uk). Usually week before Christmas.

**Harrods' After-Christmas Sale,** Knightsbridge. Call © **020/7730- 1234** (www.harrods.com) for exact dates and hours. Late December.

**New Year's Eve.** Drunken lemmings party at Trafalgar Square, where the fountains are switched off to prevent drowning and hypothermia. And lots more fun across the city. To find the hottest hotspots, contact the London Tourist Board (© **09068/663344**; www.londontown.com) or the BTA (see "Visitor Information," earlier in this chapter).

**Greenwich & Docklands First Night.** A fiesta of street theater, fireworks, music, and fun, from the afternoon right up to the big moment (© **020/8305-1818**; www.festival.org). December 31.

## 7 Insurance

## HEALTH INSURANCE

Citizens and residents of Australia and New Zealand are entitled to free medical treatment and subsidized dental care while in Britain. Americans and other nationals will usually have to pay up-front, except in accident and emergency departments (until referral). Doctors and hospitals are expensive: Even though it's not required of travelers, we recommend you take out health insurance. Most American travelers are covered by their hometown policies in the event of an accident or sudden illness on vacation. Also, some credit-card companies offer free, automatic travel-accident insurance, up to $100,000, when you buy tickets on their cards. Before spending money on additional protection, check to see that your health maintenance organization (HMO) or insurance carrier will cover you in foreign countries.

## OTHER TRAVEL-RELATED INSURANCE

You can also protect your travel investment by insuring against lost or damaged baggage, and trip cancellation or interruption costs. These are often combined into a single comprehensive plan and sold through travel agents and credit-card companies. Contact the following for more information: **Access America** (© 800/284-8300; www.accessamerica.com); **Travelex** (© 888/457-4602; www.travelex-insurance.com); **Travel Guard International** (© 877/216-4885; www.travel-guard.com); and **Wallach & Co** (© 800/237-6615; www.wallach.com).

## 8 Tips for Travelers with Special Needs

### FOR TRAVELERS WITH DISABILITIES

Before you plan a trip, consider joining **The Society for Accessible Travel & Hospitality (SATH)**, 347 Fifth Ave. Suite 610, New York, NY 10016 (© 212/447-7284; www.sath.org). It costs $45 annually, $30 for seniors and students, to gain access to the society's vast network of connections in the travel industry. It provides information sheets on travel destinations and referrals to tour operators that specialize in traveling with disabilities. The quarterly magazine, *Open World,* is full of good information and resources. New SATH members get a year's free subscription, which would otherwise cost $18 ($35 outside the United States).

For information on traveling in Britain, contact **Holiday Care Services,** 2nd floor, Imperial Buildings, Victoria Road, Horley, RH6 7PZ (© 01293/774535; www.holidaycare.org.uk), between 9am and 5pm on weekdays. The organization publishes 120 information sheets on different topics and regions, for which it charges 50p per sheet. Pay £17.50 ($25.40) to become a U.K. member, £35 ($50.75) if you live overseas, and you'll receive a newsletter and holiday discounts. **Tripscope** (© 08457/585641, or 020/8580-7021 from outside the U.K.) is a very helpful transport-information service for people with disabilities, open Monday to Friday 9am to 4:45pm.

London's major museums and tourist attractions should all now be fitted with wheelchair ramps, but call **Artsline** (© 020/7388-2227) for free advice on accessibility to theaters, galleries, and events around the city—including youth-oriented info. The phone line is open Monday to Friday from 9:30am to 5:30pm. It's common for theaters, nightclubs, and attractions to offer discounts, called "concessions," to people with disabilities. Ask for these before paying full price.

For additional local contacts, check out the **London Tourist Board's** website (www.londontown.com/london forall.phtml).

### FOR GAY & LESBIAN TRAVELERS

**The International Gay & Lesbian Travel Association (IGLTA),** (© 800/448-8550 or 954/776-2626; www.iglta.org), links travelers up with the appropriate gay-friendly service organization or tour specialist. With around 1,200 members, it publishes quarterly newsletters, marketing mailings, and a membership directory updated quarterly. A lot of members are gay or lesbian businesses, but

IGLTA is open to individuals, too, for $150 yearly, plus a $100 joining fee. Contact IGLTA for a list of agencies tied into its information resources. The purely online www.gaytoz.com, www.rainbownetwork.com, and www. queercompany.com are also very comprehensive.

When you get to London, look out for the free *Pink Paper* at gay bars, bookstores, and cafes—head straight for Old Compton Street in Soho. *Boyz* and *QX* are excellent for city listings, gossip, and scenes, and glossy magazine pin-ups. *Time Out* (www. timeout.com) also has a good gay section. And lastly, for advice on pretty much anything, including accommodations, call the 24-hour **Lesbian & Gay Switchboard** (© **020/7837-7324**; www.llgs.org.uk).

We've also reviewed the gay Philbeach Hotel: see "Earl's Court," in chapter 4. And you'll find information on "Gay & Lesbian London," in chapter 8, "London After Dark."

## FOR SENIORS

In Britain, "senior citizen" usually means a woman at least 60 years old and a man at least 65. Seniors often receive the same discounts as students. Some are restricted to British citizens only, but check at all attractions, theaters, and other venues.

Membership of AARP is open to anyone over 50. It costs $10 a year and gives you access to a purchase privilege discount program on hotels, car rentals, tours, and other travel facilities. For information, contact the **American Association of Retired Persons (AARP)**, 601 E St. NW, Washington, DC 20049 (© **800/424-3410**; www.aarp.org). If you're 55 or older, why not check out the educational programs sponsored by **Elderhostel**, 11 Ave. de Lafayette, Boston, MA 02111 (© **877/426-8056**; www.elderhostel.org). It sends thousands of people to school abroad

every year. Courses on literature, art, music, and many other topics last 1 to 4 weeks. Package prices include airfare, meals, lodging, daily instruction, and admission fees. For instance, a 14-night trip called Definitive London cost $2,859 in peak season last year.

## FOR STUDENTS

The **American Institute for Foreign Study,** River Plaza, 9 West Broad St., Stamford, CT 06902 (© **800/727-2437**; www.aifsabroad.com) offers 3- to 12-week study/travel programs, costing from $3,700 to $7,000, including meals and housing. The **Institute for International Education,** 809 United Nations Plaza, New York, NY 10017 (© **212/883-8200**; www.iie.org) also administers student applications for study-abroad programs in England and other European countries. The **Council on International Educational Exchange** (CIEE), International Study Programs, 603 Third Ave., 20th floor, New York, NY 10017 (© **212/822-2755**; www.ciee.org) can offer a term or a whole year at its London study center, which combines Goldsmith College and Imperial College, both parts of the University of London, and the University of Westminster. It is also possible to enroll in summer courses at **Oxford University** (© **01865/270360**; www.ox.ac.uk), and **Cambridge** (© **01954/280398**; www.cam.ac.uk). For the latter, also contact Dr. Joann Painter, 714 Sassafras St., Erie, PA 16501 (© **814/456-0757**).

The **International Student Identity Card (ISIC)** is the only officially acceptable form of student identification, good for discounts on rail passes, plane tickets, theaters, museums, and so on. It has a partnership with eKit (see tip 12, earlier in this chapter) to offer a "communications solution" called ISIConnect for cheap phone calls and free email. You also get basic health and life insurance and a 24-hour help line. If you're no longer a student but are still under 26, you can buy an **International Youth Travel Card,** which will get you the insurance and some of the discounts (but not student admission prices in museums). Both passes cost $22 and are available from CIEE's travel arm, **Council Travel** (© **800/2COUNCIL;** www.counciltravel.com), the biggest specialist agency in the world. Ask for a list of offices in major cities so that you can keep the discounts flowing (and aid lines open) as you travel.

The International Student Travel Confederation website (**www.istc. org**) is a useful source of advice and directions to member organizations all over the world. In London, your best bet is **USIT Campus:** to find out which of its six branches in the capital is the nearest, call © **0870/240-1010** (www.usitcampus.co.uk).

The **University of London Student Union** (**ULU**), Malet Street, WC1 (© **020/7664-2000;** www.ulu. lon.ac.uk), caters to more than 70,000 students and may be the largest of its kind in the world. In addition to a gym and fitness center with squash and badminton courts, the Malet Street building houses several shops, bars, restaurants, a bank, a ticket-booking agency, and an STA travel office. And there's an action-packed schedule of gigs and club nights. Stop by or phone for information on university activities. The student union building is open Monday to Thursday from 8:30am to 11pm, Friday 8:30am to 1am, Saturday 9am to 1am, Sunday 9am to 10:30pm. It is sometimes closed on August weekends. Take the Tube to Goodge Street.

London's youth hostels are not only some of the cheapest sleeps, they're also great spots to meet other student travelers and pick up discounts to local attractions. You have to be a member of **Hostelling International** (**International Youth Hostel Federation**), which you can join at any hostel for $25 adults, $15 for seniors (55-plus), or free if you're under 18. To apply in the United States and make advance international bookings, contact Hostelling International (AYH), 733 15th St. NW, Suite 840, Washington, DC 20005 (© **202/783-6161;** www.hiayh.org). You can also book dorm-beds online and e-mail hostels about other options through the English website (www.yha.org.uk).

## 9 Holiday Packages

Package deals rarely undercut what you'll pay by hunting down the deepest discounts for each separate component of your holiday. However, writing one check after someone else has done all the planning work is a lot less hassle. And the discounts that tour operators and airlines can get with their buying power means you'll be staying in at least a 2- or 3-star hotel, rather than risking the vagaries of a guesthouse. So check the ads in your newspaper's travel section.

Fully shepherded tours—where a group travels together and shares the same preplanned activities—are not only unnecessary for a holiday based mainly in London, but will probably make it harder for you to get the best out of this very vibrant city. Happily, packages don't have to be that regimented. Last year, "budget" tour operator **Cosmos** (© **800/556-5454;** www.globusandcosmos.com) was offering a London at Leisure deal, including Saturday flights, 6 nights accommodation, a ½-day tour, discount vouchers, a London VisitorCard giving a day's free travel on buses and Tubes, and a helpful "host service." It cost $1,430 for two people in January, rising to $2,446 in peak season.

**Tips** **E-Package Deals**

Lots of Frommer's surfers have reported good holiday experiences and good deals from **go-today.com**. So I thought I'd check out how the online holiday company compared to its "regular" terrestrial rivals. Pretty well, is the answer! A 2001 summer special, comprising flights, airport transfers, hotel room and breakfast, plus a dinky welcome pack, came to $1,398 for two people. The site pitches itself at folks who want to drop everything and go, but you can book well in advance. And should, as the price clearly rises with demand (or waning supply, perhaps). When I checked back a week later, the same holiday had gone up to $1,498.

For more information about online travel bargains, consult "Planning Your Trip Online," later in this chapter.

Airline packages can be competitive, too, if you avoid the plushest partner hotels. And they are flexible as to the day and time you can travel and what's included in the deal. You decide whether to buy from the menu of extras, such as tours, sightseeing, theater tickets, and so on. Then you go it alone—no having to dodge irritating new friends at breakfast. The packages below are representative prices quoted at press time for summer season—the two-person price drops by around $600 between October and March—with midweek flights from JFK, airport transfers, taxes, and 6 nights in a hotel with breakfast: **Virgin Atlantic Vacations** (© 888/YESVIRGIN; www.virgin. com/vacations) had an excellent $1,598 deal; **United Airlines** (© 888/ 854-3899; www.unitedvacations. com) sweetened its $1,678 package with a London for Less discount card and guidebook; **British Airways Holidays** (© 800/359-8722; www. britishairways.com/usa) was charging $1,885; **Continental Airlines**

**Vacations** (© 800/772-4622; www. coolvacations.com) was pricier at $2,109; **American Airlines Vacations** (© 800/321-2121; www.aavacations. com) was charging $2,142. **Qantas** sells Jetabout Holidays through travel agents or online (www.qantas.com.au).

**British Travel International** (© 800/327-6097; www.britishtravel. com) can build you a package of discount deals and passes on planes, trains, automobiles, and buses, as well as accommodations. In Australia, contact **Explore Holidays** (© 02/9857-6200; www.explore holidays. com.au). The excellent U.K. travel agent **Trailfinders** (www. trailfinders.com.au) also has five Australian offices and claims to be able to offer up to 75% discount on standard prices when it tailor-makes a vacation. The offices are in Sydney (© 02/9247-7666); Melbourne (© 03/9600-3022); Cairns (© 07/ 4041-1199); Brisbane (© 07/3229-0887); and Perth (© 08/9226-1222). And try Qantas, too (© 1300/ 360-347).

## 10 Getting There

### BY PLANE
More than 90 scheduled airlines serve London, more if you count Gatwick as well as Heathrow. They include these major North American carriers: **American Airlines** (© 800/433-7300;

www.aa.com), **Continental** (✆ **800/ 231-0856**; www.continental.com), **Delta Airlines** (✆ **800/241-4141**; www.delta.com), **Northwest Airlines** (✆ **800/447-4747**; www.nwa.com), **TWA** (✆ **800/892-4141**; www.twa. com), **United Airlines** (✆ **800/ 538-2929**; www.ual.com), and **Air Canada** (✆ **888/247-2262**; www.air canada.ca).

**British Airways** (✆ **800/AIR- WAYS** in North America, 300/ 134011 in Australia, 800/BRITISH in New Zealand; www.britishairways. com) is the largest U.K. airline and goes everywhere, including Australia and New Zealand. **Virgin Atlantic Airways** (✆ **800/862-8621**; www. virgin-atlantic.com) flies from New York and Newark, New Jersey, as well as from Chicago, Boston, Las Vegas, Los Angeles, San Francisco, Orlando, Miami, and Washington, D.C. **Qantas** (✆ **1300/131313**; www.qantas. com) is the national Australian carrier, also serving New Zealand, and it code-shares with many foreign carriers. **Air New Zealand** (✆ **0800/ 737000**; www.airnz.com) flies daily to Heathrow.

## FINDING THE BEST AIRFARE

London's popularity and the number of airlines flying there mean heavy competition for customers. So check local and national newspapers for special promotions and always shop around to find the cheapest seat.

The lowest-priced standard cattle-class fare usually carries some restrictions like advance-purchase, minimum stay, or a Saturday stopover, as well as penalties for altering dates and itineraries. Note, too, that weekday flights are slightly cheaper than weekends, and early mornings cheapest of all.

Make sure to check alternative ticket sources before buying direct from the airline. For instance, consolidators buy blocks of seats and sell them at a discount. Tickets are restrictive, valid only for a particular date or flight, nontransferable, and nonrefundable except directly from the consolidator, and they may also not earn frequent flier miles. There are rarely set advance-purchase requirements; if space is available, you can buy just before you fly. Always pay with a credit card, though, to protect yourself in case the consolidator goes belly up.

The lowest-priced bucket shops are usually local backroom operations with low profiles and overheads. Look for their tiny ads jam-packed with cities and prices in the travel or classified section of your local newspaper. Those that advertise nationally are rarely as competitive, but they often have toll-free telephone numbers and may be more reliable. In 2001, with a reliable consolidator, you could get a high-season, midweek, round-trip ticket to London for **$550,** including taxes. Air India seemed to be most of these guys' hottest deal: **Arrow Travel** (✆ **212/889-2550**); **Cheap Tickets** (✆ **212/570-1179,** 800/377-1000; www.cheaptickets.com); **TFI Tours International** (✆ **212/736-1140** in New York State, or 800/745-8000; www.lowestairprice.com); **Travel Land International Inc.** (✆ **212/ 268-6464**); and **Up & Away Travel** (✆ **212/889-2345**).

*Note:* In this wonderful new electronic world, it's tempting to dispense with human contact altogether. But do call these guys, because I found the instant verbal quote often undercut what I found on their websites.

**CHARTERS**    Another cheap way to cross the Atlantic is on a charter flight. Most operators advertise and sell their seats through travel agents, making them your best source of information on the deals available. **Travac** is a well-known charter company that does deal directly with passengers: it came up with a **$540** (including taxes) midweek, peak-season, return flight from JFK to London last year: call ℭ **800/872-8800** (ℭ 888/872-8327 for current fare quotes; www.thetravelsite.com).

## FLYING INTO HEATHROW

Heathrow is a self-contained, self-sufficient micro-town about 13 miles from the middle of London, due west. As well as shops and restaurants, the airport has every kind of visitor service. You can save a lot of time by sorting things out here before going into the city. The vast majority of flights from North America, Australia, and New Zealand arrive at Terminals 3 and 4. Call **Heathrow** (ℭ **0870/000-0123**; www.baa.co.uk) for any additional information.

**VISITOR INFORMATION** The **Airport Information** desks are at: **Terminal 3 Arrivals,** open daily from 5:30am to 10:30pm; **Terminal 3 Departures,** open daily from 7am to 9:30pm; and **Terminal 4 Arrivals,** open daily from 5:30am to 10:30pm. The **London Tourist Board** has an information center in the Tube station concourse that connects with **Terminals 1, 2, and 3,** open daily from 8am to 6pm (to 7pm, Mon–Sat, June–Sept).

**HOTEL RESERVATIONS** There are **British Hotel Reservation Centre** desks in the arrivals area of every terminal, open daily from 6am to midnight. The booth in the Terminal 4 Tube station opens daily 7am to 10:30pm. In the main Tube station concourse, the hours are 6:30am to 11:30pm. BHRC will book you into any accommodation anywhere, usually scoring big discounts. The nationwide freephone number is ℭ **0800/783-4020** (www.bhrc.co.uk).

**CURRENCY EXCHANGE** **American Express,** Terminal 4, Tube station concourse (ℭ **020/8754-7057**) is open daily from 7am to 7pm. At all other bureaux de change, **British Airports Authority,** which runs Heathrow, guarantees charges will match or beat at least one of Britain's big-four high street banks: for information on special deals, call

---

⟮**Tips**  **Make the Airline Pricing System Work for You**

Increasingly sophisticated reservations software allows the airlines to practice yield management. They juggle twin priorities: filling the plane and making as much profit as possible from each flight. So, airlines constantly adjust the pricing of each seat on a particular flight according to the immediate demand. Save big money either by trawling the Internet, or by talking to a reliable travel agent or one of the companies that specialize in searching out low airfares. The best these guys could do in 2001 for a high-season, midweek, round-trip ticket from JFK to London was **$565**, including taxes: **Air for Less** (ℭ 800/238-8371); **1-800 Fly for Less** (ℭ 800/359-4537); **1-800 Low Air Fare** (ℭ 800/569-2473; www.lowairfare.com); **FareBusters** (ℭ 800/618-0571; www.smartbusinessfares.com); **lowestfare.com** (ℭ 800/497-6678); and **1-800 Fly Cheap** (ℭ 800/359-2432; www.1800flycheap.com).

For more information, consult "Planning Your Trip Online," later in this chapter.

**Tips  Get Rid of Your Luggage**

There are lots of reasons why travelers might want to ditch their trans-atlantic Samsonite! Perhaps you've got a few hours to spare between landing at the airport and checking in to your hotel. Or maybe you've got a hot date on the way . . . Well, Baggage Direct (© **020/8564-4761**) will take up to two suitcases from Heathrow to anywhere in Greater London, for £26 ($37.70).

---

© **0800/844844.** These companies have numerous branches, open daily at both terminals: **Thomas Cook** (© **020/8272-8073** T3 or 020/8272-8100 T4) is open in T3 Arrivals from 5am to 10:30pm, and from 5:30am in T4; and in Departures from 5:30am to 10pm; **Travelex** (© **020/8897-3501,** T3 and T4) never closes in Arrivals, and from 5:30am to 10pm in Departures. There are ATMs throughout the airport.

**CAR RENTALS**  Renting a car for holidays in London is unwise (see "Getting Around," in chapter 3). If you must, however, airport pick-ups are very convenient. The big rental agencies all have branches at Heathrow: **Avis** (© **020/8899-1000**); **Budget Rent-a-Car** (© **020/8750-2511**); **Europcar** (© **020/8897-0811**); and **Hertz** (© **020/8897-2072**).

**GETTING FROM THE AIRPORT TO TOWN**  There are lots of ways to get into London from Heathrow. Children under 5 travel free on most services.

The **Underground** is undoubtedly the best value. There are two airport Tube stations on the Piccadilly Line: one for Terminals 1, 2, and 3, and one for Terminal 4. The journey takes 50 to 60 minutes. Trains leave the airport from 5:08am to 11:49pm and arrive there from 6am to 1:07am (shorter hours on Sun). Heathrow is in zone 6 and therefore not covered by most travelcards. One-way fares from zone 1, or Central London (see "Getting

Around," in Chapter 3), are £3.60 ($5.20) for adults and £1.50 ($2.20) for children aged 5 to 15. If you miss the last Tube, the **N97 night bus** leaves at 20 minutes past the hour and 10 to, from the Central Bus Station, and costs £1.50 ($2.20) for adults and children. Call **London Transport Travel Hotline** (© **020/7222-1234;** www.londontransport.co.uk) for more information.

**Heathrow Express** (© **0845/600-1515;** www.heathrowexpress.co.uk) is the super-luxury, nonstop rail service to Paddington Station. It takes 15 minutes from Terminals 1, 2, and 3, and 20 to 25 minutes from Terminal 4. Trains leave Heathrow from 5:07am to 11:52pm and arrive there from 5:30am to midnight. All major airlines offer full check-in at Paddington—get there at least 2 hours before your flight, 1 hour if you've only got hand luggage. Standard-class one-way tickets cost £12 ($17.40) for adults and £6 ($8.70) for children aged 5 to 15, with discounts for online booking.

National Express (© **08705/747777** info, 08705/808080 bookings; www.gobycoach.com) runs two airport bus services and accepts online bookings. The **Airbus** leaves twice an hour from just outside every Heathrow terminal and goes to 23 stops in Central London. Ask your hotel or B&B if there's one close by, because this may be the most convenient option. The service runs from Heathrow between 5:30am to 10:00pm, and from King's Cross (the last, or first, stop at the London end)

**Tips Smaller Airports**

If you're flying to London on a no-frills flight, you may land at **Stansted** (© 08700/000303; www.baa.co.uk). The quickest way to get into London is the 42-minute train trip on the **Stansted Express** direct from the airport to Liverpool Street station. It runs from 5am to 11pm, every 15 minutes at peak times, otherwise half-hourly, and costs £13 (18.85) one way (© 08457/444422; www.stanstedexpress.com). The National Express **Airbus** (see above) makes the journey to Victoria Station in about 1 hour and 40 minutes and costs £7 ($10.15) one-way. Charters and cheapie airlines also fly into **Luton Airport** (© 01582/405100; www. london-luton.com). The Greenline 757 bus leaves for London once an hour, takes 70 minutes, and charges £8 ($11.60) one-way (© 08706/087261; www.greenline.co.uk). The **Thameslink CityFlier** takes about half an hour from the new Luton Airport Parkway station to King's Cross. There are eight trains an hour from 7am to 6pm Monday to Saturday, then four until 10pm. On Sundays trains run every 10 minutes from 9am to 5pm, then every 15 minutes until 8pm. One-way tickets cost £9.50 ($13.80). Call National Rail Enquiries for further information (© 08457/484950).

between 4am and 8pm. One-way tickets cost £7 ($10.15) for adults and £3 ($4.35) for children ages 5 to 15. The **Hotel Hoppa** runs between each terminal and the main Heathrow hotels from 5:30am to 11:30pm. One-way tickets cost £2.50 ($3.65). One child aged 5 to 15 travels free with each adult.

**Hotelink** (© 01293/552251; www.hotelink.co.uk) is a door-to-door minibus service with desks at Terminals 3 and 4 Arrivals. It runs every 30 minutes from 6am to 2pm daily, then hourly to 10pm, calling at its passengers' hotels only, and costs £14 ($20.30) for a one-way ticket.

**Black taxis** (see "Getting Around," in Chapter 3) are always available at Heathrow. The approximate fare to London is £35 ($56), which is a good value, door-to-door cost if you can fill the cab with the maximum five passengers and still have room for luggage. The taxi desk numbers are: **Terminal 3** (© 020/8745-4655); **Terminal 4** (© 020/8745-7302). To walk smugly past the tedious taxi line,

book ahead with **Black Cab London** (© 877/405-7622 in the U.S., 020/8663-6400 from elsewhere overseas, or 0800/169-5296 in the U.K.; www.blackcablondon.com). The driver will meet you in arrivals and help carry that jumbo Samsonite. Such convenience comes at luxury prices, of course. The ride from Heathrow into Central London will cost £52 ($75.40), instead of £40 ($58).

**SPECIAL NEEDS** There are **Help Points** throughout Heathrow. Use the green telephone to ask for a Help Bus (© 020/8745-5185) to drive you around the airport, for a wheelchair, or just for general assistance. Travelers with disabilities can call the following numbers, in addition to those listed above, for advice or to make pre-arrangements: to pre-book the assistance of a **Skycap porter** (© 020/8745-6011); **Heathrow Travel-Care** (© 020/8745-7495); and **London Transport's Unit for Disabled Passengers** (© 020/7222-5600).

## FLYING INTO GATWICK

There are four ways of making the 25-mile trek into London (© **08700/ 002468**; www.baa.co.uk). The most popular is the **Gatwick Express** train, which takes around 30 minutes to reach Victoria, and costs £10.50 ($15.25) one-way. The station is below the airport, and trains depart every 15 minutes from 6am to 10pm (hourly, on the hour, at other times). The slightly cheaper option is **South Central Trains,** which charges £8.20 ($11.90) one-way and takes 35 to 45 minutes, depending how often it stops between Victoria station and the airport. For information on both, call National Rail Enquiries (© **08457/ 484950**), or pre-book through **www. thetrainline.com**.

You can also take the **Airbus** (© **08705/747777** info, 08705/ 808080 bookings; www.gobycoach. com). The 1½-hour trip costs £7 ($10.15) one-way. Buses leave for Victoria Coach Station from Gatwick's North Terminal hourly. **Hotelink** (© **01293/552251;** www. hotelink.co.uk) runs the same minibus service here as it does at Heathrow, but charging £20 ($29) to take you directly to your hotel, on the half-hour in the summer, on the hour in winter.

## BY TRAIN

Each of London's train stations is connected to a vast bus and Underground network, and there are phones, restaurants, pubs, luggage-storage areas, shops, and London Transport Information Centres at all of them.

If you're **arriving from France,** the fastest way to get to London is by taking the hoverspeed connection between Calais and Dover (see "By Ferry & Hovercraft," below), where you can pick up a train into the city. If you prefer the ease of one-stop travel, you can take the Eurostar train (see below) directly from Paris—or go there and back in a day for a very swanky excursion.

**VIA THE CHUNNEL** The **Eurostar** direct train service runs from Paris Gare Du Nord and Brussels Central Station to Waterloo in London. A fully-flexible round-trip between Paris and London costs $435, but you can cut that back to $101.50 with a 14-day advance purchase ticket (nonrefundable, stay two nights or a Saturday). And there are other options under $290. **Rail Europe** (© **800/ EUROSTAR;** www.raileurope.com) sells Eurostar tickets, but the cheapest it listed was $158 return, so cross-check any quote with Eurostar at © **08705/186186** (www.eurostar. com); in Paris, at © **08/36353535** or 01/53607000; in Brussels, at © **02/ 525-9292** (bookings only, no inquiries).

**FROM ELSEWHERE IN THE U.K.** If you're traveling to London from elsewhere in the United Kingdom,

---

### Onward! Short Hops Around Britain & Across the Channel

If you want to fly to Europe, or even up to Scotland or across to Ireland, check out these no-frills airlines, which all fly from Stansted: **easyJet** (© **0870/600-0000;** www.easyjet.com), also from Gatwick; **Buzz** (© **08702/ 407070;** www.buzzaway.com); **Ryanair** (© **08701/569569;** www.ryanair.ie), also from Luton and Gatwick; and **GO** (© **0906/302-0150;** www.go-fly. com). **Virgin Express** (© **020/7744-0004;** www.virgin-express.com) only flies from Heathrow. Keep an eye out for promotional deals in newspaper ads as lower prices are posted practically every day.

consider buying a **BritRail Classic Pass.** This allows unlimited rail travel anywhere during a set time period (**Eurailpasses** aren't accepted in Britain, although they are in Ireland). A second-class pass costs $265 for 8 days, $400 for 15 days, $500 for 22 days, and $600 for 1 month. Children under 5 travel free. One child aged 5 to 15 can travel free with each adult pass. All additional children pay half price. Seniors qualify for discounts. Travelers between 16 and 25 can purchase a **BritRail Classic Youth Pass,** which allows unlimited second-class travel: $215 for 8 days, $280 for 15 days, $355 for 22 days, or $420 for 1 month. The **Britrail Classic Senior Pass** costs $340, $510, $640, or $760. There are also passes for three or four people traveling in a group, or for people who are only going to roam close to London, the **BritRail South-East** pass (see chapter 9).

You must purchase all special passes before you leave home: in the United States, at the **British Travel Shop** next to the Manhattan BTA office, or those in Australia and New Zealand (see "Visitor Information," above). Or call ✆ **866/BRITRAIL** or 877/677-1066 (www.britrail.net).

## BY BUS

Whether you're coming from the Continent or from another part of the country, London-bound buses almost always go to (and leave from) **Victoria Coach Station,** Buckingham Palace Road, 1 block from the train station.

The **Tourist Trail Pass** is ideal for serious day-trippers and round-Britain tourers. This allows unlimited travel on a set number of days, not necessarily consecutive but falling within a fixed time period: either 2 days to be used within a 3-day period, for £49 ($71.05); 5 days travel, valid for 10, for £85 ($123.25); 8 days, valid for 30, for £135 ($195.75); or 15 days, valid for 30, for £190 ($275.50), or

valid for 60 days, £205 ($297.25). Under-25s and over-50s can buy a discount card for £9 ($13.05), which cuts pass and individual ticket prices by 20% to 30%. You can buy all passes with a credit card, online, or by phone, direct from **National Express** (✆ **08705/808080;** www.gobycoach. com); or, in person, at the Heathrow Central Bus Station and Victoria Coach Station, at National Express offices in St. Pancras station and Earl's Court Tube station, or at any travel agent displaying the National Express logo. The U.S. agent for National Express is **British Travel International** (✆ **800/327-6097;** www. britishtravel.com).

Bus connections to Britain from the Continent are not so much uncomfortable, as mind-blowingly tedious, but it is very cheap compared to the train and plane, except for the no-frills carriers (see above). National Express is part of the **Eurolines** network of 31 companies in 25 countries. Buses leave Victoria for more than 460 destinations in Ireland and mainland Europe. For a serious pilgrimage around Europe, check out the 15-day (youth only), 30-, and 60-day Eurolines Passes, which link you to 46 cities. A 30-day youth pass costs £129 ($187) in winter and £179 ($260) high season. The adult equivalent costs £162 and £222 ($235 and $321.90).

## BY FERRY & HOVERCRAFT

The shortest ferry crossings are also the closest to London: Dover to Calais, and Folkestone to Boulogne. Note that here, too, you pay less traveling out of season, on weekdays, and at unsociable hours, and if you pre-buy tickets rather than just turn up. To have any hope of squeezing on board in the summer and during public holidays, you must book ahead anyway.

Check with the BTA (see "Visitor Information," earlier in this chapter) for a full listing of ferries to the Channel Islands, Ireland, the Isle of Man, and around the host of Scottish islands. All the companies below put together stopover packages if you fancy a continental break from your London holiday. You can also get day-trip deals. And there are discounts for booking online.

**CAR & PASSENGER FERRIES** P&O Stena Line (② 0870/600-0600, or 01304/864003 from outside the U.K.; www.posl.com) operates car and passenger ferries between Dover and Calais, 35 departures a day, with a journey time of 1 hour 25 minutes: Summer one-way tickets cost £132 to £180 ($191–$261) for car and driver, or £26 ($37.70) for an adult foot passenger. **Sea France** (② 08705/711711;** www.seafrance.com) runs 15 departures a day, with a journey time of 1½ hours: One-way peak-season tickets cost £122 to £185 ($177 to $268) for car and driver, £17.50 ($25.40) for an adult foot passenger.

**HOVERCRAFT & SEACATS** Traveling by Hovercraft or SeaCat takes about half the time that a ferry does. For example, a hovercraft crossing from Calais to Dover with **hoverspeed** (② 08702/408070;** www. hoverspeed.co.uk) takes 35 minutes; they have 6 to 12 crossings per day. Their SeaCat crossings take a little longer, about 50 minutes, and there are five departures a day. One-way tickets on both cost £104 to £180

($150.80–$261) for car and driver, and adult foot passengers pay £24 ($34.80).

## BY CAR

If you plan to take a rented car across or under the Channel, check with the rental company about license and insurance requirements before you leave. Hertz runs a scheme called **Le Swap** for passengers taking Le Shuttle, which allows you to switch cars at Calais to keep the local driving position—left- or right-hand.

**LE SHUTTLE** Le Shuttle (② 08705/353535; www.eurotunnel. com) is the Channel Tunnel drive-on train service. Cars, charter buses, taxis, and motorcycles all do just that—drive on at Calais or Folkestone and off at the other end. It operates 24 hours a day, 365 days a year, running every 15 minutes during peak times and at least once an hour at night. The total travel time between the French and English highway system is about 1 hour (35 minutes from platform to platform).

In summer especially, it's sensible to book rather than just turn up, because stand-by queues can be very long and slow. Prices vary according to the season, the day of the week, and the time of day. A late-night/crack-of-dawn round-trip fare would cost you £267 ($387) in the summer. If you make the return trip within 5 days, that plummets to £180 ($261). The single fare is half the price of a round trip.

## 11  Planning Your Trip Online

With a mouse, a modem, and a certain do-it-yourself determination, Internet users can tap into the same travel-planning databases that were once accessible only to travel agents. Sites such as **Travelocity, Expedia,** and **Orbitz** allow consumers to comparison shop for airfares, book flights, learn of last-minute bargains, and reserve hotel rooms and rental cars.

But don't fire your travel agent just yet. Although online booking sites offer tips and hard data to help you bargain shop, they cannot endow you with the hard-earned experience that makes a seasoned, reliable travel agent an invaluable resource, even in the Internet age. And for consumers with a complex itinerary, a trusty travel agent is still the best way to arrange

**Frommers.com: The Complete Travel Resource**

For an excellent travel planning resource, we highly recommend **Arthur Frommer's Budget Travel Online** (www.frommers.com). We're a little biased, of course, but we guarantee you'll find the travel tips, reviews, monthly vacation giveaways, and online-booking capabilities thoroughly indispensable. Among the special features are **Arthur Frommer's Daily Newsletter,** for the latest travel bargains and inside travel secrets; and Frommer's **Destinations archive,** where you'll get expert travel tips, hotel and dining recommendations, and advice on the sights to see for more than 200 destinations around the globe. Once your research is done, the **Online Reservation System** (www.frommers.com/booktravelnow) takes you to Frommer's favorite sites for booking your vacation at affordable prices.

the most direct flights to and from the best airports.

Still, there's no denying the Internet's emergence as a powerful tool in researching and plotting travel time. The benefits of researching your trip online can be well worth the effort:

- **Last-minute specials,** known as "E-savers," such as weekend deals or Internet-only fares, are offered by airlines to fill empty seats. Most of these are announced on Tuesday or Wednesday and must be purchased online. Most are only valid for travel that weekend, but some can be booked weeks or months in advance. Sign up for weekly e-mail alerts at airline websites or check mega-sites that compile comprehensive lists of E-savers, such as Smarter Living (smarterliving.com) or WebFlyer (www.webflyer.com).

- Some sites will send you **e-mail notification** when a cheap fare becomes available to your favorite destination. Some will also tell you when fares to a particular destination are lowest.

- The best of the travel planning sites are now **highly personalized;** they track your frequent-flier miles, and store your seating and

meal preferences, tentative itineraries, and credit-card information, letting you plan trips or check agendas quickly.

- All major airlines offer **incentives**—bonus frequent-flier miles, Internet-only discounts, sometimes even free cellphone rentals—when you purchase online or buy an e-ticket.

- Advances in mobile technology provide business travelers and other frequent travelers with the ability to check flight status, change plans, or get specific directions from handheld computing devices, mobile phones, and pagers. Some sites will e-mail or page a passenger if a flight is delayed.

## TRAVEL PLANNING & BOOKING SITES

The best travel planning and booking sites cast a wide net, offering domestic and international flights, hotel and rental-car bookings, plus news, destination information, and deals on cruises and vacation packages. Keep in mind that free (one-time) registration is often required for booking. Because several airlines are no longer willing to pay commissions on tickets sold by online travel agencies, be aware that these online agencies will either charge a $10 surcharge if you book a ticket on that carrier or neglect to offer those air carriers' offerings.

The sites in this section are not intended to be a comprehensive list, but rather a discriminating selection to get you started. Recognition is given to sites based on their content value and ease of use and is not paid for—unlike some website rankings, which are based on payment. Remember: This is a press-time snapshot of leading websites—some undoubtedly will have evolved or moved by the time you read this.

- **Travelocity** (www.travelocity.com or www.frommers.travelocity.com) and **Expedia** (www.expedia.com) are the most longstanding and reputable sites, each offering excellent selections and searches for complete vacation packages. Travelers search by destination and dates coupled with how much they are willing to spend.
- The latest buzz in the online travel world is about **Orbitz** (www.orbitz.com), a site launched by United, Delta, Northwest, American, and Continental airlines. It shows all possible fares for your desired trip, offering fares lower than those available through travel agents. (Stay tuned: At press time, travel-agency associations were waging an antitrust battle against this site.)
- **Qixo** (www.qixo.com) is another powerful search engine that allows you to search for flights and hotel rooms on 20 other travel-planning sites (such as Travelocity) at once. Qixo sorts results by price, after which you can book your travel directly through the site.

## SMART E-SHOPPING

The savvy traveler is one armed with good information. Here are a few tips to help you navigate the Internet successfully and safely.

- **Know when sales start.** Last-minute deals may vanish in minutes. If you have a favorite booking site or airline, find out when last-minute deals are released to the public. (For example, Southwest's specials are posted every Tuesday at 12:01am Central Time.)
- **Shop around.** Compare results from different sites and airlines—and against a travel agent's best fare, if you can. If possible, try a range of times and alternate airports before you make a purchase.
- **Follow the rules of the trade.** Book in advance, and choose an off-peak time and date if possible. Some sites will tell you when fares to a particular destination tend to be cheapest.
- **Stay secure.** Book only through secure sites (some airline sites are not secure). Look for a key icon (Netscape) or a padlock (Internet Explorer) at the bottom of your Web browser before you enter credit card information or other personal data.
- **Avoid online auctions.** Sites that auction airline tickets and frequent-flier miles are the number-one perpetrators of Internet fraud, according to the National Consumers League.
- **Maintain a paper trail.** If you book an e-ticket, print out a confirmation, or write down your confirmation number, and keep it safe and accessible—or your trip could be a virtual one!

# 3

# Getting to Know London

London is one of the most exciting cities in the world, and arriving here can be a bit of a shock for bleary-eyed and jet-lagged visitors. Almost seven and a half million people live in a sprawl of 600 square miles or more. Everything will probably seem too noisy, too dirty, too fast. But it will also feel marvelously familiar, as the red buses and black taxis you've seen in hundreds of movies are suddenly right there in front of you. Despite the bustle, the city is very visitor-friendly:

It's laid out in distinct, manageable chunks, and traveling between them is easy on public transport.

This chapter will help you get your bearings. It provides a brief orientation and a preview of the city's most important neighborhoods. It also answers questions about how to use those lovely buses, as well as the Tube (less lovely on a sweaty summer's day!). The "Fast Facts" section covers all the essentials from navigating the phone system to where to get a cheap and chic haircut.

## 1 Orientation

### VISITOR INFORMATION

The **Britain Visitor Centre,** 1 Regent St., SW1 (no phone) is open Monday to Friday 9:30am to 6:30pm, Saturday and Sunday 10am to 4pm (Sat 9am to 5pm, June to Oct). It brings together the British Tourist Authority (www.visitbritain.com) and the English, Welsh, Scottish, and Irish Tourist Boards. There's a **Globaltickets** booking service for theater, sightseeing, and events; a bureau de change; and a **Thomas Cook** hotel and travel-reservations office. And it's very busy.

The **London Tourist Board** recorded-information service (© **09068/ 663344**) offers premium-rate lines for different topics. The system is comprehensive but infuriating, and worse, costly. You're better off spending your time and money surfing the website, which is jam-packed with everything you need to know, and more (www.londontown.com). The LTB also runs several **Tourist Information Centres,** too, offering similar services. The main one is at **Victoria Station forecourt,** SW1. It opens Monday to Saturday, from 8am to 8pm Easter through May, and to 9pm June through September. Sundays and every day during the winter, it is open from 8am to 6pm. There are also centers at **Liverpool Street Tube station,** EC2, and the **Waterloo International arrivals hall,** SE1. The **Greenwich TIC** is at Pepys House, 2 Cutty Sark Gardens, SE10 (© **0870/608-2000**). The **Southwark Information Centre** is at 6 Tooley St., SE1 (© **020/7403-8299**).

More convenient than all of these is a **new information center** within the **tkts** half-price ticket booth in **Leicester Square,** which opens from 10am to 6pm every day. The City of London runs its own **Information Centre** at St. Paul's Churchyard, EC4 (© **020/7332-1456**).

---

**⸢Fun Fact⸥ Name That Street**

The weird and wonderful street names in the City aren't really weird at all, but an intricate guide to centuries of history. The "bury" of Bucklers-bury and Lothbury comes from *burh,* the word for the stone mansions built by Norman barons. Ludgate, Aldgate, and Cripplegate really were gates, the original ones to the city. In the Middle Ages, *cheaps* were markets: hence modern street names like Eastcheap and Cheapside. As the city began to thrive as a commercial center, artisans and merchants gathered in particular streets. Today, you'll find Milk Street, Bread Street, and Friday Street, where fish was sold. South of the river in Southwark is Clink Street. There used to be a prison there, hence the expression "in the clink."

---

As you wander around the city, also look out for **i-plus** electronic booths, for touch-screen access to sightseeing information, theater bookings, and so on. You can also send short e-mails for free, though the process is rather laborious. You'll find one by Jubilee Place on King's Road (Chelsea), in Ossington Street in Notting Hill Gate, and near Kensington High Street, Bayswater, Pimlico, and Bond Street Tube stations. The budget hotel chains Travel Inn and Ibis have them, as do the London Transport Museum, Madame Tussaud's, Natural History Museum, Theatre Museum, and the V&A.

## CITY LAYOUT

Central London is like the jam in a doughnut, an amorphous blob rather than an official definition. Ask a local, and they'd probably tell you it means anything falling within the Circle Line on the Underground: the **City,** the **West End,** and a few bits west of that. Zone two of the Tube map loosely conforms to the broader definition of **Inner London. Greater London** includes the vast sprawling mass of suburbs.

The City is the oldest part of London, and it covers a scant "Square Mile." Now that's shorthand for one of the world's leading financial centers. Villages then sprang up around the original settlement—**Bloomsbury, Holborn, Kensington,** and so on. Over time, these gradually melded together and became absorbed into the city proper. But each one still has its own heart and character.

The West End is harder to pin down because it's so much more than a geographical term. Locals use it as shorthand meaning razzle-dazzle—the special streets where they shop by day and play by night. **Marble Arch** and **Hyde Park Corner,** with **Park Lane** running between them, mark the westernmost points. **Westminster** and **Victoria** stand by themselves, outside any catchall description. Then, west of the West End where the homes finally outnumber the offices, you come to **Bayswater** and **Notting Hill, Knightsbridge, Kensington,** and **Chelsea.**

This is the prime stomping ground for visitors. If you add on the best bits of Inner London—the cultural highlights close to the Thames at **South Bank, Bankside,** and **Southwark,** stretching as far east as **Greenwich,** as well as the markets of **Islington** and **Camden,** and pretty **Hampstead** village, to the north—that makes an area of around 25 square miles.

## FINDING YOUR WAY AROUND

Face it, you're going to get lost. Irrepressible organizers, the Victorians introduced the postcode system to show where a neighborhood is located in relation to the original post office in the City, itself EC1 for East Central. Moving west, the codes change from EC to WC (West Central) to W (West), and so on. Unfortunately, London expanded and boroughs began to be labeled alphabetically. Now all you can be sure of is the general direction: W4 is Chiswick, at least ¾ of an hour west of the West End.

Street names are completely random. And house numbers can work in several different ways: odd on one side of the street, even on the other; or in the right order, but up one side and back down the other. Murphy's law applies in spades: Wherever you start from, the target address is bound to be in the other direction.

**STREET MAPS**    Check the detailed foldout street map included with this book; you may find it's all you need to get around.

Otherwise, serious explorers should go for the one and only *London A to Z.* Do a bag check on most locals, and you'll find one. They come in a bewildering range of different sizes, though the smallest isn't up to much. Unless you've got poor eyesight, when this may be too fine, I recommend the *Mini A to Z,* which costs £3.95 ($5.75) and still won't spoil your pocket-line. Even the smallest newsagent in Central London stocks them.

## NEIGHBORHOODS IN BRIEF

**KNIGHTSBRIDGE**    Posh Knightsbridge is the first area you come to west of the West End and south of Hyde Park. It's very wealthy, and very fashionable in a way that is both solid establishment and gossip-column glitz. **Harrods** is the main attraction, of course. Green-liveried doormen will turn people away for having grubby clothing, ripped jeans, high-cut or cycling shorts, and bare midriffs or feet. The super-chic Harvey Nichols is 100 yards up the road toward Hyde Park Corner. Head for tea at the Lanesborough Hotel after that, because the covered central courtyard of what used to be St. George's Hospital is a delightful place to splash out on afternoon tea. Knightsbridge Barracks, on the edge of the park, is where the Household Cavalry lives.

**BELGRAVIA**    South of Knightsbridge, Belgravia reached the peak of its prestige in the reign of Queen Victoria, but for the new-moneyed and for those aristocrats whose forebears didn't blow all the family heirlooms, it's still a very chic address. The Duke of Westminster, who owns vast tracts of Belgravia and Chelsea, lives at Eaton Square. Architecture buffs will love the vanilla-ice-cream town houses, especially in the area's centerpiece, Belgrave Square. Budget travelers can hover on the verge of a smart address at the B&Bs in Ebury Street, though that is really Victoria.

**CHELSEA**    This stylish district may start from the north bank of the Thames, west of Victoria, but the river is probably the least important thing about it. The

---

**Where the Neighborhoods Are**
Flip to the map, "Central London," on p. 6 for a clear picture of how all the neighborhoods described here actually fit together.

action starts at Sloane Square, with Gilbert Ledward's Venus fountain at its center, and moves swiftly east down the dangerously captivating shopping heaven, the King's Road. The funkier high street names began to move in a few years ago, but it's still more chic than cheap, and retains a funky feel begun by Mary Quant's 1960s mini-skirt revolution and built on by the doyenne of punk, Vivienne Westwood. Chelsea has always been a favorite of writers and artists, including Oscar Wilde, Henry James, and Thomas Carlyle, whose home you can visit. Residents today include aging rock stars (Mick Jagger), aging politicians (Margaret Thatcher), wealthy young Euromigrant families, and 30-something former "Sloane Rangers" of the 1980s. Temporary residents won't find many cheap places to stay, but there are a handful of good values and a mix of cheap pop-in eats and restaurants with excellent set meals.

**KENSINGTON** This is the heart of the Royal Borough of Kensington & Chelsea. The asthmatic William III started the royal thing in 1689 when he fled Whitehall in search of cleaner air (which is long gone). Queen Victoria was born in the house that was by then renamed Kensington Palace, and which the royals now call "KP." The late Princess Diana lived here, and it's still home to a gang of family members including Princess Margaret. You can visit the palace (but not the royals, though you may see the odd helicopter landing in the park). Kensington lies between Notting Hill, to the north, and South Kensington. There are a couple of great bathless budget sleeps just off Kensington Church Street, which is lined with by-appointment-only antiques shops. Kensington High

Street is a good mix of mainstream brands and bargains.

**South Kensington** is best known as home to London's major museums, in a row along Cromwell Road: the Natural History Museum, Victoria & Albert Museum, and the Science Museum. They're all built on land bought with the proceeds of Prince Albert's Great Exhibition of 1851. He gave his name to two spectacular landmarks here, too: the Royal Albert Hall, where the famous promenade concerts are held every year, and the Albert Memorial. His devastated wife Queen Victoria commissioned the latter from Sir George Gilbert Scott, and it was completed in 1872. It was recently restored to its full and super-excessive glory. South Ken, as it is often called, is stuffed to the gunwales with surprisingly good-value, self-catering accommodations, so it's a prime holiday base for families.

**EARL'S COURT** This neighborhood has gone through many incarnations. It's west of South Kensington and was known between the wars as a staid residential district full of genteel ladies. It then became a haven for poor newcomers to Britain and young Brits buying an affordable first apartment. There are whole streets of budget hotels that really are dives. Things are changing, though. You can see it on the main street, Earl's Court Road, where the smarter cafe chains are starting to join the late-night fast-food joints with names that rip off KFC. The huge exhibition center brings in a lot of trade. Some hotels are upgrading to cater for it, providing good value budget sleeps. Earl's Court is a big gay enclave, with gay hotels, bars, and pubs.

**NOTTING HILL** It wouldn't be surprising if Notting Hill became a victim of its own hype. The inexorable rise in house prices began in the mid-1990s. The press climbed on the bandwagon and hip media, music, and fashion luvvies rode in with it. Then there was the much-puffed film *Notting Hill,* with Hugh Grant and Julia Roberts—the nail in the neighborhood's coffin or the final rocket-blast to stratospheric status, depending on your view. Richard Curtis, who wrote the movie, sold his Notting Hill house in 1999 for a rumored £1.4 million ($2.24 million). Now you could pay that much for a flat! Bye-bye boho scruffiness, hello U.S. coffee chain. Visitors flock here in hordes to visit the great Portobello Market, as you'll see if you stay at either of the good value sleeps we've found for you on this winding street. **Holland Park,** the next stop west, is a very chi-chi residential neighborhood, for fat wallets only. Richard Branson runs his Virgin empire from here. Budget travelers can get a fantastic cheap sleep at the youth hostel located in the middle of the park itself.

**PADDINGTON & BAYSWATER**
Paddington has been the terminus for trains coming into London from the west and southwest since 1836. In recent decades, the station has had the usual effect, turning prosperous Georgian and Victorian terraces into scruffy sleeps for people passing through quickly. The area is about to enjoy a massive redevelopment around the canal basin, north of the station—11 acres of offices, overpriced apartments, shops, and eateries. But there are still good B&B deals to be had here, only just west of the West End.

**Bayswater** is a generalization rather than a definable area, arising from the eponymous main road

running across the top of Hyde Park. Walk 5 minutes from Paddington, and you'll come to it. The buzziest bit is **Queensway,** a street of cheap ethnic restaurants, cheap tacky shops, and an ice-skating rink, with the old Whiteley's department store, now a shopping mall, at the northern end. That is also where Westbourne Grove starts, an increasingly funky street that links up with Notting Hill.

**MAYFAIR** Bounded by Piccadilly, Hyde Park, Oxford Street, and Regent Street, Mayfair is filled with luxury hotels and grand shops. The Georgian town houses are beautiful, but many of them are offices now—real people don't live in Mayfair. Grosvenor Square (*Grov*-nor) is nicknamed "Little America" because it's home to the U.S. Embassy and a statue of Franklin D. Roosevelt. You must visit **Shepherd Market,** a tiny, rather raffish village of pubs and popular eateries: Sofra Bistro is a good and very reasonable Turkish restaurant. The old market was banned for "fornication and lewdness," among other things. Upmarket prostitutes still cater to loose-trousered politicians here, allegedly!

**MARYLEBONE** Most visitors head to Marylebone to explore Madame Tussaud's waxworks or trudge up Baker Street in the virtual footsteps of Sherlock Holmes. Generally, this is an anonymous area, with most of the action in a strip running just north of Oxford Street. Robert Adam finished Portland Place, a very typical square, in 1780. Horatio Nelson's wife waited in Cavendish Square for the admiral to return from the arms of the sea and of Lady Hamilton. But the real must-visit is in Manchester Square: the mini–French chateau called Hertford House, which houses the

Wallace Collection, one of London's loveliest free attractions. St. Christopher's Place is a pretty piazza with some reasonable restaurants and unreasonable boutiques close to Bond Street Tube. Marylebone High Street has a gaggle of posh shops, too, now. While budget hotels are as rare as hen's teeth here, you will find good value, big-roomed splurges in Gloucester Place.

**ST. JAMES'S** Often called "Royal London," St. James's basks in its associations with everybody from the "merrie monarch" Charles II to Elizabeth II, who lives at its most famous address, Buckingham Palace. The English gentleman retreats here to his club, that traditional male-only bastion. St. James's starts at Piccadilly Circus and moves southwest, incorporating Pall Mall, The Mall, St. James's Park, and Green Park. Budget travelers must day-trip here to sample the lingering pomp. Cheap eats may be hard to find, except close to Piccadilly Circus, but the parks are prime picnic territory. You can get the necessities, or stop for tea, at the world's most luxurious grocery store, **Fortnum & Mason.** It has kept explorers, empire-builders, and the warrior classes supplied with food parcels for over 200 years.

**SOHO** Cities are rarely sleaze-free, but few have their strip joints and red lights right next door to chi-chi restaurants, delis, thriving media companies, and a traditional fruit and veg market (Berwick Street). The council is enforcing ever more stringent controls on the sex trade by forcibly buying flats used as unlicensed brothels and selling them to charities that in turn develop social housing. Other projects to spruce up the gloriously cosmopolitan Soho haven't been so successful—the council reversed its disastrous traffic ban after only 6 months because among the pedestrians were too many winos, aggressive beggars, and pickpockets. Soho is a wedge-shaped neighborhood. Its boundaries are Regent Street, Oxford Street (a mecca for mass-market shopping), Charing Cross Road, which is stuffed with antiquarian bookshops, and the theater-lined Shaftesbury Avenue. Urban streetwear stores are finally starting to push back the tide of tourist schlock on Carnaby Street, where the 1960s swung the hardest. In the middle of Soho, Old Compton Street is the heart of gay London. Cross Shaftesbury Avenue, and you come to Chinatown, which is small, yet authentic, and packed with excellent restaurants.

London's best-located youth hostel is in Soho, on Noel Street, and there are good deals at the Regent Palace near Piccadilly Circus. But that's it.

**PICCADILLY CIRCUS & LEICESTER SQUARE** Piccadilly Circus was named after the "picadil," a ruffled collar created by the 17th-century tailor, Robert Baker. It's packed with crowds morning, noon, and way past midnight, grazing on fast food. You don't need to do the same—Marco Pierre White's Criterion restaurant on Piccadilly Circus has great set menus. Then sample the delights of the Trocadero, if you dare. There's floor after floor filled with video games and noisy attractions, which the kids will love. Its huge signs are part of a whole gallery of neon that illuminates the statue of Eros.

**Leicester Square** is wall-to-wall neon, too, no longer the swish address it once was. It changed forever when the Victorians opened four towering entertainment halls, which today are cinemas. Crowds mill about until the early morning. It's tacky, but fun. Keep a tight hold on your wallet, as pickpockets cruise for careless tourists.

**BLOOMSBURY** Northeast of Piccadilly Circus, beyond Soho, Bloomsbury is the academic heart of London—much of the University of London, as well as several other colleges, are based here. All the same, it's quite a staid neighborhood. Writers such as Virginia Woolf, who lived here and put Bloomsbury into her book *Jacob's Room,* have fanned its reputation. She and her husband were unofficial leaders of a bohemian clique of artists and writers known as "the Bloomsbury Group." Russell Square is the main hub, and the streets around it are crammed with excellent value B&Bs. Most visitors come to see the treasure troves of the British Museum, and there are a few really good and good-value restaurants in the area.

Nearby is **Fitzrovia,** bounded by Great Portland Street, Oxford Street, and Gower Streets (lots of B&Bs there). Goodge Street is the main Tube and the village-like heart, with many shops and restaurants. It was the stomping ground of Ezra Pound, Wyndham Lewis, and George Orwell. The knobbly British Telecom Tower on Cleveland Street is one of London's best-recognized landmarks, but it's closed to the public. Broadcasting House, in Portland Place, is another landmark. It's the old BBC HQ and you could still come here if you get tickets to the recording of a radio show.

**HOLBORN** This is the heart of legal London, where the ancient Inns of Court and Royal Courts of Justice lie. Dickens was a solicitor's clerk here when he was 14 and used the experience to good effect in *Little Dorrit.* Once you're off the traffic-laden High Holborn, time rolls back. The Viaduct Tavern, 126 Newgate St., was built over the notorious Newgate Prison. Holborn Viaduct was the world's first overpass. This is too business-like to be a hotel zone, stuck oddly between the West End and the City, and northeast of Covent Garden. But you'll get a great cheap sleep at the Holborn Residence student dorm.

**COVENT GARDEN & THE STRAND** The fruit and flower market moved to an unromantic modern shed south of the river in 1970, and Professor Higgins would find today's young women in Covent Garden far too fashionable for Eliza Doolittle–style experiments. This is a very fashion-oriented neighborhood, with more shopping and general razzle-dazzle than Soho, and certainly more tourists. It's quite pricey, too. The restored market hall is in the middle of a big pedestrian piazza and filled with little boutiques. The character of Covent Garden owes a lot to its long theatrical history, which is why there are so many great pre-theater deals at the restaurants. The Theatre Royal Drury Lane was where Charles II's mistress Nell Gwynne made her debut in 1665. And the actors' church designed by Inigo Jones, St. Paul's Covent Garden, holds memorials to many famous names from Ellen Terry to Boris Karloff to Vivien Leigh. The Royal Opera House is open again and is a glorious place to stop for coffee. Stay with visiting performers and fans at the eccentric Fielding hotel, just round the corner.

The **Strand** is a windy thoroughfare, lined with theaters and hotels, including the Savoy, where the art of cocktail mixology was born. Head to the American Bar there. Or, for a cheaper concoction, go next door to the newly restored Somerset House. The riverside Palladian mansion has three galleries and a 50-jet courtyard fountain. The Strand runs northeast out of Trafalgar Square toward the City, and marks the southern border of Covent Garden. **Trafalgar Square** is a visitor must-see all by itself. Nelson's Column—the triumphal memorial to England's victory over Napoleon in 1805—is in the middle, and the National Gallery is on the northern side. Plans to pedestrianize the space between them could finally see ground broken in spring 2002 . . . allegedly.

**WESTMINSTER** Edward the Confessor launched Westminster's rise to political power when he moved out of London to build his royal palace there in the 11th century. Dominated by the Houses of Parliament and gothic Westminster Abbey, it runs along the Thames east of St. James's Park. Whitehall, which has long been synonymous with the armies of civil servants who really wield the power, is the main thoroughfare from Trafalgar Square to Parliament Square. Visit Churchill's Cabinet War Rooms, then peer through the gates shutting off Downing Street. *Chez* Blair is actually No. 11 because the Prime Minister's family wouldn't fit into No. 10, even before the surprise addition of little Leo.

Westminster also takes in **Victoria,** a strange area that is both businessy and, because it's dominated by the station, full of cheap hotels. Go carefully because a lot of them are very nasty. The classiest ones are in Ebury Street on the

fringes of Belgravia. Art lovers come here to visit Tate Britain.

**THE CITY** The City is where London began. Now it's one of the world's leading financial centers, and its institutions are recognized everywhere: the Bank of England (or the Old Lady of Threadneedle Street), the London Stock Exchange, and Lloyds of London. Much of the City was destroyed in the Great Fire of London, the Blitz, and later in the 1990s with some help from the IRA. Nowadays, it's a patchwork of the ancient and the very modern. You'll see some of the most outstanding or outlandish modern architecture here, depending on your viewpoint, alongside such treasures as St. Paul's Cathedral. The Museum of London is home to 2000 years of history, including objects found during work on the Underground's Jubilee Line extension. If you go to the Barbican cultural center, take a ball of string with you—following the painted walk-this-way lines is hopeless in this concrete jungle. **Fleet Street** was home to Britain's newspapers before the "brave new world" of remote printing prompted a move out, mostly to Docklands.

**CLERKENWELL** London's first hospital was here, and then Clerkenwell evolved into a muck-filled 18th-century cattle yard, home to cheap gin distilleries. In the 1870s, it became the center of the new socialist movement: John Stuart Mill's London Patriotic Club was in Clerkenwell, as was William Morris's socialist press later in the 1890s. Lenin lived here while he edited *Iskra.* Neither West End nor City proper, its fortunes then dwindled, but they're on the up and up again today as old commercial buildings turn into chic lofts and new restaurants open. Art galleries and shops run by small designers line Clerkenwell Green. Gritty working life goes on as meat lorries rumble into Smithfield Market. London's oldest church is here, too, the Norman St. Bartholemew-the-Great.

**DOCKLANDS**   Since the London Docklands Development Corporation was set up in 1981, billions of pounds have gone into the most ambitious regeneration scheme of its kind in Europe. **Canary Wharf** is the jewel of this nascent river city, which runs east from Tower Bridge. Its 800-foot tower, designed by Cesar Pelli, is in the center of a covered piazza filled with shops. New skyscrapers are sprouting up around it now, and guesstimates say 60,000 new workers will be needed over the next few years. It has taken two decades but the once-bleak and isolated Canary Wharf estate is finally full and developers are moving on to the World Trade Centre, five more skyscrapers in a gang of eight planned for Millennium Wharf nearby.

While the new Museum of Docklands may not be enough reason to draw you here, it is worth taking a trip on the Docklands Light Railway. Up on elevated rails, it snakes past historic buildings, grotty empty spaces, and 21st-century shrines to big business, like an architectural theme park still is. Or take the Jubilee Line: Canary Wharf station is one of the most striking of all the hi-design stops on the new extension.

**THE EAST END**   This collection of boroughs, east of the City, has long been one of the poorest areas of London. Now, though, it's hoped that the construction of a big Channel Tunnel rail interchange at Stratford will drag development eastwards. The Huguenots, fleeing religious persecution in France during the 16th century, were the first of successive waves of immigrants right up to the large Bengali population today. Yet, it's also home to the ultimate Londoner, the Cockney born within the sound of Bow Bells. This referred to the bells of St. Mary-le-Bow church, which rang the city curfew until the 19th century. The current ones are postwar replicas. Close to the docks, the East End was bombed to blazes during the Blitz. The most famous, or infamous, residents were the mad, bad, and very dangerous gangsters, the Kray twins—Reggie joined Ronnie in the hereafter last year. Nudging Clerkenwell on the western edge is **Hoxton,** the hottest hotbed of Young British artists and the entrepreneurs who know how to hype them. Otherwise, the few draws for visitors include the amazing Columbia Road flower market.

**SOUTH BANK**   This is a loose definition, devised by Londoners on the north bank of the Thames, to define the only bit south of the river they're really interested in. As more and more redevelopment takes place, the definition widens. The core is the **South Bank Centre,** now the largest cultural complex in Europe and still planning a big expansion and redevelopment. It houses the National Theatre, Royal Festival Hall, Hayward Gallery, National Film Theatre, and the Museum of the Moving Image (currently closed awaiting news of said redevelopment), as well as several eateries. There's a great second-hand book market on the riverside walk there. Upriver, facing the Houses of Parliament, are the landmark observation wheel, the British Airways London Eye, and County

Hall. Once home to the Greater London Council, this is now part luxxy Marriott hotel and part budget Travel Inn, with the London Aquarium in the basement. Go downriver (east), and you come to Tate Modern and the new Millennium Bridge, linking **Bankside** with the City. It closed after a day, swaying dangerously under the hordes of people trying to walk across, and wasn't due to reopen until at least the end of 2001. With Shakespeare's Globe Theatre only a stone's throw away, this is a really exciting neighborhood. The London School of Economics student dorm, Bankside House, offers good quality, cheap accommodation.

Still farther west, you come to London Bridge and **Southwark.** Known as the outlaw borough, the city's medieval fathers banished the prisons, prostitutes, theaters, drinking dens, and so on to here. Pilgrims rested here, too, on their way to Thomas à Becket's shrine, as recorded in Chaucer's *Canterbury Tales.* There's a feast of history to revisit in this run-down area that is starting to revive. To the east of the bridge, the glass-walled HQ for the London Mayor and the assembly, designed by Norman Foster, is due to be completed in 2002.

**ISLINGTON** Islington is just north of Clerkenwell. It's always had a hint of raffishness: Kenneth Halliwell killed his playwright lover Joe Orton here in 1967. The Almeida, which has attracted such illustrious names as Ralph Fiennes, Kevin Spacey, and Rachel Weisz, is camping in King's Cross for much of 2002 while its home here gets a big refurb. Gentrification is fairly recent, though, and still patchy despite the much-publicized influx of the New Labour "chattering classes." Or the outflux of residents such as Tony and Cherie Blair (who went straight to 11 Downing St.). Visitors should head for the antiques market at Camden Passage, to look even if they can't afford to buy.

**CAMDEN** This is another North London must-visit. The Victorian slums that grew up around the canal have now transformed into a hip, if still patchily seedy, neighborhood, first attracting artists such as Lucien Freud and Frank Auerbach, and later the burgeoning Indie music industry. The biggest draw, and it is very big, is Camden Market. This isn't just a couple of stalls selling fruit and vegetables, but a whole village of off-beat streets, covered areas, and old buildings, specializing in everything from new-age crystals to cheap clothes, bootleg tapes, arty-crafty bits and bobs, and so on. Come early on a Sunday to beat the bumper crowds.

**HAMPSTEAD & HIGHGATE** People who live in Hampstead live in Hampstead, not in London. This delightful village-style almost-burb northwest of Regent's Park has its own 800-acre patch of countryside, Hampstead Heath. Everybody from Sigmund Freud to D. H. Lawrence to Anna Pavlova to John Le Carré has lived here, and last year Eminem's granny said he was looking for a house in NW3. The wealthy, residents still number a host of A-list celebs, who joined the less famous locals a few years ago to try to fight off an invasion of a certain well-known U.S. burger chain. Hampstead makes a delightful daytrip and isn't that far by Tube.

**Highgate** is on the northeastern edge of the Heath, and almost as villagey. It's well worth a visit, if only to go to the famous Highgate Cemetery where Karl Marx and George Eliot are buried. There are marvelous mausolea, typically Victorian in their desire to show off.

**PUTNEY & HAMMERSMITH**
It's a bit lazy to lump these boroughs together. But they're among the best bits of riverbank in London. There are boathouses all along this stretch of the Thames. The leafy path going westward along the south bank from **Putney** takes you past a bird sanctuary called WWT Wetland Centre, and it could be in the middle of the countryside. The famous Harrods Depository, a huge Victorian warehouse turned into chi-chi apartments, is just by Hammersmith Bridge. Cross over there, and continue along the north bank, with its succession of hugely popular pubs.

**GREENWICH** This charming port village is just about as far as you can go east along the south bank of the river without leaving London. It's ground zero for the reckoning of terrestrial longitudes, and a UNESCO World Heritage site. Greenwich is used to fame, having enjoyed its first heyday in Tudor days, but it really didn't enjoy having its name bracketed with doom, gloom, and wasted millions at the disastrous Dome, still empty at the time of writing. So don't say the "D" word when you visit the many historic delights of Greenwich—the 1869 tea clipper, *Cutty Sark;* the National Maritime Museum; and the markets.

## 2 Getting Around

### BY PUBLIC TRANSPORTATION

The London Underground operates on a system of six fare zones. These radiate out in rings from the central zone 1, which is where visitors spend most of their time. It covers an area from the Tower in the east to Notting Hill in the west, and from Waterloo in the south to Baker Street, Euston, and King's Cross in the north. You will need a zone 2 ticket, though, for a trip to Camden, Hampstead, and Greenwich. Note that all single tickets, round-trip, and one-day passes are valid only on the day you buy them. The city's buses used to share this system but **London Transport** (LT) simplified it last year: into zone 1 and the rest for single tickets, and four fare zones for passes.

Tube, bus, and river service maps should be available at all Underground stations, or you can download them from the excellent website, **www.londontransport.co.uk**. This also has a new A-to-B journey planner: if your journey is too complicated for it, you can email in specific queries. Or call the 24-hour **travel hotline** ✆ **020/7222-1234.** There are **LT Information Centres**

---

### Escalator Update

The Tube is the oldest underground system in the world and also one of the deepest. Station escalators need millions of pounds' worth of upgrading. They are frequently closed for repair or have one side turned off forcing passengers to walk down to the platform. The London Transport hot line (✆ **020/7222-1234;** www.thetube.com) provides up-to-the-minute recorded information at standard local phone rates, as well as the option to speak to a live human being for detailed queries. Call if you have **restricted mobility** of any kind. The website also carries right-now escalator information.

**Tube Tales**

The genius behind **www.goingunderground.net**, "Annie Mole," posts irreverent observations on everything from Tube etiquette to celebrity-spotting on her site. The site has drawn an audience keen to participate and escalate the grumbling about the service.

This is a must-visit site for a passenger-eye view of the Underground. And, by the time your holiday is over, you may have tales to tell, too. Perhaps some more nutty, but oh-so everyday, driver announcements to add to this selection.

- On the Hammersmith & City Line   "I apologize for the delay but the computer controlling the signalling at Aldgate and Whitechapel has the Monday morning blues!"
- On the Waterloo & City Line   "Good evening ladies and gents, and welcome to the Waterloo & City line. Sights to observe on the journey are, to your right, black walls and to your left, black walls. See the lovely black walls as we make our way to Waterloo. We will shortly be arriving at Waterloo where this train will terminate. We would like to offer you a glass of champagne on arrival and you will notice the platform will be lined with lap-dancers for your entertainment. Have a good weekend."
- On a Central Line   "Mind the doors. Yes you, the woman in the long brown coat, love. I suggest you should shave your legs in future: it'll stop the hairs getting caught in the doors. Look at her everyone, mingin'! . . . Anyway, have a safe journey. Please, mind the doors. The doors are closing."

at several major Tube stations: Euston, King's Cross, Liverpool Street, Piccadilly Circus, Victoria, St. James's Park, and Oxford Circus. They're all open daily—except for the last two, which close on Sundays—from at least 9am to 5pm.

**FARES**   Kids up to age 4 travel free on the Tube and buses. From 5 to 15, they qualify for children's fares, generally around 40% less than adults (children must pay full rates after 10pm on buses). Parents should bring recent pictures of their offspring, plus proof of their age, to the nearest Tube station (just in case, most have photo booths) and get a Child Photocard. It costs nothing, but kids must carry one. Adults will also need passport-size photographs if buying any travel pass valid for more than 1 day (see below), except the bus-only ones.

London Transport puts up its fares once a year in early January, usually adding 10p to every one-way ticket. The 2001 prices were as follows:

Single tickets within zone 1 on the Underground cost £1.50 ($1.20) for adults and 60p (87¢) for children. Simply double that for a return fare. The price of a book of 10 single tickets, a **Carnet,** is two-thirds that of the same number bought individually. This is available for travel only within zone 1 and costs £11.50 ($16.70) for an adult and £5 ($7.25) for children. Adult bus fares range from £1 ($1.45) for any journey including zone 1, otherwise 70p, £1.50, and £1 ($1, $2.20, and $1.45) respectively on night buses. The flat daytime rate for children is 40p (58¢); they pay adult fares on night buses. A **Saver 6** gives you six journeys for the price of five, zone 1 adult fares only (£3.90/$5.65).

**TRANSPORTATION DISCOUNTS**   Anyone planning to use public transport should check out the big range of passes that are valid across all public transport: the Underground, buses, and the Docklands Light Railway. These make travel cheaper, and also get you **a third off all river service tickets.**

**One-Day Travelcards** can be used for unlimited trips after 9:30am Monday to Friday, and all day on Saturday, Sunday, and holidays, and on N-prefixed night buses. Adults traveling within zones 1 and 2 pay £4 ($5.80). Children, however, have to buy an all-zone at £2 ($2.90). If you want to beat the tourist crowds and start before 9:30am, a **One-Day LT Card** is available for zones 1 and 2 for £5.10 ($7.40) per adult, and £2.50 ($3.65) per child.

**Weekend Travelcards** are valid for one weekend, or any two consecutive days if Monday is a national holiday, and on night buses. These cost £6 ($8.70) for adults in zone 1 and 2, and £3 ($4.35) for children (again, this is all-zone).

**One-Week Travelcards** really are unlimited: any amount of trips, any hour of the day, and night buses. It costs adults £15.90 ($23.05) for zone 1 and £6.60 ($9.55) for a child; the prices rise for a zone 1 and 2 pass to £18.90 and £7.70 ($27.40 and $11.15).

**Family Travelcards** are available to groups that include up to two adults, plus one to four children, and it is only valid when they travel together. These, too, can be used only after 9:30am during the week. They cost £2.60 ($3.75) per adult in the group, and 80p ($1.15) per child, for zone 1 and 2.

**Bus passes,** valid for travel only on London Transport buses, are available for all zones for 1 day at £2 ($2.90) per adult and £1 ($1.45) per child, and for 1 week at £9.50 and £4 ($13.80 and $5.80).

You can buy all these, as well as monthly and annual passes for longer stays, at Tube stations but not on buses. They are also available at tobacconists and newsagents with a **Pass Agent** sticker in their window.

## THE UNDERGROUND

The Tube map is very easy to use. Every line has a different color: navy blue for the Piccadilly Line (the one that runs in from Heathrow), red for the Central Line, and so on. Station signs directing you to the different platforms refer to eastbound and westbound, or northbound and southbound, for each line as

---

*Tips* **Buy a Travelcard Before You Fly to Save Pounds**

If you plan to use public transport a lot, think about buying a **London Visitor Travelcard** before you leave home. This special tourist deal, which includes discount vouchers for some major attractions, isn't available in the United Kingdom. You don't need a passport picture, as you do for longer lasting travelcards bought in the United Kingdom. All zone adult passes cost $29 for 3 days, $39 for 4, and $58 for 7; child equivalents cost $13, $16, and $25. Zone 1 and 2 passes cost $20, $25, and $30 for adults, $9, $10, and $13 for kids. An extra bonus: there are no time restrictions, and you can use it on night buses. Contact the nearest BTA or BritRail office (see "Visitor Information" and "Entry Requirements & Customs," in chapter 2 for addresses and phone numbers). The visitor section of www.londontransport.co.uk also lists international agents.

appropriate, and the front of the train and the electronic notice boards on the platforms refer to the final destination, so get to know the names of stations at or near the ends of the lines you use most often. The **Docklands Light Railway** is an extension to the main system. Its driverless trains run on raised tracks east from Bank Tube station and Tower Gateway, close to Tower Hill. It operates daily at similar hours.

Except for Christmas Day, Tube trains run every few minutes from about 5:30am Monday to Saturday and 7am or so on Sunday. The Underground winds down between 11:30pm and 1am, as trains head back to home base, with stations closing behind them. The time of the last train is usually scribbled on a board in each ticket hall. Signal failures, conked-out trains, and general lunacy permitting, you can calculate how long a tube journey will take by allowing 3 minutes per stop, adding in a bit extra if you have to change lines. In 2000, a scout leader set a new record by visiting all 282 Tube stations in 19 hours, 59 minutes, and 37 seconds. Even more amazing, he only suffered a 30 minute delay.

There are two ways of buying tickets: at the station ticket window or using one of the push-button machines. Queuing at the window can be phenomenally time-consuming, particularly at West End stations during the summer. Elsewhere, the rush hour clogs things up, especially on a Monday when lots of people renew weekly travel passes. You will have to go to the window, though, if you want to buy a pass valid for longer than a day. There are two kinds of machines: The first takes only coins, and the buttons are marked with little more than the price. There should be a poster listing fares to every other station close by. The other machine has a button for each station and type of ticket, and will tell you the price of your choice. It accepts credit and debit cards, coins, and notes up to £10. The machines make change until they run out of spare coins, which tends to happen at busy times.

Hold onto your ticket throughout your ride because you'll need it to exit and LT inspectors make random checks. No excuse, however imaginative or heartrending, will get you out of the rigidly imposed £10 ($14.50) penalty fare.

## LONDON BUSES

London buses go places the Tube can only dream of. But such a comprehensive system makes for a very bewildering map. Most locals know only two of the 500-plus routes: from home to work and to the West End, and often that's the same thing. If the map foxes you completely, call the LT Travel Line (see above), and they'll tell you how to get from A to B. And ask the driver or conductor to let you know when the bus has reached your destination.

To stop a bus when you're on it, press the bell (or tug the wire running the length of the ceiling in an old bus). Without any signal, the driver won't stop unless passengers are waiting to get on the bus. If you're the one waiting, make sure to note whether it is a compulsory (white background on the sign) or a request stop (red background). At the latter, give a big wave or the bus won't stop.

Traveling by bus is a great way to see London, but it can be frustratingly slow, particularly in rush hour and along Oxford Street. Normal buses run until around midnight when night buses, with an N in front of the number, take over for the next 6 hours. On most routes, there's one every half-hour or hour, and those to, from, and through the West End all go via Trafalgar Square, so if in doubt, head there. Some travel passes are *not* valid on night buses.

You buy single-trip bus tickets on the bus itself. On the old Routemasters, a conductor comes around, but many new buses are now driver-only, including the little one-deck Hoppers, and you pay as you get on. In either case, proffering a note bigger than £5, unless you're only expecting small change, is likely to produce some very fruity language, particularly from the notoriously eccentric conductors. If inspectors find you without a ticket, the on-the-spot fine is £5 ($7.25).

## BY BOAT

Tony Blair and his government tried to use the millennium as the spur to regenerate the Thames and restore regular public transport services, long since reduced to pleasure cruising. But grand plans for an all-day Central London Fast Ferry ran aground, never offering more than a limited rush-hour commuter service. The building of new piers and tarting up of old ones has continued apace, though, to reach a grand total of 25 between Hampton Court and Gravesend. Last year, Westminster got an amazing £5 million pier, linked by a walkway to the Tube station, and Millbank Pier, near Tate Britain, finally got the go-ahead. This symphony in steel should complete in spring 2002 and transport bosses are hoping it will act as a spur to regular river services, as well as hoppa boats traveling downriver to Tate Modern.

Like buses and Tubes, boat operators now come under London mayor Ken Livingstone's control. He has already persuaded them to take part in an excellent deal, giving passengers with any travelcard a third off fares. You will find river service booklets at most Tube stations. There are maps, timetables, and fare details on **www.londontransport.co.uk**. Or call the travel hotline ℂ **020/ 7222-1234.**

## BY CAR

Please don't rent a car for a holiday in Central London. Parking is an expensive nightmare. Gas (petrol in the U.K.) is stratospherically expensive—around 80p ($1.15) a liter, or $4.35 *a gallon.* It takes a while to get to know the city well enough to drive from A to B without going via Z, even with a navigator in the car. It takes more than a while to get anywhere as the average speed is 10mph. And London drivers are a combative, unforgiving lot. By comparison, even the most hellish public transport experience looks like nirvana! The only reason to rent a car is for a day-trip into the countryside (not a city visit) or an around-Britain tour.

### RENTING A CAR

Most car-rental companies in Britain will accept U.S., Canadian, Australian, and New Zealand driver's licenses, provided you've held it for more than a year. You'll also need a passport. Many companies have a minimum age requirement, of either 23 or 25. Anyone with a record for drunk-driving will have a problem renting a car.

You can save money by booking a car in your home country before you travel, usually at least 48 weekday hours ahead, and for periods of a week or more. But try and give more than 2 weeks' notice because some rental companies will then guarantee a home-currency rate. Obviously, you must call around to find the best quote. In each case, check if the price includes the 17½% value-added tax (VAT), personal accident insurance, and collision-damage waiver (CDW). Also remember to specify an automatic if that's what you're used to because most Brits drive stick-shifts.

Some of the big companies have North American toll-free numbers, and they're listed here, followed by the London equivalents: **Avis** (℡ **800/230-4898,** 08706/060100; www.avis.com); **Budget Rent-a-Car** (℡ **800/527-0700,** 0800/ 181-1881; www.budgetrentacar.com); **Hertz** (℡ **800/654-3001,** 08708/ 448844; www.hertz.com). But make sure to check out **Europe by Car** (℡ **800/223-1516** nationwide, 212/581-3040 in New York; www.europebycar. com), because it often undercuts the majors. As does British broker **Holiday Autos** (℡ **800/576-1590** in the U.S., 0870/400-0099 in the U.K.; www. holidayautos.com), especially with discounts for online booking. It also has offices all over the world.

**easyRentacar** (www.easyrentar.com) is another venture from discount king Stelios Haji-Ioannou. It hires out Mercedes A-Class cars from depots at London Bridge, off King's Road, Chelsea, and near Edgware Road Tube station. You can only book online. Rates fluctuate according to demand, so the deal is always better if you book ahead: 1 day costs £9 to £28 ($13.05 to $40.60), plus a £5 ($7.25) car-cleaning fee. The downsides are you only get 75 free miles (not unlimited), above which the charge is 20p (29¢) a mile, and each car has easy's orange logo glowing along its side.

## PARKING

On-street parking is heavily regulated. Some areas are for residents with permits only. Some are for general use, either paid for at a meter next to the parking space or at an automatic Pay and Display ticket machine that covers a small length of street. Generalizations about where each is prevalent, the hours they operate, and how much they cost are very dangerous. Each local council makes different rules even for different areas within its own patch. Check the streetside notices and information on meters. Do not ever park on single or double yellow lines (or even stop for a second where there are red ones), zigzag white lines at the edge of the road, or in bus lanes.

Penalties are harsh, and any one of the following can apply whenever and wherever you break the rules. Council parking tickets/fines range from £40 to £80 ($58–$116) and police fines are currently around £40 ($58). *Warning:* All unpaid tickets eventually end up back at the rental company, which will send you a bill. If you still do not pay up, this will go on a central record and may prevent your re-entry into the United Kingdom. The **Transport Committee for London** (℡ **020/7747-4766;** www.tcfl.gov.uk/avoid.html) is the only round-up source of advice on how not to break the rules.

To get rid of a Denver Boot, which normally takes an hour from the time you call the number on the clamping sticker, you'll have to pay £60 ($87). It costs up to £135 ($195.75) to get a towed car out of the pound. If you do come back to an empty parking space, try the 24-hour **Vehicle Trace Hotline** (℡ **020/ 7747-4747**): It will tell you which pound it's gone to.

Blue signs point the way to **National Car Parks** (**NCP**), which are spread throughout the city. Prices vary, and most set a minimum stay of 2 hours. To give you an idea of how extortionate they are, that costs upwards of £7.50 ($10.90) in the West End, with 12 hours from £25.50 ($37). To find the closest, call NCP (℡ **020/7499-7050;** www.ncp.co.uk).

## DRIVING RULES

Be sensible and buy a copy of the *British Highway Code,* available at most newsagents and bookstores. Otherwise, there are a few basic things to remember, apart from driving on the left side of the road. Except where indicated, the speed limit in Central London, as in any built-up area, is 30mph (48kmph). In Britain, everyone in the car must wear a seatbelt, even passengers in the back. You may not turn right on a red light. Cars must stop as soon as a pedestrian steps onto a zebra crossing—the black-and-white-striped crosswalk. These are in the middle of the block, not at the corner, and are well-lit.

## BY TAXI

Black cabs carry up to five people and can make sound economic sense. All the drivers are licensed and have to pass a test called The Knowledge first, so they know London very well. Look for the yellow "For Hire" sign lit up on the roof and wave wildly. Before you get in, tell the driver where you want to go. Except in the West End, many drivers go home at midnight. You can order a black cab but you'll have to pay an extra charge for the time it takes the taxi to get to you—up to £3.80 ($5.50). These two companies are both 24-hour: **Dial a Cab** (© 020/7253-5000) and **Radio Taxis** (© 020/7272-0272).

The average cost of a taxi ride is said to be £8 ($11.60)—they must mean daytime, within central London, and no unusual traffic jams. The minimum charge is £1.40 ($2.05), and the meter goes up in increments of 20p (29¢). Ken Livingstone has talked about changing the surcharge system but, at the moment, you'll pay 60p to 90p (87¢ to $1.30) depending on the time of day: generally after 8pm and between midnight and 6am on weekdays, and slightly different times at weekends, or public holidays. Other extras on the basic fare include 40p (58¢) for every passenger after the first one and 10p (15¢) for every piece of luggage over 2 feet long or that has to go in the driver's cab. If you have any complaints, call the **Public Carriage Office** (© 020/7230-1631).

Minicabs are generally cheaper than black cabs. But drivers don't have to have a special license, and many won't know their way around any better than you do. Technically, they must operate from a sidewalk office or through phone bookings, and are not allowed to cruise for fares. The dodgy operators do, of course, particularly at main railway stations and late night in the West End—there are none of the guarantees you get with a black cab, and I would refuse the offer. Minicabs don't have meters. Always negotiate the fare with the office, and confirm it with the driver. Most firms are open round the clock, and you can pre-book for later, or for the next morning if you've got an early start. They tend to be locally based, so ask your hotel or B&B to recommend a reputable one. **Addison Lee** (© 020/7387-8888) does operate citywide.

## BY BICYCLE

Serious cyclists should check out the **London Cycling Campaign,** Unit 228, 30 Great Guildford St., SE1 OHS (© 020/7928-7220; www.lcc.org.uk), for information, maps, and advice on city two-wheeling. We have also suggested a place to rent bicycles in the section on "Organized Tours," in chapter 6.

 **FAST FACTS: London**

*Airport*  See "Getting There," in chapter 2.

*American Express*  American Express has over a dozen city center offices. The branch at 30–31 Haymarket, SW1 (© 020/7484-9610; www. americanexpress.com; Tube: Piccadilly Circus) has the longest opening hours: Monday to Friday 8:30am to 7pm, Saturday 9am to 6:30pm, and Sunday 10am to 5pm. Cardholders and anyone with American Express traveler's checks can receive mail there, but weekends are currency-exchange-only. The company has a 24-hour toll-free lines to report lost or stolen cards (✆ **0800/550011**) and traveler's checks (✆ **0800/521313**).

*Babysitters* Many hotels and B&Bs can arrange babysitting for you (see the reviews in chapter 4). **Universal Aunts** (✆ **020/7386-5900**) has been up and running for 17 years. It charges £6.50 ($9.45) per daytime hour, and £5 ($7.25) after 6pm. The minimum booking is 4 hours, and the agency fee is £3.50 ($5.60) for up to 5 hours, and £6.50 ($10.40) thereafter. You will also pay the sitter's travel both ways.

*Business Hours* Minimum bank opening hours are Monday to Friday 9:30am to 3:30pm, but most close at 4:30pm. Some are also open Saturday 9:30am to noon. Offices are generally open Monday to Friday from 9am until 5 or 5:30pm. By law, pubs can open Monday to Saturday 11am to 11pm, and noon to 10:30pm on Sunday, and most London ones do keep these hours. Some bars in the city center have late licenses that let them close up to 4 hours later. Restaurants, other than cafes and really cheap eats, serve lunch from noon to 2:30pm, and dinner 6 to 10:30pm (see chapter 5). A few go on later. Stores are generally open Monday to Saturday from 10am to 6pm. Many stay open for at least 1 extra hour on a Wednesday or Thursday, depending on the neighborhood (see chapter 8). Some around touristy Covent Garden don't close until 7 or 8pm nightly. Supermarkets and many of the stores in busy shopping areas now also open for 6 hours, usually starting at 11am, on Sundays.

*Car Rentals* See "Getting Around," earlier in this chapter.

*Climate* See "When to Go," in chapter 2.

*Credit Card Hotlines* For lost or stolen cards, call Mastercard ✆ **0800/ 964767**; Visa ✆ **0800/895082**; Diners Club ✆ **0800/460800**. Also see "American Express," above.

*Currency* See "Money," in chapter 2.

*Dentists* Try the **Dental Emergency Care Service**, Guy's Hospital, St. Thomas's St., SE1 (✆ **020/7955-2186**), a first-come, first-served clinic on the 23rd floor, Monday to Friday 8:45am to 3pm.

*Doctors* The National Health Service now runs a telephone help line, **NHS Direct** (✆ **0845/4647**), which is a useful first port of call for noncritical illnesses. Otherwise, London has five private walk-in **Medicentres**, offering the same services as a GP: those at Victoria Station and the Plaza mall at Bond Street Tube station are open every day: call for times and directions (✆ **0870/600-0870**). **Medcall**, 2 Harley St., W1 (✆ **0800/136106**) operates a late-night practice and 24-hour call-out.

*Documents* See "Visitor Information," under "Entry Requirements & Customs," in chapter 2.

*Driving Rules* See "Getting Around," earlier in this chapter.

*Drugstores* The Brits call them chemists. **Bliss Chemist**, 5 Marble Arch, W1 (✆ **020/7723-6116**), is open daily 9am to midnight. **Zarfash Pharmacy,**

233–235 Old Brompton Rd., SW5 (© 020/7373-2798) never closes. In day-time hours, there are branches of **Boots** and **Superdrug** everywhere.

*Electricity* British appliances operate on the EU standard of 240 volts. If you're bringing a hair dryer, travel iron, shaver, and so on, bring a trans-former too. British sockets take different three-pronged plugs than those in America and on the Continent. London department stores and most branches of **Boots** sell adapters, in case you arrive without one. Some hotels and B&Bs may have one you can borrow.

*Embassies & High Commissions* This list will help you out if you lose your passport or have some other emergency:

- **Australia** The **High Commission** is at Australia House, Strand, WC2 (© 020/7379-4334; www.australia.org.uk), and is open Monday to Friday from 9am to 5pm. Tube: Holborn, Temple.
- **Canada** The **High Commission** is at 38 Grosvenor St., W1 (© 020/ 7258-6600; www.dfait-maeci.gc.ca), and is open Monday to Friday from 8am to 11am. Tube: Bond St.
- **New Zealand** The **High Commission** is at **New Zealand House**, Haymar-ket, SW1 (© 020/7930-8422; www.newzealandhc.org.uk), and is open Monday to Friday from 10am to noon, and 2 to 4pm. Tube: Piccadilly Circus.
- **The United States** The embassy is at 24 Grosvenor Sq., W1 (© 020/ 7499-9000; www.usembassy.org.uk), is open for walk-in enquiries 8:30am to 12:30pm, 2 to 5pm (to 5:30pm for phone calls). Tube: Marble Arch, Bond Street.

*Emergencies* Dial © **999** free from any phone for police, fire, and ambulance.

*Holidays* See "When to Go," in chapter 2.

*Hospitals* Around a dozen city hospitals offer 24-hour walk-in emergency care. The most central is **University College Hospital,** Grafton Way, WC1 (© 020/7387-9300). The two best alternatives are **Chelsea & Westminster Hospital,** 369 Fulham Rd., SW10 (© 020/8746-8000) on the Chelsea/ Fulham border; and **St. Mary's Hospital,** Praed St., W2 (© 020/7886-6666) in Paddington.

*Hot Lines* Anyone who is distressed about anything can call the **Samari-tans** (© 08457/909090; www.samaritans.org.uk) at any time to hear a friendly voice. **Alcoholics Anonymous** runs a help line from 10am to 10pm every day (© 020/7833-0022; www.alcoholics-anonymous.org.uk), and **Narcotics Anonymous** does the same (© 020/7730-0009; www.ukna.org).

*Information* See "Visitor Information," earlier in this chapter.

*Internet Access* Britain has got the surfing bug. There are **easyEverything** cyber cafes all over London, and we've listed their addresses in chapter 5. A few budget hotels will send and receive e-mails for you, and access is available in all hostels (see chapter 4). You can also send short e-mails for free from the many **i-plus** information booths around the city (see "Visitor Information," above).

*Liquor Laws* The government has promised to update the antiquated Eng-lish and Welsh licensing laws, but probably not before the end of 2002. In the meantime, no one under 18 can buy or consume alcohol, with one exception: 16- and 17-year-olds may purchase "beer, porter, or cider," with a table meal. Under-14s may enter some pubs, but only when accompanied by an adult. Adults can buy beer, wine, and spirits in supermarkets, liquor stores (called "off-licences"), and many local grocery stores, during the same opening hours as pubs (see "Business Hours," above). Admission-charging nightclubs are allowed to serve alcohol to patrons until 3am or so. After 11pm, hotel bars may serve drinks to registered guests only. Do not drink and drive because the police are eagle-eyed and the penalties very stiff.

*Lost Property* If you lose something on the bus or Tube, wait 3 working days before going to the **Transport for London Lost Property Office,** 200 Baker St., NW1 (© **020/7486-2496** recorded information), open Monday to Friday 9:30am to 2pm. For buses, you need to call and find out which depots are at either end of that particular line (© **020/7222-1234**). There are also lost-property offices at all train stations and at Victoria Coach Station. **Taxi Lost Property** (© **020/7918-2000**) is also at Baker Street. It is open weekdays, 9am to 4pm, but only for things left in black cabs.

*Mail* Stamps cost 45p (65¢) for airmail letters weighing up to 10 grams and 40p (60¢) for postcards to anywhere outside Europe. Budget travelers can get more post for the pound by buying aerograms for 40p (60¢) each. The deal gets even sweeter at £2.20 ($3.20) for six plain aerograms and £2.70 ($3.90) for hard-to-find pictorial ones. For more information, call the **Post Office Counters Helpline** (© **08457/223344**; www.postoffice.co.uk).

*Maps* See "City Layout," earlier in this chapter.

*Newspapers/Magazines* The *Guardian, Independent, The Times,* and *Daily Telegraph* are the so-called quality national daily newspapers, listed here from left to right across the political spectrum. The *Daily Mail* and *Express* are supposedly middle-of-the-road, but very right-wing, tabloids. All have Sunday editions. (The *Guardian* has a sister paper, *The Observer.*) The *Evening Standard* is the only paid-for citywide local paper—it has a freebie sister, *Metro,* carried on Tube trains in the morning—and publishes updated editions from 10am to around 5pm. On Thursdays, it has a what's-on supplement, *Hot Tickets.* Most Sunday broadsheets produce entertainment guides, too. But the bible is the weekly *Time Out* magazine (www.timeout.com).

*Optician* For eye treatment, try the 24-hour **Opticall** © **020/7495-4915.**

*Post Office* The **Trafalgar Square Post Office,** 24–28 William IV St., Trafalgar Square, WC2, is open Monday to Friday from 8am to 8pm, opening at 9am on Saturday. Travelers can receive mail, marked "Poste Restante," here and must bring identification to collect it. Most other post offices are open Monday to Friday from 9am to 5:30pm, and Saturday 9am to noon. Look for the red signs. To contact the Trafalgar Square Post office or find the nearest local one, call the **Post Office Counters Helpline** (© **08457/223344**; www.postoffice.co.uk).

*Restrooms* The Brits have three printable words for restrooms: toilet, lavatory, and loo. Some "Public Toilets" are free—St. Christopher's Place, near Bond Street, and the uninviting but well-maintained subway facilities at Tottenham Court Tube station—but keep a few 20p coins handy for the many paid-for ones. There are top shop loos (no charge) at John Lewis (Oxford Street), Waterstone's (Piccadilly), Harvey Nichols (Knightsbridge), and Peter Jones (Sloane Square, Chelsea). You'll get a glare and often a telling off if you use a pub restroom without buying a drink, so be discreet and act natural! The same goes for non-guests popping into loos at posh hotels.

*Safety* Violent crime is no more common in Central London than any other big city, and much less common than in many. But don't take risks—keep wallets and purses hidden, bags held tightly to you, and never leave possessions unattended, even on the floor between your feet. And don't flash your cash, credit cards, or jewelry.

*Salon* A really great budget deal is the **Vidal Sassoon School,** 53 Davies Mews, W1 (*©* **020/7318-5205**), which trains recently qualified hair-dressers. Men and women can get a classic or creative cut for £8.50 ($12.35), a fraction of the cost of one at Vidal Sassoon's world-famous salons. The academy is open Monday to Friday, with appointments at 10am and 3pm.

*Smoking* You cannot light up anywhere on the Underground or on buses. Most restaurants have nonsmoking sections, and some even ban it completely. Things are also starting to change in budget hotels and B&Bs. A few don't allow smoking at all. More are now keeping some rooms as nonsmoking.

*Taxes* There are no separate county or city sales taxes in Britain. The national 17.5% value-added tax (VAT) is levied on most goods and services, and is included in the price. Takeaway food is exempt, hence the two price lists at those eateries that offer both. Hotels usually include VAT in quoted prices, but check their policy, which should be written on tariff information (all rates in this book include tax). Foreign visitors can reclaim the VAT on goods they're taking out of the U.K. Ask for a form from the sales clerk at those stores participating in the scheme—they will usually have a notice up about it. Then show it and the goods at the VAT desk at the airport. Refunds cannot be processed after you arrive home. For more information, see chapter 7.

*Taxis* See "By Taxi," earlier in this chapter.

*Telephones* Telephone dialing info at a glance:

- To call London from home, dial the international access code: & 011 from the United States and Canada, & 0011 from Australia, and & 00 from New Zealand. Follow that with 44, and then the area code minus its initial zero, and finally the number.

- To call home from London, the international codes are *©* **001** for the **United States** and **Canada,** *©* **0061** for **Australia,** and *©* **0064** for **New Zealand.** Then add the area code minus any initial zero, and the number. Or, you can use these **long-distance access codes:** AT&T USA Direct (*©* **0800/890011**), MCI Worldphone (*©* **0800/890222**), USA Sprint Global (*©* **0800/890877**), Canada Direct (*©* **0800/890016**), Telstra Direct for Australia (*©* **0800/890061**), and New Zealand Direct (*©* **0800/890064**).

- When you're in London, dial ℂ **100** for the U.K. national operator, ℂ **155** for the international operator, ℂ **192** for Directory Enquiries to find out a U.K. telephone number, and ℂ **153** for International Directory Enquiries.
- Free dial-a-directory **Scoot** (ℂ **0800/192192**) can give you the name, address, and phone number of any service you might need in London.

Several companies operate London phone boxes, each branded differently, but BT is still the largest. There are also pay phones in most large public buildings. Most accept any coin upward of 10p. Others take credit cards and pre-paid BT phonecards, which are available in post offices and newsagents. Look for the green sign.

Pay-phone **call rates** are the same every day, all day. The minimum cost is 20p (29¢) for the first 67 seconds of a local call and 43 seconds of all other calls. The pro-rata cost works out, respectively, at 9p (13¢) and 15p (22¢) per minute. Pay phones accept up to four coins at a time. They don't make change so, unless you're calling long-distance, use small denominations.

Private businesses, such as pubs and B&Bs, can calibrate their pay-phones to charge any rate they want—it's an accepted money-spinner—but they must advertise that rate on the phone. Also check the rates before using the **in-room phone** because these will often include massive surcharges.

In Britain, the main **toll-free** code is **0800,** but not all customer-service, information, or central-reservations lines use it. There are dozens of other special codes, which may be charged at the local rate (the 0845 numbers you'll see throughout the book), regional, or national rate (0870). Calls to premium-rate 090-prefixed lines cost at least 60p a minute (87¢)—by law, the operator must warn you about the charges at the start of the call. You can check any code with the operator (ℂ **100**) to avoid nasty shocks.

*Time Zone* London's clocks are set on Greenwich Mean Time—5 hours ahead of U.S. Eastern Standard Time, 10 hours behind much of Australia, and 12 hours behind New Zealand. To find out the time, dial **Timeline,** (ℂ **123**). Daylight saving time is used in Britain, too. The clocks move 1 hour back, to British Summer Time, on the last weekend of March and forward to GMT again on the last weekend of October.

*Tipping* The more expensive restaurants tend to add a service charge of 12½% to the bill. Cheaper ones sometimes do, more often if you're a big group. All should write their policy on the menu. If in doubt, ask. And make sure to check the bill before filling in the gap for a gratuity. In Britain, it is usual practice to tip cab drivers, staff in restaurants, hairdressers, some bars with table service, and hotels, but never pubs. Budget hotels and B&Bs will rarely add a percentage to the bill, so it's up to you. The usual amount on any occasion is 10%.

*Weather* Surf **www.bbc.co.uk/weather** for 5-day forecasts. Weathercall charges 60p (87¢) a minute for 7-day forecasts (ℂ **09068/505301**).

# 4

# Accommodations You Can Afford

Spend the night in a cupboard. Wash in a bucket, then dry yourself with a face cloth. Pump up the volume on the stairmaster. Whatever it is, do something to prepare yourself for the accommodations you'll find in London. The London Tourist Board (LTB) has done a great job with its campaign to create thousands more beds in the capital, but for every newly built hotel another opens in an historic building. And while the picture-postcard architecture of the latter is certainly appealing, the comforts inside won't win awards for luxury. Authorities are strict about alterations. Bedrooms are small and often old-fashioned. Private bathrooms are mainly an afterthought and tiny. And there's rarely an elevator to bypass the precipitous stairs. But, the rates will take your breath away.

There are plenty of decent double rooms for up to £80 ($116) a night, but quite a scarcity after that until around the £150 ($217.50) mark. And even at that over-splashy price,

you won't have attained a nirvana of luxury. So I have limited my splurge choices mainly to budget neighborhoods where you get more for spending more but you don't have to break the bank. Otherwise, you'd do better to try out the hot tips below and score a properly posh room at a discount. It isn't that hotels and B&Bs are out to rip you off (at least not many of them!), rather that space in London is at a super-premium. Who'd have believed someone would pay £110,000 ($159,500) just for a garage to park their car in, even if it was in tony Kensington. I hate to be such a killjoy, but forewarned is forearmed.

Whatever you think of the quality of accommodation in London, demand is strong and the average B&B so small that you should book ahead. Most places guard against no-shows by charging 1-night's stay as a nonrefundable deposit. Some ask for full payment on arrival. A very few charge for accepting credit cards. And even fewer, the really sneaky ones, quote rates

---

*Tips*  **A Tip for the Bedless**

Adrenaline junkies who arrive in London without a bed for the night can call the **London Tourist Board's** new accommodation reservation hotline (*©* **020/7932-2020;** www.londontown.com/stay). There is a £5 ($7.25) booking fee and you may get finger strain hitting the redial button as the number seems to be permanently engaged. Alternatively, staff at tourist information offices can book hotels and B&Bs—just walk in (see "Visitor Information," in chapter 3). The LTB no longer runs these offices itself and the charges vary depending on which organization does.

without VAT. Check all this out when you call. You could also ask if they have earned any quality awards. The English Tourist Board, AA, and RAC now adhere to a common set of standards. Hotels win stars: To qualify, they must have a restaurant, liquor license, lounge, and private bathrooms in 75% of their rooms. Guesthouses, B&Bs, and self-catering accommodations—most of the places we've reviewed—are rated with up to five diamonds.

## 1 How to Save on Sleeping

If you know where to look and what to ask for, you can find bargains in London. If you are not booking accommodation as part of a package deal (see "Holiday Packages," in chapter 2), read on. And don't forget to check "Fifty Money-Saving Tips," in chapter 2 for more ideas on how to save.

- **Play the supply-and-demand game.** Avoid high season. Most hotels make their annual rate increase in April and drop down again in October. See the box "The Bargain Business," later in this chapter.
- **Go native.** Many Londoners offer bed-and-breakfast in their homes. The Bed & Breakfast and Hosts Association sets quality standards and the following three members are all well established. Rates are per night and for two people sharing a room: **At Home in London** (© 020/ 8748-1943; www.athomeinlondon.co.uk) from £63 ($91.35) Central London and from £52 ($75.40) West London; **Host and Guest Service** (© 020/7385-9922; www.host-guest.co.uk) from £90 ($130.50) Central London and from £40 ($58) West London; **Uptown Reservations** (© 020/7351-3445; www.uptownres.co.uk) from £90 ($130.50) Central London.
- **Consider apartment hotels or rooms with kitchens.** Staying in self-catering accommodation can cut down on expensive restaurant bills. Agencies to try include **Emperors Gate Short Stay Apartments**, SW5 (© 020/ 7244-8409; www.apartment-hotels.com); **The Independent Traveller** (© 01392/860807; www.gowithIT.co.uk), run by the very friendly and experienced Mary and Simon Ette; **Residence Apartments** (© 020/ 7727-0352; www.residence-apartments.com); and the super-budget **Acorn Management Services** (© 020/8202-3311; www.acorn-london.co.uk).
- **Go back to school.** During the summer and sometimes at Easter, you can find accommodations starting at around £22 ($31.90) per person at the dozens of university dorms in London. We've reviewed a handful of the top options. For fuller details of what's on offer, try **Venuemasters** (© 0114/ 249-3090; www.venuemasters.co.uk), which promotes academic conference and vacation facilities all over the U.K. Or contact the three central London universities directly: **University of London** (© 020/7862-8880; www.lon.ac.uk/accom); **University of Westminster** (© 020/7911-5796; www.westminster.ac.uk/comserv/halls.htm); or **City University** (© 020/ 7477-8037; www.city.ac.uk/ems/accomm1.htm).
- **Sleep super-cheap.** Hostel dorm beds cost from £14 to £20 ($20.30–$29) per night, and many of them have cheap twin rooms, too. There are also seven **Youth Hostel Association** sites (© 020/7373-3400; www. yha.org.uk), the best of which are reviewed below. For a full list of British YMCAs, call the **National Council of YMCAs** (© 020/8520-5599; www.ymca.org.uk).

# Index of London Hotel Maps

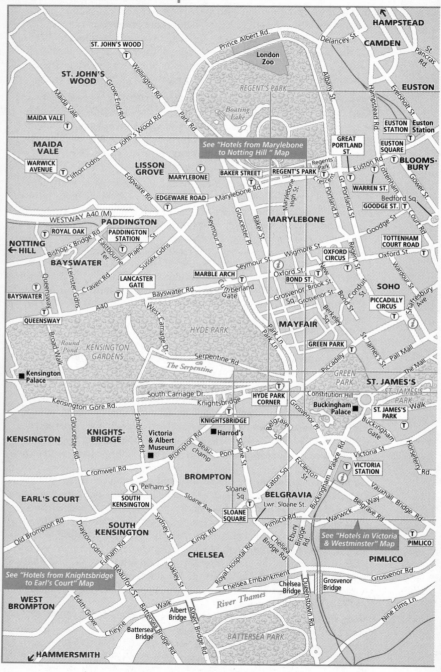

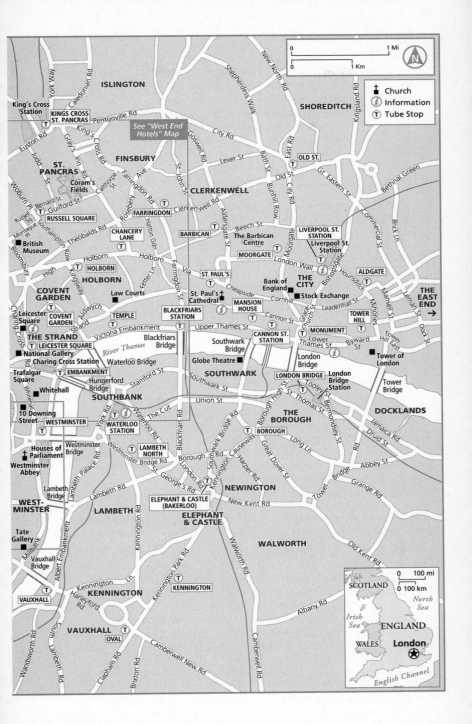

Church

ⓘ Information

Ⓣ Tube Stop

0          1 Mi
0          1 Km

ISLINGTON

SHOREDITCH

King's Cross
Station

KINGS CROSS
ST. PANCRAS

See "West End
Hotels" Map

Pentonville Rd.

City Rd.

OLD ST.

ST.
PANCRAS

FINSBURY

CLERKENWELL

Coram's
Fields

RUSSELL SQUARE

FARRINGDON

LIVERPOOL ST.
STATION

The Barbican
Centre

Liverpool St.
Station

CHANCERY
LANE

BARBICAN

MOORGATE

ALDGATE

British
Museum

HOLBORN

ST. PAUL'S

THE
CITY

THE
EAST
END

COVENT
GARDEN

HOLBORN

St. Paul's
Cathedral

Bank of
England

Law Courts

Stock Exchange

Leicester
Square

COVENT
GARDEN

TEMPLE

BLACKFRIARS
STATION

MANSION
HOUSE

MONUMENT

TOWER
HILL

THE STRAND

LEICESTER SQUARE

CANNON ST.
STATION

Tower of
London

National Gallery

Charing Cross Station

River Thames

Blackfriars
Bridge

Southwark
Bridge

London
Bridge

Trafalgar
Square

EMBANKMENT

Waterloo Bridge

Globe Theatre

LONDON BRIDGE

Tower
Bridge

Whitehall

Hungerford
Bridge

SOUTHBANK

SOUTHWARK

London
Bridge
Station

DOCKLANDS

10 Downing
Street

WESTMINSTER

WATERLOO
STATION

The Cut

Union St.

THE
BOROUGH

Houses of
Parliament

Westminster
Bridge

LAMBETH
NORTH

BOROUGH

Westminster
Abbey

Lambeth
Bridge

WEST-
MINSTER

LAMBETH

NEWINGTON

Tate
Gallery

ELEPHANT & CASTLE
(BAKERLOO)

ELEPHANT
& CASTLE

New Kent Rd.

Vauxhall
Bridge

WALWORTH

Old Kent Rd.

KENNINGTON

VAUXHALL

KENNINGTON

VAUXHALL

OVAL

0          100 mi
0          100 km

SCOTLAND

North
Sea

Irish
Sea

ENGLAND

WALES

London

English Channel

*Tips* **Net Savings**

The **British Hotel Reservation Centre** (© 020/7828-0601; www.bhrc.co.uk) site is simple to navigate, with the BHRC price next to the rack rate for more than 120 hotels and B&Bs all over London. There are big savings to be had through **www.laterooms.com**, which publishes comparable prices, for bookings up to 3 weeks in advance. It does self-catering accommodation, too. If you can bear the tension, wait until a few days before you fly and then scan **www.lastminute.com**. You should check these sites before booking if you find a hotel you like the sound of.

## 2 Kensington & Chelsea

In addition to the Trafalgar Square location (see below) **Citadines** (© 0800/ 376-3898; www.citadines.com) also has an apartment hotel on Gloucester Road near the Tube station. Studios start at £104 ($150.80) a night if you stay 1 week. Meanwhile, you'll get an even better deal at **Nell Gwynn House** ✴, Sloane Ave., SW3 3AX (© 020/7589-1105; fax 020/7589-9433; www.nghapartments. co.uk), where rates start at £425 ($616.25) per week for a small two-person studio. The downside is that bookings are only taken for whole weeks, the upside that the longer you stay the lower the price.

**Abbey House** ✴    There are no private bathrooms at Abbey House, which is why it can charge these rates in such a posh part of town. It's only a short walk up to Notting Hill, or downhill to Kensington High Street. Abbey House, owned by Albert and Carol Nayach, is a gem set in a gracious Victorian square. The bright hallway has a checkerboard floor and wrought-iron staircase lined with lithographs of glum-faced royals. The bedrooms are simple, attractive, and big for London. The second-floor room at the front gets the balcony above the front door. The bathrooms are Laura Ashley style and impeccable; there's one for every three bedrooms. And there's a kitchenette, where you can make tea and coffee for free. The staff treat you terribly well here, whether you need a hair dryer, babysitting, or restaurant advice.

11 Vicarage Gate, London W8 4AG. © 020/7727-2594. Fax 020/7727-1873. www.abbeyhousekensington. com. 16 units, none with bathroom. £45 ($65.25) single; £74 ($107.30) double/twin; £90 ($130.50) triple; £100 ($145) quad. Rates include full English breakfast. Discount available off-season. No credit cards. Tube: High St. Kensington, Notting Hill Gate. **Amenities:** Babysitting arranged. *In room:* TV, no phone.

**Prince's Gardens Halls, Imperial College** ✴    Prince's Gardens is like a holiday camp. The maze of rooms is decorated in the usual student style, and most are singles, so book early if you want a twin. There are no private bathrooms, but only four rooms share each public facility. Because Prince's Gardens is part of the campus at Imperial College, you get to use all the on-site amenities. There is a bank as well as a bureau de change, a tourist information desk and travel agency, a medical center, and so on. Guests also pay a discount rate at the sports center. The Basics restaurant does pizza for half the price you'll pay anywhere

## The Difference Between Singles, Twins & Doubles

In British English, a **single** is a room with one bed for one person. A **twin** has two beds, each for one person. A **double** has a bed big enough for two.

else, and you can do a bar crawl without even leaving the complex. You will want to leave, though, because this is a fantastic location. Harrods, the Victoria & Albert Museum, the Natural History Museum, Kensington Gardens, Hyde Park, and the Royal Albert Hall are all within a short walk.

Accommodation Link, Watts Way, Prince's Gardens, London SW7 1LU. ℂ 020/7594-9507. Fax 020/7594-9504. www.ad.ic.ac.uk/conferences. 608 units. £38 ($55.10) single; £61 ($88.45) twin. Rates include full English breakfast. MC, V. Open Easter and summer vacations. Tube: South Kensington. No children under 10. **Amenities:** Restaurant; bar; sports center with pool; game room; tour desk; salon; coin-op washers and dryers. *In room:* no phone.

**Swiss House Hotel** ℛ    If you've just gotta have your space, man, then Swiss House could be the answer to your prayers. Peter Vincenti lets out his huge family rooms to two people for £99 ($143.55). But you don't have to splurge because the standard doubles are a good size, too, and this is a lovely place. Guests walk past a curtain of greenery—plants hang from every window ledge, railing, and balcony—and under an old-fashioned canopy to the front door. Inside, chintz, dried flowers, and original fireplaces create a homey, country-style atmosphere. Traffic noise can be a problem on Old Brompton Road, so keep your fingers crossed for a room at the back looking over the peaceful communal garden, which guests are not invited to use. The proprietor is an extremely welcoming and helpful host, providing room service of soups and "monster" sandwiches from midday until 9pm. You can also pay a £6 ($8.70) supplement for a full English breakfast. Someone will carry your bags up and buy your favorite newspaper. Swiss House is popular with families, but around 80% of its guests are middle-aged U.S. tourists.

171 Old Brompton Rd., London SW5 0AN. ℂ 020/7373-2769. Fax 020/7373-4983. www.swiss-hh.demon. co.uk. 16 units, 15 with bathroom (most with shower only). £48 ($69.60) single without bathroom; £68 ($98.60) single with bathroom; £85–£99 ($123.25–$143.55) double/twin with bathroom; £114 ($165.30) triple with bathroom; £128 ($185.60) quad with bathroom. Rates include continental breakfast. Discount of 5% for 1-wk. stay and cash payment (U.S.$ accepted). AE, DC, MC, V. Tube: Gloucester Rd. **Amenities:** Secretarial services; limited room service; babysitting arranged; laundry service; nonsmoking rooms. *In room:* TV, hair dryer.

## SUPER-CHEAP SLEEPS

**Holland House Youth Hostel** ℛ    This hostel is in a really magical setting, right in the middle of a leafy public park that used to be the grounds for Holland House (1607). Sadly, incendiary bombs destroyed half of the redbrick and white-stone Jacobean mansion in World War II. The youth hostel splits its accommodation between what's left of the house and a second, not-so-vintage, 1950s building. In the summer, open-air opera is staged in the ruins (see "Performers in the Park," p. 245), and if you're staying at the hostel, there's no need to buy a ticket. Residents can sit in the courtyard and enjoy the music for free. The hostel has all the normal useful stuff like a kitchen, TV room, quiet room, and Internet access. The cafeteria has a liquor license and serves cheap meals from 5 to 8pm. The only drawback is that a lot of school groups stay here. Some dorms sleep 6 to 8, but most sleep 12 to 20 people, and there are no family bunkrooms. But you're only a 10-minute walk from two stations and a quick ride into the middle of town.

Holland Walk, Holland Park, London W8 7QU. ℂ 020/7937-0748. Fax 020/7376-0667. www.yha.org.uk. 201 units, none with bathroom. £20.50 ($29.75) per adult; £18.50 ($26.85) per person under 18. Rates include full English breakfast. MC, V. Tube: Holland Park, High St. Kensington. **Amenities:** Restaurant; game room; coin-op washers and dryers; communal kitchen; Internet access; garden. *In room:* no phone.

# Hotels from Knightsbridge to Earl's Court

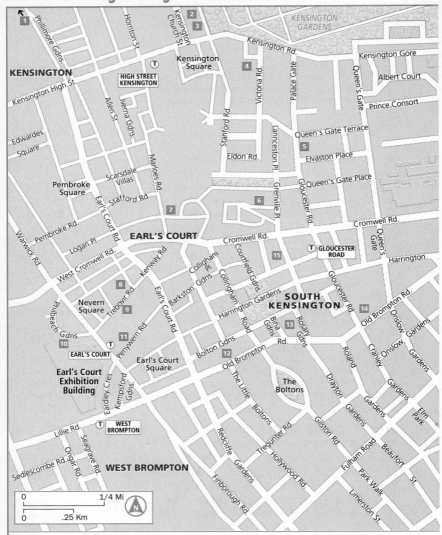

Abbey House **2**

The Amber Hotel **7**

Ashburn Gardens Apartments **15**

Astons Apartments **13**

Citadines, South Kensington **5**

Clearlake Hotel **4**

Earl's Court Youth Hostel **12**

Emperors Gate Short Stay Apartments **6**

Holland House Youth Hostel **1**

Mayflower Hotel **9**

Mowbray Court Hotel **11**

Nell Gwynn House **17**

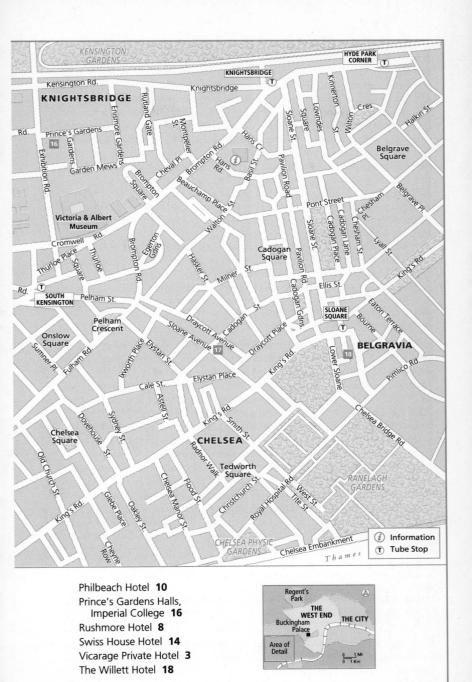

Philbeach Hotel **10**
Prince's Gardens Halls,
  Imperial College **16**
Rushmore Hotel **8**
Swiss House Hotel **14**
Vicarage Private Hotel **3**
The Willett Hotel **18**

## DO-IT-YOURSELF DEALS

**Ashburn Gardens Apartments** ⚡ *Kids*    Staying here off-season is one of the best deals in London. One-bedroom apartments undercut the B&Bs in tony South Kensington. And the bigger ones beat rates in budget neighborhoods, even accounting for guests having to fry their own bacon in the morning. It's little hardship to fill the generous rooms to capacity. For instance, using the sofa bed, you can fit four people in a one-bedroom and six people in a two-bedroom. Ashburn Gardens is a small street that joins Cromwell Road midway between a big Sainsbury supermarket and London's museum row. Though it isn't busy itself, anyone sensitive to traffic noise should ask to be at the back and above the first floor to get more of a view. Mr. Aresti and his family have owned the business since 1974. Behind the Georgian facade and entrance hall, you'll find that everything has been refurbished and modernized. The beds were all new in 1998, as were the bathrooms and open-plan kitchens in 1999 and 2000. Great maid service is part of the deal—more frequent than at a Citadines. They'll clean up every weekday, change the linen once a week, and the towels on alternate days. These apartments are popular with families, so there's a whole cupboard of cribs, high chairs, and strollers at the reception desk.

3 Ashburn Gardens, London SW7 4DG. ℂ **020/7370-2663.** Fax 020/7370-6743. www.ashburngardens. co.uk. 24 units. £525–£686 ($761.25–$994.70) per wk. 1-bedroom apt.; £875–£1,260 ($1,268.75–$1,827) per wk. 2-bedroom apt. Higher rates apply Apr–Oct. Minimum stay 1 wk. MC, V. Tube: Gloucester Rd. *In room:* TV, kitchen, fridge, coffeemaker, hair dryer, iron.

**Astons Apartments** ⚡⚡    Behind the redbrick facade of these three Victorian townhouses, you'll find the very model of a modern apartment hotel. Maids swoop through every day. The reception desk is manned around the clock. Laundry, dry cleaning, secretarial help, and a ticket-booking service are all on tap. Prices verge on being a splurge for budget travelers, but you do get good value for your money and the website often has hot deals—10% off when I looked. If money is tight, forget the singles and the great family room in the basement with its proper open-plan kitchen and a sofa bed for the kids. You can do better elsewhere. But the rest of the studios—"apartments" is a misnomer— should impress even the most exacting guests. The bathrooms were new during the massive refurbishment three years ago. The kitchenettes, behind foldaway doors, are fully equipped right down to cafetières, those mod glass coffeemakers. What's really nice is that the refurb actually enhanced Rosary Gardens' historic appeal—you can see your face in the lovely, polished, wood handrail on the stairs. Some studios do feel a bit small. My favorite is the second-floor twin with a balcony overlooking the quiet street.

31 Rosary Gardens, London SW7 4NH. ℂ **800/525-2810** or 020/7590-6000. Fax 020/7590-6060. www. astons-apartments.com. 54 units, all with bathroom (shower only). £65 ($94.25) single; £90 ($130.50) double; £125 ($181.25) designer double; £95 ($137.75) twin; £125 ($181.25) triple; £165 ($239.25) quad. Discount available for Frommer's readers; inquire when booking. Children stay free in parents' room. AE, DISC, MC, V. Tube: Gloucester Rd. **Amenities:** Tour and activities desk; business center; nonsmoking rooms. *In room:* TV w/pay movies, dataport, kitchenette, coffeemaker, hair dryer.

**Clearlake Hotel** ⚡ *Kids*    This splendidly ramshackle hotel offers a range of fantastic-value, self-catering options. It's located on Prince of Wales Terrace, a quiet street opposite the park at the eastern end of Kensington High Street. Several of the big Victorian houses need repainting, but this is a solid-gold area. What really sells the Clearlake is the huge amount of space you get, except where modern partitions cut into the gracious proportions to make single rooms or toe-to-toe twins. It's ideal for families. Despite some recent redecoration, many of the apartments resemble student digs—a junk-shop jumble of smart gilt mirrors, next to a host of 1970s horrors, and even theater props left over from plays the owner puts on. The studios are much tidier but still idiosyncratic. Stay 5 days, and you get maid service, although washing up and oven-cleaning cost is extra. Staff can lend you cribs, strollers, and high chairs, as well as arrange babysitting. Clearlake also has a few, cheaper, rooms without a kitchenette.

18–19 Prince of Wales Terrace, London W8 5PQ. ✆ 020/7937-3274. Fax 020/7376-0604. clearlake@talk21.com. 25 units, all with bathroom (some with shower only). £65–£70 ($94.25–$101.50) double/twin studio; £80 ($116) triple studio; £98–£110 ($142.10–$159.50) 1-bedroom apt.; £115–£125 ($166.75–$181.25) 2-bedroom apt.; £197 ($285.65) 3-bedroom apt. Weekly rates and long-stay discounts available. AE, DC, MC, V. Tube: High St. Kensington, Gloucester Rd. **Amenities:** Babysitting arranged; laundry and dry cleaning service; nonsmoking rooms. *In room:* TV, kitchen, coffeemaker, hair dryer.

## WORTH A SPLURGE

**Vicarage Private Hotel** 🏛   Eileen Diviney, who runs Vicarage Private Hotel, added en suite bathrooms to first floor in 1999 and the second last year, following up by redecorating the rooms. An en suite twin is a big splurge. The ground-floor one at the back, number 3, is marvelous—high-ceilinged and furnished with a pretty painted tables and old-fashioned metal bedsteads. But you really don't have to splash out here. Most of the rooms are big, the ceilings are high up to the fourth floor, and all are done in a Victorian country style. Four bedrooms share each public bathroom, and there are separate toilets. If you're trying to weigh this B&B up against Abbey House right next door, then there are other things to consider apart from the fancier decor here and marginally higher price. Vicarage Private Hotel has a TV lounge, instead of putting sets in the rooms. Hair dryers are standard, instead of at the reception desk. And you don't have to leave your room to make tea or coffee. Oh, and there are kippers (smoked herring) and porridge on a breakfast menu fit for warriors.

10 Vicarage Gate, London W8 4AG. ✆ 020/7229-4030. Fax 020/7792-5989. www.londonvicaragehotel. com. 18 units, 2 with bathroom (shower only). £47 ($68.15) single without bathroom; £76 ($110.20) double/twin without bathroom, £102 ($147.90) double/twin with bathroom; £93 ($134.85) triple without bathroom; £102 ($147.90) family room without bathroom. Rates include full English breakfast. No credit cards. Personal checks from U.S. banks accepted if received at least 2 mo. ahead of visit. Tube: High St. Kensington, Notting Hill Gate. **Amenities:** Babysitting arranged. *In room:* Coffeemaker, hair dryer, no phone.

**The Willett Hotel** 🏛🏛   The Willett is in a quiet redbrick terrace, complete with mansard roof, bay windows, and a host of the other excesses beloved by the Victorians. This is the dream location for shopaholics, just off Sloane Square and a 5-minute walk to Chelsea's King's Road. The Willett has been refurbished throughout in a ponderous traditional style to match the building. Deluxe rooms have canopies over the beds, voluptuous swagged curtains, and matching armchairs. The bathrooms don't get much bigger though. The tiny standard twins are the ones to avoid, because you sleep head to head along one wall, but the small double is a fantastic value for this swanky area. The porter will stagger upstairs with your bags. Reception can lay on your favorite newspaper. And, best of all, guests can relax in the secluded communal garden. It's all just so civilized.

32 Sloane Gardens, London SW1 8DJ. ✆ 800/270-9206 in the U.S., or 020/7824-8415. Fax 020/7730-4830. www.eeh.co.uk. 19 units, all with bathroom (shower only). £90 ($130.50) small double/twin; £100 ($145) standard double/twin, from £145 ($210.25) deluxe double/twin; £155 ($224.75) triple. Rates include full English breakfast. AE, DC, MC, V. Tube: Sloane Sq. **Amenities:** Secretarial services; limited room service; babysitting arranged; laundry service; dry cleaning; garden. *In room:* TV, fridge, coffeemaker, hair dryer.

## 3 Earl's Court

**Mayflower Hotel** ✦   The Mayflower has always been like a woman wearing her posh frock at the five 'n' dime so that nobody thinks she has to shop there. With its black pillars and showy window boxes, this hotel is determined to look a cut above cut-price Earl's Court. Fortunately, the inside lives up to the promise. Or, at least, it has in the past. I can't really comment about 2002 as the owners will have just refurbished every bedroom and bathroom. They are promising a more neutral, minimal elegance, with lots of natural fibers, to replace the vibrant colors. Generally, the rooms aren't a bad size for London. There's a lovely second-floor family room that leads onto the front porch, and there is an elevator. Every room has double-glazed windows, and the traffic on Trebovir Road dies down before midnight. The staff have always been solicitous, lending out irons, hair dryers, and adapter plugs, and making life easy for their guests. Now, the owners are aiming for even smoother service, "like Holiday Inn." Mmm, it sounds like a good deal all round, especially at this budget price.

The Mayflower also has 35 attractive self-catering accommodations, the **Court Apartments,** on busy Warwick Way. Studios start at £69 ($100.05) per night, or £420 ($609) per week.

26–28 Trebovir Rd., London SW5 9NJ. ✆ 020/7370-0991. Fax 020/7370-0994. www.mayflower-group.co.uk. 48 units, all with bathroom (some with tub only). £53–£65 ($76.85–$94.25) single; £69–£89 ($100.05–$129.05) double/twin; £89–£109 ($129.05–$158.05) triple; £99–£119 ($143.55–$172.55) family room. Rates include continental breakfast. Discount available for 3-day and weekday stays. AE, MC, V. Tube: Earl's Court. **Amenities:** Secretarial services; limited room service; dry cleaning; nonsmoking rooms. *In room:* TV, coffeemaker.

**Mowbray Court Hotel** ✦✦ *Kids*   Brothers Tony and Peter Dooley run this hotel, which the family opened 37 years ago. It's one of the few cheap places in Earl's Court where it's safe to spend the night without a biohazard suit. The staff are the ones who need protection: When I visited, they were attacking the bathrooms with some hideously pungent substance, which is presumably why everything is so spotlessly clean. Mowbray Court is a very friendly, very good value, old-fashioned, budget hotel, which even has a bar and lounge. Four bedrooms share every public bathroom. There's a von Trapp family room with seven beds in the basement of the main building and a triple with a little kitchen in the annex. Rooms at the back face the overground Tube line, but double-glazing keeps out the noise. And—get this—there's even a Vidal Sassoon–trained visiting hairdresser.

28–32 Penywern Rd., London SW5 9SU. ✆ 020/7373-8285. Fax 020/7370-5693. www.m-c-hotel. mcmail.com. 82 units, 70 with bathroom (most with shower only). £45 ($65.25) single without bathroom, £52 ($75.40) single with bathroom; £56 ($81.20) double without bathroom, £67 ($97.15) double with bathroom; £69 ($100.05) triple without bathroom, £80 ($116) triple with bathroom; £84 ($121.80) quad without bathroom, £95 ($137.75) quad with bathroom; £100–£115 ($145–$166.75) family room without bathroom, £110–£125 ($159.50–$181.25) family room with bathroom; £145 ($210.45) 7-bed room. Rates include continental breakfast. AE, DC, MC, V. Tube: Earl's Court. **Amenities:** Bar; babysitting arranged; laundry/dry cleaning; 15 nonsmoking rooms. *In room:* TV, hair dryer, safe, pants press.

**Philbeach Hotel** ✦✦   The Philbeach is a one-stop entertainment bonanza for gay travelers and somehow manages to do it at budget rates. The conservatory restaurant, Wilde about Oscar, serves delicious French cuisine from about £16 ($23.20) for two courses, and residents get a 20% discount. The hotel has a chic, Soho-style basement bar, and the weekend club nights are a blast. There's a terrace, a dance floor, and a dressing service—wigs, clothes, shoes, and make-up—for transvestites (℗ **020/7373-4848**). The Philbeach is a really friendly place and attractive, too. As you go in, the gothic decor makes it look like an arts club, with chandeliers, navy walls printed with fleur-de-lis, and dark-painted dado rail. Last year, the whole building was recarpeted and most of the rooms got new beds. None of them are very smart and some of them are small so go for one of the little mezzanine doubles. They share a terrace overlooking the lovely garden. One is en suite, and the other shares a bathroom. It's about four bedrooms to every public facility. The Philbeach gets rowdier the higher you go up the house. This isn't the place to come if you want to escape.

30–31 Philbeach Gardens, London SW5 9EB. ℗ **020/7373-1244**. Fax 020/7244-0149. www.philbeachhotel. freeserve.co.uk. 40 units, 15 with bathroom (most with shower only). £35–£50 ($50.75–$72.50) single without bathroom, £60 ($87) single with bathroom; £65 ($94.25) double without bathroom, £90 ($130.50) double with bathroom; £75 ($108.75) triple without bathroom, £100 ($145) triple with bathroom. Rates include continental breakfast. Discount available for 1-wk. stays. No 1-night stays on Sat. AE, DC, MC, V. Tube: Earl's Court. **Amenities:** Restaurant (20% discount for hotel guests); bar; garden. *In room:* TV, coffeemaker, hair dryer, iron, safe.

**Rushmore Hotel** ✦✦    This gracious hotel makes art directors at interiors magazines go weak in the knees. Italianate paint effects decorate the hallway: classical scenes and cloudy ceilings. The breakfast room is stunning, too, paved in limestone, with wrought-iron furniture and lighting that flatters even after a heavy night. Every bedroom is a different exuberant stage set. One has gothic looping curtains and a canopy over the bed, like Count Dracula's castle. In another, you'll find a chandelier and Louis XIV pale-blue walls, with panels sketched out in gold. There's a marvelous family room under the eaves, and a porter will carry up your bags. The Rushmore will take bookings for specific rooms (there are four for nonsmokers) and you can preview some of them on the website. They all had new carpet last year, and the bathrooms had a posh make-over, too. The welcoming staff will let you send a fax and pick up e-mail. There are irons at reception and safety deposit boxes. Thank goodness it is in Earl's Court, or the Rushmore would certainly bust the budget.

11 Trebovir Rd., London SW5 9LS. ℗ **020/7370-3839**. Fax 020/7370-0274. www.rushmorehotel.co.uk. 22 units, all with bathroom (most with shower only). £59 ($85.55) single; £79 ($114.55) double/twin; £89 ($129.05) triple; £99 ($143.55) family room. Rates include continental breakfast. Discount available for 1-wk. stays. 10% discount for seniors. Under-12s stay free in parents' room. AE, DC, MC, V. Tube: Earl's Court. **Amenities:** Laundry services; dry cleaning; nonsmoking rooms. *In room:* TV, coffeemaker, hair dryer.

## SUPER-CHEAP SLEEPS

**Earl's Court Youth Hostel**    If you're going to stay somewhere cheap in Earl's Court, you're far better off going to the youth hostel than one of the dozens of super-budget hotels. At least you know what you're getting, and the location is great. This garden square is just north of Old Brompton Road. On the other side of the street, the millionaires' mansions in the Boltons mark the beginning of posh South Kensington. Earl's Court is backpacker central, and they flock to this very lively international hostel. The big, half-stuccoed Victorian building has a good mix of pretty basic dorms, from a few twins up to some with nine beds or more. There are kitchen facilities so you can always supplement the shockingly meagre, packed continental breakfast. Keep your fingers crossed for fine weather when you can take your plate out to the hostel's courtyard garden. When it comes to an evening chow-down, Earl's Court is packed with cheap and often super-nasty restaurants. There are lots of late-night shops, too. If the pennies aren't too tight, head for the more upmarket Gloucester Road, which is almost as close.

38 Bolton Gardens, London SW5 0AQ. © 020/7373-7083. Fax 020/7835-2034. www.yha.org.uk. 159 units, none with bathroom. £19.95 ($28.95) per adult; £17.95 ($26.05) per person under 18. Rates include bed linen and continental breakfast. MC, V. Tube: Earl's Court. **Amenities:** Game room; travel desk; coin-op washers and dryers; communal kitchen; Internet access; garden. *In room:* no phone.

## WORTH A SPLURGE

**The Amber Hotel** ⭐    Staff at the Amber regret that Earl's Court is their nearest Tube stop and quickly add that the hotel is actually in Kensington. You can see why. This rather refined and professionally run establishment, on an elegant 1860s street north of Cromwell Road, bears very little relationship to some of the riff-raff closer to the station. But guests who stay off-season get an excellent deal, many pounds lower than the published rack rate. The private overseas owners recently funded the redecoration of the rooms and bathrooms on the mezzanine and fourth floors. Ask for a standard double on either, and you'll look out at the charming, private, terrace garden. There's even a top-whack, executive double, one of the few nonsmoking rooms, which has its own terrace. The rooms are small to medium-size but the decor is very pulled together and comfortable, with firm modern beds and the complimentary toiletries that most budget travelers can only dream of. And the continental breakfast is a free-for-all banquet—boiled eggs, cheese, salami, cucumber, yogurt, croissants, muffins, olive bread . . . and on and on.

101 Lexham Gardens, London W8 6JN. © 020/7373-8666. Fax 020/7835-1194. 38 units, all with bathroom (some with shower only). £95 ($137.75) single; £120 ($176.90) twin; £110 ($159.50) double; £130 ($188.50) triple. Rates include continental breakfast. AE, DC, MC, V. Tube: Earl's Court. **Amenities:** Bar; dry cleaning; nonsmoking rooms; garden. *In room:* TV, coffeemaker, hair dryer, safe, radio, pants press.

## 4 Notting Hill

Imperial College charges the same rates at the spartan **Pembridge Gardens Halls** (© **020/7594-9407;** www.ad.ic.ac.uk) as at its main Prince's Gardens campus. That's because the gracious, sculpted ice-cream houses on this quiet side street sell for multi-millions. And the location, between Portobello Market and Kensington Gardens, is fantastic. Bathless singles cost £38–£43 ($55.10–$62.35), or £48.50 ($70.35) with a shower; bathless twins are £61 ($88.45), £68 ($98.60) with a shower. Guests can use all the campus facilities, three Tube stops away from Notting Hill Gate at South Kensington.

**Comfort Inn Notting Hill** ⭐ *Value*    This is rather a sneaky good deal. Comfort Inn is a franchise but the owners of this hotel actively urge you to book direct with them and not through central reservations. And so do I, because it gets you the dynamite rates we've listed, which are always at least 10% lower than the official ones, and often lower still. These guys will make deals based on occupancy levels, so the quoted offer can change up to twice a week. In a quiet street off Notting Hill Gate, the hotel stretches across five terrace houses—hence the long corridors, with their series of little half-steps to trip the unwary. The rooms are on the three upper floors (there is a lift) and are a fair size for London. Rear windows look across fire escapes and rooftops, while second-floor rooms on the front have access to an east-facing balcony. In the last year, they've all been redecorated with a business feel, and equipped with firm new beds. Around 20 have external modems. The bathrooms are also newly renovated. The Comfort

Inn is a practical choice in a superb location. Breakfast is a self-service pocket-filling buffet, or you can pay £5.95 ($8.65) for full English.

6–14 Pembridge Gardens, London W2 4DU. ℂ 020/7229-6666. Fax 020/7229-3333. www.lth-hotels.com. 64 units, all with bathroom (some with shower only). £49–£72 ($71.05–$104.40) single; £58–£94 ($84.10–$136.30) double/twin; £75–£115 ($108.75–$166.75) triple; £92–£129 ($133.40–$187.05) quad. Rates include continental breakfast. Lower rates apply mid-July to Aug, Dec–Feb. Discount available for 1-wk. stays. AE, DC, MC, V. Tube: Notting Hill Gate. **Amenities:** Bar; babysitting arranged; laundry service; dry cleaning; nonsmoking rooms. *In room:* TV, dataport, coffeemaker, hair dryer, safe.

### The Gate Hotel ★
Portobello Road is the hottest tourist spot in London because of its market and antiques shops. Which makes The Gate a fun place to stay, if you don't mind crowds of people marching past as though aliens had control of their brains. The effect is even more marked from inside, because double-glazing cuts out the chatter, leaving an eerie hush. The present owner—the rather gruff "just call me Debbie"—has run the hotel for 22 years, but it has been here since 1932. Look for a tiny, late-Georgian house, with a parrot living in the caged-in basement area in front. Guests eat breakfast in their rooms, which have all been refurbished. The look is attractive, with paneled furniture and blue carpet and linen, and ceiling fans. The bigger rooms each have a small sofa bed for an extra person. There are hair dryers at reception. And if she likes you, Debbie will do your washing.

6 Portobello Rd., London W11 3DG. ℂ 020/7221-0707. Fax 020/7221-9128. www.gatehotel.com. 6 units, 5 with private bathroom (most with shower only). £55 ($79.75) single with bath and separate WC, £70 ($101.50) single with bathroom; £75–£90 ($108.75–$130.50) double with bathroom; £95 ($137.75) triple. Rates include continental breakfast. MC, V. Tube: Notting Hill Gate. *In room:* TV, fridge, radio.

### Manor Court Hotel
This quiet cul-de-sac is just off Notting Hill Gate where it turns into Bayswater Road. At the edge of Kensington Gardens, on the other side of the main road, is the gated enclave known as Embassy Row. The neighborhood gentrification is only just reaching Clanricarde Gardens, and most of the Victorian stucco-fronted houses need repainting. Manor Court recently put in new windows, which has tidied up its front a lot. The hotel is popular with families on holiday from the Continent. The decor is basic but most of the rooms are a fair size for London. Check out the huge second-floor double room, which has deep ceiling moldings and access to the balcony through floor-to-ceiling windows. My choice would be one of the triples—they're a squash at full capacity, but a bargain for two people, and you'll get a tub-shower, too. The bathrooms are clean, though some of the tiling shows signs of patching. There are hair dryers at the reception desk. This a great deal and only 10 minutes' walk from the funky Portobello Road.

7 Clanricarde Gardens, London W2 4JJ. ℂ 020/7792-3361. Fax 020/7229-2875. 20 units, 16 with bathroom (shower only). TV TEL. £35 ($50.75) single without bathroom, £40–£50 ($58–$72.50) single with bathroom; £50–£65 ($72.50–$94.25) double/twin with bathroom; £60–£75 ($87–$108.75) triple with bathroom; £85 ($123.25) family room with bathroom. Rates include continental breakfast. Discount of 10% for 1-wk. stays. AE, DC, MC, V. Tube: Notting Hill Gate. *In room:* TV.

### InterneSt@Portobello Gold ★ *Finds*
Whatever you do, do not try to make it to InterneSt until at least 6pm if you're arriving on Saturday. The road closes during the day for Portobello Market, and there's zero chance of forcing intercontinental luggage through the solid crowds, let alone past the antique stalls set up across the front of the building. The conservatory restaurant, with its romantic dining platform, is a local institution and a great deal: two courses could cost you as little as £15 ($21.75). The bar menu is almost as long, and

dishes rarely top £6.50 ($9.45). And Web time is £1.50 ($2.40) per ½ hour, with free coffee, at the second-floor buzzbar. Guests pay a minimal £5 ($7.20) set-up charge to have a computer in their room, then surf all they want for free. The rooms are tiny but they're freshly decorated. The higher bathless price listed below is for a shower but no WC. Portobello Road is quiet during the week, and the double-glazing should cut out the noise on Saturday. If you like to wallow under the covers, ask for the 7-foot-long Captain's bed. For a very special treat (£60/$87 for up to five people), make like a movie star, and tour London in Portobello Gold's 1952 Buick convertible.

97 Portobello Rd., London W11 2QB. ✆ **020/7460-4910**. Fax 020/7460-4911. www.portobellogold. com. 5 units, 3 with bathroom (shower only). £50–£60 ($72.50–$87) single without bathroom, £70–£75 ($101.50–$108.75) single with bathroom; £65–£70 ($94.25–$101.50) double without bathroom, £80–£85 ($116–$123.25) double with bathroom. Rates include continental breakfast. Lower price Sun–Thurs. Discount for 1-wk. stays. MC V. Tube: Notting Hill Gate. **Amenities:** Restaurant; bar. *In room:* TV, Internet access.

## 5 Paddington & Bayswater

**Ashley Hotel** ⍟  The Davies brothers started this place in 1967 when many British still didn't holiday abroad. They called it Tregaron to appeal to the Cornish and Welsh who arrived by train at Paddington. By 1975, they had bought two adjoining B&Bs and kept the names Oasis and Ashley so as not to scare off the regulars. The brothers only simplified matters by choosing just one name in 1999, but this is an old-fashioned place and proud of it. Most guests are still British, and the young Matthew Davies, who has now taken over, is as choosy as his father and uncle about who he lets in. The newly refurbished bedrooms are comfortable, and traditional. The washbasins are in the rooms, because the bathrooms are tiny. Rooms on the front, six of which have balconies, face Norfolk Square's pretty public garden, a rare oasis of calm in the Paddington bustle. At the back, ask to be above the second floor to avoid looking out on a wall (the hotel does not have a lift). Kids will enjoy the unusual bunks in the basement family room, a single above a double. And reception can lend you hair dryers, irons and adapter plugs.

15–17 Norfolk Sq., London W2 1RU. ✆ **020/7723-3375**. Fax 020/7723-0173. www.ashleyhotels.com. 53 units, 43 with bathroom (shower only). £36.50 ($52.95) single without bathroom, £49 ($71.05) single with bathroom; £73 ($116.80) double/twin with bathroom; £89–£96 ($129.05–$139.20) triple with bathroom; £99–£115 ($143.55–$166.75) family room. Rates include full English breakfast. Discount available for children sharing parents' room. £1 surcharge for 1-night stays. DISC, MC, V. Tube: Paddington. *In room:* TV, coffeemaker, radio.

**Dolphin Hotel** ⍟  Don't let the dread phrase "continental breakfast" turn you away from the Dolphin. It simply doesn't do justice to the extravaganza Mr. Moros lays on every morning—a buffet with cheese, fairy cakes, yogurt and honey, eggs cooked any way, and more. If that really isn't enough, it will only cost you £2.50 ($3.65) for full English. Mr. and Mrs. Moros have run the Dolphin for 22 years. It's a charming place, vying with Norfolk Court (see below) for the best deal in Norfolk Square and certainly better value than most B&Bs in Sussex Gardens. These are Victorian houses, so the bedrooms do vary widely in size. But all are comfortably decorated, with a table and chairs to write your postcards at, and some have lovely moldings. Paddington is packed with pubs and restaurants, but the fridge in every room is still handy for storing supplies. Reception will help you rent a car or book a tour.

If there's no room at this particular inn, ask about their place next door: **Shakespeare Hotel,** 22–28 Norfolk Sq. (*©* **020/7402-4646;** fax 020/7723-7233; www.shakespearehotel.co.uk).

34 Norfolk Sq., London W2 1RP. *©* **020/7402-4943.** Fax 020/7723-8184. www.dolphinhotel.co.uk. 32 units, 18 with bathroom (most with shower). £42 ($60.90) single without bathroom, £55 ($79.75) single with bathroom; £55 ($79.75) double/twin without bathroom, £70 ($101.50) double/twin with bathroom; £69 ($100.05) triple without bathroom, £80 ($116) triple with bathroom; £80 ($116) quad without bathroom, £94 ($136.60) quad with bathroom. Rates include continental breakfast. AE, DC, MC, V. Tube: Paddington. *In room:* TV, fridge, coffeemaker, hair dryer, safe.

## Dylan Hotel ✦

Huge care and pots of money have clearly gone into this B&B, which makes this next remark rather uncharitable: The Dylan looks like a Victorian bordello. Dark red, mock-damask wallpaper lines the hallways below the dado rail, with red and gold flock above. And the stair-rods are painted gold. The style fits the date of the house but is very dramatic. And Mr. Felfeli, who has run the Dylan for 12 years, seems such a shy, retiring man. It took him 2 years to renovate from top to bottom. The bedrooms are bright and more restrained, but still carefully put together. All the en suite rooms also have a fridge—relatively rare in this price range and very handy for keeping picnic provisions fresh. No bathroom worries here, either: They really do sparkle. Try to avoid the top of the house because the stairs go on forever. All in all, the Dylan is a fantastic value. One of the cheaper B&Bs in Paddington, it's off the main drag facing a quiet public square and still only 5 minutes from the Tube station.

14 Devonshire Terrace, London W2 3DW. *©* **020/7723-3280.** Fax 020/7402-2443. www.dylan-hotel.com. 18 units, 9 with bathroom (some with shower only). £35 ($50.75) single without bathroom; £52 ($75.40) double without bathroom; £72 ($104.40) double with bathroom; £80–£85 ($116–$123.25) family room. Rates include full English breakfast. Discount for 3-night stays. AE, MC, V. Tube: Paddington, Lancaster Gate. *In room:* TV, coffeemaker, hair dryer, electric fan.

## Fairways Hotel ✦

This is a large, half-white, late-Georgian house, built in the style of John Nash. The inside is charming. Jenny Adams, who runs the B&B with her husband Steve, is quite a magpie, hence the collection of thimbles and Spode china in the breakfast room. The strong personal touch throughout Fairways—the halls and tiny lounge are recently redone—makes it a home away from home. There's a lovely first-floor double at the back, which has the biggest closet in London—great for style queens on tour. Two boudoir chairs flank a little lace-covered table, decorated with a vase of flowers, and the bathroom has posh brass fittings. The basic twin is a good deal. The decor is a bit more mix 'n' match, but it's a nice-size room and only shares the bathroom with a single. Fairways may not throw in as many extras as other local B&Bs, but there are compensations. As well as the friendly atmosphere, guests renting a car to travel out of London can park it for free at the front. The Mitre Hotel next door is the only other place to offer that.

186 Sussex Gardens, London W2 1TU. *©* **020/7723-4871.** Fax 020/7723-4871. www.fairways-hotel.co.uk. 17 units, 10 with bathroom (some with shower only). £48 ($69.60) single without bathroom; £65 ($94.25) single with bathroom; £68 ($98.60) twin without bathroom, £75–£78 ($108.75–$113.10) double/twin with bathroom; £90 ($130.50) triple with bathroom; £105 ($152.25) family room with bathroom. Rates include full English breakfast. MC, V. Tube: Paddington. *In room:* TV, hair dryer, no phone.

## Garden Court ✦

Edward Connolly's grandfather opened Garden Court almost 50 years ago. I fell for it from the moment I saw the jar of Everton mints at the newly refurbished reception. The welcome is really warm. There are cheaper B&Bs in Bayswater but what you won't find elsewhere is such out-and-

# Hotels from Marylebone to Notting Hill

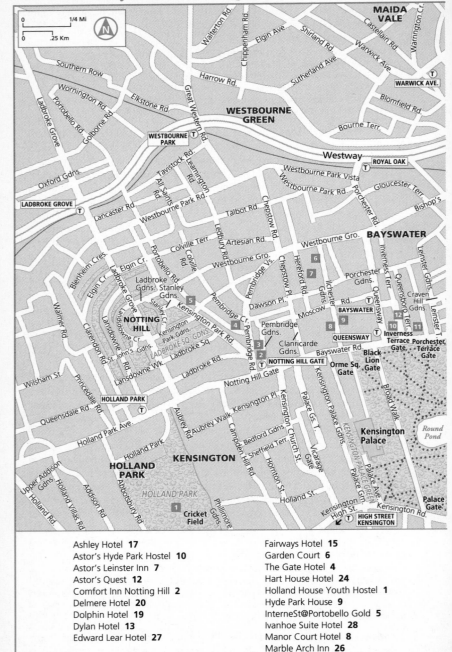

Ashley Hotel **17**
Astor's Hyde Park Hostel **10**
Astor's Leinster Inn **7**
Astor's Quest **12**
Comfort Inn Notting Hill **2**
Delmere Hotel **20**
Dolphin Hotel **19**
Dylan Hotel **13**
Edward Lear Hotel **27**

Fairways Hotel **15**
Garden Court **6**
The Gate Hotel **4**
Hart House Hotel **24**
Holland House Youth Hostel **1**
Hyde Park House **9**
InterneSt@Portobello Gold **5**
Ivanhoe Suite Hotel **28**
Manor Court Hotel **8**
Marble Arch Inn **26**

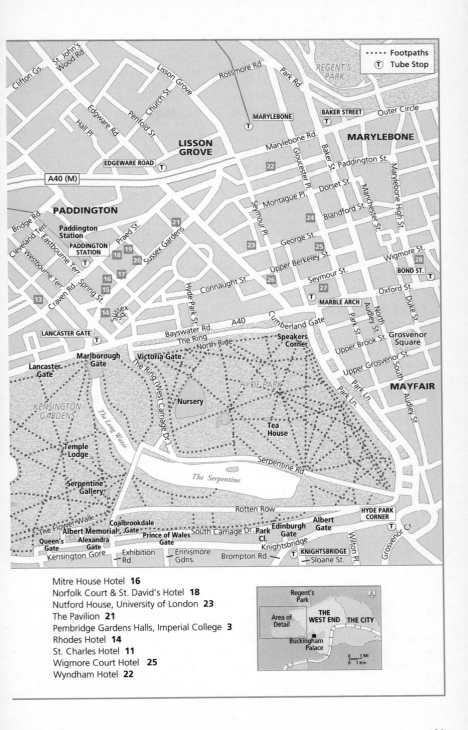

Mitre House Hotel **16**
Norfolk Court & St. David's Hotel **18**
Nutford House, University of London **23**
The Pavilion **21**
Pembridge Gardens Halls, Imperial College **3**
Rhodes Hotel **14**
St. Charles Hotel **11**
Wigmore Court Hotel **25**
Wyndham Hotel **22**

out appeal. The Victorian architect used Kensington Gardens Square to show off his full bag of tricks. The windows are a different shape on each floor, with different decorative moldings. Inside, Garden Court isn't luxxy—except for the swanky new entrance hall, it's more like a much-loved home. The main lounge has some nice old furniture, ancestral portraits, fat novels to borrow, and free hot drinks. There are only a few naff touches, like the modern paneling along the upper corridors. The best value are the rooms without private facilities (they do all have basins), because just over two share each public bathroom. Otherwise, the prices are a little high for Queensway. The rooms are all different: One has pretty yellow wallpaper and white painted furniture, another broad blue stripes that look hand-painted but aren't. Second-floor, front bedrooms lead out onto balconies. The hotel has a small private terrace at the back and access to the public garden square opposite.

30–31 Kensington Gardens Sq., London W2 4BG. © 020/7229-2553. Fax 020/7727-2749. www.gardencourthotel.co.uk. 34 units, 16 with bathroom (some with shower only). £35 ($50.75) single without bathroom; £52 ($75.40) single with bathroom; £56 ($81.20) double/twin without bathroom, £75 ($108.75) twin with bathroom but no WC, £86 ($124.70) double/twin with bathroom; £72 ($104.40) triple without bathroom, £93 ($134.85) triple with bathroom; £82 ($118.90) family room without bathroom, £120 ($174) family room with bathroom. All rates include full English breakfast. MC, V. Tube: Bayswater, Queensway. **Amenities:** Garden. *In room:* TV, hair dryer.

**Hyde Park House** *Value* This is a simple and astonishingly cheap B&B in a very tony part of town. Crown Prince Pavlos of Greece got married at the Greek Orthodox Cathedral of Saint Sophia on the opposite corner. St. Petersburgh Place is a pretty and quiet row of terrace houses, with pocket-handkerchief gardens in front. The bedroom decor is plain, the furniture mix 'n' match, and the sinks often hidden away in a cupboard. Some of the rooms are small: The second-floor triple should really lose a bed. But John and Jeanette Toygar have just repainted and put in new carpets and curtains and you do get good storage space, particularly in the second-floor twin, which has three jumbo floor-to-ceiling closets. You'll have to pant up to the double on the top floor if you want a private bathroom. The 12 other rooms share seven showers, all just redecorated. Hyde Park House doesn't have a breakfast room, so the Toygars deliver a small polystyrene tray with croissant, jams, and cheeses to your room—a nice thought, but that won't fuel a serious tourist for long. Luckily there's a fridge in each room to stock with top-up goodies.

48 St. Petersburgh Place, London W2 4LD. © 020/7229-1687. 13 units, 1 with bathroom (shower only). £30 ($43.50) single without bathroom; £40 ($58) twin/double without bathroom; £40 ($58) double with bathroom; £60 ($87) triple without bathroom; £50–£70 ($72–$101.50) family room without bathroom. Rates include continental breakfast. Discount available off-season. No credit cards. Tube: Bayswater, Queensway. *In room:* TV, fridge, coffeemaker, hair dryer, no phone.

**Mitre House Hotel** *Kids* The row of shiny 4 × 4s on the forecourt here should set off the budget-buster warning bell. Instead, it's a sign of how brilliantly the Chris brothers cater to families. There are rooms with a double bed and two singles. Family suites have a double with a private bathroom and a second bedroom with two singles—fantastic if you're traveling with teenage mutants. Mitre House stretches across four late-Georgian houses on a corner, and superior family suites face quiet, leafy Talbot Square. These have a double and a single in one room, and a double bed in the other, with the toilet and tub-shower off a little private corridor. Junior suites make a good splurge choice, with lots of extra amenities and a Jacuzzi in the bathroom. All the rooms are above average size for London and those at the back are quieter, too, though the view north across back alleys to Paddington isn't too inspiring. Mitre House may not be the cheapest deal around, but it's a good value. Hair dryers and tea-/coffeemakers are available at the reception desk. Anyone (like me) who gets cabin-fever when there's nowhere to chill out for half an hour will be delighted with the big lounge and bar, and those who travel heavy (also like me!) will drool over the elevator.

178–184 Sussex Gardens, London W2 1TU. 𝄢 020/7723-8040. Fax 020/7402-0990. www.mitrehousehotel. com. 70 rooms, all with bathroom (some with shower only). £70 ($101.50) single; £80 ($116) double/twin; £90 ($130.50) triple; £100 ($145) family room; £115 ($166.75) junior suite; £120 ($174) family suite. Rates include full English breakfast. AE, DC, MC, V. Tube: Paddington. **Amenities:** Bar; babysitting arranged; laundry service; dry cleaning. *In room:* TV, radio.

### Norfolk Court & St. David's Hotel ⭐
By January 2002, George and Foulla Neokleos will finally have finished the mammoth job of refurbishing all four of their buildings. The new look is unusual but appealing, with vanilla-painted walls and yellow picking out the moldings and original fireplaces. Norfolk Court & St. David's is a treasure trove of architectural details. One room has a domed ceiling, and there's a lovely, stained-glass window on the stairs of no. 20. These Victorian houses have balconies across the front from which guests on the second floor can admire the pretty communal gardens. In the basement, there's a truly enormous and a very good value family room that can fit five people and has a proper built-in shower. The others are sparkling drop-in units that vary in size depending on what each bedroom can cope with. When I visited, only the top floor was still waiting to have private bathrooms installed, but it was on the to-do list. Irons and hair dryers are available at reception. Full English breakfast here really does mean full, with mushrooms, tomatoes, and baked beans on top of all the rest. All in all, this is a very good and good value choice.

14–20 Norfolk Sq., London W2 1RS. 𝄢 020/7723-4963. Fax 020/7402-9061. 69 units, 60 with bathroom (most with shower only). £39 ($56.55) single without bathroom, £49 ($71.05) single with bathroom; £59 ($85.55) double without bathroom, £69 ($100.05) double with bathroom; £70 ($101.50) triple without bathroom, £80 ($116) triple with bathroom; £80 ($116) quad without bathroom, £90 ($130.50) quad with bathroom; £110 ($159.50) family room. All rates include full English breakfast. AE, DC, MC, V. Tube: Paddington. *In room:* TV, coffeemaker.

### Rhodes Hotel ⭐⭐
A couple of years ago a tourist-board inspector said that the stairs and hallways here were a little "spartan," and Chris Crias was mortally offended. Suddenly, his plan to put in some new bathrooms and spruce the place up spiraled into an £80,000 ($116,000) decorating extravaganza. He has run the Rhodes for more than 20 years, and it always did have a touch of the theatrical— witness the velvet-curtained lounge with its huge murals of Greek amphora. But now the whole place is a gallery of paint effects and angels gaze down from the cloudy ceiling halfway up the stairs to the second floor. There have been lots of other recent improvements, too. There is now air-conditioning in the main bit of the hotel, though not in the annex, which is why the rooms are cheaper there. The other reason he quotes such a wide range of rates is that he's always ready to do a deal. They have gone up a little this year as he has just put Internet access (free except for phone charges) into all the rooms. The bedroom decor is actually quite simple, and number 220 is my favorite. Halfway up the stairs, it has its own little private roof terrace, complete with table and chairs. The bunks in the family room are the poshest I've ever seen, dark wood and 3 feet wide.

195 Sussex Gardens, London W2 2RJ. 𝄢 020/7262-0537. Fax 020/7723-4054. www.rhodeshotel.com. 18 units, all with bathroom (most with shower only). £50–£65 ($72.50–$94.25) single; £65–£90 ($94.25–$130.50) double/twin; £75–£105 ($108.75–$152.25) triple; £95–£120 ($137.75–$174) quad.

Discount available for weekday and 3-day stays. Rates include continental breakfast. MC, V. Tube: Paddington. *In room:* TV, hair dryer, coffeemaker, Internet access.

**St. Charles Hotel**   The bedrooms at this B&B are plain, bright, and big. The private shower rooms are all sparkling new, and big. And yet the rates are really low. So, what's the catch? Well, the rooms don't have a TV or phone, though you can borrow an iron and hair dryer from reception. And Mrs. Wildridge, who has run the St. Charles for 20 years, had to stop offering breakfast last year—floods, pestilence and less biblical problems hit her bookings so badly that it wasn't worth paying the cook. Normal service (full English) may have resumed, so check before you go elsewhere because this place is a good value. Only the twin and the single room on the fifth floor (no lift!) don't strictly have private bathrooms, but they do have showers and the W.C. is just outside. Otherwise, the prices go up the nearer you get to ground level: for instance, a double room costs £60 ($87) on the fourth floor, but £65 ($94.25) on the second or third. Queensborough Terrace must have been very grand when it was built in 1734. The half-stuccoed houses have second floor balconies, which guests in two of the bedrooms can go out on. Inside, ornate wrought-iron banisters curve away out of the entrance hall. There are moldings and fireplaces, and the lounge is paneled like a gentleman's club.

66 Queensborough Terrace, London W2 3SH. (○ **020/7221-0022.** Fax 020/7792-8978. www.stcharleshotel. fsbusiness.co.uk. 15 units, 12 with bathroom (most with shower only). £32–£45 ($46.40–$65.25) single without bathroom; £49–£53 ($71.05–$76.85) twin without bathroom, £60–£69 ($87–$100.05) double/twin with bathroom. Rates do not include breakfast. Higher rates for 1-night stays. MC, V. Tube: Queensway, Bayswater. No children under 10. *In room:* Coffeemaker, no phone.

## SUPER-CHEAP SLEEPS

**Astor's Hyde Park Hostel** ⭐   These three Georgian terrace houses have survived with their gracious internal spaces and beautiful moldings unmolested through years as a bargain sleep. Astor's has even decreed that the crazy murals, a hallmark of its hostels, will be painted on removable boards here at Hyde Park. The company took over 4 years ago and has turned this into its London flagship. The dorms have anything from 4 to 10 bunks, hence the wide price range, and there are great discounts to be had in winter. But the changes have been much bigger than a lick of paint and new carpet. As well as replacing the bathrooms, Astor's has taken advantage of the existing commercial kitchen to open the ITA (International Travellers Association) club, bar and canteen-style cafe. Different DJs guest each night—guests get to DJ themselves on Wednesdays. Meals rarely cost more than £3 ($4.35). And beer starts at £1 ($1.45) during happy hour. If you check out the other amenities, you'll see these guys have thought of everything necessary to create a community for travelers—the 18–35 age restriction, unique in the London hostels reviewed, reinforces that spirit. Astor's has two other hostels in Queensway: **Leinster Inn,** 7–12 Leinster Sq., London, W2 4PR (○ **020/7229-9641;** fax 020/7221-5255) famed for its weekend club nights, and the smaller, more laid-back **Quest,** 45 Queensborough Terrace, London, W2 8SY (○ **020/7229-7782;** fax 020/7727-8106). There is a fourth hostel in **Victoria** (see p. 103) and the longest established **Museum Inn** in Bloomsbury (see p. 92).

2–6 Inverness Terrace, London W2 3HY. (○ **020/7229-5101.** Fax 020/7229-3170. www.astorhostels.com. 200 units, none with bathroom. £42 ($60.90) twin. £12.50–£17 ($18.15–$24.65) per person in a dorm. Rates include bed linen and continental breakfast. Discount available for 1-wk. stays off-season. MC, V. Tube:

Queensway, Bayswater. 18–35 age restriction. **Amenities:** Club, bar, and cafe; game room; coin-op washers and dryers; Internet access; communal kitchen; free valuables lock-up. *In room:* no phone.

## WORTH A SPLURGE

**Delmere Hotel** ⭐⭐    If there's one hotel website to keep an eye on, it's the Delmere's. When I looked, there was a promotion cutting high-summer rates by 10%, making it comparable to the local B&Bs. The Delmere calls itself a "boutique townhouse hotel" (pretentious or what!), hence the gold nameplates and charming window boxes along the top of the late-Georgian porch, and the real-flame fire in the lounge. It caters to a mix of business and pleasure travelers. The rooms are all recently refurbished and very comfortable, but the decor is a bit too safe for real elegance—except for the more expensive crown room, of course, which is up under the eaves and has a Jacuzzi in the bathroom. The canopied bed, frilled tablecloth, and ruched blind make this one look like a rich widow's cabin on a cruise liner. Check out the bedrooms in the annex, which feel like having your own place. The windows look onto a small courtyard, though, so you may be able to hear the music from the hotel's jazz bar. And avoid the lower floor, which is a real hole in the ground. The La Perla restaurant does three-course meals for around £19 ($27.55), but it annoyingly takes a break on Sundays as well as bank holidays and over Christmas.

130 Sussex Gardens, London W2 1UB. ☎ 020/7706-3344. Fax 020/7262-1863. www.delmerehotels.com. 36 units, all with bathroom (most with shower only). £86 ($124.70) single; £107 ($155.15) double/twin; £122 ($176.90) triple. Rates include continental breakfast (full English £6/$8.70). Discount available. AE, DC, DISC, MC, V. Tube: Paddington. **Amenities:** Restaurant; bar; tour desk, secretarial services; limited room service; dry cleaning. *In room:* TV, dataport, coffeemaker, hair dryer, safe, radio.

**The Pavilion** ⭐    Splurgin' here won't get you hot and cold running room service, except when someone brings the continental breakfast—there's no dining room. Nor a bedroom big enough to practice your golf swing. Nor even a luxurious bathroom: the showers are small, too, and rather dated, though they are well maintained. No, what you're paying for is va-va-va-voom, for a glam burlesque that makes you want to raid the costume cupboard and party. Ex-model Danny Karne and his sister Noshi took over the Pavilion nine years ago and they've created London's grooviest, affordable, townhouse hotel. Every room is decorated with paint effects, billowing fabrics, antiques and recycled junkshop finds as though by a set designer on drugs, sometimes with more dash than polish. "Honky Tonk Afro" pays homage to 1970s kitsch, with sequins and disco glitter, while "Highland Fling" has dark paneling, portraits, and acres of tartan. I love the top floor "White Day Soul Nights," a light, bright, cream-on-cream confection worthy of *Architectural Digest*. The only downside is the general scarcity of hanging space. The new sitting room, with doors out to a little courtyard, wasn't finished when I visited but it already had a working title—the Purple Parlour. The Pavilion is for people who want more than somewhere to sleep, wash, and change clothes between adventures. It is an adventure. You might even bump into a supermodel on the stairs, as this is a favorite fashion pack as well as a music business sleep—which is probably why it smells rather smoky.

34–36 Sussex Gardens, London W2 1UL. ☎ 020/7262-0905. Fax 020/7262-1324. www.msi.com.mt/ pavilion/. 27 units, all with bathroom (most with shower only, 2 with tub only). £60–£85 ($87–$123.25) single; £100 ($149) double/twin; £120 ($174) triple; £130 ($188.50) family room. Rates include continental breakfast. AE, DC, MC, V. Tube: Edgware Rd. *In room:* TV, coffeemaker.

## 6 Marylebone

**Edward Lear Hotel**   Previous reviews of this hotel talked about the pretty Georgian houses with gold-tipped railings and luxuriant window boxes; the excellent location, just behind Marble Arch; the nice people working there; and the charming lounge. Then came the "but . . .," because the standards upstairs—up five narrow flights in one house and four in the other!—never matched up to the rest. But last year, long-time owner Peter Evans finally began a 2-year renovation program. Don't expect miracles: under the terms of the lease, he is obliged to carry out certain maintenance works first. But all the bedrooms will have been redecorated by 2002. The look is drab but at least it's clean and the rooms aren't a bad size for London, with generous storage provided by the quirky built-in furniture. However, the bathrooms are scruffy and dated, and likely to stay that way until the other jobs are done. Try for room 18, a double with its bathroom down a little flight of stairs. It looks over a mews at the back, instead of busy Seymour Street—there's no double-glazing at the Edward Lear. The price range for basic rooms is because some have a cupboard-size shower but no W.C. and the rest share a bathroom between four of them. So there are good deals here, depending how laid-back you are about weird and/or shared plumbing.

28–30 Seymour St., London W1H 5WD. ℂ 020/7402-5401. Fax 020/7706-3766. www.edlear.com. 31 units, 4 with bathroom (1 with shower only). £49–£58 ($71.05–$84.10) single without bathroom; £69.50–£81.50 ($100.80–$118.20) double/twin without bathroom, £93 ($134.85) double/twin with bathroom; £83–£91.50 ($120.35–$132.70) triple without bathroom, £105 ($152.25) triple with bathroom. £99.50 ($144.30) family room without bathroom, £109.50 ($158.80) family room with bathroom. Rates include full English breakfast. Children under 2 stay free in parents' room; £9.50 ($13.80) for extra child's bed. Discount of 10% for 1-wk. stays (not July–Aug) and for Internet bookings. MC, V. Tube: Marble Arch. **Amenities:** Internet access. *In room:* TV, coffeemaker, hair dryer, radio.

**Marble Arch Inn**   Mr. Kassam likes to tease his son, who's a fanatical soccer fan. If his club, Arsenal, is due to play a crunch match when you're staying, you'll find the place festooned with the other team's memorabilia. This is an extremely reasonable B&B, especially for somewhere just behind Marble Arch. Unlike Bloomsbury, this neighborhood has no halfway house between the dives and the deluxe. The rooms at the "inn" are tiny, and the showers are all drop-in units. Only parents with saintly children should even think about staying in a family room, particularly as they'll have to eat their continental breakfast there, too, because there's no dining room. Parents who want separate rooms for older kids, or guests without any kids at all, get the best deal. Off-season, two people can take a triple and still pay less than in many other places. Anyone on a tight budget should consider foregoing a private shower because only two rooms share each public facility. Mr. Kassam knows he's got a space problem and works hard to compensate. The decor is simple but fresh. There's a fridge and satellite TV in every room, which is still quite rare in this price range.

Mr. Kassam has another B&B in Victoria: **Dover Hotel,** 42–44 Belgrave Road, SW1 (ℂ **020/7821-9085;** fax 020/7834-6425; www.dover-hotel.co.uk). The rates are similar, so that a double room with private shower costs £75 ($108.75).

49–50 Upper Berkeley St., London W1H 7PN. ℂ **020/7723-7888.** Fax 020/7723-6060. www.marblearch-inn. co.uk. 29 units, 23 with bathroom (shower only). £45–£65 ($65.25–$94.25) single/double without bathroom, £65–£75 ($94.25–$108.75) single/double/twin with bathroom; £80–£100 ($116–$145) triple with bathroom; £100–£130 ($145–$188.50) family room with bathroom. Rates include continental breakfast (full English £4/$5.80). Lower rates apply Jan–Feb. Discount of 5% for 4-night stays. AE, DC, DISC, MC, V. Tube: Marble Arch. **Amenities:** Nonsmoking rooms. *In room:* TV, fridge, coffeemaker, hair dryer, safe.

**Nutford House, University of London** ⭐ *(Finds)*    If you don't mind classic student sleeping arrangements, then this is an absolutely fantastic deal. It's hugely popular with 20-something and retired travelers. You get to stay in a quiet side street, just north of Marble Arch, for half the price of anywhere else in the neighborhood. Nutford House is a marvelous, redbrick building, put up during World War I as a hostel for distressed gentlewomen. All the rooms here are singles, basic but in good clean condition. There are kitchenettes for making snacks on all four floors—there is an elevator—and five people share each public shower or tub, all of which the university recently updated. The twin rooms are in three terrace houses knocked together over the road, which also have kitchenettes. The irony is that dining in the canteen probably works out to cost little more than DIY. Dinner is practically given away at £5 ($7.25) for two courses, or 50p cheaper if you order it when you book. An army could march for days on the breakfast menu, which changes daily. And both meals include vegetarian options. Nutford House is nonsmoking throughout and it has a blissfully peaceful walled garden at the back. Don't forget to pack a bath towel.

Brown St., London W1H 6AH. ✆ 020/7685-5000. Fax 020/7258-1781. www.lon.ac.uk/accom. 180 units, none with bathroom. £22 ($31.90) single; £34 ($49.30) twin. Rates include bed linen, hand towel, and full English breakfast. 10% discount for 1-mth stays. Minimum stay 2 nights. Open Easter and summer vacations. No credit cards. Tube: Marble Arch. **Amenities:** Restaurant; coin-op washers and dryers; nonsmoking rooms; communal kitchens; garden.

**Wyndham Hotel** ⭐ *(Value)*    Gordon Hammé used to be the world's biggest bullion dealer, based in London's Hatton Garden. He sold out, decided to buy a B&B, and took over the Wyndham in spring 1999. It was a grim and dated dump, on a pretty little terrace just off the very busy Marylebone Road. But he has restored it to full glory and, under manager Geoffrey Smith, the place is already winning quality awards. The really big construction project involved putting fantastic £1,000 showers into all the bathrooms (the toilets are still shared). Mr. Hammé got a friend, who used to work at Sotheby's, to help him find original furniture to match the Georgian building. The rooms are attractive, but very small. Luckily, the service is sufficiently solicitous to make up for this shortcoming. A basket of fruit is there to welcome arriving guests. You can call down to reception for sandwiches and salads, pick up your e-mail there, or borrow an iron or hair dryer. The Wyndham really is a charming retreat from the hard graft of sightseeing, and at absolutely giveaway rates. The breakfast room leads out into the beautiful little terraced garden. If other guests beat you to a seat in the sun, you can always look down on them from the roof terrace halfway up the stairs to the second floor.

30 Wyndham St., London W1H 1DD. ✆ 020/7723-7204. Fax 020/7723-2893. wyndhamhotel@talk21.com. 10 units, all with bathroom (most with shower only). £40–£44 ($58–$63.80) single; £52–£55 ($75.40–$79.75) double/twin; £60–£65 ($87–$94.25) triple. Rates include continental breakfast. Discount of 10% for 1-wk. stays. MC, V. Tube: Marylebone, Baker St. **Amenities:** Garden. *In room:* TV, minibar, coffeemaker, radio.

## WORTH A SPLURGE

**Hart House Hotel** ⭐    Andrew Bowden must have been the most pampered little boy in London. His parents used to run Hart House, and when he was 6 years old, maids brought him breakfast in bed to keep him out of the guests' way. This is probably why this B&B is not only extremely welcoming, but one of the most professionally run in London. A Georgian town house, the entrance is like an august gentleman's club, until the polished paneling gives way to pretty floral wallpaper. The rooms are attractive and comfortable (all nonsmoking), and have been fully refurbished over the past couple years. Double-glazing screens out the traffic roar on Gloucester Place—this is a road for folks in a hurry to get from Oxford Street to Baker Street. The top floor double used to be the best deal. Mr. Bowden was worried about persuading guests to climb up that far so he gave a discount and then carried the bags up himself. Such worries proved groundless, and he even received special requests for this peaceful high-up hideaway. The discount is off! So, I'd go for room 6, a huge twin at the back with a marvelous leaded, bay window, and its bathroom up a little flight of stairs. Reception has cots to lend out.

51 Gloucester Place, London W1H 3PE. ⓒ 020/7935-2288. Fax 020/7935-8516. www.harthouse.co.uk. 15 units, all with bathroom (some with shower only). £70 ($101.50) single; £105 ($152.25) double/twin; £130 ($188.50) triple; £150 ($217.50) quad. Rates include full English breakfast. AE, MC, V. Tube: Marble Arch, Baker St. **Amenities:** In-room massage; babysitting arranged; laundry service; dry cleaning; nonsmoking rooms. *In room:* TV, coffeemaker, hair dryer.

**Ivanhoe Suite Hotel** ⭐    This good-value sleep is a gem, but you don't have to be Daddy Warbucks to pay for it. St. Christopher's Place is a pretty piazza, just off Oxford Street, filled with designer boutiques and restaurants with tables outside. Its discreet entrance is next door to Sofra, the restaurant below the B&B, but noise shouldn't be a problem—I was there at lunchtime and couldn't hear anything from downstairs, and diners have to move inside at 11pm. Each room has its own front-door bell, and guests can check on callers via the closed-circuit TV camera linked to their television. The Ivanhoe doesn't actually offer suites, but the rooms are big enough for a table and chairs, where you eat breakfast brought up to you in the morning. The fridge is stocked with mineral water and fruit when you arrive, and the rooms all have a juice squeezer as well as a coffeemaker. The rooms are attractive and recently redecorated, with their bathrooms off a small lobby as you walk in. Some rooms face a narrow street, while others have a view over the piazza fountain. Mrs. Sofer, who was the proprietor for 29 years, sadly sold the Ivanhoe at the beginning of last year. But the atmosphere and careful service that she offered made the business so successful that the new owners had no immediate plans to change anything—other than the prices, which have gone up, of course.

1 St. Christopher's Place, Barrett St. Piazza, London W1M 5HB. ⓒ 020/7935-1047. Fax 020/7224-0563. 7 suites, all with bathroom (some with shower only). £75 ($108.75) single; £95 ($137.75) double; £120 ($174) triple. Rates include continental breakfast. AE, DC, MC, V. Tube: Bond St. **Amenities:** Limited room service; babysitting arranged. *In room:* TV w/pay movies, fridge, coffeemaker, hair dryer, pants press.

**Wigmore Court Hotel** ⭐⭐ *(Finds)*    This is a frustrating and contradictory place, which is what makes it so appealing. The owner, Najma Jinnah, knows the long climb to the fifth floor is a turn-off for a lot of guests, even though they get help with their bags, so she has introduced a reward system. Anyone who does make it to the top can sink into a four-poster bed to recover. There are two more, one each on the second and third floors. Sadly, because this is a small hotel, you'll have to soften Mrs. Jinnah's heart by saying it's your honeymoon or wedding anniversary to guarantee getting one. Budget travelers can get a very good deal here, too. There's a fourth-floor double, which is small for the hotel, but big for London because this is the gracious, Georgian Gloucester Place. It only shares a bathroom, one floor up, with a single and costs £19 ($27.55) less than the others. Though it faces the front, there is double-glazing throughout. The rooms at the back look over a mews. The decor is more relaxed than at Hart House—Wigmore Court is also a little closer to Marble Arch—and six rooms are refurbished every year. Guests can also use the kitchen and laundry facilities, a big bonus normally restricted to budget B&Bs.

23 Gloucester Place, London W1H 3PB. ℂ 020/7935-0928. Fax 020/7487-4254. www.wigmore-court-hotel.co.uk. 18 units, 16 with bathroom (some with shower only). £51 ($73.95) single without bathroom, £60–£80 ($87–$116) single with bathroom; £78 ($113.10) double without bathroom, £92 ($133.40) double with bathroom; £120 ($174) triple with bathroom; £130 ($188.50) family room with bathroom. Rates include full English breakfast. Discount of 10% for 1-wk. stays. MC, V. Tube: Marble Arch. **Amenities:** Secretarial services; laundry facilities; use of kitchen. *In room:* TV, coffeemaker, hair dryer.

## 7 Soho & Oxford Circus

### SUPER-CHEAP SLEEPS

**Oxford Street Youth Hostel**    This excellent cheap sleep is above some offices, in a location most people would kill for—the northern border of Soho. The legendary Carnaby Street, where London first took off as cult fashion capital in the swinging 1960s, is just around the corner and hip new fashion shops are finally pushing back the trashy tourist traps. All the rooms are the same size—small. So, if you've got the cash, ask to share with one other person because the four-bedders feel like a cabin on a sleeper train. Unusually, the bunks are nice sturdy wooden ones, with crisp cotton sheets. There are soft drinks and snack machines, as well as Internet access, in the lounge. The hostel is too small to have a restaurant and provides a very declinable £3.30 ($4.80) continental breakfast pack. The communal kitchen is a great excuse for a 5-minute walk to Berwick Street market. Go late on Friday afternoon, and you'll get huge scoops of vegetables at a bargain price. The hostel also changes money.

14–18 Noel St., London W1. ℂ 020/7734-1618. Fax 020/7734-1657. www.yha.org.uk. 75 units, none with bathroom. £21.80 ($31.60) per person in a twin; £20.55 ($29.80) per night for an adult or £17.50 ($25.40) for under-18s in a 3-to-4-bed dorm. Rates include bed linen. MC, V. Tube: Oxford Circus. No children under 6. **Amenities:** Coin-op washers and dryers; communal kitchen; Internet access. *In room:* no phone.

### WORTH A SPLURGE

**Regent Palace Hotel** ★ *Value*    People who want their own bathroom have to splurge here, but that's rather missing the point. The hotel was built in 1915 before the phrase "en suite" entered the dictionary. The bedrooms have basins, and only three share each block of three toilets and showers. The public bathrooms are kept locked to make sure they're spotless;if you need to use a shower, the housekeeper will ride the elevator up at any time with the key and fresh towels. That's quite a deal at a weekday price that knocks spots off many B&Bs. Breakfast is extra—around £5 ($7.25) for continental and £9 ($13.05) for full English, but the giant hotel is on the edge of Piccadilly Circus and Soho, both of which are chock-a-block with cheap eats. Granada took over 4 years ago and it has installed private showers in over half of the rooms—these also come with hair dryers, while the common bathless folk have to borrow one from reception. The decor is comfortable if a little heavy, with lots of dark, wood veneer, while the spruced-up lobby looks like an air terminal, right down to the dreadful weekend check-in queues. Granada sold the hotel last year but the management is staying put and insists there'll be no changes. The deal was going through when I called, which is why there's no new website listed. But you should try

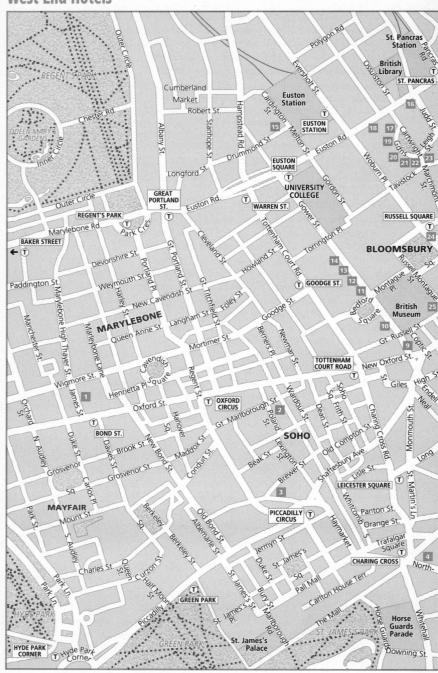

REGENT'S PARK

QUEEN MARY'S GARDENS

Outer Circle

Inner Circle

Chester Rd.

Outer Circle

Cumberland Market

Robert St.

Albany St.

Stanhope St.

Hampstead Rd.

Drummond St.

Longford St.

Cardington St.

Melton St.

St. Pancras Station

Polygon Rd.

Eversholt St.

Euston Station

British Library

ST. PANCRAS

Pancras Rd.

Ossulston St.

**15**

**EUSTON STATION**

Euston Rd.

Euston Rd.

Woburn Pl.

Cartwright Gdns.

Judd St.

Leigh St.

Marchmont St.

Tavistock

**16**

**18** **17**

**19**

**20** **21** **22** **23**

**EUSTON SQUARE**

**GREAT PORTLAND ST.**

Euston Rd.

**REGENT'S PARK**

**BAKER STREET**

Marylebone Rd.

Park Cres.

**WARREN ST.**

**UNIVERSITY COLLEGE**

Gordon St.

Gower St.

Torrington Pl.

**RUSSELL SQUARE**

**BLOOMSBURY**

Russell Sq.

Montague Pl.

Montague St.

**24**

Paddington St.

Devonshire St.

Weymouth St.

Harley St.

New Cavendish St.

Portland Pl.

Gt. Portland St.

Cleveland St.

Howland St.

Tottenham Court Rd.

**GOODGE ST.**

**14**

**13**

**12**

**11**

Bedford Square

**British Museum**

**25**

Manchester St.

Marylebone High St.

Thayer St.

**MARYLEBONE**

Queen Anne St.

Langham St.

Foley St.

Mortimer St.

Goodge St.

Berners St.

Newman St.

**10**

**9**

Gt. Russell St.

Coptic St.

New Oxford St.

**TOTTENHAM COURT ROAD**

Wigmore St.

James St.

Cavendish Square

Henrietta Pl.

**1**

Oxford St.

Regent St.

**OXFORD CIRCUS**

Gt. Marlborough St.

Poland St.

Wardour St.

Dean St.

Frith St.

Soho Sq.

Old Compton St.

Charing Cross Rd.

Giles

High

Endell

Neal

Monmouth St.

Long

**BOND ST.**

Orchard St.

N. Audley St.

Duke St.

Davies St.

Brook St.

New Bond St.

Hanover Sq.

Maddox St.

Conduit St.

Beak St.

Lexington St.

Brewer St.

**2**

**SOHO**

Shaftesbury Ave.

Lisle St.

**LEICESTER SQUARE**

St. Martin's Ln.

Grosvenor Sq.

Grosvenor St.

**MAYFAIR**

Mount St.

Park St.

S. Audley St.

Carlos Pl.

Berkeley St.

Berkeley Sq.

Queen St.

Old Bond St.

Albemarle St.

**3**

**PICCADILLY CIRCUS**

Whitcomb St.

Panton St.

Orange St.

Trafalgar Square

**CHARING CROSS**

North-

**4**

Charles St.

Curzon St.

Half Moon St.

Park Ln.

Park Ln.

**GREEN PARK**

Piccadilly

Jermyn St.

Duke St.

St. James's

St. James's Sq.

Pall Mall

Haymarket

Carlton House Terr.

**HYDE PARK CORNER**

Hyde Park Corner

HYDE PARK

GREEN PARK

St. James's Pl.

St. James's St.

Marlborough

Bury St.

**St. James's Palace**

The Mall

ST. JAMES'S PARK

Horse Guards

**Horse Guards Parade**

Whitehall

Downing St.

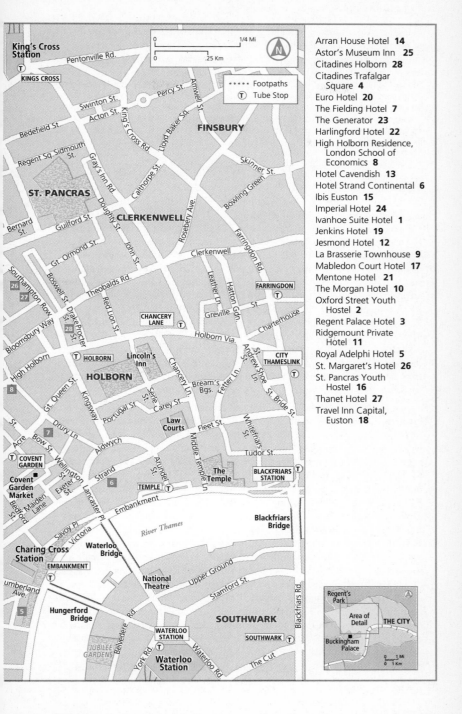

Arran House Hotel **14**
Astor's Museum Inn **25**
Citadines Holborn **28**
Citadines Trafalgar
   Square **4**
Euro Hotel **20**
The Fielding Hotel **7**
The Generator **23**
Harlingford Hotel **22**
High Holborn Residence,
   London School of
   Economics **8**
Hotel Cavendish **13**
Hotel Strand Continental **6**
Ibis Euston **15**
Imperial Hotel **24**
Ivanhoe Suite Hotel **1**
Jenkins Hotel **19**
Jesmond Hotel **12**
La Brasserie Townhouse **9**
Mabledon Court Hotel **17**
Mentone Hotel **21**
The Morgan Hotel **10**
Oxford Street Youth
   Hostel **2**
Regent Palace Hotel **3**
Ridgemount Private
   Hotel **11**
Royal Adelphi Hotel **5**
St. Margaret's Hotel **26**
St. Pancras Youth
   Hostel **16**
Thanet Hotel **27**
Travel Inn Capital,
   Euston **18**

plugging "Regent Palace" into one of the search engines—this hotel has a history of offering cheap rates through a host of accommodation sites.

Glasshouse St., Piccadilly Circus, London W1A 4BZ. © 08704/008703. Fax 020/7734-6435. 887 units, 500 with bathroom (shower only). £59–£70 ($85.55–$101.50) single without bathroom; £59–£84 ($85.55–$121.80) double/twin without bathroom; £99–£109 ($143.55–$158.05) double/twin with bathroom; £85–£99 ($123.25–$143.55) triple without bathroom; £109–£128 ($158.05–$185.60) quad without bathroom. 32 units adapted for travelers with disabilities. Lower rates apply Sun–Thurs. Discount available for long stays. AE, DC, MC, V. Tube: Piccadilly Circus. **Amenities:** Pub and coffeebar; concierge; tour desk; limited room service; laundry service; dry cleaning; nonsmoking rooms. *In room:* TV w/pay movies; coffeemaker, radio.

## 8 Bloomsbury

**Travel Inn Capital** (© 020/7554-3400; fax 020/7554-3419; www.travelinn. co.uk), reviewed under "Just South of the River," later in this chapter, has another great value hotel at 1 Dukes Rd., WC1H 9PJ. It has similar rates, decor, and amenities as its hotel in South Bank (for this one, take the Tube to Euston). For a super-cheap sleep opposite the British Library, check out the modern **St. Pancras Youth Hostel** (© 020/7388-9998; fax 020/7388-6766; www.yha.org. uk) at 79–81 Euston Rd., NW1 2QS. It costs £23.50 ($34.10) per night for adults, £19.90 ($28.85) for under-18s. Children under 3 are welcome, and cots are available. Take the Tube to Euston or King's Cross. **Astor's Museum Inn,** 27 Montague St., London WC1B 5BH (© 020/7580-5360; fax 020/ 7636-7948. www.astorhostels.com) is the company's longest established hostel, up and running for 20 years. Dorm beds cost £15 to £18 ($21.75–$26.10) per night. Because it is next to the British Museum and in a listed Georgian terrace, the Museum Inn is quieter than the Hyde Park HQ (See "Paddington & Bayswater," earlier in this chapter). Age restriction 18 to 35. Take the tube to Russell Square or Holborn.

**Arran House Hotel** ★★   It's sad to get excited by something as ordinary as a kitchen, but that's the point. Most B&Bs don't let guests use theirs, and apart from Wigmore Court in Marylebone, none of the others that do are as welcoming or as nice as this. Heat up your own supper—great for budget travelers—and dine in style in the marvelous breakfast room. The family ought to sell tickets to see this mini-museum. Swords, coats of arms, and other memorabilia line the walls, all collected by the current proprietor's father, Major Richards. After finally managing to negotiate a new lease from his landlord, the Duke of Bedford, John Richards can start his first refurbishment for years—the place had got very scruffy. Last year, he recarpeted and painted throughout—the tired showers are some way down the list. The bedrooms will still be simple, light, and homey, with new quilts to replace the covers. If you go for one with a shower, but no toilet—the higher bathless prices, below—you'll get the best deal on Gower Street. Do avoid the tiny basic twins where the beds are head to head along one wall. The front rooms are double-glazed, which cuts out the traffic hum, and reception will pipe videos through to the bedroom TVs for free. The coin-operated Internet terminal in the lounge lets you pick up your e-mails for a 50p (73¢) minimum charge. There are self-service laundry facilities. And you won't find a more beautiful garden. A top, budget sleep.

77 Gower St., London WC1E 6HJ. © 020/7636-2186 or 020/7637-1140. Fax 020/7436-5328. 28 units, 13 with bathroom (shower only). £45 ($65.25) single without bathroom, £55 ($79.75) single with bathroom; £55–£60 ($79.75–$87) double without bathroom, £75 ($108.75) double with bathroom; £73–£77 ($105.85–$111.65) triple without bathroom, £93 ($134.85) triple with bathroom; £79–£84 ($114.55–$121.80) quad without bathroom, £97 ($140.65) quad with bathroom; £88 ($127.60) 5-bed

without bathroom, £110 ($159.50) 5-bed with bathroom. Rates include full English breakfast. MC, V. Tube: Goodge St., Russell Sq. **Amenities:** Babysitting arranged; laundry facilities; garden; Internet access. *In room:* TV, hair dryer.

### La Brasserie Townhouse ★ *Finds*    Get your fingers pushing phone buttons now; deals this good are as rare as an unchatty London taxi driver. Only a tiny handful of hotels so centrally located can match the twin-room price—most are at least £10 ($14.50) a night more expensive. The singles are even more of a steal, at little more than what you'd pay to sleep at a youth hostel. That's because they really are one-person big. The other *quid pro quo* for the extraordinary price is that there is only one public bathroom for what could be six guests. But if you've gotta queue, then there are few places lovelier to do it than in one of these rooms. The furniture is all white and the decor vanilla, including the beautiful loopy curtains that ripple across the windows. The twins even get a little table and chairs to eat at. Irritatingly, you have to wait until 4pm to check in. Presumably, that's when there's a lull in the brasserie downstairs. Chef Lloyd Lewars ran the Townhouse with his wife Joanna, winning awards for his French-Caribbean cuisine. But the couple sold up just as we were going to press. Now the food is more traditionally French, and prices are £7.95 to £9.95 ($11.55–$14.45) for a fixed-price meal.

24 Coptic St., London WC1A 1NT. ⓒ 020/7636-2731. labrasserietownhouse@talk21.com. 4 units, none with bathroom. £25 ($36.25) single; £48 ($69.60) twin. Rates include continental breakfast. AE, DC, MC, V. Tube: Holborn, Tottenham Ct. Rd. **Amenities:** Restaurant; bar; limited room service; nonsmoking rooms. *In room:* TV, minibar, coffeemaker, hair dryer, iron, no phone.

### Euro Hotel ★ *Kids*    The kids' drawings that festoon the walls behind reception are a pretty heavy clue as to where the hotel's strength lies—as a favorite of families on holiday. Generally, prices are high-ish for Cartwright Gardens, a Georgian crescent in north Bloomsbury that is already more expensive than Gower Street and, while it has a more neighborhood feel, it is also farther away from the action. However, the Euro does do a good value rate for children under 16 who share a room with their parents. You pay the normal single or double price, depending on the number of adults, plus £10 ($14.50) per child: For example, a basic family room for mom, pop, and two kids would cost £87 ($126.15) a night instead of £92 ($133.40). Toddlers under 2½ stay free, and you can borrow a high chair and crib at the reception desk. The Euro was recently repainted throughout and it is an attractive place. Basic rooms only share a bathroom with one other—another good deal, especially as the public facilities have just been totally renovated. The service is very friendly—the hotel offers guests videos, use of the office safe and fax machine, and e-mail pick-up, all for free. And if the kids still need wearing out after a day on the tourist trail, you can play tennis in the gardens opposite. The Euro can lend you rackets and balls.

53 Cartwright Gardens, London WC1H 9EL. ⓒ 020/7387-4321. Fax 020/7383-5044. www.eurohotel.co.uk. 35 units, 10 with bathroom (some with shower only). £48 ($69.60) single without bathroom, £70 ($101.50) single with bathroom; £67 ($97.15) double/twin without bathroom, £87 ($126.15) double/twin with bathroom; £82 ($118.90) triple without bathroom, £102 ($147.90) triple with bathroom; £92 ($133.40) family room without bathroom, £112 ($162.40) family room with bathroom. Rates include full English breakfast. Special rates for children under 16. Discount of 10% for 1-wk. stays off-season. AE, MC, V. Tube: Euston, Russell Sq. **Amenities:** Tennis court; garden. *In room:* TV, coffeemaker, radio.

### Harlingford Hotel ★★    It takes much longer than you think to refurbish a hotel because it has to be done inch by inch without disturbing the guests. But

Andrew Davies has been hard at work on the Harlingford Hotel, a pretty, dove-gray, Georgian building on the corner of Marchmont Street and Cartwright Gardens, for over 2 years. He is the third generation of his family to run this B&B, and he's a perfectionist. I thought the bedrooms were finished, and nicely too. But Andrew sacked his designer and hired a new one to put right what he saw as mistakes. This has put back plans to renovate the lounge and breakfast rooms, which should now be finished by the end of November 2001. On either side of the front door, both rooms are a real asset with their gracious arched windows and high ceilings. Hair dryers are available on request, and guests can use the ice dispenser. You can take your drink outside into the communal gardens opposite. All you have to do is ask for the key. But you will have to bring your own tennis rackets to play on the court there.

61–63 Cartwright Gardens, London WC1H 9EL. ℂ 020/7387-1551. Fax 020/7387-4616. www. smoothhound.co.uk/hotels/harling.html. 44 units, all with bathroom (shower only). £70 ($101.50) single; £88 ($127.60) double/twin; £98 ($142.10) triple; £108 ($156.60) quad. Rates include full English breakfast. AE, DC, MC, V. Tube: Euston, Russell Sq. **Amenities:** Tennis court; garden. *In room:* TV, coffeemaker.

**Hotel Cavendish**    EMI used to book rooms at the Cavendish for try-out bands; the Beatles also slept here when there were still five of them. Eluned Edwards' mother was running the B&B then. Clean, cozy, and welcoming, Hotel Cavendish only offers bathless sleeps—there are new power-showers in all the shared facilities. No two bedrooms are the same, but Mrs. Edwards is a big fan of William Morris wallpaper, so you'll find lots of that. All the rooms have candlewick bedspreads and pretty furniture that might have come out of somebody's home. That's exactly what Hotel Cavendish looks like—a home cleverly decorated on a budget. And it's a haven for the budget traveler, who gets exactly what they're prepared to pay for. For instance, the £48 ($69.60) double is very small but why spend more if you're going to be out all day and partying all night? The pinnacle of desirability is the spacious £66 ($95.70) double at the back. Hair dryers are available at reception. Some rooms do have a TV, or guests can watch the one in the lounge. And they can sit in the garden in the summer.

75 Gower St., London WC1E 6HJ. ℂ 020/7636-9079. Fax 020/7580-3609. www.hotelcavendish.com. 20 units, none with bathroom. £38 ($55.10) single; £48–£66 ($69.60–$95.70) double; £69–£78 ($100.05–$113.10) triple; £84–£92 ($121.80–$133.40) quad. Rates include full English breakfast. Discount available for groups. AE, MC, V. Tube: Goodge St., Russell Sq. **Amenities:** Garden. *In room:* Coffeemaker, no phone.

**Ibis Euston** ✦    This chain of budget hotels, owned by the French group Accor, has cloned itself all over the country (see "Near the Airport," later in this chapter). It's a good deal for travelers who prefer up-to-date identikit accommodations and are willing to forego the quirks of a B&B. Room rates compete with those on Gower Street, though breakfast is not included—buffet continental costs £4.50 ($6.55)—and it's twice as far to walk to the West End. You'd never choose the Ibis for the beauty of its location. The "wrong" side of Euston Road is a bit bleak and businessy, but the Ibis has made its modern redbrick building very welcoming with hanging baskets and striped awnings. The inside is blandly appealing, too—the first floor has the open feel of a food court at a shopping mall. There's a railway-themed bar, and a restaurant, La Croisette, which is loosely styled as a South of France beach cafe. Supper is very reasonably priced both there and at Tracks. Upstairs, the rooms are medium-size, all with newly refurbished bathrooms. This hotel has an elevator, and you can send e-mail for free via the i-plus electronic information booth in the foyer.

3 Cardington St., London NW1 2LW. ✆ **020/7388-7777.** Fax 020/7388-0001. www.ibishotel.com. 380 units, all with bathroom (shower only). £69.95 ($101.45) double/twin. 8 units adapted for travelers with disabilities. Rates do not include breakfast. Under-12s stay free in parents' room. AE, DC, MC, V. Tube: Euston. **Amenities:** Restaurant, bar; room service; Internet access. *In room:* TV.

**Jenkins Hotel** ⭐   Sam Bellingham and his partner Felicity Langley-Hunt have just refurbished the whole of Jenkins Hotel. Budget travelers have sadly lost the cheaper bathless option, but the rate for an en suite double is still a few pounds cheaper than elsewhere in Cartwright Gardens. Rivals score points for having lounges but Jenkins offers better in-room amenities. The transformation has been achieved both by putting in upmarket shower cubicles and by shuffling a few walls about so that public bathrooms become private ones, as in the rather nice double room (no. 10) on the fourth floor. But I think the top choice is going to be the second-floor room five, where two rooms on the front, with floor-to-ceiling windows, have been knocked into one. The one to avoid is definitely the basement double. Though charmingly decorated, it is too much like troglodyte living at the price. Jenkins has been a hotel since the 1920s and once appeared in the PBS mystery series *Poirot.* Today the style is trad-lite, very English but relaxed about it. Sam's two Labradors lurk about in the kitchen which, with its huge pine table, also substitutes as reception. There are rackets and balls to borrow if you want to play tennis in communal gardens opposite. There probably won't be much competition for them either, unless it's during Wimbledon, which inspires even the most unsporting types. Jenkins is completely nonsmoking.

45 Cartwright Gardens, London WC1H 9EH. ✆ **020/7387-2067.** Fax 020/7383-3139. www.jenkinshotel. demon.co.uk. 13 units, 12 with bathroom (most with shower only). £52 ($75.40) single without bathroom, £72 ($104.40) single with bathroom; £85 ($123.25) double/twin with bathroom; £105 ($152.25) triple with bathroom. Rates include full English breakfast. MC, V. Tube: Euston, Russell Sq. **Amenities:** Tennis court; non-smoking rooms; garden. *In room:* TV, fridge, coffeemaker, hair dryer, safe.

**Jesmond Hotel**   The Jesmond's proprietors, Mr. and Mrs. Beynon, travel to the United States a lot and worry about living up to the accommodation standards there. In many ways, they can't, like anyone running a small B&B in a listed building in Central London. A lot of the rooms are small, though the choice of blonde-wood furniture helps to counteract that and the cabinets around the in-room sinks provide extra storage. And only a few have private bathrooms at the moment. However, those that do are competitively priced, and those that don't are positively cheap. And the Beynons make sure the atmosphere and welcome are top-notch—they've been working at it for over 20 years. The rooms at the front have double-glazing, which makes them pretty quiet. And the couple recently spruced up the lounge, so it really feels like home: it's got a cold-drink machine and more free tea and coffee. If you're short of something to read, there are rows of books downstairs in the breakfast room. And this is one of the few places that still puts a fruit bowl out in the morning, even though guests pocket extra portions to take with them for lunch.

63 Gower St., London WC1 6HJ. ✆ **020/7636-3199.** Fax 020/7323-4373. www.jesmondhotel.org.uk. 16 units, 5 with bathroom (shower only). £36 ($52.20) single without bathroom, £46 ($66.70) single with bathroom; £54 ($78.30) double/twin without bathroom, £68 ($98.60) double/twin with bathroom; £70 ($101.50) triple without bathroom, £80 ($116) triple with bathroom; £82 ($118.90) quad without bathroom, £90 ($130.50) quad with bathroom; £95 ($137.75) five-bed without bathroom. Rates include full English breakfast. MC, V. Tube: Goodge St., Russell Sq. *In room:* TV, coffeemaker, hair dryer, radio, no phone.

**Mabledon Court Hotel** ⭐   Dating from the 1950s, this is a modern building by local standards, but it fits in well with the Georgian and Victorian neighbors. Because it was purpose-built as a hotel, there are no nasty surprises—tiny rooms squeezed out of larger ones or hopelessly tiny bathrooms put in as an after-thought. Like the Harlingford around the corner in Cartwright Gardens, the Mabledon Court belongs to the Davies family (hence the access to the tennis court and communal garden). Last year, they completed a big refurbishment. The bedrooms have a fresh coat of paint; new carpets, beds, curtains, and bedspreads; and security chains on the doors. The bathrooms have sparkling white tiles and wooden floors, and paneling has lent the hallways a more upmarket air. There is an elevator so don't worry about ending up on a higher floor. In fact, you should probably request that, and to be at the back, because Mabledon Place is a fairly busy road. If you're feeling adventurous, the pub next door has an all-day menu that includes black pudding. I'd say that was going native, but the natives are generally too namby-pamby to touch it.

10–11 Mabledon Place, London WC1H 9BA. ✆ 020/7388-3866. Fax 020/7387-5686. www. smoothhound.co.uk/hotels/mabledon.html. 32 units, all with bathroom (shower only). £70 ($101.50) single; £80 ($116) double. Rates include full English breakfast. AE, DC, MC, V. Tube: Euston, Russell Sq. **Amenities:** Tennis court; garden. *In room:* TV, coffeemaker, hair dryer.

**Mentone Hotel** 🌟 This is the second B&B along from the south end of Cartwright Gardens. It's a bit cheaper than the neighboring Jenkins Hotel, and while the welcome is friendly and the decor newish, it doesn't have quite the same charm. The Mentone stretches across three houses and has been run by the same family for over 30 years. Simon Tyner took over from his mother in 1997, though she still looks after the hotel's hanging baskets and window boxes—she's won prizes for them in the past. Mr. Tyner has refurbished most of the bedrooms since then, and they've got nice matching quilt covers and curtains. The family has resisted chopping up the original Georgian rooms, so the only funny shapes come from the private bathrooms, also recently redone. You do get a big room here, which is not something you can say about many London B&Bs. There's enough space in some for a small sofa, and though the ceilings are lower on the top floor, the rooms don't feel cramped. You can borrow a hair dryer at the reception desk, as well as a key to get into the half-moon gardens opposite. Unlike the Euro and Jenkins hotels farther round the crescent, it doesn't lend out tennis equipment, so you'll have to bring your own to use the court.

54 Cartwright Gardens, London WC1H 9EL. ✆ 020/7387-3927. Fax 020/7388-4671. www.mentonehotel. com. 42 units, 41 with bathroom (most with shower only). £42 ($60.90) single without bathroom, £60 ($87) single with bathroom; £82 ($118.90) double/twin with bathroom; £93 ($134.85) triple with bathroom; £102 ($147.90) family room with bathroom. Rates include full English breakfast. Discount available off-season and for long stays. AE, DC, MC, V. Tube: Euston, Russell Sq. **Amenities:** Tennis court; garden. *In-room:* TV, coffeemaker.

**The Morgan Hotel** 🌟🌟 It's a real treat to find a B&B with air-conditioning and double-glazing, particularly in an elegant, 18th-century terrace house. It makes staying at the Morgan Hotel completely painless, though Bloomsbury Street is at the busy southern end of Gower Street—a 10-minute walk to Covent Garden. It's more expensive than other local B&Bs (still cheaper than Cartwright Gardens), but then, period-style decoration does tend to bump the price up. There are pretty floral bedspreads and decorative borders on the walls, and every room is different. If there are two of you, go for the first-floor room that opens onto the garden at the back, which no one else gets to use. The beds in one of the twins can be zippered together to make a king-size bed. But don't come here for a basic single room—the owner claims to get requests for the one on the first floor, but it's absolutely tiny, and there are much better deals else-where. The downside to the hotel is that it can't accommodate families larger than three in the same room. Otherwise, it's almost worth staying there just to see the breakfast room, oak-paneled room with all the seating in wooden booths. Just up the road, Morgan has four one-bedroom apartments, which go for £115 ($166.75) a night including breakfast, or £160 ($232) to have a foldaway bed, and sleep three.

24 Bloomsbury St., London WC1B 3QJ. © 020/7636-3735. Fax 020/7636-3045. 15 units, all with bathroom (most with shower only). £58–£68 ($84.10–$98.60) single; £85 ($123.25) double/twin; £130 ($188.50) triple. Rates include full English breakfast. MC, V. Tube: Goodge St., Tottenham Court Rd. *In room:* A/C, TV, hair dryer.

**Ridgemount Private Hotel** *Value*   Royden and Gwen Rees, the Welsh proprietors, have a reputation for providing a warm-hearted welcome. They've run this B&B for 35 years, and some of their guests go back a long way, too. It's 14 years since one U.S. college started sending students to stay here every January during their exchange trips. Smiling group pictures are pinned up all over the breakfast room. If you want to stay at the Ridgemount, or any of the nicer Bloomsbury B&Bs, you will have to book ahead. A large part of the University of London is here, which guarantees an endless supply of customers. The Ridgemount stretches across two buildings, one of which still has all the original fireplaces and cornices. The decor is simple, with homey candlewick covers on the beds, and some of the rooms are quite small, particularly the basic twins. But if you're looking for a double room with a private bathroom—several of which are brand new—you're unlikely to find a cheaper rate anywhere else on Gower Street. All the rooms on the front are double-glazed against the traffic noise. Free coffee and tea are available in the lounge, and you can borrow an electric fan at reception. Mr. and Mrs. Rees will even do laundry. And like most of the B&Bs on Gower Street, you can use the garden in the summer.

65–67 Gower St., London WC1E 6HJ. © 020/7636-1141. Fax 020/7636-2558. 32 units, 13 with bathroom (shower only). £33 ($47.85) single without bathroom, £45 ($65.25) single with bathroom; £50 ($72.50) double/twin without bathroom, £65 ($94.25) double/twin with bathroom; £66 ($95.70) triple without bathroom, £78 ($113.10) triple with bathroom; £76 ($110.20) quad without bathroom, £88 ($127.60) quad with bathroom; £82 ($118.90) five-bed without bathroom, £92 ($133.40) five-bed with bathroom. Rates include full English breakfast. MC, V. Tube: Goodge St., Russell Sq. **Amenities:** Laundry facilities. *In room:* TV, no phone.

**St. Margaret's Hotel** *✿*   The welcome here inspires devoted loyalty. One lady guest stayed for 28 years. Mrs. Marazzi is the second generation of her family to run the B&B, which rambles over four houses. Take a ball of string if you want to find your room again. The rooms are simple, and no two are the same—short stays usually get the smaller ones. They are also all nonsmoking. You can borrow a fan from the reception desk and a hair dryer if you're staying in one of the rooms without one. Budget travelers should go for the cheap en suite double, which has the toilet just outside. However, the Marazzis recently created some beautiful extra public bathrooms, so it's easy to survive the sharing experience. If you can afford it, room 53 is a marvelous, first-floor triple, which normally costs £110.50 ($160.25) but which two people can take for £95 ($137.75). It has a king-size bed, a single bed, and a gray-tiled, private bathroom with a corner tub. And off it is a small private conservatory, looking onto the quiet communal garden that all the guests can use. St. Margaret's has two lounges, one with a TV and the other for guests who prefer peace and quiet. Newspapers are delivered.

26 Bedford Place, London WC1B 5JL. © 020/7636-4277. Fax 020/7323-3066. 65 units, 10 with bathroom (most with shower only). £48.50 ($70.35) single without bathroom; from £60.50 ($80.75) double without bathroom, £75–£90 ($108.75–$130.50) double with bathroom. Rates include full English breakfast. MC, V. Tube: Russell Sq., Holborn. **Amenities:** Babysitting arranged; nonsmoking rooms; garden. *In room:* TV.

**Thanet Hotel**    This quiet Georgian terrace links Russell Square, which is like a London bus merry-go-round, with the more peaceful Bloomsbury Square and is the closest of all the streets listed here to Covent Garden and the rest of the West End. It had gotten a little scruffy in recent years but the Bedford estate has taken back in hand seven houses that had become a hostel for the homeless in order to do them up. It has also granted the proprietors, the Orchards, a new long lease, so last year they began to refurbish. The bedrooms have been repainted and have new carpet, curtains and bedcovers. If you can, ask for the second-floor double room, which has huge windows looking over the back garden, and is a bit bigger than some of the others. The Orchards have also redone the rather tired bathrooms with bright white tiles. It is easy to spot this guesthouse, with its blue awning and exuberant window boxes. It has won plaudits as a good budget bet for a long time, but prices have crept up. Thanet is a bit more expensive than St. Margaret's Hotel, across the way, which has two lounges and offers guests the use of the garden. But the Orchards are a really charming couple and Lynwen really has hotelkeeping in her blood—she grew up at the Harlingford.

Last year, they took over the former University of Iowa student hostel next door and began to tidy it up a bit—the bathrooms were shocking! **Pickwick Hall** (© 020/7323-4958; pickwickhall@aol.com) is a friendly place, with no age restrictions and space for 35 weary heads. It costs £25 ($36.25) for a single, £40 ($58) for a twin, and £15–£18 ($21.75–$26.10) per person in a dorm.

8 Bedford Place, London WC1B 5JA. © 020/7636-2869. Fax 020/7323-6676. www.freepages.co.uk/thanet_hotel/. 16 units, all with bathroom (shower only). £67 ($97.15) single; £88 ($127.60) double/twin; £99 ($143.55) triple; £108 ($156.60) quad. Rates include full English breakfast. AE, MC, V. Tube: Russell Sq., Holborn. *In room:* TV, coffeemaker, hair dryer, radio.

## SUPER-CHEAP SLEEPS

**The Generator**    This hostel is hidden away through a scruffy hole in the wall in tidy Tavistock Place. It opened in 1995 in what used to be a police section house; inside, it's like a cross between the set of *Alien* and a hip Soho coffee bar. Aluminum pipes and blue neon lights snake across the ceiling in reception. The different floors are called Level 01, 02, and so on. And all the signage, including room numbers, is spray-stenciled, packing-crate-style. There's a nut on the door of the women's bathrooms and a bolt on the men's. The Spartan bedrooms, all nonsmoking and with bunks, are equipped with funky metal basins, and it's about eight people to every shower. The 800-bed Generator is more expensive than its private sector rivals, except in the biggest dorms. Breakfast is self-service in the Fuel Stop canteen. There is no self-catering, which is a bit of a bind when you're traveling on this kind of budget. The bar is very Soho, but prices are lower than even a local pub's, and it stays open until 2am. In fact, the only real drawback to The Generator is that it caters for a lot of groups, so be prepared for hordes of kids on tour. (Unlike at any of the Astor's hostels, where the lower age limit is 18.)

Compton Place, off 37 Tavistock Place, London WC1H 9SD. © 020/7388-7666. Fax 020/7388-7644. www.the-generator.co.uk. 217 units, none with bathroom. £40 ($58) single; £53 ($76.85) twin; £67.50 ($97.90) triple; £15–£21.50 ($21.75–$31.20) per person in a dorm. Rates include bed linen, towels, and continental breakfast. Discount available for 5-night stays and for groups. MC, V. Tube: Russell Sq. **Amenities:** Bar; game room; nonsmoking rooms; Internet access. *In room:* no phone.

## WORTH A SPLURGE

**Imperial Hotel**  ★  *Value*    A few pounds more expensive than Bloomsbury's toniest B&Bs, the Imperial is both a splurge and a very good deal. The decor isn't particularly plush. In fact, it's rather dated. What you do get, though, is an affordable, full-on, full-service hotel, just a stone's throw from Covent Garden and Soho. It's a complete monstrosity from the outside—a huge, corrugated, concrete box taking up half the eastern side of Russell Square with a row of shops at street level. Some are useful, like Hertz and American Express, but others sell cheesy souvenirs. There are nine floors of bedrooms, and the third is nonsmoking. The hotel does a lot of tour-group business, but the rooms have stood up pretty well to the traffic. They're all a decent size and have excellent storage space. Some also have pants presses, minibars, and hair dryers. Everything is sparkling clean. In most of the doubles and twins, the en suite toilet and tub/shower are handily separate. The Imperial has a vineyard to make the Bordeaux house wine and a farm just outside London, which delivers produce every day to be served up in the rather grim Elizabethan room. Otherwise, the Day & Night Bar, an oasis of up-to-the-minute style, is open for light food and drinks until 2am. If you'd rather forego the amenities and pay a few pounds less, check out the website because the company owns five other Bloomsbury hotels.

Russell Sq., London WC1B 5BB. ⓒ 020/7278-7871. Fax 020/7837-4653. www.imperialhotels.co.uk. 448 units. £73 ($105.85) single; £97 ($141.40) double/twin. Rates include full English breakfast. AE, DC, DISC, MC, V. Tube: Russell Sq. **Amenities:** Restaurant, cafe/bar; access to nearby health club; concierge; car-rental desk; limited room service; babysitting; laundry service; dry cleaning; nonsmoking rooms. *In room:* TV, coffeemaker, radio.

## 9 Covent Garden, the Strand & Holborn

**High Holborn Residence, London School of Economics** ⭐ *Kids*   Some rooms at the back of this hall look out over the topless sunbathers around the pool at the Oasis Sports Centre next door. But don't even think about requesting one, or the view you'll have is the one most people do, of the Shaftesbury Theatre and the traffic pouring down High Holborn—not roaring, though, because the whole place is double-glazed. This is a tip-top residence in a tip-top location. Turn a corner, and it's a 5-minute walk to Covent Garden, which is why it can charge B&B hotel rates. That, and the fact that the beds have the fattest, most civilized mattresses I've ever seen in a student hall. It's very popular with moms and pops, who pay £5 ($7.25) a night for a foldaway bed plus the same again for an extra breakfast, making this one of the cheapest family rooms in town—and one of the cheapest triples, of course. Blocks of six rooms lock together and share a toilet, shower, and kitchen—bring your own utensils. Every second floor has two extra shared tubs, and everything is in very good shape. Downstairs, there's a huge breakfast room-cum-lounge, where one of the vending machines sells Häagen-Dazs. And, hey, check out that open-air pool: It only costs £2.90 ($4.20) for adults, or £1.10 ($1.60) for kids.

178 High Holborn, London WC1. ⓒ 020/7379-5589. Fax 020/7379-5640. www.lsevacations.com. 428 units, 24 with bathroom (shower only). £35 ($50.75) single without bathroom; £57 ($82.65) twin without bathroom, £67 ($97.15) twin with bathroom. 4 units adapted for travelers with disabilities. Rates include continental breakfast. Open summer vacation. MC, V. Tube: Holborn. **Amenities:** Game room; coin-op washers and dryers; communal kitchen; Internet access. *In room:* no phone.

**Hotel Strand Continental** *Finds*   This place is like the set of an art-house movie about the dying days of the British Empire. The hotel is part of the India Club, which Krishna Mennon, the first Indian High Commissioner to Britain, set up after independence. The members may be third generation, but little else has changed—the cash register in the bar looks like a manual typewriter. It certainly isn't posh, but this little hotel has become an exceptional deal since a charming Indian couple, Mr. and Mrs. Marker, took over in 1998. They've

## ⎛Tips⎞ The Bargain Business

Business hotel chains need to fill their beds when lucrative corporate customers go home so they offer special take-a-break rates. These put city-center 3-star sleeps on a par with a pricey B&B and may even make posher hotels an affordable splurge. What you'll actually pay will fluctuate according to seasonal demand, from the top leisure price quoted in the branded brochures to discounted promotional rates, so always ask for best deal. **Choice Hotels** (ⓒ **0800/444444**; www.choicehotels. com) claimed to have a myriad of offers running all the time at its Comfort Inns [£50/$72] a night B&B in a newspaper hook-up last summer!), rather than offering a branded leisure package. But the agent did admit that there is a so-called promotional rate available all year round as a rebuttal offer to any caller whose reaction to the rack rate is: "Oh, that's too expensive." I call that sneaky! Many chains also do special interest packages including theater tickets or admissions to attractions (for out of town options, see chapter 9). And savvy bargain hounds know it's always worth surfing hotel chain websites for e-deals. The rates below are per night, for two people sharing a room, and bed-and-breakfast. But, remember, you can probably do even better!

• **Best Western** (ⓒ **0800/393130**; www.bestwestern.com): 2-night Getaway Breaks any day; from £88 ($127.60). The best value Best Western hotel is Raglan Hall in Highgate. Only 15 minutes by Tube from the West End, it's in a quiet residential area and has a delightful garden and terrace.

• **Hilton** (ⓒ **08705/909090**; www.hilton.com): EscapeAways; from £105 ($152.25). This is the lowest rate, only available in May and from mid-July through August. But several of the hotels do great

repainted and recarpeted everywhere, except the utilitarian linoleum-covered stairs, and refurnished the bedrooms. At the moment, up to six share a tub and a shower, but the Markers want to put in private bathrooms. This has been on their to-do list for a while, but they promise there'll be around 10 en suite rooms by spring this year. I don't know how they'll squeeze them in. The bedrooms, with their simple decor and 4½-foot-wide double beds, are tiny. But if you've a taste for the quirky, pay the extra to get a little more space in a triple, still virtually given away. Choose one at the back for an amazing view, through the middle of fountain courtyard of Somerset House (see "London's Top Attractions," in chapter 6). The club's canteen-style restaurant is one of those food critics' "secrets"—two courses are a steal at around £8 ($11.60). Don't worry, the delicious smells are pretty well-contained.

143 Strand, London WC2R 1JR. ⓒ 020/7836-4880. Fax 020/7379-6105. 22 units, none with bathroom. £32 ($51.20) single; £45 ($72) twin; £40 ($64) double; £50 ($80) family room. Rates include continental breakfast. Discount of 10% for 1-wk. stays. MC, V. Tube: Temple. **Amenities:** Restaurant, bar. *In room:* TV, no phone.

**Royal Adelphi Hotel**    This hotel is a favorite with London Marathon runners, so you'll have to book early to stay here in April. The first thing the athletes do when they arrive, even before slipping on the Lycra, is book their lucky room for the year ahead. The Royal Adelphi is almost a splurge, especially one-night Sunday Specials all year round: for instance, £90 ($130.50), or £120 ($174) with dinner thrown in, at the fab 4-star Hilton Hyde Park, which has Nintendo consoles in every room if the notorious British weather turns against you.

- **Holiday Inn** (© 0800/897121; www.basshotels.com/holiday-inn): Weekender-Plus; maximum two adults and two children sharing, free dinner for children under 12; from £77 ($111.65) in a non-suburban Holiday Inn Express. The cheapest central Holiday Inn is £115 ($166.75), in Kensington. Then prices jump by at least a fifth, as they do for the swanky Garden Court and Crowne Plaza.

- **Jarvis Hotels** (© 01494/436264; www.jarvis.co.uk): Jarvisbreaks any day; from £79.20 ($114.85); higher rates for one-night stay. The Jarvis Hotel, next to Marylebone Tube and train station, is only a stone's throw from Madame Tussaud's and the Planetarium.

- **Radisson Hotels** (© 0800/374411; www.radisson.com): Weekend Breakaways; from £115 ($166.75). This hotel group aims for classic English style. Go for the good value Savoy Court, which is right in the thick of things by Marble Arch. And ask about theater packages—oddly, they seem to be cheaper sometimes than a basic bed-booking.

- **Thistle Hotels** (© 0800/181716; www.thistlehotels.com): Leisure Breaks any day; minimum 2 nights; from £116 ($168.20). For the best deal but scant aesthetic stimulation, go for the modern London Ryan Hotel in King's Cross. For a few pounds more, though, you can buy a more traditional sleep at the brilliantly located Bloomsbury Park (between Russell Square and Holborn).

as breakfast is not included. Full English is £8 ($11.60) and continental £4 ($5.80), but it is a self-service buffet so you can pile your plate high. But the location is fantastic. The street was named after the 17th-century courtier, George Villiers, Duke of Buckingham. It's a little pedestrian enclave, packed with sandwich shops and restaurants, linking the river to the Strand just by Trafalgar Square. Office workers flood here to buy lunch before going to sunbathe in Victoria Embankment Gardens. In the evening, it gets the overflow crowd from Covent Garden. The only downside is the noise—Buckingham Street, on the other side of the hotel, is much quieter. There's double-glazing throughout, and some windows look onto a lightwell in the center of the building, a dubious plus. The rooms are modest, too, and there's no air-conditioning, so they do get hot in summer. The decor is respectable rather than plush, with heavy wood-veneer furniture built in, and the lounge and hotel bar (open 24 hours) show distinct signs of wear and tear. But who's going to notice when there's so much going on outside?

21 Villiers St., London WC2N 6ND. © 020/7930-8764. Fax 020/7930-8735. www.royaladelphi.co.uk. 47 units, 34 with bathroom (some with shower only). £50 ($72.50) single without bathroom, £68 ($98.60) single with bathroom; £68 ($98.60) double/twin without bathroom, £90 ($130.50) double/twin with bathroom; £120 ($174) triple with bathroom; £15 ($21.75) extra bed/cot. AE, DC, MC, V. Tube: Embankment, Charing Cross. **Amenities:** Bar. *In room:* TV, coffeemaker, hair dryer, radio.

## DO-IT-YOURSELF DEALS

Citadines Trafalgar Square ✪    This French company pioneered the concept of an "aparthotel" chain in London. It opened its Trafalgar Square flagship in 1998 after totally gutting the *Ghost Busters*–style 1930s building, which used to be the members' hotel for the Commonwealth Club next door. The inside is all marble-tiled and corporate now, with an impeccable 24-hour welcome. The studios sleep two on a deluxe sofa bed—double or twin—and there's enough room to move around if you can't be bothered to fold it away in the morning. The sparkling white kitchenettes are fully equipped, down to a dishwasher and the essential extractor fan. The apartments have the same arrangement, with the tub-shower and toilet separate to cut down on awkward traffic jams. Four people sharing a one-bedroom make the rate very competitive for the area. Fill a bigger duplex and you'll get a real bargain. Every unit controls its own heating and air-conditioning, and the phones have handy voice-mail. Reception can lend you a crib, bottle warmer and changing mat. It will also organize extra maid services, otherwise it's one towel change a week. Citadines has a deal with the Commonwealth Club, so you can have breakfast there. It's expensive, £7.50 ($10.90) for continental and £9.50 ($13.80) for full English, but it's worth doing once just to see the stunning modern restaurant. For a cheaper central sleep, try the clone: **Citadines Holborn**, 94–99 High Holborn, London, WC1V 6LF (✆ **020/ 7395-8800;** fax 020/7395-8789; Tube: Holborn). Studios cost from £94 ($136.30) a night if you stay 1 week.

18–21 Northumberland Ave., London WC2N 5BJ. ✆ **0800/376-3898**, or 020/7766-3700. Fax 020/7766-3766. www.citadines.com. 187 units. £104–£135 ($150.80–$195.75) studio; £153–£199 ($221.85–$288.55) 1-bedroom apt.; £193–£229 ($279.85–$332.05) 2-bedroom apt. Lower rates apply to 1-wk. stays. 16 studios and a 1-bedroom apt. suitable for travelers with disabilities. AE, DC, MC, V. Tube: Charing Cross, Embankment. **Amenities:** Coin-op washers and dryers; dry cleaning; nonsmoking rooms. *In room:* A/C, TV, kitchenette, fridge, coffeemaker, iron, safe.

## WORTH A SPLURGE

The Fielding Hotel ✪    This hotel should exist only on film. And it almost did, as a gangster's bedroom in *Mona Lisa,* the British hit starring Bob Hoskins about a prostitute and her protector. The crew couldn't use the room because the hapless former manager rushed out and redecorated. The Fielding did keep a hilariously kitsch painting from the set, and it fits right in. The whole hotel is a clean, tidy, and regularly-renovated 1970s time warp—clearly a good decade for the owner, who keeps an iron grip on decor decisions. Despite the best efforts of his charming manager, Graham Chapman, the very narrow hallways and stairs are brown and orange, and metallic glam-rock pictures and chocolate-box alpine scenes cover the walls. Other than that, the bedrooms are attractive with comfortable new beds and faded coverlets and curtains. And the Fielding has finally upgraded its famously antiquated electrics and plumbing—there are lovely new bathrooms throughout. Breakfast is not included. As Mr. Chapman says, the hotel doesn't score marks for extra bits-and-bobs. But it is in a pretty, pedestrian street just around the corner from the Royal Opera House—the source of many of its guests, both performers and Placido Domingo's female fans. And it really is one of a kind. I defy anyone staying here not to have a grin on their face.

4 Broad Court, Bow St., London WC2B 5QZ. ✆ 020/7836-8305. Fax 020/7497-0064. www.the-fielding-hotel.co.uk. 24 units, all with bathroom (shower only). £76 ($110.20) single; £100 ($145) double/twin; £115 ($166.75) superior double/twin; £130 ($188.50) double suite with sitting room. Rates do not include breakfast. No 1-night bookings on Sat. AE, DC, MC, V. Tube: Covent Garden. No children under 13. *In room:* TV, coffeemaker.

## 10 Victoria & Westminster

Astor's also has a small hostel here, the **Victoria Hotel** on Belgrave Road, SW1 (℃ **020/7834-3077;** fax 020/7932-0693), where it costs £14 to £16 ($20.30–$23.20) per night to sleep in a 5- to 8-bed dorm. For more information on Astor's, see "Paddington & Bayswater," earlier in this chapter.

**Collin House** ✪   You could easily walk straight past the discreet slate nameplate announcing Collin House. That would be a real shame because it's one of the best B&Bs on Ebury Street. For a start, it's well worth foregoing a private bathroom, even though all the showers are new, because there are never more than two bedrooms sharing each public facility. As well as having more money to go out on the town with, you'll get a room at the back, which is blissfully quiet. All the en suites look out onto Ebury Street, and there is no soundproofing. However, if you don't mind traffic noise, go for the unusually big twin on the second floor. Most of the rooms have been redecorated over the past couple of years and there is new carpet on the stairs, where the original Victorian banisters curve outward like ribs on a skeleton. Last year, Mr. Thomas was in the middle of converting the first-floor bedroom at the front into a very attractive lounge. None of the other Ebury Street B&Bs listed here have got one, as the buildings are quite small. Let's hope he's as clever about it as he has been with the basement breakfast room. The look there is half-canteen, half-chapel, which disguises the cramped space. Collin House is nonsmoking throughout.

104 Ebury St., London SW1W 9QD. ℃/fax **020/7730-8031.** collin.house@faxvia.net. 12 units, 8 with bathroom (shower only). £55 ($79.75) single with bathroom; £68 ($98.60) double/twin without bathroom, £82 ($118.90) double/twin with bathroom; £95 ($137.75) triple without bathroom. Rates include full English breakfast. No credit cards. Tube: Victoria. **Amenities:** Nonsmoking rooms. *In room:* Hair dryers, no phone.

**Harcourt House**   Step through the door of Harcourt House, and you'll think the clock has spun back to the last century. This early Victorian townhouse has been a gentleman's lodgings since the late 1880s and the Woods have just spent 4 years lovingly redecorating the whole place to recapture the original style and atmosphere. It's fantastically theatrical. Heritage junkies will love it, so long as they're not too pedantic about details, but other guests may find it rather dark. And it is a fraction cheaper than the other Ebury Street B&Bs listed. The rooms have reproduction brass bedsteads, and are two-tone maroon and rich yellow. The only place where modern decoration is allowed to intrude is in the bright-tiled bathrooms. The Woods are clearly avid antiques hunters. The hall and stairs are lit with crystal chandeliers and decorated with junk-shop finds like the framed montage of Titanic memorabilia. The breakfast room has a real-flame fire and a restored wood-and-slate floor. Don't worry, no nasty Victorian cold cuts have made it onto the full English breakfast menu.

50 Ebury St., London SW1W 0LU. ℃ **020/7730-2722.** Fax 020/7730-3998. www.harcourthousehotel.co.uk. 10 units, all with bathroom (shower only). £60 ($87) single; £80 ($116) double/twin; £95 ($137.75) triple. Rates include full English breakfast. Minimum 3-night stay Apr–Dec. Discount available off-season. AE, MC, V. Tube: Victoria. No children under 8 except by prior arrangement. *In room:* TV, coffeemaker, hair dryer, no phone.

**James & Cartref House** ✪✪   Ebury Street calls itself Belgravia, but this is no hushed tycoon's enclave. Instead, it's a bustling road, with traffic zooming toward Victoria, a 10-minute walk away. There are dozens of places to stay either side of the junction with Elizabeth Street. Confusingly, James House and Cartref House are separate B&Bs on opposite sides of the road, both run by the very welcoming Derek and Sharon James. The main difference between them is in the number of private bathrooms. Most of them are in James House, but they're very small, so you might be better off without one—especially since only three rooms share public facilities. One thing: Kids have to be over 12 to stay in the top bunk in the James House family room. All the bedrooms are very nicely decorated: Mrs. James makes the curtains and bedcovers herself. And the couple recently put in proper permanent fans, giving you the coolest night's sleep on the whole of Ebury Street. Ask for a room with a wall-mounted one, as they've got more puff than those blowing down from the ceiling. Derek James is very proud of them, as he is of the zapper-controlled fans in his delightful conservatory dining rooms. Late-sleepers ought to be warned—breakfast stops at 8:30am, horribly early, at least by my slug-a-bed standards. Both houses are totally nonsmoking.

108–129 Ebury St., London SW1W 9DU. (C) 020/7730-7338 or 020/7730-6176. Fax 020/7730-7338. www. jamesandcartref.co.uk. 20 units, 11 with bathroom (shower only). £50 ($72.50) single without bathroom, £60 ($87) single with bathroom; £68 ($98.60) double/twin without bathroom, £82 ($118.90) double with bathroom; £90 ($130.50) triple without bathroom, £105 ($152.25) triple with bathroom; £130 ($188.50) family room with bathroom. Rates include full English breakfast. AE, MC, V. Tube: Victoria. **Amenities:** Nonsmoking rooms. *In room:* TV, coffeemaker, hair dryer, no phone.

**Luna Simone Hotel** ⚡ This family-run hotel stands out by a mile on this scruffy terrace. The outside of the big stucco-fronted house gleams bright white like the icing on a wedding cake and glass panels, etched with the hotel name, now partly shield the sides of the entrance porch. Usually, this sort of gentrification is the early warning sign of a bid for a posher class of guest. So it's reassuring to find the Luna Simone prices pegged at B&B levels, especially as the Desiras have splashed out on the inside, too. They have renovated all the bedrooms, and each year they put in more private bathrooms. Some are extremely small—you might just fit both hands in the washbasin. The rooms vary widely in size, which explains the price range for every option. Personally, I'd always go for a larger £60 double without in preference to a smaller £60 double with bathroom because there are now only nine rooms that have to share the six public facilities. The reception area is all-new, as is the breakfast room, now totally nonsmoking. The look of both is light and simple, with modern curves, a refreshing change in Victorian building.

47–49 Belgrave Rd., London SW1V 2BB. (C) 020/7834-5897. Fax 020/7828-2474. www.lunasimone hotel.com. 35 units, 27 with bathroom (shower only). £35–£40 ($50.75–$58) single without bathroom, £45–£55 ($65.25–$79.75) single with bathroom; £50–£60 ($72.50–$87) double/twin without bathroom, £60–£75 ($87–$108.75) double/twin with bathroom; £80–£100 ($116–$145) triple with bathroom. Rates include full English breakfast. MC, V. Tube: Victoria, Pimlico. *In room:* TV, coffeemaker, hair dryer, safe.

**Melbourne House Hotel** Hotel bathrooms are expensive and hard work to maintain, so many small budget hotels really let guests down. Not so Melbourne House. In one of the bathrooms, the gleaming gray tiles that I thought were brand-spanking-new turned out to be 6 years old. The actual shower units were all replaced in 1999. John Desira and his wife have run this B&B for 26 years—John is the cousin of Peter Desira, who owns Luna Simone up the road. Everything is spotless, and there is no smoking allowed. Don't come here if you're looking for frills and fancy fabrics, though. The rooms are quite a good size for central London, but the decor is very simple—plain, newly painted walls and candlewick bedspreads. The Desiras have recently replaced the carpets, beds, and furniture (a desk and ample storage space). There's a good family room for parents traveling with two teenage children, which combines a double, a twin, and a private bathroom. The lounge has had a face-lift, too. In fact, the only

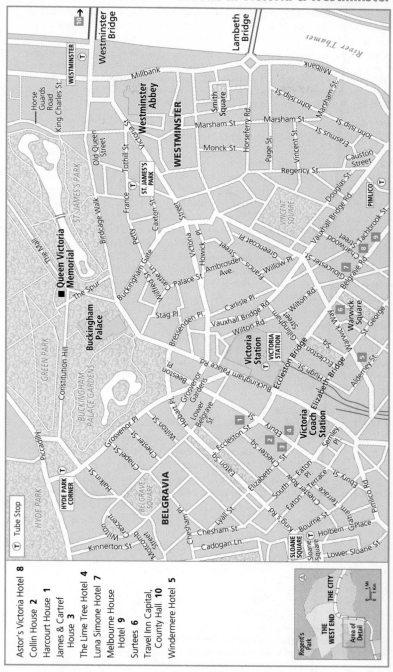

Astor's Victoria Hotel **8**

Collin House **2**

Harcourt House **1**

James & Cartref
House **3**

The Lime Tree Hotel **4**

Luna Simone Hotel **7**

Melbourne House
Hotel **9**

Surtees **6**

Travel Inn Capital,
County Hall **10**

Windermere Hotel **5**

disappointment at Melbourne House is that the full English breakfast isn't all-you-can-eat, as it is in some B&Bs. Mrs. Desira looked appalled at the thought, so don't try asking for more.

79 Belgrave Rd., London SW1V 2BG. ℭ **020/7828-3516.** Fax 020/7828-7120. melbourne.househotel@ virgin.net. 17 units, 15 with bathroom (most with shower only). £30 ($69.60) single without bathroom, £55 ($79.75) single with bathroom; £75 ($108.75) double/twin with bathroom; £95 ($137.75) triple with bathroom; £110 ($159.50) family room. Rates include full English breakfast. MC, V. Tube: Pimlico, Victoria. **Amenities:** Nonsmoking rooms. *In room:* TV, coffeemakers, hair dryers.

**Surtees** ⍟ Warwick Avenue is a rather pretty street of small Victorian terrace houses, so it's a bit of a shame that traffic thunders down it from early morning until nearly midnight. That's partly why the B&Bs here are around £10 ($14.50) a night cheaper than those in posher (but still busy) Ebury Street. Ahmed Akoudad has owned Surtees for 16 years and now runs it with his wife. The B&B stands out from its too-often grotty neighbors because it is one of the few buildings on the block festooned with hanging baskets. Inside, too, it's very clean and well cared for. Mr. Akoudad does much of the decorating work himself and has spruced up most of the rooms, each one in a different style, and the bathrooms. The basic triple is a good choice for friends traveling together: the only other room sharing the shower and two toilets is a single. There are also good deals to be had in the basement family rooms, as long as you don't mind looking out onto an internal courtyard. There's one that combines a single room with a triple. You get quite a lot of bang for your buck in terms of in-room amenities and there are cribs and VCRs to borrow at reception.

94 Warwick Way, London SW1V 1SB. ℭ **020/7834-7163** or 020/7834-7394. Fax 020/7460-8747. www. surtees-hotel.co.uk. 10 units, 8 with bathroom (shower only). £45 ($65.25) single without bathroom, £50 ($72.50) single with bathroom; £50 ($72.50) double/twin without bathroom; £65 ($94.25) double/ twin with bathroom; £70 ($101.50) triple without bathroom, £80 ($116) triple with bathroom; £90 ($130.50) family room without bathroom, £120 ($174) family room with bathroom. Rates include full English breakfast. AE, DC, DISC, MC, V. Tube: Victoria, Pimlico. *In room:* TV, coffeemaker, hair dryer, iron, radio.

## WORTH A SPLURGE

**The Lime Tree Hotel** ⍟ David and Marilyn Davies ran Ebury House, across the road, until 1994 when they moved to The Lime Tree Hotel. Mr. Davies is hugely competitive when it comes to winning prizes for his window boxes, and there are twice as many here as on any other house in the street. The Lime Tree is just as attractive inside. There are deep cornices in the hall, and statues and flowers sit in the alcoves up the stairs. The more expensive rooms are quite luxurious—swagged curtains, canopies, cushions on the beds, and pretty furniture. There is one on the first floor that leads out to a table and chairs on its own little terrace. The lower price applies to doubles and twins on the upper floors, which are more restrained but still very attractive. Don't expect a lift as part of your splurge, though. The authorities are very stringent about what they'll let people do to listed Victorian houses. The bathrooms are squeaky clean with glass-doored showers. The dining room is on the first floor, and in the summer, many guests take their breakfast out into the rose garden.

135–137 Ebury St., London SW1W 9RA. ℭ **020/7730-8191.** Fax 020/7730-7856. www.limetreehotel.co.uk. 26 units, all with bathroom (shower only). £75 ($108.75) single; £105–£115 ($152.25–$166.75) double/twin; £145 ($210.25) triple; £165 ($239.25) quad. Rates include full English breakfast. AE, DC, MC, V. Tube: Victoria. No children under 5. **Amenities:** Garden. *In room:* TV, coffeemaker, hair dryer, safe.

**Windermere Hotel** ⍟ *Finds* My favorite sleeps in Victoria are the pair of wedge-shaped rooms right at the top of this house—with windows on two sides, it feels like sleeping in a lighthouse and the view is amazing. The Windermere dates from 1857, and it became one of the first-ever B&Bs in the area 24 years later. You can spot it today by the pale blue-painted stucco porch and pillars, a much grander architecture than the cluster of rivals down the street. Owner Nicholas Hambi and his wife have completely refurbished over the past 6 years. The big top-price double on the second floor is more like a minisuite—that's why it's the same price as a triple—with a canopied bed, sofa, and armchairs, and really expensive-looking curtains. Now the Hambis have extended a toned-down version of the look into the rest of the hotel. Budget travelers get fair deal at the Windermere, too: The so-called basic double comes with a key to a hallway bathroom that no one else can use. Every room is double-glazed and eight are nonsmoking, as are all the public areas. The Hambis run an evening restaurant, called the Pimlico Rooms after the original B&B's name, serving modern British and European food; two courses cost from £14 ($20.30).

142–144 Warwick Way, London SW1V 4JE. ✆ 020/7834-5163. Fax 020/7630-8831. www.windermere-hotel.co.uk. 22 units, 20 with bathroom (some with shower only). £69 ($100.05) single without bathroom; £84–£96 ($121.80–$139.20) single with bathroom; £89 ($129.05) double without bathroom, £104–£139 ($150.80–$201.55) double with bathroom; £139 ($201.55) triple with bathroom. Rates include full English breakfast. AE, MC, V. Tube: Victoria. **Amenities:** Restaurant, bar; limited room service; nonsmoking rooms. *In room:* TV, dataport, coffeemaker, hair dryer, safe.

## 11  Just South of the River

**Bankside House, London School of Economics** ✦    Culture buffs are falling over themselves to book in to this student hall, so make sure to call as far ahead as you can. Imagine finding somewhere to stay right behind the new Tate Modern at Bankside and Shakespeare's Globe Theatre. It's also a 5 minutes' walk to the new Southwark Tube station on the Jubilee line, which links the maritime village of Greenwich (a UNESCO World Heritage site) to Bond Street and shopping heaven. Like High Holborn Residence, this isn't a super-cheap sleep, but then you do get rather more than a souped-up camp bed and a pin-board. Bankside House is a new building and more like a hotel—for a start, the mattresses are that lovely fat sort. When it began welcoming tourists in 1996, it mostly catered to youth groups, but the guest list is much more varied now that this historic, but once very run-down, neighborhood has become one of the most vibrant in London. There are even four rooms especially designed for families, with cribs and high chairs available at the reception desk. Although Bankside House does not have the usual student kitchenettes, staying there will help people on tight budgets to keep their food bills down: three courses at the cheap and cheerful restaurant can cost as little as £8 ($11.60).

24 Sumner St., London SE1 9JA. ✆ 020/7633-9877. Fax 020/7574-6730. www.lse.ac.uk/vacations. 564 units, 306 with bathroom (shower only). £28 ($44.80) single without bathroom; £41 ($59.45) single with bathroom; £56 ($81.20) twin with bathroom; £73 ($105.85) triple with bathroom; £84 ($121.80) family room with bathroom. 32 units adapted for travelers with disabilities. Rates include full English breakfast. MC, V. Open summer vacation only. Tube: Southwark. **Amenities:** Restaurant, bar; game room; coin-op washers and dryers. *In room:* coffeemaker.

**Travel Inn Capital, County Hall** ✦✦ (Kids)    No budget hotel ever had a more astonishing location. County Hall is a mammoth 1920s monument to civic pride, across the Thames from the Houses of Parliament. It used to be home to the Greater London Council until Margaret Thatcher abolished it in 1986. Now millionaires at the Marriott, which occupies the plum parts of County Hall, enjoy *the* London view. Guests at the Travel Inn, sadly, do not. Some rooms look downriver—though you can't see much water these days because the British Airways London Eye, the 135-foot-high observation wheel, is parked right next door. Most face into a big central courtyard or out at luxury apartments behind. Inside there are six floors (five nonsmoking) of bland identical corridors, but that's what budget chains do. The rooms are quite big, the decor good quality, and the price is an absolute steal. Family rooms mean just that: Maximum capacity is two kids under 16 on the sofa bed, one toddler under 2 in a crib, and two grown-ups. There are no adult-only triples or quads. Breakfast is not included. Continental costs £4.50 ($6.55), full English is £6.50 ($9.45), and under-10s can eat what they want for £3 ($4.35). The restaurant also serves a children's dinner menu. Or there's a McDonald's and a Yo! Sushi down below in County Hall, as well as the London Aquarium and the new Dali Universe exhibition.

There are several other Travel Inn Capitals, of which the best located is **Euston. Putney Bridge** is near the river in quite a chi-chi bit of West London. **Tower Bridge** is less sexy than it sounds, too far into no man's land south of the river to be convenient.

Belvedere Rd., London SE1 7PB. ⓒ **0870/242-8000** or 020/7902-1600. Fax 020/7902-1619. www. travelinn.co.uk. 313 units. £74.95 ($108.70) single, double/twin, and family room (max. 4 people). Units adapted for travelers with disabilities. Rates do not include breakfast. AE, DC, MC, V. Tube: Waterloo, Westminster. **Amenities:** Restaurant, bar; nonsmoking rooms; Internet access. *In room:* TV, coffeemaker, hair dryer, radio.

## SUPER-CHEAP SLEEPS

**St. Christopher's Village** ⭑⭑    Only Astor's is cheaper, but even its swanky Hyde Park hostel can't boast a hot tub as part of the deal. In 1999, St. Christopher's gutted some marvelous old buildings on busy Borough High Street and turned them into what it calls a hostel with attitude—PR puff, but you can see what they mean. The American diner-style bar called Belushi's puts on endless low-rent alcohol-fuelled entertainment, from guest DJs to quiz nights. The hostel lounge has a dance floor too. Or you can chill out on the rooftop deck— did I mention that's where the hot tub and sauna are? Instead of the usual self-catering arangements, St. Christopher's subsidizes the food (£1.50/$2.20 for cooked breakfast) and drink. The company has two other hostels on Borough High Street. The first is above the historic St. Christopher's Inn (no. 121) where the floors are wonky, the rooms are clean, and the showers are all new. (Don't stay here for the weekend if you're an early-bedder, because the pub goes ballistic and the floors are paper-thin.) The second is above the Orient Espresso coffee bar just up the road (no. 59). This is much quieter and suits post–Generation X-ers and families with children under drinking age. Southwark is still a bit grotty, but it's on the rise, with the mouthwatering Borough Market, Tate Modern, and Shakespeare's Globe only a few minutes away.

St. Christopher's also has hostels in **Camden, Greenwich,** and **Shepherds Bush.** You can book them all through the telephone number and website below.

165 Borough High St., London SE1 1NP. ⓒ **020/7407-1856.** Fax 020/7403-7715. www.st-christophers.co.uk. 164 units, none with bathroom. £14–£18.50 ($20.30–$26.85) per person in a 4-to-12-bed dorm. Full facilities for travelers with disabilities. Rates include linen and continental breakfast. Discount available off-season and for 1-wk. stays. MC, V. Tube: London Bridge, Borough. **Amenities:** Two bars; hot tub; sauna; coin-op washers and dryers; Internet access. *In room:* no phone.

## 12  Near the Airport

**Hotel Ibis Heathrow** (© **020/8759-4888;** fax 020/8564-7894) is on Bath Road, at the end of a long row of more expensive sleeps. Just refurbished, the amenities and decor replicate the Ibis Euston (see "Bloomsbury," earlier in this chapter), without the railway theme! An en suite double/twin is £59.95 ($86.95) during the week, but a bargain £39.95 ($57.95) at weekends. Breakfast is £4.50 ($6.55) extra. To get here from the airport, take the Hotel Hoppa bus: H3 from Terminals 1 to 3, H13 from Terminal 4.

**Harmondsworth Hall** ★★ *Finds*    Harmondsworth is the perfect place to get over jet lag or catch a last glimpse of picture-book England before you go. This pretty little village has two pubs, an old-fashioned post office, and an 800-year-old church mentioned in the Domesday Book. It takes only 15 minutes to get to one of the world's busiest airports, yet the village isn't even under the flight path. Harmondsworth Hall is a rambling, 17th-century, redbrick house, with wrought-iron gates leading into a lovely country garden where there's even a Tudor cannon. The inside is beautiful, with a checkerboard floor in the hall, coffered ceiling in the wood-paneled breakfast room, an elegant drawing room, and Turkish carpets everywhere. It may sound like a museum, but it feels more like a cherished home. The rooms have lovely old furniture, and each one is decorated differently. Number 6 is my favorite—a huge double with a polished wood floor. Try and avoid the rooms in what was originally a separate cottage, because they're relatively modern. Elaine Burke will organize your transport to and from Heathrow if you give her enough warning. She has run Harmondsworth Hall for 5 years and warns new guests to book in early as she has a lot of loyal regulars—and I can quite see why.

Summerhouse Lane, Harmondsworth, Middlesex, UB7 OBG. © **020/8759-1824.** Fax 020/8897-6385. www.harmondsworthhall.com. 10 units, 7 with bathroom (shower only). £40 ($58) single without bathroom, £45 ($65.25) single with bathroom; £50–£60 ($72.50–$87) double/twin with bathroom; £70 ($101.50) family room with bathroom. Rates include full English breakfast. Discount available for longer stays. V. Bus: U3 from Heathrow Terminals 1–3 or West Drayton train station. **Amenities:** Garden. *In room:* TV, coffeemaker, hair dryer.

# 5

# Great Deals on Dining

The Brits get really bored by the constant slurs cast on their cooking. It can even cause them to forget their manners. And rightly so. That old cliché is about as accurate as the one that says the city is permanently enveloped in a pea-soup fog. The last 2 decades have seen an explosion of new eateries, new tastes, and new celebrities in the kitchen. Today, London is one of the great food capitals of the world.

Indian entrepreneurs have been hatching the hottest ideas: now Mela and Masala Zone are pioneering a new downwardly mobile trend toward cheap authentic street food. It's all a far cry from the late-night, lager-fuelled, curry binges that Great Train Robber Ronnie Biggs so nostalgically recalled after 35 years on the lam in Brazil. It's also a far cry from the chicken tikka masala, hailed by one electioneering politician as Britain's true national dish. Ironically, this concoction was unknown on the Sub-Continent until British tourists started asking for it. Legend has it that a London chef whipped it up in the early 1970s from some spices, cream, and a can of Campbell's tomato soup to satisfy a difficult customer who was demanding gravy.

The curry house is not the only place undergoing a makeover. Great institutions all over the city are ditching institutional grub long past its sell-by date. First came the transformation of nicotine-stained "boozers" into innovative bare-boards restaurants, rather unfortunately called "gastropubs"—though locals will look at you very strangely if you ask for directions to the nearest one. And now London's lottery-revamped attractions—the museums and galleries, and even Southwark Cathedral—are also serving posh contemporary nosh, as you'll see in chapter 6.

The same company, Digby Trout, caters many of the new gourmet cultural eats, which is typical of the gremlin-ization happening in London. Cheap eats and posher restaurants are turning into chains. Others try to repeat successes with similar establishments—like the "school of . . ." paintings that came out of the Old Masters' studios. Sometimes it works, especially in the faster cheaper versions of highly-regarded eateries, as you'll see in the reviews. Sometimes it doesn't, which is why you won't see any Conran establishments.

## MEALTIMES AND RESERVATIONS

Restaurant hours vary, but lunch is usually noon to 2:30pm and dinner 6 to 10:30pm. Some eateries shut down on Sundays or, if not, for one weekday meal. You'll never go hungry, though, because the city is stuffed with all-day cafes and diners. Except for these super-cheapies, most restaurants accept reservations and it is always wise to call ahead, especially from Thursday night through the weekend.

It may be quaintly old-fashioned, but I still pick up the phone to book a table—you get a quick yes or no, with no fiddling about. But there's one website that comes close to changing my mind. The chatty and user-friendly

**www.toptable.co.uk** has overcome the fierce independence natural to restaurateurs, and persuaded over 1,000 of them to accept it as a reservations middleman. Its searchable database is much more comprehensive than just listing the usual e-friendly suspects—those marketing-savvy splurges and dodgy local eateries. Even if you don't use it to book, Toptable is a top information source, not only publishing menus but also giving a 360-degree photographic view inside many of the restaurants so that you can check the place out before you go. It also offers regularly changing special deals, e-mailed so that you can plan ahead. And there's no reservation fee.

## 1  How to Eat Without Losing £s

## Index of London Restaurant Maps

Seasoned bargain-hunters will recognize many of these dining tips, but it never hurts to have a checklist. Especially as a meal for two with wine in Central London is now reckoned to cost around £80 ($116)!

- **Net Savings.** The reservations site mentioned above, **www.toptable.co.uk**, is a good source of special offers. Also surf **www.5pm.co.uk**.
- **Sign Up for Discount Deals.** The **London for Less** card gets you 25% off the final bill, for food and drink, at 90 restaurants. The **London Pass** has a scant handful of offers. For information on both, see "Fifty Money-Saving Tips," in chapter 2.
- **Check the Charges.** Left to their own devices, Brits tip 10%, and so should you. However, some restaurants automatically add an "optional" 12% to 15% service charge. Knock it off if you're at all dissatisfied.
- **Bring Your Own Booze.** There are still a few unlicensed eateries left in London. You can take your own drink, saving pounds on inflated restaurant prices. Some charge a small fee per bottle, known as "corkage." Here's a BYOB directory: Mandola (see the "Notting Hill" section of this chapter), Patogh (see the "Marylebone" section), Centrale (see the "Soho & Chinatown" section), Diwana Bhel Poori House and October Gallery Café (see the "Bloomsbury & Fitzrovia" section), and Food for Thought (see the "Covent Garden & the Strand" section).

## 2  Restaurants by Cuisine

### AFTERNOON TEA

Brown's Hotel ★★ (Mayfair, p. 157)

Dorchester ★ (Mayfair, p. 158)

Fountain Restaurant at Fortnum & Mason (St. James's, p. 158)

The Orangery ★★ (Kensington, p. 157)

Waldorf Meridien ★★ (Covent Garden, p. 159)

### AMERICAN

Blues Bistro & Bar ★ (Soho & Chinatown, p. 136)

Arkansas Café ★★ (The City, p. 151)

Hard Rock Cafe (Chain, p. 156)

Joe Allen (Covent Garden & the Strand, p. 147)

Planet Hollywood (Chain, p. 156)

### BELGIAN

Belgo Centraal (Covent Garden & the Strand, p. 146)

### BRITISH DINER

Café in the Crypt (Covent Garden & the Strand, p. 145)

Café Grove (Notting Hill, p. 125)

Chelsea Kitchen (Kensington & Chelsea, p. 122)

# Index of London Restaurant Maps

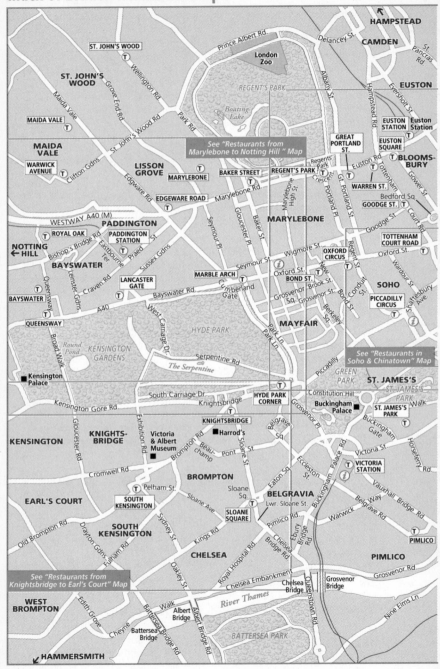

HAMPSTEAD

CAMDEN

Prince Albert Rd.

Delancey St.

St. Pancras Rd.

EUSTON

ST. JOHN'S WOOD

London Zoo

REGENT'S PARK

Albany St.

EUSTON STATION
Euston Station

Eversholt St.

Hampstead Rd.

Wellington Rd.

Grove End Rd.

St. John's Wood Rd.

Maida Vale

Park Rd.

MAIDA VALE

Boating Lake

GREAT PORTLAND ST.

EUSTON SQUARE

BLOOMS-BURY

WARWICK AVENUE

MAIDA VALE

Clifton Gdns.

Edgware Rd.

LISSON GROVE

MARYLEBONE

BAKER STREET

REGENT'S PARK

Regent's Park Crescent

Gt. Portland St.

Euston Rd.

WARREN ST.

Tottenham Court Rd.

Gower St.

Bedford Sq.

GOODGE ST.

Court Rd.

EDGWARE ROAD

Marylebone Rd.

*See "Restaurants from Marylebone to Notting Hill" Map*

Marylebone High St.

Portland Pl.

Regent St.

Goodge St.

TOTTENHAM COURT ROAD

WESTWAY A40 (M)

PADDINGTON

MARYLEBONE

Oxford St.

Wardour St.

NOTTING ← HILL

ROYAL OAK

PADDINGTON STATION

Bishop's Bridge Rd.

Eastbourne Ter.

Praed St.

Sussex Gdns.

Seymour Pl.

Gloucester Pl.

Baker St.

Wigmore St.

OXFORD CIRCUS

Oxford St.

SOHO

BAYSWATER

Leinster Gdns.

Craven Rd.

LANCASTER GATE

MARBLE ARCH

Seymour St.

Oxford St.

BOND ST.

New Bond St.

Conduit St.

PICCADILLY CIRCUS

Shaftesbury Ave.

BAYSWATER

Queensway

A40

Bayswater Rd.

Cumberland Gate

Grosvenor St.

Brook St.

Grosvenor Sq.

Bond St.

Berkeley Sq.

QUEENSWAY

Broad Walk

West Carriage Dr.

HYDE PARK

Park Ln.

Park Ln.

MAYFAIR

Round Pond

KENSINGTON GARDENS

Serpentine Rd.

The Serpentine

Piccadilly

GREEN PARK

*See "Restaurants in Soho & Chinatown" Map*

ST. JAMES'S

ST. JAMES'S PARK

Kensington Palace

South Carriage Dr.

Knightsbridge

HYDE PARK CORNER

Constitution Hill

Buckingham Palace

ST. JAMES'S PARK

Kensington Gore Rd.

KNIGHTSBRIDGE

Grosvenor Pl.

Buckingham Gate

Buckingham Walk

KENSINGTON

KNIGHTS-BRIDGE

Exhibition Rd.

Victoria & Albert Museum

Harrod's

Brompton Rd.

Beau-champ Pl.

Pont St.

Sloane St.

Belgrave Sq.

Victoria St.

Horseferry Rd.

Cromwell Rd.

Gloucester Rd.

Pelham St.

BROMPTON

Sloane Ave.

Sloane Sq.

Eaton Sq.

Eccleston St.

VICTORIA STATION

Vauxhall Bridge Rd.

EARL'S COURT

SOUTH KENSINGTON

Sydney St.

Fulham Rd.

SOUTH KENSINGTON

Kings Rd.

SLOANE SQUARE

Lwr. Sloane St.

BELGRAVIA

Pimlico Rd.

Ebury Bridge Rd.

Buckingham Palace Rd.

Warwick Way

Belgrave Rd.

PIMLICO

PIMLICO

Old Brompton Rd.

Drayton Gdns.

CHELSEA

Royal Hospital Rd.

Chelsea Bridge Rd.

Chelsea Embankment

Grosvenor Rd.

PIMLICO

WEST BROMPTON

Edith Grove

*See "Restaurants from Knightsbridge to Earl's Court" Map*

Oakley St.

Cheyne Walk

Battersea Bridge

Albert Bridge

Albert Bridge Rd.

River Thames

Chelsea Bridge

Queenstown Rd.

Grosvenor Bridge

Nine Elms Ln.

← HAMMERSMITH

Battersea Bridge Rd.

BATTERSEA PARK

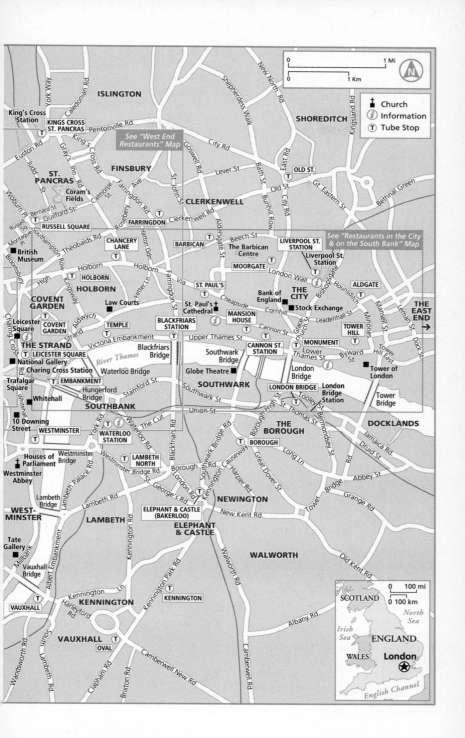

## INDIAN/SOUTH
Diwana Bhel Poori House (Bloomsbury & Fitzrovia, p. 143)

Malabar Junction ✦ (Bloomsbury & Fitzrovia, p. 143)

## INTERNATIONAL
The Bar at Villandry ✦ (Bloomsbury & Fitzrovia, p. 139)

Cork & Bottle Wine Bar (Soho & Chinatown, p. 134)

Giraffe ✦ (Marylebone, p. 129)

Portobello Gold ✦ (Notting Hill, p. 124)

## IRANIAN
Patogh (Marylebone, p. 130)

## ITALIAN
Aperitivo (Soho & Chinatown, p. 132)

Carluccio's Caffè ✦✦ (Bloomsbury & Fitzrovia, p. 142)

Centrale (Soho & Chinatown, p. 134)

Vasco & Pierro's Pavilion ✦ (Soho & Chinatown, p. 136)

## JAPANESE
Tokyo Diner ✦ (Soho & Chinatown, p. 133)

## JAPANESE NOODLES
Wagamama ✦ (Bloomsbury & Fitzrovia, p. 142)

## LEBANESE
Al Waha ✦✦ (Paddington & Bayswater, p. 128)

## MEDITERRANEAN
The Atlas ✦✦ (Earl's Court, p. 123)

## NORTH AFRICAN
Mô Tearoom ✦ (Mayfair, p. 138)

Moro ✦✦ (Clerkenwell, p. 152)

## PAN-ASIAN
Itsu ✦✦ (Kensington & Chelsea, p. 120)

Pan-Asian Canteen @ Paxton's Head ✦ (Knightsbridge, p. 116)

## PIZZA & PASTA
Ask (Chain, p. 156)

Oliveto ✦ (Victoria, p. 150)

Pizza Express (Chain, p. 156)

Pizza on the Park ✦ (Knightsbridge, p. 116)

La Spighetta ✦✦ (Marylebone, p. 130)

## POLISH
Wódka (Kensington & Chelsea, p. 123)

## SANDWICHES
EAT (Chain, p. 157)

Pret a Manger (Chain, p. 157)

## SCOTTISH
Boisdale ✦ (Victoria, p. 150)

## SEAFOOD
Back to Basics ✦ (Bloomsbury & Fitzrovia, p. 143)

Fish! ✦✦ (Just South of the River, p. 154)

Livebait ✦ (Covent Garden & the Strand, p. 148)

Lou Pescadou (Earl's Court, p. 124)

## SOUP
EAT (Chain, p. 157)

Quiet Revolution ✦ (Clerkenwell, p. 152)

Soup Opera (Chain, p. 157)

SOUP Works (Chain, p. 157)

## SPANISH
Cambio de Tercio ✦✦ (Kensington & Chelsea, p. 123)

Moro ✦✦ (Clerkenwell, p. 152)

## SUDANESE
Mandola ✦ (Notting Hill, p. 124)

## SUSHI
Itsu ✦✦ (Kensington & Chelsea, p. 120)

YO! Sushi ✦ (Soho & Chinatown, p. 133)

## THAI
Bangkok (Kensington & Chelsea, p. 120)

Tawana ✦ (Paddington & Bayswater, p. 128)

**THAI-FRENCH**
Vong ✪✪ (Knightsbridge, p. 120)

**TURKISH**
Sofra (Covent Garden & the
Strand, p. 148)
Tas ✪ (Just South of the River,
p. 152)

**VEGETARIAN**
Food for Thought (Covent Garden
& the Strand, p. 145)

Mildred's ✪ (Soho & Chinatown,
p. 132)
The Place Below ✪ (The City,
p. 151)

**WINE BAR**
Cork & Bottle Wine Bar (Soho &
Chinatown, p. 134)
Ebury Wine Bar & Restaurant
(Victoria, p. 149)

## 3 Knightsbridge

**Pan-Asian Canteen @ Paxton's Head** ✪ *Finds* GASTROPUB/PAN-ASIAN
There's been a pub on this spot since 1632 but the present one dates from the
turn of the last century. Every inch of it, inside and out, is paneled in polished
mahogany. So the new Pan-Asian Canteen upstairs comes as a bit of a surprise.
The cool, modern, Bangkok-green dining room has three big teak tables, which
can seat 12 people each, eating communal style. Depending on the day and
time, you could have one to yourself or be elbow-to-elbow with businessmen,
backpackers, and babes on a shopping break. The fixed-price dinner is four
courses, which is a brilliant value, and the regular prices make this a perfect light
meal break. The menu is very strong on seafood, from the fishcake starter to
clams, red snapper and deliciously juicy king prawns revved up with chili. But
there's lots to tempt vegetarians and carnivores, too. The pork ribs sprinkled
with sesame seeds made a very tasty starter and there's always a chicken curry.
The pub has several real ales on tap.
153 Knightsbridge, SW1. ✆ 020/7589-6627. Reservations not accepted. Main courses £5.50–£7.25
($8–$10.50). Fixed-price dinner £16 ($23.20). AE, MC, V. Mon–Sat noon–10:30pm; Sun 12:30–10pm. Tube:
Knightsbridge.

**Pizza on the Park** ✪ PIZZA & PASTA    This is one of the most popular jazz
venues in London and pulls all the big names. Sadly, you do have to pay extra
for the basement gigs—from £16 ($23.20) depending who's playing—and you
must book ahead. But come here Sunday lunchtime, and there's live background
music (not usually jazz) upstairs as well. This is a very superior pizza joint, with
high ceilings, dramatic pillars, and tables set with fresh flowers. It used to be part
of the Pizza Express chain, and the food still harks back to those days: lots of
tomato on the base and interesting toppings. My long-time favorite is the
*Quattro Formaggi,* but anyone prone to cheese-induced nightmares ought to
avoid it because it is very rich. The restaurant loses form a bit when it comes to
pasta. Pizza on the Park also does breakfast until 11:30am—great after a dawn
start and all-in wrestling session at Harrods. The nicest view is from the inside
looking out at the park. Pavement tables are a bit too close to heavy traffic.
11 Knightsbridge SW1. ✆ 020/7235-5273. Reservations required for music room. Breakfast menu
£4–£4.95 ($5.80–$7.20); main courses £6–£10 ($8.70–$14.50). AE, DC, MC, V. Daily 8:30am–midnight. Tube:
Hyde Park Corner.

## GREAT DEALS ON FIXED-PRICE MEALS
**Brasserie St. Quentin** ✪ FRENCH BRASSERIE    I've always thought
Brasserie St. Quentin was a bit of a rip-off, but then it is right on the border
between Knightsbridge and South Kensington. Local wallets are designer label,

**Moveable Feasts**

There's nothing more blissful on a sunny summer's day than dining alfresco. London is full of green spaces that are great for picnics. Get there early at lunchtime and mark out your patch, because the locals grab any chance to leave their desks. At the weekend, the parks look just like flesh-toned penguin colonies, with barely an inch of lawn visible.

That's particularly true of Soho Square, a grassy oasis right in the heart of the West End (Tube: Tottenham Court Rd.). There are lots of nearby places to pick up the necessary stuff. The **Marks & Spencer Food Hall,** 458 Oxford St., W1 (✆ 020/7935-7954), has deli fare and pre-chopped veggies and salads for busy yuppies. It sells sandwiches to huge queues of people, too. I'd also recommend I **Camisa & Son,** 61 Old Compton St., W1 (✆ 020/7437-7610), which is a scented heaven of Italian sausages, cheeses, and olives. Then pop around the corner to **Berwick Street market** for salad ingredients and great bread.

Kids will love Coram's Fields, on the eastern edge of Bloomsbury (Tube: Russell Sq.). Adults need to be accompanied by a young one for admittance. It's a wonderful inner-city farm with hens, horses, sheep, and pigs on the site of the old Foundling Hospital. **Bloomsbury Cheeses,** 61b Judd St., WC1 (✆ 020/7387-7645), will sort you out with a mammoth range of cheeses, obviously, and wine, olives, and delicious bread. **Alara Wholefoods,** 58–60 Marchmont St., WC1 (✆ 020/7837-1172), is great for salads and sandwiches. A little further west, stock up for a lazy day in Regents Park at the **Villandry Foodstore,** which is part of the restaurant of the same name (see p. 139)

**Fortnum & Mason,** 181 Piccadilly, W1 (✆ 020/7734-8040), is the only place to go before setting off to Green Park (Tube: Green Park or Hyde Park Corner). Its food halls will demand iron self-control. The obvious supply store for a picnic by the Serpentine in Hyde Park or, if you don't mind the walk, the Round Pond in Kensington Gardens, is another famous food hall: **Harrods,** 87–135 Brompton Rd., SW1 (✆ 020/7730-1234).

Walking to Kensington Gardens from Notting Hill Gate, pop in and buy a cheap takeaway bite at **Café Diana,** 5 Wellington Terrace, Bayswater Rd., W2 (✆ 020/7792-9606). It's like a shrine to the princess, with barely an inch of wall not covered by photographs. Diana brought one in herself, with her signature scrawled across the bottom.

If you pick **Holland Park** as your picnic spot, take the Tube to Holland Park and shop for lunch at one of the two French patisseries, the deli, or the pricey grocery store that are all in a row right by the station.

*Note:* You should also take a picnic if you go to the **Royal Botanic Garden Kew** or **Hampton Court Palace** to enjoy on the banks of the Thames (see "London's Top Attractions," in chapter 6).

as you'll see from the affluent clientele (there's a reassuringly high number of French, too). But the brasserie has excellent value fixed-price meals, two or three courses, both at lunch and pre-theater. These offer a blend of classic and updated

# Restaurants from Knightsbridge to Earl's Court

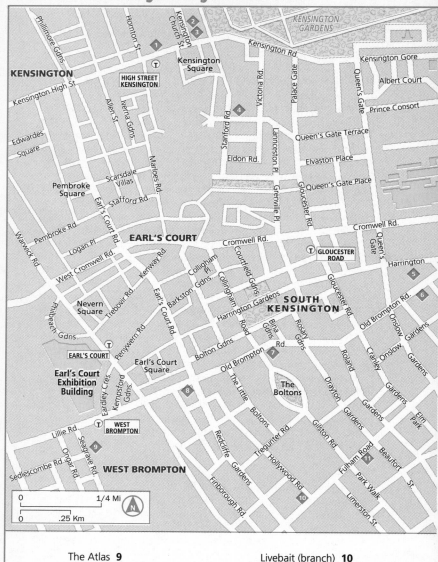

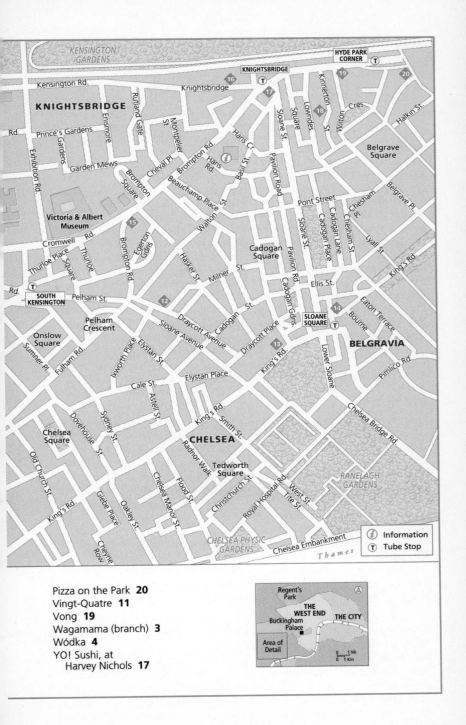

French fare, from roast rack of lamb with parsley crust, to moist pan-fried salmon with sorrel sauce. Vegetarians get a run at most of the starters but are oddly left out in the cold when it comes to a la carte main courses—which is a shame, because this is a very attractive place with its chandeliers, etched mirrors, and well-starched tablecloths.

243 Brompton Rd., SW3. ℂ 020/7589-8005. Reservations recommended. Main courses £12.25–£22 ($17.75–$31.90). Fixed-price lunch/pre-theater menus £11.95–£15.95 ($17.35–$23.15), £11 ($15.95) vegetarian. AE, DC, MC, V. Daily noon–3pm; Mon–Sat 6–11:30pm, Sun 6:30–10:30pm. Tube: Knightsbridge, South Kensington.

## WORTH A SPLURGE

**Vong** ★★ THAI-FRENCH   This is the London outpost of Jean-Georges Vongerichten. You'll either curl up in embarrassment or feel like a million dollars walking down from the reception area into this chic, basement dining room—so make sure to dress up for the occasion. Vong is a visual feast, with flashes of orange-mandarin, single-stem orchids on the tables, and plates you want to take home. The Thai-French cuisine includes a delicious lobster daikon roll with rosemary ginger dip. This is one of the five appetizers that make up the black plate pre- and post-theater menu. You'll also get a crab spring roll with tamarind dipping sauce, prawn satay with fresh oyster sauce, tuna and vegetables wrapped in rice paper, and quail rubbed with Thai spices and served with a cress salad. Seafood lovers can ditch the quail and take salmon slices in a scallion pancake with green peppercorns instead. Vegetarians can swap selections, too. If you can, add on the divine warm Valrhona chocolate cake with lemongrass ice cream.

Berkeley Hotel, Wilton Place, SW1. ℂ 020/7235-1010. Reservations essential. Main courses £16–£32 ($23.20–$46.40); fixed-price lunch £18.50–£20 ($26.85–$29); black plate menu pre-/post-theater £22.50 ($32.65). AE, DC, DISC, MC, V. Daily noon–2:30pm; Mon–Sat 6–11:30pm, Sun 6–10:30pm. Tube: Hyde Park Corner, Knightsbridge.

## 4 Kensington & Chelsea

**Bangkok** THAI   This is a veteran neighborhood restaurant. It's tiny, blandly decorated, and only has about 10 dishes on the menu, but the food is good and the service very friendly, which is why it has such a fiercely loyal clientele. The staff will describe each dish in English to Thai novices—I was very grateful not to have to point at the menu as you do when you're too embarrassed to order out loud. My spicy beef with basil and chili was delicious but my pal's prawns were too hot to be much fun. She wished she'd chosen one of the noodle dishes temptingly close on the next-door table. Bangkok isn't in anywhere near the same league as Tawana in Bayswater, but it is a great budget choice in this very tony neighborhood—not to mention a great way to meet the tony neighbors.

9 Bute St., SW7. ℂ 020/7584-8529. Reservations essential. Main courses £7–£13 ($10.15–$18.85). MC, V. Daily 12:15–2:30pm; Mon–Sat 6:45–11pm. Tube: South Kensington.

**Itsu** ★★ PAN-ASIAN/SUSHI   This is the brainchild of Julian Metcalfe, who created Pret a Manger, the chain of hip and healthy sandwich shops that revolutionized the British lunch market. Itsu has the super-fashionable conveyor belt, with circling food on white, red, black, and gold plates to show the different prices. The menu subverts tradition with pan-Asian and Western influences. On the cheapest white plates you'll find salmon sushi, a sweet omelet roll with chives, and the vegetarian Californian roll. Salmon has a big part on the menu, from the smoked variety with avocado and flying fish eggs, to some marinated with chives, or turned into sashimi. The £3.75 gold plates include tasty grilled chicken with green soba noodles. Itsu is evangelically healthy, except for the oddball crème brûlée on the black-plate list. So have a last cigarette in the bar upstairs as the restaurant is nonsmoking. A new Soho branch opened last year at 103 Wardour St., W1 (℗ **020/7479-4794;** Tube: Leicester Square, Piccadilly Circus).

118 Draycott Ave., SW3. ℗ **020/7590-2401.** Sushi £2.50–£3.75 ($3.65–$5.45) per dish. AE, MC, V. Mon–Sat noon–11pm; Sun noon–10pm. No smoking in the restaurant. Tube: South Kensington.

**Maggie Jones's** ⭐ TRADITIONAL BRITISH   This 40-year veteran bistro has a charming staff and a quirkily cozy atmosphere that pulls in a diverse clientele. Maggie Jones's is like a dusty junkshop crammed with farmhouse kitchen ephemera—copper warming pans, toddlers' rocking horses, and sheaves of dried corn hang down from the ceiling. The food is hearty farmhouse-style, too—big portions, not much finesse—from slices of eggy quiche, to wild boar sausages and mash, as well as duck, venison, guinea fowl, and rabbit. And the menu tosses avocado about with 1970s abandon. The three-course Sunday lunch is a classic, offering such national culinary treasures as roast beef with Yorkshire pudding and, my favorite, apple crumble. There's only a cover charge in the evening, but the bill includes a 12.5% service charge, so watch for the total left cheekily blank on your credit card slip.

6 Old Court Place, off Kensington Church St., W8. ℗ **020/7937-6462.** Reservations essential at dinner and for Sunday lunch. Main courses £5–£15 ($7.25–$21.75). Fixed-price Sunday lunch £14.75 ($21.40). Cover charge at dinner £1 ($1.45). AE, DC, MC, V. Daily 12:30–2:30pm; Mon–Sat 6:30–11pm, Sun 6:30–10pm. Tube: Kensington High St.

**Oriel** FRENCH BRASSERIE   Oriel is in a fantastic location, right on the corner of Sloane Square, and everyone knows it. It's always hopping, so if you're planning to eat rather than grab a coffee-stop or a quick drink (wine by the glass is very reasonably priced), try to arrive a little ahead of normal mealtimes. The upstairs is classic brasserie, with big mirrors, square-topped tables, and high ceilings. There are a few pavement tables for people-watching. Downstairs, marshmallow sofas make you never want to leave. The food is a good value, from *moules marinières* (mussels) to salads or sausage and mash. Oriel has vegetarian dishes and will provide reduced-price portions for the kids.

50–51 Sloane Sq., SW1. ℗ **020/7730-2804.** Main courses £8.45–£12.25 ($11.95–$17.75). AE, DC, MC, V. Mon–Sat 8:30am–10:45pm; Sun 9am–10pm. Tube: Sloane Sq.

**Vingt-Quatre** ⭐ MODERN BRITISH   This is a proper restaurant that serves proper food 24 hours a day. It's a West London institution and pretty unique across the whole city. Bedraggled partygoers, all untucked and blurring at the edges, roll in here hour by hour, whether to finish off the night with steak and fries or to mark the achievement of a *nuit blanche* with a rip-roaring English breakfast. Vingt-Quatre recently had a refurb, smartening up its diner image— the seating is certainly a lot bum-friendlier—and adding healthy options to the menu. Of course, you don't have to stay up all night to eat here. It's a great spot for a standard supper that isn't standard at all. The menu changes regularly, but might include the delicious Caesar salad with quail eggs, or black tagliatelle with chili oil and grilled baby squid. If you do come for a session in the wee small hours, Fulham Road is one of the more reliable places for finding a taxi.

325 Fulham Rd., SW10. ℗ **020/7376-7224.** Main courses £7–£10 ($10.15–$14.50); £1 ($1.45) cover charge 10:30pm–7am. AE, MC, V. Open 24 hours. Tube: Gloucester Rd., South Kensington. Bus: nos. 14 and N14.

> ### ⎛Tips⎞   Where to Go for a 24-Hour Munchie Fix
>
> However cosmopolitan London gets, it still can't grasp the round-the-clock thing. There are a few places to assuage the munchies if they strike at an inconvenient hour but only a very few. The top spot is the legendary Soho diner, **Bar Italia,** 22 Frith St., W1 (✆ **020/7437-4520; Tube:** Tottenham Court Rd.). The simple food ranges from hot panini specials to mouthwatering pastries and cakes. There are two more Soho never-closers: the mainly gay **Old Compton Café,** 34 Old Compton St., W1 (✆ **020/ 7439-3309;** Tube: Leicester Sq.), is good for sarnies and caffeine; and **1997,** 19 Wardour St., W1 (✆ **020/7734-2868**) is a friendly Chinese restaurant, cheekily decked out with posters of Mao and Deng Xiaoping. Otherwise, there's the omelet and shake place, Clerkenwell's **Tinseltown,** 44–46 St. John St., EC1 (✆ **020/7689-2424;** Tube: Barbican, Farringdon); the nearby multi-ethnic snack shop, **The Knosherie,** 12–14 Greville St., EC1 (✆ **020/ 7242-5190**); the **Brick Lane Beigel Bake,** 159 Brick Lane, E1 (✆ **020/ 7729-0616;** Tube: Shoreditch); and **Vingt-Quatre** (reviewed in section 4).

## SUPER-CHEAP EATS

**Chelsea Kitchen** BRITISH DINER   This is a sister to the Stockpot chain, which also has a diner on King's Road. The Chelsea Kitchen is a lot more convenient, and the food is marginally less reminiscent of the dreadful school dinners the Brits grow up on. The cuisine is still not haute by any stretch of the imagination, but it is a fantastically good deal. The menu never ever changes. It runs from omelets and burgers to salads and more substantial hot dishes, such as goulash, spaghetti bolognese, and braised lamb chops. Chelsea Kitchen is no-frills on the decor side, too, with polished wooden tables and bottom-numbing booths. The service sometimes sorely lacks a smile. But the prices are so "Old World" that it gets screamingly busy, particularly in the evening.

98 King's Rd., SW3. ✆ 020/7589-1330. Main courses £2.60–£5.10 ($3.75–$7.40); fixed-priced meal £4.90 ($7.10). No credit cards. Mon–Sun 8am–11:30pm. Tube: Sloane Sq.

## GREAT DEALS ON FIXED-PRICE MEALS

**Café Lazeez** ⚜ INDIAN   A two-times winner of Carlton TV's Best Indian Restaurant award, this is another place that has ditched flock wallpaper and canned ethnic music for a cool modern approach, evolving new dishes but losing nothing of its authenticity in the kitchen. There's a bar/brasserie on the ground floor with the dining room upstairs. In summer, diners hang out on a terrace framed with flower boxes. There's so much good stuff to choose from and at such a range of prices, that you'd have to go back several times to work out which is the best deal. The £30 ($43.50) fixed-price menu for two is a great value. It starts with delicious barbecued meat: kebabs and chicken tikka with naan bread. The main course includes spicy sautéed chicken, lamb, aubergines, cumin potatoes, dhal, rice, more naan, and coffee. Alternatively, the £15.50 ($22.50) House Feast—a host of different meats cooked in the tandoor oven—could easily feed two people. Just ask for extra cutlery. There are two other branches: at 88 St. John St., EC1 (✆ **020/7253-2224;** Tube: Barbican, Farringdon) and at the Soho Theatre, 21 Dean St., W1 (✆ **020/7434-9393;** Tube: Tottenham Court Rd.).

93–95 Old Brompton Rd., SW7. ✆ 020/7581-9993. Reservations recommended. Main courses £6.95–£14.50 ($11.10–$23.20); fixed-price meals £10 ($14.50) 11am–5pm, £12.75 ($18.50). AE, DC, MC, V. Mon–Sat 11am–1am; Sun 11am–10:30pm. Tube: South Kensington.

**Wódka** POLISH   This friendly Kensington restaurant takes a new look at classic Polish dishes, served amid the simple modern decor. The two- and three-course fixed-price lunches are a great value. You might start with a meal-in-itself, such as *zur* (sausage and sour rye soup), or light fluffy blinis with aubergine mousse. The main courses are likely to include at least one Western European dish, the delicious fishcakes probably, so don't worry if Eastern has never been your bag. If you've got a bit of spare cash, then come in the evening instead. It's a much better time to enjoy Wódka's real specialty: the mile-long menu of vodkas, served by the shot or carafe. There's every flavor under the sun, from bison grass to rose petal, or a honey one that's served hot. Wódka is a firm favorite with locals and not-so-locals who want to kick up their heels.

12 St. Alban's Grove, W8. ✆ 020/7937-6513. Reservations recommended. Main courses £10.90–£13.50 ($15.80–$19.60); fixed-price lunch £10.90–£13.90 ($15.80–$20.15). AE, DC, MC, V. Tube: High St. Kensington, Gloucester Rd.

## WORTH A SPLURGE

**Cambio de Tercio** ✰✰ SPANISH   Several changes of chef have done nothing to dent the standards or the popularity of the stylish Cambio de Tercio. The dramatic interior is decorated in a rich yellow with damask-spread tables and chairs swathed in burgundy cloth. The walls are hung with pictures of bullfights and a matador's cloak and swords. The charming Spanish staff guides you through a menu of regional delights. Ham is the house specialty—from the expensive plate of ham Jabugo, made from acorn-fed black pig, to the suckling pig Segovia style. Contrarily I went for the brilliantly conceived poached eggs with grilled asparagus, Basque wine mousseline, and sautéed foie gras. Not only should you dress up a bit for this place, but starve yourself beforehand.

163 Old Brompton Rd., SW5. ✆ 020/7244-8970. Reservations required for dinner. Main courses £10.50–£15 ($15.25–$21.75). AE, MC, V. Daily 12:30–2:30pm; Mon–Sat 7–11:30pm, Sun 7–11pm. Tube: Gloucester Rd., South Kensington.

## 5 Earl's Court

**The Atlas** ✰✰ GASTROPUB/MEDITERRANEAN   The doors open for drinkers at noon here, and that's when you should come if you want to get a table (especially one outside). The Atlas is incredibly popular, and rightly so: the food is delicious, the ambiance laid-back, and it has a real neighborhood feel generated by the clearly very regular clientele. The Manners brothers run the place, with George as the chef and grand creator of grilled Tuscan sausages with Puy lentils, or pan-fried calves liver. While he is big on balsamic vinegar, pancetta, and parmesan, the rich flavors characteristic of Spanish and North African cooking spice up both starters and main courses made from the freshest of whatever's in season. And do leave space for a pudding, because George's are some of the baddest in town. Choose from the menu chalked up on the board and order at the bar. The Atlas has several ales on tap and around ten wines available by the glass.

16 Seagrave Rd., SW6. ✆ 020/7385-9129. Main courses £7–£11 ($10.15–$15.95). MC, V. Food served daily 12:30–3pm; Mon–Sat 7–10:30pm, Sun 7–10pm. Tube: West Brompton.

## GREAT DEALS ON FIXED-PRICE MEALS

Lou Pescadou SEAFOOD/TRADITIONAL FRENCH  You can't miss Lou Pescadou's porthole front window. The fishy theme carries on inside, with scallop ashtrays, marine-blue oilcloths on the tables, and boat pictures hanging on the walls. Service is enthusiastic but often chaotic. Food standards can be patchy. Yet the restaurant has a loyal local clientele, mostly slightly older, and it is handy for anyone staying in Earl's Court. You can sit out on the pavement during the summer. I definitely wouldn't go a la carte, but the weekend fixed-price menu is a pretty good value for three courses. If you get a shellfish option, make sure it comes with Lou Pescadou's velvety mayonnaise. Main courses are sturdy and old-fashioned, from whole seabass grilled with fennel to smoked haddock with juniper butter. I'd actually go for one of the meat dishes, also classically French—the chef really knows how to cook a steak, with shallot sauce, *saignant.*

241 Old Brompton Rd., SW5. © 020/7370-1057. Reservations essential. Main courses £7.80–£13.40 ($11.30–$19.45); weekday fixed-price lunch £9.90 ($14.35); weekend fixed-price meal £13.50 ($19.60). AE, DC, MC, V. Daily noon–3pm; Mon–Fri 7pm–midnight, Sat–Sun 6:30pm–midnight. Tube: Earl's Court.

## 6 Notting Hill

Mandola ★ SUDANESE  The secret of this little local restaurant is out. Mandola started out as the half-hearted annex to the take-out joint next door. Now it has grown into an attractive and mildly eccentric restaurant. The food is very good, but the service can be unbelievably slow. The best deal is the £10.50 ($15.25) starter, which gives two diners free run at everything the salad bar has to offer—though to call it just a "salad bar" doesn't do it justice. Options include white cabbage in peanut sauce, aubergine *salata aswad,* and Sudanese falafel. Each would cost over £2 ($2.90) on its own, and you get pita bread to accompany them. Main courses are just as simple, from super-tender lamb and chicken in pungent sauces to the vegetarian stews. Mandola is unlicensed, so you can bring your own wine for £1 corkage per bottle.

139–143 Westbourne Grove, W11. © 020/7229-4734. Reservations recommended for dinner. Main courses £6–£9.50 ($8.70–$13.80). AE, MC, V. Mon–Sun noon–midnight. Tube: Notting Hill Gate.

Portobello Gold ★ Finds INTERNATIONAL  This is the place Bill Clinton popped into in December 2000, and popped out of again without paying, while Hillary Christmas-shopped in Portobello Market. I wish I'd seen the ramshackle pub-restaurant swarming with men in black wearing sunglasses and wired for sound! I hear they stuck to the all-day bar menu—none of the jumbo sandwiches, salads, nibbles and dips, patés, or sweet temptations tops £6.50 ($9.45). I'd try the restaurant, though, because it has one of the most romantic dining

---

**Finds  Much More Than Just a Bookshop**

The first muffins come out of the oven at 10am, filling **Books for Cooks** with heavenly smells. This mecca for gastronomes, which stocks nearly 12,000 titles, has a little test kitchen at the rear and a handful of tables where browsers can settle down for a cup of coffee and a freshly-baked cake. Light lunches are a steal at £5 ($7.20)—hot soup and bread in the winter, a salad or homemade savory tart in the summer. I adore this place. It's just off the Portobello Road at 4 Blenheim Crescent, W11 (© 020/7221-1992; Tube: Ladbroke Grove, Notting Hill Gate).

---

### Moments  Heavenly Smells

The simplest pleasures are often the greatest. I'm a sucker for the ambrosial aromas of really good street food. At Notting Hill Farmers' Market, the gourmet-mushroom man sautés his wares, with herbs and lashings of garlic, right there on a little camping stove. His ciabatta sandwiches cost £2 ($2.90). Stand there a moment and inhale.

---

spots in town. The "hippy balcony," as long-time owner Mike Bell describes it, is under the conservatory greenery, with a low Indian table and squashy cushions. Starters are fishy or vegetarian, unless you count the bacon in the tasty smoked eel and anchovy salad. The hearty main courses make up for it, though. My calves liver was a little over-cooked but it went very well with basil and parmesan polenta. Portobello Gold also has an Internet cafe and five B&B bedrooms (see p. 78). It's happy hour in the bar every day from 5:30 to 7pm. This is a nutty, chaotic place, but great fun, especially on Saturdays.

95–97 Portobello Rd., W11. ✆ 020/7460-4918. Reservations recommended for dinner and Sunday lunch. Main courses £7.95–14.75 ($9.45–$21.40). DC, MC, V. Restaurant Mon–Sat noon–5pm, 7–11:15pm; Sun 1–5pm, 7–9:30pm. Tube: Notting Hill Gate.

## SUPER-CHEAP EATS

Café Grove BRITISH DINER   This is the perfect refueling spot after a morning at Portobello Market. In the summer, diners sit out on the roof terrace, enjoying the bustle below. It naturally gets a lot quieter during the week and in winter. Café Grove looks like a scruffy campus hangout from the 1970s, despite the freshly painted walls, and the menu is a mixture of the worthy and the wicked. You can breakfast your way around the world here—on huevos rancheros, perhaps, or pancakes. The very ungreasy breakfast, served all day in winter and until 12:30pm in summer, could stop a truck: it's a huge plate of bacon, sausages (vegetarian or "carnivorous"), tomato, fried eggs, mushrooms, baked beans, potatoes, and toast. For those who like their lunch to look like lunch, there are salads, build-your-own sandwiches, melts, Mexican wraps, and homemade cakes. Café Grove serves Victorian lemonade, wine and beer (including organic brands), but not Coke or Pepsi. And prepare for a dirty look if you smoke.

253a Portobello Rd., W11. ✆ 020/7243-1094. Sandwiches and light meals £2–£7 ($3.20–$11.20). No credit cards (but soon). Winter 9:30am–5pm; summer Mon 8:30am–6pm, Tues–Sat 8:30am–11pm. Tube: Ladbroke Grove.

Costas Fish Restaurant 🦞 FISH & CHIPS   My dad had his office in Hillgate Street while I was growing up and it used to be a big treat to go and meet him after work for a bumper supper at Costas. And, supposedly, I didn't even like fish then! It has always seemed an unlikely place, really—a tiny, timewarp Cypriot restaurant peddling the English national dish. But the battered haddock was delicious, even if the portion was smaller than some rivals dish out (it was cheaper, too!), and so were the crunchy chips. The Greek influence is evident in the side orders, which include hummus, and in desserts such as baklava. But I much prefer this nuttiness to another local institution, Geales, round the corner, which has ideas above its chippie station and fails to live up to them. Don't confuse this place with Costas Grill, which is at nos. 12 to 14 Hillgate Street.

18 Hillgate St., W8. ✆ 020/7727-4310. Reservations recommended for dinner. Main courses £4–£7 ($5.80–$10.15). No credit cards. Daily noon–2:30pm; Tues–Sat 5:30–10:30pm. Tube: Notting Hill Gate.

# Restaurants from Marylebone to Notting Hill

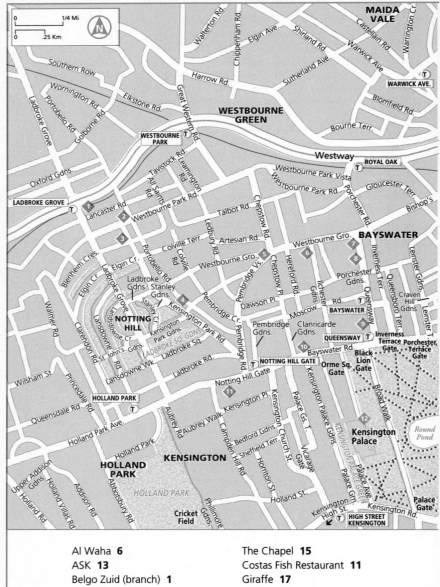

Al Waha **6**

ASK **13**

Belgo Zuid (branch) **1**

Books for Cooks **3**

Café Diana **10**

Café Grove **2**

Carluccio's Caffè **21**

The Chapel **15**

Costas Fish Restaurant **11**

Giraffe **17**

La Spighetta **16**

Mandola **5**

The Orangery **12**

Patogh **14**

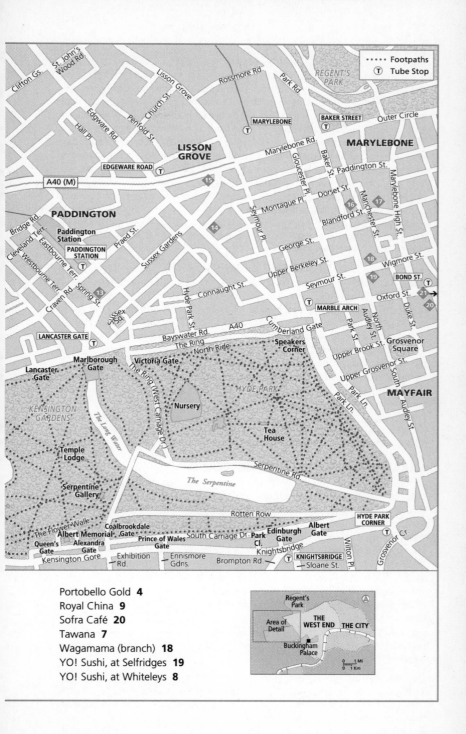

St. John's Wood Rd.

Clifton Gs.

Lisson Grove

Rossmore Rd.

Park Rd.

REGENT'S PARK

Edgware Rd.

Penfold St.

Church St.

Hall Pl.

MARYLEBONE

BAKER STREET

Outer Circle

MARYLEBONE

LISSON GROVE

Marylebone Rd.

Paddington St.

EDGWARE ROAD Ⓣ

A40 (M)

**15**

Montague Pl.

Dorset St.

**16**

**17**

Manchester St.

Marylebone High St.

PADDINGTON

Paddington Station

Praed St.

Seymour Pl.

Blandford St.

Bridge Rd.

Cleveland Terr.

Eastbourne Terr.

Westbourne Terr.

PADDINGTON STATION

Sussex Gardens

George St.

**18**

Wigmore St.

Craven Rd.

Spring St.

**13**

Upper Berkeley St.

**19**

BOND ST.

Sussex Sq.

Hyde Park St.

Connaught St.

Seymour St.

Oxford St.

**21**

LANCASTER GATE

Bayswater Rd.

A40

Ⓣ MARBLE ARCH

**20**

The Ring

North Ride

Cumberland Gate

North Audley St.

Duke St.

Lancaster Gate

Marlborough Gate

Victoria Gate

Speakers Corner

Park St.

Upper Brook St.

Grosvenor Square

KENSINGTON GARDENS

The Ring (West Carriage Dr.)

Nursery

HYDE PARK

Upper Grosvenor St.

South Audley St.

Park Ln.

MAYFAIR

The Long Water

Tea House

Temple Lodge

Serpentine Gallery

The Serpentine

Serpentine Rd.

Rotten Row

HYDE PARK CORNER

The Flower Walk

Albert Memorial

Coalbrookdale Gate

South Carriage Dr.

Edinburgh Gate

Albert Gate

Grosvenor Cr.

Queen's Gate

Alexandra Gate

Prince of Wales Gate

Park Cl.

Wilton Pl.

Kensington Gore

Exhibition Rd.

Ennismore Gdns.

Knightsbridge

Brompton Rd.

Ⓣ KNIGHTSBRIDGE

Sloane St.

Regent's Park

Area of Detail

THE WEST END

THE CITY

Buckingham Palace

0    1 Mi
0    1 Km

## 7 Paddington & Bayswater

**Al Waha** ★★ LEBANESE   I visited Al Waha with some cynicism. It had been dubbed the best Lebanese cooking in London and the critics were so excited that you couldn't help speculating about brown envelopes being passed under restaurant tables. Slapped wrists for such an uncharitable thought: Al Waha delivers spectacularly, and elegantly. Bad Middle-Eastern cooking can be very brown, like compost, but all the dishes here taste as fresh as their ingredients must have been. I can't decide whether to recommend mixing and matching the starters, of which the miniature lamb sausages and the grilled halloumi cheese are particularly good, or to say save yourself and go straight to a main course. There are lots of grills and then the daily specials, chicken stuffed with prune and pine nuts perhaps, and always fish on Fridays.

75 Westbourne Grove, W2. ℂ 020/7229-0806. Reservations recommended. Main courses £8.50–£14 ($12.35–$20.30). Fixed-price meal £18 ($26.10). Cover charge £1.50 ($2.20). AE, DC, MC, V. Daily noon–midnight. Tube: Bayswater, Queensway.

**Royal China** ★★ CHINESE   The plaudits keep rolling in for Royal China's dim sum, which is reckoned by many to be the best in London. The decor is marvelously over-ornate, with Hong Kong casino-style, black-and-gold paneling. But you don't have to be a high roller to dine here: A dim sum extravaganza is unlikely to set you back much more than £10 ($14.50). The most popular dish, and deservedly so, is the roast pork puff—crisp pastry holding a wonderfully sumptuous filling. The touch is always light as air, whether on the standard menu dumplings or daily specials, such as a delicate mangetout combination. No wonder Sundays here are as big a scrum as the Harrods sale. Come during the week when it's a lot more peaceful, and the staff are more likely to have their happy faces on—but not that much more likely!

13 Queensway, W2. ℂ 020/7221-2535. Reservations recommended. Main courses £6–£40 ($8.70–$58); fixed-price dinner £25 ($36.25). AE, DC, MC, V. Mon–Thurs noon–11pm; Fri–Sat noon–11:30pm; Sun 11am–10pm; dim sum to 5pm daily. Tube: Bayswater, Queensway.

## GREAT DEALS ON FIXED-PRICE MEALS

**Tawana** ★ THAI   Elbow room is squeezed to a minimum in the weekend crush at this very popular restaurant. Yet Tawana maintains a certain cool charm that sets it apart from the string of garish cheap joints on Queensway. And the food is the real thing. The hot and sour chicken soup, made with coconut milk, was so filling that I wished I'd eaten with more restraint—but I still found room for curry. Tawana has none of the namby pamby Western attitude to chili so it rendered me temporarily speechless, a very rare condition. But once the shock wears off, the flavors are subtle and delicious. If heat isn't your thing, get one of the friendly staff to guide you past the menu danger points. As at many Thai restaurants, puddings are pretty missable, unless you need a sorbet to cool down your taste buds.

3 Westbourne Grove, W2. ℂ 020/7229-3785. Reservations recommended. Main courses £5.50–£17.95 ($8–$26.05). Fixed-price meal £15.95 ($23.15). AE, DC, MC, V. Daily noon–3pm, 6–11pm. Tube: Bayswater, Queensway.

## 8 Marylebone

**The Chapel** ★ GASTROPUB/MODERN EUROPEAN   The Chapel more than earns the epithet of gastropub. The food is ambitious, beautifully executed, and primarily modern European. The blackboard scrawl lists a handful of daily

---

*Tips*   **Good Old-fashioned Pub Grub**

---

Swapping nicotine-stained wallpaper for chi-chi minimalist restaurant walls makes gastropub cuisine a lot pricier than honest no-frills pub grub. But budget travelers and traditionalists needn't despair. There are still lots of great British boozers serving up great pub grub.

For a really hearty homemade pie, for about £6.50 ($10.40), try the **Salisbury,** 90 St. Martin's Lane, WC2 (© 020/7836-5863). You can get hot food from 11am until 11pm (Sunday noon–10:30pm). Farther north, in Bloomsbury, there's a great place to stop after a visit to the British Museum. The **Museum Tavern,** 49 Great Russell St., WC1 (© 020/7242-8987), can fix you up with a very decent beef-and-ale pie, or a ploughman's lunch for £5 to £7 ($7.25–$10.15) at any time of the day. Built as a jail in 1780, the **Nag's Head,** 53 Kinnerton St., SW1 (© 020/7235-1135), is supposed to be the smallest pub in London. Wash down the shepherd's pie or gourmet sausages with one of the big range of on-tap real ales. The food will cost you £5 to £6.75 ($7.25–$9.80), a bargain in Belgravia. Meanwhile bar food really is pub grub at the **George Inn,** a 17th-century coaching inn owned by the National Trust at 77 Borough High St., SE1 (© 020/7407-2056). Sausage and mash or a ploughman's lunch will set you back £5 ($7.25), and there's an excellent range of real ales with which to wash it down. Head south from London Bridge Tube station and it's on the left down a little alley.

*Note:* For more Great British Boozers, check out "The Drinking Game: Pubs & Wine Bars," in chapter 8, "London After Dark."

---

starters, from brie en croute to parma ham and Tuscan bean salad in a filo basket. Main courses may sound traditional (many don't) but have a very modern twist, like the pork with caramelized apples. But it was the fluffy fishcakes that won my vote of confidence. Don't graze too enthusiastically at the complimentary basket of delicious breads because the desserts are extremely wicked, and deserve close attention. The interior is bright and spacious, but the bare-board floor does make it rather noisy. In the summer, head out to the garden where there are 15 tables where you can escape the cigarette smoke and sip a glass of wine (25 are available by the glass) or a pint of London Pride.

48 Chapel St., NW1. © 020/7402-9220. Main courses £8–£12.50 ($11.60–$18.15). AE, DC, MC, V. Daily noon–2:30pm and 7–10pm. Tube: Edgware Rd.

**Giraffe** ✦ INTERNATIONAL   The first thing staff see when they turn up at this hard-working restaurant is a queue of eager eaters, and that's at 8 o'clock in the morning! I defy anyone not to leave Giraffe in a warm glow of contentment, not only because of the delicious food, but also because of the friendly atmosphere. Filling lunchtime snacks start at £3.50 ($5.10), and though there's no fixed-price menu, you needn't spend more than £15 ($21.75) in the evening. Go with a group and you could all be eating in a different country, from English herby sausages, to Moroccan-spiced meat dishes, to something with enough garlic to win you honorary French nationality. Giraffe is also at 46 Rosslyn Hill,

NW3 (© **020/7435-0343;** Tube: Hampstead); and at 29 Essex Rd., N1 (© **020/ 7359-5999;** Tube: Angel).

6–8 Blandford St., W1. © **020/7935-2333.** Reservations recommended; not accepted for weekend lunch. Main courses £6.95–£10.95 ($10.10–$15.90). AE, MC, V. Mon–Fri 8am–11pm; Sat 9am–11pm; Sun 9am–10:30pm. No smoking. Tube: Baker St., Regent's Park.

**La Spighetta** 🗲🗲 PIZZA & PASTA   This little basement restaurant is the better-value sister of Spiga in Covent Garden. It was "created," as the higher echelons of the restaurant world say, by Giorgio Locatelli, who is chef and part owner of Knightsbridge's illustrious Zafferano. The menu is as authentic and uncomplicated as the decor, using an Italian wood-fired oven for the pizzas. The ingredients are simple—mozzarella, artichoke, spicy salami, *pecorino* cheese, and so on, all melting together on superbly crispy bases. There are nine main pasta dishes—I'd go for one with fresh and sundried tomatoes—and lots of meat and fish main courses. The menu changes every week but I hope you'll find the marvelous wind-dried tuna starter, one of several that show La Spighetta's posh pedigree. Cheaper children's portions are available on request, though I doubt the kids would thank you for sparing them even one mouthful of the heavenly homemade ice cream. This place is justly popular for working lunches and for R&R after the day is done.

43 Blandford St., W1. © **020/7486-7340.** Reservations recommended. Main courses £7–£11 ($10.15–$15.95). AE, MC, V. Mon–Sat noon–2:30pm; Mon–Sat 6:30–11:30pm, Sun 6:30–10:30pm. Tube: Baker St.

## SUPER-CHEAP EATS

**Patogh**IRANIAN   If you like simple Persian cooking, you'll love Patogh. The kebabs are legendary. Left to marinate overnight, the organic lamb or chicken melts in the mouth. The skewers come on a huge circle of seeded bread, with yogurt dips and Middle-Eastern salad. You'll never want to have a kebab made by anyone else again. If they're not your thing, there are plenty of other choices, from chicken pieces to a whole host of ready-prepared salads and starters under the glass counter. There's hummus, marinated tomato, and other *meze* (small entrees). You could stack a plate high without coming close to busting the budget. Patogh is unlicensed, too, so you can bring your own bottle of wine or beer, and you won't even be charged any corkage.

8 Crawford Place, W1. © **020/7262-4015.** Reservations recommended. Main courses £5–£7.50 ($7.25–$10.90). No credit cards. Daily noon–11:30pm. Tube: Edgware Rd.

## 9 Soho & Chinatown

**Andrew Edmunds** 🗲 *Finds* MODERN BRITISH   This charming eaterie hates to think of itself as a stop on the tourist trail. In fact, it asked to be taken out of the guide. But this is such a good deal that we pretended we hadn't heard. Andrew Edmunds has grown organically, from an early start as a wine bar, and is attached to the print gallery next door. Popular for business lunches by day, it becomes the haunt of young couples on romantic candlelit dinners in the evening. They have to whisper their sweet nothings because the tables are pretty close together. The handwritten menu changes frequently but always offers modern European cuisine in healthy portions: I thought the avocado, roasted onion and walnut salad was a bit dull. Luckily, it was my friend who chose that! I had a delicious white bean and lemon soup, then roasted free-range chicken

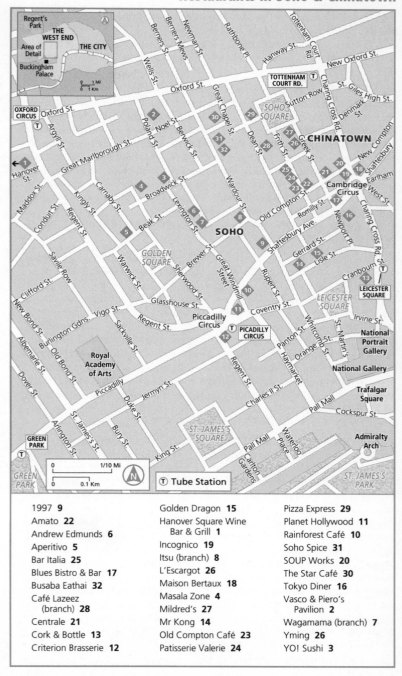

T Tube Station

1997 **9**

Amato **22**

Andrew Edmunds **6**

Aperitivo **5**

Bar Italia **25**

Blues Bistro & Bar **17**

Busaba Eathai **32**

Café Lazeez
  (branch) **28**

Centrale **21**

Cork & Bottle **13**

Criterion Brasserie **12**

Golden Dragon **15**

Hanover Square Wine
  Bar & Grill **1**

Incognico **19**

Itsu (branch) **8**

L'Escargot **26**

Maison Bertaux **18**

Masala Zone **4**

Mildred's **27**

Mr Kong **14**

Old Compton Café **23**

Patisserie Valerie **24**

Pizza Express **29**

Planet Hollywood **11**

Rainforest Café **10**

Soho Spice **31**

SOUP Works **20**

The Star Café **30**

Tokyo Diner **16**

Vasco & Piero's
  Pavilion **2**

Wagamama (branch) **7**

Yming **26**

YO! Sushi **3**

with "crushed" potatoes. The desserts are delicious classics, from tiramisu to almond tart. Finish up with a portion of Stilton.

46 Lexington St., W1. ℭ **020/7437-5708.** Reservations recommended. Main courses £8.25–£13.50 ($11.95–$19.60). AE, MC, V. Mon–Sat 12:30–3pm and 6–10:45pm; Sun 1–3pm and 6–10:30pm. Tube: Oxford Circus, Piccadilly Circus.

**Aperitivo** ITALIAN   This new restaurant is the baby sister of the much-lauded Assaggi in Notting Hill, which I haven't included because it is so over-priced. Aperitivo certainly isn't that. The menu works like Middle-Eastern meze or Spanish tapas, only here you accumulate small dishes of multi-regional Italian cuisine—meat, fish, vegetables, and salads. It's a budget heaven in the form of rather a stylish restaurant. You can drop in at any time of day and spend as much or as little as you like. The idea is to order up lots of dishes and share them, reckoning on about two per person. The most unusual is poached egg and tomato baked in a parcel of that poppadom-like Sardinian bread called carta da musica. Finish off with panna cotta, which is delicious.

41–45 Beak St., W1. ℭ **020/7287-2057.** Main courses £3.75–£6.75 ($5.45–$9.80). AE, DC, MC, V. Mon–Sat noon–11pm. Tube: Oxford Circus, Piccadilly Circus.

**Golden Dragon** ★★ CANTONESE   The crowds of local Chinese diners who come here back up the claim that the Golden Dragon serves up some of the best dim sum in town. There can be nothing but praise for the honey-glazed spare ribs, steamed eel with black-bean sauce, and sliced marinated duck with garlic dipping sauce. The service is variable but often because the staff is so busy rather than any deliberate rudeness. And the Golden Dragon is an appealing place, decked out in Chinese-holiday style. If you decide on dim sum, make sure to try the steamed scallop dumplings and prawn cheung fen. A real blowout shouldn't cost you more than £15 ($21.75), but you'll have to get here before 5pm. And do book, especially on Sundays when the place is packed.

28–29 Gerrard St., W1. ℭ **020/7734-2763.** Reservations recommended. Main courses £6–£18 ($8.70–$26.10); fixed-price menus £12.50–£22.50 ($18.15–$32.65). AE, DC, MC, V. Mon–Thurs noon–11:30pm; Fri–Sat noon–midnight; Sun 11am–11pm. Tube: Leicester Sq.

**Incognico** ★★ MODERN FRENCH   The £12.50 set menu comprises three courses, with a choice of two dishes at each stage, which is great value in itself, but even better when you realize it offers the superlative French cooking of Nico Ladenis. He won three Michelin stars in 1995 for his place in Park Lane, where the prices are beyond even a lifetime treat for budget diners. If you want to see what you've been missing, the dish Ladenis has perfected for 20 years, pan-fried foie gras with brioche and caramelized orange, is on the a la carte menu here as a starter for £11 ($15.95). Otherwise, Incognico is much lower key and a more modern enterprise, though it looks like bourgeois brasserie meets New York, with its bar, heavy paneling, and starched white tablecloths. Skate wing was delicious, as was my vegetarian choice of Parmesan risotto with mushrooms. Unlike many of London's eateries, where the food is only part of the entertainment, eating here feels like a very special gastronomic experience.

117 Shaftesbury Ave., WC2 ℭ **020/7836-8866.** Reservations essential. Main courses £9–£15 ($13.05–$21.75). Fixed-price lunch and pre-theater meal £12.50 ($18.15). AE, DC, MC, V. Daily noon–3pm; Mon–Sat 5:30–midnight. Tube: Leicester Sq., Tottenham Ct. Rd.

**Mildred's** ★ VEGETARIAN   Mildred's is a smashing lunch spot that's open in the evenings, too, though not the best one for a long linger. This is a small cafe, and you may have to share a table. But with the very continental-style *paseo* that takes over Soho's streets at night, who'd want to stay inside? Mildred's may look like a product of the current trend for healthy eating in London, but it's been around since the days when vegetarian meant lunatic fringe to most people and few restaurants offered meatless options. All the vegetarian ingredients are naturally grown—or laid, in the case of the free-range eggs—and used in the right season wherever possible. Legumes cooked every which way are a firm fixture, as are stir-fries. The menu changes every week and becomes very wicked when you get to dessert. And Mildred's also stocks organic wines.

58 Greek St., W1. ✆ 020/7494-1634. Reservations not accepted. Main courses £5.10–£6.90 ($7.40–$10). Mon–Sat noon–11pm. No credit cards. No smoking. Tube: Tottenham Court Rd.

**Mr Kong** ★★ CANTONESE   This rather shabby restaurant is so popular that it's busy until 3am every night of the week. The cheaper fixed-price menu includes soup, a choice of three main courses—beef with black bean sauce, for instance—and rice. The more expensive one covers four courses and is a lot better value. Go with either, however, and you may get a visit from the green-eyed monster when you see what others have ordered from over 150 dishes listed on three different menus. The Chef's Specials could be Mandarin chicken with jellyfish, or frog's legs in ginger wine, or fish lips. The daily specials are generally a bit cheaper and less exotic. Or you can choose from the regular selection: Sliced pork, salted egg, and vegetable soup is a house specialty. The service is friendly (really!) and the menu translated into English.

21 Lisle St., WC2. ✆ 020/7437-7341. Reservations required for weekend dinners. Main courses £6–£18 ($8.70–$26.10); fixed-price dinner £9.30–£22 ($13.50–$31.90). AE, DC, MC, V. Daily noon–3am. Tube: Leicester Sq., Piccadilly Circus.

**Tokyo Diner** ★ JAPANESE   This 3-story restaurant on the edge of Chinatown is the diametric opposite of somewhere like YO! Sushi. There's no talk of brand values here, simply great value fast food in traditional, Japanese-diner style. And it has lots of Japanese customers. The wooden tables are small and cramped, but nobody seems to mind. The bento boxes are a great value at around £10 ($14.50), and they include rice, noodle salad, salmon sashimi salad, and a main dish, which might be pork or chicken *tonkatsu,* or chicken, salmon, or mackerel teriyaki. If you really want to save money, make a meal from the *donburi*—boxes filled with rice topped with seasoned egg and chicken, perhaps, or chicken flambéed in teriyaki sauce. You can get sushi and sashimi, too. Tea is free, and Japanese beer is slightly cheaper here than at pubs.

2 Newport Pl., WC2. ✆ 020/7434-1414. Reservations only accepted on weekdays and for more than 6 people. Main courses £6–£13 ($8.70–$18.85). MC, V. Daily noon–midnight. Tube: Leicester Sq.

**YO! Sushi** ★ *Kids* SUSHI   It's like being mugged by a marketing manager, one friend said of YO! Sushi. In the 5 years since it opened, the relentless self-congratulation of the fast expanding chain has become rather a turn off. But I still love this original Soho sushi bar: you will too if fade to black on the blitz of brand messages and just enjoy what is still a novel experience. Founder Simon Woodroffe used to design rock-n-roll stages, and he's won countless awards for this venture. YO! Sushi rivals NASA for hi-tech gadgets. Talking drink trolleys circle the restaurant like R2D2, and diners pick out what they want. Sushi-making robots turn out 1,200 pieces an hour, which circle around on a 60-meter conveyor belt. The different colored plates indicate the price. Diners tuck into tuna, sashimi, and so on, until full enough to ask for a plate count. Do keep a running tally, or this could turn out to be a budget-buster—unless you come half an hour before closing when all food is flogged off for £1 ($1.45). Kids eat for free from Monday to Friday and they'll love it. There are scaled down and toned-down dishes for them, from chicken nuggets to cigar-shaped fish fingers.

Other good lunchtime deals are the £5 ($7.25) bento box and a beer at **YO! Below,** the Japanese beer and sake hall downstairs at Poland Street (*C* **020/ 7439-3660**), and below the new YO! Sushi at 95 Farringdon Rd., EC1 (*C* **020/ 7841-0785** restaurant, 0790 YO! Below; Tube: Farringdon). This latter is now the biggest YO! and it has a kids eating zone. So does the one at the Harvey Nichols store in Knightsbridge, SW1 (*C* **020/7235-6114**). Others useful to know about are at Selfridges on Oxford Street, W1 (*C* **020/7318-3944**); the Whitelys shopping center in Queensway (*C* **020/7727-9293**); at Bloomsbury's Myhotel, 11–13 Bayley St., WC1 (*C* **020/7667-6000;** Tube: Goodge St., Tottenham Ct. Rd.); and at County Hall on the South Bank by the London Eye (*C* **020/7928-8871;** Tube: Waterloo, Westminster), which is the only that accepts reservations.

52 Poland St., W1. *C* **020/7287-0443.** Sushi selections from £1.50–£3.50 ($2.20–$5.10) per plate; children's dishes £1.50–£2 ($2.20–$2.90). AE, DC, MC, V. Daily noon–midnight. Tube: Oxford Circus. No smoking.

## SUPER-CHEAP EATS

**Centrale** ITALIAN    This ought to be the ideal choice for diners who've splurged on theater tickets and want a cheap eat. But beware: The portions at Centrale are so huge that a tired traveler might fall asleep halfway through the first act. This isn't a spot for a romantic assignation, or for people who don't like people, but the old-fashioned no-frills restaurant has a great deal of charm and a very loyal clientele. People in their night-out finery mix with students on a shoestring and business people snatching a bite, all crammed together on black vinyl banquettes at narrow, red Formica-topped tables. The starters are traditional budget menu items like minestrone soup. You can eat meat for the main course. But forget all that, and do what everyone else does and plump for pasta. Often you'll get more pasta than whatever's supposed to go with it, so go for a sauce with cheap ingredients—mushroom is a good choice. And don't forget to bring a bottle of wine with you (corkage is £1/$1.60).

16 Moor St., W1. *C* **020/7437-5513.** Main courses £3.50–£7 ($5.10–$10.15). No credit cards. Daily noon–9:45pm. Tube: Leicester Sq., Tottenham Ct. Rd.

**The Star Café** *C* BRITISH DINER    This ex-pub has been run by the same family for 66 years and is proud to boast of being the oldest cafe in Soho. The walls of the main floor are hung with old, enamel, shop signs and, would you believe it, radio sets. The no-frills menu includes staples like jacket potatoes, toasted sandwiches, and pasta, with daily luncheon specials such as roast chicken with crispy bacon stuffing, steak and onion pie, or salmon filet with broccoli. Most people come for the all-day, full English breakfast, including vegetarians, who get a very superior spread with peppers and diced roast potatoes. The service is so smooth that you'll probably fall off your chair if your last meal was in Chinatown. Sadly, The Star Café closes after lunch and at the weekends.

22 Great Chapel St., W1. *C* **020/7437-8778.** Reservations recommended. Main courses £4.95–£6.50 ($7.20–$9.45). No credit cards. Mon–Fri 7am–3:30pm. Tube: Tottenham Court Rd.

## GREAT DEALS ON FIXED-PRICE MEALS

**Cork & Bottle Wine Bar** INTERNATIONAL/WINE BAR    The leafleting has stopped. Aki, the Nigerian head chef at the Cork & Bottle, has convinced the wildlife lobby that he hasn't got a team of big-game hunters doing the dodgy

**Sinful Soho: Dens of Delicious Iniquity**

Whoever said the Brits are po-faced in public and only sin behind closed doors had obviously never been to Soho. I'm not talking about sleazy strip joints, but the wicked delights of the neighborhood's famous patisseries. The French had to show them how to do it, but supposedly stodgy Londoners have taken to sweet flaky pastries, tarts, and cakes with a vengeance. Just watch the shameless hordes that flock here on a Sunday.

The most venerable patisserie is **Maison Bertaux,** 28 Greek St., W1 (© **020/7437-6007**), and I defy you to pass by its delectable window without wanting to dunk a brioche in a cup of coffee. **Patisserie Valerie,** 44 Old Compton St., W1 (© **020/7437-3466**), is *the* place to gawk at greedy film and theater types who've fallen for its chocolate truffle cake. The crowds are smaller at **Amato,** 14 Old Compton St., W1 (© **020/7734-5733**) but its alcoholic chocolate-and-coffee mousse cake is to die for.

for him. The kangaroo, crocodile, emu, and other exotic meats are all from farmed animals. The menu spans Pacific Rim, Afro-Caribbean, with some good British and European staples, too—Aki spent a few weeks in Australia training with the owner Don Hewitson's brother Iain, a famous TV chef. And it's a good value in the evening, as well as with the fixed-price lunch. This very unusual wine bar is in a cozy basement bar in the heart of London's theater district—don't go until after 8pm if you want a seat. There are about 25 wine selections available by the glass, all with chatty tasting notes written by Don. His other West End wine bar is closed on the weekends: **The Hanover Square Wine Bar & Grill,** 25 Hanover Sq., W1 (© **020/7408-0935;** Tube: Oxford Circus).

44–46 Cranbourn St., WC2. © 020/7734-7807. Main courses £6.95–£11.95 ($10.10–$17.35); bistro lunches £10–£12 ($14.50–$17.40). Mon–Sat 11am–11pm; Sun noon–10:30pm. Tube: Leicester Sq.

**Masala Zone** ★★ *Kids* INDIAN Like Mela in Shaftesbury Avenue, Masala Zone reacts against the determined upward mobility of London's Indian restaurants—never mind that its owners run one of the poshest of the lot, Veeraswamy. As the *Times of India* put it, Masala Zone will "introduce Britain to the way India really eats at home—off *thalis* and often, before dinner, at the roadside chaat stall." A thali is a fixed-price meal on a tray, including a curry, bowls of vegetables, dal, yogurt curry, rice, popadum, chapatis, chutneys and raita. The street food apes that found in Lucknow, like the anglo-influenced comfort food, gosht dabalroti—lamb curry with white bread mixed in and topped by crispy fried noodles. Masala Zone is in the bottom of a concrete block near Carnaby Street. Two Indian tribal artists came all the way from Maharashtra to decorate the inside, their white paint drawings telling the story of—guess what?—the journey from their rural village to London to decorate the walls of this otherwise minimalist restaurant. Long teak tables invite shared eating, Wagamama style. There's also a takeaway counter.

9 Marshall St., W1. © 020/7287-9966. Reservations not accepted. Main courses £4.75–£7 ($6.90–$10.15). Fixed-price meals £6–£9 ($8.70–$13.05); children's meal, available at weekends, £3.50 ($5.10). MC, V. Daily noon–3pm; Mon–Sat 5:30–11:30pm, Sun 6–10:30pm. Tube: Oxford Circus. No smoking.

**Soho Spice** 🌶 INDIAN   The food at this successful modern 100-seater restaurant is as stylish as the decor. Antique spice jars and brilliantly colored powders line the window, and there's a story-telling spice card attached to each menu. Waiters wearing brightly colored kurtas serve diners seated at wood tables. The list of familiar favorites—chicken *tikka,* tandoori lamb, and spicy prawn curry—is supplemented by a seasonal three-course menu focusing on a particular Indian regional cuisine. Punjabi, for example, means such dishes as *rara gosht,* lamb cooked in the tandoor and then stir-fried with cardamon and dried ground ginger *masala.* The two-course lunch or pre-theater deal offers a choice of appetizers like *aloo palak Bhaji* (potatoes and spinach blended with spicy graham flour) or crisp fried chicken drumsticks, followed by a choice of three main dishes. One is always vegetarian. Happy hour at the basement bar runs Monday to Saturday from 5 to 7pm, when cocktails are all £2.50 ($3.65) instead of £4.95 ($7.20). Try a Bollywood Buzz, a combination of apricot brandy and sweet vermouth spiced with a ginger-stuffed apricot and topped with ginger ale. There's a D.J. on Friday and Saturday nights. Reservations are only taken for groups of six people or more.

Amin Ali is also a partner in a cheap eat, **Busaba Eathai,** 106–110 Wardour St., W1 (© **020/7255-8650;** Tube: Piccadilly Circus, Tottenham Court Rd.), where tasty bowls of Thai noodle soup cost around £5 ($7.25).

124–6 Wardour St., W1. © **020/7434-0808.** Main courses £8–£14 ($11.60–$20.30); fixed-price lunch and pre-theater menu £7.50 ($10.90); 3-course seasonal menu £16.95 ($24.60). AE, DC, MC, V. Mon–Thurs 11:30am–12:30am; Fri–Sat 11:30am–3am; Sun noon–10:30pm. Tube: Leicester Sq., Tottenham Court Rd.

**Vasco & Piero's Pavilion** 🌶 ITALIAN   This cozy comfortable restaurant attracts a business and sophisticated older crowd who consider it their secret favorite hideaway—folks like "Call me Ken" Livingstone, London's mayor. Unfortunately, so many of them have written glowingly about it in newspaper columns that you must book ahead. The Matteucci family has run the restaurant for 31 years, and the welcome is one of the warmest around—and Vasco still does much of the cooking. The unpretentious cuisine is light on butter and cream, with flavors clear as a bell, whether in marinated anchovies or asparagus that has been perfectly cooked al dente. Many of its ingredients come from local producers in Umbria, except for the pasta, which they make themselves. The fixed-price menus change daily, and you can choose either two or three courses from a fantastic selection of seven or eight of each. Ask what's best that day, and order it. Calves' liver, allegedly the best in London, is a house specialty.

15 Poland St., W1. © **020/7437-8774.** Reservations recommended. Main courses £9.50–£15.50 ($13.80–$22.50) at lunch; fixed-price dinners £18.50–£22.50 ($26.85–$32.65). AE, MC, V. Mon–Fri noon–3pm and 6pm–1am; Sat 7–11pm. Tube: Oxford Circus.

## PRE-THEATER BARGAINS

**Blues Bistro & Bar** 🌶 AMERICAN   This sleek Soho joint is frequented by media types and a very friendly party crowd. The slim-line Art-Deco-ish dining room is like the Orient Express, but the cuisine is up-to-the-minute American. It also has possibly the best deal in town for early birds. If you come on the right day—and you'll be p*@@ed if you don't—you can have three courses for £10 ($14.50). And not just any old nosh chucked together for no-account paupers, but fragrant onion soup with a Gruyère crouton, followed by a succulent salmon filet, and a wicked chocolate marquise to finish. But that ain't the end of the temptations. If you do go a la carte, have a starter for between £5 and £8 ($7.25

and $11.60), plus a pudding for £4.95 ($7.20). The serpentine front bar is a great place to meet for an aperitif, though you might not want to leave once you see the menu there: crostini (posh baby open sandwiches) for £1 ($1.45), hot canapes up to £3 ($4.35), or a plate of hot tartlets only £6.50 ($9.35). Think of all this as an excuse to come back and back.

42–43 Dean St. W1. ℂ 020/7494-1966. Reservations recommended. Bistro main courses £7.50–£16 ($10.90–$23.20), pre-theater menu Mon–Tues, Sat–Sun £10 ($14.50); bar food £1–£6.50 ($1.45–$9.45). AE, MC, V. Mon–Thurs noon–midnight; Fri noon–1am; Sat 5pm–1am; Sun 5pm–midnight. Tube: Leicester Sq., Tottenham Court Rd.

**L'Escargot** ★★ TRADITIONAL FRENCH   Dining in a Michelin 1-star restaurant for £14.95 ($21.70) is a fantastic value. We've put L'Escargot in the pre-theater section because this is serious food, in seriously elegant surroundings, and you ought to make a real occasion of it. Cut the gallery tour because you'll still get your art fix here: The walls are hung with works by Marc Chagall, Joan Miró, and David Hockney. The first-floor restaurant's *Du Jour* fixed-price menu changes every week. Diners get to choose from three starters, main courses, and desserts, all classic French dishes perfectly executed. For example, you could have paupiette of smoked salmon with pickled cucumber, followed by stuffed rabbit leg; or swap one of those for chocolate tart with praline ice cream. Pure bliss. Choices are limited for vegetarians. Prices are higher in the upstairs Picasso Room, but the service is uniformly impeccable.

48 Greek St., W1. ℂ 020/7437-2679. Reservations recommended. Main courses £12.95 ($18.80); fixed-price lunch and pre-theater menu £14.95–£17.95 ($21.70–$26.05). AE, DC, MC, V. Mon–Fri 12:15–2:15pm; Mon–Sat 6–11:30pm. Tube: Leicester Sq., Tottenham Court Rd.

**YMing** ★ NORTHERN CHINESE   Light and airy like a hotel dining room, YMing is a tranquil antidote to more in-your-face local rivals. The large tables are prettily set, the service is smooth and unobtrusive, and the food is superb northern Chinese cuisine. Even though a la carte prices aren't outrageous, we recommend the pre-theater menu, which includes three courses. The dishes change regularly but will include a choice of appetizer (crispy won ton, spring roll, tofu, or aubergine in spiced salt, for example), followed by a main course like fish slices in Chinese wine sauce or braised tofu. If duck, prawn, or lamb are on the list, go for it. The sizzling dishes are very popular—prawns with fresh mango, or lamb with fresh leek or with ginger and spring onion. You can finish up with coffee or sip YMing's excellent tea all the way through.

35–36 Greek St., W1. ℂ 020/7734-2721. Main courses £6–£12 ($8.70–$17.40); fixed-price menu (served noon–6pm) £10 ($14.50). AE, DC, DISC, MC, V. Mon–Sat noon–11:45pm. Tube: Leicester Sq.

## WORTH A SPLURGE

**Criterion Brasserie** ★ MODERN FRENCH   This used to be the only place where diners could sample the cooking of Michelin 3-star bad boy Marco Pierre White without remortgaging their homes. Now his superlative restaurant Mirabelle, in Curzon Street (see section 10, "Mayfair," below), offers a fixed-price lunch for a similar price. But it is still well worth coming to the Criterion. Right on Piccadilly Circus, the inside is like a Byzantine palace with its fantastic gold vaulted ceiling. The staff is often pressed for time. And our wine waiter was so over the top in his Gallic superciliousness we suspected he might be a 'resting' English actor, but we didn't dare to ask. But the cuisine is superb. Don't try the three-course early dinner, unless you eat at the speed of lightning. Save the Criterion for a lunchtime blowout. Big favorites are ballottine of salmon with herbs and *fromage blanc*, and risottos are always real star performers.

224 Piccadilly, W1. © 020/7930-0488. Reservations essential. Main courses £12–£15 ($17.40–$21.75); fixed-price lunch £14.95–£17.95 ($21.70–$26.05); fixed-price dinner £17.95 ($26.05), order before 6:30pm. AE, DC, MC, V. Mon–Sat noon–2:30pm, 5:30–11:30pm; Sun 5:30–10:30pm. Tube: Piccadilly Circus.

## 10 Mayfair

**Browns** TRADITIONAL BRITISH  Browns takes the brasserie idea and makes it terribly English. The most famous one is in Oxford, where mummies and daddies take their student children for tea. The food is pretty predictable, but it's robust, generally well put together, and a good value for the money. That's a rare treat in Mayfair, where restaurants tend to cater to the super-affluent and child-free. Browns is divided into two sections, filled with wood paneling and mirrors. The restaurant is at the back beyond the bar, which is a popular after-work meeting point—during happy hour, between 5 and 7pm, cocktails start at £3.95 ($5.75). The food ranges from pastas, salads, and sandwiches, to honest-to-goodness main courses such as steak, mushroom, and Guinness pie. There are lighter, more modern dishes, too. I went for char-grilled chicken breast with tarragon butter. It could have had more tarragon, but then I'm an herb fiend. For dessert, bread-and-butter pudding is a firm favorite. There are six other branches: the most central is at 82 St. Martins Lane, WC2 (© 020/7497-5050).

47 Maddox St., W1. © 020/7491-4565. Hot sandwiches and main courses £6.95–£13.95 ($10.10–$20.25). AE, DC, MC, V. Mon–Sat noon–10pm. Tube: Oxford Circus.

## SUPER-CHEAP EATS

**Mô Tearoom** 🌟 NORTH AFRICAN  This delightful eaterie is the sister of the more famous and much pricier Momo next door. It too has exuberantly Moorish decor, crammed with jewel-colored glass lights and copper urns like a bazaar—many of the objects are for sale—but with the soothing calm of a fantasy oasis. Mô Tearoom straddles the gap between daytime cafe and evening restaurant, serving alcohol and staying open late. And the food is both delicious and an astonishingly good value, especially for rip-off Mayfair. Four dishes, combined as little tasters on a single plate, cost £5.80 ($8.40). There are 14 to choose from, spanning the traditionally Moroccan hummus or eggplant puree, light pastries, salads, and so on. For a more substantial meal, I tacked on a tailor-made sandwich to start with and honey-laden pancakes to end. The teas are a bit sweet for me, but my friend and I were very glad most other diners didn't share that opinion so that the scent of mint filled the air. A wonderful place.

**Momo,** at no. 25 Heddon Street, is wonderful too. Beaded curtains add a casbah mystique and the swathes of fabrics are pure sensuality. Main courses cost £9.75 to £14.50 ($14.15–$21.05), while the fixed-price lunch is £17 ($24.65). You must book ahead, on the number below.

23 Heddon St., W1. © 020/7434-4040. Reservations not accepted. Light meals £2–£5.80 ($2.90–$8.40). AE, DC, DISC, MC, V. Mon–Sat 11am–11pm. Tube: Piccadilly Circus.

## GREAT DEALS ON FIXED-PRICE MEALS

**Veeraswamy** 🌟 INDIAN  This will surely prove the most extraordinary Indian restaurant you've ever encountered. It's hip, painted in vibrant colors, with frosted-glass panels dividing up the sections, and ultra-modern furniture. Only a few pictures remain from the old days. Established in 1926 by a general and an Indian princess, Veeraswamy claims to be the oldest Indian restaurant in London. Over the years, it has been the haunt of princes and potentates, from the Prince of Wales to King Hussein and Indira Gandhi. The clientele are still pretty prosperous if less august today, and they're certainly well-fed by the time they leave. For starters, the stir-fried oysters with coconut and Kerala spices are sublime. For an exotic, and only mildly sweaty, choice, try the shanks of lamb curried in bone stock and spices. Unless you're in the mood to splurge, this isn't the place to sample lots of different dishes. Go for a great-value fixed-price menu instead for a real treat in new Indian cuisine. **Masala Zone** is a new sister restaurant in Soho, much cheaper and much praised: see p. 135.

99–101 Regent St., W1. ℂ 020/7734-1401. Reservations recommended. Main courses £9.75–£13.50 ($14.15–$19.05); lunch and pre-/post-theater menu £11.75–£14.75 ($17.05–$21.40); Sun menu £15 ($21.75). AE, DC, MC, V. Mon–Sat noon–2:30pm and 5:30–11:30pm; Sun 12:30–3pm and 5:30–10:30pm. Tube: Piccadilly Circus.

## WORTH A SPLURGE

**Mirabelle** ⭐⭐ MODERN EUROPEAN   As long as you don't get a primeval urge to wash your meal down with a £30,000 bottle of 1847 Chateau d'Yquem, this is the best value mouthful of Marco Pierre White you will ever eat. The lower priced, two-course, fixed-price lunch may be a splurge but it costs less than most of his main courses. And the food is sensational, made with tricky ingredients timed perfectly. The entrance to Mirabelle is pretty nondescript but behind it lies a lounge decorated with tongue-in-cheek murals, then the long bar, and finally the brasserie-style restaurant. Diners are a little cramped, but who cares. And on sunny days, you can sit out on the terrace. The menu changes seasonally but includes MPW classics. The two courses could be terrine of duck with foie gras and potatoes, in a beetroot dressing, and then hot smoked salmon with horseradish cream. A few extra pounds will get you a dessert or a selection of oozing French cheeses. This offer is only on at lunchtime.

56 Curzon St., W1. ℂ 020/7499-4636. Reservations essential. Main courses £14.50–£25 ($21.05–$36.25); fixed-price lunch £16.50–£19.95 ($23.95–$28.95). AE, DC, MC, V. Daily noon–2:30pm, 6–11:30pm. Tube: Green Park.

## 11 Bloomsbury & Fitzrovia

**The Bar at Villandry** ⭐ INTERNATIONAL   This new offshoot of the famous gourmet hotspot is a godsend for budget travelers, who no longer have to dig deep to fund restaurant main courses starting at a splurgiferous £13.50 ($19.60). And you can swing by any time of day, without having to make plans or reservations. The menu changes every week and picks the best of everything in season—in the early evening, the bar raids the Villandry foodstore for produce to make its snacks. A friend, who was visiting from overseas, chose the typically English ploughman's lunch with farmhouse Stilton and onion marmalade. It was pricier than the average pub version, but the cheese was creamy and moist. I was half-heartedly weight-watching and went for tiger prawns with chili and lemon dipping sauce, which could have done with a little more oomph. Unlike my Red Hot Villandry cocktail, an explosive mix of tomato juice and tequila. Wow, or was it "Ow?" I really like Villandry. It's an exuberant place where you can feel wicked and wholesome at the same time.

The refectory-style restaurant serves Modern British cuisine at lunch every day and dinner from Monday to Saturday. It is totally nonsmoking, unlike the

# West End Restaurants

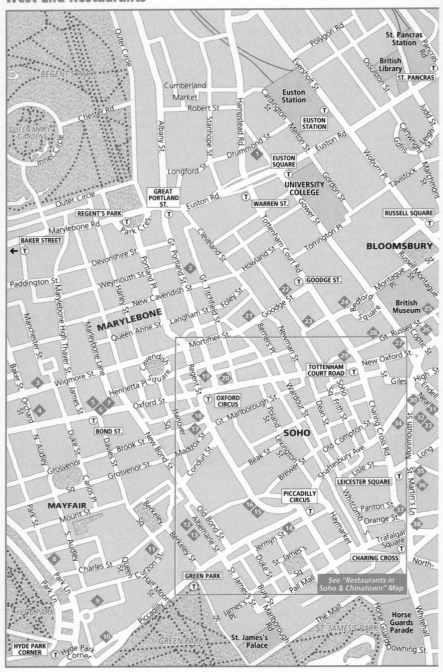

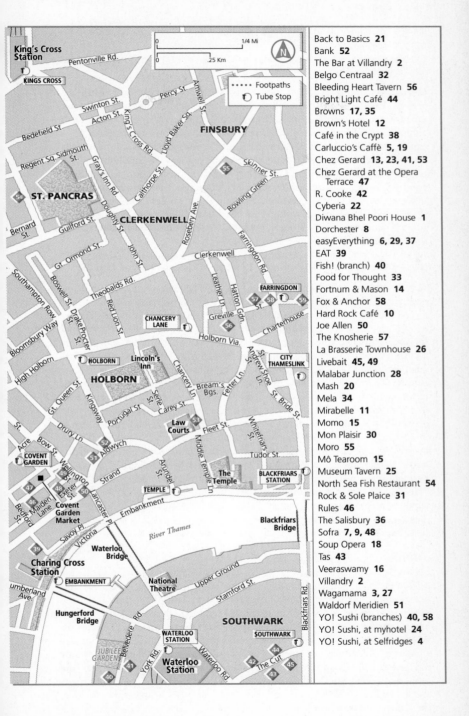

smoky bar. The Villandry foodstore closes an hour earlier than the bar (same time on Sunday).

170 Great Portland St., W1. ℂ 020/7631-3131. Main courses £3.95–£11.50 ($5.75–$16.70). AE, DISC, MC, V. Mon–Sat 8am–11pm; Sun 11am–4pm. Tube: Great Portland St.

**North Sea Fish Restaurant** ★★ FISH & CHIPS   Locals love North Sea's version of what is, of course, the national dish. Here the look is deliberately upmarket country-cozy, even down to the stuffed fish. Diners at the rear of the chippie sit on velvet-covered chairs at wooden tables. You'll find a good mix of cabbies on a tea break, local academics, and tourists here. Dining in, you could do two starters—smoked mackerel and scampi, perhaps—or one and a portion of deliciously crispy fat chips, for under £6 ($8.70). The best deal, though, is the enormous seafood platter, which comes with bite-size, battered pieces of lots of different sorts of fish and seafood. You can go for straight cod, of course, or skate, haddock, plaice, all brought in fresh from Billingsgate every morning. And I'll salute any diner who's got room for one of the traditional puddings after that. North Sea also does take-away.

7–8 Leigh St., WC1. ℂ 020/7387-5892. Reservations recommended for dinner. Main courses £6.95–£15.95 ($10.10–$23.15). AE, DC, MC, V. Mon–Sat noon–2:30pm, 5:30–10:30pm. Tube: Russell Sq., King's Cross.

**Wagamama** ★ JAPANESE NOODLES   This endures as a London hot spot even though the absolute novelty has worn off. Stone stairs lead down to a dining room set up with ranks of long shared tables like a traditional Japanese noodle bar—this not a place for private conversations or shyness. Staff punch the orders into handheld electronic keypads that send a radio signal to the kitchen. The thread noodles come in soups, pan-fried, or else served with various toppings. This place is kid heaven: The menu actually tells you to slurp because the extra oxygen adds to the taste. For a hearty dish, try the chili beef ramen—char-grilled sirloin, chilies, red onion, parsley, and spring onions served in a chili-soup base. It's up to you to add as much or as little parsley, pickled pepper, bean sprouts, and lime, as you want. Each dish is cooked and served immediately, so if you're dining with a group, be prepared for individual meals to arrive at different times. And don't expect to linger too long in the bus-station bustle. Wagamama is also in the basement of Harvey Nichols (see p. 226); at 10a Lexington St., W1 (ℂ 020/7292-0990); 101a Wigmore St., W1 (ℂ 020/7409-0111); 26a Kensington High St., W8 (ℂ 020/7376-1717); and 11 Jamestown Rd., Camden Town, NW1 (ℂ 020/7428-0800).

4a Streatham St. (off Coptic St.), WC1. ℂ 020/7323-9223. Main courses £4.70–£7.50 ($6.80–$10.90). AE, DC, MC, V. Mon–Sat noon–11pm; Sun 12:30–10pm. Tube: Tottenham Court Rd. No smoking.

## SUPER-CHEAP EATS

**Carluccio's Caffè** ★★ Kids ITALIAN   Antonio Carluccio was one of the first celebrity chefs in Britain. That the locals no longer think of Italian cuisine simply as pizza and soggy lasagna is largely due to him. The cafe uses many imported ingredients and still manages to be a mega-cheap eat. Make a quick lunch stop for soup and antipasti starting at £3.60 ($5.22), or come for an evening reviver. Even if you choose the most expensive items for each course—a huge plate of antipasti, followed by moist grilled swordfish, then a cheesy tour of regional Italy—and have the most expensive aperitif, glass of wine with the meal, and coffee, you'd still spend under £30 ($43.50). Choose the cheapest, and it'd be £16.50 ($23.95), including drinks. There are cheaper dishes for kids; the deli can provide top picnic pickings; and Carluccio's will even sell you a

Vespa! A new branch opened last year in St. Christopher's Place, W1 (© 020/
7935-5297; Tube: Bond St.)

8 Market Place, W1. © 020/7636-2228. Main courses £4.50–£7.50 ($6.55–$10.90). AE, MC, V. Mon–Fri
8am–11pm; Sat 11am–11pm; Sun 11am–10pm. Tube: Oxford Circus.

**Diwana Bhel Poori House** SOUTH INDIAN   It's hardly worth pulling out
your credit card to pay for a meal at Diwana Bhel Poori House, which absolutely
disproves the cliché that cheap means nasty—except in the 1970s decor. The
buffet lunch is still under a fiver and tummy-tinglingly good if you avoid the
oilier dishes. At other times, you'll be hard pressed to spend more than £10
($14.50) a head and can set up your own buffet of South Indian vegetarian
dishes for everyone to share. The dosas—semolina pancakes filled with spicy
potato and vegetables—are a delight; there are several to choose from. If you go
for the fixed-price *thali,* hold back from ordering anything else, because it's a
bonanza of breads, bhajees, dahl, rice, vegetables, and pickles. Diwana Bhel Poori
House has a sister restaurant across the road, Chutney's, but it's more expensive.
And this one is unlicensed: you can bring wine and there's no corkage fee.

121 Drummond St., NW1. © 020/7387-5556. Main courses £4–£6.20 ($5.80–$9); buffet lunch £4.50
($6.55); fixed-price menu £6.20 ($9). AE, DC, MC, V. Daily noon–11:30pm. Tube: Euston, Warren St.

## GREAT DEALS ON FIXED-PRICE MEALS

**Malabar Junction** ✦ SOUTH INDIAN   After a bar meal here, I defy anyone
not to come back. Okay, so the choice is minimal—chicken, lamb, or
vegetarian—but a bumper plate of curry for just £3.50 ($5.10)? This attractive
restaurant serves South Indian cuisine, specifically from Kerala. Behind an
unprepossessing entrance, the domed dining room is furnished with elegant
potted palms, and a languid tropical air hangs over the whole place. The four-
page menu starts with a long list of house specialties, which I like to mix and
match: a *masala dosa,* a traditional Kerala pancake, filled with potato *masala* and
served with *sambar* and chutney; and *rasa vada,* a lentil doughnut in a hot spicy
tomato and tamarind broth. There are dozens of vegetarian, chicken and lamb
main courses, but fish is another specialty, cooked in combinations of coconut,
turmeric, ginger, chili, garlic, cumin and curry leaves. Every dish is a taste sensation: Do try the green bananas flavored with spices and onions. After 7pm, the
minimum check is £10 ($14.50).

107 Great Russell St., WC1. © 020/7580-5230. Reservations essential. Fixed-price bar meal (served
noon–5pm) £3.50 ($5.10); main courses £7.50–£9.50 ($10.90–$13.80). AE, MC, V. Daily noon–3pm,
6–11:30pm. Tube: Tottenham Court Rd.

## WORTH A SPLURGE

**Back to Basics** ✦ SEAFOOD   You don't have to splurge to eat at here, but
that does mean forgoing a fishy main course because these start at £12.75
($18.50). The daily-changing menu, chalked up on the blackboard, always lists
at least 12 dishes dictated by what leaped out of the crate that day at market.
The flavors are modern European, from pesto and sundried tomatoes, to chili,
saffron, ginger, melted goat cheese, or honey mustard. I'd recommend going to
this relaxed storefront restaurant with a gang of friends and making everyone
order something different because it's so difficult to choose between the
delicious-sounding concoctions. The vegetable of the day is included with the
sausage platters, lamb, chicken, and beef (but not with fish), making these a very
good value, as well as useful for consoling fish-hating companions. Strict

**Surf 'n' Slurp @ the Best Internet Cafes**

The handy **www.netcafeguide.com** has a pretty good London listing, including the pioneering **Cyberia**, 39 Whitfield St., W1 (© 020/ 7681-4245; www.cyberiacafe.net; Tube: Goodge St.). This place charges £1 ($1.45) for half an hour's surfin', while sandwiches and snacks start at £2. It's open from 9am to 9pm Monday to Saturday, closing at 6pm on Sunday.

Cyberia was London's first Internet cafe—it's still one of the best—logging on in 1994. In e-volutionary terms, that's like the invention of the wheel. Now we're entering the Henry Ford phase, only this time the color is **easyEverything** orange. There are five of these giant Internet cafes in the capital—cafe is a misnomer, really, as the hundreds of screens make them look like telesales sweat shops. The charging system is radical because surfers buy credit, not minutes. The minimum spend is £2 ($2.90), and the amount of time you get for that is in inverse proportion to how busy the branch is. The rate is adjusted every 5 minutes and posted on video screens, a bit like a money market. Your ticket has a user-ID, which notes the current rate when you first log on. That becomes your rate. You'll never pay more, but if things quiet down your credit will buy more time—a pound could be worth up to 6 hours, or so they claim. easyEverything never closes so avoid afternoons and early evenings, and surf with the creatures of the night. Check www.easyeverything.com for new branches to add to this list: 358 Oxford St., W1 (© 020/7491-8986; Tube: Bond St.); 9–16 Tottenham Court Rd., W1 (© 020/7436-1206; Tube: Tottenham Court Rd.); 160–166 Kensington High St. (© 020/7938-1841; Tube: Kensington High St.); 456–459 Strand, WC2 (© 020/7930-4094; Tube: Charing Cross); and 9–13 Wilton Rd., SW1 (© 020/7233-8456; Tube: Victoria).

*Note:* You can send short e-mails up to about 90 words for **free** from any **i-plus** electronic information kiosk and you don't need to have your own e-address. But this is one-way communication, only, and the touch-screen is irritating if you're used to typing arpeggios on a keyboard. To find out where the nearest kiosk is, see "Visitor Information," in chapter 3.

vegetarians are very poorly served. If it's warm, you can sit outside—there's actually some chance of getting a pavement table here because there are about 20 of them.

21a Foley St., W1. © 020/7436-2181. Reservations essential for lunch. Main courses £7.95–£15.50 ($11.55–$22.50). AE, DE, MC, V. Mon–Fri noon–10pm. Tube: Goodge St.

**Mash** ✯ MODERN EUROPEAN   You splurge here for the buzz rather than for ambrosial food. The Love Machine at the entrance flashes romantic epigrams as people open the doors. One of the more flip is "The best way to a man's heart is to leave him." That and the video screens in the women's toilets giving glimpses into the men's are why people either love or hate Mash. Oliver Peyton opened the sleek and gargantuan resto-deli in 1998. It has one of London's first microbreweries, the huge tanks visible at the back of the first-floor cafe. Couches invite customers to linger. The cuisine is modern Mediterranean-Italian, of sorts: Paper-thin pizzas, with bizarre toppings such as crispy duck, cucumber, Asian greens, and hoisin sauce appear from a wood-fired grill. Main courses are either baked (like whole sea bass with gherkin and caper mayonnaise) or roasted (like the pork cutlet with wilted radicchio, new potatoes, French beans, and anchovy butter). This is a great place to come for a full-works brunch on the weekend: The Mash menu, American, and vegetarian all cost £10 ($14.50).

19–21 Great Portland St., W1. 𝄞 **020/7637-5555.** Main courses £9.50–£15.50 ($13.80–$22.50); brunch £10 ($14.50). AE, DC, MC, V. Restaurant: Mon–Fri noon–3:30pm, Sat–Sun noon–4pm; Mon–Sat 6–11pm. Bar: Mon–Sat 11am–2am; Sun noon–4pm. Tube: Oxford Circus.

## 12 Covent Garden & the Strand

**The Rock & Sole Plaice** ★ FISH & CHIPS   Endell Street is a peaceful oasis only one block away from Covent Garden's unrelenting crowds. But it's best to avoid The Rock & Sole Plaice in the early evenings, when it's crowded with theater-goers. It opened in 1871 and claims to be London's oldest surviving fish-and-chip shop. The decor is very Covent Garden, with theatrical posters and pavement tables. Fortunately, the prices are anything but. The Dover sole certainly has to be the cheapest in town at £11 ($15.95), and the other fish are half that price. Choose from halibut, mackerel, tuna, haddock, plaice, or cod. If you've never tried skate, then do so here-it's a moist, flaky fish with a wonderful flavor. The chips are thick and wedge-shaped, and you can add on mushy peas, pickled onions, and . . . mmm, smell that breath. For non-fish-eaters, there's steak-and-kidney and several other pies, plus sausage in batter.

47 Endell St., WC2. 𝄞 **020/7836-3785.** Reservations recommended (dinner). Eat in £7 ($10.15); take-out £5 ($7.25). DC, MC, V. Mon–Sat 11:30am–10:30pm (11:45pm for take-out); Sun noon–10pm. Tube: Covent Garden.

## SUPER-CHEAP EATS

**Café in the Crypt** BRITISH DINER   Right on Trafalgar Square, this is a great place to grab a bite to eat between a visit to the National Gallery and marching off down The Mall to Buckingham Palace. Or pop in with the kids after a session at the church's brass rubbing center. Or even for a late bite during a night out on the tiles. Simple healthy food costs a lot less here than at more commercial places. It's a self-service cafeteria, where diners pick from a big salad bar and a choice of two traditional main courses—one might be shepherd's pie. The other light-lunch options include filled rolls and delicious cups of soup. The menu changes daily, but one fixture is that most traditional of British desserts, bread-and-butter pudding (bread soaked in eggs and milk with currants or sultanas and then oven-baked). Super-light for something super-wicked. The door to the crypt is on the right-hand side of the church.

St. Martin-in-the-Fields, Duncannon St., WC2. 𝄞 **020/7839-4342.** Rolls and sandwiches £2.50–£3.10 ($3.65–$4.50); main courses £5.95–£6.50 ($8.65–$9.45). No credit cards. Mon–Wed 10am–8pm; Thurs–Sat 10am–11pm. Tube: Charing Cross.

**Food for Thought** VEGETARIAN   Food for Thought is an enduring stalwart of the vegetarian movement, which manages to lure in a broad clientele because of its unpreachy wholesome food and very cheap prices. It's a pop-in kind of a place, and you're best off popping in for brunch or maybe a strawberry scone for tea, because it's mobbed both at lunchtime when all dishes are £3.70 ($5.35) and for the £5.80 ($8.40) evening special. The decor is simple with pine tables, fresh flowers, and original art on the walls. There are a handful of outdoor tables, but you'll probably have to sit downstairs, which in summer is about the only reason to go elsewhere. The menu always features a quiche and a vegetable stir-fry. Otherwise, it will have a few salads, stews, and hot dishes along these lines, always with vegan and gluten-free options. The puddings look irresistible, and in the eating, most do manage to disguise their virtuousness. The cafe is unlicensed, so bring your own bottle: There's no corkage fee.

31 Neal St., WC2. © 020/7836-0239. Main courses £3.70–£5.80 ($5.35–$8.40). No credit cards. Mon–Sat 9:30am–8:30pm; Sun noon–5pm. Tube: Covent Garden. No smoking.

## GREAT DEALS ON FIXED-PRICE MEALS

**Belgo Centraal** BELGIAN    Blatant concept restaurants often have a very short life-span, but the Belgian national dish of *moules, frites,* and *bière,* served at long refectory tables by staff dressed as monks, has become a London dining icon. A kilo pot of mussels, prepared any one of three ways, will set you back between £10.95 and £12.95 ($15.90 and $18.80). The only quibble is that sometimes there's too much broth. There are non-seafood dishes, and you'll find them on the fixed-price lunch: either wild boar sausages served with Belgian mash and a beer, or two lighter dishes with mineral water. The pricier Belgo Complet starts with a *salade liègeoise,* then *moules,* plus either a beer or ice cream. But for sheer gluttony, nothing can outdo the Beat the Clock menu. It runs from 5 to 6:30pm on weekdays. Whatever time you order, that's what the meal will cost—£5.45 if you order at 5:45, for instance. There are three huge dishes to choose from and wash down with a free drink. This is a fun place, if you can hack the noise and pace, and it's got a Belgian beer hall, too.

Opening times and meal deals vary from branch to branch, so call ahead to check: **Belgo Noord,** 71 Chalk Farm Rd., NW1 (© **020/7672-0718;** Tube: Chalk Farm); **Belgo Zuid,** 124 Ladbroke Grove, W10 (© **020/8982-8400;** Tube: Ladbroke Grove); and the **Bierdrome,** 173 Upper St., NW1 (© **020/ 7226-5835;** Tube: Highbury, Islington, Angel).

50 Earlham St., WC2. © 020/7813-2233. Reservations recommended. Main courses £7.95–£17.50 ($11.55–$25.40); lunch £5 ($7.25); Belgo Complet fixed-price menu £14.95 ($21.70). AE, DC, MC, V. Mon–Thurs noon–11:30pm; Fri–Sat noon–midnight; Sun noon–10:30pm. Tube: Covent Garden.

**Chez Gerard at the Opera Terrace** ✰ TRADITIONAL FRENCH    From under a stylish conservatory right on top of the old market, diners look down at the throngs of people in Covent Garden Piazza—very ego-trippish! The clientele has a definite air of affluence, especially in the evening, yet the fixed-price menu is a remarkable value because Chez Gerard heads straight in with three courses and the higher price is for four. That's not counting the freshly baked bread, anchovy butter, and olives at the start of the meal, and toasted almonds at the end, paid for by the £1 ($1.45) cover charge. The cuisine is traditional French, predictable even though it is delivered in an attractive modern way. I'm always a sucker for good *gravadlax,* and the corn-fed chicken from Périgord in France will put you off the supermarket variety forever. For the budgetarily-challenged, the bar has a short but decent menu of hot dishes, platters, and salads starting at £5 ($7.25), and sandwiches from £3.75 ($5.45). It too has tables outside, but you can't make reservations.

There are eight other branches in London, including a very useful one near the London Eye and County Hall on the South Bank, at 9 Belvedere Rd., SE1 (© **020/7202-8470;** Tube: Waterloo). Otherwise, try: 31 Dover St., W1(© 020/7499-8171; Tube: Green Park); 119 Chancery Lane, WC2(© **020/ 7405-0290;** Tube: Chancery Lane); 8 Charlotte St., W1 (© **020/7636-4975;** Tube: Tottenham Court Rd., Goodge St.).

First Floor, Covent Garden Central Market, WC2. ✆ **020/7379-0666**. Reservations essential. Main courses £9.90–£19 ($14.35–$27.55); fixed-price weekend lunch and daily dinner £15.95–£21.95 ($23.15–$31.85). Cover charge £1 ($1.45). AE, DC, MC, V. Mon–Sat 11am–11:30pm; Sun noon–10:30pm. Tube: Covent Garden.

**Mela** ★★ INDIAN   This place won last year's Moet & Chandon award as best Indian restaurant in London. It claims to take its inspiration from Wali Gali, where Delhi's workers go to refuel at midday from a food stall on the street. Lunch here is a fantastic deal: curry or dahl of the day, with bread, pickle and chutney for under two quid? That's less than you'd pay for a bog-standard sandwich in this neck of the woods. Pay a little more and you can build your own version, from lots of different breads and toppings, culminating in the bargain-for-under-a-fiver, which has rice and salad thrown in too. This is a great way for curry novices to have a cheap taster—and to see it being made in the open kitchen. But do come back in the evening for a proper go at the innovative Indian country cuisine. Early birds get three courses. Fixed-price sharers have 10 dishes and accompaniments between them, with the lower prices for the vegetarian versions. The word mela means fair, and Mela the restaurant is energetic in its efforts to create a festive atmosphere.

152–156 Shaftesbury Ave., WC2. ✆ **020/7836-8635**. Main courses £6.95–£11.95 ($10.10–$17.35). Light lunches £1.95–£4.95 ($2.85–$7.20). Fixed-price meal for 2 people £24.95–£29.95 ($36.20–43.45), for 4 £44.95–£54.95 ($65.20–$79.70), for 6 £69.95–£79.95 ($101.45–$115.95). Pre-theater menu £8.95 ($13). AE, MC, V. Mon–Sat noon–11:30pm; Sun noon–10:30pm. Tube: Leicester Sq.

## PRE- & POST-THEATER BARGAINS

**Bank** ★ MODERN EUROPEAN   The chefs are part of the noisy frenetic performance here, rushing around in the kitchen behind a big glass window like fish at feeding time. Bank was a bank until an extremely hip conversion stripped bare the structural girder, put in a suspended, armor-plated ceiling, and turned it into London's most stylish brasserie. You could come here for the weekend brunch (there is a children's menu then, too), but it'll cost you an arm and a leg. Breakfast is served weekdays as well, but it's better to feast early or late on the set menu, then head to the bar where you can spy on the 100 or so other diners. Great value for either two or three courses, the seasonal cuisine brings together Continental and Southeast Asian influences in the sort of harmony the supranational organizations can only dream of: from seared rare spiced tuna with mango salad, to roast rabbit with couscous and spiced crab. The only quibbles are that the service can be too quick and the tables are close together. Bank recently replicated itself in Victoria: 45 Buckingham Gate, SW1 (same phone).

1 Kingsway, WC2. ✆ **020/7379-9797**. Reservations recommended. Main courses £12–£28; fixed-price lunch and pre-/post-theater dinner £15.50–£17.90 ($22.25–$28). AE, DC, MC, V. Mon–Fri 7:30–10am; daily noon–2:45pm; Mon–Sat 5:30–11pm, Sun 5:30am–9:30pm. Tube: Covent Garden, Holborn, Temple.

**Joe Allen** AMERICAN   This dark wood-paneled basement, with its ridiculously discreet entrance, is a thespian institution where Londoners dining late rub shoulders with the cream of West End talent. It's a great game matching the flesh-and-blood faces to those staring down from the dozens of theater posters. You'll have to splurge to join them or stick to starters and salads where the portions are pretty generous. Joe Allen does have good value pre-theater deals, though, for two or three courses. The menu changes daily, except for the perennial bowl of chili, and the cuisine is a mix of classic down-home dishes and others that look suspiciously like modern British cooking—roast guinea fowl with new potatoes roasted in balsamic vinegar, with blueberry and ginger relish.

The service is sometimes perfunctory, and the tables are too close together, but the lively atmosphere and live jazz on Sunday nights compensate.

13 Exeter St., WC2. © **020/7836-0651.** Reservations essential at weekends. Main courses £7.50–£14.50 ($10.90–$21.05); fixed-price lunch and pre-theater menu £13–£15 ($18.85–$21.75); weekend brunch menu £15.50–£17.50 ($22.50–$25.40). AE, MC, V. Mon–Fri noon–1am; Sat 11:30am–1am; Sun 11:30am–midnight. Tube: Covent Garden.

**Livebait** ⭐ SEAFOOD  If you like fish so fresh that it still looks surprised, then you'll love this very friendly, retro, white-tiled place. There's a cheap way to enjoy it, too: Settle down in the bar for a bowl of cockles and a mixed-green salad, and it'll only cost you £6.20 ($9.90). In the restaurant, you have to have a main course. The fixed-price menus are all a steal, and early booking is essential. You get two or three courses, and two dishes to choose from in each. I started with fish soup with aïoli. The garlic-laden mayonnaise was dynamite. Vacation logistics probably make a pre- or post-theater visit more achievable, and it's great to find somewhere you can eat late as well as on top of your English tea. Seafood haters should stay away because Livebait makes absolutely no concessions. It has also been spawning new branches: 43 The Cut, SE1 (© **020/ 7928-7211;** Tube: Waterloo, Southwark); 175 Westbourne Grove, W11 (© **020/7727-4321;** Tube: Bayswater, Queensway); and in Chelsea at 2 Holly-wood Rd., SW10 (© **020/7349-5500;** Tube: Earl's Court).

21 Wellington St., WC2. © **020/7836-7161.** Reservations recommended. Main courses £14–£20.75 ($20.30–$30.10); Livebait platter for two £40 ($58); fixed-price lunch and pre-/post-theater menu £13.50–£16.50 ($19.60–$23.95). AC, DC, MC, V. Mon–Sat noon–3pm, 5:30–11:30pm (10:30pm in the bar). Tube: Covent Garden.

**Mon Plaisir** ⭐ TRADITIONAL FRENCH  This is the *grande dame* of French restaurants. It has only changed hands, from one family to another, once since it opened in the 1940s. Behind the narrow glass front lies a warren of charming rooms, hung with pans and posters, where diners are packed in like sardines. Things have changed just a fraction in the past few years since chef Patrick Smith, a veteran of several well-known London restaurants, came in. He hasn't ditched the classics—*quelle idée!* You'll still find good old-fashioned coq au vin, snails, perfectly grilled entrecôte, and so on. But new dishes have crept onto the menu, such as roast duck breast with Szechuan pepper and beetroot and onion marmalade. The pre-theater menus are either two courses or three if you fancy finishing with something like profiteroles and chocolate sauce. Sadly, service is sometimes nose-in-the-air and it can get a little touristy because Mon Plaisir is such an institution.

21 Monmouth St., WC2. © **020/7836-7243.** Main courses £8.60–£15 ($12.45–$21.75); pre-theater menu plus glass of wine £11.95–£14.95 ($17.35–$21.65); fixed-price lunch £14.95 ($21.65); fixed-price dinner plus glass of wine £23.50 ($34.10). AE, DC, MC, V. Mon–Fri noon–2:15pm; Mon–Sat 6–11:15pm. Tube: Covent Garden, Leicester Sq.

**Sofra** TURKISH  This is a very modern Turkish eating-house. The cuisine is completely authentic, although the food is not as spicy as some chili fans would like, nor are the portions as generous at Sofra as they are at more basic ethnic restaurants. But the ingredients are super-fresh and so is the way they're treated. The chef goes light on the oil, chargrilling instead, which is part of what owner Huseyin Ozer promises—clean, healthy food. The fixed-price meals are a fantastic value, comprising 11 mezes and meat dishes—super-tender diced lamb, velvety hummus, the classic Middle Eastern eggplant dish, *Imam Bayildi*, and on and on. It's a great way of avoiding the perennial problem of zero self-control at the sight of a delicious menu, and then catatonic shock at the bill. This place has two little sisters: The best for stopping off mid-shopping in Oxford Street, or for dining outside, is **Sofra Cafe,** 1 St. Christopher's Place, W1 (℗ **020/7224-4080;** Tube: Bond St.). For Sunday lunch, head for **Sofra Bistro,** 18 Shepherd St., W1 (℗ **020/7493-3320;** Tube: Green Park, Hyde Park Corner).

36 Tavistock St., WC2. ℗ **020/7240-3773.** Mixed meze £5.45 ($12.60); main courses £6.95–£14.95 ($10.10–$21.70); fixed-price lunch £8.95 ($13); pre- and post-theater menu £9.95 ($14.45). AE, DC, MC, V. Daily 12pm–12am. Tube: Covent Garden.

## WORTH A SPLURGE

Rules ★★TRADITIONAL BRITISH    This ultra-British restaurant has been around for 200 years and seems likely to survive another 200. Lily Langtry and Edward VII used to tryst here, and it's about the only place in London where you'll see a bowler hat these days. But despite the hammy quaintness, Rules is a very modern restaurant operation. It supports the current "Keep Britain Farming" campaign and markets the house specialty, "feathered and furred game," as healthy, free range, additive-free and low in fat. The fixed-price mid-afternoon meal is a splurge, but it's still a great deal because you can select two courses from anything on the menu. Head straight for the biggest budget busters—lobster and asparagus salad with mango dressing, followed by fallow deer with spiced red cabbage, blueberries, and bitter chocolate sauce—and you'll save over £10 ($14.50). The food is delicious: traditional yet innovative, until you get to the puddings, which are a mix of nursery and dinner-dance classics. The wine list is pricey, but Rules does have three brown ales, so try one of them instead.

35 Maiden Lane, WC2. ℗ **020/7836-5314.** Reservations essential. Main courses £16.95–£22.50 ($24.60–$32.65); weekday fixed-price menu (served 3–5pm) £19.95 ($28.95). AE, DC, MC, V. Mon–Sat noon–11:15pm; Sun noon–10:15pm. Tube: Charing Cross, Covent Garden.

## 13 Victoria

**Ebury Wine Bar & Restaurant** MODERN EUROPEAN/WINE BAR The food here won't win any grand dining prizes, but it's a friendly, welcoming place to walk round the corner to if you're staying in Victoria. That's what its eclectic clientele does—a mix of local workers and posh Pimlico residents. The main courses should make it a splurge, but you can have an equally good meal for the price of a single dish if you stick to the 20 or so choices on the entree and salad menus. For instance, my best friend's chicken-and-bacon terrine with red onion marmalade, followed by a Caesar salad—all rousing an "mmm" of appreciation—cost £10 ($14.50). I did go for a main course, because I'm a sucker for sausages—in this case, rich mushroomy ones with mash and onion gravy, which also cost £10 ($14.50). The menu changes faster than a socialite with a full diary, except for such improbable regulars as Mars Bar spring roll. Oooh, count those extra pounds. Count them too if you decide to lubricate your meal with one of the carefully selected and very fine wines.

139 Ebury St., SW1. ℗ **020/7730-5447.** Reservations recommended. Main courses £10–£16 ($14.50–$23.20). AE, DC, MC, V. Mon–Sat noon–3pm, Sun noon–2:30pm; daily 6–10pm. Tube: Victoria.

**Jenny Lo's Teahouse** ✦ CHINESE    Jenny Lo's father was Britain's best-known Chinese chef, and this is where he had his cookery school. His restaurant, Ken Lo's Memories of China, is still going strong in nearby Ebury Street but falls on the expensive side. This teahouse, however, is very affordable. The simple but stylish decor—long shared tables, wooden chairs, and bright splashes of color—accurately mirrors the fresh cuisine. Jenny Lo doesn't use the old Chinese standard, MSG. There's a short menu, mainly rice, soup noodles, and wok noodles, ranging from the standard to ones with a southeast Asian twist (hot coconut), and from the light to quite substantial. Try the luxurious black-bean seafood noodles. Side dishes, rather than starters, include such street-food classics as onion cakes. You can't make reservations, but the staff is extremely friendly and helpful, which soothes any irritation if you have to wait for a space. Jenny Lo has also commissioned her own tonic teas from Chinese herbalist Dr. Xu. Long life and happiness are both on the menu here.

14 Eccleston St., SW1. © 020/7259-0399. Reservations not accepted. Main courses £5–£6.95 ($8–$10.40). No credit cards. Mon–Fri 11:30am–3pm, Sat noon–3pm; Mon–Sat 6–10pm. Tube: Victoria.

**Oliveto** ✮ PIZZA & PASTA   This is a cheaper offshoot spawned by Olivo, the successful Italian restaurant just 'round the corner. Oliveto offers the same quality but simpler, faster food, with the focus on pizza—that is also the cheapest main course. There are 15 different and deliciously crisp alternatives to choose from. Our favorites are the *quattro stagioni,* a revitalized old favorite made with mozzarella, tomato, sausages, prosciutto, mushroom, and squash; and one made with Gorgonzola, arugula, tomato, and mozzarella. There are always a few pasta dishes—a delicious linguine al granchio made with fresh crabmeat, garlic, and chili, for example. The daily specials, tuna or swordfish perhaps, top the price list. Oliveto has a very mixed clientele, from platinum credit-carded families who live in Belgravia and young Pimlico singles out for a relaxed supper. And Belinda Carlisle, apparently, who quoted it as one of her favorite London eateries! If you're feeling a little more flush, try **Olivo,** 21 Eccleston St., SW1 (© **020/ 7730-2505**). Main courses cost £10 to £19 ($14.50 to $27.55), and the cuisine is robust, modern Italian.

49 Elizabeth St., SW1. © 020/7730-0074. Main courses £9.50–£13 ($13.80–$18.85). AE, MC, V. Mon–Fri noon–3pm, Sat–Sun noon–4pm; daily 7–11:30pm. Tube: Victoria.

## GREAT DEALS ON FIXED-PRICE MEALS

**Boisdale** ✮ SCOTTISH   This is clan territory. Owned by Ranald Macdonald, the very model of a modern chieftain-in-waiting, the Boisdale bar boasts London's biggest range of hard-to-find single malt whiskies and a tartan menu to match. The cheaper fixed-price meal is a cultural treat you'll want to boast about at home: a hearty fish soup, then haggis made by the world famous McSween in Edinburgh, neeps (mashed swede), and tatties (mashed potato). This is the dinner that Robert Burns wrote his famous ode in praise of and which guests salute as it's brought to the table at the annual celebration of his birthday on January 25th. If centuries of tradition can't persuade you to try oatmeal and sheep's innards, then there is a more expensive fixed-price meal, with a wide choice of starters and main courses, which are bound to include venison, salmon, and Scottish beef, perhaps with a hint of the Continental in the styling. You might not want to dine here if you have a strong aversion to smoke: What else would a fat cat want to go with the single malt other than a big fat Cuban cigar?

15 Eccleston St., SW1. © 020/7730-6922. Reservations recommended. Main courses £9.90–£25 ($14.35–$36.25); fixed-price menus £14–£17.45 ($20.30–$25.30). AE, DC, MC, V. Bistro Mon–Fri noon–2:30pm; Mon–Sat 7–11pm; Sun noon–10:30pm. Bar Mon–Sat to 1am. Tube: Victoria.

ALPS                    ASPEN

AT&T Direct® Service

The easy way to call home from anywhere.

Global
connection
with the AT&T
Network

**AT&T**
direct
service

For the easy way to call home, take the attached wallet guide.

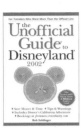
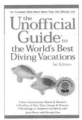
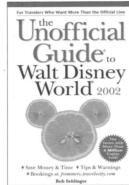

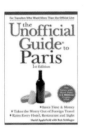
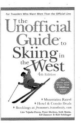
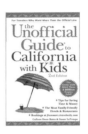
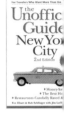

## 14  The City & Clerkenwell

# THE CITY

**Arkansas Café** ★★ AMERICAN    The U.S. Embassy swears by the barbe-cuing skills of Keir and Sarah Hellberg—if you're swish enough to get onto the Independence Day guest list there, you'll probably find them catering the party. And this is *the* place to come on Thanksgiving, sadly the only time it's open in the evening except for bookings for 25 people or more. Arkansas Café is at Old Spitalfields Market, and diners sit out in the covered central space and enjoy the sizzle and delicious smells while the Hellbergs cook steaks, lamb, sausages, ribs, and corn-fed chicken to order. My burger was so perfectly rare that I thought I heard it moo. Mr. Hellberg chooses the best cuts of meat himself from Smith-field market. Plump for a jumbo sandwich as a cheaper option or take the meat on its own. It's not really on its own, of course, because there are down-home potato and vegetable salads to have on the side and Mr. Hellberg's secret barbe-cue sauce on every table. The beef brisket and ribs are home-smoked, the pud-dings so baaad they're good enough to cue an impromptu Meg Ryan moment.

Unit 12, Old Spitalfields Market, E1. ✆ 020/7377-6999. Main courses £4.90–£13 ($7.10–$18.85). MC, V. Mon–Fri noon–2:30pm; Sun noon–4pm. Tube: Liverpool Street.

**The Place Below** ★ VEGETARIAN    St. Mary-le-Bow is a beautiful Christo-pher Wren church built on the site of a much earlier one. Today, the arched Norman vaults are home to one of the most atmospheric and delicious cheap eateries in The City. The menu changes daily but you'll always find a hot dish of the day, two salads (one dairy-free), and a quiche, which is what I chose: with roast new potatoes, rosemary, garlic, spring onions, and parmesan, it was deli-cious. Because The Place Below gets so busy at lunchtime, it offers £2 ($2.90) off all main course prices between 11:30am and noon. You'll save around the same on most dishes if you take-out rather than eat in. Soup is a dynamite deal at £2.90 ($4.20)—although my mate's mushroom bisque could have been a bit hotter. The Place Below has just had a tart up, introducing a new espresso and sandwich bar, and extending its hours to 4pm. So you could just come for a wicked chocolate brownie or pastry. There is seating for 50 outside in Bow Churchyard—good for outcast smokers.

St. Mary-le-Bow, Cheapside, EC2. ✆ 020/7329-0789. Main courses £5.50–£7.50 ($8–$10.90). MC, V. Mon–Fri 7:30am–4pm. Tube: St. Paul's, Bank. No smoking.

# CLERKENWELL

**Bleeding Heart Tavern** ★★ GASTROPUB/MODERN BRITISH    The story of Bleeding Heart Yard is every bit as gory as you hope it will be. Beautiful 17th-century it-girl Lady Elizabeth Hatton was murdered here, after walking outside with the European ambassador during her annual winter ball. Today, this is a very remarkable gastropub. The restored 1746 tavern is the London flag-ship of regional brewery and wine merchant, Southwold Adnams. It is *the* place to quaff real ale (from £2.20/$3.20 a pint) with the sort of earthy cooking you can imagine Thomas Hardy describing, were he writing today. My luscious deep-fried Somerset brie with gooseberry compote, ale-fed Suffolk pork sausages with mash and cider onion gravy, and sticky apple pie came to £15.70 ($22.75).

There are two other parts to this trencherman's heaven, with successively higher prices. Though you can drink wine in the tavern, the choice represents a mere fraction of the miraculous wine list in the bistro, from £10 ($14.50) a bottle or £2.50 ($3.65) a glass. Three courses, of a similar style cuisine, costs a couple of pounds more here. For a real splurge (£15.45/$22.45 minimum for two courses), head for the ever-so French restaurant downstairs.

Bleeding Heart Yard, off Greville St., EC1. ℂ 020/7404-0333. Reservations essential in restaurant. Main courses, tavern £6.95–£10.95 ($10.10–$15.90), bistro £7.50–£12.50 ($10.90–$18.15), restaurant £9.95–£16.95 ($14.45–$24.60); bar menu £3.50–£6.95 ($5.10–$10.10). AE, DC, MC, V. Tavern Mon–Fri 11am–11pm; bistro noon–3pm and 6–10:30pm; restaurant noon–2:30pm and 6–10:30pm. Tube: Chancery Lane, Farringdon.

## SUPER-CHEAP EATS

**Quiet Revolution** ✦ BRITISH DINER/SOUP    Originally a soup manufacturer, Quiet Revolution is approved by the Soil Association, which regulates "organic" producers. It has twice-won S.A. food awards, among a host of other trophies for concoctions like the Polska Tomato soup—suitable for vegans, 35 calories per 100g, 5g of carbohydrate, 1.3g of fat. Each variety carries this wealth of detail, plus the reassurance that the company filters the water "seconds before adding it to the stock." All very reassuring, but I'm fairly relaxed about such things and just relished the fabulous flavors. Quiet Revolution branched out into a daytime cafe-diner in 2000 to serve its super-healthy nosh direct to the public. And now it is opening in the evenings too, with an expanded but still organic menu: stews are a big feature, lamb and beef. As are squid and veggie options such as ratatouille. It was all a bit of an experiment still when we visited—there was even loose talk of a bongo club on Saturday nights!—so do call ahead. Whatever happens, this is a great place to refuel on a visit to the hot local art scene (see "Young, British, and Hung in East London," in chapter 6).

49 Old St., EC1. ℂ 020/7253-5556. Main courses £4–£10.50, soups £3–£5.50 ($4.35–$8). MC, V. Mon–Sat 9am–11pm. Tube: Old St.

## WORTH A SPLURGE

**Moro** ✦✦ NORTH AFRICAN/SPANISH    On the run-down City fringes, Clerkenwell has become a very hip neighborhood in recent years. If you didn't know that, then an evening at Moro will quickly put you in the picture. It opened 5 years ago, has amassed a pot full of awards, and gets better every day. The decor is clattery, modern minimalist—bare walls and stripped wood—with a quieter conservatory corner. The Spanish and North African cuisine is earthy and powerful. You can dine very reasonably on delicious tapas, but splurge, if you can, because the kitchen uses only the best ingredients, organic where possible, in its daily-changing menu. The charming staff will explain any of the menu's exotic mysteries. Highly recommended are the wood-roasted bream with fennel, garlic, and paprika, and the stewed long-horn beef with prunes, chard, and potatoes. Two courses will probably set you back around £20 ($29). Giving up dessert isn't too much of a sacrifice, as the choice is limited.

34–36 Exmouth Market, EC1. ℂ 020/7833-8336. Reservations recommended. Main courses £9.75–£16 ($14.15–$23.20); tapas £2.50–£4.50 ($3.65–$6.55). Mon–Fri 12:30–10:30pm; Sat 7–10:30pm. AE, DC, MC, V. Tube: Angel, Farringdon.

## 15 Just South of the River

### GREAT DEALS ON FIXED-PRICE MEALS

**Tas** ✦ TURKISH    This bright bustling restaurant must be going for the monster-est menu in town award. It lists more than 100 dishes, which is ridiculous even for a meze-style meal. So, if you want to save your brain power for

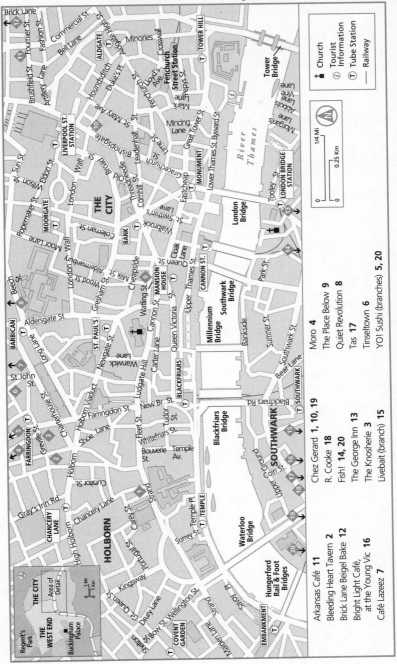

# Restaurants in the City & on the South Bank

**Map Legend:**
- ✝ Church
- ■ Tourist Information
- Ⓣ Tube Station
- ----- Railway

Tower Bridge
London Bridge
Monument
LIVERPOOL ST. STATION
LONDON BRIDGE STATION
Fenchurch Street Station
TOWER HILL
ALDGATE
THE CITY
MOORGATE
BANK
MANSION HOUSE
ST. PAUL'S
CANNON ST.
BARBICAN
BLACKFRIARS
Southwark Bridge
Millennium Bridge
Blackfriars Bridge
SOUTHWARK
FARRINGDON
CHANCERY LANE
HOLBORN
TEMPLE
Waterloo Bridge
Hungerford Rail & Foot Bridges
EMBANKMENT
River Thames

Arkansas Café **11**
Bleeding Heart Tavern **2**
Brick Lane Beigel Bake **12**
Bright Light Café,
  at the Young Vic **16**
Café Lazeez **7**

Chez Gerard **1, 10, 19**
R. Cooke **18**
Fish! **14, 20**
The George Inn **13**
The Knosherie **3**
Livebait (branch) **15**

Moro **4**
The Place Below **9**
Quiet Revolution **8**
Tas **17**
Tinseltown **6**
YO! Sushi (branches) **5, 20**

THE WEST END
THE CITY
Regent's Park
Buckingham Palace
Area of Detail
COVENT GARDEN

enjoying the London view from the Eye, or browsing the art at Tate Modern, go for one of the set menus. Even the cheapest will bring you three courses, and for well under a tenner. Bargain! And the food is very good, from the complementary appetizer, cheese and herb dip, to the homemade pita bread, and eggplant in any number of different incarnations. A "tas" is a Turkish cooking pot, and casseroles are a main course specialty—chicken and almond, for instance, which was superb with a side of apricot rice. Tas stocks Turkish wine, as well. I'm no expert but it slipped down very nicely, thank you! The great value and the fact that SE1 has hitherto been a culinary wasteland mean large crowds at lunch and in the evening. So if you hate noise, it probably isn't for you.

33 The Cut, SE1. ℂ 020/7928-1444. Reservations recommended. Main courses £4.50–£14.50 ($6.55–$21.05). Fixed-price meals £6.45–£17.95 ($9.35–$26.05). AE, MC, V. Mon–Sat noon–11:30pm; Sun noon–10.30pm. Tube: Southwark.

## SUPER-CHEAP EATS

**Bright Light Café** ★★ *Finds* MODERN EUROPEAN  So, you consulted the long-range weather forecast, crossed your fingers, prayed, and cast a voodoo spell, and still it has rained every day since you arrived! There's only one thing for it: Get down to this permanently sunny cafe. A couple of hours under its fake-sunshine lighting, the kind designed to combat Seasonal Affective Disorder, should put a smile back on your face. If that doesn't, the food certainly will because posh local deli Konditor & Cook runs this brasserie, which stretches all the way across the front of the Young Vic theater. It dishes up scrumptious quick bites, from soup to sandwiches, and good-value light meals. You might find prawn Marie Rose at the cheaper end, or a delicious citrus chicken tagine at the other. The bright lights switch off a little earlier in the evening if there's no performance, so call ahead to check.

Young Vic, 66 The Cut, SE1. ℂ 020/7620-2700. Main courses £5–£8.50 ($7.25–$12.35). MC, V. Mon–Sat noon–11pm (8pm if no performance). Tube: Waterloo, Southwark.

## WORTH A SPLURGE

**Fish!** ★★ *Kids* SEAFOOD  Tate Modern is turning Southwark into one of the hippest neighborhoods in London. Another draw is the foodie mecca, Borough Market, which is where you'll find Fish! This futuristic diner is all glass and steel,

---

### *Finds* Pie & Mash: History on a Plate

It's a curious taste but visitors who want to experience working-class London as it scarcely exists any more have got to put pie & mash on the menu. This dish is edible social history, dating back to when eels were two-a-penny in the Thames, just begging to be someone's dinner. But minced beef has long since taken their place as a cheaper substitute under the flaky pastry. That's what you get today, served with mash, liquor (a kind of green parsley gravy), and eels on the side.

Most of London's pie & mash shops are an inconvenient bus ride from East End Tube stations—they're the real deal, not packaged heritage. But the Cooke family, a big name in the business, does have one offshoot in Southwark. **R Cooke**, 84 The Cut, SE1 (ℂ **020/7928-5931**; Tube: Southwark, Waterloo) is open from 10am to 2:30pm Tuesday to Saturday and a no-frills lunch will cost you £1.80 to £3.70 ($2.60–$5.35). No credit cards.

and very noisy, especially when it's full of families at weekend lunchtimes. The restaurant has high chairs, toys, and a two-course children's menu with things like tuna bolognese that should even be able to sucker anti-fish kids. It worked with my best friend's thuggish 2-year-old. For the grown-ups, evangelical notes on the place mats detail why fish is good for you and how it should be caught. The choose-your-own menu lists 20 fish with ticks against those that are available that day, to be grilled or steamed as you like, with a choice of five accompanying sauces. Big thumbs up for my extremely tender halibut and the most tender scallops my galpal had ever had. Chips cost extra but were perfectly cooked and well worth it. The only sour note was the sour and past-it salad. There are several new branches, including one a couple of miles upriver at **County Hall;** call the central reservations number below.

Cathedral St., Borough Market, SE1. © **020/7234-3333.** Reservations recommended. Main courses £7.80–£16 ($11.30–$23.20); fixed-price children's meal £6.95 ($10.10). MC, V. Mon–Fri 11:30am–10:30pm; Sat–Sun noon–10pm. Tube: London Bridge, Borough.

## 16 Farther Afield

### ISLINGTON
#### GREAT DEALS ON FIXED-PRICE MEALS

**Granita** ⭐⭐ MODERN EUROPEAN   This used to be one of Tony and Cherie Blair's favorite dining places before they quit Islington and moved onto greater things. Superb cuisine and very friendly service have ensured that Granita draws both locals and diners from further afield. Anyone who goes a la carte will appreciate the meal-on-a-plate approach, which avoids the need to bump the bill up by adding side orders. But the short fixed-price menus, either two or three courses, are excellent value. There are about three choices at each stage, modern European dishes with nods to the Middle East and Southeast Asia. These change weekly to keep Granita's many regulars entertained. You might find sautéed calves' liver with artichokes, broad beans, sage, and lemon. Or a hearty pea and sorrel soup. Char-grilling is a favorite cooking method, particularly delicious when it comes to rump of beef with Middle Eastern spices. And the desserts would make Martha Stewart green with envy.

127 Upper St., N1. © **020/7226-3222.** Reservations recommended. Main courses £10–£15 ($14.50–$21.75); fixed-price lunch £13.50–£15.50 ($19.60–$22.50). MC, V. Wed–Sun 12:30–2:30pm; Tues–Sun 6:30–10:30pm. Tube: Angel, Highbury & Islington.

### CAMDEN

Camden is packed with hole-in-the-wall cafes and stalls selling cheap street food. Cruise any section of the market to find a bewildering array of kebabs, hot dogs, falafel, and pizza, starting at around £2.50 ($3.65) a pop.

#### GREAT DEALS ON FIXED-PRICE MEALS

**Lemonia** ⭐ GREEK   This long-established restaurant, with its classic Greek menu, is a real favorite with the locals. It's a charming place, more than living up to its name: Lemons are absolutely everywhere. The mix of polished wood and marble-topped tables cluster near the fully open front window, up on a dais, and in the conservatory. There are even a few out on the pavement. If you don't want to come this way for lunch, then the meze, which gets you a mixed bag of starters and main courses, is a fantastic deal—look around and you'll see that's what most diners are having. Otherwise, top recommendations include the moussaka, which is a triumph of eggplant, zucchini, potatoes, tomatoes, and ground beef in a creamy sauce, and the subtly flavored *afelia* (cubes of pork marinated in wine, coriander seeds, and spices), all washed down with Greek wine. Lemonia is especially crowded at the weekends when the ritual is to walk off the feast on Primrose Hill, which has one of the best views across London.

89 Regent's Park Rd., NW1. © 020/7586-7454. Reservations essential. Fixed-price lunch £6.75–£7.95 ($9.80–$11.55); main courses £7.25–£13.50 ($10.50–$19.60); meze 13.50 ($19.60). MC, V. Sun–Fri noon–3pm; Mon–Sat 6–11:30pm. Tube: Chalk Farm.

## WORTH A SPLURGE

**The Engineer** ✿ GASTROPUB/MODERN BRITISH    This was one of the gastropub pioneers, with its huge glass windows and scrubbed tables in the bar, restaurant, and garden. It is pricey, but skinny wallets can fill their stomachs with simple but delicious meals in a bowl, while the less restricted have something like lemon-scented risotto of yellow-pepper puree, Gorgonzola, and walnuts. And splurgers gorge on whole roasted sea bass. The modern British cuisine is elaborate, with a few global influences. For instance, Asian overtones take over many dishes, in the form of soy and something sauce perhaps, or wok-frying of the ingredients. Lunchtime main courses are a lot lighter than the evening fare. The menu changes every 2 weeks. And the meat is all organic. This is a delightful place and screamingly busy, particularly at the weekends as a popular local pit-stop before or after a visit to Camden market. Do book ahead.

65 Gloucester Ave., NW1. © 020/7722-0950. Reservations recommended. Main courses £9–£15.50 ($14.40–$24.80). MC, V. Mon 7am–10pm; Tues–Sun 7am–11pm. Tube: Camden Town, Chalk Farm.

## 17 Best of the Budget Chains

The past 2 decades have brought a massive explosion in restaurant chains to Britain. It began with bland, *faux*-French cafes. Now no high concept eaterie seems to be without a business plan to clone itself prolifically. London's sushi and noodle bars are a prime example, as you'll see from the reviews. Apart from them, the best budget gremlins are a mix of fast-ish food cliches and snack-stops riding the health fad.

**Pizza Express** introduced the Italian staple to Britain when even metropolitan Londoners talked about filthy foreign muck. It's still the quality benchmark, and a pizza will cost you £4.75 to £7.55 ($6.90–$10.95). There are over 60 branches across London. One of the liveliest is in Soho: 10 Dean St., W1 (© 020/7437-9595; Tube: Tottenham Court Rd., Leicester Sq). Surf the website for a full list (www.pizzaexpress.co.uk). Newcomer **ASK** is putting up a very worthy challenge. It uses chi-chi ingredients familiar in posher cuisine—goat cheese, sun-dried tomatoes, and so on. It's a restaurant, not a joint, with cool modern decor and smooth service. Yet pizza prices are very reasonable at £4 to £6.70 ($5.80–$9.70). There are about 20 ASKs—look for the blue neon signs. Two are extra handy for budget hotels: in Paddington, at 41 to 43 Spring St., W2 (© 020/7706-0707); and Victoria, at 160 to 162 Victoria St., SW1 (© 020/7630-8228).

Otherwise, there are several friendly faces for U.S. travelers—not counting the epidemic of over-priced coffee bars. Burgers cost from £7.25 ($10.50) at the original **Hard Rock Cafe,** 150 Old Park Lane, W1 (© 020/7629-0382; Tube: Hyde Park Corner); they're even pricier, starting at £9.95 ($14.45), at **Planet Hollywood,** Trocadero, 13 Coventry St., W1 (© 020/7287-1000; Tube: Piccadilly Circus). Both are noisy tourist traps and attract mega-queues! The third, and nuttiest, U.S. chain to arrive here is the **Rainforest Café,** 20 Shaftes-bury Ave., W1 (© **020/7434-3111**). Kids love this themed dining on steroids: jungly vegetation, rocks and waterfalls, tropical birds and wailing animatronic animals, thunderclaps and sudden storms—as if London needed pretend ones. There's a children's menu, and grown-ups can choose between standard fast food and more exotic Asian concoctions for £8 to £14.95 ($11.60–$21.70).

Healthy meals-in-a-cup are definitely big in London. These two are my pick of the bunch, and both are a great value. **SOUP Works** is a funky U.S.-style operation, with rows of huge metal saucepans along the counter. The flavors change regularly, but prices range from £1.50 ($2.20) to £3 ($4.35) for 8oz. (or for one of the noodle dishes). There are also 12, 16, or jumbo 32oz. pots. All four branches are in the West End. The one near Leicester Square, at 15 Moor St., W1 (© **020/7734-7687**) is great for after-dark slurps, open until 9pm Monday to Wednesday and 11pm Thursday to Saturday. Prices at **Soup Opera** include a piece of bread and fruit, and start at £3.35 ($4.85) for a 12oz. carton—this place doesn't bother with wimpy 8oz. There are 10 branches; I'd try the one near Oxford Circus at 2 Hanover St., W1 (© **020/7629-0174;** www.soupopera.co.uk).

A big cup of soup costs £1.75 to £2.85 ($2.55–$4.15) at **EAT,** a healthy cafe chain that has blossomed into 20 central London branches from the original Embankment branch: 39 to 41 Villiers St., WC2 (© **020/7839-2282**). It has won prizes for its hot sandwiches and yummy tortilla wraps (99p–£3/$1.45–$4.35), and does sushi, too. Although West End branches stay open until 7pm, this is mostly a daytime snack stop, as is **Pret a Manger.** Sandwiches are its specialty, with such luxurious fillings that you must grab a stack of napkins to catch the lateral ooze. Or grab a cappuccino, sushi box, or wicked cake. There are nearly 70 branches in London.

## 18 Afternoon Tea

The ladies at the **Chelsea Physic Garden** are demon bakers in true Women's Institute style so it's well worth making a special trip to sample their wares. The garden is open on Wednesday and Sunday afternoons, from April through October: see "Parks & Gardens," in chapter 6, "Exploring London" for more information.

### KENSINGTON

**The Orangery** ★★ *Kids* AFTERNOON TEA   The cakes here at the squidgiest of homemade English treats, from the Victoria sponge on the cheapest set menu to the Belgian chocolate heaven on the priciest one. There are three tea-time blowouts to choose from: level one gets you sandwich, shortbread, and the afore-mentioned cake; add £1 to swap the sandwich for a scone with cream and jam; and the top treat assembles all of the above, plus a luvverly glass of bubbly. The atmosphere is luvverly, too, in this elegant 18th-century conservatory by Kensington Palace. Yet the prices make most hot tea spots look like a real rip-off. Kensington Palace, Kensington Gardens, W8. © 020/7376-0239. Fixed-price teas £7.95–£12.95 ($14.45–$18.80). MC, V. Daily 10am–6pm (5pm Oct–Easter); tea served from 3pm. Tube: Kensington High St., Queensway. No smoking.

### MAYFAIR

**Brown's Hotel** ★★ AFTERNOON TEA   This quintessentially understated, oh-so English hotel (the oldest 5-star in London) is justifiably famous for its

---

*Finds* **The Best Baddest Breakfast in Town**

Playing hooky from your B&B breakfast may mean doubling up the bacon bill, but you've gotta be wicked at least once while you're here. The best budget breakfast is the bumper £5.50 ($8) special at the **Brew House,** at Kenwood House on Hampstead Heath (see p. 204). The ingredients are top-notch: free-range scrambled eggs and pork sausages, bacon, mushrooms, tomatoes, and toast. And you can tuck in from 9am every day. Make it a weekend treat, as the locals do, and bring your newspaper. During the week, head east to the **Fox & Anchor,** 115 Charterhouse St., EC1 (*C* 020/7253-5075; Tube: Barbican, Farringdon). The pub opens at 7am and the £7 ($10.15) death-by-breakfast is fittingly carnivorous for the location, just round the corner from Smithfield Market: black pudding as well as sausages, bacon, eggs, fried bread, tomatoes, and baked beans. My two top spots are **Star Café** in Soho (p. 134) and **Café Grove** in Portobello Road (p. 125).

---

country-house afternoon tea. Tailcoated waiters tend to guests reclining in armchairs in the paneled drawing room. It's a lot of money, but you certainly won't need dinner after a session here. Tea starts with a fine array of ham and mustard, smoked salmon, egg, and many other sandwiches. Scones with clotted cream and jam follow that. And then you'll have your pick of scrumptious cream cakes and pastries. Brown's serves its own blended tea, among a long list of others. You don't have to dress up, but it somehow seems part of the occasion to do so.

Albemarle and Dover sts., W1. *C* 020/7493-6020. Reservations required for 3 and 4:45pm sittings on weekdays. Dress casual. £23 ($33.35). AE, DC, MC, V. Daily 3–6pm. Tube: Green Park.

**Dorchester** *✦* AFTERNOON TEA   The Promenade may not have quite the limitless luxury of the Ritz's Palm Court, but it's a pretty close-run thing. Gold decoration and marble floors and pillars make this a very posh corridor in which to take afternoon tea. The Dorchester is famed for its pastries: The fluffy scones that follow the sandwich first course, and the strawberry tart, white chocolate parcel, coffee éclair, and the host of other cakes will send you out into the Mayfair early evening, happy but crawling on your hands and knees. The higher priced tea includes a glass of champagne.

54 Park Lane, W1. *C* 020/7629-8888. Reservations recommended. Dress smart casual, no jeans or tennis shoes. Fixed-price tea £23.50–£29.50 ($34.10–$42.80). Daily 3–6pm. AE, DC, MC, V. Tube: Hyde Park Corner.

## ST. JAMES'S

**Fountain Restaurant at Fortnum & Mason** AFTERNOON TEA   This store is world-famous, and so is its tea, so its eateries are always mobbed with tourists. The ice-cream tea at the downstairs Fountain restaurant includes a pot of own-blend tea, chocolate shells filled with scoops of vanilla ice cream, freshly baked scones with clotted cream and strawberry jam, and then a slice of one of a selection of cakes. It's great for the kids, not just because it's their kind of meal, but because there's so much noise that no one will notice if they goof around.

181 Piccadilly, W1. *C* 020/7734-8040. Ice-cream afternoon tea £12.95 ($18.80). AE, DC, MC, V. Mon–Sat 8:30am–8pm (tea 3–6pm). Tube: Green Park, Piccadilly.

## COVENT GARDEN

**Waldorf Meridien** ★★ AFTERNOON TEA    The airy Palm Court was used as the ship's lounge in the movie Titanic and it does evoke an earlier, more gracious age—especially because there's usually a harpist playing. The teas are always delicious, but the weekend tea dances are a special treat. Two-left-feet shufflers and two-step champions, young and old, happily circle together while the silver cutlery and Wedgwood china tinkles in the background. It's a marvelously old-fashioned way to work off a dozen mini-sandwiches, pastries, and squelchy cakes.

Aldwych, WC2. ✆ **020/7836-2400.** Reservations recommended, essential on weekends. Fixed-price tea £18–£25 ($26.10–$36.25); tea dance £25–£28 ($36.25–$40.60). AE, DC, MC, V. Mon–Fri 3–5:30pm; tea dance Sat 2–4:30pm, Sun 4–6:30pm. Tube: Covent Garden, Aldwych.

# 6

# Exploring London

After months of wheeler-dealering and changes to the tax regulations, the government has pulled it off: London's major national museums have just dropped their admission charges. Indulge in sci-fi fantasy at the Science Museum, for free. Inhale the aroma of cheesy socks and close-confined unwashed bodies in the Imperial War Museum's submarine simulator, for free. Experience an earthquake at the Natural History Museum, for free. Visit, but don't bounce on, the Great Bed of Ware at the V&A's lavishly poshed up British Galleries, for free. See the original model for Nelson's Column, and his bullet-pierced coat, at the National Maritime Museum, for free.

And what a time for such a privilege to kick in. There hasn't been such a museum and gallery boom since the era of the great Victorian philanthropists. All those now-free attractions have recently sprouted new extensions and wings, or had elaborate refurbs. The other big opening in 2001 was the centenary development at Tate Britain. The Museum of London is just embarking on a long and complicated tart-up.

Talking about complicated, the folks in the know didn't want to commit themselves on the dewobblification of the Millennium Bridge. Engineers hung bales of hay under the bridge last June to warn passing boats of work finally starting overhead, as dictated by the historic rules of the river. But it wasn't likely to reopen until the end of 2001.

*Note:* at time of writing, the Dome was *still* empty at the cost of £80 a minute.

## HOW TO PLAN YOUR SIGHTSEEING

The **London Tourist Board** will fall over itself to provide helpful information: if you can, surf the website rather than phoning the premium rate hotline, below, because that costs 60p (85¢) per minute (✆ **09068/663344;** www.londontown.com). For more details on where to find the capital's tourist offices, see "Visitor Information," at the start of chapter 3.

While you're online, you can check out the one-stop **www.24hour museum.org.uk**, a gateway to virtually every museum in the country. The *Evening Standard* website is useful (**www.thisislondon.com**), as is the always essential *Time Out,* both for the right-now listings in the magazine and for its electronic city guide (**www.timeout.com**).

There is always something going on in the capital—anniversaries, historic pageants, festivals, and carnivals. The really big stuff is listed in our "London Calendar of Events," in chapter 2, and you'll find lots more dates, particularly for art, craft, and antiques events, in "Top Tips for Bargain Hounds," in chapter 7. Otherwise, surf **www.artsfestivals.co.uk** and **www.londontown.com/events**, which has a very forward-looking forward diary.

Knowing the dates of the school year is also vital. Museums, galleries, and attractions put on lots of extra fun at half-term—the 1-week mini-break in the middle of each semester—and in the holidays. This is a great time for families to come to London, and for the childless who don't mind crowds double the size and 10 times as noisy—look at the bumper issues of the listings magazines and you'll see that the tours, talks, walks, exhibitions and festivals are not just for kids. Not all schools operate to exactly the same calendar but these dates for 2002 cover the spread of options: spring half-term, February 18 to February 22; Easter holidays, March 25 to April 5; summer half-term, May 27 to June 7; summer holidays, July 19 to September 4; winter half-term, October 21 to November 1; and the Christmas holiday starts on December 20.

*Note:* A family ticket usually covers two adults and two children, but sometimes you can take an extra offspring. Under-5s get free admission to most attractions, while the age limit to qualify as a child varies widely, from 15 to 18.

## 1  How to Spend Less & See More

London will never be a cheap thrill, but fortunately, in addition to the top-dollar tourist draws there are plenty of free museums, galleries, and historic buildings—as long as you hard-heartedly resist all invitations to make a donation. We've reviewed more than 40 in our listing, enough to keep even a performance-enhanced tourist happy, especially now that it includes London's major national museums.

There are lots more ways to have fun on the cheap. Take a look at the suggestions below and at "Frommer's Favorite London Moments," in chapter 1.

- **Net Savings.** As well as the surfin' suggestions above, another top site for budget travelers is **www.londonfreelist.com**. It has details of 1,500 permanently good deals and diary date specials, most of which are free, and none costing more than £3 ($4.35).

- **Check out the Discount Deals.** Special cards and passes are best for energetic travelers because you have to cram a lot into each day to get your money's worth. Check out details on the **London Pass,** the **London for Less card and guidebook,** and the **Great British Heritage Pass** under "Fifty Money-Saving Tips," in chapter 2.

- **Look for Two-Fors.** If the discount passes don't fit your holiday needs, you can still save money by grabbing any joint ticket offers: **Tower of London** and **Hampton Court,** for instance (see "London's Top Attractions," below); **London Zoo** and a **boat trip** with the London Waterbus Company on the Regent Canal (see "Especially for Kids," later in this chapter); **The Monument** and **The Tower Bridge Experience;** or a big **Bus Tour** package with entry to popular attractions like Madame Tussaud's.

## SUGGESTED ITINERARIES

Europeans often poke fun at the hectic pace of Americans, Australians, and New Zealanders trying to squeeze in as many of the "hits" as their brief vacations allow. Pay no attention. Familiarity makes the locals blasé toward their national treasures. These itineraries are designed for long-distance visitors, so skip a few stops if you'd prefer a more leisurely pace. If you're here for 2 days or more, I'd highly recommend joining a walking tour for a very cheap, efficient, and fun way to see the city.

### If You Have 1 Day

Take the Tube to Charing Cross or Embankment and cross into Trafalgar Square, London's unofficial hub. Here, the commercial West End meets The Mall, the regal

# Central London Sights

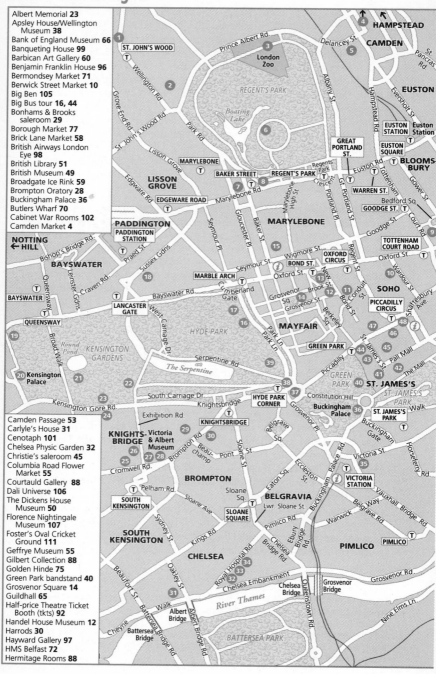

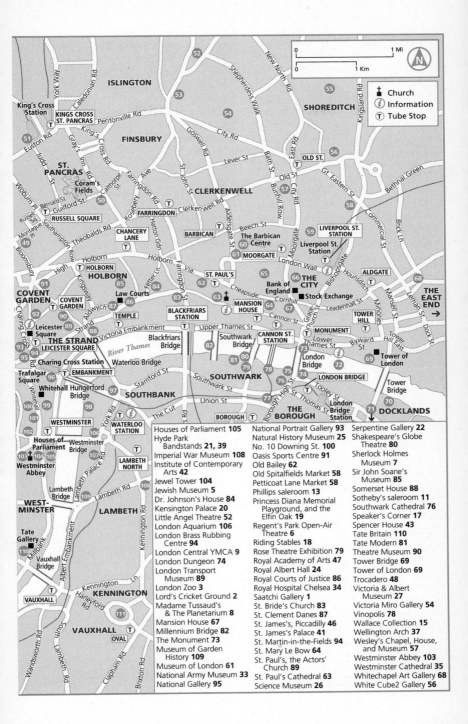

avenue that leads to Buckingham Palace, and governmental Whitehall. Nelson's Column is in the middle of the square, with the National Gallery facing it to the north and the church of St. Martin-in-the-Fields, east at about 2 o'clock.

Turn down Whitehall and visit Banqueting House to see the nine magnificent, allegoric ceiling paintings by Rubens. If you're quick, you'll be out again in time to watch the Changing of the Guard across the road at Horse Guards (at 11am Mon–Sat, 10am on Sun). Walking on down Whitehall, you'll come to the Cenotaph, the moving memorial to all those who fell in the two world wars. No. 10 Downing Street, usually the Prime Minister's official residence, is right opposite. It was too small for the Blair family, so you'll have to keep your eyes peeled on no. 11 to catch a glimpse of little Leo. Whitehall ends in Parliament Square, which is flanked by Big Ben, the spectacular Houses of Parliament, and Westminster Abbey. Then walk across Westminster Bridge and take a flight on the British Airways London Eye. The giant 443-foot-high observation wheel on the south bank will give you a 25-mile bird's-eye view of the London landmarks you haven't got time to visit.

### If You Have 2 Days

Follow the 1-day itinerary but at a more leisurely pace and in reverse. So start your Whitehall stroll from Parliament Square, cross the beautiful St. James's Park to arrive at Buckingham Palace for the 11am Changing of the Guard. Then pop into the National Gallery in Trafalgar Square. Pop out again and continue north along Charing Cross Road, turn right on Long Acre, and visit Covent Garden. You're spoilt for choice there:

shopping, street entertainment, and a late lunch. Finish off the day at Somerset House, a 10 minute stroll south on the other side of the Strand.

Make your second day the one for hitting some of "London's Top Attractions," below. The British Museum, with its new Great Court, is a must, especially as you can now visit the celebrated British Library Reading Room. At lunchtime, head east to one of the City churches for a free lunchtime concert: if it's a Tuesday or Friday, it must be St. Bride's on Fleet Street. Then carry on to St. Paul's Cathedral. From there, you won't be able to resist a visit to Tate Modern. Housed in the old power station, it looms across the Thames at the end of the Millennium Bridge (check if the bridge open first).

### If You Have 3 Days

Spend days 1 and 2 as described above, but leave out Tate Modern, and make day three a Bankside and South Bank special. You can start at either end of the Millennium Mile riverside walk, but I'd recommend a ride in the British Airways London Eye first, before queues build up. Then stroll along the Thames to the South Bank Centre for a fascinating backstage tour of the Royal National Theatre, and a bite to eat during a lunchtime concert at the Royal Festival Hall. Next stop Tate Modern. End the day, if you can, with a show at Shakespeare's Globe Theatre.

### If You Have 4 Days or More

With the big stuff done on your first 3 days, use your last one to explore other historic neighborhoods, enjoy more of the city's cultural scene, or shop. For option one, take a boat downriver to Greenwich, perhaps, or the other

*Moments*   **The Golden Jubilee**

In 2002, Queen Elizabeth II becomes only the fourth British monarch in history, after medieval Henry III, mad George III of movie fame, and Queen Victoria, to celebrate a golden jubilee.

The Whitsun bank holiday—the last Monday in May—will be postponed until the first weekend in June, turning it into a four-day festive big bang. The Golden Jubilee Celebrations kick off on Saturday June 1, 2002, with a classical concert on the famous palace lawn. The audience of 14,000 will get their tickets for free in a nationwide ballot, as they will for the pop concert on Monday June 3. Star performers at the royal gig were unconfirmed at time of writing but are likely to number such national treasures as Sir Cliff Richard, Sir Paul McCartney, Dame Vera Lynn. The BBC is staging both concerts, which it is relaying to giant screens in the parks and avenues around the palace.

Monday really is the first salvo of the celebratory big bang after Sunday's bell-ringing and Jubilee church services. Planners are encouraging local communities to put on street parties and to light beacons, the first of which will be lit by the Queen after the pop concert.

The pomp and circumstance kicks in on Tuesday with a royal procession from Buckingham Palace to a service of thanksgiving at St. Paul's Cathedral, also relayed to the giant TV screens. Then the festivities close with a Carnival Pageant along the Mall.

That is the grand finale of the Golden Jubilee weekend. But don't worry if you can't make the trip right then. The capital is the focus of a whole season of celebrations from March to December 2002, the **London String of Pearls Golden Jubilee Festival.** More than 70 great institutions and landmarks are throwing themselves open to the public, often for the first time. A full diary of events will be available from January 2002 (① **020/7665-1540;** www.stringofpearls.org.uk).

*Note:* For up-to-the-minute information on the Golden Jubilee weekend, call ① **0845/000-2002** (www.goldenjubilee.gov.uk).

way to Hampton Court. Alternatively, head for South Kensington to see the spectacularly overhauled British Galleries at the V&A and the new Welcome Wing at the Science Museum. Diana fans might want to stop at Kensington Palace, nearby in Kensington Gardens.

Turn east, instead, and walk along the edge of the park to Knightsbridge if you yearn for the Harrods experience. You should also check out the markets in chapter 7, "Shopping," because you may want to swap your days around to fit in a serious browsing session.

## 2 London's Top Attractions

**British Museum** ✦✦✦   To get the maximum visual kerpow from your first sight of the **Great Court,** use the main south entrance into the museum—the one with the too-white portico made of the wrong kind of stone. Bar that embarrassing blunder, the £100 million redevelopment of the British Museum, designed by Sir Norman Foster, has won high praise. The 2-acre Great Court used to serve as a giant store cupboard. Now covered by a stunning steel-and-glass roof, it has become the light-filled hub of the Bloomsbury complex, staying open after the galleries close, with an education center, restaurants where you can have supper Thursday through Saturday, and coffee shops. Call for details of talks, performances, and workshops.

But the real excitement is that for the first time, visitors can enter the copper-domed **British Library Reading Room.** The giant drum in the middle of the Great Court is clad in the same too-white stone, while the interior has been restored to its Victorian blue, cream, and gold glory. Designed by Robert Smirke and completed in 1857, it inspired Thomas Carlyle, Virginia Woolf, Mahatma Gandhi, Lenin, George Bernard Shaw, Karl Marx (who wrote *Das Kapital* here), and a host of other great names. It houses the museum's books on the upper floors, with a public reference library and multimedia center down below.

From a collection purchased from Sir Hans Sloane in 1753, the British Museum has grown into one of the richest storehouses of antiquities, prints, drawings, manuscripts, and *objets d'art* in the world, rivaled only by the Smithsonian in Washington, D.C. There are 2½ miles of galleries, so you'll need to weed out what really interests you and make a plan of attack. The £2.50 ($3.65) *Visit Guide* will help. Otherwise, let the museum take the stress out of deciding: the 90-minute Highlight tour takes place daily at 11am and 3pm and costs £7 for adults ($10.15), £4 ($5.80) concessions and under-11s; the 60-minute Focus tour costs £5 and £3 ($7.25 and $4.35) respectively, and takes in the most important treasures in the museum, daily at 1pm, plus 5:30 and 7pm on Thursday and Friday. There are also free single gallery tours, EyeOpeners, which take place half-hourly from 11am to 3pm.

Personally, I'd pop in to see the much fought-over **Elgin Marbles.** The Egyptian antiquities are also a must—they include the **mummies,** scarcophagi and the **Rosetta Stone.** It would also be a shame not to take in a bit of local history, like the leathery remains of garotted **Lindow Man,** or the glittering Anglo-Saxon silver and gold of the **Sutton Hoo treasure.** And then I'd wander into the new **Sainsbury African Galleries,** a modern imaginative exhibition a

---

### ⎛Kids⎞ Changing of the Guard

Looking more like toy soldiers than honed fighting machines, these poor men somehow do their duty, apparently oblivious to kids pulling silly faces and the clicking of holiday snaps. **Changing of the Guard** takes place at **Buckingham Palace** daily from April through August at 11:15am, and on alternate days September through March; at **St. James's Palace,** St. James's St., W1 (Tube: Green Park) at 11:15am, same dates; and at **Horse Guards** (Tube: Charing Cross) Monday through Saturday at 11am, and 10am on Sunday.

Appropriately, it's the Household Cavalry that mounts the guard at Horse Guards. The soldiers ride across town every day from Knightsbridge Barracks, on the edge of Hyde Park, in their shiny breastplates and plumed helmets. The smartest men at the morning inspection get the plum position, on horseback in the sentry boxes, and get to go home at 4pm. Those on foot have to stay until 8pm.

Very bad weather and state events disrupt the schedules.

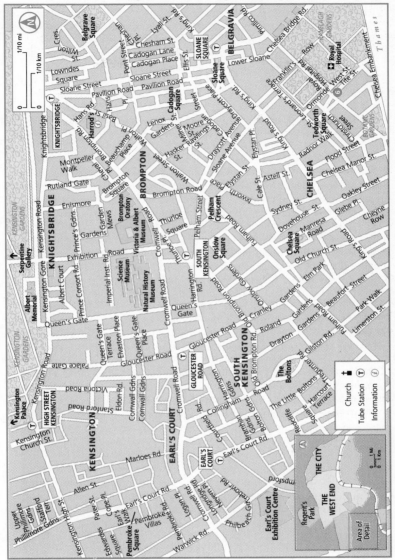

far cry from the dusty trophy rooms of empire days. Check out the fabulous 1950s fantasy coffins from Ghana: my favorite is one that looks like a white Mercedes, with the number plate RIP2000.

Great Russell St., WC1. ☎ **020/7323-8000**, or 020/7323-8299 info desk. www.thebritishmuseum.ac.uk. Main galleries free; £2 ($2.90) donation requested. Special exhibitions £4–£8 ($5.80–$11.60) adults, £2–£4 ($2.90–$5.80) concessions, free under-11s. Galleries Sat–Wed 10am–5:30pm; Thurs–Fri 10am–8:30pm. Great Court Mon 9am–6pm; Tues–Wed and Sun 9am–9pm; Thurs–Sat 9am–11pm. Tube: Russell Sq., Holborn, Tottenham Court Rd.

## The Queen's Gallery to Re-open

The £10 million refurbishment of the Queen's Gallery is the biggest building project at Buckingham Palace since George V stuck on the Portland stone facade in 1913. An imposing new Doric portico will lead into a series of new modern galleries and a much expanded range of exhibits, including photographs from the Royal Archives at Windsor. There's even going to be the first ever Buck House coffee shop—ooh, Ma'am! The grand opening is planned for early 2002, in time for the Queen's Golden Jubilee celebrations. Call Buckingham Palace for more information.

**Buckingham Palace** 👎 *Overrated*  This is Her Maj's official London residence, and supposedly the one she likes least of all her homes. You know she's there when the royal standard is flying. The palace has 600 rooms, of which the Queen and the Duke of Edinburgh only occupy a suite of 12. The rest are used by the royal household or for posh functions, banquets, and investitures.

King George III and Queen Charlotte bought the house from the Duke of Buckingham in 1762, but it was George IV who converted it into a palace. He commissioned John Nash to pump up the grandeur, which he did by adding wings at the front and extending those at the back, all for £700,000. Neither George nor his brother William IV actually lived here, and by the time Queen Victoria came to the throne, doors wouldn't close, windows wouldn't open, bells wouldn't ring, and the drains were clogged. Victoria sent Nash packing and Edward Blore completed the repairs. But it quickly became too small for an official residence. So, in 1847, the queen had the East Front built, facing The Mall, and moved Marble Arch from the palace forecourt to the top of Park Lane. Sir Aston Webb designed the facade in 1913.

The Queen first opened the 18 formal **State Rooms,** including the **Throne Room,** in 1993 to help raise money to repair Windsor Castle after the fire. Overlooking the 45-acre gardens, where she gives her famous summer parties, they contain priceless pictures, tapestries, and a little bit of furniture from the royal collections. Queen Victoria's vast ballroom—the ceilings are 45 feet high and there's room to park 35 double-decker buses—was added to the tour in 2000. This is certainly not a fly-on-the-wall glimpse of royal home life. For a start, you can only visit during August and September when the family is on holiday. And these rooms are not where they put their feet up with a reviving cuppa anyway—it could be almost any unlived in stately home or grand private collection. Tickets can be purchased in person, from 9am on the day: Eager tourists start queuing at sunrise, and an hour-long wait is the rule. Booking a fixed-time ticket by phone, or asking the Visitor Office for an application form, is less hassle, but only the £11 ($15.95) rate is available in advance.

Much better value is the **Royal Mews** 👍👍 (entrance in Buckingham Palace Road). These superb working stables house the royal carriages, including the gold state coach used at every coronation since 1831, and the horses that draw them. By tradition, the Queen always has greys.

The Mall, SW1. ℂ **020/7839-1377,** 020/7799-2331 recorded info, 020/7321-2233 credit-card bookings, 020/7839-1377 for visitors with disabilities. www.royalresidences.com. State Rooms £11 ($15.95) adults, £9 ($13.05) seniors, £5.50 ($8) under-17s, £27.50 ($39.15) family ticket. 2nd week in Aug to end Sept daily 9:30am–4:15pm. Royal Mews £4.60 ($6.65) adults, £3.60 ($5.22) seniors, £2.60 ($3.75) under-17s, £11.80 ($17.10) family ticket. Oct–July Mon–Thurs noon–4pm; Aug–Sept Mon–Thurs 10:30am–4:30pm; times are very tentative so call ahead. Tube: Victoria, St. James's Park, Green Park.

**Hampton Court Palace** ★★★ *(Kids)*    Bring a picnic because a visit to Hampton Court makes a splendid day out. You'll need 2 to 3 hours to look round the palace itself, plus time to wander through the 60 acres of gardens. And then there's the famous **maze,** with its half a mile of twisting paths—most people take 20 minutes or so to extricate themselves from its clutches.

Hampton Court is around 15 miles southwest of London on the banks of the Thames. Henry VIII's pleasure-loving Lord Chancellor, Cardinal Wolsey, took the house in 1515 as a retreat from the city's poisonous air and water. His grandiose remodeling plan called for 280 rooms, new courtyards and gardens, and 500 staff. When the cardinal fell into disfavor in 1528, the ever-grasping king confiscated his property. Henry spent a whopping £18 million in today's money and turned it into a very sophisticated palace—with bowling alleys, "real tennis" courts, a chapel, pleasure gardens, a hunting park, The Great Hall for dining, and a 36,000 square-foot kitchen.

Queen Elizabeth I planted the gardens with new discoveries, such as tobacco and potatoes, brought back by Sir Francis Drake and Sir Walter Raleigh from South America. Under the Stuarts, the palace collections grew with hundreds of new paintings and other lavish objets d'art. Charles II banished the gloom of Cromwell's brief stay here with his lively court and many mistresses. William and Mary found the palace apartments old-fashioned and uncomfortable, so they commissioned Sir Christopher Wren to make improvements and asked such artists as Grinling Gibbons, Jean Tijou, and Antonio Verrio to decorate the rooms. George III ended royal occupation—his grandfather used to box his ears in the State Apartments, so he hated the place.

The highlights for visitors to Hampton Court are the **Tudor Kitchens** and the **King's Apartments,** as well as the **Wolsey Rooms** and **Renaissance Picture Gallery.** One of Henry VIII's wives, the headless Catherine Howard, has been sighted several times in the **Haunted Gallery.** Throughout the palace, costumed guides bring the centuries of history to life—as does the full calendar of special events and festivals.

East Molesey, Surrey. ✆ **020/8781-9500** recorded info, or 020/8781-9666. www.hrp.org.uk. Admission £10.80 ($15.65) adults, £8.30 ($12.05) students and seniors, £7.20 ($10.45) under-16s, £32.20 ($46.70) family ticket. Mid-Mar to mid-Oct Mon 10:15am–6pm, Tues–Sun 9:30am–6pm; mid-Oct to mid-Mar Mon 10:15am–4:30pm, Tues–Sun 9:30am–4:30pm. Park 7am–dusk. Closed Dec 24–26. Train: Waterloo to Hampton Court. 30-min. journey time. Travel after 9:30am on cheap day-return ticket, £4.60 ($6.70) adults, £2.30 ($3.35) children. River services from Westminster pier (✆ **020/7930-2062** or 020/7930-4721; www.wpsa.co.uk, 3- to 4-hr. journey time. Leaving 10:30, 11:15am, and noon; returning from Hampton Court at 3, 4, and 5pm; all dependent on the tide; reduced schedule Oct–Mar. Tickets cost £10 ($14.50) one-way or £14 ($20.30) return; under-16s half-price.

**Houses of Parliament** ★★★    This neo-Gothic extravaganza, with its trademark clock tower, is the ultimate symbol of London. Edward the Confessor built the first palace here, and the site was home to the monarchy and court until Henry VIII's time. But, in 1834, a fire lit to burn the Exchequor's tally sticks got

---

*Tips*  **A Money-Saving Joint Ticket**

Buying a joint ticket to **Hampton Court** and the **Tower of London** (see p. 178) saves around £2 ($2.90) per person. It costs £19 ($27.55) for adults, £14.50 ($21.05) seniors and students, £12.50 ($18.15) under-16s, or £55 ($79.75) for a family ticket.

out of control, sparing only Westminster Hall (1097), which is not open to the public, and the Jewel Tower (see "Lots More to See," later in this chapter). Charles Barry designed the Houses of Parliament (1840) you see today. Augustus Welby Pugin created the paneled ceilings, tiled floors, stained glass, clocks, fireplaces, umbrella stands, and even inkwells. There are more than 1,000 rooms, 100 staircases, and 2 miles of corridors. Big Ben is not the clock tower, as many people think, but the largest bell in the chime. It weighs close to 14 tons and was named, rather unromantically, after the first commissioner of works.

The parliamentary session runs from mid-October to the end of July, with breaks at Christmas and Easter. Visitors can watch debates from the Strangers' Galleries in both houses. Most visitors are struck by how small the **Commons chamber** is. It was rebuilt in precise detail in 1950 after being destroyed during the Blitz of 1941. Only 437 of the 651 MPs can sit at any one time; on the rare occasions when most of them turn up, the rest crowd noisily around the door and the Speaker's chair. The ruling party and opposition sit facing one another, two sword lengths apart, though from the volume of the argy-bargy you'd think it was more like 2 miles. The Mace, on the table in the middle, is the symbol of Parliament's authority. The queue for the **House of Lords** is usually shorter, as debates here are less crucial and a lot more polite. The chamber is fantastically opulent, decorated with mosaics and frescoes. The Lord Chancellor presides over proceedings from his seat on the Woolsack, a reminder of the days when wool was the source of Britain's wealth. You'd think such tradition made the place sacrosanct. Yet, in 2000, New Labour made all the hereditary peers pitch to keep their privileges and ousted 600 of them. And last year it appointed the promised "people's peers," though the prominent professionals chosen seemed scarcely more representative of the general population than the aristocracy.

During the summer recess, you can take a 75-minute tour of the Houses of Parliament (© **020/7344-9966;** www.ticketmaster.co.uk) for just £3.50 ($5.10). It isn't really suitable for young children as rest-stops are limited.

Bridge St. and Parliament Sq., SW1. © 020/7219-4272 House of Commons or © 020/7219-3107 House of Lords. www.parliament.uk. Free admission, subject to recess and sitting times. House of Commons: Wed 9:30am–1:30pm, Mon–Wed 2:30–10:30pm; Thurs 11:30am–7:30pm; and Fri 9:30am–3pm. House of Lords: Mon–Thurs 9:30am–1pm (last entry noon); occasionally Fri. Queue at St. Stephen's entrance, near the statue of Oliver Cromwell. Debates usually run until 10pm and often into the night; lines shrink after 6pm. For tickets to Prime Minister's Question Time, Wed 3–3:30pm, write to your MP (overseas residents, to your embassy). Guided tours available during 6-wk. summer recess. Tube: Westminster. River services: Westminster Pier.

**Kensington Palace State Apartments and Royal Ceremonial Dress Collection** 🐒🐒  The palace has been a pilgrimage site ever since Princess Diana died in August 1997, when people flocked to the gates and carpeted the ground with flower tributes. Several of her best-known designer frocks are now on permanent display here, as are dozens of dresses, shoes, and hats worn by the Queen over the past 50 years.

The asthmatic William and his wife Mary bought this house from the Earl of Nottingham in 1689 to escape from the putrid air enveloping Whitehall. Then they commissioned Sir Christopher Wren to remodel the modest Jacobean mansion. Queen Anne, who came to the throne in 1702, laid out the gardens in English style, had the Orangery built after designs by Nicholas Hawksmoor, and died here in 1714 from apoplexy brought on by overeating. The first two Georges lived at Kensington Palace. George III abandoned it in favor of Buckingham House (now Palace, too). But his fourth son, Edward Duke of Kent, did have apartments here. Queen Victoria was his daughter. The Archbishop of Canterbury and the Lord Chamberlain roused her from sleep here on June 27, 1837, with news of the death of her uncle, William IV and her succession to the throne. That night was the first she had ever slept outside her mother's room. Three weeks later, she moved into Buckingham Palace.

Today, Princess Margaret, the Duke and Duchess of Gloucester, and Princess Michael of Kent all have apartments here. Only the **State Apartments,** filled with art treasures from the Royal Collection, and the display of court fashions and uniforms from 1760 in the **Royal Ceremonial Dress Collection** are open to the public. See the Cupola Room, where Queen Victoria was baptized, and marvel at William Kent's magnificent trompe l'oeils and paintings in the King's Drawing Room, Presence Chamber, and on the King's Staircase. And you can have lunch or tea in the Orangery.

Kensington Gardens. Ⓒ **020/7937-9561.** www.hrp.org.uk. Admission £8.80 ($12.75) adults, £6.90 ($10) seniors and students, £6.30 ($9.15) under-16s, £26.80 ($38.85) family ticket. Additional charge for temporary exhibitions. Mar–Oct daily 10am–5pm; Oct–Mar daily 10am–4pm. Tube: Queensway, High St. Kensington.

## Madame Tussaud's & the Planetarium *(Overrated* Madame Tussaud had an extraordinary life. Born Marie Grosholtz, she learnt her craft from her mother's doctor employer, who had a talent for wax modeling. Such was her renown that Louis XIV and Marie Antoinette appointed her as their children's art tutor. Gruesomely, Marie had to make the royal couple's death masks after their execution in 1793 to prove her loyalty to the revolution and get out of Laforce Prison. You can see several casts from her original molds—a spooky 3-D Voltaire, for instance—at this "museum." But most of its space is devoted to modern superstars, from Sadam Hussein to Mel Gibson, in whose pockets staff once found a pair of ladies knickers. Craftsmen take more than 200 measurements from each star sitter. And stars know they're on the wane when Tussaud's boils their figure down and uses the wax to make someone else. Actor Robert Carlyle has joined the Garden Party, wearing rather more clothes than he did in either *The Full Monty* or *The Beach*—he donated a pair of Levi's, a denim jacket, and tennis shoes. The dungeon-level Chamber of Horrors is the stuff tourist traps are made of. It "honors" Charles Manson, Jack the Ripper, and Dracula, as well as burning Joan of Arc at the stake and doing grisly unmentionables to Gunpowder Plotter Guy Fawkes. Madame Tussaud's is expensive and rather overrated, but it attracts more than 2.5 million visitors a year. So it has introduced a fast-track system whereby you pre-book time slots. Use it or you'll queue for longer than the 2 hours or so it takes to go round.

Next door, the **London Planetarium** is a much more specialist attraction, and not my cup of tea, as it happens. But if you're going to Madame Tussaud's anyway, it's worth spending the extra couple of pounds for a combined ticket. This copper-domed London landmark is the largest planetarium in Europe. Its state-of-the-art Digistar II projection system re-creates an earth-based view of 9,000 stars and planets scattered across the night sky, and takes you on a *Starship Enterprise* journey past exploding nebulae right to the edge of the universe. There are also interactive exhibits to play on.

Marylebone Rd., NW1. Ⓒ **020/7935-6861,** 0870/400-3000 booking. www.madame-tussauds.com. Madame Tussaud's £11.50 ($16.70) adults, £9 ($13.05) seniors, £8 ($11.60) under-16s. Planetarium £6.50 ($9.45) adults, £5.10 ($7.40) seniors, £4.35 ($6.30) under-16s. Combined ticket £13.95 ($20.25) adults, £10.80 ($15.65) seniors, £9.50 ($13.80) under-16s. Madame Tussaud's: opening time varies by season (9, 9:30, and 10am), closing at 5:30pm. Planetarium daily 10am–5:30pm. Shows run every 40 min., 12:20–5pm, weekends/holidays from 10:20am. Closed Dec 25. Tube: Baker St.

**National Gallery** ★★   Britain's national art collection comprises more than 2,300 paintings dating from 1260 to 1900, supplemented by masterpieces on loan from private collectors. The gallery is arranged in four time bands. The **Sainsbury Wing** ★ shows work from 1260 to 1510 by such artists as Giotto, Botticelli, Leonardo da Vinci, Piero della Francesca, and Raphael. The **West Wing** takes on the next 90 years, with El Greco, Holbein, Bruegel, Michelangelo, Titian, and Veronese. The **North Wing** holds the 17th-century masters, Rubens, Poussin, Velázquez, Rembrandt, and Vermeer. Van Dyck's *The Abbé Scaglia* entered the collection in 1999, given by a private owner in lieu of inheritance tax. Works by Stubbs, Gainsborough, Constable, Turner, Canaletto, van Gogh, Corot, Monet, Manet, Renoir, and Cézanne are all in the **East Wing.** From May to September, the National Gallery lets natural daylight illuminate many of the paintings, particularly in the Sainsbury Wing, to magical effect—the colors are truer, and it cuts down on flare and shadow from the frames. You'll need to choose a sunny day for your visit, though, because artificial help steps in if it gets too gloomy. Weekday mornings and late on Wednesday are the quietest times.

There's a free (donation invited) audio guide to every painting on the main floor, and free guided tours start at 11:30am and 2:30pm every day, plus at 6:30pm on Wednesday evenings. Most of the gallery talks are also free. There are two eateries: the Crivelli's Garden restaurant (✆ **020/7747-2869**) at the top of the Sainsbury Wing, and the Pret a Manger sandwich cafe in the basement of the main building.

Trafalgar Square, WC2. ✆ **020/7747-2885.** www.nationalgallery.org.uk. Main galleries free; Sainsbury wing, £3–£7 ($4.35–$10.15) for some special exhibitions. Wed 10am–9pm; Thurs–Tues 10am–6pm. Closed Jan 1, Good Friday, and Dec 24–26. Tube: Charing Cross, Leicester Sq.

**Natural History Museum** ★★ *Kids*   It roars. It belches foul breath. And it's the biggest hit the museum has ever had. On its first weekend, queues snaked more than 1000 yards around South Kensington to see the **robotic Tyrannosaurus Rex** in its smoky foul-smelling swamp. Now you now have to book a timed ticket for the next available half-hourly slot. Visitors shuffle through, with no time to linger. But I think it's worth it just to watch the 12-feet tall toothy beast, which is driven by motion sensors, react to the appearance of each new human meal. The huge **dinosaur skeletons** are awe-inspiring, too. And the earthquake and volcano simulations in the **Earth Galleries** hint at the terror of the real thing.

Sir Hans Sloane was such a prolific collector that his treasures overflowed the British Museum. Hence the decision to build this vast terra-cotta building (1881), with its towers, spires, and nave-like hall, fit "for housing the works of the Creator." Yet it, too, can display only a fraction of its specimens—animal, vegetable, and mineral. An exciting project is set to revolutionize all that, opening both the collection stores and the science labs, with their 300 white-coated experts, to public view. The £28 million first phase of the Darwin Centre will be ready in summer 2002. The museum already has the new Clore Education Centre, where kids can use video microscopes and bug-hunting magnifying glasses, build their own websites, and take part in regular events. Highlight and themed tours start near the entrance to the Life Galleries.

Cromwell Rd., SW7. ✆ **020/7942-5000** or 020/7942-5011. www.nhm.ac.uk. Admission free. Mon–Sat 10am–5:50pm; Sun 11am–5:50pm. Clore Education Centre Mon 10:30am–5pm (school holidays); Tues–Fri 2:30–5pm (term-time); Sat 10:30am–5pm; Sun 11:30am–5pm. Closed Dec 23–26. Tube: South Kensington.

**Royal Botanic Gardens Kew** ★★    More than 240 years of plant collecting, cultivation, and scientific research have won Kew recognition as a UNESCO World Heritage Site. Augusta, widow of Frederick Prince of Wales, started the first botanical garden here in 1759. But it was Sir Joseph Banks, made director by George III in 1772, who laid the foundations of its fame. He had voyaged to Australia with Captain Cook on HMS *Endeavour* and urged other collectors to scour the world for specimens. Today, there are more than 35,000 different plants in this magnificent park, which covers 300 acres amassed from the royal Kew and Richmond estates. Its borders, arboretum, lakes, glasshouses, follies, museums, galleries, and working buildings are a lasting testament to countless famous names from Capability Brown to architects John Nash, Sir William Chambers, and Decimus Burton. And now Shigeru Ban, who designed the eco-friendly Paper Forest Pavilion made out of recycled paper.

Look out for the oldest potted plant in the world—a Cycad brought back to Kew in the 1770s—in the 4-acre Victorian **Palm House** (1844–48). The **Princess of Wales Conservatory** (1987) is an exuberant Eden split into 10 climactic zones growing sci-fi cacti, spooky orchids, and mangrove swamps. The **Museum,** across the lake from the Palm House, is worth a visit for its wonderful oddities: a Pacific Islands newspaper printed on beaten bark, rubber dentures, and a shirt made from pineapple fiber. As for outside, the wonders are too numerous to list. Spring is magical as more than two million crocuses bloom into a sea of color, and then the bluebells take over. In summer, wheat and wildflowers flank the Broadwalk. The garden map is split into three different areas, each one keeping the visitor busy for 2 to 3 hours.

Kew has four entrances. Nearest to Kew Gardens tube station is Victoria Gate, with its visitor center and shop. This is where you catch the **Kew Explorer** road train for a 35-minute tour of the garden: there are eight stops at which to hop on and off, and it costs £2.50 ($3.65) for adults and £1.50 ($2.20) for children. Main Gate is closest to Kew Pier and Kew Bridge station, and the Orangery cafe-shop. A mile from there and nearest to the Pagoda folly and the Pavilion Restaurant, is Lion Gate. Brentford Gate is next to the car park.

Richmond, Surrey. ✆ **020/8332-5622,** 020/8332-5655 events, 020/8332-5633 tours. www.rbgkew.org.uk. Admission £6.50 ($9.45) adults, £4.50 ($6.55) late entry 45 min. before buildings close, £4.50 ($6.55) concessions, free under-17s. Feb–Mar daily 9:30am–5:30pm, buildings close 5pm; Apr–Aug Mon–Fri 9:30am–6:30pm, Sat–Sun 9:30am–7:30pm, buildings close 5:30pm; Sept–Oct daily 9:30am–6pm, buildings close 5:30pm; Nov–Jan daily 9:30–4:15pm, buildings close 3:45pm. Queen Charlotte's Cottage open summer weekends only. Kew Palace is closed for renovations. Tube: Kew Gardens. Train: From Waterloo to Kew Gardens or Kew Bridge; cheap day-return after 9:30am £3.30 ($4.80) adults, £1.65 ($2.40) concessions and children. River services: from Westminster Pier (✆ **020/7930-2062/4721;** www.wpsa.co.uk) to Kew Pier; £11 ($15.95) return adults, £5 ($7.25) children. Leaving Westminster 10:30, 11:15am, noon, and 2pm; returning from Kew noon, 1:30, 4:30, 5:30, and 6:30pm.

**St. Paul's Cathedral** ★★★    No one who saw the wedding of Prince Charles and Lady Diana in 1981 will ever forget the image of the royal carriages approaching St. Paul's. Now, 20 years later, the Queen is to process to a ceremony of thanksgiving here to celebrate her Golden Jubilee.

This magnificent cathedral is 515 feet long and 360 feet high to the cross on the dome, which dominated the contemporary skyline. Christopher Wren laid out the whole base first to thwart interference from his paymasters, who harassed him constantly over the 35 years it took to complete the building (1675–1710). Buried in the crypt, Wren's epitaph says it all: *"Lector, si monumentum requiris, circumspice"* ("Reader, if you seek his monument, look around you"). Frescoes depicting the life of St. Paul line the inner dome. You can see them best from the **Whispering Gallery,** famous for its amazing acoustics, which can project a murmur right across the void. A second steep climb leads to the Stone Gallery, and a third to the highest Inner Golden Gallery. In all, it's 530 steps to the top, with the views ever more awe-inspiring.

Many artists worked on the decoration. Grinling Gibbons carved the choir screens and stalls, and the organ case. Francis Bird sculpted the statues on the west front. Tijou was responsible for the chancel gates. Caius Gabriel Cibber carved the phoenix above the motto "Resurgam" on the south pediment. And master mason William Kempster designed the geometric staircase in the southwest tower, which holds Great Tom, the bell rung when a member of the royal family, the Bishop of London, the Dean of St. Paul's, or the lord mayor dies. In the ambulatory, the **American Memorial Chapel** pays tribute to soldiers killed in World War II.

I prefer to visit St. Paul's very early before the guide hum starts up. If you go later, join a tour so that you're part of the irritating crowd, not being irritated by it, and can enjoy the anecdotes at full pitch. "Supertours" of the cathedral and crypt take place at 11, 11:30am, 1:30, and 2pm, and cost £2.50 ($3.65) for adults, £2 ($2.90) concessions, £1 ($1.45) children, plus admission. Audio guides are available in five languages until 3pm: £3.50 ($5.10) for adults, £3 ($4.35) concessions, plus admission. "Triforium" tours take in the library, geometric staircase, the West End gallery, and Trophy Room where Wren's Great Model is on display. Tickets are £10 ($14.50), including admission. Call Monday to Friday, 9am to 4pm, to book. Also check the cathedral diary for closures, special services, talks, and concerts. There are often organ recitals at 5pm on Sunday, at no charge. Fuel up at the Crypt Café first.

St. Paul's Churchyard, EC4. ✆ **020/7246-8348** or 020/7246-8319. www.stpauls.co.uk. Admission £5 ($7.25) adults, £4 ($5.80) students and seniors, £2.50 ($3.65) under-16s. Mon–Sat 8:30am–4pm; Sun for worship only. Tube: St. Paul's, Mansion House.

**Science Museum** ⭐⭐ *Kids* The massive £45 million **Wellcome Wing** has revolutionized the museum. The striking cantilevered building houses six new exhibitions presenting the latest developments in science, medicine, and technology. Find out what the kids might look like in 30 years in the *Who am I?* gallery. For a more intimate portrait, check out the gory digital cross-sections in *The Visible Human Project.* This is fantasyland for gadget geeks, who'll love the mad interactivity. Art installations by Marc Quinn, Yinka Shonibare, Darrell Viner, and other big names on the ultra-modern scene, should pacify science-hating culture buffs. And there's a 450-seat IMAX cinema on the first floor. Another huge new gallery, **Making the Modern World,** links the Wellcome Wing to the old museum. Using some of the most iconic treasures of the permanent collection—Apollo 10, Stephenson's Rocket, and a fleece from famous Scottish clone, Dolly the Sheep—it charts 250 years of technological advances and their effects on our culture.

The new galleries are stunning, but don't let them dazzle you into forgetting the rest of this marvelous museum. It is home to many pioneering machines: Arkwright's spinning machine, for instance, and the Vickers "Vimy" aircraft, which made the first Atlantic crossing in 1919. The basement is dedicated to children, with water, construction, sound and light shows, and games for 3 to 6 year olds in the **garden,** and the **Launch Pad** for 7 to 15 year olds. Of course, the Wellcome Wing is even more ambitious: its first-floor **Pattern Pod** aims to

*Moments* **Water Magic**

Time your visit right and you can see the fountains in the Somerset House courtyard doing their balletic synchronized spouting: there's a quick 4-minute session every ½-hour from 10am to 11pm, with bumper 11-minute performances at 1, 6, and 10pm. With the water softly underlit in the city night, this finale is the most magical moment. The fountains are turned off from December through February. For a few weeks over Christmas, the courtyard transforms into an outdoor ice-rink.

convert kids to science from the age of 3 months! For info about museum sleep-overs, see "After Lights Out," on p. 201.

Although the museum introduced free admission in December 2001, it does still charge for shows at the IMAX and rides on its two simulators.

Exhibition Rd., SW7. ℂ **020/7942-4000,** or 0870/870-4771. www.sciencemuseum.org.uk. Admission free. Daily 10am–6pm. Closed Dec 24–26. Tube: South Kensington.

**Somerset House** ★★    The Queen Mother once remarked how sad it was that the courtyard at Somerset House had become an Inland Revenue car park. It was just the spur needed by the long-running campaign to open up the 1,000-room civil service palace, designed by Sir William Chambers (1724–96), to the public. The government moved its workers out and the Heritage Lottery Fund coughed up the millions needed to restore the buildings, the courtyard with its new fountains, and the river terrace, where there's now a summer cafe, cheaper than the new restaurant indoors. The "new" people's playground offers a heady mix of high culture and "street" entertainment, housing three major museums and hosting a program of open-air performances, talks, and workshops (ℂ **020/7845-4670** box office). The restoration is proceeding in phases and you can already visit the **Seamen's Waiting Hall,** where naval officers came to collect their commissions. The 45-minute tours at 11am and 3:15pm on Tuesday, Thursday, and Saturday cost £2.75 ($4).

The **Courtauld Gallery** ★ (ℂ **020/7848-2526;** www.courtauld.ac.uk) has been in Somerset House since 1989. Its chief benefactor, textile mogul Samuel Courtauld, collected impressionist and post-impressionist paintings, which are still the gallery's real strength—Manet's *Bar at the Folies Bergères;* Monet's *Banks of the Seine at Argenteuil; Lady with Parasol* by Degas; *La Loge* by Renoir; Van Gogh's *Self-Portrait with Bandaged Ear;* and several Cézannes, including *The Card Players.* But you'll find work by most great names (lots of Rubens), right up to modern greats Ben Nicholson, Graham Sutherland, and Larry Rivers. At noon on Tuesday, Thursday, and Saturday, 1-hour tours cost £7.50 adults ($10.85), £7 ($10.15) concessions.

The **Gilbert Collection** ★★ (ℂ **020/7420-9400;** www.gilbert-collection.org.uk) is also in the South Building, as well as in the vaults beneath the river terrace, originally stables and workshops, then a store for birth and death certificates. The glittering gold, silver, and mosaics were valued at £75 million when Arthur Gilbert donated the 800-piece collection to the nation in 1996. There are objects here from Princess Diana's old home, Althorp. The 1-hour tour on Tuesday, Thursday, and Saturday costs £5.50 ($8) adults, £5 ($7.25) concessions.

The last and most extraordinary of the treasures of Somerset House are the **Hermitage Rooms** 🎃🎃 (✆ **020/7845-4630;** www.hermitagerooms.co.uk). This offshoot of the State Hermitage Museum in St. Petersburg exhibits pieces from the Russian Imperial collections: until the beginning of March 2002, the subject is French drawings and paintings from Poussin to Picasso. Half the tickets are sold in advance (✆ **020/7413-3398;** www.ticketmaster.co.uk), half at the door, for half-hourly timed entry. Arrive early to bag your slot—there's always something to do if you have to wait.

Strand, WC2. ✆ 020/7845-4600. www.somerset-house.org.uk. Somerset House free. Courtauld Gallery £6 ($8.70) adults, £5 ($7.25) seniors, free under-18s. Gilbert Collection £4 ($5.80) adults, £3 ($4.35) seniors, free under-18s. Combined admission planned, call to check. Hermitage Rooms £6 ($8.70) adults, £3 ($4.35) concessions, free under-5s. Courtyard 7:30am–11pm (7pm in winter). Galleries and exhibitions Mon–Sat 10am–6pm, Sun noon–6pm. Closed Jan 1, Dec 24–26. Tube: Temple, Covent Garden, Charing Cross.

**Tate Britain** 🎃🎃    The new Tate Modern at Bankside may have been making all the noise, but the shifting around of collections has also seen a huge overhaul at the original gallery, founded in 1897 and endowed by sugar magnate Sir Henry Tate. The Centenary Development was due to open in November 2001, boosting exhibition space by 35% with a suite of airy new galleries on the lower floor of the northwest wing, refurbished ones above, and stripped-bare space at the heart of the building. That's the new home for **Art Now,** with its strong focus on new media and experimental work by foreign artists living in London and Brits based here and abroad. Having handed International Modernism over to Bankside, Tate Britain can now concentrate on British work dating back to 1500. It has ditched the chronological displays and gone, like the new gallery, for a thematic approach: **Private and Public** includes portraits and scenes of daily life; **Artists and Models** explores nudes and self-portraiture; **Literature and Fantasy** is for visionary artists such as Blake and Spencer; and **Home and Abroad** looks at the landscape artist at home and abroad. Juxtaposing very different kinds of work isn't always successful, but the vibrancy of the place can't help but give you a rush. And with more space and less artistic ground to cover, you won't have to stalk your favorite painting for months, waiting for its brief foray out of storage. Also, really important people, like Gainsborough, Constable, Hogarth, and Hockney, get a room to themselves, which should pacify the traditionalists.

Like all Britain's major arts institutions, open access is the mantra. The imposing wrought-iron gates have gone. The surrounding gardens have been transformed. And the guided tours, gallery talks (Mon–Fri 11:30am, 2:30, and 3:30pm, and Sun 3pm), auditorium lectures, and films, are mostly free—as it is to use the Art Trolley, designed to entertain kids aged 3 to 11, and available Sunday 2 to 5pm in term-time, all week during the holidays. Tate Britain also

---

**Traveling Inter-Tate**

Millbank Pier got the go-ahead last year, which means visitors will at last be able to take the most logical route, as the fish swims, between the two Tates—Bankside Pier was built ages ago. Transport bosses "hope" that inter-gallery hoppas and other river services will start from spring 2002, which is when work should complete at Millbank. Plans for the pier made it sound more like an art installation: 100 meters of welded steel, with light sculptures and fluorescent tubes underfoot, changing color with the tide.

---

**Finds  Picnic on Top of the World**

If you're not in the mood to wait in the long queue for a table at Café Level 7 at Tate Modern, smuggle in your own sarnies and sodas, ride the elevator to the seventh floor, and then walk along the viewing corridor to the opposite side of the old power station. There's a bizarrely empty room there with a stupendous three-way panorama. Nobody will bat an eyelid if you hunker down and tuck in. In fact they'll be horribly envious.

---

has shops, a good cafe and espresso bar, and a well-regarded but pricey restaurant. If you're peckish, check out Tate Modern instead.

Millbank, SW1. ✆ **020/7887-8000**, 020/7887-8888 for events. www.tate.org.uk. Permanent collection free; temporary exhibitions £6.50–£8.50 ($9.45–$12.35) adults, £4.50–£5.50 ($6.55–$8) concessions, £17.50–£22.50 ($23.40–$32.65) family ticket. Daily 10am–5:50pm. Closed Dec 24–26. Tube: Pimlico. River services: Millbank Pier.

**Tate Modern** ★★★   Perhaps the biggest fillip for this fantastic new gallery came in the form of a backhanded compliment from an old enemy across the Channel. Who'd have imagined the French press would turn on their government for not making the reopening of the famous Pompidou Centre as big a success! The furore has been phenomenal. But then, so is Tate Modern, London's first new standalone space on this scale for hundreds of years—there are already plans to double the size with a new extension. The defunct Bankside Power Station has been reborn as a cathedral of modern art. Except for a 2-story glass addition on the roof, the vast bunker-like facade looks much as it ever did, right down to the London grime. Then you enter the building, down a ramp into the old turbine hall. Left empty, its huge dimensions (500 feet long by 100 feet high) make you feel like Gulliver in *Brobdingnag*. Three floors of ultra-plain white galleries allow 60% of the collection to be on view—almost as much as used to be in storage. The work is arranged thematically rather than chronologically: **Landscape/Matter/Environment, Still Life/Object/Real Life, History/Memory/Society,** and **Nude/Action/Body.** In some rooms, paintings are next to sculptures next to installations. Others are devoted to a single artist—like the marvelous Joseph Beuys sculptures. The display concept is certainly challenging, but the themes often seem spurious, lacking the quirky spirit of a mixed private collection where one person's taste is the guide.

There's no such thing as a flash visit to Tate Modern. Set aside half a day if you can. Free guided tours start daily at 10:30, 11:30am, 2:30, and 3:30pm, each focusing one of the four themes. There's also a busy talks program (usually £6/$8.70; free talks weekdays at 1pm); music; and children's workshops and storytelling sessions. But if you only do one thing at Tate Modern, go up to the glass-roofed level seven to see the spectacular views across the Thames. The cafe there is often mobbed so time your visit for early mealtimes and during the week. It is also open for dinner until 9:30pm on Friday and Saturday but doesn't take bookings.

Bankside, SE1. ✆ **020/7887-8000**, 020/7887-8888 for events. www.tate.org.uk. Permanent collection free; temporary exhibitions £5.50–£8.50 ($8–$12.35) adults, £3.50–£6.50 ($5.10–$9.45) concessions, £17.50–£22.50 ($23.40–$32.65) family ticket. Sun–Thurs 10am–6pm; Fri–Sat 10am–10pm; galleries open at 10:15am. Closed Dec 24–26. Tube: Southwark, Mansion House, and St. Paul's (cross over Millennium Bridge). River services: Bankside Pier.

**Tower Bridge Experience** ★★ (Kids)   Here's a London landmark you must not miss—possibly the most celebrated and photographed bridge in the world, and a reminder never to underestimate the English in a business deal. A certain American tried to buy it, but asked for London Bridge by mistake, as he discovered when he unpacked his enormous parcel to find nary a tower in sight. Despite its Gothic appearance, Tower Bridge dates from 1894, and the twin towers are made of steel clad in stone. Inside, interactive exhibits trace its history and construction and, in the south tower, you can see the old (pre-1976) hydraulics used to raise and lower the bridge—not that big a thrill unless you're an engineer. It uses electrical power now, and about five ships a day pass through in the summer months. The views from the pedestrian walkways are glorious, to St. Paul's, the Tower, and the distant Houses of Parliament. There is no set schedule for raising the bridge but you can call up one day ahead to find out when large boats are due to pass beneath it.

London SE1. ✆ 020/7403-3761. www.towerbridge.org.uk. Admission £6.25 ($9.05) adults, £4.25 ($6.15) seniors and under-16s, £18.25 ($26.45). Apr–Oct daily 10am–6:30pm; Nov–Mar daily 9:30am–6pm. Last entry is 1¼ hr. before closing. Closed Dec 25–26. Tube: Tower Hill, London Bridge. River services: Tower Pier.

**Tower of London** ★★★ (Kids)   This is the most perfectly preserved medieval fortress in Britain and you'll need at least 2 or 3 hours for a maximum impact visit. Especially as the restored New Armouries building has opened as a delicious and good value cafe.

Over the centuries, the Tower has served as a palace and royal refuge; a prison, military base, and supplies depot; home to the Royal Mint and the Royal Observatory; and finally a national monument. It has only twice come into practical use since the late 19th century: in World War I, 11 spies were executed here; then, in World War II, Rudolph Hess was a prisoner here for 4 days, and another spy got his just desserts. The oldest part is the massive White Tower, built in 1078 by the Norman king, William the Conqueror, to protect London and discourage rebellion among his new Saxon subjects. Every king after him added to the main structure, so that when Edward I completed the outer walls in the late 13th century, they enclosed an 18-acre square. Walk round the top of them for a bird's-eye view of how the Tower of London would have looked in its heyday.

The **Crown Jewels,** glittering in the Jewel House in Waterloo Barracks, are the real must-see. No words can do justice to the Imperial State Crown,

---

### The Ceremony of the Keys

Every night for 700 years, the guards have secured the Tower of London with the **Ceremony of the Keys.** The chief yeoman warder marches out across the causeway at 10 o'clock precisely to lock the entrance gate, then returns with the guard to do the same at the Byward Tower. As the pair approaches the Bloody Tower, the sentry cries, "Halt, who goes there?" and the chief yeoman warder replies "The Keys." "Whose keys?" comes the demand. "Queen Elizabeth's keys." The sentry presents arms, and the chief warder raises his Tudor bonnet, yelling, "God preserve Queen Elizabeth." The ritual ends with a rousing "amen" from the whole guard. Tickets to see it are free. Write at least 1 month in advance, enclosing an International Reply Coupon, to: Ceremony of the Keys, 2nd floor, Waterloo Block, HM Tower of London, London EC3N 4AB.

encrusted with 3,200 precious stones, including a 317-carat diamond. A moving walkway is meant to keep visitors flowing through, but it can still be a long wait. The **Martin Tower** exhibition tells the stories of two of the world's most famous diamonds, the Koh-i-Noor and Cullinan II, as well as of a botched attempt to steal the State regalia in the late 17th century.

Visitors with a more ghoulish bent should start at The Chapel Royal of St. Peter ad Vincula, which contains the graves of all the unfortunates executed at the Tower. The Scaffold Site, where the axeman dispatched seven of the highest-ranking victims, including Henry VIII's wives, Anne Boleyn and Catherine Howard, is just outside. Everyone else met their end on Tower Green. Imagine their terror as they arrived by boat at the dread **Traitors' Gate.** The **Bloody Tower** was where Richard of Gloucester locked up his young nephews while he usurped his crusading brother Edward IV. The princes' bodies were later mysteriously found by the White Tower. Today, an exhibit recreates how Sir Walter Raleigh might have lived during his 13-year imprisonment after the Gunpowder Plot against James I.

The royal menagerie moved out in 1834 to form the new London Zoo—all except the **ravens.** Legend has it Charles II was told that if they ever left the Tower the monarchy would fall. Ever since, a few birds have been kept in a lodging next to Wakefield Tower, looked after by a yeoman warder. The **yeoman warders,** or Beefeaters, have guarded the Tower for centuries. Now usually retired soldiers, they lead tours every half hour from 9:30am to 3:30pm and give vivid talks at 9:30, 10:15, 11:30am, 2:15, 4:30, and 5:15pm (the first one on Sun is at 10:30am). Costumed guides also recreate historic happenings.

As well as the daily **Ceremony of the Keys** (see box), there's a diary of State events and gun salutes. Call for info. **Beating the Bounds** takes place every third year on Ascension Day, the Thursday 40 days after Easter. The Chief Yeoman Warder leads 31 choirboys around the 31 parish boundary marks in the surrounding streets, beating each one with willow wands, to signal the Tower's independence from the jurisdiction of the city.

Tower Hill, EC3. © 020/7709-0765. www.hrp.org.uk. Admission £11.30 ($16.40) adults, £8.50 ($12.35) students and seniors, £7.50 ($10.90) under-16s, £34 ($49.30) family ticket. Mar–Oct Mon–Sat 9am–5pm, Sun 10am–5pm; Nov–Feb Tues–Sat 9am–4pm, Sun–Mon 10am–4pm. Last tickets sold 1hr. before closing. Last entry to buildings 30 min. before closing. Closed Jan 1, Dec 24–26. Tube: Tower Hill. DLR: Tower Gateway. River services: Tower Pier.

## Victoria & Albert Museum 🎭🎭

Even the staff drop bread crumbs to find their way around this labyrinthine treasure house. Plans to extend the 7 miles of galleries devoted to the decorative and fine arts with an ultra-modern, and ultra-controversial, new building have hit a brick wall: the V&A has asked architect Daniel Libeskind to scale down his design for the Spiral to cut costs. In the meantime, the **British Galleries** were due to reopen in November 2001 after a £31-million overhaul. Allegedly, the patriarchal approach is history: no more dazzling the hoi-polloi with treasures protected in glass cases, not in these 15 rooms at least Instead, there'll be pieces to handle, video re-creations of how they were used, and commentaries on taste by historical figures and today's top designers. Iconic objects, such as the Great Bed of Ware, which Shakespeare mentions in *Twelfth Night,* will tell the story of Britain's 400-year rise (1500–1900) to world power and cultural authority. The V&A will also be able to show millions of objects previously stored in its West London storehouse.

Once you've "done" the British Galleries, you'll want to cherry-pick the highlights from the rest of the V&A's collections: the designer frocks in the **Costume**

**Gallery,** textiles, sculpture, furniture, prints, paintings, photographs, silver, glass, ceramics, and jewelry, from Britain and all over the world. Not only is the museum worth a good long visit, but there are so many regular activities you'll want to keep coming back. Free guided tours take place daily on the hour, 10:30am to 3:30pm, plus 4:30pm on Wednesday. Specialist gallery talks start at 1pm. There are art and craft demonstrations every Saturday from 2 to 5pm. Late View, starting at 6:30pm every Wednesday and the last Friday of the month, is a jamboree of lectures (plus £5/$8), exhibitions, entry into certain galleries, and live music. Tickets cost £8 ($11.60) adults, £5 ($7.20) students.

Cromwell Rd., SW7. ⓒ **020/7942-2000,** 020/7942-2209 events. www.vam.ac.uk. Admission free. Thurs–Tues 10am–5:45pm; Wed and last Fri each mo. 10am–10pm. Closed Dec 24–26. Tube: South Kensington.

**Westminster Abbey** ★★★    St. Peter ordered Sebert, king of the East Saxons, to build the first church here in the 7th century and then materialized at the consecration. No wonder the devout Edward the Confessor chose the site to found his new abbey (1065). This is neither a cathedral nor a parish church, but a "royal peculiar," under the jurisdiction of the dean and chapter, and subject only to the sovereign.

Largely dating from the 13th to 16th centuries, Westminster Abbey has played a prominent part in British history—most recently, with the funeral of Princess Diana. Every coronation since 1066 has taken place here. The oak **Coronation Chair** was made in 1308 for Edward I and it held the ancient Stone of Scone, on which the kings of Scotland were crowned. The English seized the stone in 1296 and refused to return it until a couple of years ago. Visit the **Norman Undercroft,** to see the replica coronation regalia. Five kings and four queens are buried near the Shrine of Edward the Confessor, which is behind the high altar. Geoffrey Chaucer sowed the seeds for **Poets' Corner** when he was buried here in 1400—in his case, because he worked for the abbey. Ben Jonson is there, as well as Dryden, Samuel Johnson, Sheridan, Browning, and Tennyson. The practice of putting up literary memorials began in earnest in the 18th century with a full-length figure of Shakespeare, but the sinner Oscar Wilde didn't get a memorial window until 1995. Now there are historical figures from every field. The **Tomb of the Unknown Soldier** honors the fallen of World War I. The nameless man lies under Belgian stone in soil brought back from the battlefields of France. Above the West Door, on the outside, you'll see the tradition of commemoration still continues with the **statues of 20th-century martyrs** such as Martin Luther King and Maximilian Kolbe, the Catholic priest who died at Auschwitz.

Guided tours of the abbey, lead by the vergers, cost £3 ($4.35). These start at 10, 10:30, 11am, 2, 2:30, and 3pm (not Fri) during the week April through October; at 10, 11am, 2, and 3pm (2:30pm on Fri) on winter weekdays; and at 10, 10:30, and 11am on Saturday year-round. It's best to book. Audio guides are only £2 ($2.90). With both, you get discounted entry to the **Chapter House** (1245–55) in the east cloister, the nearby **Pyx Chamber,** and the **Abbey Museum,** all under the care of English Heritage. Call the abbey for a diary of concerts and talks.

Dean's Yard, SW1. ⓒ **020/7222-5152,** 020/7222-5897 Chapter House, or 020/7233-0019 Pyx Chamber and Abbey Museum. www.westminster-abbey.org. Admission £5 ($7.20) adults, £3 ($4.35) seniors and students, £2 ($2.90) under-16s, £10 ($14.50) family ticket. Chamber House, Pyx Chamber, and Abbey Museum £2.50 ($3.65) adults, £1.90 ($2.75) seniors and students, £1.30 ($1.90) under-16s; reduced with Abbey admission, free with guided and audio tour. Cloisters, College Garden, St. Margaret's Church free. Abbey Mon–Fri 9:30am–4:45pm; Sat 9:30am–2:45pm; last admission 1hr. before closing, Sun for worship. Chapter House Apr–Sept 9:30am–5:30pm; Oct 10am–5pm; Nov–Mar 10am–4pm. Pyx Chamber and Abbey Museum daily

10:30am–4pm. Cloisters 8am–6pm. College Garden Apr–Sept 10am–6pm; Oct–Mar 10am–4pm. St. Margaret's Church Mon–Fri 9:30am–3:45pm; Sat 9:30am–1:45pm; Sun 2–5pm. Tube: Westminster.

## 3 Churches, Cathedrals & a Cemetery

Many of the churches listed below put on lunchtime concerts. Tickets are usually free, although it's customary to leave a small donation. The **City Information Centre**, St. Paul's Churchyard, EC4 (☎ **020/7332-1456**) can give you a full list. It's open from 9:30am to 5pm, daily April through September and weekdays October through March, and 9:30am to 12:30pm on winter Saturdays.

**Brompton Oratory** ★    The priests of the Institute of the Oratory, founded by St. Philip Neri, serve this amazing church, which architect Herbert Gribble modeled after the Chiesa Nova in Rome. Completed in 1884, its baroque extravagance marked the revival of the long disenfranchised English Catholicism. The marble statues of the apostles are by Mazzuoli and were originally in Siena Cathedral. The Oratory is famous for its beautiful musical services—the organ has nearly 4,000 pipes—and for the Latin mass, sung at 11am on Sunday.

Thurloe Place, Brompton Rd., SW7. ☎ **020/7808-0900**. Free admission. Daily 6:30am–8pm. Tube: South Kensington.

**Highgate Cemetery** ★★    Serpentine pathways wind through this beautiful cemetery, which opened in 1829 and became fashionable so fast that a new graveyard had to be consecrated on the other side of Swain's Lane only 3 decades later. You have to take a tour to visit the old western cemetery. Victorian funerary rituals were extraordinarily elaborate—witness the tomb-lined Egyptian Avenue, which leads up to the catacombs in the Circle of Lebanon. Scientist Michael Faraday, poet Christina Rossetti, and many other famous figures are buried here in an atmosphere that is part fright-night movie, part woodsy wildlife sanctuary. The grave of Karl Marx, marked by a gargantuan bust, lies in the eastern cemetery. Here you'll also find novelist George Eliot, whose real name was Mary Anne Evans, and Farzad Bazoft, the *Observer* journalist killed by Iranian terrorists. Please remember the cemetery is still very much in use. No children under 8 can enter the western side, and you have to buy a permit to use a camera—no video allowed.

Swain's Lane, N6. ☎ **020/8340-1834**. East Cemetery £2 ($2.90); West Cemetery £3 ($4.35); £1 ($1.45) to bring a small camera. East Cemetery Apr–Oct Mon–Fri 10am–5pm, Sat–Sun 11am–5pm; Nov–Mar closes at 4pm. West Cemetery tours Apr–Oct Mon–Fri at noon, 2, and 4pm, Sat–Sun also at 11am, 1, and 3pm; Nov–Mar Sat–Sun at noon, 1, 2, and 3pm. Tube: Archway. No under-8s in the West Cemetery.

**St. Bride's Church**    St. Bride's is in Fleet Street, once the heart of Britain's newspaper industry, which is why it is known as the "journalists' and printers' church." An archaeological dig, carried out after the 1940 bombing, discovered a Roman house preserved in the crypt—there's a museum there now. St. Brigit of Ireland founded the first Christian church here, and the present one is the eighth on the site. After the Great Fire, Sir Christopher Wren supervised the rebuilding, which cost £11,430. The spire was added later. This "madrigal in stone"—four octagonal tiers capped by an obelisk, itself topped off with a ball and vane—is 234 feet tall and supposedly inspired the wedding cakes of a 17th-century Fleet Street pastry cook. St. Bride's has had many famous parishioners, including writers John Dryden, John Milton, Richard Lovelace, and John Evelyn. The diarist Samuel Pepys and his eight siblings were all baptized at St. Bride's. There are half-hour concerts every Tuesday and Friday.

Fleet St., EC4. ☎ **020/7427-0133**. Free admission. Mon–Fri 8:30am–4:30pm; Sat 9:30am–4:30pm; Sun 9:30am–12:30pm and 5:30–7:30pm. Concerts at 1:15pm on Tues and Fri. Tube: Blackfriars.

**St. Clement Danes**   No one knows for certain where the "Danes" comes from, but there was a wooden Saxon church on this site. Rebuilt in stone in the late 10th century, it survived the Great Fire but was declared unsafe. Sir Christopher Wren (him again!) was commissioned to rebuild it, though James Gibbs designed the spire. Samuel Johnson attended services regularly and the wife of poet John Donne is buried here. Gutted in the Blitz, St. Clement's was rebuilt in the late 1950s and underwent another big renovation in 1999. This is the RAF's church and contains memorials to the British, Commonwealth, and American airmen who flew in World War II. It is also thought by some people to be the church immortalized in the nursery rhyme, "Oranges and lemons say the bells of St. Clement's." (In fact, the rhyme probably refers to St. Clement Eastcheap, which is on the riverfront where citrus fruits were unloaded.)

Strand, WC2. ℭ **020/7242-8282**. Free admission. Daily 8:30am–4:30pm. Tube: Temple (closed Sun), Charing Cross, Blackfriars.

**St. James's Church, Piccadilly** ✮   In the late 17th century, the thriving city expanded its western borders into a new aristocratic enclave known as St. James's. Its patrons naturally commissioned Sir Christopher Wren to build their parish church, while Grinling Gibbons carved the reredos, organ case, and font. Diarist John Evelyn wrote, "There is no altar anywhere in England, nor has there been any abroad, more handsomely adorned." As might be expected, this church has rich historical associations. William Blake, the poet and artist, and William Pitt, who became England's youngest prime minister at age 24, were both baptized at St. James's. Caricaturist James Gillray, auctioneer James Christie, and coffeehouse founder Francis White are all buried here. The church has seen some colorful weddings, too—none more so than that of explorer Sir Samuel Baker to a woman he bought at a Turkish slave auction. St. James's holds lunchtime recitals on Monday, Wednesday, and Friday, and has an irregular program of inexpensive evening concerts and talks. The market is a bit of a scrum, but worth a look for odd little gifts amid the crafty kitsch.

197 Piccadilly, W1. ℭ **020/7734-4511**. Free admission. Daily 8am–7pm. Recitals Mon, Wed, and Fri at 1:10pm. Courtyard market: antiques Tues, crafts and souvenirs Wed–Sat. Tube: Piccadilly Circus, Green Park.

**St. Martin-in-the-Fields** ✮   This church is one of the best-loved in London. The current building dates from 1726. Designed by James Gibbs, the intricate plasterwork ceiling enhances the simple nave. Curiously, the parish boundary passes through the middle of Buckingham Palace, and the names of many royal children appear on the baptismal registry. The Queen Mother, who lives at Clarence House, is a parishioner. St. Martin's is famous for its music: Handel played the organ here, though not the current 3,637-pipe instrument, which was installed in 1990. There are free concerts at 1:05pm on Monday, Tuesday, and Friday. Evening recitals take place from Thursday to Saturday. Many are by candlelight, and the program leans heavily toward the baroque. The choral music during the three Sunday services is sublime. Evensong is the most quintessentially Anglican, usually at 5pm, but call ahead for specific times.

In the crypt of St. Martin's is the **London Brass Rubbing Centre,** which has about 100 medieval and Tudor church brasses as well as unusual Celtic patterns and early woodcuts of the zodiac. Materials and instruction are provided, and it's great fun. The gift shop stocks Celtic jewelry as well as courtly mementos, and many of the artworks in the crypt gallery are also for sale. If you have time, take a break for tea or a delicious meal at **The Café in the Crypt** (see chapter 5).

Trafalgar Sq., WC2. ℂ **020/7766-1100** for church info, 020/7839-8362 for box office, or 020/7930-9306 London Brass Rubbing Centre. www.stmartin-in-the-fields.org. Free admission to church and lunchtime recitals; evening concerts £6–£17 ($13.90–$24.65). Brass rubbings £2–£15 ($2.90–$21.75), £1 ($1.45) discount under-12s. Church daily 9am–6pm (except during services); London Brass Rubbing Centre Mon–Sat 10am–6pm, Sun noon–6pm. Tube: Charing Cross, Leicester Sq.

**St. Mary Le Bow**   Traditionally, to be a true Cockney, you have to be born within the sound of Bow bells—the ones that ring at this church. St. Mary's colorful history has been marked by a series of bizarre incidents. The first happened in 1091, when a storm ripped off the roof. Then, in 1271, the church tower collapsed, killing 20 people. In 1331, Queen Philippa and her ladies-in-waiting plummeted to the ground when a wooden balcony collapsed during a joust to celebrate the birth of the Black Prince. The Great Fire destroyed the church, and it was rebuilt by the great architect Wren—not a disaster, of course. St. Mary's was rededicated in 1964 after a big restoration. As well as the Thursday lunchtime concerts, the rector holds discussions with an intriguing range of guests, from museum curators to movie directors and representatives of other faiths, every Tuesday during school terms.

Cheapside, EC2. ℂ **020/7248-5139.** Free admission. Mon–Thurs 6:30am–6pm; Fri 6:30am–4pm. Lunchtime concerts Thurs 1:05pm. Dialogues Tues 1:05pm during school terms. Closed major holidays and the week after Christmas and Easter. Tube: St. Paul's, Bank, Mansion House.

**St. Paul's, The Actors' Church**   The Drury Lane Theatre, the Theatre Royal, and the Royal Opera House are all within the parish of St. Paul's, so it's little wonder that it has become known as the actors' church. Inside, you'll find dozens of memorial plaques dedicated to such thespian luminaries as Vivien Leigh, Boris Karloff, and Noël Coward, to name but a few. It is also the last resting place of wood-carver Grinling Gibbons, writer Samuel Butler, and the doctor's daughter Margaret Ponteous, who was the first victim of the Great Plague in 1665. Famous baptisms here have included that of landscape painter J. M. W. Turner and librettist W. S. Gilbert. Despite substantial and repeated restoration work over the years, particularly after a fire in 1795, the church is still largely how Inigo Jones designed it for the Earl of Bedford in the 17th century, with its quiet garden piazza in the rear. St. Paul's celebrates the Eucharist at 11am on Sunday. Every second Sunday of the month, there is choral evensong at 4pm.

Bedford St., WC2. ℂ **020/7836-5221.** Free admission. Mon–Fri 8:30am–4:30pm; Sun 9:30am–12:30pm. Tube: Covent Garden.

**Southwark Cathedral** ⍟   Archaeological evidence proves this to have been a place of worship for more than 1,000 years. The present church dates from the 15th century, though it was partially rebuilt in 1890. And it has just had a £10 million makeover: the stonework is clean of London grime and floodlit; the riverside courtyard has been cleared of the modern offices; and an exciting new visitor center has opened to teach people about the history of Southwark. In medieval times, this was the outlaw borough "of players and poets, prostitutes, paupers and prisons, pilgrims and patients." It was also the first stop on the pilgrimage to Canterbury, as immortalized by Chaucer's Tales. Chaucer and Shakespeare both worshiped here—don't miss the Bard's carved memorial. The cathedral has seen many important historical events, from the marriage of James I of Scotland and Mary Beaufort in 1424, to the Tudor Bishop of Winchester's consistory court, which condemned seven of the Marian martyrs to death. Southwark Cathedral has a notable choir, so it's worth attending a service here just for the music. Otherwise, there are free concerts every Thursday at 1pm and a program of other events. In the summer, tables are put out in the courtyard, which makes a very nice pit-stop on a day out in Southwark and Bankside.

Montague Close, London Bridge, SE1. © 020/7367-6700. www.dswark.org. Exhibition £3 ($4.35) adults, £2.50 ($3.65) concessions, £1.50 ($2.20) children; audio tour £2.50 ($3.65) adults, £2 ($2.90) concessions, £1.25 ($2) children; joint price £5 ($7.25), £4 ($5.80), or £2.50 ($3.65), and £12.50 ($18.15) family. Mon–Sat 10am–6pm; Sun 11am–5pm. Tube: London Bridge. River services: London Bridge City.

**Wesley's Chapel, House & Museum**    John Wesley, the founder of Methodism, established this chapel in 1778 as his London base. There's a day-long service every year on November 1 to celebrate the occasion, and another on May 24 to mark his full conversion. This simple man, who traveled around England on horseback and preached in the open air, is buried in a grave behind the chapel. The building somehow survived the Blitz but later fell into serious disrepair, until a major restoration in the 1970s. The museum in the crypt traces the history of Methodism. Look out for Wesley's bizarre experimental machine for electric shock treatment. Across the road in **Bunhill Fields** is the Dissenters Graveyard where Daniel Defoe, William Blake, and John Bunyan are buried. Come here for one of the Tuesday lunchtime music recitals.

49 City Rd., EC1. © 020/7253-2262. Chapel is free; house and museum £4 ($5.80) adults, £2 ($2.90) under-18s. House (audio-guide) and museum Mon–Sat 10am–4pm (closed Thurs 12:45–1:30pm, worshippers welcome); Sun noon–2pm. Music recital every Tues at 1:05pm. Tube: Old St., Moorgate.

**Westminster Cathedral** ✪    The land this cathedral stands on once belonged to the monks of Westminster Abbey, who used it for a market and feast-day fairs. After the dissolution of the monasteries under Henry VIII, it changed hands several times until 1882, when Cardinal Henry Edward Manning bought the land for what was to become the premier Roman Catholic church in Britain. John Francis Bentley designed the massive brick-and-stone edifice (1903)— 360 feet long and 156 feet wide—in spectacular Byzantine style. The richly decorated interior uses 100 different kinds of marble, and mosaics emblazon the chapels and the vaulting of the sanctuary. The controversial Stations of the Cross are the work of famous sculptor Eric Gill. One of the biggest thrills is taking the lift to the gallery at the top of the 273-foot-tall **campanile** ✪ for a fantastic panoramic view over London. Another is attending a free Sunday organ recital or sung mass. Music is an extremely important part of cathedral life and has been since composer Sir Edward Elgar premiered his celebrated choral work, the oratorio setting of Cardinal Newman's *The Dream of Gerontius* at its opening. Call for information on the concert program.

Ashley Place, SW1. © 020/7798-9055. www.westminstercathedral.org.uk. Cathedral and Sun organ recitals free; tower £2 ($2.90) adults, £1 ($1.45) under-16s. Cathedral, daily 7am–7pm; Campanile lift Apr–Nov daily 9am–5pm, Dec–Mar Thurs–Sun 9am–5pm. Tube: Victoria.

## 4 Memorials & Monuments

Since ancient times, nations have honored their heroes with imposing public memorials. And there can be few more imposing than **Nelson's Column,** the original model for which has just gone on display at the National Maritime Museum (see p. 198). The admiral's victory at the Battle of Trafalgar in 1805 staved off the French invasion and cost him his life. It took almost 40 years to complete the 185-foot Corinthian column, a copy of one in the temple of Mars

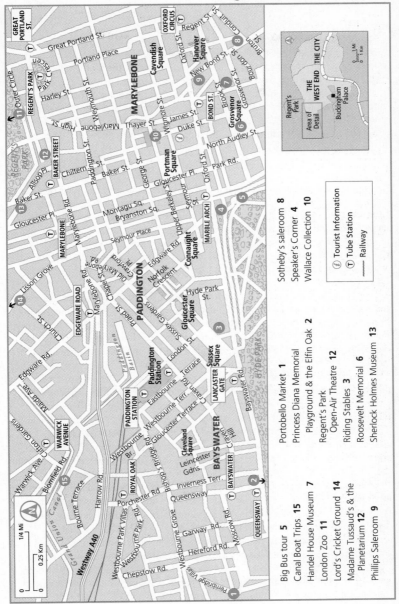

Sotheby's saleroom **8**
Speaker's Corner **4**
Wallace Collection **10**

_i_ Tourist Information
T Tube Station
—— Railway

Portobello Market **1**
Princess Diana Memorial
Playground & the Elfin Oak **2**
Regent's Park
Open-Air Theatre **12**
Riding Stables **3**
Roosevelt Memorial **6**
Sherlock Holmes Museum **13**

Big Bus tour **5**
Canal Boat Trips **15**
Handel House Museum **7**
London Zoo **11**
Lord's Cricket Ground **14**
Madame Tussaud's & the
Planetarium **12**
Phillips Saleroom **9**

Ultor (the Avenger) in Rome. Bronze reliefs on the sides of the pedestal commemorate Nelson's most famous battles. By the time Landseer's lions were added in 1867, their four empty plinths had become a standing joke, as is the one that has now been empty for 161 years while city grandees debate which famous person deserves such high-profile immortalization.

---

*Fun Fact*  **Size Matters**

Nelson's Column may be the most famous in the world, but **The Monument** is nearly 20-feet taller. Christopher Wren and Robert Hooke built it in 1677 to commemorate the Great Fire of London: the Doric column is 202 feet high, which matches the distance from Monument Street to the famous baker's shop in Pudding Lane. It is also a grueling 311-step climb to the viewing gallery at the top—not something Horatio can offer—but well worth it for the view over the City of London. Open 10am to 5:40pm daily; £1.50 ($2.20) adults, 50p (72¢). For info, call © 020/7626-2717, and take the Tube to Monument.

---

But plans to pedestrianize the north side of Trafalgar Square do seem to be moving on a pace. By 2003, you should be able to marvel at Nelson's Column from the National Gallery steps without bumper-to-bumper buses spoiling the view. This is the first phase of an urban renaissance project due to extend down to Parliament Square, sprucing up Whitehall on the way. That's where you'll find the **Cenotaph,** a very simple, but eloquent, memorial to the fallen of World Wars I and II. Designed by Sir Edwin Lutyens, it is the center of Remembrance Day ceremonies on November 11.

Last year, the Household Cavalry rode through **Wellington Arch** to celebrate the restoration of the Hyde Park Corner landmark. It was originally commissioned as a posh gateway to Buckingham Palace, and only later recycled as a memorial to Wellington's victory over Napoleon. The statue on top was ludicrously too big, so it was a huge relief when the arch had to move in 1882 to ease a bottleneck and Wellington could be sent off honorably to army HQ. The also-enormous *Peace Descending on the Quadriga of War* by Adrian Jones replaced it and looks spectacular with the bronze relieved of its wartime black paint. The arch was a police station for a while, but this is the first time the public can go inside and see the view from the top down Constitution Hill. There is also an exhibition about London's memorials and monuments. The arch is open Wednesday to Sunday from 10am to 6pm, closing earlier in winter, and tickets cost £2.50 ($3.65) adults, £1.90 ($2.75) concessions, and £1.30 ($1.90) for children (© 020 79302726; www.english-heritage.org.uk).

London's most extraordinary monument is the **Albert Memorial** in Kensington Gardens. Queen Victoria was so devastated by Albert's premature death from typhoid fever in 1861 that she withdrew from public life for more than a decade and wore her trademark black until she died in 1901. Unveiled in 1998 after a 10-year restoration, this Gothic icon is in better condition than when it was built to designs by Sir George Gilbert Scott. Gilding removed in World War I glows opulently once more, and craftsmen have carefully replaced missing statuary and mosaics. Railings protect the memorial, but you can take a guided tour behind them on Sundays at 2 and 3pm (© 020/7495-0916; www.tourguides.co.uk). Tickets cost £3.50 ($5.10) for adults, and £3 ($4.35) for concessions. No need to book.

Dedicated to Princess Diana, the **Peter Pan playground** in Kensington Gardens is a wonderland with a pirate galleon for children to scramble about on. This replaced the idea for a memorial garden, as locals feared they'd be besieged by hordes of pilgrims. **Westminster Abbey** and **St. Paul's Cathedral** both hold memorials to many famous people and events, as do the holy places listed in the section above.

## 5 Lots More Sights to See

## HISTORIC BUILDINGS

There is no charge to gawk at the notorious £300-a-roll Pugin-designed wallpaper now decorating the **Lord Chancellor's rooms** at the Palace of Westminster. But the tour waiting list is very long so you will need to call his private office (© **020/7219-4785**) and ask for a place on it 6 months ahead of your visit. A similar system operates at **Mansion House,** the official residence of the Lord Mayor of London. But, this time you must write to request tickets, to the Principal Assistant-Diary, Mansion House, London EC4N 8BH (© **020/7626-2500**). If you can't plan that far ahead, come anyway because this impressive Palladian building is well worth a look. Simply hop on the Tube to Bank.

**Banqueting House**     This is all that remains of the great Palace of Whitehall after the fire of 1698. A masterpiece of English Renaissance architecture (1619–22), it was designed by Inigo Jones for James I. The main hall was obviously for posh banqueting (as it still is today), hence the nine magnificent ceiling paintings by Rubens, depicting the Divine Right of Kings. You can also visit the undercroft (crypt), somewhere the king could get drunk with his mates. On a somber note, the bust of Charles I above the entrance reminds visitors that he was beheaded in front of the building. Combine a visit with watching the Changing of the Guard, at Horse Guards opposite (see p. 164).

Opposite Horse Guards Parade, Whitehall, SW1. © 020/7839-3787. www.hrp.org.uk. Admission £3.90 ($5.65) adults, £3.10 ($4.50) seniors and students, £2.30 ($3.35) under-16s. Mon–Sat 10am–5pm. Last admission 4pm. Closed Dec 24–Jan 1, Good Friday, and for government functions. Tube: Charing Cross, Embankment, Westminster.

**Cabinet War Rooms** ⭐⭐     This warren of underground rooms served as Churchill's nerve center and the secret HQ of the British government during World War II. It is preserved exactly as it was back then: the Cabinet Room, where the PM, his ministers, and military men made their crucial decisions; the Map Room, where they plotted out the progress of the war; the Telephone Room, where so many calls were placed to and received from FDR; even the PM's Emergency Bedroom. In 1995, the Heritage Lottery Fund bought the Churchill Papers for the nation. The core of the collection is held in Cambridge, but there are always pieces on display here—the exhibition space expanded last summer into several newly restored rooms. It is eerie and oddly exciting imagining the great man and his staff living their secret subterranean life.

Clive Steps, King Charles St., SW1. © 020/7930-6961. www.iwm.org.uk. Admission £5.40 ($7.85) adults, £3.90 ($5.65) students and seniors, free under-16s. Apr–Sept daily 9:30am–6pm (last admission 5:15pm); Oct–Mar daily 10–6pm (last admission 5:15pm). Closed Dec 24–26. Tube: Westminster, St. James's Park.

**Guildhall**     This has been the seat of government (for the City of London only, and not to be confused with Mayor Ken's mob) for more than 800 years. The Guildhall itself dates from 1411 and has the largest medieval crypt in a capital crawling with crypts. The building has been restored, with great care, on several occasions, notably after the Great Fire and the Blitz. Among the decorations are the banners of the 100 livery companies and inscriptions in the windows recording the names of all the lord mayors since 1189. Some of them also merit a monument, as do Churchill, Wellington, and Nelson. Statues of the legendary giants Gog and Magog guard the institution.

Off Gresham St., EC2. ✆ **020/7606-3030.** www.corpoflondon.gov.uk. Free admission. Apr–Sept daily; Oct–Mar Mon–Fri 9:30am–5pm, Sat 9:30am–12:30pm. Closed Jan 1, Good Friday, Easter Monday, Dec 24–26, and for ceremonial occasions. Tube: Bank.

**Jewel Tower**   Opposite the Houses of Parliament, this is one of only two sur-viving buildings from the medieval Palace of Westminster. It was built around 1365 so that Edward III had somewhere to stash his treasures. The exhibition explains how Parliament works, and runs a virtual-reality tour of both houses.

Abingdon St., Westminster, SW1. ✆ **020/7222-2219.** www.english-heritage.org.uk. Admission £1.60 ($2.30) adults, £1.20 ($1.74) seniors, 80p ($1.15) under-16s. Apr–Sept daily 10am–6pm; Oct daily 10am–5pm; Nov–Mar daily 10am–4pm. Closed Dec 24–26. Tube: Westminster.

**Rose Theatre Exhibition**   The Rose was assumed long gone until it was unearthed during the building of a new office block in 1989. Dating from 1587, it was the first-ever theater on Bankside (the medieval equivalent of the West End) and Kit Marlowe's stage. It's been preserved (under a pool of water) and opened to the public. While a video, narrated by actor Sir Ian McKellen, tells the story of the Rose, lights under the water illuminate the remains. The Trust hopes eventually to raise the money for a full excavation.

56 Park St., SE1. ✆ **020/7593-0026.** www.rosetheatre.org.uk. Admission £4 ($5.80) adults, £3 ($4.35) seniors and students, £2 ($3.20) under-16s, £10 ($14.50) family ticket. Daily 10am–5pm. Tube: London Bridge.

**Royal Hospital Chelsea**   Inspired by the Hôtel des Invalides in Paris, Charles II founded this dignified home for veteran soldiers in 1682. Hence the statue of the king, by Grinling Gibbons, in the courtyard. Sir Christopher Wren completed the buildings in 1692, and there's been little change since, except for minor work done by Robert Adam in the 18th century and the addition of Sir John Soane's stables in 1814. In the main block, you can look around the

---

*Moments*   **See British Justice Done . . . Allegedly**

You can witness mainly civil cases at the **Royal Courts of Justice,** in the Strand, WC2. Designed by G. E. Street, the neo-Gothic court buildings (1874–82) contain 3½ miles of corridors and more than 1,000 rooms. Sessions run from 10:30am to 1, and 2 to 4pm, Monday to Friday, except during August and September (✆ **020/7947-6000;** www. courtservice.gov.uk; Tube: Temple).

The nation's Central Criminal Court is in the City. Affectionately known as the **Old Bailey,** it has seen many famous trials, including those of Oscar Wilde, Lord Haw Haw, and the Yorkshire Ripper. Take a seat in one of the public viewing galleries to watch the bewigged bar-risters presenting their cases. The courts are on Newgate Street, EC4 (✆ **020/7248-3277;** Tube: St. Paul's). There's even a remnant of the original city walls down in the basement. Sessions keep the same hours as above; you can't take cameras, electronic equipment (mobile phone, pager, radio, and so on), large bags, food, or drink, and the court cannot look after anything for you, so leave all of the above at your hotel. No childen under 14.

museum, chapel, and hall, where the Duke of Wellington lay in state for a week in 1852. The east and west wings are dormitories for around 400 ex-servicemen pensioners, in blue uniforms for everyday, red on ceremonial occasions. The grounds play host to the annual Chelsea Flower Show (see p. 25).

Royal Hospital Rd., SW3. ℂ 020/7730-5282. Free admission. Mon–Sat 10am–noon and 2–4pm; Sun 2–4pm. Tube: Sloane Sq.

## MUSEUMS & GALLERIES

If you are interested in England's sporting history, check out the museums of cricket, rugby, and tennis in "Spectator Sports," later in this chapter.

**Bank of England Museum** ✪   Housed in the old Stock Office, designed in 1793 by Sir John Soane, the museum traces the history of the "Old Lady of Threadneedle Street" from its foundation by Royal Charter in 1694 to its role now as the nation's central bank. Gold glitters temptingly in ancient ingots and the modern market bar, and you can feel how heavy they are. There are also displays of bank notes, coins, and the pikes and muskets used to defend the bank. The private financial papers of such famous clients as the Duchess of Marlborough, George Washington, and Horatio Nelson are there for everyone to nosey through. One interactive presentation gives an intriguing insight into the intricacies of bank note design and production. Another lets you risk it all on the Dollar/Sterling Exchange market. Call ℂ **020/7601-5491** to find out about events at the museum, including special entry to the "inner sanctum"— the governors' and directors' entertaining rooms—during September's Open House Weekend (see "How to Plan Your Sightseeing," at the beginning of this chapter).

Threadneedle St., EC2. ℂ 020/7601-5545. www.bankofengland.co.uk. Free admission. Mon–Fri 10am–5pm, and 2nd Sat in Nov for Lord Mayor's Show. Closed bank holidays. Tube: Bank.

**Barbican Art Gallery**   This is the Barbican's main exhibition space, and from the end of February to April 2002, it will be celebrating the arts center's 20th birthday with a show on design and architecture. The gallery has an entertainingly eclectic brief, ranging from established artists to low culture surprises. Also in the diary for 2002 are: New Contemporaries, an exhibition of the hottest young art students around (May–June); Game On, which looks at Computer Graphics (July–Sept); and a show of fashion photography, Dressing Down (Sept–Oct). The Concourse Gallery on level "0" has been rechristened **The Curve**. Shows are free, tend to have a multicultural bent, and are open from 10am to 7:30pm on Monday, Wednesday, Friday, and Saturday, until 6pm on Tuesday and Thursday, and from noon to 7:30pm on Sunday.

Level 3, Barbican Centre, Silk St., EC2. ℂ 020/7382-7105. www.barbican.org.uk. Admission £6–£10 ($8.70–$14.50) adults; £4–£7.50 ($5.80–$10.90) students, seniors, and under-15s. Mon–Tues and Thurs–Sat 10am–6pm; Wed 10am–9pm; Sun noon–6pm. Tube: Barbican, Moorgate.

**British Library** ✪   This is the national research library responsible for Britain's printed archive. Legally, publishers must send in one copy of everything they produce. The new building in St. Pancras was one of the longest-running and problematic projects that London had ever seen, taking decades to come to completion. Designed by Colin St. John Wilson, critics first condemned it as an eyesore, and then changed their minds when it finally opened in 1998. It has three exhibition spaces. The **John Ritblat Gallery** displays the permanent collection of treasures brought from the library's old home, the British Museum:

the *Magna Carta,* Tyndale's *New Testament,* Shakespeare's first folio, and more (George III's library, given to the nation in 1823, is in a six-story, glass tower by the cafe). Throughout, there are audio stations where visitors can listen to poets and writers reading from their works—James Joyce from *Finnegan's Wake,* for example. Truly amazing, though, are the interactive exhibits that allow you to flip through an illuminated manuscript, such as Leonardo's *Notebooks.* A second gallery is used for temporary exhibitions, and the third, The Workshop of Words, Sounds & Images, traces the history of book production from the earliest written documents to the current digital revolution—and there are regular free book-craft demonstrations. Also in the busy events diary are free Monday lunchtime talks, based on the collections, and Friday lunchtime author visits and discussions held in the excellent British Library shop.

96 Euston Rd., NW1. ℂ 020/7412-7332. www.bl.uk. Free admission. Galleries and public areas Mon and Wed–Fri 9:30am–6pm; Tues 9:30am–8pm; Sat 9:30am–5pm; Sun 11am–5pm. Tours of public areas: Mon, Wed, Fri 3pm, Sat 10:30am and 3pm; tickets £5 ($7.25) adults, £3.50 ($5.10) concessions. Tours including a reading room: Tues 6:30pm, Sun 11:30am and 3pm; tickets £6 ($8.70), £4.50 ($6.55) concessions. Tube: Euston, King's Cross.

### Dali Universe
I love the Dali museum in his home town in Spain, but this gallery, curated by long-time friend and collector Benjamin Levi, is very underwhelming, certainly for an ignorant fan like me. The iconic pieces have a curiosity value—the voluptuous Mae West Lips sofa, now looking a little grubby, and the eyeball painting for the set of Hitchcock's *Spellbound.* Otherwise, I suspect you need to be an expert to appreciate the serried ranks of illustrations, drawings and paintings never seen before in Britain. Part of the problem is that the walls are painted black, which looks dusty and scruffy, like a nightclub during the daytime. This is also a poor backdrop for many of the metal sculptures. Surrealism works so much better in the Mediterranean sunshine!

County Hall, Riverside Building, SE1. ℂ 020/7620-2720. www.daliuniverse.com. Admission £8.50 ($12.35) adults, £6 ($8.70) concessions, £5 ($7.20) under-17s, £22 ($31.90) family. Daily 10:30am–5:30pm. Tube: Waterloo, Westminster. River services: Festival Pier.

### Dulwich Picture Gallery ★★
This is Britain's oldest public picture gallery, set up in 1817 to house a superb collection of European Old Masters—Canaletto, Gainsborough, Poussin, Rembrandt, Rubens, and Van Dyck—put together at the behest of the King of Poland for his national museum. Forced to abdicate before paying his English art dealer, he never took possession. Sir John Soane designed the beautiful original building, now linked by an airy glass cloister to a new wing, comprising extra exhibition space, a lecture hall, cafe, and working studio. Each year, three temporary exhibitions borrow important works from all over the world (contact the museum for details). Free gallery tours take place every Saturday and Sunday at 3pm. And there is a whole program of talks, concerts, evening events, and children's workshops.

Gallery Rd., SE21. ℂ 020/8693-5254. www.dulwichpicturegallery.org.uk. Admission £4 ($5.80) adults; £3 ($4.35) seniors, free concessions, students, and under-16s; free on Fri. Temporary exhibitions £2–£3 ($2.90–$4.35) plus admission. Tues–Fri 10am–5pm; Sat–Sun (bank holiday Mon) 11am–5pm. Closed Jan 1, Good Friday, and Dec 24–26. Tube: Brixton, then P4 bus. Train: West Dulwich.

### Florence Nightingale Museum ★
The reconstruction of a ward in Scutari Hospital in war-torn Crimea shows exactly the ghastly scene that fired Florence Nightingale's reforming zeal. She founded her School of Nursing here in 1860, dedicating her life to improving hospital standards and public health. You can see Nightingale's copious notebooks, as well as a bracelet she wore woven from

her mother's and sister's hair (there is more of her jewelry at the National Army Museum; see below). There are free guided tours every weekday, and entrance tickets are valid for a month.

St. Thomas' Hospital, 2 Lambeth Palace Rd., SE1. ℂ 020/7620-0374. www.florence-nightingale.co.uk. Admission £4.80 ($6.95) adults, £3.60 ($5.20) children and concessions. Mon–Fri 10am–5pm; Sat–Sun 11:30am–4:30pm; last admission 1hr. before closing. Closed Good Friday, Easter Sunday, Dec 25–Jan 2. Tube: Westminster, Waterloo.

## Geffrye Museum ★★    This gem of a museum is devoted to the home life of the English urban middle classes from 1600 to 2000. Based in the old Iron-mongers' almshouses (1715), separate rooms recreate each era down to the last detail, as though the occupant had just popped out. Time-travel past Elizabethan oak, fine Georgian aesthetics, and ornate Victoriana, to the 20th-century snapshots in the new wing. There you'll find Art Deco, post-war utility, the 1960s plastics explosion, even a 1990s loft conversion. December is magical as the rooms sparkle with festive decorations, bringing to life 400 years of Christmas tradition. As well as the original walled herb garden, a series of garden rooms trace the evolution of that green-fingered English passion. There's also a shop, restaurant, and a space dedicated to showcasing contemporary designers.

Kingsland Rd., E2. ℂ 020/7739-9893. www.geffrye-museum.org.uk. Free admission. Tues–Sat 10am–5pm; Sun and holidays noon–5pm. Closed Jan 1, Good Friday, and Dec 24–26. Herb garden and period garden rooms open Apr–Oct. Tube: Liverpool St., then no. 149 or 242 bus.

## Hayward Gallery ★★    This highly regarded modern art gallery is wedged between the Royal National Theatre and the Royal Festival Hall on the South Bank. Built in 1968 (the era of "brutalist" architecture!), it has one of the largest and most versatile spaces in Britain. Shows conform to one of four different for-mats: single artists, historical themes and artistic movements, other cultures, and contemporary. The 2002 highlights include an exhibition of Paul Klee paintings from all over the world, curated by Bridget Riley (Jan–Mar); in the summer, it will be work by American photographer Ansel Adams; and in the autumn, the first big gallery show for 1996 Turner Prize-winner Douglas Gordon. There are always linked events—talks, children's workshops, video-recorded interviews with the artist, and so on—and often live guides who are happy to chat about an exhibition. Come early on weekends, because the queues are staggering.

Belvedere Rd., SE1. ℂ 020/7960-4242. www.hayward-gallery.org.uk. Admission varies but is usually around £8 ($11.60) adults, £5.50 ($8) concessions, free under-17s out of school hours. Tues–Wed 10am–8pm; Thurs–Mon 10am–6pm. Tube: Waterloo, Embankment. River services: Festival Pier.

## Imperial War Museum ★★ Kids    The IWM excels in explaining and re-creating 20th-century conflicts, to honor those who fought in them and to make sure they never happen again. A clock in the basement keeps a grim tally of the human cost of war—over 100 million people now. The Holocaust Exhibition, opened in 2000, continues that tradition. Four years in the making, it uses historical material—a funeral cart from the Warsaw Ghetto, victims' diaries and photograph albums, part of a deportation railcar—to tell the story of Nazi persecution. Eighteen survivors have given their testimony, while other exhibits explain the spread of anti-Semitism across Europe after the First World War. This exhibit is not recommended for under-14s. Life in the trenches during that earlier conflict is the subject of another exhibit, as is the Blitz of WWII, which dramatically re-enacts an air raid with special effects, sound, and scents—clinical disinfectant, dusty old buildings, burnt wood and cooking at the tea stands serving the rescuers. The curators, who collect a lot of witness reminiscences, say

that smells are often the strongest memories. So they often use them to heighten reality, like the cheesy feet and body odor in the simulated submarine, which kids will love. The tales of espionage and dirty tricks in the excellent Secret War are thrilling too. There's a German Enigma machine and that essential bit of spy kit, invisible ink, as well as a recreation of the SAS operation to break the Iranian Embassy siege in 1980. Women in Uniform is due to open in Spring 2002. Call to find out about gallery talks, history evenings, and children's workshops.

Lambeth Rd., SE1. ✆ 020/7416-5320. www.iwm.org.uk. Admission free. Daily 10am–6pm. Closed Dec 24–26. Tube: Lambeth North, Waterloo.

**Institute of Contemporary Arts (ICA)** ✿  The publicly assisted ICA is a major forum for the avant-garde arts, with two galleries, as well as a theater, cinema, media center, cafe, bar, bookshop, and lecture program. Since it opened in 1948, many artists have held their first solo shows here. Among the more recent are Damien Hirst, Helen Chadwick, Gary Hume, and Steve McQueen. The ICA also hosts Beck's Futures, the largest art prize in the U.K., won in 2001 by Tim Stoner: the shortlist exhibition runs from March to May. The admission price is to cover the institute's day membership. If you are attending a movie or performance, you can take in the galleries at no extra cost.

The Mall, SW1. ✆ 020/7930-3647, 020/7930-6393 recorded info. www.ica.org.uk. Galleries Mon–Fri £1.50 ($2.20) adults, £1 ($1.45) seniors; Sat–Sun £2.50 ($4) adults, £2 ($3.20) seniors; free with cinema or show ticket. Daily noon–9:30pm. Tube: Piccadilly Circus, Charing Cross.

**Jewish Museum** ✿  This museum opens a window into the history and religious life of the Jewish community. The History Gallery has medieval notched, wooden tax receipts and loving cups presented to the lord mayors of London by the Spanish and Portuguese Synagogue. The exceptional Ceremonial Art Gallery houses ritual objects of great beauty like a 16th-century Italian synagogue ark, Nathan Meyer Rothschild's *Book of Esther,* and silver Torah bells crafted in London. The museum is very big on talks, family history workshops and children's events.

The sister **Jewish Museum,** The Sternberg Centre, 80 East End Rd., N3 (✆ **020/8349-1143**) traces the history of immigration and settlement in London, with displays like the reconstructions of East End tailoring and furniture workshops. A moving exhibition traces the life of one London-born Holocaust survivor. It is open 10:30am to 5pm Monday to Thursday and closes at 4:30pm on Sunday. Admission is £2 ($2.90) for adults, £1 ($1.45) concessions, and free for children. Also at the center is a shop, cafe, and a garden that grows one of every plant mentioned in the Bible.

129 Albert St., NW1. ✆ 020/7284-1997. Admission £3.50 ($5.10) adults, £2.50 ($3.65) seniors and children, £8 ($11.60) family ticket. Mon–Thurs 10am–4pm; Sun 10am–5pm. Closed Jewish and public holidays. Tube: Camden Town.

**London Transport Museum** ✿✿ *Kids*  This fantastic museum, in the old Covent Garden flower market, traces the 200-year history of public transport in London, from the days when cabs were horse-drawn and the pollution squelchy. Like a Noah's Ark for machinery, it has examples of just about everything, from omnibuses to trams to Tube trains, as well as paintings, posters, working models and interactive exhibits. Kids love it. Actors play characters like a 1906 tunnel miner and a World War II clippie (bus conductor to you). There's lots of stuff to pull and push. And the program of workshops during half-terms and holidays is usually free with admission. The museum even organizes guided London tours, with a transport bent, on the river, Tube, or bus (£10/$14.50). The shop is terrific, selling models, posters, and other original gifts.

The London Transport Museum can only display about 400 of the 370,000 items in its massive collection, so it has taken over a defunct Tube shed in West London for storage and as somewhere to work on conservation. On the last Friday of the month, there are guided tours of **The Depot.** Tickets cost £10 ($14.50), and you must book ahead. There are also a few open weekends each year, when you can explore the main shed and its vehicles, machinery, signs, and shelters, as well as enjoy the stalls and themed displays. Tickets cost £6.95 ($10.10). No need to book, just call for dates and take the Tube to Acton Town.

The Piazza, Covent Garden, WC2. ( ) 020/7565-7299 recorded info, or 020/7379-6344. www.ltmuseum.co.uk. Admission £5.95 ($8.65) adults, £3.95 ($5.75) concessions, free under-16s. Sat–Thurs 10am–6pm; Fri 11am–6pm (last admission 45 min. before closing). Closed Dec 24–26. Tube: Covent Garden, Charing Cross.

**Museum of Garden History** ⟨⟩    In a old church next to Lambeth Palace (the Archbishop of Canterbury's official residence), this museum is devoted to *the* quintessential British passion and the horticulturalists, botanists, and collectors who have nurtured it. Follow the lives of the royal gardeners to Charles I and II, John Tradescant and his son (also John), who are buried here. Or of noted English landscape designer Gertrude Jekyll (1843–1932), who is perhaps best-known through her collaboration with architect Sir Edwin Lutyens. The museum's own patch is planted in a 17th-century Knot Garden design and contains many rare plants introduced into the country by the Tradescants. Captain Bligh of mutiny fame is buried here too, and John Smith who married Pocohontas. Green-fingered enthusiasts would enjoy the weekday evening lectures, which cost £8 to £13.50 ($11.60–$19.60).

St. Mary-at-Lambeth, Lambeth Palace Rd., SE1. ( ) 020/7401-8865. www.museumgardenhistory.org. Free admission, donation invited £2.50 ($3.65) adults, £2 ($2.90) concessions. Sun–Fri 10:30am–5pm. Closed mid-Dec to late Feb. Tube: Lambeth North.

**Museum of London** ⟨⟩⟨⟩ *Kids*    The folks behind the scenes have begun a 5-year redevelopment by dusting down 2,000 objects, many previously unseen, to go into a new World City Gallery. Opening in December 2001, this traces London's development between 1789 and 1914 into the first great metropolis of the industrial age. From July 2002, London before London will rewind history to look at life before the Romans, when hippos and elephants roamed Trafalgar Square.

Not only is this the biggest and most comprehensive city museum in the world, but it is genuinely engaging and creative. Among the highlights are a reconstruction of a Roman interior; a bedroom in a merchant's house from the Stuart period; the lord mayor's coach; a brilliant, audio-visual, dioramic presentation on the Great Fire with a voiceover reading diarist Samuel Pepys' account; a Victorian barber's shop; and the original elevators from Selfridges department store. The museum's archaeologists get called in at the start of most big building projects in London and their finds generally go on display once the study and conservation process is completed. Every year, there are three big temporary exhibitions often looking at the social culture of the modern city. Many of the resident experts take part in the talks, museum tours, and workshops program (free to £5/$7.25), as well as leading London walks and outside visits (£3–£10/$4.35–$14.50). And early in 2002, the open-door policy begins at the museum's storage facility in East London. The huge former warehouse will be like a 3-D reference library, with curators explaining their work and leading tours.

150 London Wall, EC2. ℂ 020/7600-3699. www.museumoflondon.org.uk. Admission £5 ($11.60) adults, £3 ($4.35) seniors, free under-16s; free from 4:30pm. Tickets valid 1yr. Mon–Sat 10am–5:50pm; Sun noon–5:50pm. Tube: St. Paul's, Moorgate, Barbican.

**National Army Museum**   This is the British Army's own museum and tells the soldier's story, starting from 1415. It is crammed with life-size models, medals, paintings of battle scenes by Gainsborough and Reynolds, weapons, and uniforms. Among the highlights are a 420-square-foot model of the Battle of Waterloo; the skeleton of Napoleon's horse, Marengo; and the saw that was used to amputate the leg of Lieutenant-General, the Earl of Uxbridge during the battle. Even more offbeat is the now-stuffed cat brought back from Sebastopol by a sentimental officer during the Crimean War. Each exhibit aims to let you inside the soldiers' everyday lives—Henry V's archers shivering at Agincourt, Wellington's troops standing shoulder to shoulder at Waterloo, and British Tommies scrambling over the top at the Somme. Visitors can experience what it was like in a World War I trench, as well as try on an excruciatingly uncomfortable civil war helmet, or test the crushing weight of a cannonball. One exhibition focuses on the contribution women have made to the army and armed conflict. The new Modern Army Gallery focuses on today's high-tech military force. Lunchtime talks take place most Thursdays at 1pm.

Royal Hospital Rd., Chelsea, SW3. ℂ 020/7730-0717. www.national-army-museum.ac.uk. Free admission. Daily 10am–5:30pm. Closed Jan 1, Good Friday, early May, Dec 24–26, public holiday. Tube: Sloane Sq.

**National Portrait Gallery** ★★   Celebrity vanity and the paparazzo spirit are clearly nothing new, evidenced by this gallery of 10,000 paintings and 250,000 photographs. It charts the history of the nation through its famous faces. The curators have consigned Helmut Newton's portrait of Margaret Thatcher, among others, to the historical section, to make room for such right-now icons as David Beckham (Posh Spice's footballer husband) and *Harry Potter* author J. K. Rowling. The flow through the gallery is much improved by the bright white Ondaatje Wing, built in a courtyard pinched from the neighboring National Gallery. The permanent collection is displayed chronologically. You'll find Henry VII, Henry VIII, and Sir Thomas More, all painted by Holbein; the only extant portrait of Shakespeare; and T.S. Eliot by Sir Jacob Epstein. There are endearing amateur daubs, too, including one of Jane Austen by her sister. Temporary exhibitions take on big themes and single artists. Upcoming exhibitions include *Self-Portraits by Women Artists* and *Saving Faces,* portraits painted by Mark Gilbert of patients before and after reconstructive facial surgery for the charity.

The NPG puts on free lectures and events, on a huge range of topics, on Tuesday and Thursday lunchtimes and weekend afternoons. Thursday evening lectures mostly start at 7pm (free–£3/$4.35). On Friday at 6:30pm, there are free musical events. As well as the cafe, there is the stunning **Portrait Restaurant & Bar**

---

**Notice of Attractions Closings**

Sadly, the **Museum of the Moving Image,** at the South Bank Centre, is closed for redevelopment probably until 2003. Worse, the **BBC Experience** has closed down.

(© **020/7312-2490**), looking out across the rooftops from under the Ondaatje Wing's glass roof.

St. Martin's Place, WC2. © **020/7306-0055**. www.npg.org.uk. Free admission; £5 ($7.20) adults, £3 ($4.35) concessions for special exhibitions. Sat–Wed 10am–6pm; Thurs–Fri 10am–9pm. Closed Jan 1, Good Friday, May 1, Dec 24–26. Tube: Leicester Sq., Charing Cross.

**The Planetarium**   See "Madame Tussaud's & The Planetarium" under "London's Top Attractions," earlier in this chapter.

**Royal Academy of Arts** ★   Sir Joshua Reynolds and Thomas Gainsborough were founding members of The Royal Academy (1768), the nation's first art school and the first institution to hold an annual exhibition. In June to July, this is now one of the world's biggest open show of contemporary painting, sculpture, and drawing. The hanging panel's choices always excite frenzied media debate. In 2001, it was curated by pop artist Peter Blake and included a painting by Paul McCartney. The year-round stalwart is the Friends Room, which displays the recent work (often for sale) by Royal Academicians. In the last 2 weeks of June, you can see and maybe invest in pieces by hot young artists at the end of 3 postgraduate years at the Royal Academy schools.

Burlington House, Piccadilly, W1. © **020/7300-8000**. www.royalacademy.org.uk. £7 ($10.15) adults, £6 ($8.70) seniors, £5 ($7.25) students, £1.50–£2.50 ($2.20[nd$3.65) children. Sat–Thurs 10am–6pm; Fri 10am–10pm. Closed Dec 25, Good Friday. Tube: Piccadilly Circus, Green Park.

**Saatchi Gallery**   Tierney Gearon's photographs of her naked children caused so many complaints last year—the police even got involved—that the gallery decided to extend the exhibition. Charles Saatchi certainly knows how to create a sensation. The ex-adman has amassed one of the largest independent collections of contemporary British and international art in the world. He is famous for launching new homegrown artists and for creating brand names—first the Young British Artists, then Neurotic Realism. Enter through the unmarked metal gateway of what was once, appropriately, a paint warehouse.

98a Boundary Rd., NW8. © **020/7624-8299**. Admission £5 ($7.25), £3 ($4.35) seniors, under-12s free. Thurs–Sun noon–6pm. Tube: St. John's Wood, Swiss Cottage.

**Serpentine Gallery** ★   Always on a mission to stimulate and provoke, the Serpentine Gallery last year asked the controversial Daniel Libeskind (he of the V&A Spiral) to create the first temporary structure for its new Architecture Commission. From now on, every June to September, there will be a unique one-off pavilion on the front lawn, part of the exhibition program and contributing to it as a venue for talks and pre-Prom poetry readings. This delightful gallery opened over 30 years ago in a 1934 tea pavilion in Kensington Gardens and it now attracts more than 400,000 people a year to see shows of modern and contemporary art, arranged by theme or single artist.

Kensington Gardens (near Albert Memorial), W2. © **020/7402-6075**. www.serpentinegallery.org. Free admission. Daily 10am–6pm. Tube: Knightsbridge, Lancaster Gate, South Kensington.

**Shakespeare's Globe** ★★   For information on tours and the exhibition, see p. 242.

**Sherlock Holmes Museum**   The quintessential English detective "resided" at this literary address from 1881 to 1904. It's not really a museum—nothing about Sir Arthur Conan Doyle, for instance—but a re-creation of the Victorian chambers as they might have been if they had ever been. In the living room, you can pick up Sherlock Holmes's pipe, don a deerstalker, and take a photograph of

**Backstage Tours**

London is a wonderland for lovers of the performing arts and budding thespians. There are several stages where you can step behind the footlights and see what goes into creating the spectacular performances. The first **Theatre Royal Drury Lane** was built in 1663, though the present one is 150 years younger. It was here that women first appeared on stage, including Nell Gwynn, to a less than rapturous response from the critics—they thought boys in drag were better at playing the fairer sex. Professional actors bring the history of the theatre to life in one-hour tours. **Through the Stage Door** (© 020/ 7494-5091) takes place on Monday, Tuesday, Thursday and Friday at 12:30, 2:15, and 4:45pm; and on Wednesday and Saturday at 11am and 1pm. Tickets cost £7.50 ($10.90).

The **Royal National Theatre** and **Royal Opera House** also invite visitors behind the scenes (see chapter 8). So does the BBC. Its landmark West End HQ, designed by G. Val Myers in 1932, burst at the seams long ago and the corporation has shifted many of its operations to the labyrinthine **BBC Television Centre**, Wood Lane, W12 (© 0870/ 603-0304; www.bbc.co.uk; Tube: Wood Lane). You must pre-book the 1½-hour tour. It sets off at 10:30am, 1:30 and 3:15pm, and costs £7.95 ($11.55) adults, £6.95 ($10.10) seniors, £5.95 ($8.65) students and under-17s. No children under 14. (See "Freebies," at the beginning of chapter 8, "London After Dark," for information on tickets to TV and radio shows.)

yourself horsing around. Other "exhibits" include Dr. Mortimer's stick from *The Hound of the Baskervilles* and numerous letters written to Holmes asking him to solve individual mysteries and his "replies." But it's not worth the ticket unless you're a real Holmes fan.

221b Baker St., NW1. © 020/7935-8866. www.sherlock-holmes.co.uk. Admission £6 ($8.70) adults, £4 ($5.80) under-16s. Daily 9:30am–6pm. Tube: Baker St

**Theatre Museum** ★ *Kids*    The demonstrations and workshops are the best bit about this surprisingly unvibrant museum. Kids love learning how make-up artists create hideous scars, or trying on costumes made in the style of famous designers—a Versace *School for Scandal*, perhaps—to find out how they help an actor create a character. Otherwise the displays are rather static. An offshoot of the V&A, the Theatre Museum holds the national collections of everything relating to the performing arts—theater, ballet, opera, music hall, pantomime, puppetry, circus, and rock 'n' pop. It tells the story of the British stage, from Shakespeare to the present day, with models, posters, props, and souvenirs of such legendary British thespians as Garrick, Kean, and Irving. The museum also has a big Diaghilev archive, and it recently acquired the Tiller-Clowes marionettes, the last and most complete collection of Victorian puppets in Britain.

Russell St., WC2. © 020/7943-4700. theatremuseum.vam.ac.uk. Admission free. Tues–Sun 11am–6pm. Daily guided tours at 11am, 2, and 4pm; makeup demonstrations at 11:30am, 1, 2:30, 3:30, and 4:30pm; costume workshops at 12:30 and 3pm. Closed all bank holidays. Tube: Covent Garden, Charing Cross.

## Young, British & Hung in East London

The neighborhood around Hoxton Square has become a vibrant creative community, hotching with young British artists and hot new galleries in old industrial buildings. Entrepreneur Jay Jopling, who has a fine line in creating bankable stars, from Tracey Emin and Damien Hirst to Gary Hume and the Chapman brothers, has turned an old warehouse into a new gallery, **White Cube**[2], 48 Hoxton Sq., N1 (© **020/7930-5373**; www.white cube.com). It is open Tuesday to Saturday 10am to 6pm. **Victoria Miro Gallery,** 16–18 Wharf Rd., N1 (© **020/7336-8109;** www.victoria-miro.com), is also open Tuesday to Saturday 10am to 6pm. Turner prizewinner Chris Ofili, of elephant dung fame, is one of her artists. To visit both of these, take the Tube to Old Street.

**Vinopolis, City of Wine**    The soaring vaulted rooms at Vinopolis are beautiful, but the museum relies too much on wine-bottle pyramids and serried ranks of fuzzy over-blown-up photos of vineyards (yawn!). And the personal audio guides are infuriating. Each exhibit has a three-digit code to punch in to hear the information, which is the only reason why you'll find yourself spending hours here. The only light relief is getting three wine tastings, at tables set up in the relevant regional rooms, with your admission ticket. Even so, I'd counsel you not to bother. We've only included it here because it's been heavily marketed locally, and you're bound to see a few signs for it.

1 Bank End, SE1. © **0870/241-4040.** www.vinopolis.co.uk. Admission £11.50 ($16.70) adults, £10.50 ($15.25) seniors, £5 ($7.25) children. Mon 11am–9pm; Tues–Fri and Sun 11am–6pm; Sat 11am–9pm. Tube: London Bridge. River services: Bankside Pier.

**Whitechapel Art Gallery** ⭐    Canon Barnett of Toynbee Hall founded this gallery in 1901 to enlighten, and lighten the lives of the poor of the East End. Though its fortunes have fluctuated ever since, largely due to the perennial shortage of cash, the Whitechapel has maintained a determined independence from any stylistic or aesthetic pressures. Iwona Blazik took over as director last summer, hot from working on the launch of Tate Modern. It was uncertain whether she would revive the biannual Whitechapel Open, a show of jury-selected works by local artists. But from January to March 2002, the gallery is holding a big retrospective of American photographer Nan Goldin.

80–82 Whitechapel High St., E1. © **020/7522-7888.** www.whitechapel.org. Free admission. Tues and Thurs–Sun 11am–5pm; Wed 11am–8pm. Closed holidays. Tube: Aldgate East.

## 6 Maritime & Waterfront Sights

### WOOLWICH

**Firepower, The Museum of the Royal Artillery**    This museum opened in May 2001 at the Royal Arsenal in Woolwich. From the 17th century, this vast and well-guarded complex was the home base of the Royal Regiment of Artillery. Firepower will eventually fill four buildings, first the ordnance laboratories and former ammunition factories, and then the Hawksmoor military academy once it is restored. The main Field of Fire gallery simulates being in combat. Visitors can learn how to point and fire the big guns in the interactive Real Weapon gallery. Its unique collection of big guns spans nearly 300 years, including a section of the Iraqi super-gun. Sounds like Rambo heaven.

Royal Arsenal, Woolwich, SE18. © 020/8855-7755. www.firepower.org.uk. £6.50 ($9.45) adults, £5.50 ($8) concessions, £4.50 ($6.55) children. Daily 10am–5pm. Tube: North Greenwich, then bus nos. 161, 422, 472. Train: Woolwich Arsenal.

**Thames Barrier** ✯ This giant feat of engineering opened in 1982 to protect London from flooding. Like a row of mini–Sydney Opera Houses, the barrier has four 3,000-ton gates, each as tall as a 5-story building, and six smaller ones. They take 1½ hours to raise—which has happened around 60 times for real. Now, global warming is pushing water levels up and threatening to halve the barrier's projected life to 50 years. The Visitor Centre on the south bank shows how it works—and disgustingly recreates the Great Stench, which wafted up from the river before pollution control in the 19th century. Take a boat, because it's a pain to get to any other way.

Unity Way, Woolwich, SE18. © 020/8305-4188. Admission 75p ($1.10) adults, 50p (73¢) children 5–17. Daily 10:30am–4:30pm. Train: Charlton. River services: Barrier Gardens Pier.

## GREENWICH

**Cutty Sark** ✯ This 19th-century sailing clipper is one of the most famous to have survived its era. Built in Dumbarton, it launched in 1869, too late to succeed in the tea trade, which had been taken over by steamers after the opening of the Suez Canal. Instead, it carried Australian wool, circling the globe round the Cape of Good Hope on the outward journey and Cape Horn on its return. Designed for speed, the Cutty Sark could cover almost 400 sea miles a day. It was restored in 1922 and has been in dry dock since 1954. On board, you'll see how tough life was for the Victorian crew and officers. The Long John Silver Collection of merchant ship figureheads is the biggest in the country. Go below deck for hands-on activities.

King William Walk, SE10. © 020/8858-3445. www.cuttysark.org.uk. Admission £3.50 ($5.60) adults, £2.50 ($4) children. Daily 10am–5pm. Closed Dec 24–26. DLR: Cutty Sark. River services: Greenwich Pier.

**National Maritime Museum** ✯✯ Even if the closest you get to the sea is eating fish on Fridays, there'll be something to intrigue you at this museum. How about the 7 ft-tall stone model for Nelson's Column? Or the wreckage from a Zeppelin shot down in 1915 as it bombed the docks? Perhaps a 2-ton remnant salvaged from the Baltic Exchange after the 1992 IRA bomb? All of these are on display in a new gallery, Maritime London. This museum is one of the largest of its kind in the world—the ceremonial opening in 1937 was the first duty of the new King George VI after the abdication crisis. The collection contains 2,500 ship models, 50,000 charts, and 750,000 ship plans, plus hundreds of scientific and navigational instruments. It even has the bullet-pierced coat Nelson was wearing when he died. Now, with 12 new galleries, modern interactive technology looks at modern maritime issues: how pollution threatens the sea, new ways of exploring its ultimate depths, pleasure-cruising, and more. On Saturdays, a workshop in the All Hands gallery recreates seafarers' lives through the ages. It runs from 2 to 4pm, except on the first Saturday of the month when there's a guest presenter and a longer session, 12:30 to 4:30pm.

All time is measured from the Prime Meridian Line at the **Royal Observatory Greenwich,** which Charles II founded in 1675 as part of his quest to determine longitude at sea. Clockmaker John Harrison eventually solved the problem in 1763, and received £20,000 for his pains. You can stand astride the meridian (with a foot in each hemisphere) and set your watch precisely by the falling time-ball, which is how shipmasters set their chronometers from 1833 on. High on a hill above the Thames, the observatory has a collection of historic timekeepers and astronomical instruments, and Britain's largest refracting telescope. A couple of times a week, the boffins let visitors have a quick look at the stars but you'll need to call and find out when. Planetarium shows happen every weekday afternoon and on Saturdays from Easter through August.

The innovative Inigo Jones designed **The Queen's House** (1616) for Anne of Denmark, wife of James I. She died before it was completed, so Charles I gave it to his queen, Henrietta Maria. The house's cantilevered tulip staircase was the first of its kind. The royal apartments give a wry insight into the niceties of court etiquette: Only visitors of the highest rank made it through the full sequence of seven rooms to the royal bedchamber. The Queen's House has now become a quasi-art gallery, where the museum can show revolving exhibitions from its collection of 4,000 paintings.

Romney Rd., SE10. ℂ **020/8858-4422** or 020/8312-6565. www.nmm.ac.uk. Admission free; possible small charge for special exhibitions. Daily 10am–5pm. Closed Dec 24–26. DLR: Cutty Sark, Greenwich. River services: Greenwich Pier.

**Old Royal Naval College**    Sir Christopher Wren designed this complex as a naval hospital in 1696. Its four blocks, named after King Charles, Queen Anne, King William, and Queen Mary, are split into two sections so as not to block the view of the river from The Queen's House. If you're in the neighborhood, do stop in to see Thornhill's magnificent Painted Hall where Nelson lay in state in 1805. You can also visit the Georgian chapel of St. Peter and St. Paul, or come at 11am on Sunday for the choral Eucharist. The Navy moved out of the college in 1998, and it is now home to departments of the University of Greenwich and other public organizations.

King William Walk, off Romney Rd., SE10. ℂ **0800/389-3341**, or 020/8269-4747. www.greenwichfoundation. org.uk. Admission £3 ($4.35) adults, £2 ($2.90) concessions, free under-16s; free after 3:30pm and Sun. Mon–Sat 10am–5pm; Sun 12:30–5pm. Closed Good Friday and Dec 24–26. Rail: Charing Cross to Maze Hill. DLR: Cutty Sark, Greenwich. River services: Greenwich Pier.

## DOCKLANDS

The team converting the cavernous 18th-century warehouse at West India Quay into a new **Museum in Docklands** (www.museumindocklands.org.uk) were considering recreating the smells of the cargoes stored in its heyday—a head-spinning mingling of rum, sugar, and coffee! Twelve galleries will trace two millennia of watery history, from the Romans to redevelopment, through the collections of the Museum of London and the Port of London Authority. It was due to open by the end of 2001.

## TOWER BRIDGE

The iconic **Tower Bridge** is a must-visit, of course, as is the **Tower of London** (see "London's Top Attractions," earlier in this chapter for a review of both) on the north bank. Facing it across the river is the new HQ for the new Greater London Authority, designed by Norman Foster. Wander down and see how work is progressing on the giant glass display case, built in the shape of a rugby ball. It is due to complete in 2002.

**HMS Belfast** ★ (Kids)    This 11,500-ton, 32-gun battle cruiser played a vital role in World War II—during the Normandy landings, the sinking of the *Scharnhorst* in the Battle of the North Cape, and on the terrible Arctic convoy route to North Russia. HMS *Belfast* has nine decks to explore, from the Bridge to the boiler and engine rooms. Along the way visitors can operate anti-aircraft guns and imagine what life was like for the sailors in the Mess decks. Cramped but pretty boozy is the answer: from 1950 to 1952, when the ship served in the Far East, the crew consumed 56,000 pints of Navy rum, along with 134 tons of meat and 625 tons of potatoes. There are kids' events during the holidays.

Morgan's Lane, Tooley St., SE1. (C) 020/7940-6300. www.iwm.org.uk/belfast/index.htm. Admission £5.40 ($7.85) adults, £4 ($5.80) seniors, free under-16s. Mar–Oct daily 10am–6pm; Nov–Feb daily 10am–5pm. Closed Dec 24–26. Tube: London Bridge, Tower Hill. River services: London Bridge City.

## BANKSIDE

This once-scruffy neighborhood has got it all, from the very ancient to the super-modern, and enough of it to keep you buzzing for days. Check out **Tate Modern** (see "London's Top Attractions," earlier in this chapter), **Shakespeare's Globe** (see chapter 8), **Southwark Cathedral** (see "Churches, Cathedrals & a Cemetery," earlier in this chapter), and, nearby, **Borough Market** (see "Markets," in chapter 7) and the ancient **The George** (see "Pubs," in chapter 8).

The **Millennium Bridge** is the first new foot-crossing on the Thames since the 19th century and a photo opportunity to rival the best in the capital. Sir Norman Foster designed the £14-million streak of steel and light. From Bankside, it looks like a space-age causeway leading straight to St. Paul's Cathedral. Such a shame that the infamous wobble closed the bridge the very weekend it opened, and looked like it would keep it closed until the end of 2001.

**Golden Hinde** ★ *Kids*   Purists may mutter "theme park," but this meticulous replica of the galleon in which Sir Francis Drake circumnavigated the globe (1577–80) is no cardboard sham. Since her 1973 launch, the *Golden Hinde* has sailed over 140,000 miles herself, even repeating Drake's historic feat. The ship is very hot on the educational stuff. During half-terms and holidays, you can drop the kids off for a 4-hour workshop where they'll learn to load cannons, sing Tudor sailing songs, and discover the horrors of barber surgery. Prices vary, and you need to book ahead. Families and small groups can even stay overnight: see "After Lights Out," below.

St. Marie Overie Dock, Cathedral St., SE1. (C) 08700/118700. www.goldenhinde.co.uk. Admission £2.50 ($3.65) adults, £2.10 ($3.05) concessions, £1.75 ($2.55) children, £6.50 ($9.45) family ticket; pre-booked guided tour £3 ($4.35) adults, £2.60 ($3.75) concessions, £2.25 ($3.25) children. Daily, call for opening times. Tube: London Bridge. River services: Bankside

## SOUTH BANK

The twin foot-crossings flanking **Hungerford Bridge** are another millennium project: one side should be open by the end of 2001, and the other in Summer 2002. Suspended from steel pylons, they link the West End to the vibrant South Bank. There, on the upstream side, you'll find County Hall, which is home to the **London Aquarium** (see p. 206), **Dali Universe** (see p. 190), and a couple of cheap fast eats.

**British Airways London Eye** ★★★ *Kids*   "Passengers" on the Eye can see straight into the Buckingham Palace garden, much to the Queen's annoyance. And both the Ministry of Defense and Shell have spent thousands spy-proofing their offices after discovering that someone with the right gadgetry could look in and pinch their secrets. At 443 feet high, this is the world's tallest observation wheel (don't say "Ferris;" it's a dirty word to these guys). On the south bank, next to County Hall, the ½-hour, very slow-mo "flight" gives a stunning 25-mile view over the capital. It's better when the sun isn't shining, as the glare makes it difficult to see out. And the pod should have a map of the landmarks running

---

*Kids*  **After Lights Out**

One Saturday a month, February through November, families can zip back 400 years and stay on a replica of Sir Francis Drake's galleon, the **Golden Hinde** (*C* **08700/118700;** www.goldenhinde.co.uk; Tube: London Bridge). Actors play the officers and crew preparing for a voyage, while the parents and kids (6–12) join the work dressed in Tudor clothes, eat rather better food than the sailors would have done, and sleep on the lower decks. At £31.50 ($45.70) per person, it costs about the same as a bed-and-breakfast. Kids aged 8–11 can also camp out for the night with their parents at the **Science Museum** (see p. 174). The galleries become a private playground, while they learn to make slime or how to drop an egg without breaking it. A Sleepover costs £20 ($29) for adults and £25 ($36.25) for kids. To find out more, call *C* **020/7942-4747.**

---

round the inside: instead you have to pay £4.50 ($6.55) for a guide book. Book your "boarding ticket" in advance to avoid too much hanging about.

Jubilee Gardens, SE1. *C* **0870/500-0600.** www.ba-londoneye.com. Admission £9.50 ($13.80) adults, £7.50 ($10.90) concessions. Apr–Oct daily 9am–dusk; Nov–Mar daily 10am–6pm. Tube: Waterloo, Westminster. River services: Festival Pier.

## HAMMERSMITH

The path along the south bank of the Thames, between Putney and Hammersmith bridges, is one of the loveliest walks in London. The urban clatter seems miles away in the green-lit tunnel of trees—even the rowers glide by almost noiselessly on the river below. The only downside is the stream of arrogant cyclists who assume that you'll jump out of their way.

**WWT The Wetland Centre** ★★ *Kids*   This 105-acre network of lakes, lagoons, and marshes is the first created on such a scale in any capital city anywhere. The Wildfowl & Wetland Trust shifted thousands of tons of concrete and recycled 500,000 cubic meters of soil to turn the old reservoirs into a Site of Special Scientific Interest. Paths loop out in two directions from the Discovery Center, across little bridges and past observation hides. Turn one way for World Wetlands, where some of the world's rarest ducks, geese, and swans live in 14 mocked-up habitats, and for life in a native pond (Wildside). Turn the other for three eco-friendly designer gardens, a children's farmyard full of ducks, and wetland crafts in Waterlife. A great place to take a break, whether you're a bird-spotter or not. The view from the observatory is breathtaking. You can watch the wardens feed the birds at noon and 3:30pm, or take a tour at 11am and 2:30pm.

Queen Elizabeth's Walk, SW13. *C* **020/8409-4400.** www.wetlandcentre.org.uk. Admission £6.75 ($9.80) adults, £5.50 ($8) seniors, £4 ($5.80) children, £17.50 ($25.40) family ticket. Summer daily 9:30am–6pm; winter 9:30am–5pm. Tube: Hammersmith, then bus nos. 283, 33, 72, or 209.

## 7  At Home with History's A-List

London has nurtured so many famous heroes, aristos, artists, writers, musicians, scientists, and all-round superstars that every other street boasts somebody's former home. English Heritage (*C* **020/7973-3000;** www.english-heritage.org. uk) marks significant spots with a blue plaque, and there are now almost 800 stuck up on walls all over the city: at Jimi Hendrix's Mayfair lair, at

Mahatma Gandhi's student digs in Fulham, in Noel Road, Islington, where playwright Joe Orton lived until his murder in 1967. Last year, composer Benjamin Britton got plaqued, at 173 Cromwell Rd., SW5, his student digs while he was at the Royal College of Music (1931–33). Usually, that's all there is left to mark the past, but there are some exceptions.

**Apsley House, The Wellington Museum** ☆    Once known as "No. 1 London" because it was the first house outside the tollgate, Apsley House has been the magnificent city residence of the dukes of Wellington since 1817. (The name comes from its first owner, the Earl of Bathurst, Baron Apsley). Wellington moved in on his return from a triumphant military career in India, Spain, and Portugal, culminating in the victory at Waterloo. He entertained extravagantly, dining off the gorgeous Sèvres Egyptian Service that Napoléon had commissioned for Josephine, and a vast silver Portuguese service with a 26-foot-long centerpiece. Wellington's heroic military success earned him lavish gifts as well as royal respect. No wonder the original Robert Adam house (1771–78) had to be enlarged to house the duke's treasures. Today, it is crammed with silver, porcelain, sculpture (note the nude statue of Napoléon by Canova on the main staircase), furniture, medals, hundreds of paintings by Velázquez, Goya, Rubens, Brueghel, and other masters. It's one of the few great London town houses where such collections remain intact and the family is still in residence: The eighth Duke of Wellington and his son have private apartments.

149 Piccadilly, Hyde Park Corner, W1. ✆ 020/7499-5676. Admission (includes audio guide) £4.50 ($6.55) adults, £3 ($4.35) concessions, free seniors and under-18s. Tues–Sun 11am–5pm. Closed Jan 1, Good Friday, May 1, and Dec 24–26. Tube: Hyde Park Corner (exit 3).

**Carlyle's House** ☆    The bearded gent on the wall plaque is writer and historian Thomas Carlyle, who lived in this Queen Anne terrace house from 1834 until he died in 1881. Many famous friends visited the "Sage of Chelsea" here, including Chopin, Dickens, Tennyson, and George Eliot, whose house was round the corner on Cheyne Walk. Virtually unaltered, the house has the original furniture and many books, portraits, and mementos from his day. The walled Victorian garden has been restored and is a delight.

24 Cheyne Row, SW3. ✆ 020/7352-7087. Admission £3.50 ($5.10) adults, £1.75 ($2.55) under-17s. Apr–Oct only, Wed–Sun 11am–5pm. Tube: Sloane Sq.

**The Dickens House Museum**    This terraced house on the edge of Bloomsbury was home to Victorian London's quintessential chronicler for only 2 years (1837–39). In that time, though, Dickens produced some of his best-loved works, including a portion of *The Pickwick Papers, Nicholas Nickleby,* and *Oliver Twist.* His letters, furniture, and first editions are on display in rooms restored to their original appearance.

48 Doughty St., WC1. ✆ 020/7405-2127. www.dickensmuseum.com. Admission £4 ($5.80) adults, £3 ($4.35) students and seniors, £2 ($2.90) children, £9 ($13.05) families. Mon–Sat 10am–5pm. Tube: Russell Sq., Chancery Lane.

**Dr. Johnson's House**    The house is tucked away behind Fleet Street, on a little square at the end of an ancient labyrinth of alleys and passages. Samuel Johnson lived here from 1748 to 1759, while he compiled the first comprehensive English dictionary. In the top garret, six copyists transcribed the entries. Johnson sat elsewhere reading and making lists of words from the best literature of the time. You can actually see the original dictionary, published in 1755, as well as letters, prints, portraits, and other memorabilia.

## Benjamin Franklin Holds Open House

St. Paul's Cathedral was the first public building in the world to get one of Benjamin Franklin's new-fangled lightning conductors. The American scientist, philosopher, printer, writer, inventor, statesman, and creator of perfect soundbites, lived in London between 1757 and 1775. His "genteel lodgings" at **36 Craven Street,** near Charing Cross, served as the first de facto American embassy after Independence. The Friends of Franklin House formed a trust 25 years ago to rescue the great man's home. During the restoration, workmen discovered 10 dissected bodies under the basement floorboards—his landlady's son-in-law was a surgeon and seems to have operated his own anatomy school. **Benjamin Franklin House** is due to open to the public early in 2002. To find out more, call ℂ **020/ 7930-9121;** www.rsa.org.uk/franklin.

17 Gough Sq., Fleet St., EC4. ℂ 020/7353-3745. www.drjh.dircon.co.uk. Admission £4 ($5.80) adults, £3 ($4.35) students and seniors, £1 ($1.45) under-16s, free under-10s, £9 ($13.05) family ticket. May–Sept Mon–Sat 11am–5:30pm; Oct–Apr Mon–Sat 11am–5pm. Tube: Blackfriars, Chancery Lane.

**Fenton House** ✦   This lovely house, built in 1693, belonged to a merchant named Fenton (what a surprise!) in the 18th century. In the 1950s, then-owner Lady Binning handed it over to the National Trust with her fine collection of Oriental and European porcelain, needlework, and furniture. Now it is also home to the Benton Fletcher collection of early keyboard instruments, all in working order, including a 1612 harpsichord that Handel probably played. You'll feel as if you've stepped back into a much more gracious time.

Hampstead Grove, NW3. ℂ 020/7435-3471. Admission £4.30 ($6.25) adults, £2.15 ($3.10) children, £10.50 ($15.25) family ticket. Mar Sat–Sun 2–5pm; Apr–Oct Sat–Sun 11am–5pm, Wed–Fri 2–5pm. Closed Nov–Feb. Tube: Hampstead.

**Handel House Museum**   This museum was finally due to open in November 2001. Brook Street was new when composer George Frideric Handel moved here in 1723. Although he had come to England a decade earlier, this was his first proper home. Using his will and an inventory taken after he died in 1759, the Handel House Trust has painstakingly restored the interior, even commissioning a particular crimson fabric to swathe a magnificent full-tester bed lent by English Heritage and building a harpsichord to Handel's original specifications (live music will be part of the visit).

25 Brook St., W1. ℂ 020/7495-1685. www.handelhouse.org. Admission £4.50 ($6.55) adults, £3.50 ($5.10) concessions. Tues–Sat 10am–6pm (Thurs 8pm); Sun noon–6pm. Tube: Oxford Circus.

**Keats House**   The romantic poet John Keats fell in love with Fanny Brawne, his neighbor's daughter, when he lived in this charming Regency cottage in Hampstead (1818–20). Sadly, he had tuberculosis and left to winter in Italy, where he died the following year. While at the cottage, Keats penned "Ode to a Nightingale"—a first edition is on display with books, diaries, letters, memorabilia, and some original furnishings. For the next few years, the museum will close for a short period during the winter for restoration: the interiors are to be done last, by 2004. There is always a full summer diary of tours and events.

Keats Grove, NW3. ℂ 020/7435-2062. Admission £3 ($4.35) adults, £1.50 ($2.20) concessions, free under-16s. Free admission to garden. Tues–Sun noon–4pm. Call to check times and winter closure. Tube: Hampstead, Belsize Park.

*Moments*  A Bandstand with a View

A snowy constitutional on Hampstead Heath inspired C.S. Lewis to write *The Lion, the Witch and the Wardrobe.* They do feel like a parallel universe, these 800 acres of half-wild half-manicured green in northwest London. Sundays are like a fiesta: lay back and listen to the bandstand concerts on Parliament Hill, with its unparalleled view across the capital. People fly kites or wield a mean Frisbee. Others fish, swim, and race model boats in the ponds. The Heath & Hampstead Society organizes a 2-hour walk on the first Sunday afternoon of every month except January. Call Michael Welbank ✆ **020/7435-6553;** www.heathandhampsteadsociety. org.uk. Hampstead Heath has a very helpful information center (✆ **020/ 7482-7073**).

**Kenwood House & Iveagh Bequest** ★★   English Heritage has given the palatial Kenwood House a makeover. The chilly blues and grays were replaced by deep, harem-like colors that flout the core conservators' code—thou shalt remain true to the original design of a historic building—which the very same organization usually polices relentlessly. But the bold interiors are a perfect foil for the astounding art collection here, left to the nation with the house by Lord Iveagh in 1927. It includes the Rembrandt self-portrait, voted Britain's favorite picture, and Vermeer's *The Guitar Player,* among others. This wedding-white house, remodeled by Robert Adam in the late 18th century, is high on Hampstead Heath, overlooking the lake, and famous for its summer open-air concerts (see chapter 8). The Brew House is a favorite pit-stop, especially for a lazy breakfast in its walled garden (it opens at 9am year-round). And make sure to see the entrancing gypsy caravan in one of the outbuildings.

Hampstead Lane, NW3. ✆ 020/8348-1286. www.english-heritage.org.uk. Free admission. Daily: Apr–Sept 10am–6pm; Oct 10am–4pm; Nov–Mar 10am–4pm (10:30am Wed, Fri). Tube: Archway, Golders Green, Hampstead, and Highgate, then no. 210 bus from outside all stations.

**Sir John Soane's Museum** ★★   The son of a bricklayer, Sir John Soane (1753–1837) apprenticed himself to George Dance the Younger and Henry Holland before opening an architectural practice of his own. He married into great wealth and began collecting the objects displayed in this house, which he both designed and lived in. It is enchanting, stuffed full of architectural fragments, casts, bronzes, sculpture, and cork models. The sarcophagus of Seti I (Pharaoh 1303–1290 B.C.), whose £2,000 price-tag had stopped the British Museum in its tracks, is also here. Soane used colored glass and mirrors to create reflections of architectural details and other dramatic effects—magical during evening opening when the rooms are candlelit. The collection includes works by Turner, three Canalettos, and two series of paintings by Hogarth, *An Election* and *The Rake's Progress.* Others, including a wonderful group of Piranesi drawings, are ingeniously hung behind movable panels in the Picture Room. Meanwhile, the gallery displays changing exhibitions from Soane's collection of over 30,000 architectural drawings, which includes works by Dance, Sir Christopher Wren, Sir William Chambers, and Robert and James Adam. There's a tour every Saturday at 2:30pm. Tickets cost £2 ($2.90) and go on sale half an hour before. Be early as there are always more bodies than the 22 spaces.

13 Lincoln's Inn Fields, WC2. ✆ 020/7405-2107. www.soane.org. Free admission (£1 donation requested). Tues–Sat 10am–5pm; first Tues of each month also 6–9pm. Tube: Holborn.

**Spencer House** ✪  The first Earl Spencer—an ancestor of Princess Diana—married his sweetheart Georgiana Poyntz secretly at Althorp and set about building this splendid house (1756–66) in St. James. Today, it is the only 18th-century private palace in London still intact. Quite an achievement since it stopped being a home in 1927 and was then rented out to the Ladies' Army & Navy Club, Christie's, and British Oxygen Gases. The Spencers also took things like the fireplaces, doors, and moldings to safety at Althorp during the Blitz. Painstaking restoration began in 1987 and has returned the house to its original opulent splendor. The Earl and Countess were a very wealthy couple; the diamond buckles on John's honeymoon shoes alone were valued at £3,000. The eight staterooms were some of the first neoclassical interiors created in London by John Vardy and James Stuart. The Painted Room contains superb gold furniture set against an elegant mural celebrating the Triumph of Love. There is no unsupervised wandering; you have to take the 1-hour tour. Come early because you can't pre-book. On certain spring and summer Sundays, the garden is open too. Backing on to Green Park, it has recently been restocked with plants fashionable in the 18th and 19th centuries.

27 St. James's Place, SW1. ⓒ 020/7499-8620. www.spencerhouse.co.uk. Admission only on timed tour ticket: £6 ($8.70) adults, £5 ($7.25) seniors and children 10–16. Garden £3.50 ($5.10) Sun 10:30am–5:30pm (closed Jan and Aug). Tube: Green Park. No under-10s.

**Wallace Collection** ✪✪  According to the terms of Lady Wallace's bequest, this collection must remain "unmixed with other objects of art." So the collection remains a perfect time capsule of 19th-century Anglo-French taste. Sir Richard Wallace was the illegitimate heir of the Marquis of Hertford, and the fifth generation to add to the acquisitions of exquisite furniture, armor, paintings, and decorative arts in the family's London home. There's so much to delight the eye—Sèvres porcelain, Limoges enamels, 17th-century Dutch paintings, 18th-century French (Watteau, Fragonard, and Boucher) and British art, and Italian majolica. To celebrate its centenary as a national museum, the neglected basement has become a study center for lectures, workshops, and object-handling sessions. Four new galleries hold temporary shows, explain the craft of conservation, and house pieces previously in store. But the really flashy bit is the sculpture garden and cafe under a glass roof covering the internal courtyard. For free tours, come at 1pm any weekday, 11:30am on Wednesday and Saturday, or 3pm on Sunday.

Hertford House, Manchester Sq., W1. ⓒ 020/7563-9500. www.the-wallace-collection.org.uk. Free admission. Mon–Sat 10am–5pm; Sun noon–5pm. Closed Dec 24–26, Jan 1, Good Fri, May Day. Tube: Bond St.

## 8 Especially for Kids

Call the tourist board's **London Line** (ⓒ **09068/663344;** www.londontown.com/kids), then "press 7" for lots of info on how to give the kids a good time. But that costs 60p a minute, so pick up a copy of the invaluable *Kids Out,* the monthly listings magazine spawned by *Time Out.* We've tried to make life easier, too, by flagging the best-fun attractions in the reviews with the new "kids" icon.

The perennial favorites are: touring the **Tower of London,** seeing the **Changing of the Guard** at Buckingham Palace, climbing to the top of **Tower Bridge,** taking a "flight" in the **British Airways London Eye,** shivering the timbers of the pirate galleon in **Peter Pan playground** in Kensington Gardens, or feeding the ducks at **WWT The Wetland Centre.** London's museums are shaking off their dusty image, not only with interactive exhibits, but fun workshops, especially during half-terms and holidays. Topping the hit list are the **Science Museum** (see "After Lights Out," on p. 201), the **London Transport Museum,** the **Museum of London,** the **Theatre Museum,** the **British Museum,** and the **V&A.** Two more places offering sneakily educational role-playing are **Shakespeare's Globe** (see chapter 8) and the **Golden Hinde. Madame Tussaud's** is always a hit. You should also try the **London Brass Rubbing Centre** in the crypt at St. Martin-in-the-Fields.

Founded in 1948, **Unicorn** is London's oldest professional children's theater company. It stages old favorites and commissioned works for 4-to-12-year olds. The company doesn't have its own theater yet, so call the office to find out what's on and where (© 020/7700-0707; www.unicorntheatre.com).

**Little Angel Theatre**    This magical theater is the only one like it in London. It puts on a huge variety of puppet shows from fairy tales to adaptations of children's books, by its own company and visiting masters of the art. Performances take place on weekends at 11am and 3pm, from September to August, and during half-terms and school holidays. It's not for children under 3, and every show is designated for a specific age group.

14 Dagmar Passage, Islington, N1. © 020/7226-1787. www.littleangeltheatre.com. Tickets £5.50–£8 ($8–$11.60). Box office Sat–Mon 9am–5pm; Tues–Fri 9:30am–5:30pm. Tube: Angel, Highbury, Islington.

**London Aquarium** ⭐    Down in the basement of County Hall is one of Europe's largest aquariums—it has 650,000 gallons of water for the fish to slosh about in. The two main tanks contain hundreds of varieties of marine life from the Atlantic and Pacific. Kids enjoy the shallow Beach Pier where they can stroke stingrays and other fish, while there are less alarming but equally yucky things in the Touchpool. Other zones whiz you through a rainforest, mangrove swamp, coral reef, and an English stream on a summer's day. Call for details on feeding times and talks.

County Hall Riverside Building, Westminster Bridge Rd., SE1. © 020/7967-8000. www.londonaquarium. co.uk. Admission £8.75 ($12.70) adults, £6.50 ($9.45) seniors, £5.25 ($7.60) under-15s, £25 ($36.25) family ticket. Daily 10am–6pm. Closed at Christmas. Tube: Westminster, Waterloo. River services: Festival Pier.

**London Dungeon** ⭐⭐    This state-of-the-art horror chamber has huge appeal for kids with a taste for the gruesome and ghoulish, but it will frighten the little ones, so be careful. I almost had a heart attack when warty actors with wild hair leapt out at me in the dark. The dungeon re-enacts the goriest events from British history: one night in the bloody life of Jack the Ripper, the passing of a death sentence that sends you by barge through Traitors' Gate, a medieval city ransacked by invaders, a roaring red tableau of the Great Fire of London, and so

---

**_Tips_  How to Bribe a Bolshy Teen**

If your offspring are revolting against going to any more boring old museums and galleries, try bribing them with a session at the **Trocadero** in Piccadilly Circus. This trashy entertainment mall is a kid's idea of heaven, and parental hell. It's got virtual reality arcade games, dodgems, a puke-inducing ride that whips you up 9 stories and then drops like a stone, naff souvenir shops, and junk eateries. Bring lots of £1 coins and a pair of earplugs against the din. The Troc (© 09068/881100) is open Sunday through Thursday 10am to midnight, closing at 1am on Friday and Saturday.

on. Rank smells and a smoke machine ratchet up the atmosphere. Much more fun than Madame Tussaud's.

28–34 Tooley St., SE1. 📞 **09001/600-0666.** www.thedungeons.com. Admission £10.95 ($15.90) adults, £9.50 ($13.80) students, £6.95 ($10.10) under-15s (must be accompanied by an adult). Apr–Sept daily 10am–6:30pm; Oct–Mar daily 10am–5:30pm; late openings July–Aug. Closed Dec 25. Tube: London Bridge. River services: London Bridge City Pier.

**London Zoo** 🌟 Animal experts from the zoo went on safari in north London last year after a reported sighting of a Big Cat. For once it wasn't next door's moggie seen through the bottom of a wine glass, but an endangered European Lynx. They rushed it back to hospital to recover from its adventure. London Zoo already looks after more than a hundred endangered species. It also takes part in 146 breeding programs, so there are always cute baby animals to see, as well as the perennial favorites: penguins, lions, tigers, hippos, chimps, and so on. There's something going on every hour of the day, from chow-time to the elephants' bath-time, so pick up a copy of the daily guide. The newest attraction is Web of Life, a state-of-the-art education center promoting conservation and biodiversity. The zoo opened in 1827 and is like a 36-acre architectural theme park: 10 of its buildings are so distinctive as to be Grade I or Grade II listed.

Regent's Park, NW1. 📞 **020/7722-3333.** www.londonzoo.co.uk. Admission £10 ($14.50) adults, £8.50 ($12.35) concessions, £7 ($10.15) children 3–15, £30 ($43.50) family. Daily Mar–Oct 10am–5:30pm, Nov–Feb 10am–4pm. Closed Dec 25. Tube: Camden Town. London Waterbus: From Camden Lock or Little Venice; for joint boat trip/zoo entry tickets, see "Boat Trips," below.

## 9 Parks & Gardens

### PRIVATE

From April through August, enthusiastic amateurs and the not-so-amateur open their private gardens to the public to raise money for charity, organized by the **National Gardens Scheme.** This is a chance to see the British at their most passionate, allegedly, for a nominal entry fee—a pound or two at the most. You can pick up an NGS handbook, listing which garden is open on what day, from most bookstores. Or contact the NGS at Hatchlands Park, East Clandon, Guildford, Surrey, GU4 7RT (📞 **01483/211535;** www.ngs.org.uk).

Founded in 1673 by the Society of Apothecaries to teach apprentices how to identify medicinal plants, the **Chelsea Physic Garden,** at 66 Royal Hospital Rd. (enter from Swan Walk), SW3 (📞 **020/7352-5646;** www.cpgarden.demon. co.uk), is the second-oldest botanical garden in England. Behind its high walls is a rare collection of exotic perennials, shrubs, and trees, including those that gave us steroids, aspirin and other common pills and potions. The rockery (1773) has just been restored—see if you can tell the Icelandic lava from the old stones "borrowed" from the Tower of London. Admission is £4 ($6.40) for adults, £2 ($3.20) for students and children. The garden is open April through October, on Wednesday noon to 5pm, and 2 to 6pm on Sunday. It's a lovely place to stop for tea and homemade cakes. The English Gardening School holds lectures throughout the summer. Take the Tube to Sloane Square.

### PUBLIC

Behind Kensington High Street, **Holland Park** is one of the city's most entrancing parks—an oasis of woods and gardens set around the ruins of Holland House. That's where the open-air theater and opera (📞 **020/7602-7856;** see chapter 8) take place in the summer, ousting the noisy peacocks. There's an adventure playground for kids and lots of sports facilities (squash, tennis, cricket, golf nets, and football): Call ℂ **020/7602-2226** for reservations. Also worth seeking out is the Japanese Kyoto Garden. A summer ballroom is now an upscale restaurant, and there's a cafe, too. Take the Tube to High Street Kensington or Holland Park.

Regent's Park, Hyde Park, Kensington Gardens, Green Park, and St. James's Park all come under the aegis of the **Royal Parks Agency** (ℂ **020/7298-2000**). Most organize guided walks around the monuments and hidden historical byways, as well as taking part in a Summer Festival of music, theater, and children's events. Picture-postcard stripy deck chairs are ubiquitous, and fee collectors seem to appear from nowhere to startle visitors who didn't realize they had to pay to sit down—it costs £1 ($1.45) to crash out for 4 hours.

**Hyde Park** (ℂ **020/7298-2100**) is the largest and most popular of all London's parks. The aptly named Serpentine Lake, created in the 1730s, is the most notable feature in all 350 acres. Take a boat out, lounge by its side, or swim from the Lido—make sure you've had your shots if you do, though, as the guano quota is pretty high. Or go horseback riding (see "Staying Active," below) along Rotten Row, a corruption of route du roi, laid out by King William III from the West End to Kensington Palace. On Sunday the park really comes alive. People flock to the contemporary Serpentine Gallery (ℂ **020/7402-6075;** see "Lots More Sights to See," earlier in this chapter for details), while artists of dubious talent hang their works along the Bayswater Road railings. On Sundays, the northeast corner near Marble Arch becomes **Speaker's Corner.** Anyone can stand on a soapbox here and spout their opinions and grievances—anarchists, stand-up comics, religious fanatics, would-be politicians, and the deeply eccentric. This tradition is often touted as an example of Britain's tolerance of free speech. In fact, the ritual began several hundred years ago when condemned prisoners were allowed a few final words before they were hanged on Tyburn gallows, which stood on the very same spot. Take the Tube to Marble Arch.

**Kensington Gardens** (ℂ **020/7298-2117**) abuts the western perimeter of Hyde Park, and it's hard to spot the join. Laid out in the early 18th century, the trees, lawns, and criss-crossed paths stretch out to Kensington Palace (see "London's Top Attractions," earlier in this chapter) on the opposite side. There, you can wander around the edges of the sunken gardens, enjoy a bite at the Orangery, and while away the time on one of the many benches. Perhaps near the Round Pond, where enthusiasts make their model boats buzz between the ducks. Close to the northwestern entrance to the park is the Peter Pan playground, a memorial to Princess Diana, where kids can clamber about on a mock pirate galleon. And do show them the Elfin Oak. In the 1930s, Ivor Innes carved hundreds of little gnomes, goblins, and fairies peering out of the nooks and crevices in a 10-foot-high tree stump. It really is enchanting, despite being vandalized almost as soon as it was restored 4 years ago. Near the Long Water, you'll find the famous bronze statue of Peter Pan with his rabbits. And, on the south side of the park, near Queen's Gate, is the overpoweringly gothic Albert Memorial. The Pet Cemetery in Kensington Gardens was the fashionable last resting place for cats and dogs, noble and not-so-noble, from Victorian times until 1867. Call ahead for permission to visit. Take the Tube to Queensway or Bayswater.

**Regent's Park** (ℂ **020/7486-7905**) was once Henry VIII's private hunting ground—as were most of the royal parks—but it was formally laid out 1811 by the Prince Regent and John Nash as part of an elaborate remodeling of London. Now, it is the people's playground. In summer, you'll see people walking their dogs; playing cricket, soccer, and baseball; doing gymnastics; and throwing Frisbees. Besides the zoo, it's famous for the boating lake, summer open-air theater (© 020/7486-2431; see chapter 8), brass band concerts on Holme Green, and bat-watching walks. There are 30,000 blossoms and 400 different varieties in Queen Mary's rose garden. And don't miss the Italianate Avenue Gardens, the Japanese Gardens, and the wildflowers flanking the Regent's Canal. Get there by Tube to Regent's Park, Baker Street, or Camden Town.

Opposite Buckingham Palace, **St. James's Park,** The Mall (© 020/ 7930-1793), is perhaps the most beautiful of all of London's parks. It was landscaped by Le Notre and John Nash. The famous lake and Duck Island are a waterfowl sanctuary for lots of species, including coots and white and Australian black swans, which give the park a romantic atmosphere. Come at 3pm to see the keepers feeding the pelicans, descendants of a feathered present given by a 17th-century Russian ambassador. You can get a great view of Buckingham Palace from the bridge. Lots of benches and plenty of grass and shade make this an ideal picnicking place. Take the Tube to St. James's Park.

Named for its absence of flowers (except for a short time in spring), **Green Park** (© 020/7930-1793) provides ample shade from tall trees that make it a picnic bower. For other places to *déjeuner sur l'herbe,* and where to buy supplies, see chapter 5.

## 10 Organized Tours

Joining an organized tour might sound like grim death to some independent travelers, but it is a useful way both to orient yourself when you arrive and to make the most of limited time. And the guides are a mine of quirky tales, as well as historical facts.

### GUIDED WALKS

The best way to soak up the atmosphere of London's most interesting streets is to explore them on foot. **Zig Zag Audio Tours** (© 0800/195-7827, or 020/8458-5310; www.zigzagtours.com) has adapted a museum service to the outside world. It costs £10 ($14.50) to rent a walkman, delivered to your hotel, for 24 hours. There are five different commentaries, covering the City, Royal & Parliamentary London, Soho & the West End, Jack the Ripper, and Old Hampstead Village. Each could take 2 hours, unless you zigzag, get distracted by rival attractions, take a pit-stop, and other rebellious stuff not allowed on guided walks.

The pluses of a walk lead by an actual human instead of a disembodied voice is price—most cost half as much—and the leeway the guides have to digress into juicy gossip. The **Original London Walks,** P.O. Box 1708, London NW6 4LW (© 020/7624-3978, or 020/7625-9255; www.walks.com) has been going since 1965. It boasts an unrivalled schedule of themed tours, from spies, to royalty, to rock-'n'-roll legends, all led by experts, well-known actors, and top Blue Badge guides. You can even go on a historic Thames-side pub crawl. The famous "Jack the Ripper" walk leaves daily at 7:30pm from Tower Hill Tube station. Try and go when Donald Rumbelow, a retired city policeman and authority on the subject, is leading the tour—Sunday, Monday, and Tuesday, plus alternate Fridays. Tours cover up to 1½ miles and take around 2 hours: £5 ($7.20) adults, £4 ($5.80) seniors and students. No need to book. It's an even better bargain if you buy a **Discount Walkabout Card** (£1.50/$2.40): every walk after the first one then costs £3.50 ($5.10). This company also does out-of-London Explorer Day tours every Saturday (see chapter 9).

Every night is fright night with historian, ghost researcher, and Magic Circle member, **Richard Jones,** 67 Chancery Lane, London WC2A 1AF (© **020/ 8530-8443;** www.london-ghost-walk.co.uk). His hauntingly good 2-hour walking tour starts at 7:30pm at Bank Tube station (Royal Exchange exit). Tickets cost £5 ($7.20) adults, £4 ($5.80) concessions. You must book ahead.

An expert from the **Museum of London** (© **020/7600-3699;** www. museumoflondon.org.uk) tells tales of archaeological digging along the Thames foreshore, on a walk from St. Paul's Cathedral to the Tower of London. Tickets are a steal at £3 ($4.35). Similar excursions on special topics linked to exhibitions rarely cost more than £7.50 ($10.90). Tours of the royal parks are free: you just have to call and find out when they are (see "Parks & Gardens," above). **Shakespeare's Globe** also puts on Walkshops, a combined guided tour of Southwark, a hotbed of historical gossip, and a look round the theater itself (see chapter 8).

## BICYCLE RIDES
For a faster pace, try the **London Bicycle Tour Company,** 1a Gabriel's Wharf, 56 Upper Ground, London SE1 9PP (© **020/7928-6838;** www.londonbicycle. com; Tube: Waterloo, Blackfriars). You'll cover 6 to 9 miles in around 3½ hours, with pauses for historical gossip and refreshment, and it costs £11.95 ($17.35), including bike rental. If you want to go solo, the company rents out bikes for £2.50 ($3.65) an hour, or £12 ($17.40) for the first day and then £6 ($8.70) a day, or £36 ($52.20) a week, with discounts for kids. It also does 2- and 3-day weekend breaks: see chapter 9.

## BUS TOURS
If your time is more limited than your budget, then bagging all the big sites from the top of a double-decker bus may be the best bet. **The Big Bus Company** (© **020/7233-9533;** www.bigbus.co.uk) leaves from Green Park, Victoria, and Marble Arch daily, from 8:30am to 7pm (4:30pm in winter) on three different routes that take anything from 1½ to 2½ hours. Tickets include a river cruise and walking tours, and cost £15 ($21.75) for adults and £6 ($8.70) children. Valid for 24 hours, they let you hop on and off at 54 locations. Big Bus often has special offers, too, throwing in cheap theater tickets, fast-entry to popular attractions, and so on, which can be a fantastic deal: Call to get the low-down. The **Original London Sightseeing Tour** (© **020/8877-1722;** www. theoriginaltour.com) has been going since the Festival of Britain in 1951. The 2-hour tour leaves from Piccadilly Circus, Victoria, Baker Street, or Marble Arch, every 6 minutes, from 8:30am to 7pm. This one has 90 stops to hop on and off at during the day. It costs £14 ($20.30) for adults, £7.50 ($10.90) for under-16s, and you can buy tickets on board. No need to book.

## BOAT TRIPS
The fabulously loopy **London Frog Tours** (© **020/7928-3132;** www. frogtours.com) has adapted several World War II amphibious troop carriers, known as DUKWs, to civilian comfort levels, painted them screaming yellow, and now runs 80-minute road and river trips. Tours start behind County Hall, rumble through Westminster and up to Piccadilly, gathering bemused stares all the way. Then they splosh into the Thames at Vauxhall for the 30-minute cruise. The high ticket price of £15 ($21.75) for adults, £12 ($17.40) concessions, £9

---

*Tips*  **Seeing London by Bus**

Buy a **Travelcard** (see "Getting Around," in chapter 3), and you can tour all over London on the top of a red double-decker anytime you want. The no. 11 bus has one of the best routes—Liverpool Street Station to Fulham Broadway, via King's Road, Westminster Abbey, Whitehall, Horse Guards, Trafalgar Square, the National Gallery, the Strand, Law Courts, Fleet Street, and St. Paul's Cathedral. A **Riverbus** service was due to launch in October 2001, traveling from Covent Garden to the British Airways London Eye, Tate Modern (it's the only bus allowed to stop by the gallery), the Globe, and over Tower Bridge to the Tower of London. Nobody knew what number it would carry as we went to press—R1, probably—so call the London Transport hot line (© **020/7222-1234**).

---

($13.05) children, and £42 ($60.90) for families is worth it in holiday-snap value alone.

Thanks to Mayor Ken, you can now use your Travelcard to get a third off most boat trip tickets. The Thames has always served as the city's highway, and there are 23 piers along its London stretch, from Hampton Court to Gravesend in the estuary—the funky Millbank Pier, by Tate Britain, is due to open by spring 2002. At the last count, more than 10 companies were running cruises and rush-hour-only ferries. There's a full schedule on the London Transport website www.londontransport.co.uk/river; or pick up its **Thames River Services** booklet, at Tube stations and tourist information offices.

The best value pound-per-minute (even before the Travelcard discount) and for flexibility, is the **Crown River Cruises** service (© **020/7936-2033**) from Westminster to St. Katherine's Dock, stopping by the South Bank Centre and London Bridge, from 11am to 6:30pm in peak season. A return ticket costs £6 ($8.70) for adults, £3.75 ($5.45) concessions, and £3 ($4.35) under-16s. The round-trip takes 1 hour but the ticket is valid all day, so you can hop on and off to sightsee. Don't forget: You can go to Hampton Court and the Royal Botanic Gardens Kew by boat. Those trips are dearer, and there are fewer headline sights on the way, but it does make a great day out (see "London's Top Attractions," earlier in this chapter).

You can also take a boat along the Regent's Canal. From April to October, **Jason's Trip** (© **020/7286-3428**; www.jasons.co.uk; Tube: Warwick Ave.) operates a 90-minute tour from the wharf opposite no. 60 Blomfield Rd. in Little Venice. The painted narrow boat leaves at 10:30am (except in Oct), 12:30, and 2:30pm and takes you past Brownings Island (so called because Robert Browning lived there), through the Maida Hill Tunnel and Regent's Park, to Camden Lock. The round-trip price is £6.95 ($10.10) for adults, £5.50 ($8) for children, £21.50 ($31.20) for a family ticket; £5.95 ($8.65) and £4.75 ($6.90), respectively, one-way. **London Waterbus Company** (© **020/7482-2660**; Tube: Warwick Ave., Camden Town) travels the same stretch of canal, leaving every hour from 10am to 5pm. The fares are as follows: one-way £4.20 ($6.10) adult, £2.80 ($4.05) children; round-trip £5.60 and £3.60 ($8.10 and $5.20). An all-in-one ticket including admission to London Zoo costs £11 ($15.95) adults, £8.10 ($11.75) children, from Little Venice; or £10.50 and £8 ($15.25 and $11.60), respectively, from Camden Lock. A bargain, if you look at the zoo's ticket prices (see above).

## 11 Staying Active

For information on cycling, check out "Bicycle Rides," above.

### GOLF

You'll have to travel into the burbs if you want to tee off while you're here. Contact the **English Golf Union** (© **01526/354500;** www.uk-golf.com) to find out where.

### HORSEBACK RIDING

Both these stables take groups out riding in Hyde Park every day except Monday. **Hyde Park Stables,** 63 Bathurst Mews, W2 (© **020/7723-2813**) charges £35 ($50.75) an hour at weekends, £32 ($46.40) during the week, for all ages. **Ross Nye Stables,** 8 Bathurst Mews, W2 (© **020/7262-3791**) charges £30 ($43.50) an hour for adults, £25 ($36.25) for children, on any day. You can't gallop or jump, only amble rather sedately around the sandy track. Both get booked up early for weekends. Take the Tube to Lancaster Gate or Paddington.

### ICE-SKATING

They turn off the fountains at **Somerset House** (see p. 175) in December and for a few weeks the courtyard is transformed into the most romantic ice rink in the world. In fact, open-air skating is enjoying quite a revival. There have even been plans mooted to build two "pads"—for roller as well as ice-skating—on the traffic island next to Marble Arch (www.skatinginthepark.co.uk).

**Broadgate Ice Rink** ⭐    This is London's only purpose-built open-air rink that operates all winter. It is tiny, surrounded by city wine bars and skyscrapers, and the state-of-the-art sound system will knock your skates off.

Broadgate Circus, Eldon St., EC2. © 020/7505-4068. Admission £5 ($7.25) adults, £3 ($4.35) seniors and students; skate rental £2 ($2.90) adults, £1 ($1.45) students and seniors. Late Oct–Apr only, Mon–Thurs noon–2:30pm and 3:30–6pm; Fri noon–2:30pm, 3:30–6pm, and 7–10pm; Sat–Sun 11am–1pm, 2–4pm, and 5–7pm (8pm on Sat). Tube: Liverpool St.

### INLINE SKATING

The inline skating cult erupts in London's streets and parks as soon as there's the least sign of summer. It's a mass participation thing—kinda *Fame* meets *Sex in the City*. Every Wednesday from mid-May, hundreds of people meet up at 7pm on the north side of the Serpentine in Hyde Park for a 2½-hour marshalled skate. The route takes in the capital's most famous landmarks, from Big Ben to Buckingham Palace. The hardcore don't turn round until they reach Tower Bridge, while the lightweights stop for a drink on the river. Taking part in **London Skate** (© **0800/169-3889;** www.sweatybetty.com/bettyblade) is free, as is instruction on the night if you're a little nervous about keeping up. Be warned, though—neither this event, nor the **Friday Night Skate** (FNS), which also starts at 7pm on the north side of the Serpentine, are for novices. The excellent **www.citiskate.com** organizes FNS and is a one-stop info shop for everything about the sport, including where to hire skates. **Slick Willies,** 41 Kensington High St., W8 (© **020/7939-3824;** Tube: Kensington High St.) charges £10 a day ($14.50), and £15 overnight ($21.75). Prices at **Sun and Snow,** 229 Brompton Rd. (© **020/7581-2039;** Tube: South Kensington, Knightsbridge) are £7.50 ($10.90) for a weekday, £10 ($14.50) Saturday or Sunday, or overnight during the week, £15 ($21.75) for Saturday plus Sunday. Both take a big deposit.

**Tips  Where to Go for Sports Info**

The English are passionate about sports, and there's no better way to get to know and understand them than to watch them watching the play: **www.sportal.co.uk** carries fixture information for everything from football to Formula One motor-racing. Otherwise, **Sportsline** (© 020/7222-8000) will answer any questions, on where to work out as well as where to spectate, Monday through Friday from 10am to 6pm.

## SWIMMING & FITNESS

**London Central YMCA** ✿  Super-snazzy for a Y, this West End health and fitness center has a pool, weight room, squash and badminton, short tennis, cardiovascular equipment, sauna, and solarium. It's membership only, so you pay a flat fee to do as much or as little as you want. There are also beauticians, plus massage and holistic therapists.

112 Great Russell St., WC1. © 020/7637-8131. Admission £15 ($21.75) per day, £39 ($56.55) per week. Mon–Fri 7am–10:30pm; Sat–Sun 10am–9pm. Tube: Tottenham Court Rd.

**Oasis Sports Centre** ✿ *Finds*  This place has got pretty much everything and at very reasonable prices for London. But the irresistible draw is the roof-top open-air pool. Come and tune out after a hard day's sightseeing.

32 Endell St., WC2. © 020/7831-1804. Swim £2.90 ($4.20) adults, £1.10 ($1.60) under-16s. Gym £5.40 ($7.85). Sauna £6.80 ($9.85) peak times, £3.70 ($5.35) before noon and 2–4pm. Exercise classes £4.50 ($6.55) for 45min., £5 ($7.20) for 1hr. Indoor pool Mon, Wed 6:30am–6:30pm; Tues 6.30am–5:30pm; Thurs–Fri 6:30am–7:15pm; Sat–Sun 9:30am–5pm. Outdoor pool Mon–Fri 7:30am–9pm (8:30pm Thurs); Sat–Sun 9:30am–5:30pm. Tube: Covent Garden, Holborn.

## 12 Spectator Sports

## CRICKET

Lord's and the Oval are London's two cricket venues. Tickets to county games are the budget-friendliest at around £10 ($14.50), and you can just turn up on match day. Book ahead for international Test matches and 1-day games: For fixture information, call the international hotline © **0870/533-8833.** Tickets are dear at £25 to £50 ($36.25–$72). The cricket season runs from April through September.

**Foster's Oval**  Less stodgy and prettier than Lord's, except for the gasometer looming up behind it, the Oval is home to Surrey County Cricket Club. It also traditionally hosts the final game in the summer international Test series. The box office is open Monday to Friday 9:30am to 4pm.

The Oval Kennington, SE11. © **020/7582-6660,** 020/7582-7764 box office. www.surreyccc.co.uk. Tube: Oval.

**Lord's**  This hallowed ground is the home of both the ancient Marylebone Cricket Club (which governs the game) and the Middlesex County Cricket Club, which plays league matches here. The international Tests have the aura of high society, or at least corporate hospitality, events. The box office is open Monday to Friday 9:30am to 5:30pm.

You don't have to endure a cricket match to make a pilgrimage to Lord's. There are **guided tours** at noon and 2pm from October to March, with an extra one at 10am in spring and summer. These include a visit to the **museum,** which

---

*Tips*  **Go Native with Sporting Pub Crowd**

Pay-per-view TV channels own the live-broadcast rights to most of the hottest fixtures, from Premiership football to international rugby and cricket. Rather than pay to view at home, fans use this as an excuse to enjoy their two favorite things at the same time—sport and downing a pint with the lads. Find a local pub with a big-screen TV and you've got *the* authentic English experience! **Lord's Tavern,** Grace Gates, St. John's Wood Rd., NW8 (*©* **020/7266-5980)** is an upmarket version of the same thing. Just by the hallowed Lord's cricket ground, it is also the summer HQ for the most obsessive followers of the game, the Barmy Army.

---

has exhibits on legendary cricketers such as W. G. Grace and houses the Ashes trophy, for which the English and Australians compete furiously. The Marylebone Cricket Club moved here in 1816. On the tour, you'll see the pavilion, where the dressing rooms are, the "real tennis" court, and the space-pod-style media center. Then watch bowling machines fire practice balls at 100 m.p.h. in the indoor school, before popping into Lord's Tavern for a pick-me-up. It does rather good brasserie food.

St. John's Wood Rd., NW8. *©* **020/7432-1066,** or 020/7432-1033 for tours of the ground. www.lords.org/mcc. Tours & museum £6.50 ($9.45) adults, £5 ($7.25) concessions, £4.50 ($6.55) children, £19 ($27.55) family ticket. Tube: St. John's Wood.

## FOOTBALL (SOCCER)

A gilded relief of David Beckham, the Manchester United star and Posh Spice's hubbie, has taken the spot usually reserved for angels at the foot of the main Buddha statue in a Bangkok temple. Soccer attracts quasi-religious devotion here, too. Yet, whatever you may have read about English fans in the past, the violent hooliganism that marred the national game has declined with the building of all-seat stadiums. The football season runs from August to April, and matches usually kick off at 3pm on Saturdays or 7:45pm on Wednesdays. The capital has more than a dozen clubs in different leagues. Tickets cost from £8 to £30 ($11.60–$43.50), and more for gold-dust Premiership games. London's glamour clubs are: **Arsenal,** Arsenal Stadium, Avenell Rd., N5 (*©* **020/ 7704-4000,** or 020/7704-4040 for the box office; www.arsenal.co.uk; Tube: Arsenal); **Tottenham Hotspur** ("Spurs"), White Hart Lane, 748 High Rd., N17 (*©* **020/8365-5000,** or 020/8365-5050 for the box office; www.spurs.co.uk; Tube: Seven Sisters); and **Chelsea,** Stamford Bridge, Fulham Rd., SW6 (*©* **020/ 7385-5545,** or 0891/121011 for the box office; www.chelseafc.co.uk; Tube: Fulham Broadway).

## GREYHOUND RACING

**Wimbledon Stadium** ★★   This people's sport is enjoying a big renaissance as *the* alternative night out. The minimum bet is £1 ($1.45), but the results are even less predictable than horse races. You can eat, drink, and make very merry at quasi-posh restaurants, bars, and fast food stalls. A good laugh and a good value.

Plough Lane, SW19. *©* **020/8946-8000.** www.wimbledondogs.co.uk. Admission: £5 ($7.20) adults, £2.50 ($3.60) under-15s, free for children under-6. Races Tues, Fri–Sat 7:30–10:30pm (stadium open 6:30pm). Tube: Wimbledon Park.

# HORSE RACING

**Royal Windsor Racecourse** ★★ Windsor does hold sporadic afternoon race meetings during the chillier months, but the festive summer Monday evenings are by far the best fun. The relaxed crowd is a mix of champagne Charlies and regular Joes, sampling the restaurants and bars (dress code demands a tie), or diving into a DIY picnic. Even the journey is a delight. Turn right out of the train station, and follow the crowd to the Riverbus for the 35-minute trip up the Thames to the racecourse. It leaves on the hour, and at 20 and 40 minutes past, from an hour or so before the first race, to a ½ hour after the last one. Buy your ticket on board.

Maidenhead Rd., Windsor, Berkshire, SL4 5JJ. ℂ 0870/220-0024, or 01753/865234. www.windsor-race course.co.uk. Admission £5–£16 ($7.20–$23.20), under-16s free. Discount for online booking. Race meetings: Mar, Oct–Nov afternoons; May–Aug Mon evenings; start times vary, 5–6pm. Train: Windsor Riverside, then Riverbus (ℂ 01753/851900; www.boat-trips.co.uk) from nearby Barry Ave. Promenade, £4 ($5.80) return.

# RUGBY UNION

The capital's top clubs are **London Wasps,** Loftus Rd. Stadium, South Africa Rd., W12 7PZ (ℂ 020/8743-0262; www.wasps.co.uk) and **Harlequins,** Stoop Memorial Ground, Langhorn Dr., Twickenham, Middlesex, TW2 7SX (ℂ 020/ 8410-6000; www.quins.co.uk). This chest-thumpingly macho game can be very exciting. The season runs from August to May, with games on Saturday and Sunday afternoons. Tickets are relatively easy to get hold of (though it is wise to book ahead) and cost £10 to £25 ($14.90–$36.25). For full fixtures listings, surf **www.rfu.com**.

**Twickenham Stadium** The Rugby Football Union HQ hosts international games (very hard to get tickets) and cup finals (a little bit easier). The annual Six Nations battle between Scotland, Ireland, Wales, England, France, and Italy takes place from January to March, whipping up a fever of patriotism.

Take the **Stadium Tour,** and you can walk through the players' tunnel to see what they see on the big day, visit the dressing room to savor the lingering smell of socks, and hear lots of sporting stories. There's a scrum machine (a bit like a blocking sled in American football) in the **Museum of Rugby,** where you can test your own strength. You'll see lots of memorabilia, including the oldest jersey still in existence, and the best rugby moments of all time, ever, ever, on film.

Rugby Rd., Twickenham, Middlesex, TW1 1DZ. ℂ 020/8892-8877, -8892 for tours. www.rfu.com/ twickenham. Museum and/or tour £6 and £4 ($8.70 and $5.80) adults, £4 and £3 ($4.80 and $4.35) concessions, £19 ($27.55) family ticket. Stadium tours Tues–Sat 10:30am, noon, 1:30, and 3pm; Sun 3pm. Museum of Rugby Tues–Sat 10am–5pm; Sun 2–5pm; match and post-match days from stadium opening to 1hr. after final whistle. Train: From Waterloo to Twickenham, then bus no. 281.

# TENNIS

Ever since players in flannels and bonnets took to the courts in 1877, the **Wimbledon Lawn Tennis Championships** have drawn a socially prominent crowd. Now it's the people's game, too, and even anti-sport fanatics get drawn into the national tennis fever. Save up and savor the extortionately priced strawberries and cream that are part of the experience. Show court seats are mostly sold by ticket ballot. The allocation is random, so you can't request a specific court or date. To be included, write between August 1 and December 31 of the preceding year for an application form, enclosing a self-addressed envelope with an International Reply Coupon, to **All England Lawn Tennis Club,** P.O. Box 98, Church Rd., Wimbledon, SW19 5AE (ℂ 020/8944-1066 or 020/8971-2473;

www.wimbledon.org). For the first 8 days of the tournament, around 500 seats for each show court are sold on match day. People camp out in line on the pavement to get them; depending on the court and the day, prices range from £16 to £66 ($23.20–$95.70).

During the earlier rounds, you can watch lots of top-rankers playing on the outside courts if you just buy Ground Admission. Prices start at £12 ($17.40), winding down to £4 ($5.80) at the end of the 2 weeks when there's much less to see; or £7 ($10.15) falling to £1 ($1.45), if you come after 5pm to catch the tail-end of the day's play. There are two more great deals, too: People leaving the show courts are encouraged to turn in their tickets for cheap resale, with the proceeds going to charity; and on the middle Saturday of the tournament all prices are discounted, including 2,000 Centre Court tickets. The gates open every day at 10:30am and play starts at noon on the outside courts, and 1pm on Centre and No.1 Courts (except finals weekend when it's 2pm). Come early—and I mean any time from 7am—because there are 6,000 ground tickets and the gates close for the day when the crowd inside reaches capacity.

The **Wimbledon Lawn Tennis Museum** (© **020/8946-6131**) is open daily 10:30am to 5pm. Tickets cost £5 ($7.25) adults, £4.25 ($6.15) students and seniors, and £3.50 ($5.10) for under-16s. It has all sorts of memorabilia, from costumes and tennis kit (including miniscule dresses worn by Venus Williams and Anna Kournikova), to TV footage of famous matches. A visit includes a tour of Centre Court. The museum is closed Friday to Sunday before the championships, the middle Sunday, and the Monday after it finishes. During the 2 weeks, it is only open to tournament visitors. It is also closed December 24 to 26 and January 1.Take the Tube to Southfields, then a 39, 93, or 200 bus.

# 7

# Shopping

The Brits tend to think of the United States as the home of the crazy consumer, but research has shown they're a little bit odd themselves. Wouldn't you know it, embarrassment is the main reason they buy online: Men rush at the chance to avoid having to guesstimate their partner's size in a sexy lingerie store, while women gratefully sidestep the technobabble from car and electronics salesmen. Otherwise, Brits still like to see, touch, scratch, and sniff what they're buying. Shopping is a buzz and, with around 30,000 stores, nowhere is buzzier than London.

Stores are usually open from 10am to 6pm, and most add on an extra hour at least 1 night a week. There's late-night shopping, as it's called, on Wednesday in Knightsbridge, Kensington, and Chelsea, and on Thursday, in the West End. Around touristy Covent Garden, many doors don't close until 7 or 8pm every night. Shops can open for 6 hours on a Sunday, and many do, usually from 11am or noon. If you're planning to visit a particular store, always call ahead to check.

## TAXES & SHIPPING

Most goods and services, with the exception of books, newspapers, groceries, and children's clothing, carry 17.5% value-added tax (VAT) in Britain, which is included in the price. Visitors from non-EC countries can reclaim the tax on any shopping they take home. Before you buy, check whether or not the store participates in the refund scheme, as unfortunately not all do. And although there is no official minimum purchase requirement, some stores set their own, usually around £50 ($72.50).

To make a claim, you must show identification at the store and fill out a VAT reclaim form then and there. Keep the receipt, form, and goods handy to show to the British Customs office at the airport (allowing ½ hour to stand in line). If you leave the country with your form unstamped, you've blown it. There are two ways to get the money: Either mail the form back to the store, choosing a credit card refund, or go to the VAT Export desk in the departure lounge, where you will lose money on the conversion rate if you take other than sterling. For more info, call Customs' **Passenger Enquiry Point** (© **020/8910-3744;** www.hmce.gov.uk/public/travel/index.htm).

VAT is not charged on goods shipped directly out of the country by the supplier—some stores will do that for you, at a price. But you will have to pay import duty at home. If you have overshopped and need to ship stuff yourself, call **London Baggage,** Gatwick London Air Terminal, Victoria Place, Victoria, London, England SW1W 9SJ (© **020/7828-2400;** www.londonbaggageltd.co.uk), or **Excess Baggage,** which has branches in every Heathrow and Gatwick Terminal, at Paddington railway station, and at Earl's Court Tube station (© **0800/783-1085;** www.excess-baggage.com).

## 1 Top Tips for Bargain Hounds

Britain is a pricey place. But never fear—this super-shopper has pounded the capital's pavements to unearth money-saving strategies, budget-friendly stores, and ideas for affordable but quintessentially English souvenirs (see the "London's Best Buys" box, below).

- **Net Savings.** Journalist Noelle Walsh will make your mouth water with her tales of amazing savings at **www.gooddealdirectory.co.uk**. I have also heard good things about **www.whatsonsale.co.uk**, but it was being rebuilt when we went to press. *Time Out* has a shopping section at **www.timeout.com/london/serv**.
- **London for Less.** This $19.95 discount card and guidebook gets you 20% off at around 50 shops, lots of them selling cashmere: see "Fifty Money-Saving Tips," in chapter 2.
- **Traditional Sales.** January sales are as English as plum pudding—and that's one thing always reduced by 30% after the Christmas holiday. London's summer sell-offs are exciting, too, and start earlier every year—certainly by the end of June.
  *Buyer beware:* Many stores ship stuff in especially for sales, and it may be of lower quality.
- **Samples, Seconds, and Ends of Lines.** As well as the two established sale companies (see "Regular Sales" under "Fashion," later in this chapter), which put on bimonthly bargain fests, the individual fashion designers also flog off their own excess inventory. The last week of November and the first few weeks of December are packed with sample sales: check the listings magazines for details. Other labels operate sale stores (see "Discount" under "Fashion," below). If you like posh table-setting, don't miss the Villeroy & Boch Factory Shop (see "China & Glass," below).
- **High Fashion at High Street Prices.** Many chainstores now commission top designers to create exclusive collections just for them. These include **Marks & Spencer** and **Debenhams** (see "Department Stores," below), as well as **Top Shop** (see "Contemporary" under "Fashion," later in this chapter).
- **Markets.** Knowledgeable locals and bargain-hunting visitors love to cruise London's outdoor markets (see "Markets," later in this chapter) for food, clothing, furniture, books, and crafts.

### EVENTS

There are all sorts of annual fairs, festivals, and special events in London that provide bumper opportunities for bargain-hunting. The only downside is that you may have to part with £5 to £10 ($7.25–$14.50) for admission. Check *Time Out* for details, particularly around Christmas when lots of charities raise money through craft fairs.

For instance, the art world may seem a scary and expensive place, but anyone can become a collector—it is largely a matter of timing. Prices start at £100 ($145) at **Art 2002.** This takes place January 16 to 20 and brings together more than 100 of Britain's leading contemporary art galleries at the Business Design Centre, Islington (© **020/7288-6005;** www.art-fair.co.uk). The **Art School degree shows** in May and June are great for hot talent at debut prices—you could spot Charles Saatchi shopping for his famous gallery. If you're in London from February 28 to March 3, or October 17 to October 20, visit the **Affordable**

*Tips*  **London's Best Buys**

Smart shoppers stock up on specialties you can only find in Britain, or that are made better here than anywhere else. Here are just a few ideas.

- Unusual **pickles** and **preserves**. As well as the stores and markets reviewed below, **The Spice Shop**, 115–117 Drummond St., NW1 (© 020/7916-1831; Tube: Euston, Warren St., or Great Portland St.), is a hotspot for authentic Indian chutneys. **Mr Christian's**, 11 Elgin Crescent, W11 (© 020/7229-0501; Tube: Ladbroke Grove), has shelves full of unusual preserves, such as quince and rose-petal jelly.

- **Stationery** is another best buy. Try **John Lewis** (see "Department Stores," below) for leather-bound address books, and **Paperchase**, 213 Tottenham Court Rd., W1 (© 020/7580-8496; www.paperchase. co.uk; Tube: Charing Cross) for gorgeous papers and notebooks. If you know anyone who still uses a Filofax, head straight for the British HQ where you can pick up every insert made for every size of filer: **The Filofax Centre**, 21 Conduit St., W1 (© 020/7499-0457; Tube: Oxford Circus).

- **Wet weather gear.** Few things are more British than the umbrella, and **James Smith & Sons**, 53 New Oxford St., WC1 (© 020/7836-4731; www.james-smith.co.uk; Tube: Holborn, Tottenham Court Rd.) has been making them since 1830. Traditional "brollies" come in nylon or silk, stretched over wood or metal frames, and prices start from about £30 ($43.50). Then head off to the **Burberry** factory shop for the classic trench coat at a discount (see "Discount" under "Fashion," below).

- **Classic entertainment.** For suitcase-friendly gifts for Anglophiles of every age, try the **BBC World Service Shop**, Bush House, Strand, WC2 (© 020/7557-2576; Tube: Temple). It stocks recordings of drama, comedy, and book readings from Radio 4, and lots of stuff for kids.

**Art Fair** in Battersea Park. Over 100 stands display paintings, prints, and sculpture, all priced at under £2,000 ($2,900). Tickets cost £7.50 ($10.90): for details, call © 020/7371-8787; www.wills-art.com.

Meanwhile, **New Designers 2002** is a super-degree show in July for 4,000 graduates from across Britain—jewelry, textile and glass-makers, ceramicists, and so on—also at the Business Design Centre (© 020/7359-3535; www.newdesigners.com). Canny collectors of decorative arts might also plan a trip to London at the end of the year. The **Chelsea Crafts Fair** is the largest in Europe and takes place during the last 2 weeks of October: contact the Crafts Council for details (© 020/7278-7700; www.craftscouncil.org.uk). The **Hidden Art** festival (© 020/7729-3301; www.hiddenart.co.uk) runs over the last weekend in November and first in December. It mobilizes more than 300 members of East London's design community to open their studios and workshops, and sell direct to the public. There are also monthly book fairs at the Hotel Russell, Russell Sq., WC1 (© 01763/248400; www.pbfa.org).

## 2 The Shopping Scene

The **West End** is the heart of London shopping; its main artery is **Oxford Street,** a mile of mass-market chains and department stores like John Lewis, Selfridges, and Marks & Spencer. At the eastern end, St. Giles High Street is the gateway into **Covent Garden,** a warren of narrow streets lined with stores selling quirky specialties and the hottest fashion trends. The old market is home to boutiques and craft stalls, while the piazza is a nonstop street festival of mime artists, singers, and entertainers.

Oxford Circus is the first big intersection walking west along Oxford Street, where it crosses the patchily elegant **Regent Street:** Turn south for Liberty, Aquascutum, Austin Reed, and Hamleys. Sixties' hotspot **Carnaby Street** is tucked in behind Liberty. After years as a naff tourist trap, it is now a hub of street and extreme sports fashion.

The next landmark westwards is New Bond Street, which changes to Old Bond Street as it heads south through **Mayfair.** It's wonderful for designer window-shopping and for fine art and antiques. Both Regent Street and Old Bond Street run into Piccadilly, to the south of which is **St James's** and some seriously upper-crust shopping. Here you'll find Hatchard's for books; Swaine, Adeney Brigg & Sons for fine leather goods and riding equipment; and the fabulous food halls of Fortnum & Mason. Jermyn Street is famous for shirtmakers; other fine shops include Paxton & Whitfield, a specialist cheesemonger, and Floris, which has been blending perfume since 1730.

Continue west from Piccadilly and Hyde Park Corner, to posh **Knightsbridge** and the world-famous Harrods department store on Brompton Road. Off Knightsbridge (it's a street as well as a neighborhood), is Sloane Street, lined with the most rarified names in haute couture. This runs down to Sloane Square and **Chelsea's** King's Road. The latter was the center of Swinging London in the 1960s and of the punk revolution a decade or so later. Mainstream boutiques have invaded now, but there's still a healthy dose of the avant-garde.

Young fashion and outdoor sports gear flourishes on **Kensington High Street.** Nearby **Notting Hill** is crammed with funky boutiques of every kind, especially around Portobello Market, though budget-busters are pushing out the neighborhood bargains—Westbourne Grove and Ledbury Road are *Vogue's* idea of heaven. You have to travel east to find a hip shopping scene still on the way up: creative **Clerkenwell,** or **Brick Lane** in the city. As well as the market, the latter now has Dray Walk, an enclave of quirky studio-shops and galleries.

## 3 Shopping A to Z

### ANTIQUES

There are thousands of antiques stores in London—hardly surprising because the place is ancient and the Brits never throw anything away. Like husbands at a barbecue, gangs of dealers naturally gravitate together so there are several arcades on the must-visit list. Otherwise, **Kensington Church Street,** W8, offers superb aspirational browsing: the shops here are the sort where you have to ring the bell to get in. Also check out "Markets" and "Auction Houses," below.

**Alfie's Antique Market**    With 150-plus dealers crammed into this old Edwardian department store, Alfie's would fox the most expert maze-builder. You name it, you'll find it here, from Art-Deco lighting to 20th-century ceramics, and at prices below the West End. Michael Jackson popped in to buy a bit of movie

**Finds** Mick the Trolley

One man's junk is another man's nice little earner. The rag-and-bone men knew that. These wily traders used to drive their horses and carts around London, knocking on people's doors offering to take away any unwanted household items. Then they sold the best stuff. Mick the Trolley still trawls wealthy Chelsea. You can usually find him, as well as some impressive bargains, at the car boot sale that takes place every 3 weeks at Christchurch C of E School, Caversham St., SW3 (© **020/7351-5597;** Tube: Sloane Sq.). Call for dates. Entry is 50p (73¢).

memorabilia during his visit to the UK last year. Closed Sunday and Monday. 13–25 Church St., NW8. © **020/7723-6066.** www.ealfies.com. Tube: Edgware Rd., Marylebone.

**Antiquarius**    More than 120 dealers have set up shop in this Arts and Crafts–style building. They sell everything from classic luggage to Art-Nouveau sculpture and jewelry. Head for the lower-priced basement hall. Closed Sundays. 131–141 King's Rd., SW3. © **020/7351-5353.** Tube: Sloane Sq.

**Camden Passage**    Bargains are hard to find, but there's wonderful browsing at the arcades, malls, and specialty stores lining this little enclave. The outdoor stalls are open on Wednesday and Saturday, bringing the dealer-count up to 250, and these are the best days to look for affordable jewelry, silverware, and trinkets. Off Upper St., N1. © **020/7226-4474.** Tube: Angel.

**Grays Antiques Market & Grays in the Mews**    The main antiques market is home to 85 dealers and it is red hot on jewelry, but the Mews is a better bet for bargain hunters especially if they're looking for something pocket-size, like a model car or music box. **Biblion** is an enormous hall especially for books, antiquarian and merely secondhand. Grays is closed on the weekends. Call for details on regular exhibitions. 58 and 1–7 Davies St., W1. © **020/7629-7034.** www.egrays.com. Tube: Bond St.

**London Silver Vaults**    This is a marvelous place to buy a wedding or christening present. Over 40 dealers trade in modern and antique silver, with prices starting at around £20 ($29). Closed Sundays. Chancery House, 53–64 Chancery Lane, WC2. © **020/7242-3844.** www.londonsilvervaults.co.uk. Tube: Chancery Lane.

## ART

**Cork Street,** Mayfair, is nose to tail with grand commercial galleries, while **Hoxton,** on the City's northern edge, has become the stalking ground of the brash new art entrepreneurs (see "Young, British & Hung in East London," p. 197). Both are strictly for window-shopping only. If you really want to get your wallet out, head for the **Alternative Art Market,** on Sundays at Old Spitalfields Market (see p. 233).

**Will's Art Warehouse**    Will Ramsay set up his warehouse in an old motorcycle garage in 1996 to debunk art-market snobbishness and offshore-bank-account prices. The 200 pictures on display change every 6 weeks. Customers can peruse the entire collection on a computer screen and choose which piece(s) they would like to see. Prices range from £50 ($72.50) to £2,000 ($2,900), and you can buy works on Will's website too. The venture has spun off into the now biannual **Affordable Art Fair** in Battersea Park (see "Events," above). Unit 3, Heathmans Rd., SW6. © **020/7371-8787.** www.wills-art.com. Tube: Parson's Green.

## AUCTION HOUSES

A Monet sold for millions to a mystery bidder always grabs the headlines, but it's a tiny part of what passes through London's salerooms: from toys to fine wine, Roman coins to rock stars' underpants. Emotions and prices run high, so it's a great spectator sport, and the lots go on view to the public for a few days beforehand. London's four biggest auction houses first banged their gavels in the 18th century. To find out what's on (little in August), contact their main salerooms: **Bonhams & Brooks,** Montpelier St., SW7 (© **020/7393-3900;** www.bonhams.com; Tube: Knightsbridge); **Phillips,** 101 New Bond St., W1 (© **020/7629-6602;** www.phillips-auctions.com; Tube: Bond St.); and **Sotheby's,** 34–35 New Bond St., W1 (© **020/7293-5000;** www.sothebys.com; Tube: Bond St.). **Christie's** has been looking to move out of Mayfair into new headquarters but, for the meantime, try 8 King St., SW1 (© **020/7839-9060;** www.christies.com; Tube: Green Park).

**Chiswick Auctions** (Finds) This friendly local saleroom is a place where travelers on a budget can dare to raise their hands as prices start as low as £10 ($14.50). Loony lots often add to the party atmosphere: fake marble columns from a props company or 5-foot-high bronze parrots. But there's good stuff, too. Chiswick Auctions handles a lot of private libraries. Viewing runs from Sunday afternoon until the auction starts on Tuesday—small goods at 5pm, furniture from 7pm, every week. 1 Colville Rd., W3. © **020/8992-4442.** Tube: Acton Lane.

## BATH & BODY

**Lush** You've probably never seen anything quite like Lush—it's a beauty shop that takes "organic" to a whole new level. Huge slabs of soap burst with pineapple slices (good for the skin) or poppy seeds (a great exfoliator). The store whips up fresh facial masks and keeps them over ice. Just scoop some into a take-home container and keep refrigerated. Lush is a fabulous source for gifts, especially for visitors from the U.S., where the store has yet to open. The best-seller is the "bath bomb," which fizzes and scents the water. There are branches on King's Road, Chelsea, and Carnaby Street in Soho, as well as at Victoria railway station. Units 7 and 11, The Piazza, Covent Garden, WC2. © **020/7240-4570.** www.lush.co.uk. Tube: Covent Garden.

**Neal's Yard Remedies** Founded in 1981, this is still the best shop in London for herbal toiletries, homeopathic hair remedies, and alternative medicines. Most of the products come in deep-blue glass bottles, and make attractive and reasonably priced gifts. Try Remedies-to-Roll, roll-on essential oils to fit in your handbag, including one for sleep. Or create your own bespoke potions, choosing oils and extracts to add to base lotions and creams. The store is at the end of a short cul-de-sac off Short's Gardens. There is a second one at Chelsea Farmers Market in Sydney Street. 15 Neal's Yard, WC2. © **020/7379-7222.** www. nealsyardremedies.com. Tube: Covent Garden.

---

*Moments* **Take 5**

When I'm all shopped out, nerve ends fraying and feet aflame, I like to take five with a drink, a sandwich, and my book in the churchyard of St. Paul's in Covent Garden. Enclosed by buildings, it's a peaceful place with benches and rambling roses. The garden is open from 8:30am to 4:30pm Monday to Friday; enter on Henrietta Street or King Street.

---

**Penhaligon's**    Barber William Penhaligon opened for business in 1841 and the scents are still made by hand according to his formulas. This lavish store sells soaps, eau de cologne, and shaving kits. It also has a fine selection of antique scent bottles and silver accessories, such as boxes, mirrors, and manicure sets. The most famous women's scents are Violetta and Bluebell. Love Potion No. 9 is irresistible. 41 Wellington St., WC2. ✆ 020/7836-2150. www.penhaligons.co.uk. Tube: Covent Garden.

## BOOKS

London is one of the best places in the world for avid readers and bibliophiles. The city has 1,000 or so booksellers, dealing in new, not-so-new, and antiquarian volumes. Look for entire shops devoted to art, science fiction, religion, medicine, crime, politics, sport, and travel. Browsers should start from Leicester Square Tube station and walk north along **Charing Cross Road,** the heart of London's bookselling community. And don't ignore side streets like St. Martin's Court and Cecil Court. Bloomsbury (**Museum Street** in particular) also has more than 30 secondhand book shops and scholarly antiquarian dealers. Or pop into the **Biblion** book hall at Grays (see "Antiques," above).

**Books Etc.**    Given the choice, I'd always go to Books Etc. in preference to its mammoth U.S. parent, Borders, because I find the layout of Books Etc. to be much more user-friendly. It is very good on modern fiction and holds some backlist titles. And it regularly puts on readings and author signings, as does the branch at 26 James St., Covent Garden. 421 Oxford St., W1. ✆ 020/7495-5850. Tube: Bond St.

**Books for Cooks**    This store stocks nearly 12,000 cookery books: the classics, hot manifestos from celebrity chefs and recipes from virtually every ethnic cuisine. BFC has also compiled a series of little books of recipes tried out in its test kitchen—a great bargain buy. That's also where the chefs rustle up the soups, salads, and puddings that make this such a great pit-stop. Sadly, the store has stopped its famous three-course meals, but at least you don't need a reservation now. 4 Blenheim Crescent, W11. ✆ 020/7221-1992. www.booksforcooks.com. Tube: Ladbroke Grove, Notting Hill Gate.

**Borders Books, Music & Café**    This U.S. import stocks almost 250,000 titles and, allegedly, the biggest choice of newspapers and magazines in the country. The busy Café Express, where Borders holds readings and events, is on the second floor. There's a second branch in Charing Cross Road. 203–207 Oxford St., W1. ✆ 020/7292-1600. www.bordersstores.com. Tube: Oxford Circus, Tottenham Court Rd.

**Children's Book Centre**    A brilliant place for baby bookworms and their parents. There are more than 15,000 titles for every age group up to 15, from fiction to fun factual stuff. The shop is crammed with toys, CD-ROMs, and audio tapes, too. Some Saturdays, it arranges "personal appearances" by popular cartoon characters. 237 Kensington High St., W8. ✆ 020/7937-7497. www.childrensbook centre.co.uk. Tube: Kensington High St.

**Crime in Store**    This is absolutely my favorite store for a wet weekend afternoon. You can settle down on the sofa and browse through fictional whodunnits and true crime stories, knowing you're among kindred spirits. 14 Bedford St., WC2. ✆ 020/7379-3795. www.crimeinstore.co.uk. Tube: Covent Garden, Charing Cross.

**Foyles**    The famous, and famously old-fashioned, Foyles has given itself a partial makeover. It has launched a website, started opening on Sundays, and at last stacks fiction alphabetically rather than having separate sections for each publisher. Reassuringly, the store still looks chaotic, crammed with books on virtually every topic under the sun. It's the place to come for titles other shops have stopped stocking, or never did in the first place. 113–119 Charing Cross Rd., WC2. ℂ 020/7440-5660. www.foyles.co.uk. Tube: Leicester Sq., Tottenham Court Rd.

**Garden Books**   Gardening has never been funkier in Britain. The endless backyard makeovers on TV are making even those yuppies who'd rather be seen dead than with a trowel in their hand sit up and pay attention. This store opened in 1996 and now carries around 7,000 titles, including a section on interior design. If a book ain't here, then it's probably out of print. 11 Blenheim Crescent, W11. ℂ 020/7792-0777. Tube: Ladbroke Grove, Notting Hill Gate.

**Gay's the Word**   The fantastically comprehensive stock makes this Britain's biggest gay and lesbian bookshop. It has everything from literary fiction to detective novels and erotica, as well as issues-based titles, philosophy, and politics. 66 Marchmont St., WC1. ℂ 020/7278-7654. www.gaystheword.co.uk. Tube: Russell Sq.

**Hatchards**   A holder of Royal Warrants from the Duke of Edinburgh and the Prince of Wales, Hatchards has been trading since 1797. It carries popular fiction and nonfiction titles, and all the latest releases. Just climbing the creaking stairs and browsing the venerable wooden stacks makes one feel frightfully uppercrust. 187 Piccadilly, W1. ℂ 020/7439-9921. www.hatchards.co.uk. Tube: Piccadilly Circus.

**Offstage Theatre & Cinema Bookshop**   Offstage is packed with drama students and the occasional famous actor thumbing through play and movie scripts. There is every kind of specialty book here, including sections on circus, stagecraft, cinematography, and commedia dell'arte. Check out the big secondhand department, too. 37 Chalk Farm Rd., NW1. ℂ 020/7485-4996. Tube: Camden Town, Chalk Farm.

**Stanfords Map & Travel Bookshop**   Stanford's is world-renowned for its exhaustive collection of travel literature, guidebooks, atlases, and maps of every kind, from maritime to historical, for biking or hiking, and covering every region of the world. It has a good selection of globes, too. Oddly enough, though, there are few guides to London—not exotic enough, obviously. 12–14 Long Acre, WC2. ℂ 020/7836-1321. www.stanfords.co.uk. Tube: Covent Garden.

**The Travel Bookshop**   This little gem is the last of the trio of specialist bookshops in Blenheim Crescent—you'll find the cooking and gardening ones in the list above. It carries a huge variety of travel literature and guidebooks, both old and new, mainstream and more adventurous. 13–15 Blenheim Crescent, W11. ℂ 020/7229-5260. www.thetravelbookshop.co.uk. Tube: Ladbroke Grove.

**Waterstone's**   It seems a bit insulting to call this a mere bookshop when it's the largest one in Europe. Spread over seven floors in the building where posh store Simpson used to be, the Waterstone's flagship is the very model of a modern emporium. There are over 265,000 titles here, as well as Internet access, a juice bar, cafe, lounge bar, and the Red Room restaurant. It holds regular events and is a great place for a free wee if you get caught short sightseeing and need the bathroom. 203–206 Piccadilly, W1. ℂ 020/7851-2400. www.waterstones.co.uk. Tube: Green Park, Piccadilly Circus.

## CHINA & GLASS

**Reject China Shop**   Most of the very wide range of English china sold here is seconds or discontinued lines. This branch also stocks cutlery and crystal. Shoppers who know the going prices in the United States may pick up a bargain.

The other shops are in Brompton Road, Knightsbridge, and Covent Garden Piazza. 134 Regent St., W1. ✆ 020/7734-2502. www.chinacraft.co.uk. Tube: Piccadilly Circus.

**Royal Doulton**    Founded over 200 years ago, Royal Doulton is one of the most famous names from the heart of English china production in Staffordshire. The company also produces Minton, Royal Albert, and Royal Crown Derby, all stocked here. 154 Regent St., W1. ✆ 020/7734-3184. www.royal-doulton.com. Tube: Piccadilly Circus.

**Villeroy & Boch Factory Shop**    This German company has been making high-class tableware since 1748. You can find it in all the top London stores, from Harrods to Selfridges and Liberty. However, take the Tube to the wealthy suburb of Wimbledon, near the end of the District line, and you'll save a whopping 30% to 70% on seconds and discontinued ranges. 267 Merton Rd., SW18. ✆ 020/8875-6006. www.villeroy.com. Tube: Southfields.

**Waterford Wedgwood**    Waterford crystal and Wedgwood china share the same table at this upscale shop. Fine cut-glass vases, platters, and objets d'art come in a wide range of prices. You can even splash out on complete sets of the famous powder-blue and white Jasper china, and lots of other styles and patterns, too. There's a smaller branch on Piccadilly. 158 Regent St., W1. ✆ 020/7734-7262. www.waterfordwedgwood.co.uk. Tube: Piccadilly Circus.

## CRAFTS

For years, popular prejudice lauded the noble artist and dissed the craftsman. Not anymore. Britain is in the grip of a passion for great design. Ceramicists, jewelry and textile-makers, glassworkers, and others command huge respect and all-too respectable prices. Check out **Contemporary Applied Arts,** 2 Percy St., W1 (✆ 020/7436-2344; www.caa.org.uk; Tube: Tottenham Court Rd.): the organization represents more than 200 makers, with diverse skills, and exhibits their work in what is the largest specialist gallery in Britain. The independent but publicly funded **Crafts Council** has two shops, too—one is at the Victoria & Albert Museum (see chapter 6) and the other at its gallery, 44a Pentonville Rd., N1 (✆ 020/7806-2559; www.craftscouncil.org.uk; Tube: Angel). Big pieces are look-but-don't-touch, but small ceramics, jewelry, or scarves shouldn't bust the budget. The Crafts Council can also give you a schedule of open-studio days, when individual designers welcome visitors to their workshops and you can buy without paying the middleman's mark-up. Call ✆ 020/7278-7700.

## DEPARTMENT STORES

**Debenhams**    Once-dowdy Debenhams shocked the fashion pack when it became one of the first chain stores to persuade big name designers to descend to high street level. Now the list of hot-name collaborators includes **Pearce II Fionda, Maria Grachvogel, Edina Ronay, John Rocha,** and undies queen **Janet Reger. Tristan Webber** is the latest addition. Last year, chic chicks could have slipped into a floaty satin dress by **Jasper Conran** for £80 ($116). The lads had an even tastier bargain—black wool trousers designed by **Oswald Boateng** for £45 ($65.25). As well as her covetable womenswear, **Elspeth Gibson** has created the Sweet Pea range for girls aged 3 to 8. And now Debenhams is even roping some of these same designers into creating interiors ranges. 334–348 Oxford St., W1. ✆ 020/7580-3000. www.debenhams.co.uk. Tube: Bond St., Oxford Circus.

**Harrods**    Opened in 1849, Harrods claims it's the most famous department store in the world, and that anything in the world can be bought (or ordered)

---

**Tips**   **Beware the Bathroom Rip-off**

Harrods makes shoppers pay an outrageous £1 ($1.45) to use its bathrooms. Unless they've changed the system, the only way to beat the charge is to say "yes" when the attendant asks if you've been to the cafe. Otherwise, nip five minutes up the road to Harvey Nichols where there's no charge and the queues are a good deal shorter.

---

here. The incredible ground-floor food halls are a feast for all the senses. And, for sheer theme-park excess, nothing beats the Egyptian escalator and the children's department with its cartoon cafe and specialty hairdresser. On the minus side, the store layout is very frustrating. With around 35,000 visitors a day, it can become a nightmare experience, like Disney World on the 4th of July. Harrods also has a snooty dress code: no dirty or unkempt clothing, ripped jeans, high-cut shorts, athletic singlets, cycling shorts, and bare tummies or feet. Knightsbridge, SW1. ℂ 020/7730-1234. www.harrods.com. Tube: Knightsbridge.

**Harvey Nichols**   This elegant store is nicknamed Harvey Nic's by its fashion-pack and It-Girl clientele, and it could hardly be more different from its brash Knightsbridge neighbor, Harrods. Whereas the latter is crammed to opulent bursting point with everything under the sun, and much of it in dubious taste, Harvey Nichols is a cool haven of chic. It pioneered the showcasing of designer collections from London, Paris, and Milan—from Chloe to Gaultier, Tocca to Joseph—and has a decent menswear department, too. And you can't go hungry here either: as well as the food hall and fifth-floor bar, cafe, and restaurant, Harvey Nicks also has a YO! Sushi and a Wagamama (see chapter 5). 109–125 Knightsbridge, SW1. ℂ 020/7235-5000; www.harveynichols.com. Tube: Knightsbridge.

**John Lewis**   This is one of the few remaining traditional department stores that really does stock everything, from fashions and fashion fabrics, to curtain fabrics and furniture, clothing, washing machines, and lovely leather-bound diaries. John Lewis makes a big promise—"Never Knowingly Undersold." If customers find the same goods locally at a better price, the store will refund the difference. (And it employs an army of undercover shoppers to check out the competition.) Sister store **Peter Jones,** Sloane Sq., SW1 (ℂ **020/7730-3434;** www.peterjones.co.uk; Tube: Sloane Sq.), is the Sloane Ranger's spiritual home. It is having an £80-million refurb, due to be complete in 2004. 278–306 Oxford St., W1. ℂ **020/7629-7711.** www.johnlewis.com. Tube: Oxford Circus.

**Liberty**   If Selfridges is all flash, cash, marble and gold, then Liberty is baroque sensuality. London's prettiest department store may be olde worlde on the outside (neo-Tudor, in fact), but everything here is very, very stylish. As well as clothing with the famous Liberty imprint, it has a fantastic array of women's fashions by well-known and up-and-coming designers. And don't miss the world-famous furnishing and dress fabrics. Liberty is far from cheap, but you're bound to find something to take home as a small gift on the bazaar-like first floor or among the housewares downstairs. 210–214 Regent St., W1. ℂ **020/ 7734-1234.** www.liberty-of-london.com. Tube: Oxford Circus.

**Marks & Spencer**   Things have come to a pretty pass when the French protest against store closures, as they did in Paris last year, and the Brits wonder why on earth they bother. The home crowd has lost all respect for the venerable M&S. Neither the new vampy undies range, Salon Rose, nor the Autograph label, designed by Katherine Hamnett, Betty Jackson, and others, managed to reverse its plummeting fortunes. A "good value" label called George was due to launch last October. We'll just have to wait and see if that does the trick. In the meantime, those machine-washable bad-girl basques are still a bargain, and the food hall does yummy lunchtime sandwiches and salads. 458 Oxford St., W1. ℭ 020/7935-7954. www.marksandspencer.com. Tube: Marble Arch.

**Selfridges**    Chicago salesman Harry Selfridge opened this store in 1909, stunning Londoners with his marble halls and sheer variety of goods. An opulent revamp, just completed, is stunning them again. The ground-floor perfumery and cosmetics department is the biggest in Europe. Upstairs is crammed with covetable designer fashions and home accessories. And Miss Selfridge is several shops within a shop within a shop. It has its own teen-queen label—which you can also find in a chain of outlets around the country—and hosts high street names, including Oasis and Warehouse, alongside some funky young designers. Selfridges also boasts one of London's finest food halls, and the biggest choice of restaurants and cafes of all the department stores. 400 Oxford St., W1. ℭ 020/7629-1234. www.selfridges.co.uk. Tube: Bond St., Marble Arch.

# FASHION
## CHILDREN
Floaty womenswear designer Elspeth Gibson has turned to a younger clientele—girls aged 3 to 6—and created the Sweet Pea collection for **Debenhams** (see "Department Stores," above). The store also has a 0 to 3 range by **Jaspar Conran,** Junior J, and its own label. Also check out **H&M** (see below). It is virtually unique among the fashion chains in doing kids clothes—like Gap with a Euro-twist and almost half the price.

## CONTEMPORARY
No one wants to look like a chainstore clone but high street names compete so hard on quality and design nowadays, and change their stock so often, that it is easy to put together a chic and individual look. Especially if you follow our advice for nabbing bargain designer pieces to mix in with your budget imitations. Start at Oxford Circus. Near H&M and Top Shop, you'll find another favorite, **Oasis,** 12–14 Argyll St., W1 (ℭ **020/7434-1799**), where you can park the man in your life on a comfy sofa while you try on the clothes. Just opposite is **Warehouse,** 19–21 Argyll St., W1 (ℭ **020/7437-7101**). For **Miss Selfridge,** check out Selfridges in "Department Stores."

Apart from M&S, Britain's clothing stores are still pretty hopeless at catering for women of other than average size (4–10 in the US, which is 8–14 in the UK). H&M and Top Shop are rare exceptions, as is **Dorothy Perkins,** West One Shopping Centre, 379 Oxford St., W1 (ℭ **020/7495-6181;** www.dorothyperkins.co.uk; Tube: Bond St). It has both a petite range and one that goes up to size 20 (16 US).

**Accessorize**    This fabulous shop can help you turn any old frock into a knock 'em dead dazzler, and prices are so reasonable you don't have to save up to buy its wares or save them just for special occasions. Flirty little bags cost £15 to £25 ($21.75–$29). It also has sumptuous scarves, hats, and girly jewelry, in all the season's prettiest colors. 386 Oxford St., W1. ℭ 020/7491-9424. www.accessorize.co.uk. Tube: Bond St.

**H&M**    This Swedish chain has its flagship store just the other side of Oxford Circus from Top Shop. It too has been around a long time yet it has always seemed to be of the time, constantly refreshing its image. Like ice-cream flavors, different H&M labels cater to different tastes, from frontline fashion trends to clubbing skimpies, slouching streetwear to classics for work. And three cheers for a store that recognizes we're not all Hollywood lollipop-heads, a la Ally McBeal: the Big is Beautiful range goes up to size 30 (26 U.S.). H&M also does funky maternity wear, tough stuff for kids, and menswear too. All at very good value prices. 261–271 Regent St., W1. ⓒ 020/7493-4004. www.hm.com. Tube: Oxford Circus.

**Top Shop/Top Man**   The multi-floored, multi-everything Top Shop used to sell cheap tat for teenyboppers, but its funky styles have now become top wannabuys for stylists and their pop star clients. Yet, it's still amazingly cheap. The TS Design label boasts an army of A-list names: **Clements Ribeiro, Hussein Chalayan, Tracey Boyd,** plus **Markus Lupfer.** Others who haven't quite become international names yet take guest spots at Bazaar, a section that apes the feel of Portobello or Camden market. But I love Top Shop for its Tall Girl label—women's jeans with a 36" leg! You can get your clothes customized, get a haircut, and get severe brain ache because this is the kind of noisy full-on place that turns even dedicated shopaholics into shopping-phobes. 214 Oxford St., W1. ⓒ 020/7636-7700. www.tops.co.uk. Tube: Oxford Circus.

## DISCOUNT

**Browns Labels for Less**   Browns is the sort of name that wins star treatment from a designer when the buyer visits a collection. The main boutiques show-case only the best names—from Chloe to Jill Sander—and can make a hot young newcomer. All unsold stock from last season is moved across to Browns Labels for Less, where it is discounted from 30% to 70%. You never know what you'll find: Issy Miyake, perhaps, or Comme des Garcons, Dries van Noten, and Prada accessories. 50 S. Molton St., W1. ⓒ 020/7514-0052. www.brownsfashion.com. Tube: Bond St.

**Burberry's Factory Outlet**   Burberry is back from the dead. Not long ago only tourists actually wore the famous plaid, but now Britain's best-known luxury marque is also one of the hippest and best loved. And that plaid is on everything—from trench coats to trench dresses, and even knickers, eye masks, and bikinis. You have to take a local train to get to the factory shop, but savings of up to a third on samples and ends of lines will more than cover the cost of your ticket. (Burberry also has a very swanky new store at 21–23 New Bond St., W1.) 29–53 Chatham Place, E9. ⓒ 020/8328-4320. Train: Hackney Central BR station.

**Central Park**   I snapped up an aqua linen skirt and a faux Burberry bag for £15 ($21.75) each here, and few things cost more than £20 ($29). The clothes at Central Park may not be built to last a lifetime but they'll look good while they do. 22 Kensington Church St., W8. ⓒ 020/7937-3672. Tube: High St. Kensington.

**Paul Smith**   There are three floors stocking this hot British designer, mens and kidswear only, and mostly last season's. Discounts range from 30% to 70%. 23 Avery Row, W1. ⓒ 020/7493-1287. www.paulsmith.co.uk. Tube: Bond St.

## REGULAR SALES

Vivienne Westwood, Valentino, Dolce & Gabana, Elspeth Gibson, Miu Miu, Prada, Gucci, Neisha Crosland, Paul Smith, John Smedley . . . the list goes on and on. Both the sales organizers below claim to have bagged all these hot designers and dozens more.

**Designer Warehouse Sales**   For 40% to 80% discounts on cancelled orders, showroom and catwalk samples, and just-*passé* styles from nearly 100 top fashion names, check out the bimonthly Designer Warehouse Sales. These run for 3 days—menswear usually the week after womenswear—starting on a Thursday, which is when you should go for the best pickings. Register online, for free, to get advance warning of sale dates. Entry is £2 ($2.90). The Worx, 45 Balfe St., N1. © 020/7704-1064. www.dwslondon.co.uk. Tube: King's Cross.

**Designer Sale UK**  Registering online for free lets you in on the Wednesday preview day. This is hardly exclusive because anybody qualifies, but it might just give you an edge. Sales go on until Sunday and take place every couple of months. Discounts on the 150 rails of hot designer mens and womenswear and accessories sometimes go as high as 90%. Entry is £2 ($2.90). Atlantis Gallery, Old Truman Brewery, 146 Brick Lane, E1. © 01273/470880, or 020/7247-8595 on sale week. www.designersales.co.uk. Tube: Liverpool St., Aldgate East.

## SHOES
London's shoe stores almost outnumber pubs and churches. **King's Road** in Chelsea, **Neal Street** in Covent Garden, and **South Molton Street** just by Bond Street Tube are the best for hot but affordable styles.

**Clarks**  British kids have been growing up in Clarks' sensible shoes for 175 years. Now this staid brand has blossomed, selling a small collection of great-value fashion shoes. Most are for well-scrubbed eco-hippies. Some are simple but smart. But none of them will give you bunions. 260 Oxford St., W1 (© 020/ 7499-0305. www.clarks.co.uk. Tube: Oxford Circus.

**Office**  Urban warriors and dolly birds will love this store. It sells the sort of shoes you drool over in glossy magazines—for men as well as women—but for very reasonable prices. There's a branch of the sister sports shoe shop, **Offspring,** nearby at no. 60 Neal St. The **Office Sale Shop** at 61 St. Martin's Lane, WC2, has ends of lines and last year's models at up to half price. 57 Neal St., WC2. © 020/ 7379-1896. www.office.co.uk. Tube: Covent Garden.

## VINTAGE & SECONDHAND
Did you know that the cute penguin pajamas Renée Zellweger wore last year as London's favorite singleton, *Bridget Jones,* actually came from Oxfam? Her image may not have been the sleekest, but real life fashion babes Stella McCartney and Kate Moss are deep into thrift-shop chic, too. The stock can be very good quality. **Oxfam** (www.oxfam.org.uk) is Britain's fifth biggest retailer, selling Fair Trade products, gifts, furnishings, and books, as well as secondhand clothes. **Oxfam Originals** stores concentrate solely on funky, retro fashions. There are three in Central London, at 123a King's Rd., Shawfield St., SW3 (© 020/7351-7979; Tube: Sloane Sq.); 22 Earlham St., WC2 (© 020/7836-9666; Tube: Covent Garden); and 26 Ganton St., W1 (© 020/7437-7338; Tube: Oxford Circus).

---

*Fun Fact*  **Footwear Fables**

Doc Martens—those funky, clunky boots with the air-cushioned soles that are requisite street wear for cool kids the world over—were invented by Dr. Klaus Maertens in post-war Germany as a comfort shoe for old ladies. At **Dr. Marten's Department Store,** 1–4 King St., WC2 (© 020/7497-1460; www.drmartens.com; Tube: Covent Garden), you can pick up a pair of the basic shoes for £40 to £50 ($58–$72.50). Camden Market has them at a discount.

Otherwise, **Monmouth Street** in Covent Garden is a hot spot for retread fashions. For great 1970s gear, head to **Pop Boutique** (no. 6): my suede sweater cost less than £20 ($29) yet people always assume it's this season's Bond Street bank-breaker. **The Loft** (no. 35) is a dress agency handling the city girl's favorite labels. **Cenci** (no. 31) has mostly secondhand Italian stuff, for boys and girls.

**Blackout II**    This fun emporium has hidden depths—below the small store front is a basement crammed with gear. From the glamorous 1930s to the glam 1970s and 1980s, from crocodile handbags and feather boas to kitsch fake fur and bell bottoms, you'll find it here. To rent for a wild London club night, as well as to buy. 51 Endell St., WC2. ℂ 020/7240-5006. www.blackout2.com. Tube: Covent Garden.

**Cornucopia**    The stock is so huge that there are definitely bargains to be found here, it just takes a bit of rummaging to find them. But that's so much fun with this treasure trove of costumes from the 1920s on, all arranged by era. Women off to the hottest parties in town come here for entrance-making evening wear and the costume jewelry to go with it. 12 Upper Tachbrook St., SW1. ℂ 020/7828-5752. Tube: Victoria.

**Pandora**    Ladies who lunch don't throw last season's clothes away: They sell them through this Knightsbridge dress agency. Pandora is the grande dame of the secondhand scene, claiming to hold every famous designer from Armani to Zilkha (Ronit, that is). The stock is seasonally correct, and there are even sales: from July to August, and December to January. 16–22 Cheval Place, SW7. ℂ 020/7589-5289. Tube: Knightsbridge.

**Retro Man, Retro Woman, and Retro Jewellery**    There are no guarantees with secondhand stores but the gear at these three is generally good quality, with a smattering of designer names and barely-worn bargains. Both clothing stores have £5 ($7.25) bargain basements. The handbags and shoes at no. 30 would make Carrie Bradshaw flex her plastic, with names such as Gucci making a regular appearance. Part of the burgeoning Music & Video Exchange empire, these stores operate the same pricing policy: the longer an item hangs around, the further the price falls. And you can take your own stuff in to swap or sell. 30, 32, 34 Pembridge Rd., W11. ℂ 020/7792-1715, or 020/7727-4805. www.buy-sell-trade.co.uk. Tube: Notting Hill Gate.

## WOOLENS

**Westaway & Westaway**    The window mannequins at this old-fashioned store look like Hitchcock heroines frozen in time, but then the stock is very traditional, ranging from lambswool sweaters, to Shetland knits with handmade fair isle yokes, to miniature kilts for the kids. Prices are old-fashioned, too: at £35 ($50.75), the woven lambswool stoles make pashminas look prohibitively expensive as well as *passé*. 64–65 Great Russell St., WC1. ℂ 020/7405-4479. www.westaway.co.uk. Tube: Holborn.

## FOOD & DRINK
### FOOD HALLS

London's department-store food halls are a Bacchanalian feast of vibrant colors and exotic smells. Pick your treats wisely, though, or you could break the bank. **Harrods** is the king of food halls. There are close to 20 departments, of which the meat, fish, and poultry room—with its mosaics of peacocks and wheat sheaves, ceramic fish, scallop shells, boars, and more—is the most amazing. The best handbag-size buys are jams made with fruits rarely found at home, like gooseberries. Rows of food counters sell every kind of portable lunch, perfect for a picnic in Hyde Park across the road. Or try neighboring **Harvey Nichols,** lauded for its stylish branded goods. The **Selfridges** food hall is much more compact than Harrods, but it packs an awful lot in, and the wine and choccy departments are separate.

**Fortnum & Mason**    This may be a department store but few shoppers penetrate beyond the food hall—unless it's to have afternoon tea (see chapter 5). Mr. Fortnum and Mr. Mason opened their doors in 1707 and it is *the* place to find the aristocratic foods and empire-building delicacies you've only ever seen in period movies—traditional hams and pies, for instance, as well as cheeses, handmade chocolates, and preserves. Fortnum knows everything there is to know about tea: The house range is pricey but includes more than 50 blends and it's said that if you take along a sample of your tap water, they'll know which one to pair it with. 181 Piccadilly, W1. ⓒ 020/7734-8040. www.fortnumandmason.com. Tube: Green Park, Piccadilly Circus.

## SPECIALITIES

**The Chocolate Society**    The Chocolate Society uses the venerated Valrhona in all its chocolates. This is 70% cocoa solids, more than three times a normal candy bar, so when you come into this little shop, stand and inhale the mouthwatering smell. Shelves groan with truffles, chocolate-dipped fruit, cakes, and more. 36 Elizabeth St., SW1. ⓒ 020/7259-9222. www.chocolate.co.uk. Tube: Victoria, Sloane Sq.

**Condon Fishmongers** *(Finds*    This place is truly scent-sational. Salmon, haddock, eels, cod's roe, and much more pass through the traditional smokehouse in the back of the store. Herrings turn into kippers here, creating the aroma of a traditional British breakfast. The store is closed after 1pm on Thursday, and on Sunday and Monday. 363 Wandsworth Rd., SW8. ⓒ 020/7622-2934. Tube: Stockwell, then no. 77 bus.

**A. Gold** *(Finds*    Opposite Old Spitalfields Market, this store specializes in British foods, from candy to liqueurs; clotted cream to cakes that make you want to freeze time at tea-time. And it is all so much more authentic than the many so-called traditional treats packaged and priced for the tourist market. 42 Brushfield St., E1. ⓒ 020/7247-2487. Tube: Liverpool St.

**Neal's Yard Dairy**    This is *the* place for British and Irish cheeses—none of that foreign muck—from the old favorites to delicious new ones developed by farmhouse cheese-makers. Staff are delighted for you to try before you buy. Then pop 'round the corner to **Neal's Yard Bakery,** 6 Neal's Yard, WC2 (ⓒ **020/ 7836-5199**), for still-warm bread to go with your selection. There is a second dairy at Borough Market, SE1 (see "Markets," below). 17 Shorts Gardens, WC2. ⓒ 020/7379-7646. Tube: Covent Garden.

**Paxton & Whitefield**    London's most venerable cheese shop (est. 1797) concentrates on English and French farmhouse cheeses—about 200 in all— and matures each one itself. Prices are refreshingly reasonable despite the uppercrust location, and shelves groan with a big selection of wine and port, plus gourmet accessories such as olives and biscuits, to go with whichever cheese you choose. 93 Jermyn St., SW1. ⓒ 020/7930-0259. www.cheesemongers.co.uk. Tube: Green Park.

## TEA

**The Tea House**    Besides teapots and tea balls, this wonderful-smelling shop sells more than 70 varieties of tea from India, China, Japan, and the rest of the world. Available loose or in bags, traditional English blends make excellent, light, and inexpensive gifts. 15 Neal St., WC2. ⓒ 020/7240-7539. Tube: Covent Garden.

**Whittard of Chelsea**  Whittard has everything you need to make a luvverly cuppa, even pure origin teas you can blend yourself. It sells a full range of coffees, too, and colorful ceramics. There are more than 20 branches in London. 38 Covent Garden Market, WC2. ✆ 020/7379-6599. www.whittard.com. Tube: Covent Garden.

## WHISKEY

**Milroys of Soho**  Milroys has perhaps the longest whisky list in London, including the rare and collectable, from Ireland and Scotland, New Zealand, Czechoslovakia, and Japan. There are American bourbons, too, if you're feeling homesick. The store has moved into the cellar to make room for a tasting bar at street level, open Monday to Saturday, 11am to 11pm. 3 Greek St., W1. ✆ 020/7437-9311. www.milroys.co.uk. Tube: Leicester Sq.

**The Vintage House**  This little store opened just after World War II and stocks over 750 whiskies, as well as rare old bottles of other spirits, champagne, fine wines, and Cuban cigars. It is open until 11pm, and shuts on Sundays. 42 Old Compton St., W1. ✆ 020/7437-2592. www.sohowhisky.com. Tube: Leicester Sq.

## MARKETS

Farmers' markets may be old hat in the United States, but they're a new idea in London. The produce is all English, whatever's in season, and much of it chemical-free. Farmers sell only their own produce and also make the sausages, cheese, jams, and so on—even buffalo pastrami. You'll find the biggest range at **Islington Farmers' Market,** Essex Rd. opposite Islington Green, N1 (Tube: Angel), open Sundays 10am to 2pm. **Notting Hill Farmers' Market,** behind Waterstones on Notting Hill Gate, W11 (Tube: Notting Hill Gate), Saturday 9am to 1pm; **Swiss Cottage Farmers' Market,** Winchester Market, Avenue Rd., NW3 (Tube: Swiss Cottage), Wednesday 10am to 4pm. For information, call ✆ 020/7704-9659; www.londonfarmersmarkets.com.

**Bermondsey Market**  Forget Portobello Road, charming though it is. This is where serious antiques collectors and dealers come—burglary victims, too, tracking down stolen possessions. It's a dawn start with the serious business done by 9am and stalls closing from noon. The market is a bit of a trek from the Tube but it's an adventure. Bermondsey Sq., SE1. Fri only 5am–2pm. Tube: Bermondsey, London Bridge.

**Berwick Street Market**  London's most-filmed stallholder works near the top end of this little Soho market—he still shouts out his wares, so he's God's gift to TV. It's mostly fruit and veg here, with lots of £1-a-scoop bargains towards the end of the day. The biggest variety of stalls, including bread, cheese, olives, and dried herbs, spices, and fruit, turn out on Friday and Saturday. Berwick St., W1. Mon–Fri 8am–5pm. Tube: Piccadilly Circus.

**Borough Market**  Celebrity chefs are said to fill their shopping baskets at this covered food market next to Southwark Cathedral. Stalls laden with fruit and vegetables, meats (including bacon and venison), fish, olives, chocolates, bread, pies, organic beers, and much more are wickedly tempting. The third weekend of every month, twice as many producers turn out for "The Big One." Borough Sq., SE1. www.londonslarder.org.uk. Fri noon–6pm; Sat 9am–4pm. Tube: London Bridge.

**Brick Lane Market**  One of the last places you can try that oh-so English delicacy, jellied eels, yet one of the hippest markets in London. As well as fruit and veggies, cheap clothes, and lots of leather, there's the **Laden Market** at 103 Brick Lane—a covered space abuzz with young fashion and accessory designers, great for cheap unique gifts. Combine Brick Lane with a visit to neighboring Old Spitalfields Market (see below). Brick Lane, E1. General Market Sun 8am–1pm; Laden Market Mon–Sat 11am–6pm Sun 10am–4:30pm. Tube: Liverpool St., Aldgate East.

**Brixton Market**    Brixton is the heart of Afro-Caribbean London, and Brixton Market is its soul. Electric Avenue (immortalized by Jamaican singer Eddie Grant) is lined with exotic fruit and vegetable stalls. Turn right at the end for a terrific selection of the cheapest secondhand clothes in London. Granville Arcade, off the avenue, is crammed with foods, African fabrics, and reggae records. Electric Ave., SW9. Mon–Tues, Thurs–Sat 8am–6pm; Wed 8am–3pm. Tube: Brixton.

**Camden Market**    This vast market fills the streets, arcades, and courtyards, taking more money than the whole of the West End. Hundreds of stalls flog crafts, bric-a-brac, clothes, and furniture, with a big hippy-trippy contingent. The Stables concentrates on clothing, almost-junk, and 20th-century collectibles. The best vintage clothing can be found on Buck Street, Camden High Street, and in Electric Market (good for cheap Doc Martens). In an old timber yard by the canal, Camden Lock is crammed with craft workshops, stores, and cafes. It hosts a Producers' (Farmers') Market on Saturday and Sunday. Come to Camden early, particularly on Sundays, as this is one of London's biggest tourist attractions. Camden High St. and Chalk Farm Rd., NW1. Camden Market Thurs–Sun 9am–5:30pm; Camden Lock daily 10am–6pm; Stables Market Sat–Sun 8am–6pm; Camden Canal Market Sat–Sun 10am–6pm; Electric Market Sun 9am–5:30pm. Tube: Camden Town, Chalk Farm.

**Columbia Road Flower Market**    It's pure torture for gardeners and plant-lovers coming here on a spring or summer Sunday morning. The sights and smells at this heavenly flower market are so tantalizing and the prices so reasonable you'll wish it wasn't illegal to take growing plants home. But if you're looking for souvenirs, you're bound to find a pretty pot or garden accessory. Columbia Road, E2. Tube: Old St.

**Greenwich Market**    The market is an essential part of a visit to this bustling and historic maritime borough. Greenwich is pretty chi-chi, which is reflected in the quality of stuff on sale: from upscale antiques to collectors' oddities, old and new. The Central Market, which is a treasure trove of vintage clothing and music stalls, and the Food Market are on Stockwell Street, just off the high road. The Craft Market is in College Approach. From Greenwich High Rd. (opposite St. Alfege's Church), SE10. Antiques Market Sat–Sun 9am–5pm; Central Market indoor Fri–Sat 10am–5pm, Sun 10am–6pm, outdoor Sat 7am–6pm, Sun 7am–5pm; Craft Market Thurs 7:30am–5pm, Fri–Sun 9:30am–5:30pm; Food Market Sat 10am–4pm. Docklands Light Railway: Cutty Sark, Greenwich.

**Old Spitalfields Market**    Like Brick Lane, this market has burgeoned under the wave of trendoids moving into the city fringes. It's mostly antiques and crafts during the week, with designer and retro fashion stalls setting up at the week-end. On Friday and Sunday, the market turns into a cornucopia of edible delights, too. Organic producers sell pickles, relishes, cakes, fruit, and vegetables. Sunday is the busiest and definitely the best day to go as, on top of everything else, that's when the Alternative Art Market happens. This is also where new young designers come for Alternative Fashion Week, a series of free events just after the official frock fest: call ✆ **020/7375-0441.** From Lamb St. to Brushfield St., E1. Organic Market Fri, Sun 10am–5pm; General Market Mon–Fri 11am–3pm, Sun 10am–5pm. Tube: Liverpool St.

**Petticoat Lane**    This ancient market is not what it used to be now that stores open on Sunday, and other events draw the crowds. But it almost feels like discovering the real London, if you can ignore the hordes of tourists. Batteries and cigarette lighters are sold in bulk. Shoes and clothes are cheap, and rarely chic. And the jewelry glitters just as though it was gold. Middlesex St., E1. Sun 9am–2pm. Tube: Liverpool St., Aldgate.

**Portobello Market**    Portobello Market is a lot of fun, despite the seething masses. Saturday is the full-on armoires-to-lava-lamps day. More than 2,000 antiques dealers set out their stalls at the southern, uphill, end: Head for Notting Hill Gate Tube station. For retro, street-hip, and club-chic clothing, secondhand music, and junkabilia, go to Ladbroke Grove instead. Cross the road out of the station to the passage left of the bridge. Weekdays, Portobello is an old-fashioned fruit and veg market, with organic food on Thursdays. Portobello Rd., W10, W11. Antiques Market Sat 4am–6pm; General Market Mon–Wed 8am–6pm, Thurs 9am–1pm, Fri–Sat 7am–7pm; Organic Market Thurs 11am–6pm. Clothes & Bric-a-brac Market Fri 7am–4pm, Sat 8am–5pm, Sun 9am–4pm. Tube: Notting Hill Gate, Ladbroke Grove.

## MUSIC

**Denmark Street** is *the* musicians' hangout. This scruffy cut-through off Charing Cross Road is lined with shops selling everything you need to get a band on the road.

### NEW RECORDS, CDS & TAPES

Check out the stores below, and especially Tower Records, for flyers offering cheap entry into London's hippest night clubs (see "Dance Clubs & Discos," in chapter 8).

**HMV**    This HMV is a mega-megastore, so whatever you want it's probably got it. Dance music is a real strength, and the ground floor has all the new rock, soul, reggae, and pop releases. The range of world music and spoken-word recordings is huge. Last year, HMV opened a new super hi-tech branch at 360 Oxford St., W1 (*©* **020/7514-3600;** Tube: Bond St.). It's the first music store in the country where customers can create their own CDs with digital downloads. 150 Oxford St., W1. *©* **020/7631-3424.** www.hmv.co.uk. Tube: Oxford Circus.

**Tower Records**    A warehouse of sound, Tower has four floors of records, tapes, and compact discs—pop, rock, classical, jazz, bluegrass, folk, country, soundtracks, and more, all in separate departments. Downstairs you'll find a fantastic selection of international music magazines. You can also buy tickets to gigs here, and there are in-store signings. This store is open until midnight every day except Sunday. 1 Piccadilly Circus, W1. *©* **020/7439-2500.** www.towerrecords.co.uk. Tube: Piccadilly Circus.

**Virgin Megastore**    The Virgin Megastore is a microcosm of Richard Branson's ever-expanding empire. You can buy a mobile phone, an airline ticket, or an hour on the Internet, as well as hardware and software for computer games, MP3 players . . . oh, and the usual albums and singles. And it holds regular live performances and signings. 14–16 Oxford St., W1. *©* **020/7631-1234.** www.virginmega. co.uk. Tube: Tottenham Court Rd.

---

*Tips*  **Video Warning**

Britain uses the PAL broadcast standard, which is incompatible with the U.S. standard NTSC. Even if a video tape says VHS, it won't play in an American VCR.

---

## VINTAGE & SECONDHAND

**Hanway Street,** close to Tottenham Court Road, and **Berwick Street** in Soho both have lots of secondhand stores and are heaven for vinyl buffs.

**Harold Moores Records & Video**    Classical heaven, this store is full of stock ranging from 78s to LPs—70,000 of them—and CDs, some rare and precious to the tune of thousands of pounds. But it has great sales and it will do part-exchange, so surf the website to find out what the store is interested in acquiring. 2 Great Marlborough St., W1. ℂ 020/7437-1576. www.haroldmoores.com. Tube: Oxford Circus.

**Mole Jazz**    Jazz fans come here for historic recordings, whether it be New Orleans traditional, swing, or modern. You can ring up or e-mail to ask for an auction list, too, if you're on the hunt for something really rare. 311 Gray's Inn Rd., WC1. ℂ 020/7278-0703. www.molejazz.co.uk. Tube: King's Cross.

**Music & Video Exchange**    There are four stores all in a row and each specializing in something different. Together they offer bargain buys and collectible rarities; CDs, tapes, and vinyl; the classics, jazz, folk, dance music, and more. And they have an excellent policy on prices, which keep on dropping the longer something stays on the shelf. 36–42 Notting Hill Gate, W11. ℂ 020/7243-8573. www. buy-sell-trade.co.uk. Tube: Notting Hill Gate.

## TOYS

**Hamleys**    William Hamley founded Noah's Ark, as it was called then (in 1760), and it's one of the largest toy stores in the world. There are seven floors stuffed with more than 26,000 toys, games, models, dolls, cuddly animals, and electronic cars—even executive toys at very adult prices. Recently refurbished, the store is easier to get around, but you still have to navigate around the crowds watching toy demonstrations. 188–196 Regent St., W1. ℂ 020/7494-2000. www. hamleys.com. Tube: Oxford Circus, Piccadilly Circus.

**London Dolls House Company**    Girls little and big will love this store. Collectible dollhouses can fetch a breathtaking £5,500 ($7,250), but kits start at £65 ($94.25) and miniature furnishings at 50p (70¢). Just like the real-life property market, it's a matter of tailoring your aspirations to meet your budget. 29 Covent Garden Market, WC2. ℂ 020/7240-8681. www.londondollshouse.co.uk. Tube: Covent Garden.

**Science Museum**    I turn into an enthusiastic nerd every time I visit the shop here. It's got mini-robots, oddball clocks and telescopes, books, high-tech games, puzzles, and other gimmickry—glow-in-the-dark t-shirts or a baby hot-air balloon. The museum also has a small concession at Selfridges. Exhibition Rd., SW7. ℂ 020/7942-4499. www.sciencemuseum.org.uk/shop. Tube: South Kensington.

# 8

# London After Dark

The biggest shock of 2001 was that the Royal Shakespeare Company is leaving home. It will no longer base itself at the Barbican, but hot-stage it around the West End. I wonder whether the Theatre Royal Haymarket is in the RSC's little black book? Possibly not after the stalls bar flooded, and on a press night, sending merciless hacks scampering upstairs to save their interval snifters. London's water table is rising and several of the West End's ancient theaters are built so deep that they regularly find themselves sloshing about in a temporary Thames!

Luckily, though, most recent talk of sloshing has referred to an influx of government cash into the performing arts. From this year, the capital's off-West End and fringe scene will divvy up an extra £15 million, the biggest increase ever. The Soho Theatre, Almeida, and the children's Unicorn Theatre are all set to benefit. This comes on top of the millions of pounds of lottery funds that have poured into old venues, improving facilities and restructuring ticket prices. Now it is the turn of the Royal Albert Hall and the London Coliseum to tart themselves up. They're even putting in air-conditioning.

The news coming out of the club scene was a weird mixed bag. On one hand, intimate club bars took over the hot spot from the mouthy gargantuan superclubs. On the other, the biggest phenomenon of 2001 was SchoolDisco.com—a Saturday nighter for which 2,000 allegedly cool dudes dressed up in school uniforms to recreate their teenage snogs without the spots. Only in England!

**BUY BEFORE YOU FLY** West End shows, opera, ballet, big festivals, rock concerts, and other spectaculars all sell out very fast. If getting in is more important to you than getting a great deal, just hand over the cash, and as far ahead as possible. Ticket-agency fees vary according to the event and seat quality. There's usually a handling charge, too. **Globaltickets** (© 800/223-6108) adds up to 20% to box offices prices. The office is open from 9am to 8pm Monday through Saturday, and noon to 7pm on Sunday. In London, the agency operates out of the Britain Visitor Centre, 1 Regent St., SW1 (© 020/7734-4555). **Ticketmaster** (© 020/7316-4709; www.ticketmaster.co.uk) takes phone and e-bookings around the clock for a fee of £1 to £5.50 ($1.45–$8), plus a variable handling charge. It has branches in Tower Records and HMV (see chapter 7). **Firstcall** (© 0870/906-3838; www.firstcalltickets.com) charges £1 to £5.65 ($1.45–$8.20), plus a £1.50 ($2.20) handling charge, and never sleeps. Pop concert specialist **Stargreen** (© 020/7734-8932; www.stargreen.co.uk) just imposes a £2 to £5 ($2.90–$7.25) fee, and takes calls Monday through Saturday 10.15am to 6pm.

**WHERE TO GET YOUR CULTURE INFO** Even if you have zero intention of actually buying a ticket from them, surf the ticket agencies' websites for far-advance notice of what's going on. You will find more useful e-directories at the start of each section of this chapter. Once you get here, make sure to buy a copy of the listings bible *Time Out* (www.time-out. com), which comes out on Wednesdays. The *Evening Standard* (www.thisislondon.com) produces a supplement, *Hot Tickets,* on Thursdays. You'll also find good guides in the weekend broadsheet newspapers.

## 1 Entertainment on a Shoestring

Having a blast is a lot more affordable here than in other swinging cities. If you put in the legwork, join a few queues, and time your foray just right, you can cruise around town on a wave of dynamite deals. Below are our favorite London freebies and cheapies, as well as some money-saving strategies.

### FREEBIES

- **Holland Park Theatre** (see p. 245)   Don't buy a ticket; just sit on the grass outside and soak up the music for free.
- **Royal Festival Hall** (see p. 250)   Come for hot **Commuter Jazz** in the foyer on Fridays from 5:15 to 6:45pm.
- **Lamb & Flag** (see p. 259)   Fantastic free jazz at a fantastically traditional pub in Covent Garden every Sunday night.
- **Bar Rumba** (see p. 253)   Between 5 and 9pm, Monday through Thursday, drinks are two for the price of one *and* there's no cover charge, so come early and stay late for free clubbing.
- **Notting Hill Arts Club** (see p. 255)   Come before 8pm, or 6pm on Sundays, for some wicked live music and DJ nights at this tiny basement bar.
- **The Social** (see p. 255)   There's no cover charge at the downstairs dance-club bar, except for Wednesday nights when the two indie bands perform Acoustically Heavenly music. Then, it's a bargain at only £3 ($4.35).
- **Popstarz** (see p. 256)   At the Scala now, and still packing them in, the original gay indie club night is free before 11pm with a flyer or Web ad.
- **Heaven** (see p. 256)   London's most famous gay club is free with a flyer before 11:30pm on a Friday. Other nights that'll get you in for £1($1.45).
- **National Portrait Gallery** (see p. 194)   Many of gallery's side events are free, but you never have to pay to listen to the early Friday evening concerts.
- **Summertime Inline Skate-athons** (see p. 212)   You'll need to hire the kit, but joining the crowd for Wednesday's London Skate and the Friday Night Skate is free. Both start at 7pm on the north side of the Serpentine in Hyde Park.
- **Borders** (see p. 223)   No reservations so come early for live music, readings, and talks at this mammoth bookstore, usually at 6:30pm.
- **Waterstone's** (see p. 224)   This bookstore is so big there are even function rooms. Events tend to start around 7pm and most are free (or £1–£2/$1.45–$2.90). Booking recommended.
- **BBC TV and Radio Recordings**   The Beeb is always looking for audiences for its radio and TV shows, and tickets are free. For more information, contact **BBC Audience Services** (© **020/8576-1227;** www.bbc.co.uk/tickets).
- **Street Entertainment**   Fire-eaters, mime artists, musicians playing Andean nose flutes, all throng at the Piazza at Covent Garden.

### CHEAPIES

Below are the most gobsmacking entertainment deals, plus a few alternative nights out that you might not have thought of.

- **Royal Court Theatre** (see p. 239)    The cutting edge of contemporary theater for £5 ($7.25) a ticket every Monday night. Last-minute standbys at the Theatre Downstairs cost a token 10p (15¢).
- **Shakespeare's Globe** (see p. 242)    Just as the Bard did it, both the stage and production style. Stand in the raucous central yard for only £5 ($7.25).
- **Soho Theatre** (see p. 243)    Monday nights, all tickets are £5 ($7.25) at this recently re-launched hotbed of new writing and community theater.
- **The English National Opera** (see p. 244)    Get here early for £3 ($4.35) day-of-performance balcony tickets to see one of Britain's finest opera companies.
- **Comedy Café** (see p. 250)    The cover is only £3 ($4.35) on Thursdays. You can go for free on Wednesday, but that's when new acts try out.
- **Rumba Pa'Ti** (see p. 253)    Elder Sanchez teaches uptight Brits to be sinuous Latinas in a 2-hour salsa class (6:30–8:30pm) at Bar Rumba. Then the pa'ti really starts, with guest DJs and live bands. You don't need a partner and it only costs £6 ($8.75).
- **G.A.Y. at the Astoria** (see p. 256)    Pick up a flyer to have fabulous fun at this club for just £1 ($1.45).
- **After-Dark Walking Tours** (see p. 209)    Discover Jack the Ripper's haunts or the city's most haunted streets on a £5 ($7.25) walking tour . . . whooo!
- **Windsor Racecourse** (see p. 215)    Take a boat up the Thames from the train station to see Monday evening horse racing, summer only: Tickets start at £5 ($7.25).
- **Wimbledon Greyhound Stadium** (see p. 214)    A lot less posh than horse racing but doggone fun (sorry!). Admisison is £5 ($7.25). Starts at 7:30pm.

## SIX MONEY-SAVING STRATEGIES

1. **Net Savings.** Scan **www.lastminute.com** for fab short-notice discounts of up to 50% on theater, musicals, comedy, cinema, concerts, and even VIP entry to nightclubs. The online ticket brokers, listed above, usually have a few enticing deals, too, particularly **Ticketmaster** and **Firstcall.**
2. **Flock to a Festival.** Time your trip to coincide with any one of a host of festivals for a blitz of entertainment, often at giveaway prices. See our "London Calendar of Events," in chapter 2. There are 20 London festivals covered in the brochure and e-listing compiled by the **British Arts Festivals Association** (② **020/7247-4667;** www.artsfestivals.co.uk). Also check with *Time Out* (www.timeout.com), which produces a summer festival guide each year. Again, the ticket brokers are good sources of information—it's in their interest to fill in the info gaps.
3. **Interrogate the Box Office.** Most performing-arts venues follow a few basic charging rules: Tickets may be cheaper on certain nights of the week, Monday especially, and for matinees; it's cheaper to see a preview; same-day tickets and standbys cost a fraction of normal prices; so do bad views and standing up; and seniors, students, and children almost always pay less.
4. **Buy a London for Less Card and Guidebook.** It can't guarantee ticket availability but an investment of just $19.95 does get you 20% to 25% off at West End theaters, and up to 80% (rarely that high) on concerts, opera, and ballet. See "Fifty Money-Saving Tips," in chapter 2.
5. **Theater Bargains.** For West End shows, go to the half-price ticket booth on the south side of Leicester Square, W1. Run by the Society of London Theatre (SOLT), **tkts** charges a £2.50 ($3.65) per seat booking fee for day-

of-performance tickets, a maximum of four per person, and no returns allowed. It is open Monday through Saturday from 10am to 7pm, Sunday noon to 3:30pm for matinees. It only accepts cash and credit cards.

*Note:* Scalpers cluster around the official booth. Don't succumb, and report any that try to rip you off to **SOLT**, 32 Rose St., WC2 (✆ **020/7557-6700**).

6. **Go out Early for Some Discount Dancin'.** Nightclubs are keen to catch punters early and keep them as late as they can, so the cover is often cheaper at either end of the evening. Look for discount flyers inside the main door of Tower Records on Picadilly Circus (see chapter 7) and on club websites. *Time Out* also has a weekly cut-out-and-keep Privilege Pass on its club pages, which will get you a couple of quid off at selected venues.

## 2 London's Theater Scene

Ticket prices at London's 40 or so West End theaters range from £10 to £35 ($14.50–$50.75). That's a bargain compared to rip-off Broadway: the cheapest standard seat for an evening performance of *Mamma Mia!* is $26.85 (£18.50) at the Prince Edward Theatre (✆ **020/7447-5400**), but $60 at the Winter Garden in New York.

There are two fantastic websites for finding out all the theater goss'. Like the half–price ticket booth in Leicester Square, **www.officiallondontheatre.co.uk** is run by the Society of London Theatres. Listings include summary, cast, times, prices, and the date a show is guaranteed to run until. For pretty good reviews of West End shows, surf **www.whatsonstage.com**.

### MAJOR COMPANIES

**Royal Court Theatre**    The 10p standby is a spectacular deal, so naturally there's a catch. Not only do you have to rely on a less-than-full house, but it doesn't even apply to every show. But the Bloomberg-sponsored £5 Mondays are a regular feature, and a real steal. The 400-seat proscenium arch theater and upstairs studio of the Royal Court are home to the English Stage Company. Since premiering the plays of the angry young men of the 1950s (John Osborne, Arnold Wesker, and so on), it has built a world-class reputation as a forum for challenging new writing, nurturing such talents as Conor McPherson, whose play The Weir moved into the West End and onto Broadway, as many do once the ESC has taken the "risk." The Royal Court recently had a £26 million tart-up, including digging out a new restaurant under Sloane Square. Sloane Sq., SW1. ✆ 020/7565-5000. www.royalcourttheatre.com. Jerwood Theatre Downstairs tickets £8–£22.50 ($11.60–$32.65) matinee; £10–£24.50 ($14.5–$35.55) evening; £5 ($7.25) restricted view; concessions £9 ($13.05) pre-booked, £5 ($7.25) on day of performance; all tickets unsold 1hr. before performance 10p (15¢). Jerwood Theatre Upstairs tickets £12.50 ($18.15) matinee; £15 ($21.75) evening; concessions £9 ($13.05). Mon evening, all seats in both theaters are £5 ($7.25):

---

(*Value*  **Stealing the Show . . . And Dinner, Too!**

Mondays at the Royal Court are really rather special. Two people can enjoy a 5-star night out for less than it costs to buy just one Broadway ticket. Not only are all seats £5 ($7.25), but the sexy new Royal Court dining room also serves a rather good modern European three-course meal for only £10 ($14.50). Royal Court Bar & Food is open Monday through Saturday from 11am to 11pm (✆ 020/7565-5061).

pre-bookable for Downstairs; in person at the box office from 10am for Upstairs (limit of 2 tickets per buyer). Tube: Sloane Sq.

**Royal National Theatre**    The core repertory company and ever-changing guest stars perform in three auditoria in this concrete bunker on the South Bank. The large open-stage **Olivier,** the traditional proscenium of the **Lyttelton Theater,** and the smaller, studio-style **Cottesloe** put on dozens of productions a year: reworked classics, cutting-edge premieres, musicals, and shows for young people. Beyond the productions, there's so much else going on. **Platforms** are talks and readings by hot names in the performing arts. They take place at lunchtimes in the Terrace Café and on stage in the early evening. Tickets are practically given away at £3.50 or £2.50 ($5.10 or $3.65) for students and seniors. From the end of June through August, the Theatre Square and the National's terraces are abuzz with **Watch This Space,** a free alfresco festival of music, mime, street theater, acrobats, and magic from all over the world. There's something going on every day but Sunday, mostly in the early evening. Try and make it one Saturday for a Waterloo Sunset spectacular (10:15pm). For events info, call ✆ **020/7452-3327.** Otherwise, the box office is open Monday through Saturday 10am to 8pm.

The 1-hour **backstage tour** is a fascinating docu-soap glimpse into day-to-day theatrical life. Tours take place Monday through Saturday at 10:15am, 12:30 (12:15pm on Olivier matinee days), and 5:30pm, and cost £5 ($7.25) or £4.25 ($6.15) students and seniors. Do book because there are only 30 places on each tour. South Bank, SE1. ✆ 020/7452-3400, 020/7452-3000 box office. www.nt-online.org. Tickets £10–£32 ($14.50–$46.40); matinee £10–£28 ($14.50–$40.60); seats with restricted view in Cottlesloe are £13 ($18.85); all tickets unsold 2hr. before performance in the Olivier and Lyttleton theaters £15 ($21.75); student standby may also be available for £8 ($12.80) 45 min. before curtain at all 3 theaters. Tube: Waterloo, Embankment (cross over Hungerford Bridge). River services: Festival Pier.

**Royal Shakespeare Company**    The RSC dropped a considerable bombshell last year by announcing it would not be renewing its contract with the Barbican, where it's spent 8 months a year since 1982. From May 2002, when its last season there ends, the RSC will be without a London base for the first time in its 41-year history. Though the Barbican Theatre will still be on its list of performance venues, the company plans to build on its already frequent side-trips into the West End proper. Artistic director Adrian Noble says he wants to place each production on the stage best suited to it. Also, actors will no longer have to sign up for 18 months or 2 years, which has hampered the RSC's star pulling powers. Ralph Fiennes and Kenneth Brannagh have both apparently agreed to perform with the company this year. Meanwhile, the RSC is also launching an Academy for young actors in Stratford-upon-Avon, the first embryonic fruits of which will be on view during the 2002 summer festival season at The Other Place.

All this is rather muddlesome for visitors to London. Until the end of April, there will be shows as usual at the Barbican (see listing details below), but after that, who knows what, where, or when! The RSC certainly didn't when I asked. And it didn't even have a number to call in the future for information. I can only suggest you surf the website (**www.rsc.org.uk**). Barbican Centre, Silk St., EC2. ✆ 020/7638-8891 for box office. Barbican Theatre £8–£29 ($11.60–$42.05); matinees and previews £5–£25 ($7.25–$36.25); bench seats or standing £5 ($7.25). The Pit £15–£22 ($21.75–$31.90); previews £10 ($14.50). Standbys on both stages for concessions £12 ($19.20). Tube: Barbican, Moorgate.

# Central London Theaters

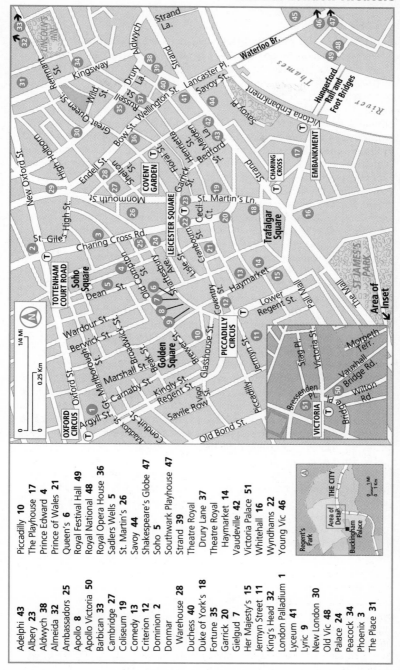

---

**_Kids_   Parent Alert!**

**ChildsPlay** at Shakespeare's Globe is a parent's dream. A drama workshop and story-telling session keep the kids (8–11 years old) happy and elsewhere, while you enjoy the Saturday matinee in peace. Tickets cost £10 ($14.50).

---

**Shakespeare's Globe Theatre**   Academics and historians will always chew over the authenticity of the reconstructed theater and the re-staged drama. Critics will sniff at crowd-pleasing performances and the theme park atmosphere. But a night out at the Globe is a really fun experience. The replica stands on the site of Shakespeare's original amphitheater, which burned down in 1613. Constructed from the same materials, four tiers of banked benches encircle the stage where the company performs the Bard's great works as their predecessors would have done in his day. The Elizabethan set shuns lighting and scenery. There are no little luxuries like cushions on the wooden bench seats, many of which are backless, or protection from the elements, hence the summer-only season. At some point, winter performances may be staged in the **Inigo Jones Theater,** now used for rehearsals. Hawkers selling food and drink roam through the audience standing in the central yard—no sitting allowed, not even on "shooting sticks"! The box office is open Monday through Saturday from 10am to 6pm.

The excellent **Shakespeare's Globe Exhibition,** ✶ in the undercroft below the Globe, is open daily, May to September 9am to noon and October to April 10am to 5pm. Tickets include a theater tour, unless matinees throw off the schedule (✆ **020/7902-1500**), and cost £7.50 ($10.90) adults, £6 ($8.70) seniors and students, £5 ($7.25) children, £23 ($33.35) family ticket.

And call to find out about the huge range of workshops (stage fighting, voice work, and so on), lectures, staged readings, and Walkshops—guided tours of the historical sights of Southwark and a quick look round the Globe. Most take place on weekends, others on weekday evenings. Usually £5 to £13 ($7.25 to $18.85), tickets are free one mid-June weekend to celebrate the birthday of the man with the vision to rebuild the Globe, Sam Wanamaker.

You can dine here, with superb river views: Shakespeare's Globe Café (✆ **020/ 7902-1576**) is open May to September from 10am to 11pm, October to April from 10am to 6pm; Shakespeare's Globe Restaurant (✆ **020/7928-9444;** reservations essential) has pre- and post-theater menus costing from £17.50 ($25.40) during the season and is open noon to 2:30pm, and 6 to 11pm throughout the year. 21 New Globe Walk, Bankside, SE1. ✆ **020/7401-9919.** www.shakespeares-globe.org. Tickets £11–£27 ($15.95–$39.15) adults; £9–£23 ($13.05–$33.35) concessions; £5 ($7.25) yard-standing tickets. Price ranges reflect 4 levels of restriction to view. Season runs end April–Sept; booking from mid-Feb. Tube: Mansion House and St. Paul's (cross over Millennium Bridge), Southwark. River services: Bankside Pier.

## OFF–WEST END & FRINGE THEATER

Listings magazine _Time Out_ carries details for around 60 off-West End theaters and fringe venues, where you'll see some of the most original drama in London—and some of the dodgiest, so do consult the reviews! Some of the best are reviewed below. Also check out the Canal Café Theatre under "Comedy," later in this chapter.

**Almeida Theatre**   The Almeida has moved house while its old science lecture hall in Almeida Street, Islington, gets an all-out massive makeover. Until autumn 2002, the theater is using an old bus depot in King's Cross—look for a building covered in a carpet of fleshy house leeks. It's quite a tricky space, causing questions about why it was chosen over a "proper" auditorium—is the Almeida being different just for the sake of it? But, its mission, however high-brow, is to provoke: last year, Anna Friel starred in a revival of Wedekind's 19th-century erotic tragi-comedy *Lulu*, and Neil LaBute's play *Bash*, with Rachel Weisz, won high praise. The Almeida has built such a hot reputation that A-list actors gladly play leading roles for £300 a week. Meanwhile, the annual Festival of Contemporary Music, a.k.a. Almeida Opera, takes place in June and July. The box office is open Monday to Friday 5:30am to 7pm, and from 1pm on Satur-day. Omega Place, off Caledonian Rd., N1. ℭ 020/7359-4404. www.almeida.co.uk. Tickets £10–£27.50 ($14.50–$39.90); £6 ($8.70) restricted view; £8–£10 ($11.60–$14.50) concessions, Mon–Thurs eves and Sat matinee. Tube: Angel, Highbury & Islington.

**Donmar Warehouse**   Anyone shocked that a first-timer could have directed the smash hit *American Beauty* and won an Oscar for it should look at Sam Mendes's track record. He was only 24 when he took over the Donmar, now one of the hippest and most highly rated theaters in London. Under his artistic direction, this Covent Garden stage produces a huge range of old and new shows, including performances by visiting companies and a cabaret season, Divas at the Donmar, which last year featured Michael Ball. And, yes, this was where Nicole Kidman got her kit off in *The Blue Room*. Runs last for 2 or 3 months. The box office is open from 10am to 8pm, but phone booking is round the clock. The 20 standing tickets go on sale once there's a full house. 41 Earlham St., WC2. ℭ 020/7369-1732. www.donmar-warehouse.com. Tickets usually £15–£25 ($21.75–$36.25), but vary for each show; standing tickets £5 ($7.25). Tube: Covent Garden.

**The King's Head**   London's oldest pub-theater produces new writing and neg-lected classics, some of which have gone on to the West End and Broadway. It also trains up 12 young directors each year. But, sadly, the King's Head was fac-ing a bleak future at press time, after having its funding withdrawn. If it's still here by the time you arrive, come for a pint before you see the tiny stage where Hugh Grant and Gary Oldman started their careers. The box office is open Monday to Saturday 10am to 8pm, Sunday 10am to 4pm. 115 Upper St., N1. ℭ 020/7226-1916. Tickets £14 ($20.30); £10 ($14.50) concessions Sun–Thurs evenings, £15 ($21.75) Sat–Sun matinee; Fri–Sat evenings, no concessions. Tube: Angel, Highbury & Islington.

**Soho Theatre**   The mission (and it is that evangelistic) at this newly built the-ater and smaller studio is to foster new writing and new talent. It has been very successful at both, winning a reputation for high-quality drama. Shows tend to have a one-month run, alongside Soho Nights—late-pm stand-up comedy every Thursday through Sunday. There is also a Café Lazeez downstairs (see chapter 5): two courses in the bar costs £7.50 ($10.90). The box office is open from 10am to curtain-up. 21 Dean St., W1. ℭ 020/7478-0100. www.sohotheatre.com. Tickets £12–£14 ($17.40–$20.30), £7.50–£10 ($10.90–$14.50) concessions; Mon all tickets £5 ($7.25). Tube: Tottenham Court Rd.

**Young Vic**   The Young Vic has a large main auditorium and a smaller studio, where tickets are no pricier than going to the movies. It not only puts on its own productions, with guest stars for bankability, but hosts touring companies too. Even before the Barbican shake-up, the RSC spent a large part of its London season here. The faded decor and inadequate loos are somewhat redeemed by the delicious brasserie menu at its Bright Light Cafe (see "Just South of the River," in chapter 5). The box office is open Monday to Saturday 10am to 7pm. 66 The Cut, SE1. © 020/7928-6363. www.youngvic.org. Main House tickets £18 ($26.10), £12 ($17.40) concessions, £9 ($13.05) students; preview performances £9 ($13.05), £7 ($10.15) concessions. Studio £8–£9 ($11.60–$13.05), £5 ($7.25) concessions. Tube: Waterloo, Southwark.

## 3 The Performing Arts

### OPERA & BALLET

Opera audiences have flocked to Covent Garden ever since the mid-18th century. All the world's great singers, from the legendary Adelina Patti and Maria Callas to the three tenors, have appeared at what is now the **Royal Opera House,** and an Honours List of famous British composers has premiered works there: Sir Arthur Bliss, Sir Ralph Vaughan Williams, Sir Benjamin Britten, Sir Michael Tippett, and Sir William Walton. The **Royal Opera Company** moved in after music publishers Boosey & Hawkes bought the lease of the building after World War II. The other big opera venue is the beautiful **London Coliseum,** on nearby St. Martin's Lane, which is the home of the **English National Opera.** It sings in English, is generally more cutting edge, and sets almost-affordable ticket prices.

After WWII, the Royal Opera House also invited Lilian Baylis and her ballet company to take up residence. But it was not until the big ROH refurb that **The Royal Ballet,** as it is now known, got a custom-made performance space. Also newly renovated, **Sadler's Wells** no longer has its eponymous performers: Baylis's second company left there for Birmingham a few years ago. But the touring **Rambert Dance Company** usually has a Sadler's Wells season, as the **English National Ballet** does at the London Coliseum.

London is also a regular stop for international dance companies, both classical and contemporary. See "Dance," below for more on the sizzling modern scene.

### MAJOR COMPANIES

**The English National Opera**    The ENO thrills enthusiasts and rocks traditionalists with newly commissioned works and lively, theatrical reinterpretations of the classics. Upcoming productions include Mozart's *Così fan tutte* and the ENO's first ever staging of *Lulu* by Berg, based on Wederkind's erotic play. The company is also embarking on a mammoth production of Richard Wagner's four-opera Ring Cycle, due to culminate in 2005. The ENO performs in the 2,350-seat London Coliseum, always in English, during a season lasting from September to July. Pre-performance talks are free (you must book) and start at 4:45pm. At Christmas and during the summer, the English National Ballet takes over the auditorium. If you're prepared to put in a bit of effort (hang around for standbys and so forth), tickets here are an incredible deal. The box office is open 10am to 8pm (9:30am–8:30pm, by phone), Monday through Saturday. London Coliseum, St. Martin's Lane, WC2. © 020/7632-8300. www.eno.org. Tickets £6–£58 ($8.70–$84.10). Discounted day-of-performance tickets Mon–Fri, Sat matinee: £29 ($42.05) in Dress Circle, £3 ($4.45) in the Balcony; on sale at the box office at 10am or by telephone from noon for matinees and 2:30pm for evening performances. Tickets unsold 3 hr. before performance: £28 ($40.60) in Dress/Upper Circle, Sat evening; £18 ($26.10) concessions and £12.50 ($18.15) students any day. If house is full, £3 ($4.35) standing tickets may be available. Each adult buying a full-price ticket can buy one half-price seat for a child under 18. No under-5s. Tube: Charing Cross, Leicester Sq.

**The Royal Ballet**  Britain's leading ballet company is now firmly ensconced back at the Royal Opera House, but last year saw more than logistical upheavals. Long-time director Anthony Dowell has retired, to be succeeded by Ross Stretton, a former stalwart of the American Ballet Theater, then artistic director of The Australian Ballet. The company's repertoire is very varied but tilts toward the classics and works by its earlier choreographer-directors, Sir Frederick Ashton (*A Month in the Country*) and Kenneth Macmillan (*Romeo and Juliet*). From July 25 to August 30, 2002, the evening performance will celebrate the Royal Ballet's founder in a *Tribute to Ninette de Valois*. No specific ticket prices, only ranges, had been released as we went to press. Royal Opera House, Bow St., WC2. ℂ 020/ 7304-4000. www.royalballet.org. Tickets evening £3–£66 ($4.35–$95.70); matinee £3–£42 ($4.35–$60.90); 67 discounted seats for each show sold from 10am on day of performance. Tube: Covent Garden.

**The Royal Opera**  Despite promises to bring opera to "the people," the Royal Opera House only sells 20% of its seats through the box office—the rest are filled by prosperous debenture holders and the corporate entertainment crowd. And it's a master at smoke and mirrors when discussing prices. They weren't fixed for next season when we went to press, yet the ROH confidently promised that "over half the house for all opera performances will cost under £50," that "more than 480 seats for any performance of standard opera will cost £20 or less," and that "almost 400 seats for any performance of standard opera will cost £12 or less." Hope that helps! The combined talents of the Orchestra of the

 **Performers in the Park**

It might sound like utter lunacy in a place as rain-tossed, allegedly, as Britain, but there's a very strong tradition of open-air theater, music, and dance in London's parks. The **Open Air Theatre**, Inner Circle, Regent's Park, NW1 (ℂ **020/7486-2431;** www.open-air-theatre.org.uk; Tube: Baker St., Regent's Park), has been staging summer drama, from June to early September, since 1932. Tickets cost £8.50 to £23 ($12.35–$33.35). **Holland Park Theatre**, Holland Park, W11 (ℂ **020/ 7602-7856;** www.operahollandpark.com; Tube: Holland Park), has opera, and a week of ballet, to the accompaniment of the Royal Philharmonic Orchestra, from June to August under a temporary canopy in the ruins of the Jacobean Holland House. Tickets cost £28 ($40.60). Savvy bargain hounds listen to the music for free while relaxing on the lawn outside. Perhaps the most famous open-air concerts are during July and August at the Robert Adam mansion, **Kenwood House,** Hampstead Lane, NW3 (ℂ **020/7413-1443;** www.picnicconcerts.com). This is a magical scene, on Hampstead Heath, by a lake that reflects the spectacular firework finales—a favorite with unstuffy types enjoying popular classics. Tickets are £17 to £20 ($24.65–$29) for a deckchair, or £14.50 to £16.50 ($21.05–$23.95) to promenade. Take the Tube to East Finchley, and catch the courtesy bus. For more details on **Kenwood House & Iveagh Bequest,** see chapter 6. Also call **Somerset House** (see p. 175) about open-air concerts and theater in the stupendous courtyard.

Royal Opera House, the Chorus of the Royal Opera, and the dozens of guest artists and conductors are sublime. Operas are usually sung in the original language, and projected supertitles translate the libretto for the audience. This year's program is the last under the musical direction of Bernard Haitink. And it is full of operatic supernovas, from Luciano Pavarotti in Puccini's *Tosca* and Bryn Terfel in Mozart's *Don Giovanni* (both Jan), to Willard White in Bartók's *Duke Bluebeard's Castle* (Mar), and Roberto Alagna in Puccini's *La Rondine* (May). Plácido Domingo in Tchaikovsky's *Queen of Spades* (June) will be one of three BP-sponsored live relays into Covent Garden piazza. Royal Opera House, Bow St., WC2. ✆ 020/7304-4000. www.royalopera.org. Tickets £3–£155 ($4.35–$224.75); 67 discounted seats for each show sold from 10am on day of performance. Tube: Covent Garden.

## CLASSICAL MUSIC

The city supports several major orchestras—the **London Symphony Orchestra** at the Barbican Centre, the **London Philharmonic** and **Philharmonia Orchestra** at the Royal Festival Hall, on the South Bank, and the wandering **Royal Philharmonic,** which wanders into the Holland Park over the summer (see above). Then there's the host of choirs, chamber groups, and historic instrument ensembles, and the highly regarded but smaller venues (see below), where they often perform. Look out for the modernist **London Sinfonietta,** the **English Chamber Orchestra,** and the **Gabrieli Consort.** Lastly, London also draws top-name international musicians to its top-name venues, including the Royal Albert Hall (see "Major Arts Venues," below).

The **British Music Information Centre,** 10 Stratford Place, W1 (✆ 020/7499-8567), is *the* resource center for new British classical music, including upcoming concerts. Phone or stop by from noon to 5pm, Monday to Friday. It also holds recitals (£6/$8.70 adults, £4/$5.80 seniors and students), usually on Tuesday and Thursday at 7:30pm. Call for exact times, then take the Tube to Bond Street.

**London Symphony Orchestra**    You'll know the LSO already if you've seen *Star Wars, Episode 1: The Phantom Menace*—it worked on the soundtrack with John Williams at the famous Abbey Road Studios. London's top orchestra is a major international force under the direction of principal conductor Sir Colin Davis. It stages 85 concerts a year at the Barbican Hall, which had a big refurb last year, including an improvement to the acoustics. Reduced-price student standby tickets are sometimes on sale 90 minutes before a performance. Barbican Centre, Silk St., EC2. ✆ 020/7638-8891. www.lso.co.uk. Tickets £6.50–£35 ($9.45–$50.75); £3 ($4.35) under-16s, up to 2 child tickets per accompanying adult; 20% discount for buying ticket to 3 or more concerts in a series. Tube: Barbican, Moorgate.

## RECITAL VENUES

Don't forget to check out the magical candlelit concerts at **St. Martin-in-the-Fields** (see chapter 6).

**St. John's Smith Square**    This baroque masterpiece, designed by Thomas Archer, is slightly bigger than Wigmore Hall, but a lot less comfortable. It hosts chamber groups, choirs, and voice soloists. From September to July, on alternate Thursdays, there are lunchtime concerts, which are a steal at £5 ($7.25). The box office is open Monday to Friday, from 10am to 5pm. Smith Square, SW1. ✆ 020/7222-1061. www.sjss.org.uk. Tickets £5–£18 ($7.25–$26.10). Tube: Westminster, St. James's Park.

**Wigmore Hall**  This vaulted auditorium, which celebrated its centenary in 2001, is London's foremost venue for lieder and chamber music. Even the cognoscenti don't mind the cheap seats at the back of the stalls, as the acoustics are excellent. All tickets at The Sunday Morning Coffee Concerts, and those recorded for BBC Radio 3 on a Monday lunchtime, are £8 or £9 ($11.60 or $13.05)—a great deal. The box office is open Monday to Saturday from 10am to 8:30pm, Sunday 10:30am to 8pm (5pm from Nov to mid-Mar). 36 Wigmore St., W1. © 020/7935-2141. www.wigmore-hall.org.uk. Tickets £7–£20 ($10.15–$29). Discounted standbys sometimes available for concessions. Tube: Bond St., Oxford Circus.

## DANCE

Set up in 1998, the publicly-funded **London Dance Network** aims to build audiences and win support for creating a National Dance House. It revamped its website last year (**www.londondance.com**), so this should be a one-stop info shop on everything that's going on in the capital. Contemporary dance is certainly thriving here. Top international companies like Merce Cunningham, Twyla Tharp, and Trisha Brown appear at the Barbican Centre, Royal Festival Hall, and Sadler's Wells Theatre (see "Major Arts Venues," below). While smaller venues, like **The Place** (see below), focus on the even more avant-garde. Also worth checking out for the occasional dance events in their programs are: **ICA,** The Mall, SW1 (© **020/7930-3647;** www.ica.org.uk; Tube: Piccadilly Circus, Charing Cross); and **Riverside Studios,** Crisp Rd., W6 (© 020/8237-1111; www.riversidestudios.co.uk; Tube: Hammersmith).

Many of these are among the host of venues for **Dance Umbrella** (© 020/ **8741-4040;** www.danceumbrella.co.uk), the internationally acclaimed fall showcase of contemporary dance. It runs for 6 weeks from October into November. Seats are usually available on the day of performance, and cost as little as £8 ($11.60), depending on the venue.

**The Place**  This is *the* showplace for contemporary dance and has been since it was founded in the late 1960s by Robert Cohan of the Martha Graham Company. Now The Place is the permanent home of the Richard Alston Dance Company and the London Contemporary Dance School. The box office is open Monday to Friday (and Sat performance days) from 10am to 6pm. 17 Duke's Rd., WC1. © 020/7387-0031. www.theplace.org.uk. Tickets £10 ($14.50), £8 ($11.60) concessions. Tube: Euston.

### 4 Major Arts Venues

**Barbican Centre**  What a way to celebrate your 20th birthday. The Barbican claimed to welcome the Royal Shakespeare Company's desertion in favor of hot-staging around the West End. It would be a challenge, said the jilted arts complex, to see if it could run its two theaters more economically than the £1.4 million RSC management fee. The other £1 million paid for the RSC productions would now boost the Barbican International Theatre Event (BITE). To date, this festival of drama, music-theater, and dance, as well as foyer and outdoor events has filled the gap between RSC seasons (May to Sept). Tickets have tended to range from free to £30 ($48). No one knew how all that would work in 2002.

The Barbican opened in 1982. Reputedly the largest arts complex in Europe, it is so maze-like that yellow lines have been painted across its brick-paved walkways and piazzas to help visitors find their way around. The architecture

---

**Finds   Fantasy on Folgate Street**

American artist Dennis Severs spent nearly 20 years, until his death in 2000, turning his Georgian terrace house in Spitalfields into a "still-life drama." Each of the 10 rooms is dedicated to a different era in the life of a family of Huguenot weavers, between 1754, when the house was built, and 1914. The half-eaten supper, the wig on the back of the chair, smells, sounds, and flickering candlelight are meant as shamanistic triggers to transport you back in time. The house is open every Monday evening: the time varies depending when dusk falls. Tickets are £10 ($14.50) and you must call to book: **Dennis Severs' House,** 18 Folgate St., E1. (© **020/ 7247-4013;** www.dennissevershouse.co.uk; Tube: Liverpool St.). Children are not welcome.

---

may be the object of derision, but even detractors agree that the facilities inside are superb. As well as the Barbican Theatre and The Pit, it has two art galleries, three cinemas, and several restaurants, bars, and cafes. The newly refurbished concert hall is home to the London Symphony Orchestra (see "Classical Music," above), and hosts other festivals and large-scale events between LSO performances.

**Barbican Plus** is the program of talks and workshops, often linked to major productions, some costing £5 to £8 ($7.25–$11.60), but many are free. Call the box office, open daily from 9am to 8pm, for tickets and to find out what's on. Silk St., EC2. © **020/7638-8891.** www.barbican.org.uk. Tube: Barbican or Moorgate.

**London Coliseum**   Built in 1904, this is one of London's most architecturally spectacular houses. But it has fallen into grim disrepair. So, in 2000, the Coliseum started a £41 million facelift. This will really glam up the public spaces—and double the number of ladies loos, yippee—and improve conditions backstage in time for the centenary year in 2004. The Coliseum is home to English National Opera and hosts touring companies when the ENO is resting or away. English National Ballet has a fleeting Christmas season and comes back during the summer. The box office is available by phone around the clock. St. Martin's Lane, WC2. © **020/7632-8300.** www.eno.org. Tube: Leicester Sq., Charing Cross.

**Ocean**   Three different performing spaces, with a total capacity of 2,700. Acoustics adjustable at the flick of a switch to suit any kind of music. Wired for live webcasts. It is little wonder Ocean cost £23 million. It is in Hackney, North-East London, and is part of a big regeneration push, which is why it has a strong community education program. That's also why the musical calendar is so eclectic—it had to reflect the local melting pot culture. Ocean's proud boast is that it hosts everything from bhangra to blues, classical to country, rock to reggae, jazz, soul, rap, latin, dance, and world music. Since opening in February 2001, it has already pulled in world-renowned percussionist Evelyn Glennie, the Fun Lovin' Criminals, and a pan-European live broadcast by MTV. It also has six bars and one cafe-bar. 270 Mare St., E8. © **020/8533-0111,** 020/7314-2800 box office. www.ocean.org.uk. £5–£18 ($7.25–$26.10). Tube: Bethnal Green, then 8-minute ride on nos. 106 or 253 bus.

**Royal Albert Hall**   A £3 ($6.95) standing ticket to one of the Sir Henry Wood Promenade Concerts at the Royal Albert Hall has to be one of the best buys of the summer cultural season (www.bbc.co.uk/proms). Every year, from mid-July to mid-September, the daily changing performances cover every conceivable spot on the classical music spectrum. During the festival, the hall takes out all the central orchestra seats to leave an open unregulated space for the promenaders. They take over the show on the Last Night of the Proms, a national institution broadcast live into Hyde Park, with wild jingoistic flag waving to the sounds of Elgar's *Pomp and Circumstance*. The rest of the year, it puts on a huge range of entertainment, including the 80th birthday concert for Prince Philip in 2001. Joaquin Cortes, Robbie Williams, Sheryl Crow, Burt Bacharach, Tony Bennett, B.B. King, Cirque du Soleil, and the world's top stand-up comedians, tennis players, sumo wrestlers, amateur choirs—they've all appeared here. The Royal Albert Hall is going through a big refurbishment until 2003, but it is not closing. The box office opens daily from 9am to 9pm. Kensington Gore, SW7. ℂ 020/7589-8212. www.royalalberthall.com. Tube: South Kensington, Kensington High St.

**Royal Opera House**    The ROH reopened at the end of 1999 in a new guise as the "people's pleasure palace." The Royal Ballet has new performance and rehearsal spaces. The backstage area is crammed with high-tech equipment. The main auditorium now has air-conditioning. The Vilar Floral Hall—a stunning, Victorian, glazed atrium—has been restored. And a new "indoor street" called The Link runs through the ROH to the piazza colonnade, finally completed to Inigo Jones's design.

Ticket prices have come down, but still only a small proportion of them are affordable: last year, top prices for the visiting Kirov Ballet reached £145 ($210.25). However, the ROH does seem to have picked up a few tips on open access from the Barbican and the South Bank Centre. The new Linbury Studio Theatre stages unusual repertory—this year, the English Bach Festival, Opera Restor'd, the Classical Opera Company, Music Theatre Wales, the Rambert Dance Company, Unicorn Children's Theatre, the British Youth Opera, Gospel swingers Citizen K, the National Youth Music Theatre and from Japan, the Hosokawa Opera Company. Together with the Clore Studio Upstairs, it also hosts talks and workshops. Tickets only cost £8 to £25 ($11.60–$36.25), but many events are free. And there are free lunchtime concerts every Monday at 1pm during the season. Tickets are available from 10am on the day of performance at the information desk next to the box office. Pre-performance talks are also free. You can tour backstage, usually at 10:30am, 12:30, and 2:30pm, for £7 or £6 ($10.15 or $8.70) for concessions. For tour information only, call ℂ **020/7212-9389.** No children under 7.

The Link, its coffee bar, and the box office are open to the public Monday to Saturday from 10am to 8pm, the Vilar Floral Hall from 10am to 3pm. The Amphitheatre restaurant (ℂ **020/7212-9254**), with its terrace overlooking Covent Garden, serves modern European cuisine to the public as well as theatergoers at lunchtime. But it's a splurge, with main courses costing around £12.50 ($18.15). Bow St., WC2. ℂ 020/7304-4000. www.royaloperahouse.org. Tube: Covent Garden.

**Sadler's Wells Theatre**    Recently rebuilt, this is one of the busiest stages in London and also one of the best, with superb sight lines. It hosts top visiting opera and dance companies from around the world. Each May, Sadler's Wells is one of the venues for the Covent Garden Festival. It is dedicated to making dance accessible, so there are always some seats within reach of the budget traveler (£8.50–£35/$12.35–$50.75). Students, kids, and seniors can sometimes get standbys 1 hour before a performance. Prices are much the same at The Peacock

Theatre in Holborn, initially a temporary home during the rebuild and now a permanent satellite venue staging more populist musical theater and dance. The ticket office is open Monday to Saturday 9am to 8:30pm. Rosebery Ave., EC1. ℂ 020/7863-8000. www.sadlers-wells.com. Tube: Angel.

**South Bank Centre**    This is one of the most controversial redevelopments in London, and the story is going to run and run. Due to be completed in 2001, the SBC has moved on to yet another architect and yet another plan. It wants to re-landscape the neighboring Jubilee Gardens, which is where the London Eye is now, and build shops, a new concert hall, a home for the Museum of the Moving Image (currently closed), and a multiplex cinema to add to the existing **National Film Theatre,** hub of November's London Film Festival (www.lff.org.uk). That's as well as bringing the **Hayward Gallery** (see chapter 6) and RFH up to millennial standards, and making the existing brutalist playground fit for humans to enjoy. The **Royal National Theatre** has already had a few millions spent on it (see "London's Theater Scene," above).

The **Royal Festival Hall** comprises three music and dance venues: **RFH1** is the usual venue for big populist orchestral performances. The smaller **RFH2,** which used to be the Queen Elizabeth Hall, is known for chamber music, semi-staged opera, and special events. And the intimate **RFH3** usually hosts advanced students and young performers making their professional debut. All three stages are lit almost every night of the year, with ballet (including the Royal Ballet), jazz, pop, and folk concerts in the diary as well as classical music. If you can, try to make it over for Meltdown in June. The RFH invites a different performer each year to devise their fantasy arts festival, so this 3-week event is uniquely diverse (or perverse, perhaps).

The RFH foyer must be one of London's hardest-working venues. Free informal recitals take place in front of the Festival Buffet cafe, from Wednesday to Sunday, 12:30 to 2pm. On Friday evenings, it's Commuter Jazz from 5:15 to 6:45pm. **Summer on the South Bank** is a fest of mostly free events in the foyers and outdoors on the terraces, from mid-July through August. Booking is not usually required, but check with the box office, open daily from 9am to 9pm. Belvedere Rd., SE1. ℂ 020/7960-4242. www.sbc.org.uk. Tube: Waterloo, Southwark, Embankment (cross over Hungerford Bridge). River services: Festival Pier.

## 5 The Club & Music Scene

### COMEDY & CABARET

The blessed *Time Out* lists comedy gigs, or surf **www.chortle.co.uk** for longer-winded reviews. Do be careful when you see laughably low-ticket prices as they may be for open-mike, talentless spotting sessions. However, some deals really *are* too good to miss. At the **Comedy Café,** 66 Rivington St., EC2 (ℂ 020/7739-5706; Tube: Old St.), there's no admission charge on Wednesday, when new acts perform, and it's only £3 ($4.35) on Thursday. Some pubs also have highly rated, regular comedy nights: **Bound & Gagged,** Tufnell Park Tavern, Tufnell Park Rd., N7 (ℂ 020/8450-4100; Tube: Tufnell Park), kicks off at 9:30pm on Saturdays, with a £7 ($10.15) cover, plus £1 ($1.45) membership. Otherwise, the **Soho Theatre** (see p. 243) pulls big names in the laughter game for its late-pm weekend shows, Soho Nights, for which tickets are £6 to £10 ($8.70–$14.50).

Since its revamp, **Madame JoJo's** has de-vamped into being a club with a DJ instead of a drag cabaret. The divas only do their stuff on Saturdays now: for more information, see "Dance Clubs & Discos," below.

**Canal Café Theatre**    For a really lovely evening out, come early and stroll along the canal in this very pretty part of Maida Vale. The Canal Café Theatre is a small but long-established fringe venue above a pub. Performances range from drama to cabaret, but the most famous is the topical sketch show *Newsrevue* (Thurs–Sat at 9:30pm, Sun at 9pm). You can buy tickets in person up to 45 minutes before the show, or book on the office line above, which is sometimes manned by an answering machine. Food is served until 10pm. The Bridge House, Delamere Terrace, W2. ✆ **020/7289-6054.** Cover £7 ($10.15), or £5 ($7.25) concessions, plus £1 ($1.45) membership. Tube: Royal Oak, Warwick Ave.

**The Comedy Store**    Launched in 1979, The Comedy Store has nurtured such talents as Rik Mayall, Keith Allen, Dawn French, Ben Elton, Paul Merton, Jack Dee, and Eddie Izzard. Tuesday night it's the topical satirical revue, Cutting Edge. An improv group, The Comedy Store Players, takes the stage on Wednesday and Sunday. Best in Stand-Up is on Thursday (with an open spot), Friday, and Saturday. Shows start at 8pm, Tuesday to Sunday, with extra midnight performances on Friday and Saturday. The box office opens at 6:30pm and 100 of the 400 tickets are always held back to be sold on the night. Haymarket House, 1A Oxendon St., SW1. ✆ **020/7344-0234.** www.thecomedystore.co.uk. Cover £12–£15 ($17.40–$21.75), or £8 ($11.60) concessions. Tube: Piccadilly, Leicester Sq.

## ROCK & POP

London has hundreds of live music venues hosting rock legends, pre-fab boy and girl bands, and the sharpest indie sounds. The newest is the technologically marvelous **Ocean,** in Hackney (see "Major Venues," above). For big name gigs, you'll need to book well ahead—sometimes several months. The website **www.aloud.com** is an excellent source of advance info, as are the ticket agencies mentioned at the start of this chapter. But contact the box office directly to avoid the booking fee.

The ever-expanding Mean Fiddler Group—it's king of the music festival scene, too—owns three of London's premier venues: **Astoria** and next door **Mean Fiddler W1** (the ex-LA2), 157–165 Charing Cross Rd., WC2 (✆ **020/ 7434-9592;** Tube: Tottenham Court Rd.); and **Forum,** 9–17 Highgate Rd., NW5 (✆ **020/7344-0044;** Tube: Kentish Town). Tickets cost £8 to £20 ($11.60–$29) and find out what's on where at **www.meanfiddler.com.** Two more to keep an eye out for are **Brixton Academy,** 211 Stockwell Rd., SW9 (✆ **020/7771-2000;** Tube: Brixton); and **Shepherds Bush Empire,** Shepherds Bush Green, W12 (✆ **020/7771-2000;** Tube: Shepherds Bush). Tickets to both are £10 to £25 ($14.50–$36.25).

Camden's legendary **Bull & Gate,** 389 Kentish Town Rd., NW5 (✆ **020/ 7485-5358;** Tube: Kentish Town) could hardly be more different. Small and scruffy, this is the unofficial headquarters of London's pub music scene. Unsigned indie bands play back-to-back, sometimes three or four a night, starting at 8:30pm. Nirvana and Manic Street Preachers are alumni! You'll pay around £5 ($7.25) for a night at the bottom end of the fame chain (no credit cards).

Also check out the live music nights at the club bars, reviewed below.

## FOLK

**Cecil Sharp House**    This was the focal point of the 1960s folk revival. The English Folk Dance and Song Society is based here and continues to document and foster this music. Concerts range from traditional English music, to Cajun, Irish, and anything else that's danceable. Tuesday nights are the Sharp's Folk

Club "singaround" sessions with guest artists: 8pm, no need to book. 2 Regent's Park Rd., NW1. ✆ **020/7485-2206.** www.efdss.org. Cover £3–£8 ($4.35–$11.60). Tube: Camden Town.

## JAZZ

There is a superb gig guide at **www.jazzservices.org.uk**; otherwise trawl the listings magazines. A big freebie favorite is **Commuter Jazz** from 5:15 to 6:45pm on Fridays at the Royal Festival Hall (✆ **020/7960-4242**). The **Lamb & Flag** in Covent Garden (see "Pubs," below) also puts on free jazz on Sunday night from 7:30pm. So does **The 100 Club** noon to 3pm on Friday (see below).

**Jazz Café**    The Sunday lunchtime Jazz Jams are the most fun. Aspiring musicians pitch up and get in the groove with the resident band, Tomorrow's Warriors, from noon to 4pm and the cover is £1 ($1.45). On a regular night, the sounds are very contemporary, from rap to Latin jazz. You must book a table ahead of time, but try to avoid going upstairs; the restaurant is pricey. Music starts at 7pm. Open Monday through Thursday until 1am, until 2am on Friday and Saturday, and midnight on Sunday. 5 Parkway, NW1. ✆ **020/7916-6060.** www.jazzcafe.co.uk. Cover £8–£17.50 ($11.60–$25.40). Tube: Camden Town.

**The 100 Club**    The smoky basement stage hosts jazz sets, swing, jive, rhythm and blues, as well as funk and soul. Every night is different, so give them a ring-a-ling to find out what's on. Don't miss the fab Friday Lunchtime Jazz— admission is free. Open Monday to Thursday 7:30 to 11:30pm, Friday 11:15am to 3pm and 8:30pm to 2am, Saturday 7:30pm to "late," Sunday 7:30 to 11:30pm. 100 Oxford St., W1. ✆ **020/7636-0933.** Cover £8–£10 ($11.60–$14.50). Tube: Tottenham Court Rd.

**PizzaExpress Jazz Club**    Unlikely though it sounds, the basement of this chain restaurant is one of the city's most popular jazz venues. The house band, the PizzaExpress All-Stars, shares the stage with leading traditional and contemporary names. Doors open at 7:45pm, with the first set at 9pm. Also check out the more expensive Pizza on the Park (see "Knightsbridge," in chapter 5). 10 Dean St., W1. ✆ **020/7439-8722.** www.pizzaexpress.co.uk. Cover £12.50–£20 ($18.15–$29), plus food. Tube: Tottenham Court Rd.

**Ronnie Scott's**    Since it opened in 1959, London's best-known jazz room has featured all the greats, from Ella Fitzgerald and Dizzy Gillespie to Hugh Masekela and Charlie Watts. Book a week ahead for a Saturday show. On Sunday, an independent promoter puts on contemporary and world music. Ronnie Scott's is open Monday to Saturday 8:30pm to 3am, Sunday 7:30 to 11pm. There's a separate entrance for clubbers to get Upstairs@Ronnies. On Wednesdays and Sundays, the Ratt Club spins some R&B, soul, and hip hop; 1970s jazz, funk, and soul takes over on Thursday at Starsky & Hutch (no sneakers); on Friday and Saturday, it's Club Latino and the first hour is a salsa lesson. Upstairs opens 10pm to 3am except on Sunday, on which it opens 6pm to midnight. 47 Frith St., W1. ✆ **020/7439-0747.** www.ronniescotts.co.uk. Cover £15–£20 ($21.75–$29); Upstairs@Ronnies £3–£7 ($4.35–$10.15). Tube: Leicester Sq., Tottenham Court Rd.

## DANCE CLUBS & DISCOS

Okay, so urban clubbers don't have quite the same mass urge to mate that characterizes party animals on islands like Ibiza and Cyprus, but in every other respect, the London scene is kicking. Even hardcore hedonists will find their heads spinning at the choice.

The hot spots change from week to week, so it's crucial to consult *Time Out* for the latest roster. The magazine's **Privilege Pass,** printed weekly, will buy you cheap entry at a number of venues: for more money-saving tips, see "Entertainment on a Shoestring," earlier in this chapter. Also check **www.burnitblue.com** for thorough listings and been-there, sweat-sheened reviews of bars, venues, and specific club nights.

*Note:* Always check the dress code because many clubs ban trainers (sneakers).

## GROOVY SATURDAY CLUB NIGHTS

- **Blow Up** 1960s R&B, funk, and soulful jazz for a stylish post-pubescent crowd, at The Syndrome, 54 Berwick St., W1 (© **020/7437-6830;** www.blowup.co.uk). Cover £8 ($11.60) before 11pm, £10 ($14.50) until 2:30am, then £3 ($4.35). Open 10pm to 5am. Tube: Piccadilly Circus.
- **Carwash** Glam disco night, so dress sexy like Sindy-does-fetish (no wigs), at Sound, 10 Wardour St., W1 (© **020/7403-8585**). Cover £12 ($17.40) before 2am, then £5 ($7.25). Open 10pm to 4am. Tube: Leicester Sq.
- **Garage City** Underground garage, disco house, and dressy gear, at Bar Rumba, 36 Shaftesbury Ave., W1 (© **020/7287-2715**). Cover £7 ($10.15) before 11pm, then £12 ($17.40). Open 9pm to 4am. Tube: Piccadilly Circus.
- **Headstart** Techno club with open-doors attitude to guest DJs— big names and newcomers—and live acts, at Turnmills, 63 Clerkenwell Rd., EC1 (© **020/7250-3409**). Cover £8 ($11.60). Open 9pm to 5am. Tube: Farringdon.
- **Rulin** U.S. and U.K. house, and designer streetwear, at the monster clubland brand Ministry of Sound, 103 Gaunt St., SE1 (© **020/7378-6528;** www.ministryofsound.co.uk). Cover £15 ($21.75). Open midnight to 9am. Tube: Elephant & Castle.
- **SchoolDisco.com** Sad glimpse into English psyche as 2,000 naughty girls and boys turn up in mandatory school uniform to relive their best teenage snogging moments, or worst, at Po Na Na, 230 Shepherds Bush Rd., W6 (© **020/8699-9983;** Tube: Hammersmith). Cover £10 ($14.50). Open 10pm to 3am.

## GREAT VENUES

Also check out the upstairs nightclub at **Ronnie Scott's** under "Jazz," above.

**Bar Rumba** This club is a classy favorite. It travels through the whole musical spectrum every week—from Latin sounds to cosmic disco house and garage (see "Groovy Saturday Club Nights," above). And get this: Drinks are two-for-one during weeknight happy hour, *and* there's no cover charge, so come before 9pm and you can club it up later for free. Except on Tuesdays, when a night of Latin mayhem starts with a salsa class (6:30–8:30pm). Open Monday to Thursday 5pm to 3:30am, Friday 5pm to 4am, Saturday 7pm to 6am, Sunday 8pm to 1am. 36 Shaftesbury Ave., W1. © 020/7287-2715. www.barrumba.co.uk. Happy hour Mon–Thurs 5–9pm. Cover £3–£12 ($4.80–$19.20). Tube: Piccadilly Circus.

**The End** At this beautifully designed, cutting-edge club, the main sounds are techno, house, garage, and drum 'n' bass. Monday is Trash: dress code "make an effort"; music, anything excessive from 1980s electronica to hi-NRG; cover, a super-cheap £4; and cheap drinks too! Thursday night is the gay-ish Atelier (see below). Be prepared for long lines any night. Open Monday 10am to 3pm, Thursday 7pm to 1am, Friday 11pm to 5am, Saturday 10pm to 6am, and

Sunday 8pm to 3am. 18 West Central St., WC1. ✆ **020/7419-9199.** Cover £4–£15 ($7.25–$24). Tube: Holborn, Tottenham Court Rd.

**Fabric** The 15 Victorian brick arches of this minimalist superclub (capacity 2,500) used to be the old cold-store for Smithfield meat market. There are three rooms, various bars, a roof terrace, and chill-out rooms. A hi-tech sound system pumps the beat from some of the city's best house, garage, techno, and drum 'n' bass up through the main dance floor. One grumble: Fabric is notorious for its mile-long lines, both to get in and for the *Ally McBeal*–style unisex bathrooms. Sunday is the gay DPTM night (see below). Open Friday 10pm to 5am and Saturday 10pm to 7am. 77a Charterhouse St., EC1. ✆ **020/7336-8898.** www.fabriclondon. com. Cover £12–£15 ($17.40–$21.75). Tube: Barbican, Farringdon.

**Hanover Grand** Here's the scene: A dress-conscious crowd cavorts around a renovated theater to a maelstrom of musical styles. It's the home of youth, glitter, and glam—the kind of place to pack your high heels and sequins for, next to the comfy slacks and sightseeing shoes. Wednesday's Fresh 'n' Funky is a great cheap mid-weeker, £5 to get in before 11pm, then £7. Open Wednesday and Thursday 10pm to 4am, Friday 11pm to 4am, and Saturday 10:30pm to 4:30am. 6 Hanover St., W1. ✆ **020/7499-7977.** www.hanovergrand.com. Cover £5–£15 ($7.25–$21.75). Tube: Oxford Circus.

**Madame JoJo's** Paul Raymond, of Revue Bar fame, opened this drag cabaret club in 1986. Madame Jojo's changed hands recently. The revamp has stayed true to the tarted-up interior used in countless movies, including *Eyes Wide Shut*, but it has turned itself into a straight dance club, spinning a bit of everything from nu-jazz to breakbeats, funk, and deep soulful house, and the clientele is mainly straight, too. The divas only do their stuff on Saturdays now: cabaret tickets are pricey and you must pre-book. Open Wednesday 10pm to 2am, Thursday 9:30pm to 3am, Friday 10pm to 3am, Saturday 10:30pm to 3am, and Sunday 9am to 3pm (yes, really!) and 9:30pm to 2:30am. 8 Brewer St., W1. ✆ **020/ 7734-3040.** Cover £5–£10 ($7.25–$14.50); £37 ($53.65) cabaret, Sat. only. Tube: Piccadilly Circus.

**Scala** This is the smallest of the so-called superclubs (capacity 800) and it is certainly the quirkiest. The shabby old independent cinema reopened in March 1999 as a live music venue, gallery, sometime film-house and nightclub. Surf the website because the schedule of DJs, promoters, and special events is very eclectic. It's the gay Popstarz on Fridays. Open Thursday 9pm to 3am, Friday 10pm to 5am, and Saturday 9pm to 5am. 278 Pentonville Rd., N1. ✆ **020/7833-2022.** www. scala-london.co.uk. Cover £6–£12 ($8.70–$17.40). Tube: King's Cross.

**Velvet Room** This basement joint is a rare treat, low lit almost every night of the week. It's the reason so many clubbers turn up for work looking like the living dead. U.K. garage celeb Neutrino must have seen his life flash before him in May 2001 when he was shot after leaving the club. He was the victim of an "ordinary" robbery and the gun went off in the scuffle. Neutrino then drove himself to the hospital! Open Monday and Thursday 10pm to 3am, Tuesday 10:30pm to 3pm, Wednesday 10pm to 2:30am, Friday 10pm to 4:30am, and Saturday 10pm to 4am. 143 Charing Cross Rd., WC2. ✆ **020/7439-4655.** www.velvetroom. co.uk. Cover £4–£10 ($5.80–$14.50). Tube: Tottenham Court Rd.

## CLUB BARS

For every action there is a reaction. And the reaction to superclubs has been the rise of the club-bar. These are more intimate spaces, but with live music and specialist DJs. Nights tend to end earlier and the cover charge is much cheaper.

**Cargo**    The three interconnecting brick arches at Cargo are billed as a bar with live music and DJs, not a club, but it has the feel of a nightclub in the decades up to the 1950s. Venues were smaller then and it was quite the thing to combine bands and singers, with dancing, drinks, and food, just as Cargo does. Friday's Barrio, which is latin house, funk, nu-jazz, and soul, is the only weekly fixture. Otherwise the diary spans every kind of music style. Cocktails are £5 ($7.25). That's also the highest price for any dish on the international street food menu. Cargo is open Monday to Friday from noon to 1am, Saturday 6pm to 1am, and Sunday noon to midnight. Kingsland Viaduct, 83 Rivington St., EC2. ℂ 020/7739-3440. www.cargo-london.co.uk. Cover £3–£7 ($4.35–$10.15). Tube: Old St.

**Notting Hill Arts Club**    Come before 8pm (6pm on Sun) and it's free to get in. Come early any way or you'll have no chance at all of getting in to this cupboard-sized basement bar that hosts a mix of DJ and live music nights. Wednesday night is Radio4, a live music line-up put together by Alan McGee, ex of Creation Records fame. Bands take the sort-of stage on Saturday too, at RoTa. But the hottest spot on the dial is Sunday's hard dancing at Lazy Dog. NHAC is open Tuesday to Friday 6pm to 1am, Saturday 4pm to 1am, Sunday 4 to 11pm. Oh, and the art is minimal and doubtful! 21 Notting Hill Gate, W11. ℂ 020/7460-4459. Cover £5 ($7.25). Tube: Notting Hill Gate.

**The Social**    The upstairs bar is just a bar. Downstairs is where the action is, from DJs laying on some soulful house, hip hop, and funk, to the live Acousti-cally Heavenly night every Wednesday. That's the only time there's a cover charge, but it's worth it because there are always two indie bands or singer-songwriters in the line-up. The stage is high above the hole-in-the-ground dance floor and you'll have to get there early to get a table. The Social downstairs is open Monday to Saturday 7pm to midnight, closing at 10:30pm on Sunday. 5 Little Portland St., W1. ℂ 020/7636-4992. www.thesocial.com. Cover £3 ($4.35) Wed. Tube: Oxford Circus.

## 6 Gay & Lesbian London

Old Compton Street in Soho is the epicenter of gay London life. But there are plenty of bars and clubs elsewhere. To find out what's going on and where, pick up one of the free newspapers you'll find at most of the places listed below: the *Pink Paper* and *Boyz*, for instance. *QX* magazine is another top guide, and there are gay listings in *Time Out*. Lastly, for purely online help, check out the com-prehensive **www.gaytoz.com** or **www.rainbownetwork.com**. Otherwise, the **Lesbian & Gay Switchboard** (ℂ **020/7837-7324;** www.llgs.org.uk) is a round-the-clock information source on absolutely everything.

*Note:* Clubbers should check out the gay bars (see below) for discount flyers and jump-the-queue tickets.

### GROOVY CLUB NIGHTS

- **Atelier**    Groovy laid-back house for loungers from the media, music, fash-ion, and film industries at The End, 18 West Central St., WC1 (ℂ **020/ 7419-9199**). Cover £5 ($7.25). Open Thursday 10pm to 4am; happy hour 10 to 11pm. Dress: "Make an effort." Tube: Holborn, Tottenham Court Rd.
- **Coco Latté**    Get queue-jump tickets at The Box (see below) and join the mixed crowd for a hot, hot night of garage, techno, and 1970s sounds, at the Velvet Room, 143 Charing Cross Rd., WC2 (ℂ **020/7439-4655**). Cover £10 ($14.50). Open Friday 10pm to late. Tube: Tottenham Court Rd.

- **Crash**  Gaining an international reputation as "the dog's bollocks," music and muscle on two dance floors in a Vauxhall railway arch, at Crash, Arch 66, Goding St., SE11 (𝄐 **020/7820-1500**). Cover £10 ($14.50) or £8 ($11.60) with a flyer. Open Saturday 10:30pm to late. Tube: Vauxhall.
- **DPTM**  Three dance floors of latino house, funky grooves, hip hop, R&B, soul and jazz, and a few Sunday celebs, at new superclub Fabric, 77a Charterhouse St., EC1 (𝄐 **020/7439-9009**). Cover £13 ($18.85). Open Sunday 10pm until late. Tube: Barbican, Farringdon.
- **Popstarz**  Kitsch 1970s and 1980s, plus indie and alternative sounds, at the Scala, 278 Pentonville Rd., N1 (𝄐 **020/7738-2336**). Cover £8 ($11.60), free with a flyer before 11pm. Open Friday 10pm to 5am. Tube: King's Cross.
- **Trade**  Late-night techno, lasers, and the seriously body beautiful, at Turnmills, 63 Clerkenwell Rd., EC1 (𝄐 **020/7250-3409**). Cover £12 with a flyer, or £15 ($17.40–$21.75). Open from 4am Saturday to 1pm Sunday. Tube: Farringdon.

## GREAT VENUES

**G.A.Y.**  This colossal club is less about posing and more about a young unpretentious crowd having fun. The biggest night is strictly gay-only Saturday, when there are always some special surprises—big-name personal appearances, for instance. Five hundred queue-jump tickets go on sale at the Astoria box office from the Monday before, with some available on Saturday afternoon at Ku Bar (see below). G.A.Y. is open Monday 10:30pm to 3am, Thursday 11pm to 4am, Friday 11pm to 4am, and Saturday 10:30pm to 5am. Astoria and Mean Fiddler, 157–165 Charing Cross Rd., WC2. 𝄐 **0906/100-0160**. www.g-a-y.co.uk. Cover £3 ($4.35) or £1 ($1.45) with a flyer, Sat £10 ($14.50) or £8 ($11.60) with a flyer. Tube: Tottenham Court Rd.

**Heaven**  The 2,000-capacity Heaven is London's most famous gay club, though its popularity has drawn a lot of heteros, too. It's like a self-supporting space colony, with three floors of separate bars and dance floors. Big name DJs power up the volume across the full musical spectrum. On a Monday, you'll get cheap drinks, with happy pop, disco trash, and dance downstairs, and indie upstairs. Wednesday is soul and heavy funk, Friday techno and hard house. Saturday is the one strictly gay-only night. Surf the website, and you can print off "flyers" to save pounds getting in. Open Monday and Wednesday 10:30pm to 3am, Friday 10:30pm to 6am, and Saturday 10pm to 5:30am. The Arches, Craven St., WC2. 𝄐 **020/7930-2020**. www.heaven-london.com. Cover £4–£12 ($5.80–$17.40), free with a flyer before 11:30pm on Friday and £1–£6 ($1.45–$8.70) other nights; £1 ($1.45) with printable Web voucher. Tube: Embankment, Charing Cross.

## PUBS, BARS & CAFES

These places keep regular pub hours—Monday through Saturday 11am to 11pm, Sunday noon to 10:30pm—unless otherwise stated.

**The Box Bar**  A friendly, comfortable, and recently redesigned cafe-bar where people hang out and graze during the day, and gather for drinks in the evenings. This is one of the places to pick up queue-jump tickets to Saturday night at Heaven (see above). Seven Dials, 32–34 Monmouth St., WC2. 𝄐 **020/7240-5828**. Tube: Leicester Sq.

**Candy Bar**  Britain's first-ever 7-night lesbian bar opened its doors 3 years ago and has been such a hit that it has moved to bigger and better premises around the corner. There's more outdoor lounging, but otherwise the same principles

---

**Finds** Trannie Heaven

Saturday nights at the chic basement bar of the **Philbeach Hotel** (see chapter 4) are a clubby megaton blast. So call the transvestite dressing service (**⌀ 020/7373-4848**) and get the full works—wigs, clothes, shoes, and make-up.

---

apply: great beer, great cocktails, and great club nights. Gay men are welcome as guests. Open Monday to Thursday noon to 1pm, Friday and Saturday noon to 3am, and Sunday noon to 11pm. 23–24 Bateman St., W1. ⌀ 020/7437-1977. Cover Fri–Sat £5 ($7.25) after 9pm. No credit cards. Tube: Tottenham Court Rd.

**Central Station**    A pub with a difference—later hours and a laid-back crowd here for the cabaret, sports bar, roof terrace, and cruising at the basement's club nights (Mon and Thurs, men-only). Open Monday to Wednesday 5pm to 2am, Thursday 5pm to 3am, Friday 5pm to 4am, Saturday noon to 4am, and Sunday 11am to midnight. 37 Wharfedale Rd., N1. ⌀ 020/7278-3294. Happy hour Mon–Fri 5–9pm. Cover free–£5 ($7.25). Tube: King's Cross.

**Ku Bar**    Great place to start a night on the town as you'll find lots of discount flyers for clubs at this hip West End bar. You can also buy advance tickets on Saturday afternoon for that night's G.A.Y. (see above). All the beer is bottled, so no cheap pints. But there's another hot seller, schnapps shots—try asking for one after you've had a few! On Sundays, Ku Bar doesn't open until 1pm. 75 Charing Cross Rd., WC2. ⌀ 020/7437-4303. Happy hour daily noon–9pm. Tube: Leicester Sq.

**Kudos**    A well-groomed pampered party crowd gather at what many think is the best boys' bar in London. Kudos certainly tries hard, with big video screens downstairs for semi-real music nights, and DJs on Wednesday and Saturday (no cover). It's also a good place to pick up club flyers and advance tickets. 10 Adelaide St., WC2. ⌀ 020/7379-4573. Happy hour Mon–Fri 4–6pm, Sat–Sun 6–8pm. Tube: Embankment, Charing Cross.

**West Central**    Is it a pub? Is it a club? Yes, to both of those. There's a decibel and energy level to suit any mood at the three-storied West Central, with some kind of entertainment every night for eyes, ears, and dancin' feet. The basement bar stays open latest, Wednesday and Thursday 10:30pm to 2am, Friday and Saturday 10:30pm to 3am. The main bar opens at 3pm and the plush velvety Theatre Bar upstairs at 5pm. 29–30 Lisle St., WC2. ⌀ 020/7479-7980. Cover (basement bar only) £3 ($4.35). Tube: Leicester Sq.

**The Yard**    This is a friendly spot, attracting a laid-back mixed clientele and a big after-work crowd. There's a blissfully secluded courtyard, behind a set of iron gates, and two bars inside. The Yard opens at noon and is closed on Sundays. 57 Rupert St., W1. ⌀ 020/7437-2652. Tube: Piccadilly Circus.

## 7 The Drinking Game: Pubs & Wine Bars

The antiquated licensing laws in England and Wales restrict the sale of alcohol in pubs, bars, restaurants, and shops to between 11am and 11pm, Monday to Saturday, and noon to 10:30pm on Sunday. Proprietors must make a special application if they want to extend their hours, put on entertainment, and so on, which is why late-openers often charge for entry.

The government has promised to overhaul the whole system, but no one could tell me when. In the meantime, and probably at least until the end of 2002, assume the old rules apply.

## PUBS

There's nothing more British than a luvverly local boozer. But it takes more than a formula of polished wooden bar, beer on tap, big ashtrays, and a few pictures of Queen Victoria to make a true British pub—the atmosphere of the real thing is unique. We've listed public houses as evening entertainment, but the locals go almost any time—to meet their mates, swap stories, tell jokes, and put away quite a lot of booze. Pubs serve every sort of alcohol, except fancy cocktails, but beer is the national drink. Expect to pay £1.80 to £2.70 ($2.60–$3.90) for a pint, depending on what and where you're drinking. It would be absurd to try and review all the great pubs in London, or even the merely good—surf **www.goodpubs.com** for another 160 or so to add to our list.

*Note:* In pubs, you order food as well as drinks at the bar; there's no table service and there's no tipping, either.

**Cittie of Yorke**   This soaring high-gabled room must have the longest bar in England. You can still see the huge vats originally used to dispense wine and liquors. All along one wall are private wood-carved cubicles, supposedly designed for lawyers from the dozens of chambers in the neighborhood to meet discreetly with clients. The pub dates from 1430, though it was rebuilt in 1923. 22–23 High Holborn, WC1. ✆ 020/7242-7670. Tube: Chancery Lane, Holborn.

**The Dove**   A perfect riverside pub at Hammersmith, with a terrace perfect for watching the rowers from the local boathouses. Along with what must be one of the smallest bars in the world, it has a series of comfortable oak-paneled rooms with copper tables and settle seating. Get here early on sunny weekends. 19 Upper Mall, W6. ✆ 020/8748-5405. Tube: Ravenscourt Park.

**French House**   This Soho institution became the center of French life in London during World War II when de Gaulle and his circle gathered here. It still attracts a lot of French-speaking visitors. Beer is only sold in half pints—myths abound but no one really knows why. 49 Dean St., W1. ✆ 020/7437-2799. Tube: Tottenham Court Rd.

**Grenadier**   This cozy mews pub is always crowded. It was an officers' mess in the Duke of Wellington's time. Come to see the military memorabilia and the resident ghost of a soldier flogged to death for cheating at cards. 18 Wilton Row, SW1. ✆ 020/7235-3074. Tube: Hyde Park Corner.

**Jamaica Wine House**   This is one of the oldest bars in the City, where Caribbean merchants met to make deals over coffee and rum. Today, young bankers gather at the first-floor bar or downstairs in the cozier cellar to sip good wines, port, or beer. St. Michael's Alley, off Cornhill, EC3. ✆ 020/7626-9496. Tube: Bank (Exit 5).

**Jerusalem Tavern**   This pub pulls a mean pint, supplied by the St. Peter's Brewery in Suffolk. So it's no surprise that the tiny Georgian-style bar, with its open fire, is always packed and getting more so as Clerkenwell zooms up the list of London's coolest neighborhoods. 55 Britton St., EC1. ✆ 020/7490-4281. Tube: Farringdon.

**The Lamb**   The etched and hinged glass screens stretching round the bar here are called snob screens; they were put in so that customers didn't have to see the bartender. Apparently, they were the cat's pajamas at the turn of the last century

**Shakin' Cocktails**

Last seen several decades ago sporting a kitschy paper umbrella and a glacé cherry, the cocktail is making a huge comeback in London, but this time, it's very, very classy. Also check out the Bar at Villandry and Soho Spice, in chapter 5.

- **A White Lady at the American Bar of the Savoy**   Best for paying homage to London's first 'mixologist,' American barman Harry Craddock, who invented the delicious mix of gin, lemon juice, and Cointreau. A splurge at £10 ($14.50). Dress very elegantly. Open 11am to 11pm. Savoy Hotel, Strand, WC2 (*(C)* **020/7836-4343;** Tube: Charing Cross).

- **Pimms on the River Terrace of Somerset House**   Best for some enchanted evening, weather permitting, and if you can ignore the embankment traffic noise, as you sip the quintessential English summer tipple of Pimms, lemonade, ginger ale, fresh fruit, and mint for £6 ($8.70). Open 10am to 11pm, April to September. Somerset House, Strand, WC2 (*(C)* **020/7845-4600;** Tube: Charing Cross).

- **A Dekamron at the Lab**   Best for hangin' with the 20-somethings tasting Soho's finest fruity flavors, like this mix of Myer's and coconut rums, with papaya, fresh lime, and apple juices, cream and sugar. One's enough at £5.90 ($8.55). Open Monday to Friday noon to midnight, Saturday 4pm to midnight, Sunday 4 to 10:30pm. 12 Old Compton St., W1 (*(C)* **020/7437-7820;** Tube: Leicester Sq., Tottenham Court Rd.).

- **A YO! Qualude at YO! Below**   Best for drinking horizontally on the 30ft-wide bed at this crazy beer and sake hall, as the mix of Wyborowa vodka, sake, Baileys, and Frangelico puts you in the mood for a Japanese neck massage or tarot reading. Given away at £3.50 ($5.10). Open noon to 11pm. 95 Farringdon Rd., EC1 (*(C)* **020/ 7841-0790;** Tube: Farringdon).

when such Victorian niceties really mattered. 94 Lamb's Conduit St., WC1. *(C)* **020/ 7405-0713.** Tube: Oxford Circus.

**Lamb & Flag**   This old timber-framed pub is in a short cul-de-sac off Garrick Street, Covent Garden. The poet Dryden dubbed it the "Bucket of Blood" after he was almost beaten to death here. The Lamb & Flag can be hard to find, but the friendly atmosphere and list of 30 whiskies are ample reward for the effort. The food is good traditional pub grub, and there's free live jazz from 7:30pm on Sunday evenings. 33 Rose St., WC2. *(C)* **020/7497-9504.** Tube: Leicester Sq.

**Market Porter**   This pub opens from 6 to 8:30am, as well as at the usual times, to cater for the weird working hours of the porters at Borough Market. It's the place to come for an alcoholic reviver after a dawn start trawling the antiques at the other almost local market, Bermondsey. Purists bewail the recent makeover but it still has a good selection of real ales. 9 Stoney St., SE1. *(C)* **020/ 7407-2495.** Tube: London Bridge.

**Prospect of Whitby**   Named after a coal barge that operated between York-shire and London, this is an atmospheric pub with a fine view of the river. Once frequented by smugglers, thieves, and "Hanging" Judge Jeffries, it dates back to 1520. Take a cab from the Tube station, or turn right and walk along the river. 57 Wapping Wall, E1. ℂ 020/7481-1095. Tube: Wapping.

**Punch Tavern**   Charles Dickens and a bunch of his friends founded the satir-ical magazine *Punch* at this pub next to St. Bride's Church. It is one of the pubs in London, though it's known now for its brilliant plush Victorian gin-palace interior and Punch & Judy memorabilia. 99 Fleet St., EC4. ℂ 020/7353-6658. Tube: Blackfriars.

**Spaniards Inn**   This romantic Hampstead Heath pub has a lovely garden in summer and hearthside drinking in winter. Part of it dates back to 1585, and many a famous drinker has dallied here—from Keats and Shelley to Dickens and the highwayman Dick Turpin, who stabled his horse across the road. Spaniards Rd., NW3, Hampstead. ℂ 020/8731-6571. Tube: Hampstead, then no. 210 bus.

**Toucan**   This pub is so tiny that drinkers can barely raise their elbows to sup their Guinness, so they spill out onto the street. As well as pints of the black stuff, Toucan has a selection of fine Irish whiskeys and Galway Bay oysters on the bar menu. 19 Carlisle St., W1. ℂ 020/7437-4123. Tube: Tottenham Court Rd.

**Windsor Castle**   It's a risky business meeting a friend at the Windsor Castle—the maze of small wood-paneled rooms are always crowded, and you can circle round hopelessly for hours. Come in the summer and enjoy a drink in the lovely walled garden. 114 Campden Hill Rd., W8. ℂ 020/7243-9551. Tube: Notting Hill Gate.

## WINE BARS

Wine lovers will thank their lucky stars for an alternative to the pub, where plonk predominates over fine bouquet. A bottle of house red or white generally costs £10 to £15 ($14.50–$21.75), a great deal to share between two or three people, and most wine bars sell a selection by the glass (from £2.50/$3.65). You can almost always eat there, which is why the full reviews are in "Great Deals on Dining," in chapter 5. For great wine lists at more than manageable prices, try: **Bleeding Heart,** Bleeding Heart Yard, off Greville St., EC1 (ℂ **020/ 7242-8238;** Tube: Chancery Lane, Farringdon); and **Cork & Bottle,** 44–46 Cranbourn St., WC2 (ℂ **020/7734-7807;** Tube: Leicester Sq.).

# 9

# Easy Excursions from London

Spur-of-the-moment escapes may be great fun, but you won't be laughing when you realize how much you could have saved by making plans at the same time you booked the whole holiday—especially if you're traveling to a hot spot at a hot time in the summer when discount deals are snapped up very quickly. You can arrange tours, trains, and coaches, as well as get helpful advice, at the **Britain Visitor Centre,** 1 Regent St., SW1 (no phone; **www.visitbritain.com**), open Monday to Friday 9:30am to 6:30pm, Saturday and Sunday 10am to 4pm (Sat 9am–5pm, June–Oct).

All the excursions in this chapter are doable in 1 day. But it might be rather a long day if you choose Oxford, where there's so much to see and do, or Bath and Stratford-upon-Avon, which also offer lots of entertainment and take longer to get to. So, why not pack a toothbrush? Local tourist offices can book you a bed and you'll find some tips on bagging a cheap sleep in "How to Save on Day-Trippin'," below. To help you pick a trip, we've put together a calendar of the must-see annual events ("Calendar of Events for London Excursions," below). Again, the tourist offices can fill in any gaps. Also, have a browse through *Frommer's England from $70 a Day,* by Darwin Porter and Danforth Prince.

## 1 How to Save on Day-Trippin'

Don't forget to check out additional ideas and information on special passes under "Fifty Money-Saving Tips," in chapter 2.

- **Play the Train Fare Game**  Avoid traveling on Fridays when prices soar to profit from the mass exodus of city dwellers. There are dozens of different fares with varying restrictions (see "The Train Ticket Dictionary," below). So always ask for the cheapest, and then decide if it suits your travel plans.

---

### Tips  The E-List for Side-Trip Surfing

I've bookmarked a handful of really handy websites for anyone planning a London-plus kind of holiday. The very comprehensive U.K. guide and travel e-zine, **www.britannia.com**, is only marred by the high prices of its short-break packages and by such sloppiness as leaving in some old London telephone numbers 6 months after the code-change. Lovers of stately homes must surf **www.nationaltrust.org.uk** and **www.english-heritage. org.uk**, the sites for the leading custodians of Britain's heritage. Gateways like **www.cathedrals.org.uk**, **www.24hourmuseum.org.uk**, and **www. goodpubs.com** take out a lot of the legwork (sorry, fingerwork!). Like a nationwide local newspaper, **www.localtoday.co.uk** posts details of every kind of event from car-boot sales to glass-blowing demonstrations.

**The Train Ticket Dictionary**

These are the fares most likely to suit budget-travelers on an excursion from London. You can hunt down fares and book online at **www.thetrainline.com**.

- **Cheap day returns** For journeys under 50 miles, leaving London after 9:30am. No need to book specific train times. An ordinary **day-return** ticket allows travel during peak times.

- **Network Away Break** No need to book specific trains, but not available on some peak services. Return journey must be within 5 days.

- **Super APEX** Selected services only, off-peak. Must be bought 14 days before departure with fixed dates and times for both halves of the journey.

- **APEX** Selected services only, mostly off-peak. Must be purchased a week in advance with fixed dates and times for departure and return.

- **Super Advance** Must be bought by 6pm the day before departure with fixed times and dates, mostly off-peak.

- **Supersaver return** Walk on, but only outside the morning (after 9:30am) and evening rush hours. Not available on a Friday.

- **Standard return** A no-restriction splurge.

- **Train Passes** If you expect to make several trips out of London, call **BritRail** (📞 **866/BRITRAIL** or 877/677-1066; www.britrail.net) about the **SouthEast Pass**—before you leave home, as it is only available outside Britain. This flexipass gets you to Windsor, Cambridge, and Oxford, which we've suggested as excursions, as well as to Brighton, Canterbury, and so on. It's $73 for 3 days and $106 for 4 days travel within an 8-day period, or $142 for 7 days travel within a 15-day period. Child passes are $21. One big benefit: there are no time-of-day restrictions on these passes.

- **Bus Deals** The leading long-haul bus line is **National Express** (📞 **08705/808080;** www.gobycoach.com). The **Tourist Trail Pass** allows unlimited travel on a set number of days falling within a fixed time period: either 2 days to be used within a 3-day period, for £49 ($71.05); 5 days travel, valid for 10, for £85 ($123.25); 8 days, valid for 30, for £135 ($195.75); or 15 days, valid for 30, for £190 ($275.50), or valid for 60 days, £205 ($297.25). Under-25s and over-50s can buy a discount card for £9 ($13.05), which cuts pass and individual ticket prices by 20% to 30%.

- **Car Deals**—I beg people on bended knee not to drive in London, but the deals at **easyRentacar** are so good that it does make sense for a puttering-about kind of excursion into the English countryside—for ideas, check out the AA's top 30 circular driving tours (**www.theaa.com/getaway/tour_home. html**). Daily rates fluctuate according to demand, so book early and you might only have to pay £14 ($22.40) to have a Mercedes A-Class for a day. You only get 75 free miles. After that, there's a charge of 20p (29¢) a mile. Booking is online only (www.easyrentacar.com).

- **Take an Escorted Tour** The **London for Less** discount card gets you 20% off **Frames Rickards** (☎ 020/7837-3111) 1-day coach tours, or 10% on longer trips and specialist trips such as garden tours. **Trafalgar Tours** (☎ 020/7976-5363; www.trafalgartours.com) coach trips cost £47.50 ($68.90) per person to Bath and Stonehenge, and £28 ($40.60) to Windsor—just as a couple of examples. Both companies include entry to attractions in their prices.
- **Foot-Following** The **Original London Walks** (☎ 020/7624-3978; www.walks.com) can get you a discount on a cheap day-return train ticket. It offers **Explorer Days** every Saturday to places like York, Oxford, Bath, Salisbury, and Stonehenge.
- **Cheap Sleeps** Several of our hot tips for finding a budget London also apply to stopovers. You can make net savings at the excellent **www.laterooms.com**. Mary and Simon Ette, at **The Independent Traveller** (☎ 01392/860807; www.gowithIT.co.uk), broker self-catering accommodations, both urban and rural. For leisure deals at chain hotels, check out "The Bargain Business," on p. 100. Outside London, youth hostel dorm beds cost £11 to £18 ($15.95–$26.10) a night for adults. For addresses countrywide, including in each of our side-trip destinations, and booking, call ☎ 0870/870-8808 (www.yha.org.uk).

## CALENDAR OF EVENTS FOR LONDON EXCURSIONS

### February

**Cambridge University Rag Week.** Students dress up and play the fool to raise money for charity. February 23 to March 3.

### March

**Festival of Easter Walks.** Hundreds of themed walks all over the country, exploring local heritage, landscapes, and wildlife, and led for free by members of the Ramblers Association. Call the London HQ for regional contact details (☎ 020/7339-8500; www.ramblers.org.uk). March 29 to April 1.

### May

**Oxford Eights Week.** Intercollegiate rowing championship. Usually end of May.

### June

**Cambridge Strawberry Fair.** Free fest of music, arts, and crafts on Midsummer Common (☎ 01223/560160; www.strawberryfair.org.uk). Usually 1st Saturday of June.

**Encaenia.** Begowned university bigwigs and lucky dignitaries process at noon through **Oxford** to the Sheldonian Theatre for the bestowing of honorary degrees. June 19.

### July

**Cambridge Shakespeare Festival.** Open-air performances of uncut texts in beautiful grounds of ancient colleges (☎ 01223/357851 box office; www.cambridgeshakespeare.com). Early July to late August.

**Cambridge Folk Festival.** Tents go up in the wooded grounds of Cherry Hinton Hall on the edge of Cambridge for one of the oldest folk festivals in Europe, going since 1965. Very family-friendly celebration of blue grass, gospel, jazz, ceilidh, and world music (☎ 01223/857851; www.cam-folkfest.co.uk). Usually from Thursday through last weekend in July.

### September

**St. Giles' Fair.** Street mayhem in Oxford, usually the first weekend in September.

**Windsor Festival.** Concerts and events in Windsor Castle, Eton College, and the Wren-designed Guildhall. For information, write to the Secretary, Windsor Festival, 4 Park Street, Windsor, SL4 1JS. Last 2 weeks in September.

## 2 Windsor & Eton

21 miles W of London

Surrounded by gentle hills and lush valleys, this pretty riverside town—which the ancient Britons called Windlesore—is famous for two things: an enormous luxe fortress and a very posh private boys school. You'll need at least 1½ hours to look around Windsor Castle, and that's at a bit of a trot. Take it easy, and make sure to see St. George's Chapel and Queen Mary's Doll House, too, at a pace that lets you really enjoy them. Then take a well-earned lunch break to refuel before one of these three great afternoon options: visit Eton College, for free unless you look round the museum or take a tour; take a boat trip that goes past the school for a smallish fee; or splurge and head for the amazing Legoland theme park.

## A WEEK AT A GLANCE

**Monday:** Summer evening meetings at **Royal Windsor Racecourse** (© 01753/ 865234; www.windsor-racecourse.co.uk). Admission £5 to £16 ($7.20–$23.20), under-16s free. Take the Riverbus to the racecourse from just west of Windsor Bridge, paying your £4 ($5.80) return fare on board. **Saturday:** in the afternoon, Eton boys change out of tailcoats and wing collars, into "mufti." **Sunday:** no Changing of the Guard; St. George's Chapel open for services only; Eton boys in "mufti" after church.

## ESSENTIALS

**GETTING THERE** Trains depart from Waterloo for Windsor & Eton Riverside and take about 50 minutes. A standard return costs £11.60 ($16.80); a cheap day return is £6.20 ($9). If you have a London Transport travelcard that covers zone 4, you can hop on the same train, a few minutes into its journey, at Richmond—the District Line Tube and proper trains use the same station. Standard return is £8.70 ($12.60); cheap day return is £5 ($7.25). Trains to Windsor Central, very near Riverside station, start from Paddington and, inconveniently, you have to change at Slough. Call **National Rail Enquiries** (© 08457/484950). **Green Line buses** (© 08706/087261) leave from Bulleid Way, near Eccleston Bridge behind Victoria Station, and take around 1 hour. Day-return tickets cost £7.50 ($10.90), £4 ($5.80) children. If you're driving, take the M4 west out of London to exit 6.

**ORIENTATION** Windsor is one place where there's little chance of getting lost. The castle is so enormous that you can always take your bearings from it. Eton is just on the other side of the river.

---

### More Side Trips from London

Bath, Brighton, and Stratford-upon-Avon are also popular side trips from London, but unfortunately we don't have room to cover them here. For details on how to get to these towns and what to do once you're there, check out *Frommer's England from $70 a Day*, or browse the "Destinations" section of our website, **www.Frommers.com**.

**VISITOR INFORMATION** Turn right out of the station, and follow Datchet Road round the walls of Windsor Castle. It turns briefly into Thames Street and then High Street. The **Royal Windsor Information Centre** is at no. 24 (© **01753/743900;** www.windsor.gov.uk). It's open daily 10am to 5pm. Windsor is a perfect day-trip, but if you fancy staying overnight, call the center's **Accommodation Hotline** (© **01753/743907**). It charges £5 ($7.25) to make reservations.

## CASTLE HILL

Windsor Castle ★★   It took 1.5 million gallons of water and 15 hours to put out the fire at Windsor Castle in 1992. The repair bill was so huge that it prompted the Queen to open Buckingham Palace to the public for the first time as a way of raising the necessary funds. In 2002, this spectacularly restored fortress is likely to be the upstream pearl in the String of Pearls festival—a calendar of special events and openings at riverside attractions and working institutions— to celebrate the Queen's Golden Jubilee (**www.stringofpearls.org.uk**).

Windsor Castle lies on a bend in the Thames, surrounded by 4,800 acres of lawn, woodlands, and lakes. With more than 1,000 rooms, it claims to be the largest inhabited castle in the world and it is certainly one of the oldest, dating back over 900 years. The **State Apartments** are open to the public as long as the Queen isn't in residence—if you see the Royal Standard flying, then you're out of luck. Room after room is filled with fabulous furnishings, tapestries, and paintings by Rembrandt, Canaletto, van Dyck, Rubens, and Holbein. **St. George's Hall** was one of the most laborious parts of the restoration, decorated with the heraldic arms of more than 800 Knights of the Garter going back to the founder, the Black Prince. The painter of the extraordinary pagan feast on the **King's Dining Room** ceiling got ideas above his station and put himself into the picture. See if you can find his face, or ask one of the guards to point it out.

But my favorite of all the treasures at Windsor Castle is the spectacular **Queen Mary's Doll House.** Designed by Sir Edwin Lutyens, it took 1,000 craftsmen more than 3 years to create. Everything in it actually works, from the plumbing to a tiny electric iron. Even the bottles in the cellar contain a drop of by-now vintage wine.

The **Changing of the Guard,** when soldiers march to a military band through the town to the castle's Lower Ward, takes place at 11am, from Monday to Saturday between April and June, and on alternate days the rest of the year. So, call the castle before you decide which day to visit.

Edward IV founded **St. George's Chapel** (© **01753/865538**) in 1475. Within the castle precincts, it's one of the finest examples of late Gothic architecture in Britain. This is where Prince Edward and Sophie got married. Ten sovereigns have left their bones here, including Henry VIII, who completed the chapel, and his third wife Jane Seymour. St. George is patron saint of the Most Noble Order of the Garter, Britain's highest chivalric order. You can see the banners, swords, helms, and crests of each current member, as well as more than 700 metal stall plates, the oldest of which dates back to about 1390. Sadly, many have been lost, including those of the original founders in 1348. Visitors are welcome at Sunday services and also at daily Evensong, at 5:15pm during school terms. Go to the Henry VIII Gate.

© **01753/868286.** www.royalresidences.com/frWindsor.htm. Admission £11 ($15.95) adults, £9 ($13.05) seniors, £5.50 ($8) under-17s; if the State Apartments are closed, admission discounted to £5.50 ($8), £4.50 ($6.55), and £2.70 ($3.90). Castle Mar–Oct daily 9:45am–5:15pm (last entry 4pm); Nov–Feb daily

9:45am–4:15pm (last entry 3pm); closed when Queen in residence (call to check). St. George's Chapel Mon–Sat 10:45am–4:15pm (last entry 4pm).

## . . . AND BEYOND

Have a wander through the cobbled streets, known as Guildhall Island, opposite the castle gates. Then turn down the High Street toward the river, which is where all the afternoon options start. Eton is across the bridge. You can catch the shuttlebus for Legoland from either Windsor Central Station on the left, or back at Windsor & Eton Riverside. And boat tours start just upriver from the bridge on the Windsor bank.

It's about a 10-minute walk from the bridge, past browsable antiques stores, to the most prestigious "public school" in England, **Eton College** (★ (✆ **01753/671177;** www.etoncollege.com). Prince William is now at St. Andrew's University in Scotland but you might still see Harry wandering through the streets between lessons, in wing collar and tailcoat. Eton has educated many members of the British establishment, including 19 prime ministers. The **Lower School** has one of the oldest classrooms in the world (1443). It costs £3 ($4.35) for adults, £2 ($2.90) for under-15s, to look round the Schoolyard, College Chapel, Cloisters, and Museum of Eton Life. The 1-hour tour includes all these, as well as an ambulatory history lesson from the founding of the school in 1440 to the present day. It starts at 2:15 and 3:15pm, and costs £4 ($5.80). No need to book, but call to make sure of the schedule and opening times: end March to mid-April, and July through August, 10:30am to 4:30pm; mid-April through June, and September, from 2 to 4:30pm.

For a more leisurely peak at Eton, as well as several river islands, posh houses, and Royal Windsor Racecourse, take a **French Brothers boat trip** (★ up the Thames from Barry Promenade. The bumper 2-hour cruise starts at 1:30 and 2:30pm, every day from Easter to the end of October. Tickets cost £6.30 ($9.15) for adults and £3.15 ($4.55) for children. Cheaper quickie tours, lasting 35 minutes, leave every ½ hour from 11am to 5pm, and cost £4 ($5.80) for adults and £2 ($2.90) for children. Call (✆ **01753/851900** (www.boat-trips.co.uk) for info.

Few theme parks are as extraordinary or impressive as **Legoland** (★★, Windsor Park ((✆ **08705/040404;** www.legoland.co.uk), although visitors from California could probably give it a miss as there's another one at Carlsbad north of San Diego. It took 20 million of the famous Danish Toy company's little plastic building bricks just to create Miniland, one of seven different zones offering over 50 attractions and rides—wet ones, high ones, fast ones, scaled-down ones for little kids. The shuttlebus from either train station is free with a pre-booked Legoland ticket. And it is essential to book, not only to get the £1 ($1.45) discount on turn-up ticket prices, but because queues can be terminally long on school holidays. You can buy over the phone, online, and at train stations between Waterloo and Windsor.

One-day admission is £18.50 ($26.85) adults, £15.50 ($22.50) under-16s (under-3s free), and £12.50 ($18.15) seniors. Legoland is open Friday to Monday 10am to 6pm, shutting at 5pm Tuesday to Thursday. It often stays open late during summer holidays. The park closes for the winter from early-November to mid-March.

## WHERE TO EAT

**Peascod Street** and **Church Lane,** Windsor, are both good cruising grounds for cafes, delis, and good old-fashioned public houses.

**Gilbey's Bar & Restaurant** ✿ WINE BAR   This specialist importer sells its French wines at shop prices alongside bottles from its own English vineyard. The bar menu is delicious and reasonable—perhaps a starter of soup with crusty bread, for around £3.50 ($5.10), followed by a double-size portion of smoked haddock fishcakes. Or, the set menu is an excellent value and will save you a few pennies off the heavier restaurant prices. In the summer, you can eat out in the garden.

82–83 High St., Eton. ✆ 01753/854921. Bar main courses £7.95 ($11.55); 2-course set menu £10.95 ($15.90). AE, DC, MC, V. Mon–Fri noon–2:30pm, Sat–Sun noon–3pm; daily 6–11pm.

## 3 Cambridge

55 miles N of London

Cambridge and Oxford compete fiercely in everything. Oxford is grander and older. A thriving town before the first college opened its doors, it has a busy industrial area, now centered around the Science Park. Cambridge has a much more somnolent air and an immediately captivating beauty. But behind the lazy romance of this town on the banks of the Cam is a dot-com business boom. Ever since Microsoft set up its European research center here, Cambridge has become known as "Silicon Fen."

Settled by the Romans, the city did not begin to flourish until the 13th century when the first college was founded. Cambridge University now has 31 colleges, the grounds of which are open to the public year-round. Some are worth visiting, others less so, and admission fees can quickly add up. We recommend a trip to the Fitzwilliam Museum, Kettle's Yard, and then one or two of the colleges, before taking a punt out on the river. During the summer holidays, the colleges are crowded with visitors.

*Note:* Cambridge University **term dates** for 2002 are: January 15 to March 15; April 23 to June 14; and October 8 to December 6.

### A WEEK AT A GLANCE

**Monday:** Fitzwilliam Museum and Kettle's Yard closed. **Saturday:** craft market takes over All Saints Passage, opposite Trinity Hall. **Sunday:** farmers' market in Market Square, plus an art, craft, and antiques market.

*Note:* There is a general market, selling everything from fish to fruit to fripperies, every day but Sunday in Market Square.

### ESSENTIALS

**GETTING THERE**   Trains depart from King's Cross station and take 55 minutes. The day-return fare is £17.70 ($25.65); cheap day return £15 ($21.75). From Cambridge station, take the Cityrail bus to Market Square, in the middle of Oxford. Call **National Rail Enquiries** (✆ 08457/484950). **National Express buses** (✆ 08705/808080) leave from London's Victoria Coach Station, take 1 hour and 55 minutes, and cost £13.50 ($19.60) return, £9.50 ($13.80) same-day return. If you're driving from London, take the M11 motorway to Exit 11.

**ORIENTATION**   Cambridge (pop. 111,000) has two main streets. **Trumpington Road**—which becomes Trumpington Street, King's Parade, Trinity Street, and finally St. John's Street—runs parallel to the River Cam. It's close to several of the city's colleges. **Bridge Street,** the city's main shopping zone, starts at Magdalene Bridge; it becomes Sidney Street, St. Andrew's Street, and finally Regent Street.

**VISITOR INFORMATION** The **Tourist Information Centre** (TIC), Wheeler St. (© **01223/322640;** www.cambridge.gov.uk/leisure/tourism.htm), is behind the Guildhall. It'll tell you everything you need to know about transportation and sightseeing, and has useful maps as well. The office is open all year Monday to Friday 10am to 5:30pm, Saturday 10am to 5pm, Sunday 11am to 4pm. To find out more about Cambridge University, it's best to surf the rather dry website as the administration is very decentralized (© **01223/337733;** www.cam.ac.uk).

The TIC **Accommodation Booking Service** (© **01223/457581**) charges a £3 ($4.35) fee for advance and phone reservations—£5 ($7.25) if you turn up and need a bed that night—and 10% deposit. It operates from 9:30am to 4pm Monday to Friday.

## WALKS & TOURS

Walking tours leave from the Tourist Information Centre at least twice a day, at 11:30am and 1:30pm, from April to October—more often at the height of the summer, less in the fall and winter. Tickets are £7 ($10.15) and include entrance to King's College Chapel. For more info on guided tours, call © **01223/457574.**

## VISITING THE COLLEGES

You won't have time to see all the colleges. And some are frankly not worth the admission charges of between £2 and £3.50 ($2.90 and $5.10), so below are a few recommendations. A great way to see a lot more of them, from the outside, is to take a stroll along the Backs—the meadows between the colleges and the Cam. This swath of green takes you up to **St. John's Bridge,** a replica of the Bridge of Sighs in Venice.

The undoubted must-visit is **King's College** ★★ (© **01223/331100,** or © 01223/331155 for the chapel), founded by Henry VI in 1441. The chapel is internationally famous for its choir and the traditional Festival of Nine Lessons and Carols, which is broadcast every Christmas Eve. It has incredible fan vaulting, stained-glass windows, and a screen given by Henry VIII that bears his initials and those of his queen at the time, Anne Boleyn. Behind the altar is Rubens's *Adoration of the Magi,* painted in 1634. A small exhibition hall holds a display about the chapel's history.

Go for a choral service (Mon–Sat at 5:30pm, Sun at 10:30am and 3:30pm, call to check) for the full experience, but only during university terms and during the first half of July. Then, the chapel is open Monday through Saturday 9:30am to 3:30pm, Sunday 1:15 to 2:15pm. During vacation, it's open Monday through Saturday 9:30am to 4:30pm, Sunday 10am to 4:30pm. The chapel is closed December 26 through January 1, and often without notice for recording sessions and rehearsals. Admission is £3.50 ($5.10) for adults, £2.50 ($3.65) for students and children.

Founded by Henry VIII in 1546, **Trinity College** (© **01223/338400**) is the largest and wealthiest of Cambridge's colleges. It has produced 29 Nobel Laureates. Famous alumni include the scientist Sir Isaac Newton; poets and writers Francis Bacon, Lord Tennyson, Lord Byron, Andrew Marvell, and John Dryden; and philosopher Bertrand Russell. Traditionally, students try to run around the two-acre courtyard in the time it takes the clock to strike 12, a scene you may remember from the movie *Chariots of Fire.* More rakishly, it's said that the poet Byron used to bathe naked in the large central fountain. Note the statue of

# Cambridge

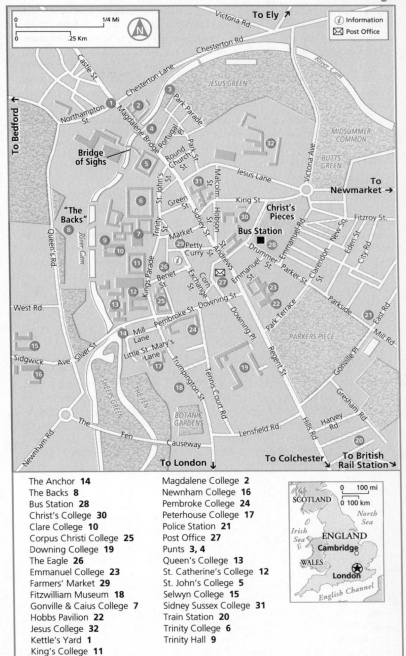

*Information*
*Post Office*

To Ely ↗
Victoria Rd.
Chesterton Rd.
Castle St.
Chesterton Lane
JESUS GREEN
River Cam
MIDSUMMER COMMON
To Bedford ←
Northampton St.
Magdalene Bridge
Portugal Pl.
Park Parade
Park St.
Round Church St.
BUTTS GREEN
Bridge of Sighs
Jesus Lane
Victoria Ave.
To Newmarket →
Malcolm St.
King St.
St. John's St.
Green St.
Sidney St.
Hobson St.
Fitzroy St.
"The Backs"
Christ's Pieces
New St.
Eden St.
City Rd.
Queen's Rd.
River Cam
Trinity St.
Market
St. Andrews St.
Bus Station
Emmanuel Rd.
Clarendon Rd.
Petty Curry
Drummer St.
Emmanuel St.
Parker St.
West Rd.
Kings Parade
Benet St.
Corn Exchange St.
Downing St.
Park Terrace
Parkside
East Rd.
Pembroke St.
Downing Pl.
PARKERS PIECE
Mill Rd.
Mill Lane
Silver St.
Little St. Mary's Lane
Regent St.
Gonville Pl.
Sidgwick Ave.
Trumpington St.
Tennis Court Rd.
Gresham Rd.
Harvey Rd.
Hills Rd.
SHEEPS GREEN
THE FEN
BOTANIC GARDENS
Lensfield Rd.
Newnham Rd.
The Fen Causeway
To London ↓
To Colchester ↘
To British Rail Station ↘

| | |
|---|---|
| The Anchor **14** | Magdalene College **2** |
| The Backs **8** | Newnham College **16** |
| Bus Station **28** | Pembroke College **24** |
| Christ's College **30** | Peterhouse College **17** |
| Clare College **10** | Police Station **21** |
| Corpus Christi College **25** | Post Office **27** |
| Downing College **19** | Punts **3, 4** |
| The Eagle **26** | Queen's College **13** |
| Emmanuel College **23** | St. Catherine's College **12** |
| Farmers' Market **29** | St. John's College **5** |
| Fitzwilliam Museum **18** | Selwyn College **15** |
| Gonville & Caius College **7** | Sidney Sussex College **31** |
| Hobbs Pavilion **22** | Train Station **20** |
| Jesus College **32** | Trinity College **6** |
| Kettle's Yard **1** | Trinity Hall **9** |
| King's College **11** | |

SCOTLAND
North Sea
Irish Sea
ENGLAND
Cambridge
WALES
London
English Channel

0    100 mi
0    100 km

Henry VIII on the Great Gate clutching a chair leg instead of a sword—the result of a student prank. The impressive **Wren Library** was designed by Sir Christopher himself and holds many original works by famous former students. Admission is £2 ($2.90) for adults, or £1 ($1.45) for concessions.

**Queens' College** (✆ **01223/335511**) is arguably the prettiest of them all. Founded in 1448, it is named for Margaret of Anjou, the wife of Henry VI, and Elizabeth, wife of Edward IV. The most spectacular parts are the 16th-century **President's Lodge** and the Tower, where the great scholar, Erasmus, lived from 1510 to 1514. Other places to stop in include **Magdalene** (pronounced "*Maud*-len"), to view the Pepys Library, the diarist's collection of 3,000 volumes; and **Jesus College,** for the chapel's stained-glass windows designed by Edward Burne-Jones and its ceiling by William Morris.

### . . . AND BEYOND

"Punting," or pole-boating, is a Cambridge tradition, and the venerable **Scudamore's Punting Company** (✆ **01223/359750;** www.scudamores.com) has been operating since 1910. It costs £12 ($17.40) an hour to hire a punt, and you have to leave a £50 ($72.50) refundable deposit. Head for the Mill Lane punting station, next to the Anchor pub (see below), or the one by Magdalene Bridge. Both are open daily, from 9am to dusk, April through September, and from 10am in February, March, October, and November; weekends only from 10am to dusk in December and January. The main boatyard, also in Mill Lane, keeps the same summer schedule, and opens at weekends only, 10am to dusk, in March and October. The Jesus Green punting station operates June through August, 10am to 6pm, and weekends only, from 10am to dusk, in April, May, September, October. Scudamore's also organizes "chauffeured" punting tours.

If you enjoy museums and galleries, there are two exceptional **freebies** to visit here in Cambridge. The **Fitzwilliam Museum**, Trumpington Street (✆ **01223/332900;** www.fitzmuseum.cam.ac.uk), is an eclectic treasure house of Chinese jades and bronzes, pages from beautiful Books of Hours, and the first draft of Keats's "Ode to a Nightingale," as well as china, glass, majolica, silver, clocks, and a superb Egyptian collection. The paintings range from medieval and Renaissance works to contemporary canvases. Feast your eyes on Titian's *Tarquin and Lucretia,* Rubens's *The Death of Hippolytus,* brilliant etchings by van Dyck, rare Hogarths, 25 Turners, works by William Blake, the impressionists, and more recent artists Paul Nash and Sir Stanley Spencer. Expect to see a few hard hats on your visit: building was to start in January 2002 on the Courtyard Development, which will provide new exhibition, education, and shopping space! Open Tuesday to Saturday 10am to 5pm, and Sunday 2:15 to 5pm.

**Kettle's Yard,** Castle Street (✆ **01223/352124;** www.kettlesyard.co.uk), is a very different kettle of fish. Jim Ede was the curator at the Tate during the 1920s and 1930s. He and his wife Helen acquired this collection of artworks, furniture, and decorative objects, displayed as he arranged them in his home. You'll find work by Ben Nicholson, Christopher Wood, and Alfred Wallis, and sculptures by Henry Moore, Henri Gaudier-Brzeska, Brancusi, and Barbara Hepworth. The gallery, meanwhile, holds exhibitions of 20th-century art. The house is open Tuesday to Sunday 1:30 to 4:30pm (2–4pm in winter), and the gallery Tuesday to Sunday 11:30 to 5pm.

### WHERE TO EAT

Ram-raid the market for picnic provender then head to the Backs for an idyllic stolen moment by the Cam. Magical!

**The Anchor** PUB   Looking out on a raft of punts and the willow-fringed river, the Anchor is loaded with atmosphere—beams, sloping ceilings, and filled with odds and ends like cider pots and prints. It serves traditional homemade English pub grub from battered cod and plaice, to lamb-and-vegetable or leek-and-potato pies, or sausage, egg, and chips. Come here for real ale, as well as the usual selection of lagers and bitters.

Silver St. (C) **01223/353554**. £1.95–£5.50 ($2.85–$8). MC, V. Food served Mon–Thurs noon–7:45pm; Fri–Sat noon–3:45pm; Sun noon–2:30pm.

**The Eagle** 🔫 PUB   This ivy-covered pub has a lovely galleried courtyard that serves as a beer garden. Inside are two bars and three sitting areas with scrubbed wood tables. Burned into the ceiling of the Air Force bar are the names and numbers of wartime officers. The Eagle has culinary aspirations—its five daily specials range from shark steak to cajun chicken.

Benet St. (C) **01223/505020**. Lunch £3.25–£4.95 ($4.70–$7.20); evening main courses £4–£9.95 ($5.80–$14.45). Food served Sun–Thurs noon–9pm; Fri–Sat noon–8pm.

## 4 Oxford

57 miles NW of London

Oxford contrasts dramatically with Cambridge. It's a modern, crowded, and busy place where town seriously competes with gown. After all, people were living here 2 centuries before the founding of the first college. Although scholars and students began to congregate as early as the 12th century, Oxford University didn't receive its charter from the Papal Legate until 1214. From 1249, colleges began popping up like mushrooms, starting with University, then Balliol in 1263, and Merton in 1264. Originally, they were men only. The first one for women, Lady Margaret Hall, was established in 1878. In 1975, some of the men's colleges began admitting women, and the rest reluctantly followed.

Wedged between the Thames and Cherwell rivers, Oxford has more than 600 buildings listed for historical or architectural interest. If you really want to uncover the nooks and crannies, the history and personalities, then read *Oxford* by Jan Morris.

### A WEEK AT A GLANCE

**Monday:** Ashmolean Museum and Museum of Modern Art closed. **Wednesday:** general market at Gloucester Green. **Thursday:** flea market, same place; also farmers' market the first Thursday of the month. **Saturday:** additional official tour of Oxford at 1:45pm, starting at Carfax Tower and usually including a visit to Christ Church. **Sunday:** same additional tour as Saturday; Sheldonian Theatre closed; no tours of the Bodleian Library.

### ESSENTIALS

**GETTING THERE**   Trains depart from London's Paddington Station and make the trip to Oxford in about 1 hour. A cheap day return is £15.30 ($22.20) and a Network Away Break £19.50 ($28.30). Call **National Rail Enquiries** ((C) **08457/484950**). **National Express buses** ((C) **08705/808080**) take 1 hour and 40 minutes, and round-trip fares from Victoria Coach Station are £10 ($14.50), with day returns for £8 ($11.60). If you're in a car, take the M40 to the A40, to the A420. Don't drive into the city center, however, as parking and traffic are horrific. There are free **Park and Ride** car parks on the main approaches to the north, south, and west sides of the city. Buses run regularly from there into the heart of the city (there's a small charge).

**ORIENTATION**    Known as **Carfax,** the city center ripples out around the crossroads where Cornmarket Street, St. Aldate's Street, Queen Street, and High Street meet. Most of the colleges are to the east, with **Magdalen Bridge** beyond the eastern end of High Street. The bus station and the tourist information center are in the northwest corner of Carfax, while the train station is further west, across the canal.

**VISITOR INFORMATION**    The **Oxford Information Centre** is in The Old School, Gloucester Green (© **01865/726871;** www.visitoxford.org), and opens Monday to Saturday 9:30am to 5pm, Sunday 10am to 3:30pm. As well as providing maps and brochures for local sights and attractions, the center has an accommodation booking service, which charges a £2.50 ($3.65) fee and takes a 10% deposit. Cheap sleeps are scarce in the middle of Oxford, but the main roads out of town are lined with affordable B&Bs—fine if you don't mind a bus ride or healthy walk.

For more information and a handy what's-on guide, surf **www.oxfordcity. co.uk**. Otherwise, **Oxford University's** website (www.ox.ac.uk) is refreshingly visitor-friendly and better than the phone (© **01865/270000**) as a one-stop info shop on all the colleges and museums, what to see and when.

## WALKS & TOURS

Two-hour tours, costing £5.85 ($8.50) for adults or £3 ($4.45) for under-12s, leave from the center daily at 11am and 2pm. The 1:45pm tour, from Carfax Tower, only happens on Saturday and Sunday and usually includes free admission to Christ Church: it costs £6.50 or £3.50 ($9.45 or $5.10). You can pick up more details at the information center.

## THE DREAMING SPIRES

**The Oxford Story,** 6 Broad St. (© **01865/728822;** www.oxfordstory.org.uk), claims to be the longest "dark ride" in Europe, trundling around the inside of a converted book warehouse. The animatronics are pretty creaky but they will help put in context what you see during your visit, telling the history of Oxford and student life from the first town and gown riots in the 14th century. Open daily: July and August from 9:30am to 5pm; otherwise Monday to Saturday 10am to 4:30pm, and from 11am on Sunday. Admission is £6.10 ($8.85) adults, £4.90 ($7.10) concessions, and £18.50 ($26.85) for a family of four.

A cheaper way to plot out Oxford's dreaming spires is to scale the 97 steps to the top of **Carfax Tower** ❀ (© **01865/792653**). The attendant will give you a map identifying the individual rooftops. It's open daily from 10am to 5:15pm but closes at 3:30pm in winter. Admission is £1.20 ($1.75) adults, 60p (87¢) children, or half price with the official walking tour.

Today there are 41 colleges scattered throughout the city. Most open their quads and chapels in the afternoon only, except for Christ Church, Hertford, New College, St. Hugh's, and Trinity College, which are open in the morning, too. Obviously you can't and probably wouldn't want to visit all of them, so we've picked the best of the bunch.

Founded in 1458, **Magdalen** ❀❀ (© **01865/276000;** pronounced "*Maud-len*") is one of the largest and most beautiful of the colleges—the hall has some particularly lovely carved wood paneling. Its tower (1492–1509) is a city landmark from which, on May mornings, you can hear the glorious pealing of bells. Magdalen alumni include Thomas Wolsey, Edward Gibbon, Oscar Wilde, and Edward, Prince of Wales. The college is open daily from 2 to 6pm. The

# Oxford

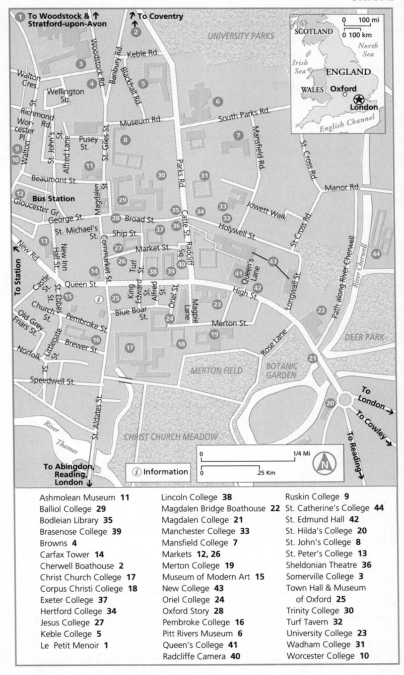

To Woodstock &
Stratford-upon-Avon

To Coventry

UNIVERSITY PARKS

Keble Rd.

Walton
Cres.

Wellington
Sq.

Richmond
Rd.

Wor-
cester
Pl.

Museum Rd.

South Parks Rd.

Pusey
St.

Beaumont St.

Bus Station

Gloucester Gr.

George St.

St. Michael's
St.

Broad St.

Ship St.

Market St.

Holywell St.

Jowett Walk

New Rd.

New Inn
Hall St.

Cornmarket St.

Turl
St.

Queen St.

Castle
St.

St. Ebbes
St.

King
Edward
St.

Alfred
St.

Oriel
St.

High St.

Church
St.

Pembroke St.

Blue Boar
St.

Magpie
Lane

Merton St.

Old Grey
Friars St.

Brewer St.

Norfolk
St.

Speedwell St.

MERTON FIELD

BOTANIC
GARDEN

DEER PARK

To
London

To Cowley

To Reading

River
Thames

CHRIST CHURCH MEADOW

To Abingdon,
Reading,
London

Information

0        1/4 Mi
0        .25 Km

SCOTLAND

North
Sea

Irish
Sea

ENGLAND

WALES  Oxford

London

English Channel

0    100 mi
0    100 km

St. Aldates St.

Manor Rd.

St. Cross Rd.

River Cherwell

Path along River Cherwell

Rose Lane

Longwall St.

Mansfield Rd.

Parks Rd.

Catte St.

Radcliff
Sq.

Queen's
Lane

Woodstock Rd.

Banbury Rd.

Blackhall Rd.

St. Giles St.

Magdalen St.

St. John's St.

Alfred Lane

Walton St.

Littlegate

> **Fun Fact   Time for Bed**
> At 9:05pm every evening, the 7-ton "Great Tom" bell at Christ Church tolls
> 101 times. The tradition dates from the time when each chime repre-
> sented a scholar and the tolling marked the closing of college.

admission charge of £2 ($2.90), or £1 ($1.45) for concessions, is only collected
from Easter to the beginning of October—"who wants to be bothered standing
out in the cold to take tickets?" laughed a college staffer. The Botanic Gardens,
meadows, and Grove (where deer have roamed since the 1700s) that surround
the college make it a very peaceful retreat.

Built on the site of St. Frideswide's Monastery, **Christ Church** ⊛ (© **01865/
276150**) dates from 1546 and is both college and cathedral. The latter contains
some beautiful medieval stained glass, including a depiction of the martyrdom
of Thomas à Becket, and the St. Frideswide and St. Catherine windows by
Edward Burne-Jones. Charles I took up residence in the Deanery during the
civil war, when Oxford was his military headquarters. Sir Christopher Wren
designed **Tom Tower** (1682), at the college gate.

The dining hall at Christ Church has a fine collection of portraits, including
those of notable graduates William Penn, W. E. Gladstone, John Wesley,
Anthony Eden, and Lewis Carroll. The college is open year-round from 9:30am
to 5:30pm Monday to Saturday, and from 11:30am on Sunday. You can visit the
dining hall from 10:30am to noon, and 2:30 to 4:30pm. Times at the cathedral
vary depending on choir practices, concerts, and services, of which there are four
on Sunday. Evensong is at 6pm weekdays. Admission to Christ Church is £4
($5.80) adults, £3 ($4.35) concessions—£1 less if any parts of the college are
closed to visitors.

The chapel at **New College** (1379) is one for culture buffs: It has some very
famous artworks, including Epstein's *Lazarus* and El Greco's *St. James,* as well as
fine stained-glass windows and woodwork, particularly the carving of the choir
stalls. The paneled hall is the oldest in Oxford, while the gardens are some of the
most beautiful.

**Corpus Christi** (1517) is a small college. Somehow it managed to retain most
of its silver and other plate. It also has a charming sundial topped by a pelican
in the middle of the Front quad and an altarpiece in the chapel, *The Adoration
of the Shepherds,* attributed to Rubens. **Hertford** (1874) has its own Bridge of
Sighs. Capability Brown laid out the gardens at **St. John's** (1555). And if you
want to tread in Bill Clinton's footsteps, visit **University College** where he was
a Rhodes Scholar in 1968.

## . . . AND BEYOND

The attractions below are ranked subjectively by entertainment value. It is up to
you how to mix and match them. Bear in mind that the Pitt Rivers Museum is
only open for a few hours in the afternoon. The bustling **covered market** ⊛,
which links Market Street and High Street, has fed the burghers of Oxford since
1774. It's a great place to take a breather from earnest sightseeing, as well as to
grab food for a picnic out on the river.

Punting, or pole-boating, is as traditional in Oxford as it is in Cambridge.
Both the hire companies below are on the River Cherwell and operate every day
from March to October only. The **Magdalen Bridge Boathouse** ⊛

(✆ **01865/202643**) hires out punts, rowing boats, and pedalboats for £9 to £10 ($13.05–$14.50) an hour, plus £25 ($36.25) deposit, from 10am to dusk. **Cherwell Boathouse,** Bardwell Road (✆ **01865/515978**) charges £8 to £10 ($11.60–$14.50) an hour for a punt, with a £40 to £50 ($58–$72.50) deposit, from 10am to 6pm.

Back on the history trail, let's start with a fabulous **freebie.** Founded in 1683, the **Ashmolean Museum** ⚜⚜, Beaumont Street (✆ **01865/278000;** www. ashmol.ox.ac.uk), is England's oldest public museum. It's the sort of place where you don't quite believe what you're seeing is for real—things like Guy Fawkes's lantern, Henry VIII's stirrups and hawking gear, and the mantle said to have belonged to Powhattan, father of Pocohontas and King of Virginia. It has a terrific archaeology collection, too, with Egyptian mummies, casts of Greek sculptures, silver, ceramics, and bronzes. The paintings include works by da Vinci, Raphael, and Rembrandt. The Ashmolean is open Tuesday through Saturday 10am to 5pm, Sunday 2 to 5pm. Hours extend June through August, to 7pm on Thursdays, and from noon on Sunday.

Sticking to the haunts of academe, just off Broad Street you'll find the famous 1602 **Bodleian Library** (✆ **01865/277224;** www.bodley.ox.ac.uk), which contains more than 5 million books. The **Radcliffe Camera** (1748) is England's earliest round reading room, designed by James Gibbs. The only way Joe Public can look around is to take a tour, at 10:30, 11:30am, 2, and 3pm from Monday to Friday, April through September; and mornings only during summer weekends and over the winter. This is a working library and it is also often closed for university ceremonies, so call ahead to make sure the schedule isn't disrupted. Tickets cost £3.50 ($5.10).

To see where the university bestows honorary degrees during the Encaenia ceremony (June 26), visit the **Sheldonian Theatre** (✆ **01865/277299**). This concert hall was Sir Christopher Wren's first commission, completed in 1669. The interior is made entirely of wood except for the ceiling, which consists of 36 panels painted by Robert Streeter, court painter to Charles II. It's open Monday to Saturday 10am to 12:30pm and 2 to 4:30pm (to 3:30pm mid-Nov to Mar), but call ahead to check. Admission is £1.50 ($2.20) adults, £1 ($1.45) children.

The **Pitt Rivers Museum** ⚜ on Park Street (✆ **01865/270949;** http://units.ox.ac.uk/departments/prm/) is free, and it's like a 3-D tour through the pages of *National Geographic*. General Pitt Rivers gave his collection of ethnic artifacts to the university in 1884 and there are now more than half a million objects. The spookiest section is on magic; there's a 17th-century silver phial said to have a witch trapped inside. Most redolent of adventure are the 150 pieces collected during Captain Cook's second voyage, from 1773 to 1774, including a Tahitian mourner's costume. Arranged by type, rather than geography or date, the exhibits demonstrate how different peoples tackled the same tasks. The Pitt Rivers is open Monday to Saturday 1 to 4:30pm, and from 2pm on Sunday. To get to it, walk through the courtyard of University Museum.

The **Museum of Modern Art** on Pembroke Street (✆ **01865/722733;** www.moma.org.uk) could hardly be more of a contrast. This leading center for contemporary visual arts holds ever-changing exhibitions of sculpture, architecture, photography, video, and other media. It's open Tuesday through Sunday 11am to 6pm (until 9pm Thurs). Admission is £2.50 ($4) adults, £1.50 ($2.40) seniors, free for under-16s. Café MOMA is a great place for a breakfast, lunch, or tea-time snack-stop. It opens at 9:30am from Tuesday to Saturday and nothing costs much more than £5 ($7.25).

## WHERE TO EAT

**Browns** TRADITIONAL BRITISH   This large, casual, upbeat brasserie is one of the best places to eat in Oxford. It serves hearty food, including a good traditional cream tea, and has a large convivial bar and a very pleasant outdoor terrace. Mummies and daddies come here with their high-achieving offspring when they come to visit them at the university. There is also a Browns in London (see "Mayfair," in chapter 5).

5–11 Woodstock Rd. ✆ **01865/311415.** Main courses £6–£15 ($11.60–$21.75). AE, MC, V. Mon–Sat 11am–11:30pm; Sun noon–11:30pm.

**Le Petit Manoir** ★★ MODERN FRENCH   This sleek brasserie offers budget diners a slice of affordable heaven. It's an offshoot of Raymond Blanc's much-lauded restaurant, Le Manoir aux Quat'Saisons. You'll find such delicious signature dishes as deep-fried goats' cheese, olive tapenade, French beans, and tomato chutney (yum!), or chargrilled Scottish ribeye steak with frites and bearnaise sauce, or the wicked chocolate fondant with pistachio ice cream. But you won't have to sell your children to eat here as prices are a third of what you'd pay at HQ. The children have their own very good value menus too. Do book because this place is justifiably very popular.

71–72 Walton St. ✆ **01865/510999.** Main courses £8–£13 ($11.60–$18.85). Fixed-price meal £12.50–£15 ($18.15–$21.75). Children's menu £5.95–£7.95 ($8.65–$11.55) AE, DC, MC, V. Open Mon–Sat 11am–11pm; Sun 11am–10pm.

**The Turf Tavern** PUB   Tucked away down a cobblestone alley, this delightful pub, gets very crowded. It has several bars in a series of long, low-ceilinged rooms decorated with rowing crew portraits and other Oxford memorabilia. The food is traditional grub, ranging from steak-in-ale pie, and fish and chips, to sandwiches and salads. It also has a good selection of cask ales and a pleasant beer garden.

4 Bath Place. ✆ **01865/243235.** Main courses £4–£5.75 ($5.80–$8.35). Daily noon–7:30pm.

# Appendix:
# London in Depth

London is the place to see history in the making. Two thousand years of continuous habitation have left their mark on the city's architecture, cuisine, politics, and just about any aspect of culture you care to mention. The city is like an ever-expanding time capsule, to which each generation adds its own contribution—from modern streets that still follow the arrow-straight Roman highways, to chic new-wave Indian cuisine that is the legacy of the Empire, and the ebb and flow of social mores. This appendix will help you to see beyond the superficial and immerse yourself in a truly 3D London experience.

## 1 London Today

The capital is on the cusp of enormous change. The population has jumped to 7.4 million and is forecast to top 8 million by 2016. The economy has grown by more than 35% since 1993. The public transport system is grinding under the pressure of too many bodies and too little investment. Traffic is at a standstill. Housing is in short supply. Aaargh! Cue Mayor Ken Livingstone and his 20-year plan for London: more skyscrapers, new Tube lines, and pushing new development East, balancing the city up by redistributing some of the wealth from West London.

Mayor Ken's 103-page wish-list was still in draft form at the time of writing. And while Londoners may admire the sentiments, they ain't holding their breath. The wheels of change grind so slowly here that the movement is imperceptible. But Ken's scrappy little chap, ready to take anyone on. He's had lots of practice, getting up Tony Blair's nose. The PM wants to privatize the Underground. Mayor Ken says oh, no, you don't.

British governments have an expiration date, rather than a set date, for re-election. The Prime Minister and party pundits read the runes, sniff the air, and poll thousands of voters to find the most propitious moment within their allotted 5-year term to "go to the country." Sniffing the air was a bad idea in 2001, unless you wanted a noseful of cow smoke. Foot and mouth ran rampant round the country, running roughshod over New Labour's election plans. Instead of sucking up to the voters, he was sucking up to stay-away tourists, and persuading Hugh Grant to tell his mates that Britain was open for business. It was an annus horribilis all-round on that score. Dissenting politicians have forced the dissolution of the Northern Ireland Assembly, but members of a dissident IRA group still plant the occasional bomb in London—most notably last year outside the BBC. You have only to look at the state of Blair's once-bouffant locks, now deflated and graying, to see what hard work it's been.

But somehow, despite farmers using his election poster as a dartboard, he still managed to annihilate the Conservatives, the first time Labour has ever won a second term with an outright majority. So it's back to no. 11 Downing Street—no. 10 couldn't accommodate the abundant Blair family even before the shock arrival of baby Leo.

On the royal front, after officially meeting the Queen in 2000, Camilla Parker-Bowles attended a posh reception at Holyrood Palace as Prince Charles' pseudo-wife. Could it be that the Royal family is loosening up? Prince William asked not to be called HRH yet, and revealed a royal talent for cooking when he voluntarily broke the media blackout on his 18th birthday, just before leaving Eton. Property prices around the Scottish university town of St. Andrew's soared in anticipation of his arrival. And the Queen called in the two men behind Britain's most successful breakfast TV show to advise her how to click with Britain's youth.

Democratization is the buzzword among the once elitist cultural institutions that have scooped up lottery millions. The government has persuaded the national museums to ditch their admission charges, a rare example of successful political meddling in the arts. Witness the contrasting fortunes of the Dome and Tate Modern: The latter was a roaring success from the moment it opened; the former made a fat mark in red on New Labour's popularity balance sheet and was *still* empty at the time of writing at the cost of £80 a minute.

The commercial entertainment scene is just as hot, hot, hot as ever. Restaurant pioneers turn into empire-builders, leaving space at the bottom of the heap for yet more new ideas. The new club-bars provide an intimate antidote while giving the stage to new bands: the live music scene is hotching in a way it hasn't done since Britpop first hit the world-tour arenas. Meanwhile young British artists—not called that any more, of course—seem to have moved en masse to pump up the excitement in East London. You know the East is where it's at when arch-art marketer, the entrepreneur Jay Jopling, chooses that neighborhood for his second gallery, White Cube². The city's streets have become the center of the shopping universe, particularly for anything to do with the twin national obsessions: gardening and home decoration.

This DIY obsession is tangled up with soaring property prices. It's said you have to be earning at least £50,000 a year ($72,500) even to buy a shoebox, while rumor has it Madonna paid over £10 million for her townhouse. The government has had to promise help to "key workers"—nurses and teachers, particularly—to stop a mass migration out of town.

That is just part of a wider, and unfortunate, problem—the polarization of society. Like any big multicultural city, London suffers from homelessness, poverty, drugs, crime, and violence. Even in Southwark—which Tate Modern has turned into one of the most visited boroughs and developers have yuppiefied by turning warehouses into apartments—the deprivation is still evident.

## 2 A Look at the Past

### EARLY ROMAN, SAXON & DARK AGE LONDON

London is very old by any measure. Archaeologists have unearthed evidence of settlements from as far back as 2500 B.C. Scholars hotly debate the origin of the city's name, but most believe it comes from the Celtic words *Llyn Din,* meaning "lakeside fortress."

The British Isles began to feel the heat of Roman attention in A.D. 43. The invaders were great engineers and

### Dateline

- A.D. 43 Londinium settled by Roman invaders.
- 50 London Bridge built across the Thames.
- 61 Boudicca sacks London.
- 190–220 City walls built.
- 350 Saxons invade.
- 410 Romans retreat.
- 457 Londoners take refuge behind city walls.

*continues*

put in an impressive infrastructure throughout the empire. Some of London's modern streets follow their original roads—Oxford Street, Bayswater Road, and Edgeware Road, for example. As the Romans settled Britain, they transformed what began as a military base into an important trading center, putting up buildings with tiled roofs and mosaic floors. To see what it looked like then, visit the Museum of London, which has a very effective reconstruction.

Two hundred years later, though, the Empire began to crumble and the Romans pulled out of Britain. The vacuum created by the sudden loss of a national governing force led to inevitable turmoil. The local tribes had to fend for themselves against Anglo-Saxon invasions.

From the 7th to the early 9th centuries, the tribal kingdoms of Kent, Mercia, Northumbria, and the West Saxons fought each other for control of Britain. Meanwhile, the Viking hordes descended, occupying the Saxon suburb that had grown up around Charing Cross, outside the walls (871–872). The Saxon king Alfred the Great fought back, then in 886 made peace with the Danes. Londoners abandoned the settlement and moved back inside the Roman walls. The population had grown by then to around 12,000.

The rapacious Vikings began raiding again in the late 10th century. London resisted at first, but finally had to accept Sweni as king in 1013, and later his son Canute. After the latter's death, Edward, the son of Ethelred the Unready, came to the throne. It was he who moved the court out of the city, to a new purpose-built palace on the site of today's Westminster Hall. He also spent a tenth of his income rebuilding the nearby abbey of St. Peter. Not for nothing was the king known as Edward the Confessor. When his beloved wife Eleanor of

- 604 First St. Paul's built. Mellitus appointed Bishop of London.
- 886 Alfred the Great takes London from the Danes.
- 1066 William of Normandy (the Conqueror) crowned king.
- 1078 Construction of White Tower begun.
- 1097 William Rufus builds Westminster Hall.
- 1123 St. Bartholomew's Hospital founded.
- 1176–1209 London Bridge built of stone.
- 1192 Henry FitzAilwin elected first mayor of London.
- 1214 King John grants city a charter.
- 1215 Magna Carta signed.
- 1348–49 Black Death sweeps London.
- 1381 Peasants' Revolt.
- 1397 Richard Whittington, a wealthy merchant, elected lord mayor.
- 1401 Water piped in from Tyburn.
- 1455 Wars of the Roses begin.
- 1461 Edward of York crowned king.
- 1483 Richard, Duke of Gloucester, imprisons (and possibly murders) Crown Prince Edward V and his brother; crowns himself Richard III.
- 1485 Henry Tudor defeats Richard at Bosworth. Henry VII launches Tudor dynasty.
- 1509 Henry VIII succeeds to the throne. Marries first of six wives.
- 1513 Henry VIII builds Navy and opens dockyards at Deptford and Woolwich.
- 1536–40 Dissolution of the monasteries. Church of England established, with king at head.
- 1553 Mary Tudor made queen. Lady Jane Grey, the "Nine Days' Queen," is executed.
- 1558 Elizabeth I (1558–1603) succeeds to throne.
- 1588 Spanish armada defeated.
- 1599 Globe Theatre built.
- 1600 London expands south of the Thames.
- 1605 Guy Fawkes and his Gunpowder Plot to blow up King James I and Parliament are foiled.
- 1631 Inigo Jones builds Covent Garden.

*continues*

Castile died in Nottinghamshire, her funeral cortege traveled slowly back to London and Edward had a cross erected at every overnight stop. Only one survives in London—at Charing Cross, the last stop on the sad journey. You can visit his tomb in Westminster Abbey.

Edward's death on January 6, 1066, sparked a raging battle for the throne between the Saxons and the Normans—his mother's people. The city's merchants and barons sold their support to the Saxon Harold for the promise of certain rights and privileges. But he fell at the Battle of Hastings and William the Conqueror marched on London, burned Southwark, and forced a surrender.

**MEDIEVAL LONDON**  William had himself crowned in Westminster. He was smart enough to understand the power the bigwigs wielded, and he fulfilled Harold's promises—though that didn't stop them from fighting for more independence. William granted favored Norman barons tracts of land on which they built huge, fortified, stone houses, known as *burhs*. None survive, but street names such as Bucklersbury and Lothbury tell us where they once stood.

Throughout the 11th century, the old Saxon London of wood and thatch slowly transformed into Norman stone. William began the massive, impregnable White Tower (of the Tower of London) in 1078, not only as a fortification against invaders, but also to intimidate his new London subjects.

But the City fathers went on wielding influence in later battles for the throne. King Stephen (1135–54) only held onto his because Londoners attacked Matilda, daughter of Henry I, and prevented her coronation at Westminster. Later, they kept the rebel William Longchamp in the Tower, and King John (1199–1216) in power. That earned them formal right, later

- 1637 Hyde Park opens to the public.
- 1642–58 Oliver Cromwell leads Parliamentary forces during Civil War and later Protectorate.
- 1649 King Charles I beheaded before the Banqueting House in Whitehall.
- 1660 Monarchy restored under Charles II.
- 1665 Great Plague strikes 110,000 Londoners.
- 1666 Great Fire destroys 80% of the medieval city.
- 1675–1710 Wren rebuilds 51 churches, including St. Paul's.
- 1688 Bloodless Revolution: James II banished; William and Mary invited to throne.
- 1694 Bank of England established.
- 1725 Mayfair developed.
- 1739–53 Mansion House built.
- 1759 British Museum founded.
- 1780 In Gordon Riots, mobs protest against Papists.
- 1801 First census. Population: 959,000.
- 1802 West Indian Dock opens.
- 1826 University College established.
- 1829 Metro Police established.
- 1832 First Reform Bill enfranchises some property owners.
- 1837 Victoria, 18, succeeds her uncle, William IV.
- 1840s Influx of Irish immigrants, fleeing famine and political repression.
- 1847 British Museum opens.
- 1851 Hyde Park hosts the Great Exhibition, which finances development of South Kensington.
- 1858 The Great Stink. Royal Opera House opens.
- 1861 Prince Albert dies, sending Victoria into deep mourning and 10 years out of the public eye.
- 1863 The first Underground connects Paddington to the City.
- 1877 First Wimbledon Tennis Championship.
- 1882 Law Courts built in the Strand.
- 1888 London County Council established.
- 1889 Great Dock Strike.
- 1894 Tower Bridge opens.
- 1900 Coca-Cola arrives in Britain.
- 1901 Queen Victoria dies. Edward VII ascends throne.

*continues*

enshrined in the Magna Carta and still in place today, to elect their own leader, the Lord Mayor of London. Which is why the monarch has to ask permission to enter the City.

Wars dominated the whole of the 12th, 13th, and 14th centuries: abroad, in the Crusades and the Hundred Years' War with France; at home, with the Wars of the Roses, between the House of Lancaster and the House of York for the English throne. Despite all this strife, London continued to grow and thrive, through trade largely, even though London Bridge was the only way across the Thames. The original wooden bridge was replaced several times, then work started on a stone version in 1176: It was to take 33 years to complete and cost 200 lives. It was 940 feet long, with 20 arches, and had a chapel on top of it, dedicated to Thomas à Becket. Timbered houses lined the 12-foot-wide cobbled roadway. It was across the new London Bridge that the medieval kings of England set out to Crécy, Poitiers, and Agincourt. And they impaled the heads of traitors on the gate at the southern end (one foreign visitor in the 16th century counted 30 on display).

The River Thames was the city's main highway. It cost only 2p to travel from London to Westminster in 1372. Wharves lined the banks, each one assigned a particular type of cargo. There were a few roads wide enough for 16 knights to ride abreast (dubbed royal roads), but most were narrow, unpaved, and badly maintained.

London's wealth grew out of the wool trade, in particular: Sheep outnumbered people 300 to 1. A handful of merchants controlled the market, which was exporting a million yards of cloth to Europe by the 1480s. Other industries flourished, too. In 1422, the clerk of the Brewers Company

- 1907 Central Criminal Court (the Old Bailey) constructed.
- 1910 King Edward VII dies and is succeeded by George V.
- 1914–18 World War I. London bombed from planes and airships.
- 1922 BBC begins broadcasting.
- 1936 King George V dies. Prince of Wales succeeds to throne as Edward VIII, but abdicates to marry Wallis Simpson.
- 1937 Edward's younger brother crowned King George VI.
- 1939–45 World War II. Air raids and rocket attacks destroy much of the city: 30,000 killed; 50,000 injured.
- 1947–48 New influx of Commonwealth immigrants.
- 1948 London hosts Summer Olympics.
- 1951 Royal Festival Hall opens.
- 1952 King George VI dies.
- 1953 Queen Elizabeth II crowned in first nationally-televised coronation ceremony.
- 1955 Heathrow Airport opens.
- 1956 Clean Air Act passed to cut through famous pea-soup smog.
- 1960s Swinging London—Mary Quant, the Beatles, et al. The controversial Centre Point Tower built. England beats Germany in the Football World Cup in 1966, and dines out on it ever after.
- 1965 Churchill (b. 1874) dies. Greater London Council formed.
- 1973 Britain joins the European Common Market, despite opposition from the old foe France.
- 1974 Covent Garden Market moves out to Nine Elms.
- 1976 Royal National Theatre opens.
- 1979 Margaret Thatcher becomes Britain's first woman prime minister, heading a Conservative government.
- 1981 Charles, Prince of Wales, marries Lady Diana Spencer in St. Paul's Cathedral. Docklands Development Corporation established.
- 1982 The Thames Flood Barrier is completed downstream at Woolwich. Barbican Arts Centre opens.

*continues*

recorded 111 city trades—drapers, soapmakers, cordwainers, goldsmiths, vintners, haberdashers, and many more. The guilds set standards, trademarks, and prices, and arranged pensions for their members. As prosperity grew, they built impressive halls. Many survive today, though often in 19th-century incarnations: Drapers' Hall, Fishmongers' Hall, and Goldsmiths' Hall, for instance. You can see the companies' banners flying in the Guildhall.

Daily life was hard for most. The Great Plague killed 30% to 40% of the population between 1348 and 1349. At the height of the epidemic, one London cemetery buried 200 dead each day. Drink and religion were the common escape from the grind and the terrors. In 1309, there were 1,334 taverns, each brewing its own individual ale. London had 106 churches in 1371 and several monasteries. Holy Days, royal celebrations, and fairs, like the famous St. Bartholomew fair, provided blessed relief.

The Court had its own pleasures. Jousting tournaments took place in Smithfield and Cheapside and the king went hunting for deer, boar, and hare in what are now our favorite London parks. Among the wealthy classes, chess was so popular that *The Rules of Chess* was the second book Caxton printed.

Westminster was the center of government, linked to London by Whitehall and the Strand (but primarily via the Thames). From the early 14th century on, the king summoned

- **1986** Margaret Thatcher abolishes the Greater London Council after battling for years with its bolshy left-wing leader, Ken Livingstone.
- **1990** Tories oust Margaret Thatcher and vote for John Major to replace her. Paparazzi shots of a possibly-tearful Maggie leaving Downing Street shoot round the world.
- **1992** Royal family rocked by scandals, and Windsor Castle fire. Queen agrees to pay income tax and opens Buckingham Palace to the public.
- **1994** Channel Tunnel officially opens.
- **1996** IRA bombs Docklands in first attack for 17 months. Two die. Prince Andrew and Sarah Ferguson's divorce becomes final. Charles and Diana divorce, too.
- **1997** Tony Blair wins election for New Labour. Princess Diana killed in Paris car crash; nation mourns with huge outpouring of grief.
- **1999** Scotland and Wales win partial self-government. Monica Lewinsky chooses Harrods to launch her book, *Monica's Story*, written by Diana biographer Andrew Morton. Prince Edward and Sophie Rhys-Jones marry at Windsor. New Labour makes hereditary lords pitch for parliamentary privileges, and ousts 600 of them.
- **2000** First Universal Day of new millennium starts at Greenwich. Dome's fortunes go downhill from there. Ken Livingstone elected as first London mayor. First official meeting between the Queen and Camilla Parker-Bowles. Prince William leaves Eton.
- **2001** Foot and mouth disease ravages Britain. Tony Blair trounces the Tories, again, to win Labour a second term with an outright majority for the first time ever.
- **2002** Queen Elizabeth II celebrates her Golden Jubilee.

his nobles to council there. The courts and the treasury were in Westminster Hall, where the exchequer kept the accounts with tally sticks. Notches marked out the money owed along the stick, which was then split in half, one part kept by the exchequer and the other by the debtor. It was burning old sticks that destroyed the original buildings at Westminster in 1854.

By the early 14th century, the population had reached 50,000 and living conditions were abysmal. Pigs, chickens, packhorses, and dogs roamed the city and the streets were open sewers. Many people scraped a living as rakers and gong farmers—digging through the garbage and excrement. There was no clean water supply: It came straight out of the Thames at the Great Conduit in Cheapside. And fires were frequent.

**TUDOR & ELIZABETHAN LONDON**   The modern history of London begins with the Tudors, who ascended the throne at the end of the 15th century. The first was Henry VII, who laid the solid administrative foundations on which his successors built a great nation and a strong monarchy.

Between 1500 and 1600, the population of London rocketed from 50,000 to 200,000. The city got wealthier and wealthier, due largely to the English Company of Merchant Adventurers. They traded wool to the Dutch in Antwerp and shipped back to England all kinds of things, from tennis balls, licorice, and Bruges silks, to warming pans, thimbles, and dye for cloth. These 800 or so wholesale traders were the richest men in England. It was they who, in 1571, founded the first financial institution in the city, the Royal Exchange, which went on operating until 1939.

Under the Tudors, England grew in economic and political power. Henry VIII was a powerful Renaissance prince who competed fiercely with archrival Francis I of France. It was Henry who laid down the foundations of the British Army and the Navy.

But Henry's most significant legacy was separating the English church from Rome in furious response to the pope's refusal to grant him a divorce. It was a huge step, and a very lucrative one, because the king went on to dissolve the monasteries and confiscate church wealth and lands. Frustrated in his desire for a male heir, Henry married six times, executing two of his wives and divorcing two. One died of her own accord and one outlived him. Anne Boleyn passed through Traitor's Gate at the Tower in 1536 on the way to her beheading. Catherine Howard was beheaded too, but she tested the block first and died proclaiming her love for Culpepper, who'd already got the chop for dallying with her.

Patronage of the arts and architecture was an important way to display power, and Henry VIII invited great painters like Holbein to his court. He built Nonsuch Palace (long gone), and embellished St. James's and Whitehall. Henry's reputation for extravagance was well earned. The kitchen at Hampton Court Palace, which you can visit, was 100 feet long and 38 feet wide, and had ceilings 40 feet high. He spent £300,000 a year on food and £50,000 on drink. What is surprising is that, despite his ever-expanding waistline, the king had boundless energy for manly pursuits: He enclosed Hyde, St. James's, and Green Parks for his own hunting and other pleasures.

Henry VIII may have plundered Catholic coffers and estates, but it was his fanatical protestant son, Edward VI (1547–53), who wreaked the greatest physical destruction on London's parish churches. He presided over the wholesale stripping of sculptures and decoration: One church lost 100 tombs and monuments. The Lord Protector Somerset demolished the cloister of St. Paul's in 1549 and used the materials to build Somerset House in the Strand. In 1550, Edward dissolved the bishopric of Westminster. The church returned to the Dean, but part of its revenues were transferred to St. Paul's; hence the English saying, "robbing Peter to pay Paul." Henry VIII's elder daughter Mary reestablished Catholicism in 1553. She was as hard-line as her brother had been, though of the totally opposing view, and many public executions took place at Smithfield.

Her sister Elizabeth ascended the throne in 1558, ushering in not only Protestantism again, but a period of unprecedented colonial expansion and economic growth. A popular queen and master politician, she held England at peace for

30 years while she advanced the nation's interests against those of Catholic France and Spain. In 1588, her Navy defeated a large Spanish armada that had set out to invade. Elizabeth gave thanks for this victory at St. Paul's.

Literature and the arts also flourished. Edmund Spenser dedicated his epic poem, *The Faerie Queene,* to Elizabeth. And the statesman and philosopher Francis Bacon; the soldier, explorer, and poet Sir Walter Raleigh; and others of equal versatility wrote pivotal books on history, science, and philosophy. At the same time, the English theater came into its own. James Burbage built the first playhouse, called simply "The Theatre," in Shoreditch in 1576, then the Rose on Bankside in 1587, the Swan in 1595, and the Hope in 1614. Play-going became a central part of London life, with as many as 40 productions a year at the Rose, including works by Christopher Marlowe, John Webster, Ben Jonson, Thomas Middleton, and William Shakespeare, of course, who joined Burbage's company in 1599. Today, Bankside is experiencing another cultural flowering, with the rebuilding of the Globe Theatre and opening of Tate Modern.

**STUART LONDON**    Elizabeth's death destroyed the longstanding political stability as an increasingly assertive, and largely Puritan, Parliament sought to build its power and limit that of the monarch. Known as the Virgin Queen, she had no direct successor and the throne passed to James VI of Scotland, who then became James I of England. James believed absolutely in the divine right of absolute monarchy, so couldn't help but fight with Parliament. He persecuted the Puritans, despite an avowed intention to begin a new era of religious tolerance. And, though it was Catholic-led, he won no friends during the Gunpowder Plot when Guy Fawkes tried to blow him up at the state opening of Parliament.

If the conflict had simmered under James I, it exploded under his son Charles I, who was forced to dissolve several parliaments. In response, Parliament put the king's ministers on trial. It charged Thomas Wentworth, Earl of Strafford, with 28 crimes and he fought for 18 days in Westminster Hall to defend himself. Charles fled to York. In 1642, he raised his standard at Nottingham and London prepared for a Royalist attack. Parliament called out trained bands of men. Armed boats patrolled the Thames. And 100,000 men were pressed into digging 18 miles of trenches to link up the 24 bastions. The attack never came. The Royalist and Parliamentary troops waged their battles all over the country instead— at Edgehill, Oxford, Marston Moor, Naseby, and Preston.

Finally defeated, Charles I stood trial in Westminster Hall in 1649 and was condemned to death. He took his last walk through St. James's Park on January 30, flanked by guards with a troop of soldiers in front and behind, colors flying and drums pounding. The procession crossed a gallery at what is now Horse Guards Parade and entered the Banqueting House of Whitehall Palace. Four hours later, the king stepped out of the window onto the wooden scaffold. After saying his prayers, he pulled off his doublet, laid down his head, and the executioner wielded his ax. His last words were: "To your power I must submit, but your authority I deny." Today, a statue of a horseman stands looking down to the spot where he died. At the other end of Whitehall, outside Westminster Hall, there's a statue of Oliver Cromwell, the Puritan general who ruled England from 1649–1658, as Lord Protector, after Charles's execution.

Charles I had been a great patron of the arts and invited Van Dyck and Rubens to his court. In 1621, the latter painted the ceilings of the Banqueting House in Whitehall for £3,000 and a gold chain. Under Cromwell, the arts died. He closed the theaters and the city fell under a pall of fear and Puritan gloom. Diarist John Evelyn described Cromwell's funeral in 1658 as the "joy-fullest . . . that ever I saw." The crowds impaled his head and those of his generals Ireton and Bradshaw and stuck them up on the roof of Westminster Hall. It's said Cromwell's remained there for 25 years until the wind blew it down and a sentry stole it.

The Restoration brought the Merry Monarch, Charles II, to the throne and brought the city back to life. The theaters reopened and the king kept a lavish court at Whitehall Palace. Political and social climbers flocked there to curry favor, either directly or with one of the many royal mistresses.

Two major catastrophes interrupted the merrymaking—another Great Plague (1665) and the Great Fire of London (1666). The first victim of Black Death died on April 12, 1665; by December, 110,000 had died. The king and his court left for Hampton Court, and most of the nobility dismissed their servants and fled. The unemployed roamed the city looting and pillaging. Men worked day and night digging mass graves, but couldn't keep up with the corpses, which piled up in mounds. The stench of death was horrific. When someone succumbed to the swellings in the groin and armpit (buboes), officials locked up their whole household for 40 days, and marked a red cross on the door, which multiplied the death rate. The innocent-sounding nursery rhyme "ring a ring o' roses" refers to the first telltale marks on the victim's skin.

Eventually, the rat-born plague ran its course and, in February 1666, the king deemed it safe enough to return to London. In the early morning of September 2, 1666, the Great Fire broke out at the bakery of Robert Farriner in Pudding Lane. It raced through the city, fanned by strong easterly winds. Samuel Pepys describes the flames leaping 300 feet into the air, warehouses blazing, and people jamming the river and roads in a vain attempt to flee.

The Duke of York (later James II) was put in charge of firefighting, and the king himself helped too. The flames raged for 4 days, over 400 acres within the city walls and 60 more outside. It wiped out medieval London, destroying 87 churches, 44 livery halls, and 13,000 half-timbered houses. Ten thousand people were left homeless. From then on, it was decreed that all buildings must be constructed of stone and brick.

Although Charles II realized this was an opportunity to create an elegantly planned city, and even invited architects to submit plans, London needed rebuilding immediately. The medieval layout had to stay: To this day, London's streets follow the same routes as in the Middle Ages, hence the traffic jams and average speed of 10mph. The streets were widened, though, and pavements laid for the first time. The king appointed six commissioners to mastermind the city's reconstruction. Wren was one of them: He rebuilt 51 churches (23 survive today, along with the towers of 6 others) and designed the 202-foot Monument commemorating the fire. St. Paul's was his greatest achievement.

In 1688, England went through a "Bloodless Revolution." James II had succeeded his brother Charles and, after converting himself, tried to bring the whole nation back to Catholicism. It was too bitter a pill for the people to swallow. So, they asked his Protestant daughter Mary and her husband, the Dutch Prince William of Orange, to take the throne. The couple did so, first signing a new bill of rights, fixing limits to a sovereign's power. England had taken its first step on the path to constitutional monarchy.

London went through a property boom between 1660 and 1690, especially in Piccadilly, the Strand, and Soho. In 1656, Covent Garden Market opened as a temporary arrangement in the Earl (later the Duke) of Bedford's garden. In their headlong flight from fire and plague, many of the aristocracy had suddenly woken up to the advantages of living outside London, in the villages north and west of the city—Bloomsbury, Kensington, Hackney, Islington, and Hampstead. As they developed their estates, London began to take on its current form. They built houses and laid out formal squares, like Bloomsbury (1666) and St. James (1665).

**18TH-CENTURY LONDON**   During the 18th century, London's population continued to multiply explosively, from 490,000 in 1700 to 950,000 in 1800. The city transformed in the process, as Mayfair and the West End began to develop. Private and corporate landowners laid out squares as the focal points of their estates.

Wealth flowed back from overseas colonies in America and from those established in the 17th century by the East India Company, the Royal Africa Company, and the Hudson's Bay Company. The Port of London boomed, trade tripling between 1720 and 1780. Because of the congestion on the Thames, it sometimes took 3 or 4 weeks to unload one vessel. As the century progressed, though, the pivotal role of the river as a main trade and general highway began to decline. Other forms of transport, from the stage and hackney coach to the sedan chair, took over and more and more bridges began to span the river, like the one built at Westminster in 1749.

Other social developments helped change the face of the city, too. Greater wealth brought philanthropy and a growing concern for the poor. This led to the establishment of major public institutions like the Foundling Hospital (1742), Chelsea Hospital (1692), and Greenwich Hospital (1705); the British Museum (1755); and the Royal Academy of Arts (1768). The authorities set up a rudimentary fire department. And, by 1710, there were already 3,000 pupils at various charity schools, including St. Paul's, Westminster, and Christ's Hospital.

The major social institution, other than the church, was the coffeehouse, where literary and powerful men gathered to debate and gossip about politics and society. Addison, Steele, and Swift all met at Burtons in Russell Street; Samuel Johnson was a regular at the Turks Head at no. 142 the Strand; East India Company merchants thronged the Jerusalem Coffeehouse in Cornhill; and the first ever stock exchange started informally at Jonathan's Coffeehouse in 1722. In 1702, London got its first newspaper, the *Daily Courant,* which was reaching 800 readers by 1704. Later in the century the *Guardian, Spectator,* and *Rambler* all published regular editions. Grub Street hacks would anonymously fire off any kind of libel or satire for a fee—a tradition some might say the tabloids uphold to this day.

One word sums up the politics of the age—corruption. Hogarth pictured the scene most acidly in his series, *The Election.* Votes were bought and sold. Politicians stole from the public purse. Riots were common; during the worst, the Gordon Riots in 1780, the mob torched several prisons and attacked the Bank of England and Downing Street.

Life was grim in the 18th century for the poverty stricken. Silk weavers in Spitalfields hired out looms, employing female and child labor. Workhouses and prison workshops were common, too. To see the seamier side of London life, just take a look at Hogarth's *Gin Lane* or *The Rake's Progress.*

Those who could afford it took their leisure at Vauxhall Gardens (1660) or at Ranelagh Pleasure Gardens (1742). Their favorite fun was horse racing, archery, cricket, bowling, and skittles, as well as less salubrious pastimes like bullbaiting and prizefighting. Freak shows were very popular, too, at Don Saltero's Coffee House in Chelsea. And people flocked to Mrs. Salmon's waxworks in Fleet.

Though the prudish Victorians later hushed it up, London's sex industry has never been bigger than it was behind the elegant Georgian facades. Indeed, it funded much of the building. One in eight women (25,000) in the city was a prostitute in 1796, each one making more in a night than the average man earned in a fortnight. It was no big deal for celebs and wealthy Londoners to go to brothels, half-heartedly disguised as Turkish baths. As well as the wealthy courtesans of Marylebone, streetwalkers did brisk trade in Covent Garden, adding to the louche atmosphere of this theatrical neighborhood.

David Garrick and Richard Brinsley Sheridan were the best-known actor-managers, both at Drury Lane. Musicians and composers were feted at the courts of the Hanoverian kings (Georges I, II, and III): Johann Christian Bach, Franz Joseph Haydn, and Mozart all performed there. Handel is the composer most closely identified with the London of this period: It was during the reign of George III that the annual performance of his *Messiah* began. Beyond court and the church, Thomas Britton fired a new musical tradition in the city, arranging weekly concerts from 1678 to 1714 in a loft above his Clerkenwell coal house.

Under the Georges, a great many artists rose to prominence, among them Sir Joshua Reynolds (who became head of the Royal Academy of Arts, founded by George III in 1768), Thomas Gainsborough, William Turner, and William Hogarth. Literature burgeoned too: The celebrity cast list includes the great lexicographer and wit Samuel Johnson, his biographer James Boswell, poet Alexander Pope, and the novelists Samuel Richardson and Henry Fielding. Edward Gibbon's multivolume *History of the Decline and Fall of the Roman Empire*, one of the great achievements of English literature, caused George III to remark, "Always scribble, scribble, scribble. Eh, Mr. Gibbon?"

**19TH-CENTURY LONDON**   In the 19th century, London became the wonder of the world—a wonder based on imperial wealth and power. In 1811, at the age of 58, the Prince of Wales became regent for his father, mad George III. He set up an alternate court at Carlton House and at his extravagant palace in Brighton. At both, the prince entertained his mistresses openly and lavishly. He treated his wife Caroline abominably, banning her from his coronation, which took place in 1820 at the massive cost of £238,238. Though lambasted for his dissolute behavior, George IV did contribute to London's development, working with architect John Nash to introduce urban planning. Together they laid out Regent Street, a grand avenue from Carlton House to Piccadilly, and Regents Park.

Plump as a partridge, Victoria ascended the throne in 1837. As the century progressed, the city's transformation into a modern industrial society proceeded apace, shaped by the growing power of the bourgeoisie and the queen's strict moral stance. The raciness of the preceding three centuries seemed to disappear, but it actually just went underground.

Extremes of wealth and poverty marked life in Victorian London. Children worked long hours in factories and sweatshops, or as chimney sweeps. Immigrants—Irish and European—poured into the foul, overcrowded slums. Thirty percent of the population lived below the poverty line, in the appalling conditions graphically described in many of Charles Dickens' novels. The consumption of gin was huge in the 1820s. In an effort to reduce it, the government abolished tax on beer, and scores of ale houses opened as a result—probably why there are so many pubs in London today.

Parliament passed the first Reform Bill in 1832 and social campaigners pressed for better conditions: Lord Shaftesbury strove for improvements in labor and education, Elizabeth Fry in prisons, and Florence Nightingale in hospitals. In 1870, the Education Act made elementary education compulsory.

The Victorians revolutionized public transport, too. In 1829, Shillibeer launched his horse-drawn omnibus. Underground trains started running from Paddington to Farringdon in 1863, carrying 12,000 passengers that year. And the first electric Tube ran on the Northern Line in 1890. Vast railway networks spread out across the country, all terminating at impressive Central London stations—Victoria, Charing Cross, St. Pancras, and Euston—several of which are virtually unchanged today.

In 1851, Prince Albert put his weight behind a celebratory Great Exhibition, housed in an astonishing iron-and-glass construction, Crystal Palace, built in Hyde Park. More than 6 million people flocked to see this showcase of the industrial and technological wonders of the age. Albert was a great promoter of new advances, like the revolutionary electric lighting that began to replace traditional gas lamps in London houses in 1880.

The middle class enjoyed a fantastic nightlife. By 1850, London had more than 50 stages, producing everything from popular blood-and-thunder melodramas to pageants at Christmas and Easter. The repertoire began to get more upmarket toward the end of the century, with works by Oscar Wilde, Arthur Wing Pinero, James Barrie, and George Bernard Shaw. Actor-manager Henry Irving and actress Ellen Terry lit up the Lyceum in the Strand. But music halls were even more popular—there were over 400 in 1870. People flocked to the Hackney Empire and the London Coliseum to hear Marie Lloyd, Dan Leno, and other stars belt out Cockney tunes and ribald variety shows.

Eating out became an upper-middle-class pastime, too. Once an exclusively male domain, mores slowly relaxed to let women in on the fun. The opening of the first Joe Lyons corner house in 1894 made eating out something the masses could enjoy, too. There were 98 in London by 1910, serving everything from a snack to a five-course meal.

Spectator sports took off in a big way in the 19th century—football, rugby, and especially cricket. The All England Croquet Club put in tennis courts in 1874 to revive its sinking fortunes. The ploy was so successful that the club held its first Wimbledon Championship in 1877. The manufacture of the safety bicycle in 1885 launched a craze, which gave women a taste of liberation: The "New Woman" of the 1890s took to the road on two wheels without a chaperone. Shopping, too, was becoming a national pastime. Department stores opened up to satisfy the urge to splurge—Whiteleys in Queensway (1863, now converted into a shopping mall), Harrods (1860s), Liberty (1875), and Selfridges (1909).

Victoria celebrated her golden jubilee in this energetic capital, before ushering in the 20th century.

**THE EARLY 20TH CENTURY** The early 1900s, during the reign of Edward VII (1901–10), were filled with confidence. Britain was at the height of its power and Londoners looked forward to a radiant future. Looking back, though, some historians pinpoint this as the start of the economic decline, arguing that Britain was already losing markets and trade to the United States.

At home, the trade union movement gained recruits and women campaigned vigorously for the vote. They chained themselves to railings and protested at the

Houses of Parliament. The courts sent 1,000 suffragettes to Holloway Prison between 1905 and 1914, and it took World War I, with its social ramifications, to help women gain the franchise.

Rivalry with Germany had been festering for years, and war eventually broke out in 1914. British men marched off to do their duty, expecting certain and rapid victory. Instead, the war bogged down in the trenches and the slaughter wiped out a whole generation. Back home, 900 bombs fell on London, killing 670 people and injuring almost 2,000. The Great War shattered the liberal middle class's illusion that peace, prosperity, and social progress would continue indefinitely.

The peace imposed on the Germans at Versailles led inexorably to economic dislocation, and ultimately to both the Crash of 1929 and the Great Depression of the 1930s. An unprecedented constitutional crisis further threatened Britain's stability in 1936, when the new and hugely popular king, Edward VIII, abdicated after refusing to renounce his love for the American divorcee, Wallis Simpson. His brother succeeded him as George VI.

Meanwhile, fascism was rising in Germany and threatening the peace with its expansionist ambitions. British and French attempts at appeasement failed. Hitler marched into Poland. And, in 1939, World War II began. The Blitz of 1940–41 and again in 1944–45 killed over 20,000 people in London and destroyed vast areas of the city, but Londoners' spirit proved indomitable. They dug trenches in public parks to resist the expected invasion. Night after night, they ran for their shelters as waves of German bombers flew overhead. One hundred and fifty thousand slept in the Underground, others stayed home, and the defiant continued partying. The royal family remained in London despite the dangers.

Recordings of Winston Churchill's speeches still evoke pride, even among people who weren't born at the time. But for many who were there, the memories are bittersweet: Britain won the war but lost the peace. Unlike Germany and Japan, which received American aid under the Marshall Plan, Britain was impoverished, and her industrial plants antiquated. Dissolution of the empire and a plummeting of national morale followed swiftly.

**POSTWAR & CONTEMPORARY LONDON**     Postwar London was a glum place. Rationing continued until 1953. Only the coronation of Queen Elizabeth II in June 1953, watched by 20 million on their TV screens, seemed to lift the city's spirits. Heathrow formally opened in 1955, the same year Mary Quant launched her boutique on the King's Road. The coffee bar, rock 'n' roll, the new Mini (relaunched in 2001 as the BMW Mini at 20 times its original £499 price-tag), and antinuclear protests all arrived in the 1950s, setting the stage for the Swinging London of the following decade. It was then that young people all over the world went bananas over the Beatles, the Kinks, the Rolling Stones, The Who, Eric Clapton's Yardbirds, and the Animals. Sixties London was suddenly the fashion and arts capital of the world.

The swinging slacked off a bit in the 1970s when the Beatles disbanded. But the trendy movement continued as Terence Conran launched Habitat, Anita Roddick created the Body Shop, and the Saatchi & Saatchi advertising empire were born. In 1976, London finally got its Royal National Theatre, first conceived of in 1848. The Barbican Arts Centre opened in 1982.

Other less-heartwarming developments also took place during the postwar years. The number of West Indians heading for Britain each year rose from

**What'd Ya Say?**

Many Americans are shocked to discover that there's such a thing as British English. Believe it or not, the gulf between the two languages is wide enough to cause some embarrassing and entertaining exchanges. The English use words and phrases you may think you understand, but their meaning is often quite different from the U.S. equivalent.

**Troublesome Slang**    "Mean" is a playground word for nasty, an adult word for "stingy," and a once-cool term of praise. And "homely," isn't "ugly" or "plain," but "cozy and comfortable." Other slang can get you into much worse trouble. In England "pissed" is "drunk," "pissed off" is "angry;" a "rubber" refers to an "eraser," and "fag" means a "cigarette" as well as being a homophobe's term of abuse. "Fanny" in English is definitely not what you think it means. *Fanny Hill* might give you a clue—let's leave it at that.

**Problematic Pronunciation**    The letter Z is pronounced "zed." Zero can be "zero," but is more often "nought," or interchanged with the letter "O," especially when people are telling you their phone number. French words can cause hiccups (or "hiccoughs," sometimes), too. The Brits put the emphasis on the first half of "*croi*-ssant" and "*ba*-llet."

**Local Customs**    If you don't line up in London, you're a pariah. Except that the Brits "queue" instead.

**Public Transport**    Whereas a "subway" is an underground pedestrian walkway, the actual subway system is "the Underground" or "the Tube."

**Automobiles**    Very little is the same, except for the word "car": A truck is called a "lorry"; a station wagon is an "estate car." The hood is the "bonnet," the windshield the "windscreen," and the trunk is the "boot." Drivers "hoot" the horn and "indicate" before they turn. Oh, and gas is "petrol."

**Groceries**    In a supermarket, canned goods become "tins," potato chips "crisps," eggplants "aubergines," green squash "courgettes," while endive is "chicory" (and, conversely, chicory is "endive"). Both cookies and crackers become "biscuits." A Popsicle is called an "iced lolly," candy is "sweets," and a soda is a "fizzy drink." If you want diapers, ask for "nappies."

**Clothes Shopping**    This is a real red-face territory. Repeat after me: Undershirts are called "vests" and undershorts are "pants" to the English. Long pants are "trousers," their cuffs are called "turnups," and, unless you're looking for lacy things that hold up ladies' stockings, ask for "braces," not suspenders. Panties are "knickers" and pantyhose are "tights." Pullovers can also be called "jumpers," "jerseys," or "sweaters."

**At Home**    Most of us know that an English apartment is a "flat," unless it's over two floors, which much-reviled estate agents (realtors) describe as a "maisonette," rather than a duplex. An elevator is a "lift." And the first floor is always the ground floor, the second floor the first, and so on.

1,000 to 20,000 after 1952 when the United States closed its doors to them. Ultra-conservative politicians like Enoch Powell called for a slowdown in immigration, and London experienced its first-ever race riots in Notting Hill in the summer of 1958. Parliament responded by restricting entry to Britain, but prohibiting discrimination in housing and employment. More riots followed in 1981 and 1985, and the race issue continues to fester as the second and third generations still find themselves treated as second-class citizens.

In the 1950s and 1960s, immigrants also began arriving from India and Pakistan. Their communities have also been under attack, but successful Asian entrepreneurs and businesspeople are fighting back and demanding justice. In contrast to other European countries, though, the shocking violence of the 1980s does seem to have helped mold a more honest cross-cultural society than most, despite tabloid references to "frogs" and "krauts" that might suggest the contrary.

The post-war economic decline was initially masked by Britain's continuing reliance on preferential trade with former colonies. Most Commonwealth exports flowed through London, making its port one of the busiest in the world. But many of these countries gained full independence in the 1960s and began to build their own industries and diversify. Germany, Japan, and the United States were tough competitors, too. Most dockyards closed, and manufacturing jobs went as big companies like Thorne-EMI and Hoover relocated to other areas. Unemployment in the poorer boroughs of London, like Tower Hamlets and Southwark, soared from 10,000 in the 1960s to 80,000 in the 1980s.

The Conservatives rose to power in 1979, with Britain's first woman prime minister at the helm, on the promise of revitalizing the economy. Margaret Thatcher's reforms were ground-shaking: privatization of major industries, from insurance companies to British Airways and British Rail. Maggie also squashed the trade unions and dismantled parts of the welfare state. At the height of her power in the early 1980s, she mobilized British forces to rescue the Falkland Islanders from the Argentine invasion. The return to gunship diplomacy reignited English pride and won the Tories the next election.

Later, fiercely protective of British sovereignty, Maggie refused to agree to a German-backed monetary union within the European Community and opposed moves toward the creation of a federal entity. She angered many backbenchers in her own party in doing so. And, in 1990, the party rebelled and ended the longest tenure of any modern British prime minister, voting to replace her with the Chancellor of the Exchequer, John Major. His tired government limped along, but the Furies were on their tail.

The Tories couldn't seem to keep their hands off dodgy money and dodgy women. They fought amongst themselves, very publicly, about Britain's role in Europe. In 1994, the Channel Tunnel opened. Though considered an astonishing feat of engineering and a success now, then it was a money-pit that had to seek repeated refinancing. And the monarchy, of which the political right has

---

## Impressions

*"Every city has a sex and age which have nothing to do with demography. London is a teen-ager and urchin, and, in this, hasn't changed since the time of Dickens."*

—John Berger, *Guardian*, March 27, 1987

always been a loyal supporter, was in such disarray that it prompted louder calls for a republic than at almost any time since the Protectorate.

In 1992, Windsor Castle lit up the night sky as workers struggled for 15 hours to put out the blazing fire. Angry political debate about freeloading royals prompted the Queen to agree to pay income tax for the first time. And both her elder sons' marriages crumbled in the full lip-smacking glare of media attention. The next year brought her yet more grief in the shape of published transcripts of taped almost–telephone sex between Charles and Camilla Parker-Bowles. The Royal marital farce reached its climax in 1996 with the divorces of Prince Charles and Diana, and Prince Andrew and Sarah Ferguson.

The British people were more than ready for change. Tony Blair moved the Labour Party way up the sexiness scale and to the political center, reassuring Middle England that it was no longer the party of high taxation. It worked, and the blessed Tony led his gang to a massive victory in 1997.

After 18 years of Tory rule, it felt like throwing off a particularly smelly and oppressive old dog blanket. The government promised so much to so many, in a new inclusive society: help for the disadvantaged, powerful support to British business, a revitalized education system and health service, backing for the arts, and so on. Blair's golden glow lit up their efforts, even surviving the misjudged sucking up to arts and media luvvies.

A year later, Britain had its dreadful Kennedy moment. Ask any local and they'll be able to tell you where they were when they heard about the death of Princess Diana: I'd fallen asleep with my radio on and awoke before dawn to hear a shocked journalist reading an unconfirmed bulletin. The nation plunged into mourning and turned on the royal family for their hidebound reaction. With the PM volunteering advice, they have been trying to "get real" ever since.

## 3 Recommended Books & Films

## BOOKS

Why not set the scene with a little light background reading about the country as a whole. The very funny *Notes from a Small Island* tells the tale of Bill Bryson's final walking tour around Britain, where he lived for 20 years, before moving home to the U.S. He really knows the place and its people, yet he maintains the weathered eye of the outsider. *The English: A Portrait of a People* is the mirror opposite—an exploration of the national quirks, without the humor, by arch-tiger BBC journalist Jeremy Paxman.

**GENERAL**    Peter Ackroyd's 800-page *London: The Biography* treats the city as an organism, an entity with a life of its own, whose current state of health is inextricably linked to its past. John Russell's *London* is a very personal portrait filled with anecdotes, observations, color photographs, and illustrations. Novelist and literary critic V. S. Pritchett's *London Perceived* (Hogarth, 1986) is another favorite.

Coming right up to date with a rapier-sharp eye on recent events, particularly Thatcherism, read novelist Julian Barnes' *Letters from London,* a set of essays originally printed in the *New Yorker.*

Then there's a great book to take with you. *Americans in London* (William Morrow, 1986) by Brian N. Morton is a great street-by-street guide to the clubs, homes, and favorite pubs of more than 250 famous Americans.

**FICTION**    Of all the arts, England is probably richest in literature. This sounds dreadfully like a school reading list, but every age has its headline chronicler.

## Impressions

*It was a great way to get straight to where you were going in a cab, and not go by Harrods four times. At first, I was like, "So there are three Harrods in London?"*
— Renée Zellweger, on speaking with an English accent while living in London to prepare for being *Bridget Jones,* March 2001

Chronologically, start with Chaucer's bawdy portrait of medieval London in his *Canterbury Tales.* Follow with Shakespeare and Ben Jonson. Pepys and Evelyn are wonderful friends with whom to explore 17th-century London. For the 18th century, take Fielding, Swift, and Defoe. Anything by Dickens or Thackeray will unlock Victorian London for you. The period from the turn of the century to the 1920s and 1930s is best captured in the works of Virginia Woolf, Henry Green, Evelyn Waugh, P. G. Wodehouse, and Elizabeth Bowen. Contemporary authors who provide insight into London society are, particularly, Muriel Spark, Iris Murdoch, Angus Wilson, V. S. Naipaul, Martin Amis, Angela Carter, Ian McEwan, Jeanette Winterson, Graham Swift, Anita Brookner, Kazuo Ishiguro, Hanif Kureishi, Allan Hollinghurst, Nick Hornby, and a legion of others.

Michael Moorcock's novel *Mother London* was shortlisted for the U.K.'s prestigious Whitbread Prize. It's a magical epic, interweaving the stories of three outpatients from a mental hospital from the Blitz to the present day. Moorcock's *King of the City* and *London Bone* (short stories) come highly recommended too.

Almost-child prodigy, and hot name on the literary scene, Zadie Smith was still at university when she wrote the hugely successful *White Teeth,* about tangled immigrant lives in North London from World War II to now.

**BIOGRAPHY**    The biography is definitely back in fashion. Amanda Foreman's *Georgiana, Duchess of Devonshire,* the story of an 18th-century political and social siren, fashion icon, and chronic gambler, propelled the thirty-something blonde to media stardom. *Bosie, A Life of Lord Alfred Douglas* is by another just-ex student, Douglas Murray—a companion read to Richard Ellman's *Oscar Wilde* (Knopf, 1988).

And there are so many others to choose from. Among the greats are Jackson Bate's study of Samuel Johnson, the many royal portraits written by Antonia Fraser, as well as her book on Oliver Cromwell, and Blake's *Disraeli.* For a portrait of Disraeli's opponent Gladstone, see those written by Richard Shannon or H. C. Matthews. When it comes to Winston Churchill, you can read his autobiography, or turn to Martin Gilbert's *Churchill: A Life* (St. Martin's, 1991). Also rated as a good read are the stories of Tory infighting and the substantial ghost of Maggie in John Major's *The Autobiography* (surprisingly), and the roaring indiscretions in the *Diaries* of Alan Clark, a minister for two terms under the Iron Lady.

As for the tabloid-harried royals, several books dredge up all the lurid details—Anthony Holden's *The Tarnished Crown* (Random House, 1993), A. N. Wilson's *The Rise and Fall of the House of Windsor* (W. W. Norton & Company, 1993), and the very sleazy *Elizabeth: Behind Palace Doors,* by investigative hack Nicholas Davies. For Diana's perspective on the whole family and her role in it, read *Diana: Her True Story* (Simon & Schuster) by Andrew Morton. Trevor Rees-Jones tells of paparazzi-dodging on the dreadful day of the crash in *The Bodyguard's Story*. And Fergie sets the record straight, as far as she sees it, in *My Story, Duchess of York*, by Sarah Mountbatten-Windsor and Jeff Coplon.

## FILMS

Get out the popcorn, take the phone off the hook, and settle down for a big preview night of London at the movies. Oooh, it'll be like that scene out of *Bridget Jones*, the spot-on exposé of single life in London.

Pierce Brosnan takes a rather speedy river cruise past some of the city's major landmarks to Docklands and on to Greenwich as James Bond in *The World is Not Enough*. You'll even get to see the Millennium Dome, which Tony Blair may have wished the special effects guys really had blown up. The film goes perfectly back-to-back with the classic gangster movie *The Long Good Friday*, with Bob Hoskins.

Merchant Ivory chose Mansion House for the new adaptation of Henry James's *The Golden Bowl*, starring Nick Nolte and Uma Thurman. *Patriot Games* showcased the Royal Naval College at Greenwich.

To tread in Gwyneth Paltrow's footsteps, head for the Church of St. Bartholemew's the Great in Spitalfields, where much of *Shakespeare in Love* was made. *Sliding Doors* sent the lovely Gwyneth and John Hannah all over London, but the rainy shot in the boat took place just by Hammersmith Bridge; and most of the cafe scenes were shot at Mas Café in All Saints Road, at the bottom of Portobello. *Notting Hill* really put this neighborhood on the map.

Spotty-dog fans will recognize Burlington Arcade, in Piccadilly, as the location of several scenes in *101 Dalmatians*. Movie director Neil Jordan had to wheel out the smoke machines to create just the right grimly gloomy London day outside the Savoy for *The End of The Affair*.

Don't just restrict your preview pleasures to London-specific movies. Think of the following as British Culture 101. Start with the 1997 hit *The Full Monty*. Then add *Secrets and Lies, Naked, Trainspotting, Four Weddings and a Funeral, The Crying Game, Mona Lisa, My Beautiful Laundrette, Educating Rita,* and *A Clockwork Orange*. Oh, and the full Merchant Ivory backlist!

# Index

See also Accommodations and Restaurant indexes, below.

## FROMMER'S® MEMORABLE WALKS

| | | |
|---|---|---|
| Chicago | New York | San Francisco |
| London | Paris | |

## FROMMER'S® GREAT OUTDOOR GUIDES

| | | |
|---|---|---|
| Arizona & New Mexico | Northern California | Vermont & New Hampshire |
| New England | Southern New England | |

## SUZY GERSHMAN'S BORN TO SHOP GUIDES

| | | |
|---|---|---|
| Born to Shop: France | Born to Shop: Italy | Born to Shop: New York |
| Born to Shop: Hong Kong, Shanghai & Beijing | Born to Shop: London | Born to Shop: Paris |

## FROMMER'S® IRREVERENT GUIDES

| | | |
|---|---|---|
| Amsterdam | Los Angeles | San Francisco |
| Boston | Manhattan | Seattle & Portland |
| Chicago | New Orleans | Vancouver |
| Las Vegas | Paris | Walt Disney World |
| London | Rome | Washington, D.C. |

## FROMMER'S® BEST-LOVED DRIVING TOURS

| | | |
|---|---|---|
| Britain | Germany | New England |
| California | Ireland | Scotland |
| Florida | Italy | Spain |
| France | | |

## HANGING OUT™ GUIDES

| | | |
|---|---|---|
| Hanging Out in England | Hanging Out in France | Hanging Out in Italy |
| Hanging Out in Europe | Hanging Out in Ireland | Hanging Out in Spain |

## THE UNOFFICIAL GUIDES®

| | | |
|---|---|---|
| Bed & Breakfasts and Country Inns in: | Florida with Kids | New Orleans |
| California | Golf Vacations in the Eastern U.S. | New York City |
| New England | The Great Smokey & Blue Ridge Mountains | Paris |
| Northwest | | San Francisco |
| Rockies | Inside Disney | Skiing in the West |
| Southeast | Hawaii | Southeast with Kids |
| Beyond Disney | Las Vegas | Walt Disney World |
| Branson, Missouri | London | Walt Disney World for Grown-ups |
| California with Kids | Mid-Atlantic with Kids | Walt Disney World for Kids |
| Chicago | Mini Las Vegas | Washington, D.C. |
| Cruises | Mini-Mickey | World's Best Diving Vacations |
| Disneyland | New England & New York with Kids | |

## SPECIAL-INTEREST TITLES

Frommer's Adventure Guide to Australia & New Zealand
Frommer's Adventure Guide to Central America
Frommer's Adventure Guide to India & Pakistan
Frommer's Adventure Guide to South America
Frommer's Adventure Guide to Southeast Asia
Frommer's Adventure Guide to Southern Africa
Frommer's Britain's Best Bed & Breakfasts and Country Inns
Frommer's France's Best Bed & Breakfasts and Country Inns
Frommer's Italy's Best Bed & Breakfasts and Country Inns
Frommer's Caribbean Hideaways

Frommer's Exploring America by RV
Frommer's Gay & Lesbian Europe
Frommer's The Moon
Frommer's New York City with Kids
Frommer's Road Atlas Britain
Frommer's Road Atlas Europe
Frommer's Washington, D.C., with Kids
Frommer's What the Airlines Never Tell You
Israel Past & Present
The New York Times' Guide to Unforgettable Weekends
Places Rated Almanac
Retirement Places Rated

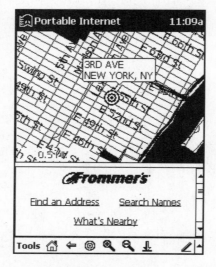